# Emerging Trends in Computation Intelligence and Disruptive Technologies

## *(Volume 2)*

## *Demystifying Emerging Trends in Machine Learning*

Edited by

**Pankaj Kumar Mishra**
*Hi-Tech Institute of Engineering and Technology*
*Ghaziabad, U.P.*
*India*

&

**Satya Prakash Yadav**
*School of Computer Science*
*Engineering and Technology (SCSET)*
*Bennett University, Greater Noida, U.P.*
*India*

# Emerging Trends in Computation Intelligence and Disruptive Technologies

*(Volume 2)*

*Demystifying Emerging Trends in Machine Learning*

Editors: Pankaj Kumar Mishra and Satya Prakash Yadav

ISBN (Online): 978-981-5305-39-5

ISBN (Print): 978-981-5305-40-1

ISBN (Paperback): 978-981-5305-41-8



First published in 2025.

**Bentham Science Publishers Pte. Ltd.**
80 Robinson Road #02-00
Singapore 068898
Singapore
Email: subscriptions@benthamscience.net

BENTHAM SCIENCE

# CONTENTS

# PREFACE

Artificial intelligence (AI) and machine learning (ML) are revolutionizing the way we approach healthcare and various industries. AI and ML are being used to improve patient outcomes, reduce costs, and increase efficiency in the healthcare industry. AI is also used in medical devices to predict and identify diseases, classify data for disease outbreaks, and optimize medical therapy.

In this book, we explore the role of neural networks in AI and ML in the medical and health sector. Neural networks are being used in oncology to train algorithms that can identify cancerous tissues at the microscopic level with the same accuracy as trained physicians. Various rare diseases may manifest in physical characteristics that can be identified in their premature stages by using facial analysis on patient photos.

The book also explores the role of AI and ML in various industries such as finance, retail, manufacturing, and more. AI is being used to improve customer experience by providing personalized recommendations based on customer data. In manufacturing, AI is being used to optimize supply chain management by predicting demand and reducing waste.

This book is a comprehensive guide for anyone interested in learning about the role of AI and ML in medical, health sectors, and various industries.

**Pankaj Kumar Mishra**
Hi-Tech Institute of Engineering and Technology
Ghaziabad, U.P.
India

&

**Satya Prakash Yadav**
School of Computer Science
Engineering and Technology (SCSET)
Bennett University, Greater Noida, U.P.
India

# List of Contributors


**Ayush Gandhi** Centre for Interdisciplinary Research in Business and Technology, Chitkara University Institute of Engineering and Technology, Chitkara University, Punjab, India

**Ansh Kataria** Centre for Interdisciplinary Research in Business and Technology, Chitkara University Institute of Engineering and Technology, Chitkara University, Punjab, India

**Akhilesh Kalia** Centre for Interdisciplinary Research in Business and Technology, Chitkara University Institute of Engineering and Technology, Chitkara University, Punjab, India

**Abhinav Mishra** Centre for Interdisciplinary Research in Business and Technology, Chitkara University Institute of Engineering and Technology, Chitkara University, Punjab, India

**Abhishek Singla** Centre for Interdisciplinary Research in Business and Technology, Chitkara University Institute of Engineering and Technology, Chitkara University, Punjab, India

**Amarpal Yadav** Department of AI, Noida Institute of Engineering & Technology, Greater Noida, Uttar Pradesh, India

**Dikshit Sharma** Centre for Interdisciplinary Research in Business and Technology, Chitkara University Institute of Engineering and Technology, Chitkara University, Punjab, India

**Deepak Minhas** Centre for Interdisciplinary Research in Business and Technology, Chitkara University Institute of Engineering and Technology, Chitkara University, Punjab, India

**Darleen Grover** Centre for Interdisciplinary Research in Business and Technology, Chitkara University Institute of Engineering and Technology, Chitkara University, Punjab, India

**Dhiraj Singh** Centre for Interdisciplinary Research in Business and Technology, Chitkara University Institute of Engineering and Technology, Chitkara University, Punjab, India

**Himanshu Makhija** Centre for Interdisciplinary Research in Business and Technology, Chitkara University Institute of Engineering and Technology, Chitkara University, Punjab, India

**Jaspreet Sidhu** Centre for Interdisciplinary Research in Business and Technology, Chitkara University Institute of Engineering and Technology, Chitkara University, Punjab, India

**Jagmeet Sohal** Centre for Interdisciplinary Research in Business and Technology, Chitkara University Institute of Engineering and Technology, Punjab, India

**Jatin Khurana** Centre for Interdisciplinary Research in Business and Technology, Chitkara University Institute of Engineering and Technology, Chitkara University, Punjab, India

| | |
|---|---|
| **Jagtej Singh** | Centre for Interdisciplinary Research in Business and Technology, Chitkara University Institute of Engineering and Technology, Chitkara University, Punjab, India |
| **Jaskirat Singh** | Centre for Interdisciplinary Research in Business and Technology, Chitkara University Institute of Engineering and Technology, Chitkara University, Punjab, India |
| **Mridula Gupta** | Centre for Interdisciplinary Research in Business and Technology, Chitkara University Institute of Engineering and Technology, Chitkara University, Punjab, India |
| **Madhur Taneja** | Centre for Interdisciplinary Research in Business and Technology, Chitkara University Institute of Engineering and Technology, Chitkara University, Punjab, India |
| **Manpreet Singh** | Centre for Interdisciplinary Research in Business and Technology, Chitkara University Institute of Engineering and Technology, Chitkara University, Punjab, India |
| **Manish Nagpal** | Centre for Interdisciplinary Research in Business and Technology, Chitkara University Institute of Engineering and Technology, Chitkara University, Punjab, India |
| **Madhur Grover** | Centre for Interdisciplinary Research in Business and Technology, Chitkara University Institute of Engineering and Technology, Chitkara University, Punjab, India |
| **N. Sengottaiyan** | School of Computer Science and Engineering, JAIN (Deemed-to-be University), Bangalore, India |
| **Pratibha Sharma** | Centre for Interdisciplinary Research in Business and Technology, Chitkara University Institute of Engineering and Technology, Chitkara University, Punjab, India |
| **Pavas Saini** | Centre for Interdisciplinary Research in Business and Technology, Chitkara University Institute of Engineering and Technology, Chitkara University, Punjab, India |
| **Prabhjot Kaur** | Centre for Interdisciplinary Research in Business and Technology, Chitkara University Institute of Engineering and Technology, Chitkara University, Punjab, India |
| **Prakriti Kapoor** | Centre for Interdisciplinary Research in Business and Technology, Chitkara University Institute of Engineering and Technology, Chitkara University, Punjab, India |
| **Preetjot Singh** | Centre for Interdisciplinary Research in Business and Technology, Chitkara University Institute of Engineering and Technology, Chitkara University, Punjab, India |
| **Prateek Garg** | Centre for Interdisciplinary Research in Business and Technology, Chitkara University Institute of Engineering and Technology, Chitkara University, Punjab, India |
| **Pratik Mahajan** | Centre for Interdisciplinary Research in Business and Technology, Chitkara University Institute of Engineering and Technology, Chitkara University, Punjab, India |

| | |
|---|---|
| **Rohaila Naaz** | College of Computing Science and Information Technology, Teerthanker Mahaveer University, Moradabad, Uttar Pradesh, India |
| **Rahul Mishra** | Centre for Interdisciplinary Research in Business and Technology, Chitkara University Institute of Engineering and Technology, Chitkara University, Punjab, India |
| **Rajat Saini** | Centre for Interdisciplinary Research in Business and Technology, Chitkara University Institute of Engineering and Technology, Chitkara University, Punjab, India |
| **Siddharth Sriram** | Centre for Interdisciplinary Research in Business and Technology, Chitkara University Institute of Engineering and Technology, Chitkara University, Punjab, India |
| **Sidhant Das** | Centre for Interdisciplinary Research in Business and Technology, Chitkara University Institute of Engineering and Technology, Chitkara University, Punjab, India |
| **Sorabh Sharma** | Centre for Interdisciplinary Research in Business and Technology, Chitkara University Institute of Engineering and Technology, Chitkara University, Punjab, India |
| **Sukhman Ghumman** | Centre for Interdisciplinary Research in Business and Technology, Chitkara University Institute of Engineering and Technology, Chitkara University, Punjab, India |
| **Sulabh Mahajan** | Centre for Interdisciplinary Research in Business and Technology, Chitkara University Institute of Engineering and Technology, Chitkara University, Punjab, India |
| **Sakshi Pandey** | Centre for Interdisciplinary Research in Business and Technology, Chitkara University Institute of Engineering and Technology, Chitkara University, Punjab, India |
| **Simran Kalra** | Centre for Interdisciplinary Research in Business and Technology, Chitkara University Institute of Engineering and Technology, Chitkara University, Punjab, India |
| **Shubhansh Bansal** | Centre for Interdisciplinary Research in Business and Technology, Chitkara University Institute of Engineering and Technology, Chitkara University, Punjab, India |
| **Sover Singh Bisht** | Department of DS, Noida Institute of Engineering & Technology, Greater Noida, Uttar Pradesh, India |
| **Saniya Khurana** | Centre for Interdisciplinary Research in Business and Technology, Chitkara University Institute of Engineering and Technology, Chitkara University, Punjab, India |
| **Saket Mishra** | Centre for Interdisciplinary Research in Business and Technology, Chitkara University Institute of Engineering and Technology, Chitkara University, Punjab, India |
| **Sahil Suri** | Centre for Interdisciplinary Research in Business and Technology, Chitkara University Institute of Engineering and Technology, Chitkara University, Punjab, India |

**Sourav Rampal** Centre for Interdisciplinary Research in Business and Technology, Chitkara University Institute of Engineering and Technology, Chitkara University, Punjab, India

**T. R. Mahesh** Department of Computer Science and Engineering, JAIN (Deemed-to-be University), Bangalore, India
Department of Computer Science and Engineering, Galgotias University, Greater Noida, Uttar Pradesh, India

**Tarang Bhatnagar** Centre for Interdisciplinary Research in Business and Technology, Chitkara University Institute of Engineering and Technology, Chitkara University, Punjab, India

**Tarun Kapoor** Centre for Interdisciplinary Research in Business and Technology, Chitkara University Institute of Engineering and Technology, Chitkara University, Punjab, India

**Vaibhav Kaushik** Centre for Interdisciplinary Research in Business and Technology, Chitkara University Institute of Engineering and Technology, Chitkara University, Punjab, India

CHAPTER 1

# A Method Based on Machine Learning to Classify Text for the Field of Cybersecurity

**Siddharth Sriram**[1,*]

[1] *Centre for Interdisciplinary Research in Business and Technology, Chitkara University Institute of Engineering and Technology, Chitkara University, Punjab, India*

**Abstract:** Rapid advancements in networks and computer systems have opened a new door for immoral acts like cybercrime, which threaten public safety, and security, as well as the global economy. The purpose of this proposal is to analyse IP fraud and cyberbullying as two distinct types of cybercrime. The primary goals of this study are to use instances of cybercrime to provide a short examination of cybercrime activities, and the family member principles, and propose a pairing schema. Using the Naive Bayes (NB) & Support Vector Machine (SVM) artificial intelligence techniques, cybercrime instances are categorised according to their ideal qualities. The Twitter data in the Kaggle database has been clustered using K-means. User ID, sign-up date, referral, browser, gender, and age as well as IP address are just a few of the most useful information used to educate the computer. Total 151,113 datasets were used for experimental analysis of the suggested algorithm's performance. The accuracy of the suggested approach, 97%, is higher than that of the current method (NB). The challenge of regression may be easily surmounted with the use of the random forest method for the categorization of the resultant cybercrimes. The planned study uses age categories as the foundation for identifying the different offenses.

**Keywords:** Cyber security, Machine learning techniques, Text classification.

## INTRODUCTION

In order to collect energy from the wake created by oscillating foils, a machine-learning model is constructed. For array deployments of oscillating foils, the function of the wake structure is crucial because the unstable wake significantly affects the performance of downstream foils. User sentiment is gleaned from social media using sentiment analysis [1, 2]. It is a way of organizing the text's ideas into positive, negative, and neutral categories. The outcomes of training and classifying the Twitter dataset have varied depending on the strategy utilized by

* **Corresponding author Siddharth Sriram:** Centre for Interdisciplinary Research in Business and Technology, Chitkara University Institute of Engineering and Technology, Chitkara University, Punjab, India;
E-mail: siddharth.sriram.orp@chitkara.edu.in

**Pankaj Kumar Mishra and Satya Prakash Yadav (Eds.)**

the researchers. The algorithm is crucial, especially in time-sensitive industries like airlines and retail [3, 4]. Smartphones, tablets, and other Internet of Things (IoT) devices are frequently used in settings as diverse as the household and the factory. Bluetooth Low Energy (BLE) is used by many of these gadgets as a control or data transmission mechanism [5, 6]. These devices are susceptible to simple attacks because of their lack of robust security mechanisms and the inherent weaknesses in their software as well as communication components. Machine learning is often used for classification purposes [7]. In order to classify images and other remote sensing data, GIS experts often use deep neural network-based classification methods. Graph neural networks (GNNs) can be utilized for identifying geographical features by taking their topology into account, which is useful for data represented as a graph, such as line or polygonal spatial data [8, 9]. Using GNNs to group spatial objects into several categories is suggested in this article. Three alternative methods were tested, two of which depended only on the classification of text and one which combined text classification with a matrix of adjacency. The suggested method's application case was the categorization of planning zones in LSPs [9]. The outcomes of the trials demonstrated the importance of object topological information in enhancing GNNs' classification accuracy. Input characteristics including document length, training data representation format, and network architecture all need to be considered for optimal model performance [10].

## RELATED WORK

In this study, we look at 46 different kinematics of oscillation foils to find vortex wakes in pictures of vorticity fields and to adjust the wake parameters according to the input kinematic elements. There are three types of wakes that are classified using a network of convolutional neural networks (CNN) that has lengthy short-term memory units. Utilizing an unsupervised convolutional auto-encoder with [Formula: see text]-means++ clustering, four separate wake patterns are identified, which corroborate the differences in foil kinematics. Future research might use these patterns to predict how foils positioned in the wake would behave and to build optimal foil combinations for tidal energy collecting [11].

In this paper, we provide an optimisation-based machine-learning method for tweet classification. The process consisted of three distinct steps. The process begins with gathering and organising data, then moves on to improving it *via* feature extraction, and then concludes with reclassifying the revised training set using machine learning methods. Different algorithms provide different results. Sequential minimal optimising with decision trees has been proven to have a high degree of accuracy (89.47%) when compared to other machine learning techniques [12].

In the first part of this essay, we saw how to get unprocessed information on network traffic while simultaneously launching a MitM assault on BLE devices. Second, we investigate the possibility of using machine learning—and specifically a combination of unsupervised and supervised methods—to identify this kind of assault. We reconstructed the model of BLE interactions using two unsupervised approaches and utilised those models to spot suspicious data batches. The packets within each batch were then categorised as either normal or attack using a classification approach based on the Text-CNN technology. The results of our model reconstruction demonstrate that our classification approach is very accurate (0.99), with a low false positive rate (0.03) [13].

We used LIME to explain the model's predictions and a conglomeration of deep learning algorithms (CNN-GRU) to categorize four distinct cardiac arrhythmia kinds as part of this study. A 1D convolutional neural network (CNN) served as the basis for training the model. A well-liked local explanation method, LIME can simulate the behavior of every machine learning system and provide an explanation for it. Unfortunately, LIME is limited to explaining data in tabular, textual, and visual formats. In order to better illustrate LIME on the signal dataset, we advocated for a heat map to be used to draw attention to relevant regions of the heartbeat signals. Our approach also allows for more accurate heartbeat segmentation by accurately extracting characteristics such as the QRS Complex, P Wave, and T Wave from electrocardiogram, or ECG, records. Tests for recall, accuracy, precision, f1 score, as well as area under the receiver operator curve of characteristic (AUC-ROC) were conducted using ECG lead II from the MIT-BIH datasets to evaluate the proposed hybrid model. We directly compare the suggested model to the independent CNN and GRU algorithms to show that it is more accurate and has a better ROC [14].

Corona Virus and Conspiracies Multimedia Analysis Task of the MediaEval 2021 Challenge is dedicated to investigating claims of wrongdoing in relation to the COVID-19 pandemic. Our HCMUS group takes several methods based on various pre-trained models to handle 2 separate jobs. We provide 5 iterations of Task 1 and 1 of Task 2 based on our experiments. While the BERT [5] trained model is included in both runs, the first run also incorporates a subjective assessment for acquiring semantic features prior to training. Our third and fourth runs will be more method-diversified with the use of naïve Bayes classifiers [4] as well as a long short-term memory framework [8]. By combining many ML and DL models, Run 5 is able to perform a multimodal analysis of textual data [3]. A single-run Bayesian categorization approach is used in the final phase of subtask 2. In the end, our approach yields scores of 0.5987 on task 1 as well as 0.3136 on task 2. The author's copyright for this article is valid until 2021 [15].

## PROPOSED WORK

### Preliminary Knowledge

As a machine learning strategy, text classification aims to automatically classify texts using tags or categories. NLP (natural language processing) text classifiers can quickly sort through massive volumes of text according to user intent, emotions, and themes, far faster than humans can. Emails, chats, websites, social media, reviews on the internet, support tickets, survey results, you name it: they all contribute to an overwhelming amount of data that is difficult for people to process. Imagine attempting to manually handle even a small percentage of the staggering 20 billion messages sent each month between businesses and individuals on Facebook Messenger. It would take an extremely long time and a lot of money. Businesses may get a wealth of knowledge from any and all communication channels, but it can be difficult to sift through the information they receive and identify actionable insights. This is prompting businesses to look at automated options, such as text classification. Text categorization, driven by machine learning, allows you to categorise text in a dependable, scalable, accurate, as well as economical manner. Fig. (**1**) represents the System Architecture.

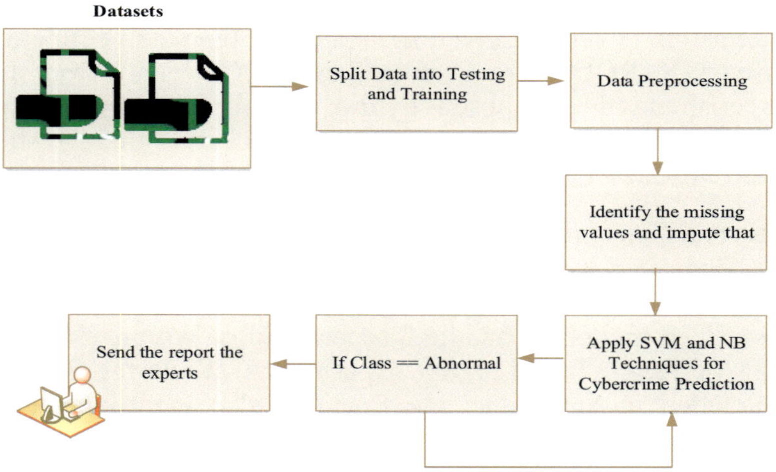


**Fig. (1).** System Architecture.

### Dataset Description

Since we could not find a Spanish-language dataset, we used Facebook's API to compile data on three forms of cyber-aggression in Latin America: racism, violence against women, and violence according to gender identity. We gathered a total of 5,000 comments, but only 2000 were usable since they were free of spam (which we define as texts including uncommon characters, visuals of expression, or hilarious ideas like memes, blank spaces, or irrelevant remarks). Afterward, we classified the feedback (instances) as follows: 700 comments related to sexual orientation-based violence; 700 comments related to violence against women; and 600 comments related to racism.

The act of labelling. We noticed that some academics utilised the Amazon Mechanical Turk website to hire unidentified online employees to manually categorise various types of data (*e.g.*, comments, reviews, words, photographs). Amazon's Mechanical Turk employees found that 2.5% of reviews flagged as "no cyber-bullying" should really be labelled as such, therefore the company reached out to psychology majors at the graduate and undergraduate levels for help with the tagging process.

In light of the above, we opted to have a team of three educators versed in machine-learning algorithms to manually tag the remarks with the help of psychologists versed in assessing and treating incidents of bullying in secondary schools. The psychologists went through the three types of cyber-aggression with the faculty and how to classify comments into the appropriate categories. Each remark was assigned an offensive value based on the criteria of cyber-aggression and a predetermined number scale as part of the labelling procedure. We utilised a scale from 0 to 2 to rank the offensiveness of statements that included sexual assault against women. The same four-point-six-point scale was applied for statements concerning sexual orientation-based violence, with the lowest number indicating the least obscene remarks. Last but not least, racist statements were ranked from least offensive to most offensive using a scale from zero to 10. To this end, we collected a dataset of abusive posts and fed it into our feature selection and training processes. The first column of this data set held the comment or instance, while the second column provided an objectionable value for each comment. In the following, we detail the feature-selection technique and training process algorithms and methodologies employed in this study.

## Machine Learning Algorithms for Text Classification

Machine learning classifier training begins with converting text into a machine-readable format. In many cases, this is accomplished with the help of a "bag of words," a set of words whose frequency in a given set of words is represented by a vector. After information is vectorized, vectors of features for every word sample and tag are used to train a text classification model. The more data it has to learn from, the more precise its forecasts will be. The most popular algorithms for text categorization are waiting, so let's have a look at them:

### *Naive Bayes*

The Naive Bayes approach uses Bayes' Theorem, a classifier based to forecast a text's label using prior information about potentially related circumstances. After determining the likelihood of every tag for the input text, it makes a prediction based on the tag having the greatest likelihood.

Naive Bayes may also be made more effective with the use of other methods:

- Getting rid of filler words that nobody ever uses. Words like "able to," "either," "else," "ever," "*etc*".
- To lemmatize a term is to classify its many derivations under the same heading. Words like "draught," "drafted," "draughts," "drafting," *etc.*
- N-grams: The n-gram denotes the likelihood of occurrence of a single word or a series of words of 'n length' inside a text.
- TF-IDF: A measure of a word's significance in a text or group of documents, TF-IDF is an abbreviation for "term frequency-inverse document frequency." It has great potential for scoring words, in that its value rises with the frequency with which a given word occurs in a document rises, but its value falls as the quantity of documents containing that word falls.
- Forecasters: [X1, X2] and Board: Y To get the posterior probability, one uses the following formula -

$$P\left(\frac{Y}{X1,X2}\right) = \frac{\mathrm{P}(Y)*P\left(\frac{X1,X2}{Y}\right)}{\mathrm{P(X1,X2)}} \quad \textbf{(1)}$$

- Accepting the Offer of Limited Responsibility for *P(X1,X2/Y=1)*,

$$P\left(\frac{Y}{X1,X2}\right) = \frac{\mathrm{P}(Y)*P\left(\frac{X1}{Y}\right)*P\left(\frac{X2}{Y}\right)}{\mathrm{P(X1,X2)}} \quad \textbf{(2)}$$

- Naive Bayes Classifier's posterior probability calculation formula.

### *Support Vector Machines*

The classification system known as Support Vector Machines (SVM) excels in situations when there is a small quantity of data to work with. For each given category, it evaluates all possible vectors and selects the best one. For example, let us pretend that there are two attributes (x and y) and two labels (expensive and cheap) in the data set. There has to be a way to tell which of the two sets of variables (x, y) is more expensive. The support vector machine (SVM) does this by creating a boundary (the decision boundary) between the data points and classifying everything on either side as expensive or cheap. The subspace of a group and the subspace of an outgroup are created when a space is divided in half by a decision boundary. Training text is represented by vectors, and each tag is represented by a set. SVM has the advantage of not needing a large amount of training information to provide correct results, but it does demand more processing power than Naive Bayes to do so. It is a machine learning method that may be used for Regression and Classification, and it is supervised. The number of features, n, determines the number of dimensions in which data points are shown in SVM. The next step in classification is to choose an appropriate hyper-plane that clearly separates the two groups. The hyper-plane has (n minus 1) dimensions in n-dimensional space.

$$\beta 0 + \beta 1X1 + \beta 2X2 + \cdots + \beta nXn = \beta 0 + \sum_{i=1}^{n} \beta iXi \quad (3)$$

We presume that categories may be divided into linear subsets. Classification is facilitated by the sign in the equation, while the scale of the equation clarifies the extent to which the observation deviates from the hyper-plane. If the magnitude is large, we may more confidently place it in a certain category. Margin is defined as the minimal distance of points of data from the hyper-plane to either class. For it to be very significant, we need a large safety margin. Therefore, the name "Maximum Margin Classifier" is applied to this hyper-plane. The observations that fall on or outside the boundary and cause the hyper-plane to deform are known as support vectors. The hyper-plane is propped up by the support vectors.

## RESULTS AND DISCUSSION

Seventy percent, ten percent, and twenty percent of the whole sequence dataset were used for training, validation, and testing, respectively.

To evaluate the models, we used accuracy and macro-weighted F1. The article's claimed accuracy is based on conclusions drawn from the test set. Since it gives an average F1 score while considering the corresponding frequency of each label, the macro-weighted F1 statistics is used when assessing the efficacy of a model on a dataset. Fig. (**2**) displays comparison analysis of accuracy.

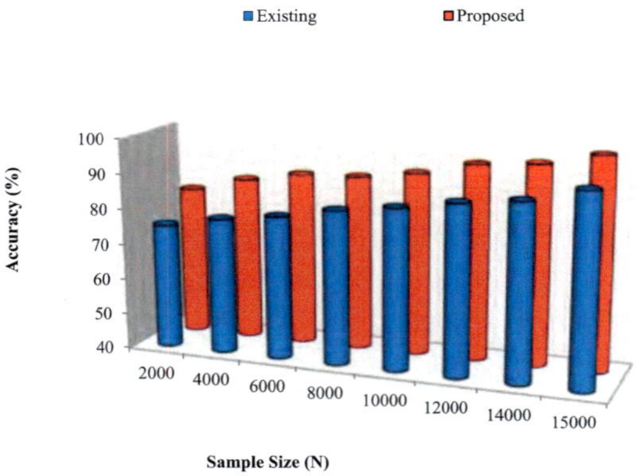


**Fig. (2).** Comparison analysis of accuracy.

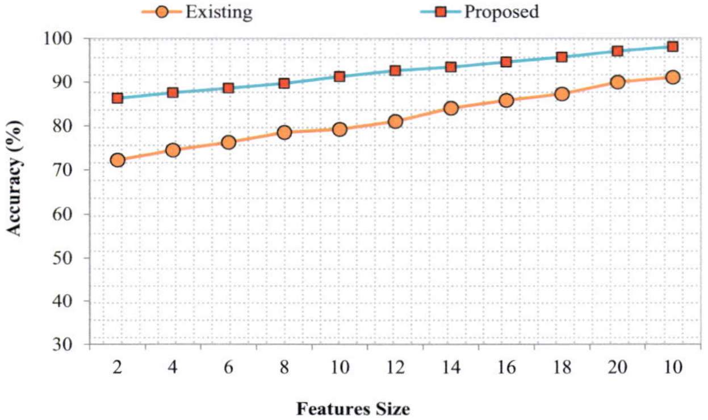


**Fig. (3).** Accuracy (**a**). Sample Size, and (**b**). Feature Size.

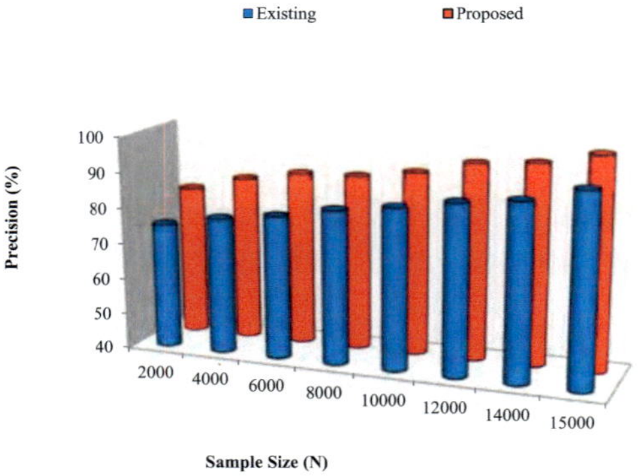


**Fig. (4).** Comparison analysis of precision.

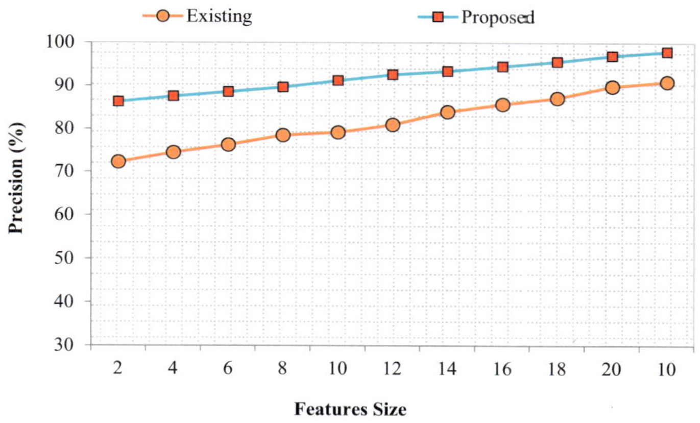


**Fig. (5).** Precision (**a**). Sample Size, and (**b**). Feature Size.

Fig. (**3**) depicts accuracy (a). sample size and (b). and feature size. Fig. (**4**) displays comparison analysis of precision. Fig. (**5**) represents precision (a). sample size, and (b). feature size, Fig. (**6**) portrays comparison analysis of recall. Fig. (**7**) displays recall (a). sample size, and (b). feature size, Fig. (**8**) shows comparison analysis of F-score, Fig. (**9**) shows F-score (a). sample size, and (b). feature size. Cross-validation is often used as a measure of a text classifier's effectiveness. The training data are randomly split into sets of equal size. The remaining sets are used to train the text classifier and test its predictions for each set of the same length. By comparing their predictions with human-tagged data, classifiers may reduce the likelihood of producing false positives and negatives.

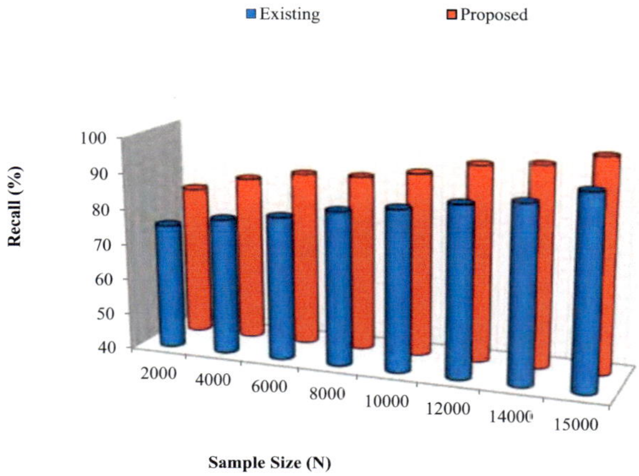


**Fig. (6).** Comparison analysis of Recall.

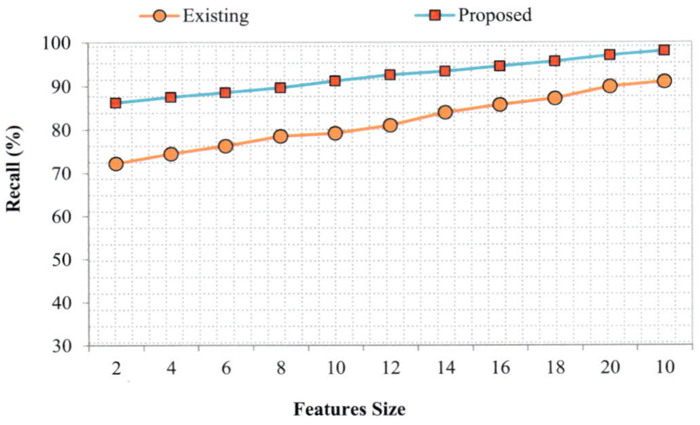


**Fig. (7).** Recall (a). Sample Size, and (b). Feature Size.

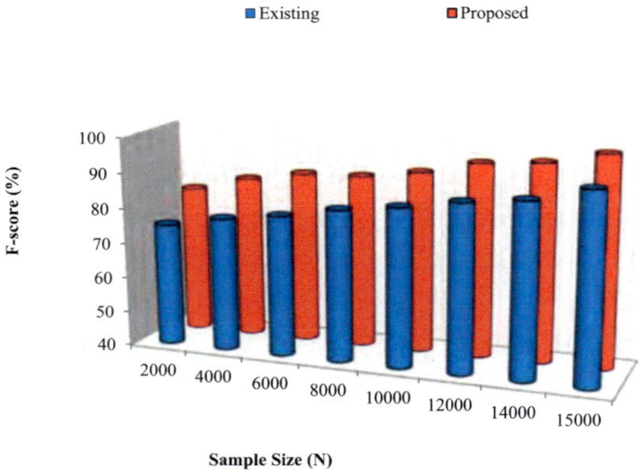


**Fig. (8).** Comparison analysis of F-score.

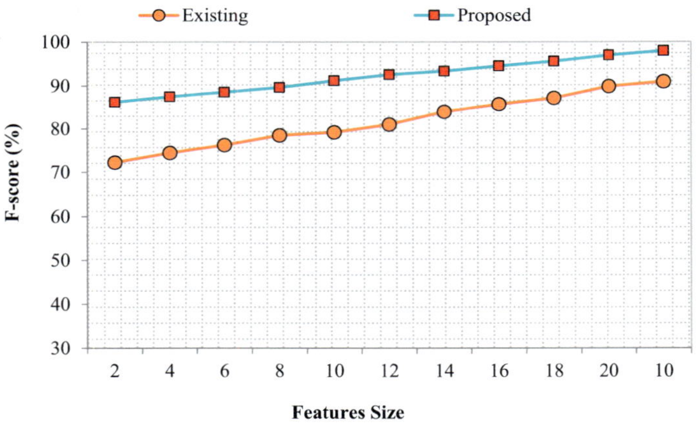


**Fig. (9).** F-score (**a**). Sample Size, and (**b**). Feature Size.

Measures of a classifier's efficacy may be derived from these outcomes:

- **Accurateness:** Proportion of correctly predicted texts with tags.
- **Exactness:** Numbers of texts the classifier's prediction for a tag's total number of instances was within the margin of error.
- **Recallotion:** The proportion of instances out of the overall amount of cases for which it might have made a prediction, the classifier made a prediction for a given tag.
- **F1 Score:** The optimal balance between precision and recollection.

## CONCLUSION

Cybercrime poses a danger to humanity's security, and the global economy because of the quick advancements in networks and computer networks that have opened up new avenues for immoral actions. The proposed work's objective is to categorise cybercrimes into IP fraud analysis and cyberbullying. The main goals of this work are to provide a brief inspection of cyber activities, and their respective underpinnings, and supplying a matching schema *via* cybercrime occurrences. Cybercrime episodes are grouped based on their ideal qualities using data mining methods called Naive Bayes (NB) as well as Support Vector Machine (SVM). Data from Twitter is extracted from the Kaggle databases using K-means clustering. In order to provide appropriate computer training, it is necessary to collect the majority of relevant data, including customers ID, sign-up time, source, web browser, gender, age, as well as IP address. There are 151,113 data points used in the studies that test how well the approach works. With an accuracy rate of 97%, the suggested approach outperforms the current technique (NB). When it comes to cybercrime categorization, the random forest method is superior to novelty regression. The proposed method classifies the different crimes according to a number of age groups.

## REFERENCES

[1] I. Kaczmarek, A. Iwaniak, and A. Świetlicka, "Classification of Spatial Objects with the Use of Graph Neural Networks", *ISPRS Int. J. Geoinf.,* vol. 12, no. 3, p. 83, 2023. [http://dx.doi.org/10.3390/ijgi12030083]

[2] S. Maguen, E. Madden, O.V. Patterson, S.L. DuVall, L.A. Goldstein, K. Burkman, and B. Shiner, "Measuring Use of Evidence Based Psychotherapy for Posttraumatic Stress Disorder in a Large National Healthcare System", *Adm. Policy Ment. Health,* vol. 45, no. 4, pp. 519-529, 2018. [http://dx.doi.org/10.1007/s10488-018-0850-5] [PMID: 29450781]

[3] A.K. Nikhath, K. Subrahmanyam, and R. Vasavi, *Building a K-Nearest Neighbor Classifier for Text Categorization,* 2016.

[4] M. Benitez, J. Tian, M. Kelly, V. Selvakumaran, M. Phelan, M.A. Mazurowski, J.Y. Lo, G.D. Rubin, and R. Henao, *Combining deep learning methods and human knowledge to identify abnormalities in computed tomography (CT) reports" Medical Imaging,* 2019.

[5] M.A. Pedro, R. Baker, O. Montalvo, A. Nakama, and J.D. Gobert, *Using Text Replay Tagging to*

*Produce Detectors of Systematic Experimentation Behavior Patterns.* Educational Data Mining, 2010.

[6] S. Sutha, M.C. Kandasamy, and M.N. Prakash, *Image Retrieval with Relational Semantic Indexing Color and Gray Images*, 2020.

[7] M.A. Sanglikar, and D.C. Kothari, *Named Entity Recognition System for Hindi Language: A Hybrid Approach*, 2011.

[8] S.P. Yadav, S. Zaidi, C.D.S. Nascimento, V.H.C. de Albuquerque, and S.S. Chauhan, "Analysis and Design of automatically generating for GPS Based Moving Object Tracking System", *International Conference on Artificial Intelligence and Smart Communication (AISC),* 2023 pp. 1-5 Greater Noida, India.
[http://dx.doi.org/10.1109/AISC56616.2023.10085180]

[9] A. Almuhareb, W.A. Almutairi, H. Al-Tuwaijri, A. Almubarak, and M. Khan, "Recognition of Modern Arabic Poems", *J. Softw.,* vol. 10, pp. 454-464, 2015.
[http://dx.doi.org/10.17706/jsw.10.4.454-464]

[10] S. P. Yadav, and S. Yadav, "Mathematical implementation of fusion of medical images in continuous wavelet domain", *Journal of Advanced Research in dynamical and control system,* vol. 10, no. 10, pp. 45-54, 2019.

[11] B.L. Ribeiro, and J.A. Franck, "Machine Learning to Classify Vortex Wakes of Energy Harvesting Oscillating Foils", *AIAA J.,* 2022.

[12] A. Naresh, and P. Venkata Krishna, "An efficient approach for sentiment analysis using machine learning algorithm", *Evol. Intell.,* vol. 14, no. 2, pp. 725-731, 2021.
[http://dx.doi.org/10.1007/s12065-020-00429-1]

[13] A. Lahmadi, A. Duque, N. Heraief, and J. Francq, *MitM Attack Detection in BLE Networks Using Reconstruction and Classification Machine Learning Techniques.* PKDD/ECML Workshops, 2020.
[http://dx.doi.org/10.1007/978-3-030-65965-3_10]

[14] T.A. Abdullah, M.S. Zahid, T.B. Tang, W. Ali, and M. Nasser, "Explainable Deep Learning Model for Cardiac Arrhythmia Classification", *2022 International Conference on Future Trends in Smart Communities (ICFTSC),* pp. 87-92, 2022.
[http://dx.doi.org/10.1109/ICFTSC57269.2022.10039860]

[15] T. To, N. Nguyen, D. Vo, N. Le-Pham, H. Nguyen, and M. Tran, "HCMUS MediaEval 2021: Multi-Model Decision Method Applied on Data Augmentation for COVID-19 Conspiracy Theories Classification", *Proceedings of the MediaEval Workshop 2021,* vol. 15, no. 2, pp. 123-130, Dec. 2021.

CHAPTER 2

# A Practicable E-commerce-Based Text-Classification System

**Sidhant Das**[1,*]

[1] *Centre for Interdisciplinary Research in Business and Technology, Chitkara University Institute of Engineering and Technology, Chitkara University, Punjab, India*

**Abstract:** This article examines the features of the dealer's brush list evaluation material in light of research findings on misleading assessment and identification of online purchasing. A Gated Recurrent Unit (GRU) model using keyword weighting is presented as a solution to the issue that it is challenging for the DL model to collect the feature data of the whole assessment text in a false evaluation identifying job. The TF-IDF technique is first used to generate the list of keywords, and then that list's weight is applied to the word vector. Finally, a weighted vector of words is categorised using this method of the model to finish the recognition job of erroneous evaluation, replacing the pooling component of the GRU model with a constrained Boltzmann machine. By using a variety of text categorization algorithms and comparing their results in terms of correctness and performance, this research aspires to represent the practical benefits of applications that use machine learning in the real world. We built a system that can run several text classification algorithms, and we used that system to create models that were educated using actual data taken from E-Commerce, a virtual fashion e-commerce platform. The Convolutional Neural Network technique achieved the greatest mean accuracy of 96.08% (with a range of 85.44% to 99.99%) with an average deviation of 5.65%.

**Keywords:** Feature extraction with machine learning, Text classification, Text mining.

## INTRODUCTION

E-commerce platforms should prioritize pre-sale customer support since it helps improve the purchase experience for potential consumers. We propose AliMe KG, a domain knowledge graph in E-commerce that contains user issues, POIs, item information, and linkages there between [1, 2] to better serve consumers. It is

* **Corresponding author Sidhant Das:** Centre for Interdisciplinary Research in Business and Technology, Chitkara University Institute of Engineering and Technology, Chitkara University, Punjab, India;
E-mail: sidhant.das.orp@chitkara.edu.in

useful for gauging user interest, preparing for sales conversations, and writing up guides. Trading online is not a novel idea [3]. By removing the need for physically stored papers and replacing them with digital ones, businesses may save time and money [4, 5]. E-commerce, or electronic commerce, is a kind of business transaction that takes place *via* the open Internet. It has become a major part of people's daily routine. Therefore, businesses of all sizes must work quickly to create a reliable E-commerce system [6, 7]. The primary components analysis (PCA) is a statistical method used to examine the impact of key variables and attributes on the growth of electronic commerce [8]. The findings are calculated using the PCA model and expert ratings. Primary components and factor analysis (PCFA) are used to examine the effectiveness of the security mechanism used in E-Commerce transactions. The analysis findings represent the major function indexes of assessment in security methods in E-Commerce affairs [9], and are based on the PCFA model and the ratings by experts. Based on the results of the case study, it is clear that some indices play a crucial part in the analysis and assessment of the primary function indices, and that all evaluations should be considered. Using logic and reasoning, we may deduce that using PCFA to evaluate security techniques in E-Commerce business is feasible, given the goal of reducing data loss [10].

The following is the outline for this paper. The experimental setup is described briefly in Section 2, our study is described in depth in Section 3, along with the datasets, evaluation metrics, and features used in our analysis, and the results are evaluated, a conclusion is drawn, and future work is discussed in Section 4.

## RELATED WORK

The goal of this research is to help AirAsia better serve its online shoppers by analysing the influence of e-commerce sites on the airline's customers' purchasing habits. This study used a qualitative approach based on in-depth interviews. E-commerce websites have an influence on consumers' purchasing habits, and this report will help the organisation better understand this effect and implement successful ideas. AirAsia has to learn more about its customers' purchasing habits if it wants to succeed. As a result, AirAsia has to invest time and energy into studying customer preferences to better serve them [11].

We used AliMe KG in a number of real-world use cases, including shopping guides, property inquiry answering, and the creation of selling points, and saw significant financial returns. In this work, we systematically explain our method for building a domain knowledge graph out of unstructured text, and we show its commercial usefulness *via* a number of examples. Our results demonstrate the viability and potential benefit of extracting structured information from unstructured text in the vertical domain [12].

This research investigates the ways in which women have established themselves in various sectors of the online economy. How has the rise of online shopping affected the status of women in society? And how can governments encourage e-commerce growth in low-income regions? Most examples of businesses run by women that have found success in business-to-consumer (B2C) e-commerce focus on selling niche goods to affluent customers. The government plays a pivotal role in stimulating the growth of e-commerce by actual realistic actions [13], even if it is widely recognised that the private sector should take the main role in the creation and usage of e-commerce.

In this paper, a.NET-based e-commerce framework is proposed. It provides examples of the most frequent E-commerce system functions, a system enclosure, designing concepts for the system's levels, and the most pressing technical issues associated with the system. The standard features of an E-commerce platform have been implemented on this one. As has been shown in the real world, this kind of E-commerce platform may fulfill the requirements of several typical businesses such as Electronic market, .NET framework, purchases, temporary storage, and subscriptions [14].

Evidence from case studies demonstrates that some features and qualities have a significant impact on the growth of the e-commerce industry; nevertheless, all of these elements must be considered in order to achieve a successful outcome. Analysis and debate lead to the conclusion that using PCA to analyse the impact of E-Commerce development is feasible [15], predicated on the assumption that data loss can be kept to a minimum.

## PROPOSED WORK

### Problem Formulation

Instead of basing their decisions on the semantic resemblance of words, text classification algorithms take into account the closeness of term vectors in the vector space using different approaches (such as cosine similarity). However, the similarity score suffers when words with distinct forms owing to suffixes, prefixes, or tenses are evaluated as separate vectors. We devised a procedure called "Stemming" to remove suffixes, prefixes, and tenses from words and return them to their root forms so as to circumvent this issue. Next, we use a process called "Vectorization" to convert every sentence in our data set into a numerical value. Words are converted into machine-readable values (such as integers or floating-point numbers) inside a limited vector space. Vectorization assigns a numerical value (vector) to each distinct word, and then prediction algorithms employ these vectors to address classification issues. CountVectorizer iteratively counts every phrase in a text and provides a vector containing the counted words and the frequency with which they occur in the document.

Our experimental technique continues with the creation of the dataset utilised for training, which consists of linearized features and target classes, following the "Vectorization" process outlined above. The last stage is to use the trained model with the vectorized input query to choose the proper machine-learning techniques and make sufficiently accurate predictions. Fig. (**1**) uses a realistic scenario that we anticipate encountering to demonstrate the aforementioned general approach and procedures.

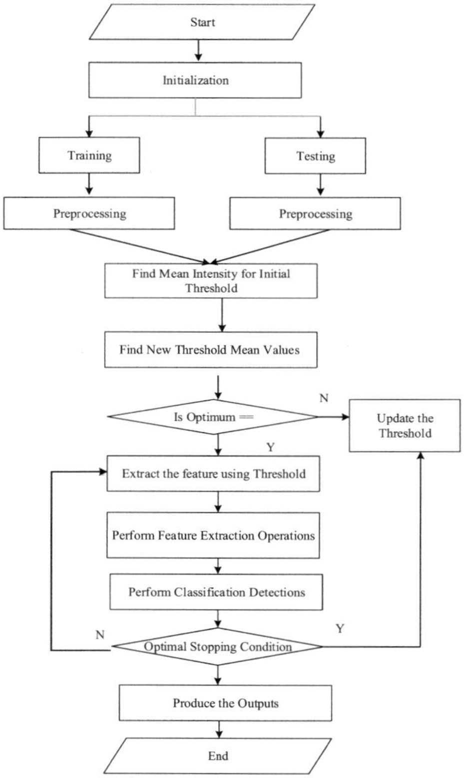


**Fig. (1).** System Flowchart.

## Dataset Description

Classification-based E-commerce text database for "Electronics," "Household," "Books," and "Clothing and Accessories," which together account for about 80% of all products sold on any E-commerce website.

There are two columns in the ".csv" file: the first contains the class name, and the second contains the corresponding data point. The item and its description from an online store provide the data point.

The characteristics of the dataset are as follows:

- Multivariate data set characteristics.
- 50425 total occurrences.
- The Course Load: 4.
- Part: Computer science.
- Distinctive Features: Real.
- Attribute Count: 1.
- Allied Errands: Classification.
- Lost Morals? No.

## System Model

In this research, we present a keyword-weighted evaluation text classification system. The results of the experiments suggest that (1) keywords weighting may prioritise the high-discrimination key evaluation, provide an improved feature expression of assessment text, and better correct the erroneous evaluation. Two SOFTGRU models can extract more semantic features from e-commerce evaluation texts, have better classification performance, and offer more benefits for the false evaluation under a variety of commodity evaluation sets and sentence vector dimensions.

Information content, how evaluation phrases are used, and the diversity of the fake evaluation in comparison to the genuine shopping evaluation are all different between the real as well as the false evaluation in the text data from e-commerce product reviews. Real consumers prefer to assess fewer words when trying to produce the impact of enhancing or smearing products. This work offers a TF-IDF method driven on keyword weighting to improve the degree of false assessment in accordance with the features of evaluation data. A vocabulary is formed from the language used in the keywords, improving the model's classification accuracy by giving more weight to keyword vectors that score over a threshold. Fig. (**1**) represents the System Flowchart.

### *Procedure*

Calculation of textual density by TF-IDF.

### *Intake*

E-commerce assessment text set $T = \{T_1, T_2, ..., T_N\}$.

1 Word frequency count $f(T,x)$ of each word in set of text $T = \{T_1, T_2, ..., T_N\}$
2 Sets of words with a frequency greater than the mean $C = \{C_1, C_2, ..., C_N\}$
3 Find out how much each word is worth TF-IDF in $C$
4 Recollected words with a mathematical expectation score above and above, compositional keyword set $X = \{X_1, X_2, ..., X_N\}$ And $T$, $C$ correspondingly vectorized through Word2Vec $T' C'$
5 for every $T_i'$ do
6 Using the text set, find the i-th word vector $t_i'$
7 for every $X_i'$ do
8 Using the text set, find the i-th word vector $X_i'$
9 Calculation of the value $\text{sim}_i = \frac{c_i s_i}{\|c_i\| \|s_i\|}$, join the collection Sim = {$\text{sim}_1$, $\text{sim}_2$,…,sim $\text{m}_n$}
10 end for
11 Select $maxsim_n$ in the set Sim as the weight $w_n$ of the word vector $t_n$, add the weight set $W = \{w_1, w_2, ..., w_n\}$
12 end for
13 Normalized weight $w_i = \frac{\exp(w_i)}{\sum_{j=1}^{n} \exp(w_j)}$
14 return $W_i$

After texts pass through the notice based deep GRU model, they have been effectively preprocessed. Word Embedded layers, Dropout layers, GRU layers, Tanh layers, Attention Layers, and Softmax Layer are only few of the layers that make up the proposed Attention oriented Deep GRU.

Fasttext, a word-based embedding approach, is used for feature extraction. Each Letter Here Is (ϖ)is broken down into a string of words in the tweet. To ensure accurate rare-word recognition, this process is carried out. The process of dividing words into smaller units is predicated on a previously determined value for k. In this notation, the root word is written as the sum of all of its morphemes,

$$s(\varpi, \epsilon) = \sum_{h \in H_{\varpi}} g_h \, v_{\epsilon} \quad \textbf{(1)}$$

Where, $h$ indicates each component word, and $H\varpi$ indicates the group of sub-words. εdenotes the context and $v_\epsilon$represents the context vector in each case. For better regularisation, the embedding layer's output is sent to a dropout layer, whose job it is to avoid overfitting by randomly removing certain units. The GRU layer receives the encoded words and generates the output $y_t$ with intake $v_t$ and $y_{t-1}$ as formulated below,

$$rs_t = \sigma(J_r v_t + D_r y_{t-1}) \tag{2}$$

$$ud_t = \sigma(J_u v_t + D_u y_{t-1}) \tag{3}$$

$$\tilde{y}_t = tanh\big(J_c v_t + D(rs_t \odot y_{t-1})\big) \tag{4}$$

$$y_t = (1 - ud_t) \odot y_{t-1} + ud_t \odot \tilde{y}_t \tag{5}$$

Where $rs_t$, $ud_t$, and $y_t$ are, in order, a concealed gate, an update gate, and a reset gate in dimension d. σ is the sigmoid function's symbol, $J_r$, $J_u$, $J_c$are $D_r$, $D_u$, $D$some risky GRU layer settings. Non-linear categorization boundaries for making difficult judgements may be learned using the Tanh function. In particular, we have retrieved characteristics related to intensifiers, diminuers, negation, morphemes, semantics, and syntax. SentiWordNet is a lexical repository used for studying the semantic connections between words. Each word is given a good and negative score based on the synsets, which may be expressed as, Fig. (**2**). represents the Attention GRU-based Text Classification.

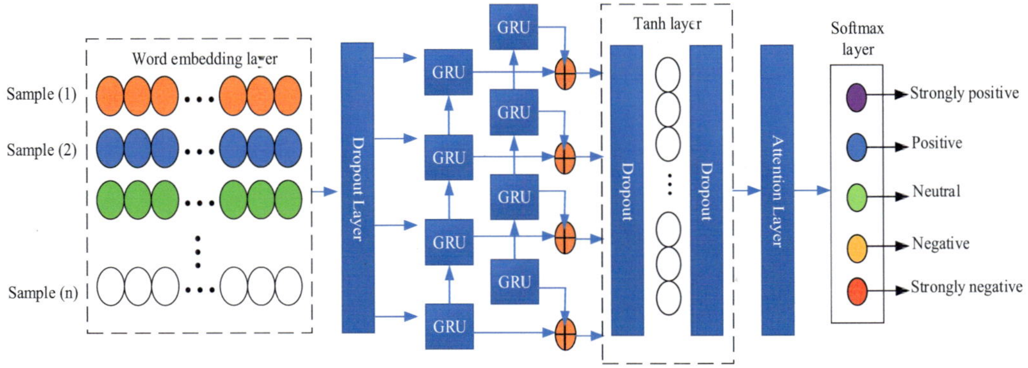


**Fig. (2).** Attention GRU based text classification.

$$P_s = \frac{1}{b} \sum_{st \in Z} Sp(st) \tag{6}$$

$$N_s = \frac{1}{b} \sum_{st \in Z} Sn(st) \tag{7}$$

Where *Sp* and *Sn* Senti Word Net's favourable and negative ratings are shown. $P_s$, and $N_s$ indicate the word's favourable and negative evaluations in terms of synsets.

*b* means that there are a lot of synonyms for that term $\varpi$. The attention layer receives these features and their scores, predicts the relevance of each feature, and then removes duplicate features to deal with dimensionality reduction. It is possible to calculate the feature vector using the weighted sum method, as,

$$y^{(k)} = \sum_{n=1}^{P_k} \gamma_i^{(k)} y_i^{(k)} \quad \textbf{(8)}$$

Where $y_i^{(k)}$ is the output of the GRU layer at *i*, and the weight $y_i^{(k)}$is expressed as

$$\gamma_i^{(k)} = aj_i^{(k)} + b \quad \textbf{(9)}$$

Where, *a, b* represent the network settings in a corresponding manner. In the softmax layer, feature vectors are sorted into one of five categories based on the attention layer's output: Strongly Positive, Positive, Negative, Strongly Negative, and Neutral. The pre-processed tweets serve as input to the proposed Focus based GRU model for sentiment classification, and the resulting classifications are shown in Fig. (**2**).

## RESULTS AND DISCUSSION

Experiments on classification and comparison are conducted using the SVM method, the SOFTGRU model, and the DBN model provided in this study. Only the earphone assessment dataset was utilised here, and the 7:3 split between the training and the test data was chosen at random. Fig. (**3**) displays the experimental outcomes.

The above graphics demonstrates the fact that SOFTGRU algorithm maintains consistency across four performance measures of accuracy, precision, recall, and F1-Measure. There is a lot of variation. The method exhibits a general rising trend as the number of training samples grows, suggesting that the accuracy of classification grows in tandem with the training learning. The efficiency of each method presented in this research is also clearly superior than that of competing algorithms.

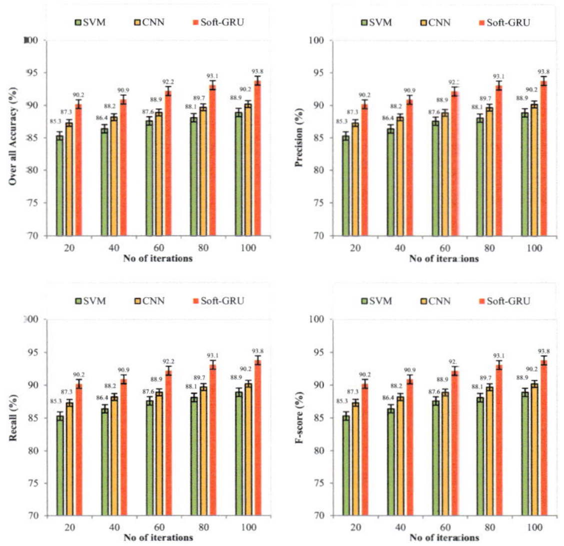


**Fig. (3).** Performance analysis.

## CONCLUSION

In this research, we offer a keyword-weighted approach for evaluating texts for categorization. The results of the experiments suggest that (1) keyword weighting may prioritise the high-discrimination key evaluation, provide a better classification feature manifestation of the evaluated text, and better perform the erroneous evaluation. (2) Comparing the classification models' performance across multiple commodity evaluation sets as well as sentence vector dimensions reveals that the SogtGRU model is better equipped to extract semantic qualities of e-commerce assessment text, resulting in better classification performance and more benefits for the false evaluation.

## REFERENCES

[1] Q. Zhi-ming, and L. Jinxian, "Application of PCFA in Assessing Security Technique in E-Commerce Affairs", *2009 Second International Symposium on Electronic Commerce and Security,* pp. 413-417, 2009.
[http://dx.doi.org/10.1109/ISECS.2009.25]

[2] L. Liu, "Investigation on E-Commerce Based on Suffix Trees and Moore's Law", *2009 International Conference on Environmental Science and Information Application Technology,* pp. 527-529, 2009.

[3] C-P. Wei, P.J. Hu, and Y-X. Dong, "Managing document categories in e-commerce environments: an evolution-based approach", *Eur. J. Inf. Syst.,* vol. 11, no. 3, pp. 208-222, 2002.
[http://dx.doi.org/10.1057/palgrave.ejis.3000429]

[4] D. Zhang, and M. Zhang, "The Enterprises Logistics Information Platform Framework based on E-Commerce", *2007 IEEE International Conference on Automation and Logistics,* pp. 880-883, 2007.
[http://dx.doi.org/10.1109/ICAL.2007.4338689]

[5] L. Jian-ning, "Security scheme for mobile agent-based e-commerce", *Journal of Naval University of Engineering,* vol. 16, no. 4, pp. 45-50, 2024.

[6] D. Da-ke, "Establish E-commerce Platform Based on Mobile Agent", *Anhui Nongye Daxue Xuebao,* 2005.

[7] S.P. Yadav, K. Baalamurugan, S.R. Kumar, A. Kumar, V. Kumar, and S. Padmanaban, "Blockchain Security", *In Blockchain Security in Cloud Computing, EAI/Springer Innovations in Communication and Computing, Cham: Springer,* pp. 1-20, 2021. [http://dx.doi.org/10.1007/978-3-030-70501-5_1]

[8] M. Khan, "Fingerprint Biometric-based Self-Authentication and Deniable Authentication Schemes for the Electronic World", *IETE Tech. Rev.,* vol. 26, no. 3, pp. 191-195, 2009. [http://dx.doi.org/10.4103/0256-4602.50703]

[9] V.D. Dang, *Coalition formation and operation in virtual organisations,* 2004.

[10] D. Xiao, X. Liao, G. Tang, and C. Li, "Using Chebyshev chaotic map to construct infinite length hash chains", *2004 International Conference on Communications, Circuits and Systems (IEEE Cat. No.04EX914),* vol. 1, no. 1, pp. 11-12, 2004.

[11] P.D. Singh, G.K. Wen, D.M. Kee, G.S. Yee, L.C. Ying, F.K. Ling, M. Shammas, G.R. Tandra, and L.G. Sin, "The impact of AirAsia's e-commerce websites on its consumer buying behavior", *Int. J. Tourism Hosp. Asia Pac,* vol. 5, no. 3, pp. 112-125.

[12] F. Li, H. Chen, G. Xu, T. Qiu, F. Ji, J. Zhang, and H. Chen, "AliMeKG: Domain Knowledge Graph Construction and Application in E-commerce", *Proceedings of the 29th ACM International Conference on Information & Knowledge Management,* 2020. [http://dx.doi.org/10.1145/3340531.3412685]

[13] S.P. Yadav, S. Zaidi, C.D.S. Nascimento, V.H.C. de Albuquerque, and S.S. Chauhan, "Analysis and Design of automatically generating for GPS Based Moving Object Tracking System", *2023 International Conference on Artificial Intelligence and Smart Communication (AISC),* 2023 pp. 1-5. Greater Noida, India. [http://dx.doi.org/10.1109/AISC56616.2023.10085180]

[14] H. Longjun, Z. Caiying, D. Li-ping, and H. Minghe, *Research and Implementation of E-commerce Platform Based on.* NET Framework, 2009.

[15] S. Sanyuan, and W. Xiaoli, "Investigation of primary components analysis in influential factors of E-Commerce development", *2009 ISECS International Colloquium on Computing, Communication, Control, and Management,* vol. 2, pp. 399-402, 2009. [http://dx.doi.org/10.1109/CCCM.2009.5267453]

CHAPTER 3

# AI Model for Text Classification Using FastText

**Sorabh Sharma**[1,*]

[1] *Centre for Interdisciplinary Research in Business and Technology, Chitkara University Institute of Engineering and Technology, Chitkara University, Punjab, India*

**Abstract:** The purpose of text categorization, a machine learning technique, is to automatically assign tags or categories to texts. Natural language processing (NLP)-based text classifiers can quickly analyse vast volumes of text and classify it based on emotions, themes, and human intent. FastText was created by Facebook's AI Research team and is available to the public as a free library. Its primary goal is the efficient and accurate processing of big datasets in order to provide scalable remedies for the problems of text categorization and representation. Traditional machine learning techniques used in most text categorization models suffer from issues including the curse of dimensionality and subpar performance. This research offers a fastText-based AI text classification model to address the aforementioned issues. The fastText approach allows our model to create a low-dimensional, continuous, and high-quality representation of text by mining the text for relevant information through feature engineering. The experiment uses Python to define the text dataset, and the results demonstrate that our model outperforms the baseline model trained using classic ML methods in terms of accuracy, recall, and F values.

**Keywords:** Emotional polarity judgment, Feature engineering, Machine learning, Text classification.

## INTRODUCTION

As a result of the COVID-19 pandemic, all global activity ceased. Taking care of one's mental and emotional well-being is as crucial as taking care of one's physical well-being under such circumstances. Since telecommuting has become the norm, users now make use of Twitter to express how they're feeling about the situation, and their tweets may be analysed in this way [1, 2]. Sentiment analysis of text is a necessary part of many NLP tasks. The use of sentiment analysis to sift through Internet data for useful insights is becoming more important as social media platforms grow in popularity [3]. In light of recent developments, we're considering using models based on deep learning to manage sentiment categori-

* **Correspondending author Sorabh Sharma:** Centre for Interdisciplinary Research in Business and Technology, Chitkara University Institute of Engineering and Technology, Chitkara University, Punjab, India;
E-mail: sorabh.sharma.orp@chitkara.edu.in

**Pankaj Kumar Mishra and Satya Prakash Yadav (Eds.)**

zation. As a result of the service malfunction that happened on July 20, 2019, Bank Mandiri's share price plummeted 0.95 percent at the start of trade on July 22, 2019, compared to its opening price [4, 5, 6]. Looking for a connection between Twitter or online media coverage attitudes or views and the price of the stock of Bank Mandiri (BMRI) [7], the fall proceeded to reach 1.27 percent from the previous price. The use of text mining to acquire data, optimisation of the model using Logistic Regression, as well as feature expansion with FastText are used for predicting sentiment by decreasing lexical discrepancies [8]. Then, at the year's conclusion, a Pearson Correlation Coefficient test is conducted to see whether sentiment forecasts are correlated with stock prices from May through September. Connectivity to Bank Mandiri's stock price data in order to learn how satisfied customers are with a certain service offered by Bank Mandiri [9]. Automated text classification tasks have been proven to improve to a fair degree when combining efficient word representation methods (word embeddings) with contemporary machine learning models. However, in terms of inadequate word vector representations for training, the efficacy of such methods has not yet been assessed. When it comes to pattern identification, picture analysis, and text categorization, Convolutional Neural Networks have been shown to be very effective [10].

## RELATED WORK

The goal of our research system is to analyse user emotions over time by collecting data from Twitter and processing it based on keywords. Fasttext, a text categorization tool developed by Facebook, does this by categorising tweets into the following states of mind as quickly and accurately as possible: angry, relieved, bored, happy, hateful, fun, loving, surprised, enthusiastic, sad, and empty. FastText is a popular Natural Language Processing (NLP) Library for representing and categorising text. Classifying emotions across time sheds light on the state of mind of the general public and how it has evolved [11].

A text emotion classification model using FastText & multi-scale DPCNN is presented to enhance the effectiveness of Chinese text emotion classification. The FastText model is first used to build a text vector matrix. After that, a multi-scale filter is used to extract numerous feature maps from the content vector matrix. At last, the DPCNN model is fed the combined feature maps for sentiment analysis. Tests are conducted using the Chinese sentiment mining corpus (ChnSentiCorp) data set, and the findings from various sets of tests that compare the accuracy of text sentiment classification using the proposed model with other techniques [12] demonstrate its efficacy.

In this research, we introduce the use of a Convolutional Neural Network (CNN) inside a framework we call fastText. To kick things off, we feed a CNN using word vector representations generated by fastText. The goal of FastText is to both create an automatic model of a single word and accurately represent word distance. This one allows the parameters to be set at a good CNN point, which improves the effectiveness of neural networks in this setting. Second, we develop a Convolutional Neural Network structure tailored to emotional analysis. In this architecture, we combine two groups of convolutional layers with pooling layers. To the best of our knowledge, this is the initial occasion that a 9-layer design and architecture model based on fastText and CNN have been utilized to evaluate the sentiment of sentences. To make our model more precise and adaptable, we employ the Normalisation and Dropout methods alongside Rectified Linear Unit (ReLU) regression. For this experiment, we used a publicly accessible dataset consisting of excerpts from movie reviews labelled as either "negative," "slightly negative," "neutral," "moderately positive," or "positive" to evaluate our methods. With a test precision of 96.4%, ourReLU paired network outperforms other neural network models on this dataset [13].

Applying Logistic Regression and including feature expansion in the FastText scenario with a split of 90% of training and 10% of testing yields 71.8% efficiency in the model improvement scenario. Using an optimisation model on both positive and negative sentiment, we find that negative sentiment correlates most strongly with changes in BMRI stock from May 2019 to the close of September 2019 [14].

In this research and experiments, we look at how the CNN model may be used to solve text classification issues. We used six publicly accessible benchmark datasets—Ag News, Amazon Full & Polarity, Yahoo Question choice Yelp Full, & Polarity—to train our classification model utilising the popular word embedding generation methodology, Fast Text. In addition, the suggested model has been evaluated using a non-benchmark dataset including tweets about U.S. airline companies. Fast Text as embedding words was shown to be a promising method in this study [15].

## PROPOSED WORK

### System Model

Fig. (**1**) illustrates the overarching concept of the approach we suggest in our study to categorise text as harmful, non-toxic, or ambiguous. To get started with this study, we integrated two separate datasets into one larger one. Following this first stage, we use ML classifiers and then DL-based algorithms for further breakdown.

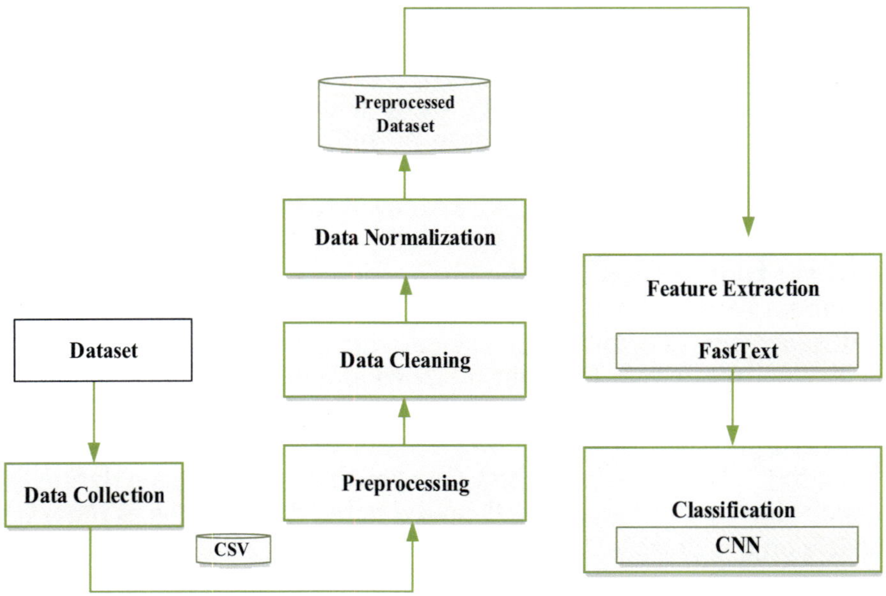


**Fig. (1).** FastText with CNN for text classification.

## FastText Model

Although the time investment in training the model is high, the networks excel in a wide range of NLP-related activities. In 2016, Facebook Researchers made available the tool FastText, which can be used to produce word vectors and text classification. Fig. (**1**) shows the overall structure of the fastText model.

The input portion of the fastText model, in contrast to the standard bag-of-words model, employs the n-gram characteristic of the sentence as input in addition to the word representations matching each syllable in the sentence. Input for a standard bag-of-words model, such as "I like play basketball," would consist of "I," "like," "play," and "basketball," with fasText serving as the model's foundation. In addition to the aforementioned, the n-gram feature is implemented. If there are just two observations, then the average of the terms "I like," "like playing," and "playing basketball" is the supplementary feature. By using n-gram characteristics, fastText is better able to produce a more precise sentence representation than was previously possible with conventional bag-of-words models. FastText takes an average of the input layer's word representation with n-gram characteristics in the hidden layer. FastText predicts the input text label using a hierarchical softmax model in the output layer. Additionally, model training time is drastically cut down when hierarchical softmax is used.

- Learning rate - A setting in an optimisation algorithm that affects the amount of the steps taken between iterations while the algorithm attempts to minimise a loss function.
- Epoch - Adjust the iteration algebra for the model's parameters.
- Window size - Adjusts the current context window's width and height.
- Bucket - The large number of n-gram characteristics necessitates the use of the hash approach for mapping. It is possible for many n-grams to be placed in the same category.
- Loss - In this study, we use the hierarchical softmax loss function.
- Dim - How many words are in the vector that determines the fastText setting.

In multi-class classification issues, an activation function is often a Softmax function, which returns the probability that a given input belongs to one of the k classes. When there is a high number of subcategories and a class imbalance in the data, hierarchical Softmax performs very well. As opposed to a flat, list-like structure, the classes here are presented in a tree distribution. The Huffman code tree is the foundation of the hierarchy softmax layer's structure, with shorter trees used to represent more common classes and longer trees used to represent less common classes. A depth-first search through the nodes of the various branches is performed to determine the likelihood that a particular text matches a class. As a result, improbable branches (or classes) may be eliminated. As a consequence, the classification time for data with a large number of classes is drastically lowered in comparison to more conventional approaches.

Polynomial logistic regression is another name for softmax regression. The training set for softmax regression may be represented as (1).

$$\{(x^{(1)}, y^{(1)}), \ldots, (x^{(m)}, y^{(m)})\}, y^{(i)} \in \{1, 2, \ldots, K\} \tag{1}$$

Each member of the K-dimensional vector the model generates as a result of taking x as input reflects the chance that x corresponds to the current categorization. In particular, we may express the model as $h_0(x)$, as shown in (2).

$$h_\theta(x) = \begin{bmatrix} P(y = 1 \mid x; \theta) \\ P(y = 2 \mid x; \theta) \\ \cdots \\ P(y = K \mid x; \theta) \end{bmatrix} = \frac{1}{\sum_{j=1}^{K} e^{\theta(nr x}} \begin{bmatrix} e^{\theta(1)rx} \\ e^{\theta(2)rx} \\ \cdots \\ e^{\theta(K)rx} \end{bmatrix} \tag{2}$$

The loss function for the relevant paradigm is shown in (3).

$$J(\theta) = -\left[\sum_{i=1}^{m} \sum_{k=1}^{K} 1\{y^{(i)} = k\} \log \frac{e^{\theta(kTt_{x^{(i)}}}}{\sum_{j=1}^{K} e^{\theta\left(//T^{(i)}\right.}}\right] \quad (3)$$

After the aforementioned methods have been used to generate work embeddings, the embeddings are used as input into algorithms for deep neural networks such as MLP, CNN, and LSTM.

- Multi-Layer Perceptron (MLP): In case of tabular datasets like images, texts, or time series, these conventional neural networks have shown to be incredibly useful. More than three distinct layers of neurons make up these structures. They are not helpful in settings that need spatial data related to the data to be considered, and they may lead to repetition with high-dimensional input.
- Convolutional Neural Networks (CNN): This subclass of neural networks outperforms the more popular MLP variant. These showcase its usage in NLP and were originally popular for image processing. Text pattern detection is much improved because of the deeper, sparsely connected layers here, particularly in the presence of noise or outliers.
- LSTM: This RNN variant is capable of learning both text dependence and text context. Because they employ memory cells to gradually update the buried layers, they excel at successively learning complex text relationships.

## RESULTS AND DISCUSSION

The tests were conducted using a laptop outfitted with an Intel (R) Intel (TM) i5-8250u 1.60GHz CPU, 8GB of RAM, and Windows 10 (64-bit personal Chinese version). The algorithm is written in Python 3.7 and utilised by the software. The popular frameworks sklearn and fastText are two examples. Fig. (**2**) depicts the comparison of classification performance.

**Table 1. Outcomes (Samples).**

| Sample | Exactness | Recollection | F-value |
|---|---|---|---|
| MLP | 0.9142 | 0.9249 | 0.9156 |
| CNN | 0.8813 | 0.6339 | 0.6713 |
| LSTM | 0.8637 | 0.8831 | 0.8526 |
| Our typical | 0.9275 | 0.9301 | 0.9286 |

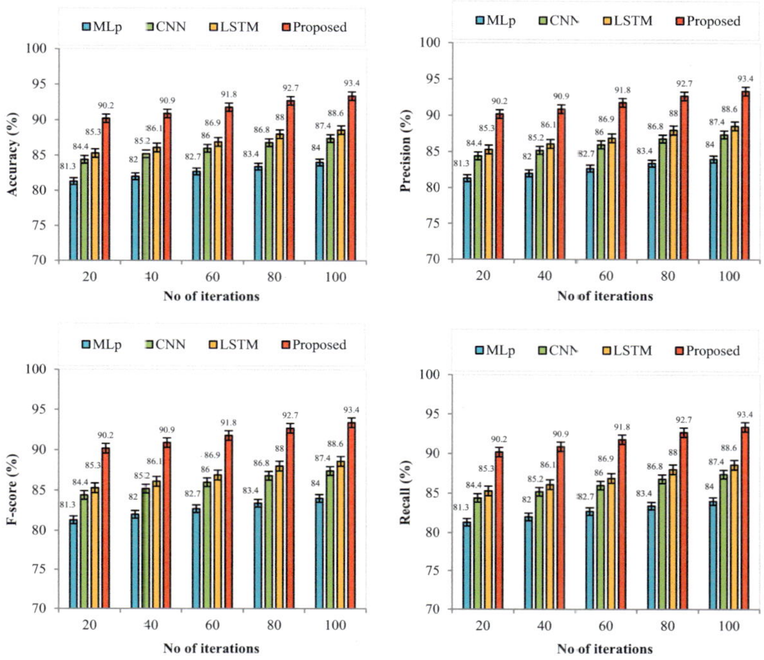


**Fig. (2).** Comparison of samples.

In this research, we use the support vector machine, 1 o-nearest algorithm, as well as the naive Bay to carry out text classification and comparative tests to determine which method produces the best results. When testing the efficacy of a text categorization model built using fastText, each model was tested ten times with no crossover between runs. The dataset was randomly split between a set for training and a test set in each experiment using a 4: 1 split. The model was then taught using the training set, and its performance was evaluated using the test set. Ten separate tests were averaged to determine each model's F value, recall percentage, and accuracy. Table **1** displays the outcomes of the experiments. The experimental findings show that the k-neighbor technique has the worst overall performance among all four text- text-categorization models, with the lowest F value derived by the classification results. One possible explanation is that there are a disproportionately high number of samples that are positive. compared to those that are either neutral or negative. However, the performance of a model will also suffer if a huge quantity of training data is provided since the k-nearest method model is rather simplistic. The Naive Bayes method has a higher F value and greater recall than the 1 o-neighbors approach. The algorithm developed by Naive Bayes also outperforms the k-neighbors strategy in terms of precision. In a user polarisation of sentiment classification job, support vector machines outperformed k-neighboring algorithms and Naive Bayes algorithms, and their F-values were much higher. In terms of accuracy, recall, and F value, the fastText-based text categorization model was superior than the other three. This demonstrates that, in comparison to a traditional machine learning classification algorithm, the fastText-based text classification model is better able to collect as well as utilise attributes tied to emotional polarity in the input text, thereby producing more accurate judgments on the affectionate polarity of user evaluations (Fig. **3**) and Table **3** illustrates the comparison analysis of Accuracy, Precision, Recall, and F-score with respect to the number of iterations.

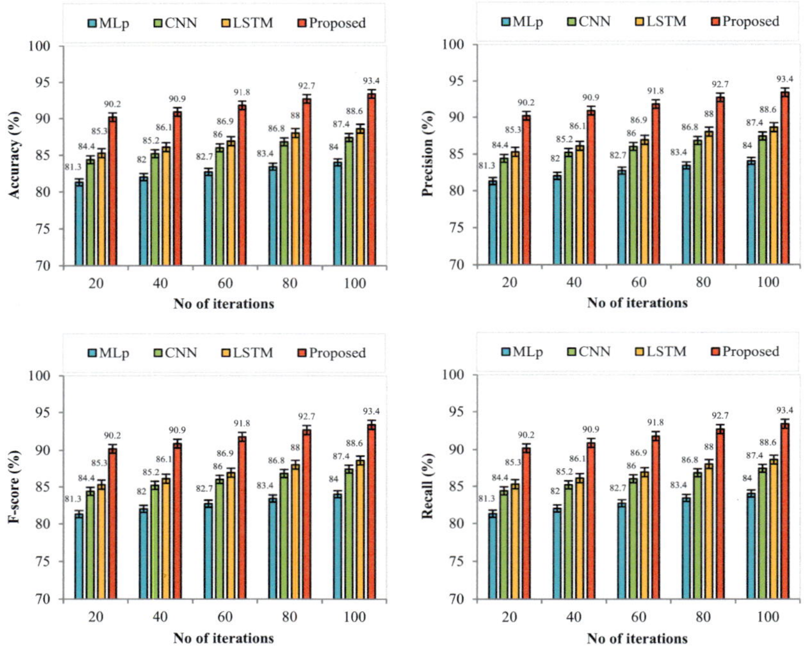


**Fig. (3).** Comparison of iterations.

**Table 2. Outcomes (Iterations).**

| Sample | Exactness | Recollection | F-value |
|---|---|---|---|
| MLP | 0.9142 | 0.9249 | 0.9156 |
| CNN | 0.8813 | 0.6339 | 0.6713 |
| LSTM | 0.8637 | 0.8831 | 0.8526 |
| Our typical | 0.9275 | 0.9301 | 0.9286 |

## CONCLUSION

In this study, we provide a fastText-based text classification algorithm that makes effective use of the cheap-dimensional, ongoing, and high-quality sentence representation produced by fastText to harvest the most crucial information in the data. The fastText-based text categorization model benefits greatly from the use of both. The superior performance of the fastText-based text classification model is shown by comparing it to other popular classification techniques. Classifier efficacy is also profoundly impacted by text preparation and feature engineering. Some tokenization findings fall short of expectations when conducted during the text preprocessing step, making improvements to tokenization accuracy a promising area for further study. In addition, feature engineering has been successful, but it has not yet been investigated how various features affect the classification accuracy. Assigning varying weights to characteristics using machine learning will allow for improved text categorization models in the future.

## REFERENCES

[1] H.A. Chowdhury, M.A. Imon, and M.S. Islam, "Authorship Attribution in Bengali Literature Using fastText's Hierarchical Classifier", *2018 4th International Conference on Electrical Engineering and Information & Communication Technology (iCEEiCT),* 2018 pp. 102-106. [http://dx.doi.org/10.1109/CEEICT.2018.8628109]

[2] Z. Ibrahim, S. Haidar, and I. Sbeity, "Large-scale Text-based Video Classification using Contextual Features", *European Journal of Electrical Engineering and Computer Science,* 2019.

[3] N.R. Aljohani, A. Fayoumi, and S.U. Hassan, "A novel focal-loss and class-weight-aware convolutional neural network for the classification of in-text citations", *J. Inf. Sci.,* vol. 49, no. 1, pp. 79-92, 2023. [http://dx.doi.org/10.1177/0165551521991022]

[4] M.R. Hossain, M.M. Hoque, M.A.A. Dewan, N. Siddique, M.N. Islam, and I.H. Sarker, "Authorship Classification in a Resource Constraint Language Using Convolutional Neural Networks", *IEEE Access,* vol. 9, pp. 100319-100338, 2021. [http://dx.doi.org/10.1109/ACCESS.2021.3095967]

[5] Y. Dai, H. Hua, C. Ma, H. Zhang, and L. Yang, "A Fusion Method for Word Vector Based on Fasttext-KdTree", *2019 Seventh International Conference on Advanced Cloud and Big Data (CBD),* pp. 229-234, 2019. [http://dx.doi.org/10.1109/CBD.2019.00049]

[6] A.V. Kurtukova, A.S. Romanov, A.M. Fedotova, and A.A. Shelupanov, "Application of machine learning methods and feature selection based on a genetic algorithm in solving the problem of determining the authorship of a Russian-language text for cybersecurity", *Proceedings of Tomsk State University of Control Systems and Radioelectronics,* 2022.

[7] S.L. Vaikole, and S. Holkar, "Audio and Video Toxic Comments Detection and Classification", *Int. J. Eng. Res. Technol. (Ahmedabad),* p. 9, 2020.

[8] S.P. Yadav, S. Zaidi, C.D.S. Nascimento, V.H.C. de Albuquerque, and S.S. Chauhan, "Analysis and Design of automatically generating for GPS Based Moving Object Tracking System", *2023 International Conference on Artificial Intelligence and Smart Communication (AISC),* 2023 pp. 1-5. Greater Noida, India. [http://dx.doi.org/10.1109/AISC56616.2023.10085180]

[9] S. Tabashum, M.M. Hossain, M.A. Islam, M.Y. Mahafi Taz Zahara, and F.N. Fami, "Performance Analysis of Most Prominent Machine Learning and Deep Learning Algorithms in Classifying Bangla Crime News Articles", *Proceedings of the IEEE Region 10 Symposium (TENSYMP),* pp. 496-501, June 2020. [http://dx.doi.org/10.1109/TENSYMP50017.2020.9230785]

[10] Z. Wang, "Study on Chinese Text Classification for FastText Combining TF-RF and Improved Random Walk Model", *Proceedings of the 2021 14th International Conference on Signal Processing (ICSP),* pp. 987-992, Dec. 2021. [http://dx.doi.org/10.1109/ICSP51882.2021.9408910]

[11] A. Kulai, M. Sankhe, S. Anglekar, and A. Halbe, "Emotion Analysis of Covid Tweets using FastText Supervised Classifier model", *2021 International Conference on Communication information and Computing Technology (ICCICT),* pp. 1-6, 2021. [http://dx.doi.org/10.1109/ICCICT50803.2021.9510156]

[12] S. Tsai, and L. Shi, "Chinese Text Sentiment Classification Model Based on FastText and Multi-scale Deep Pyramid Convolutional Neural Network", *2022 International Conference on Computation, Big-Data and Engineering (ICCBE),* pp. 75-77, 2022. [http://dx.doi.org/10.1109/ICCBE56101.2022.9888185]

[13] S. P. Yadav, and S. Yadav, "Mathematical implementation of fusion of medical images in continuous wavelet domain", *Journal of Advanced Research in dynamical and control system,* vol. 10, no. 10, pp. 45-54, 2019.

[14] M.F. Putra, and E.B. Setiawan, "Influence of Sentiment on Mandiri Bank Stocks (BMRI) Using Feature Expansion with FastText and Logistic Regression Classification", *2022 International Conference on Advanced Creative Networks and Intelligent Systems (ICACNIS),* pp. 1-7, 2022. [http://dx.doi.org/10.1109/ICACNIS57039.2022.10055450]

[15] M. Umer, Z. Imtiaz, M. Ahmad, M. Nappi, C. Medaglia, G.S. Choi, and A. Mehmood, "Impact of convolutional neural network and FastText embedding on text classification", *Multimedia Tools Appl.,* vol. 82, no. 4, pp. 5569-5585, 2023. [http://dx.doi.org/10.1007/s11042-022-13459-x]

## CHAPTER 4

# An Algorithm for Textual Classification of News Utilizing Artificial Intelligence Technology

**Rahul Mishra**[1,*]

[1] *Centre for Interdisciplinary Research in Business and Technology, Chitkara University Institute of Engineering and Technology, Chitkara University, Punjab, India*

**Abstract:** The rate at which technology is improving is increasing all throughout the world. Every day, a tremendous amount of textual data is produced as a result of the Internet, websites, business data, medical information, and the media. Extraction of interesting patterns from text data with varied lengths such as views, summaries, and facts is a challenging issue. This work provides a deep learning (DL) algorithm-based approach to news text classification to address the issues of large amounts of text data and cumbersome features obtaining value in news. Although the relationship among words as well as categories has a significant impact on the categorization of news text, previous approaches to text classification relied solely on the knowledge of the connections between words to make their classification decisions. This research uses the idea of a tailored algorithm to provide a CNN, LSTM, and MLP-based customizable ensemble framework for categorising news text data. The proposed model is based on a parallel representation of word vectors and word dispersion. We feed the term vector to the CNN module to convey the relationship between words, as well as nourish the discrete vector corresponding to the relationship between words and categories into the MLP module to achieve deep learning of the spatial data on features, the time-series feature information, and the connection words and categories in news texts. Extensive experimental study confirmed the dependability and efficacy of the proposed approach. The experimental results demonstrated that the proposed method improved the most - in terms of precision, recall rate, and comprehensive value, while also addressing the problems of text length, extraction of features issues with the news text, and classification of news text.

**Keywords:** Artificial intelligence, CNN, LSTM and MLP, Text classification.

* **Corresponding author Rahul Mishra:** Centre for Interdisciplinary Research in Business and Technology, Chitkara University Institute of Engineering and Technology, Chitkara University, Punjab, India;
E-mail: rahul.mishra.orp@chitkara.edu.in

**Pankaj Kumar Mishra and Satya Prakash Yadav (Eds.)**

## INTRODUCTION

Cystoscopy clinical documentation consists of both written and visual information. However, inadequate data handling in ordinary clinical practice continues to restrict secondary applications of visual judgment data for educational as well as research reasons [1]. Methods: Three main components—data management, annotation management, and utilisation management—make up the conceptual framework developed for standardised cystoscopy documentation. For quality assurance and problem-solving, the Swiss-cheese paradigm was presented [2]. With FAIR (findable, readily available interoperable, and reusable) principles in mind, we outlined the supporting infrastructure that would be needed to put the framework into action. To guarantee conformity with FAIR principles [3, 4], we used two scenarios illustrative of data sharing for educational and research uses. Academic activity around adversarial instances in the picture area has exploded in recent years, after their discovery [5]. With the rise of AI in recent years, scientists have been more interested in studying rival samples in the written sector [6]. Given the rapidly growing amount of electronic resources [7], automated categorization of certain resources has become critically vital. Artificial intelligence (AI) was used to glean people's thoughts from social media. Despite this, most ongoing studies concentrate on extrapolating characteristics from texts. Due to the increased complexity of giving a single label to each text fragment and the sheer volume of accessible data, multi-label textual data categorization has emerged as a pressing issue. You may see this in the media and in emails [8]. Building a classification system that can categorise fresh data based on labelled online documents is a primary goal of automated web page classification research in web mining [9]. In order to solve text classification challenges, such as the categorization of online documents, machine learning techniques are adopted. Artificial immune systems of Computational intelligence use cues from biological immune systems to address a wide range of challenges in artificial intelligence, including categorization [10].

Nevertheless, the aforementioned combination of depth learning research only considers the relationship among words and ignores the relationship among words and categories, despite the fact that this is a crucial factor in the categorization of news text. The following are a few of the paper's most fundamental contributions: (i) This study chooses CNN, LSTM, and MLP models to present a custom MLP algorithm for news text categorization based on double input mixed depth learning, in line with the research concept of the combination of DL approaches based news text classification. (ii) Word vector and word dispersion are used in tandem to describe the suggested model. To achieve deep learning of news text's spatial data on features, time-series data feature information, as well as the connection between words and categories, we feed a word vector representing the relationship between words into the CNN module, and a discrete vector representing the relationship between words as well as categories into the MLP module. (iii) Many experiments were performed to test the reliability and effectiveness of the strategy under consideration. The experimental findings demonstrate that the suggested technique significantly outperforms the alternatives in terms of the accuracy of predictions as well as other performance metrics, hence (iv) The method is a clear winner.

The remaining sections of the paper are laid out as follows. The relevant literature is presented in Section 2, and the suggested model for news material categorization is shown in Section 3. In Section 4, we provide the findings and analyses of our experiments, and in Section 5, we draw a conclusion.

## RELATED WORK

In order to shed light on the causes of the observed fluctuations in the direct ownership and market liquidity in the United States, this article employs a text-based sentiment indicator. Market sentiment is taken from 66,070 news stories on the US real estate market in the research firm S&P Global Market database using an artificial neural network. The network is trained using a remote supervision technique and labelled data from Seeking Alpha, a crowdsourced financial advising portal, totaling 17,822 investment ideas. The derived textual emotions indicator is significantly associated with the depth as well as resilience aspects of liquidity in the market (proxied by Amihud's (2002) price impact measure) and the breadth dimensions (proxied by transaction volume), as determined by self-regressive distributed lag models that include contemporary as well as lagged sentiment as variables that are independent. These findings point to the existence of a long-term relationship between market mood and direct property market liquidity. This impact should be taken into consideration by market players when making investment choices and when pricing liquidity risk. Not only does this research add to the body of knowledge on text-based emotion indices in property, but it is additionally the first to use AI to extract sentiment from news stories in the context of market liquidity [11].

Successful implementation of the framework is carried out according to FAIR guidelines. The resulting cystoscopy atlas could be featured on a website dedicated to education; 68 full-length subjective videos and their annotation data were made available for use in AI projects addressing frame segmentation and classification issues at the case, lesion, and frame levels. Results from our research indicate that the suggested architecture makes it possible to save visual records in a standardised format and provides FAIR data for use in training and studying AI [12].

Utilising a specific word deletion scoring mechanism, this paper proposes an adversarial sample generations algorithm for use in a black box scenario; the algorithm searches the HowNet vocabulary for synonyms of keywords that have an important effect on the classifier's decision and then generates a set of adversarial data sets that are conceptually in line with the original samples. Then, a genetic algorithm is used in tandem with the created samples to find the optimal solution. Experimental findings on sentiment classification and news categorization datasets using LSTM and CNN demonstrate that the algorithm may significantly lower the accuracy of an intended model if there is little interference [13].

Arabic text categorization using multiple labels is the topic of this study. Several different designs were put to the test once the datasets were collected. With an F-score of 86.6 on the development set and an F1-score of 82.24 on the leaderboard of the Mowjaz competition, bidirectional long short-term memory networks (BiLSTM) proved to be the most effective [14].

In this research, we take a look at how artificial the immune system's based methods fare when applied to the problem of online page categorization. Therefore, the Immunos-1 and Immunos-99 algorithms, both based on the artificial immune system, are compared against the C4.5 decision tree classifier and the Naive Bayes classification, two conventional machine learning approaches. Fifty datasets acquired from the Open Directory Project (DMOZ) are used to empirically assess the methods. Predictive performance for website categorization is improved experimentally using artificial immunity-based systems [15].

## PROPOSED WORK

### System Model

In this part of the research, the suggested model utilised to categorise the latest information in textual data is presented and illustrated. The suggested paradigm involves many sequential procedures. Here we describe how DL approaches may be used to classify news texts when they first emerge online:

#### *Level 1*

Feed the text into a CNN model and have it forecast whether it is related to a news event. It is not necessary to keep an eye on the answer or forecast if it is not.

### *Level 2*

Second-level text preprocessing as well as feature expression includes stop-word filtering, word-vector extraction using the word2vec model, and dispersion-vector computation. Word-category connections are reflected in the discreteness-based input vector. A higher numerical number indicates a more significant aid in categorization. The word-vector-based input accurately captures the context in which individual words are used. Two types of feature expression may help the model pick up as many of the text's underlying characteristics as feasible.

### *Level 3*

When learning the text's temporal features, first feed the word vector into an Ensemble CNN (multiple CNN) component to get the spatial characteristics through two pooling and convolution processes. A discrete matrix is then sent into the MLP module, where the submerged neuron is trained to make connections between words and classes. For the scaling of features and news prediction category output, the function of softmax activation is fed the combined values from the MLP and LSTM modules' outputs.

## Preprocessing

Unlike regular writing, news content includes few keywords and yet has a high degree of relevance to the topic at hand. The word "earthquake" in a news article's headline or body indicates that the article covers an earthquake-related occurrence. In order to represent information in news texts and to differentiate regular texts from event news, this article employs key feature terms with significant connection. To ignore the relative importance of speech in the content and the association data among words and categories, DL techniques like the word vectors method and the one that uses heat use spatial distance for expressing the degree of similarity of word meaning. Fig. (**1**). depicts the System Model. Some examples of levels that include the specified situation are as follows:

### *Level 1*

The word frequency vector for a category may be calculated by counting the amount of texts that include a given term. The quantity vector VI of the term I in the selected set of n categories is where VIM is the total quantity of texts containing the letter I in the m"th " category.

$$V_I = (v_{I1}, v_{I2}, \dots, v_{In}) \quad \textbf{(1)}$$

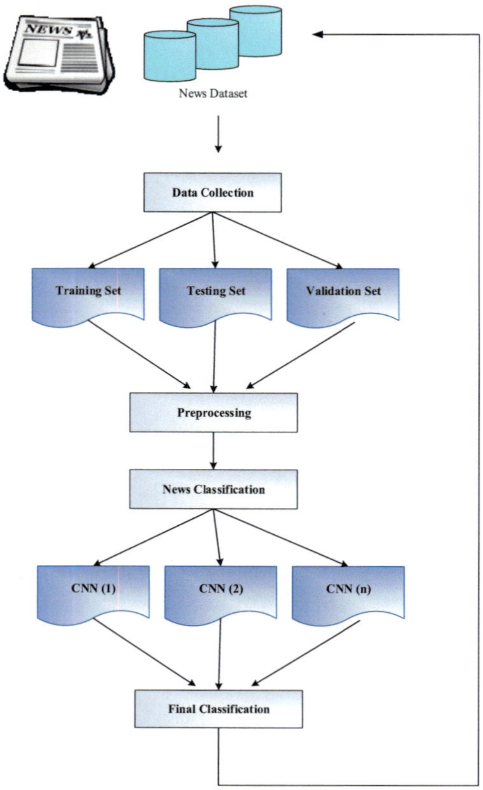


**Fig. (1).** p>System Model

## *Level 2*

The chance of a word appearing in a given class is determined by taking into account the shift in the class frequencies vector due to differences in the total quantity of texts in each category. Let Qi be the sum of all texts of type I, and $P_I$ be the following category probability vector:

$$P_I = \left(\frac{v_{I1}}{q_1}, \frac{v_{I2}}{q_2}, \ldots, \frac{v_{In}}{q_n}\right). \quad \textbf{(2)}$$

## *Level 3*

Determine the standard deviation of $P_I$ similar to how the word "I" might wander. The more the variance, the higher the dispersion, and the clearer the feature information in the categorization. Let $\bar{p}_I$ be the mean probability of the letter I and $ó_I^2$ be the variance of the probabilities associated with the letter I, then the distribution formula is as follows:

$$\bar{p}_I = \frac{\sum_{i=1}^{n} v_{Ii}/q_i}{n},$$
$$\sigma_I^2 = \sum_{i=1}^{n} \left(\frac{v_{Ii}}{q_i} - \bar{p}_I\right)^2. \quad (3)$$

Level 4: Height is the total amount of words, whereas width is the privacy of each individual word in the text. The variation value of a word is the word sequence that goes along with its occurrence. If not, it would be 0. If we define Z as the total quantity of words in the dataset and d as the text dispersion vector, we get the following expression:

$$D = (\sigma_1^2, \sigma_2^2, \ldots, \sigma_Z^2) \quad (4)$$

## News Text Classification

Ensemble Cnn takes a word vector as input including interword feature information and one of five convolution kernels. The local features of the word vector are then extracted using different convolution kernels, and a vector of text area feature data is generated for each kernel. Fig. (**2**) illustrates the proposed CNN model using ensemble learning.

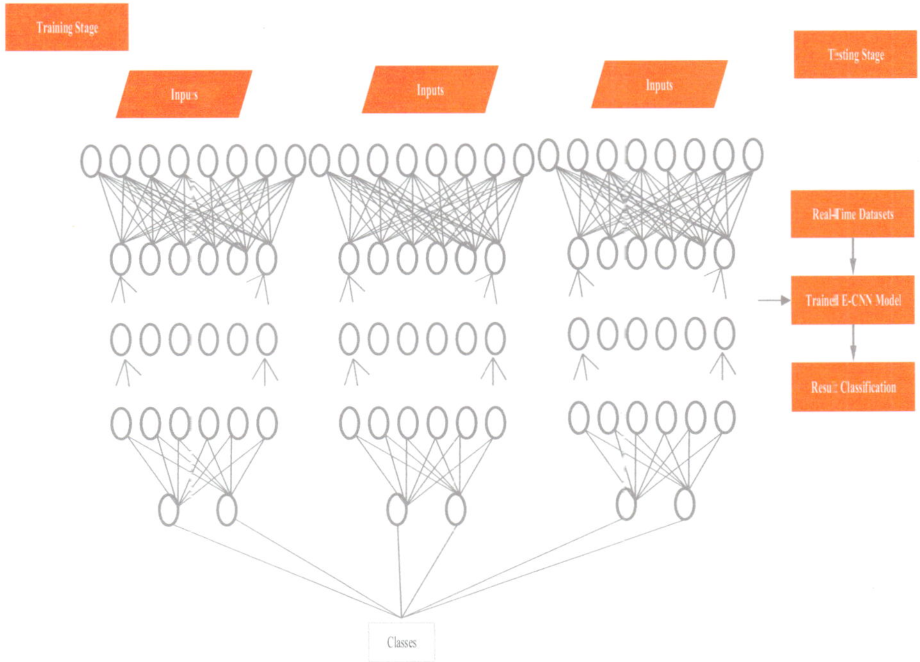


**Fig. (2).** Ensemble CNN Model.

One time segment is represented by the vector of features extracted by a single convolution kernel, while multiple time segments are represented by the feature information obtained by multiple convolution kernels, all of which are suggestions to the layer with a full connection, which learns the time-series feature data pertaining to multiple time segments and, ultimately, outputs the complete spatial feature vector. A new feature data vector is constructed from the output feature vectors and sent into the entire relationship layer for re-learning. The re-learned feature extraction is then sent into a softmax layer for scaling features, and the text subcategory is ultimately determined.

## RESULTS AND DISCUSSION

Here, we report the findings of our various experiments and the subsequent analysis of those findings. The tests were run on a laptop running Microsoft Windows 10 with the operating system and an Intel Core i7, 9th generation CPU, clocked at 2.7 GHz, and 12 GB of RAM. The simulations were run with the help of the IDE Anaconda, Jupyter Notebook. Both the code and the generated simulation results were written in Python. Pandas, Numpy, Matplotlib, Keras, Tensorflow, seaborn, and Sklearn were some of the Python tools utilised in this research.

In this part, we compile the textual data on events reported in the news. First, we have public health news, followed by social security news, accidents and catastrophes, and finally, natural disasters. We use the crawler technology to search Baidu news for the keywords "storm," "rainstorm," "Blizzard," "earthquake," "tsunami," "flood," "debris flow," "forest fire," "sandstorm," and "landslide," and we found 5477 news case texts related to these 10 types of natural disasters. Using the same methodology, we also explored the open-source daily news event text collection, which includes 2815 news texts (including economic, artistic, and political news texts).

There are a total of 8292 messages included in the sample, made up of 5477 event news articles and 2815 regular news texts. The suggested CNN framework is fed the training set of 6699 texts from the samples set, while the test set of 1593 texts is fed into the model for evaluation. The number of synapses in the complete connection layer, the number of layers of convolution, the duration of the first mock test, and the size of the word vector are the main setting parameters of a CNN equation. The accuracy and recall of the model, as well as the mean of the composite value, are derived by running the simulations three times for each variation of the single model parameters.

We tested several algorithms, including LSTM, CNN, and MLP, and found that CNN was the most effective. Dense layers of 128 & 256 LSTM units were utilised after a convolutional layer of 50 LSTM units. CNN uses the following architecture. The tweets' embedding from the previous stage produced an e s-dimensional word vector. The convolution layer received this vector as input. The features obtained by the convolution layer were subjected to max pooling in order to extract the most valuable feature. As a consequence, the convolution layer was used to learn the 1024 most relevant characteristics. The data was then sent into a hidden layer consisting of 256 perceptrons, which produced another set of 256 features at a greater granularity. The output layer, which consists of a single perceptron, takes as its input the freshly created higher-level features. We utilised a ReLU activation function for the hidden layers, and a sigmoid activation function for the output layer. We anticipated better results using LSTM since it is a popular model for NLP applications and effectively keeps tabs on the most crucial vocabulary. However, we found that CNN performed marginally better than LSTM, suggesting that it can recognise a subset of crucial words and correct them for the noise in those words. In the below Table, we detail the accuracy, precision, recall, and F1-score of each approach.

**Table 1. Evaluation of results.**

| **Proposed CNN** | | | | | |
|---|---|---|---|---|---|
| **Presentation** | **SP** | **P** | **NT** | **N** | **SN** |
| Accurateness (%) | ≃91.85 | ≃ 92.02 | ≃92.15 | ≃91.79 | ≃92.04 |
| Exactness (%) | ≃93.13 | ≃92.98 | ≃92.85 | ≃92.78 | ≃93.45 |
| Recollection (%) | ≃92.65 | ≃92.28 | ≃92.19 | ≃92.49 | ≃92.88 |
| F-value (%) | ≃91.39 | ≃91.63 | ≃91.72 | ≃91.95 | ≃91.57 |
| **CNN** | | | | | |
| **Presentation** | **SP** | **P** | **NT** | **N** | **SN** |
| Accurateness (%) | ≃88.85 | ≃87.94 | ≃88.22 | ≃88.76 | ≃88.17 |
| Exactness (%) | ≃87.93 | ≃88.38 | ≃87.24 | ≃89.02 | ≃87.69 |
| Recollection (%) | ≃87.88 | ≃88.53 | ≃86.93 | ≃88.33 | ≃87.92 |
| F-value(%) | ≃86.64 | ≃86.82 | ≃87.35 | ≃86.96 | ≃86.48 |
| **Bi-LSTM** | | | | | |
| **Presentation** | **SP** | **P** | **NT** | **N** | **SN** |
| Accurateness (%) | ≃87.58 | ≃87.22 | ≃86.99 | ≃87.36 | ≃87.07 |
| Exactness (%) | ≃86.33 | ≃86.91 | ≃87.66 | ≃87.28 | ≃87.48 |
| Recollection (%) | ≃86.32 | ≃87.54 | ≃86.85 | ≃87.15 | ≃87.33 |
| F-value (%) | ≃85.73 | ≃85.99 | ≃86.22 | ≃85.33 | ≃85.47 |
| **LSTM** | | | | | |

*(Table 1) cont.....*

| Proposed CNN | | | | | |
|---|---|---|---|---|---|
| **Presentation** | **SP** | **P** | **NT** | **N** | **SN** |
| **Performance** | **SP** | **P** | **NT** | **N** | **SN** |
| Accurateness (%) | ≃84.69 | ≃83.98 | ≃84.13 | ≃84.28 | ≃84.58 |
| Exactness (%) | ≃83.64 | ≃84.25 | ≃84.68 | ≃84.15 | ≃83.82 |
| Recollection (%) | ≃84.33 | ≃83.71 | ≃84.24 | ≃84.08 | ≃83.69 |
| F-value (%) | ≃82.78 | ≃83.13 | ≃82.48 | ≃82.55 | ≃82.82 |

## CONCLUSION

Understanding the evident differences between the keywords in various types of event news articles and the keywords in everyday texts is a crucial and difficult task. The aforementioned issues are addressed, and three new developments are presented in this work. To begin, we created a model for two-tiered categorization. The primary model detects news occurrences, while the secondary model categorises them. Second, In order to effectively communicate textual characteristics, this article suggests a standalone vector, as opposed to the existing research's use of vectors of words to express text include information, and it does so while taking into account the involvement of each word in classification. Finally, the text characteristics are expressed using a word vector and a dispersion vector in the suggested model. Word vectors contain semantic information hidden in words, whereas dispersion vectors show how words relate to classes. Strong identification and categorization skills for news events are demonstrated by an experiment and comparison with the two-level system of classification suggested in this paper, with the rate of recognition of 99.5% in the first-level model as well as a success rate of 99.82% for a second-level model. As a drawback, this paper relies on a public stop word list for its text preprocessing rather than a news-specific one; as a result, some feature information is lost in the process. However, a news-specific stop word list can be established in the future. However, the model's poor efficacy is due to the small amount of sample sets and the unequal distribution of different forms of news. Later on, while conducting tests, larger sample sizes are required. Future research is necessary to address the limitations of this report.

## REFERENCES

[1] M.D. Giovanni, L. Corti, S. Pavanetto, F. Pierri, A. Tocchetti, and M. Brambilla, *A Content-based Approach for the Analysis and Classification of Vaccine-related Stances on Twitter: the Italian Scenario.* ICWSM Workshops, 2021.

[2] N. Channawar, and S.B. Kishor, "Intrinsic Plagiarism Detection Approach Utilizing Support Vector Machine in Text Classification", *J. Emerg. Technol. Innov. Res.,* 2019.

[3] V. Silva-Rodríguez, S.E. Nava-Muñoz, L.A. Castro, F.E. Pérez, H.G. Pérez-González, and F. Torres-

Reyes, "Machine Learning Methods for Inferring Interaction Design Patterns from Textual Requirements", *International Conference on Ubiquitous Computing and Ambient Intelligence,* 2019. [http://dx.doi.org/10.3390/proceedings2019031026]

[4] M.A. Saloot, N. Idris, R. Mahmud, S. Ja'afar, D. Thorleuchter, and A. Gani, "Hadith data mining and classification: a comparative analysis", *Artif. Intell. Rev.,* vol. 46, no. 1, pp. 113-128, 2016. [http://dx.doi.org/10.1007/s10462-016-9458-x]

[5] S. P. Yadav, and S. Yadav, "Mathematical implementation of fusion of medical images in continuous wavelet domain", *Journal of Advanced Research in dynamical and control system,* vol. 10, no. 10, pp. 45-54, 2019.

[6] T. Dinushika, L. Kavmini, P. Abeyawardhana, U. Thayasivam, and S. Jayasena, "Speech Command Classification System for Sinhala Language based on Automatic Speech Recognition", *2019 International Conference on Asian Language Processing (IALP),* pp. 205-210, 2019. [http://dx.doi.org/10.1109/IALP48816.2019.9037648]

[7] D.C. Akalya, R.D. Karthika, T. Harisudhan, V.K. Jeevanantham, J. Jhanani, and V.S. Kavi, "“Text emotion recognition using fast text word embedding in bi-directional gated recurrent unit” i-manager's", *J. Inf. Technol.,* 2022.

[8] D. Alnahas, F. Aşık, A. Kanturvardar, and A.M. Ülkgün, "Opinion Mining Using LSTM Networks Ensemble for Multi-Class Sentiment Analysis in E-Commerce", *Proceedings of the 2022 International Conference on Intelligent Information Systems and Engineering (IISEC),* pp. 245-250, Nov. 2022. [http://dx.doi.org/10.1109/IISEC56263.2022.9998264]

[9] S.P. Yadav, S. Zaidi, C.D.S. Nascimento, V.H.C. de Albuquerque, and S.S. Chauhan, "Analysis and Design of automatically generating for GPS Based Moving Object Tracking System", *2023 International Conference on Artificial Intelligence and Smart Communication (AISC),* pp. 1-5, 2023.Greater Noida, India. [http://dx.doi.org/10.1109/AISC56616.2023.10085180]

[10] Z. Wang, Z. Hu, F. Li, S.B. Ho, and E. Cambria, "Learning-Based Stock Trending Prediction by Incorporating Technical Indicators and Social Media Sentiment", *Cognit. Comput.,* vol. 15, no. 3, pp. 1092-1102, 2023. [http://dx.doi.org/10.1007/s12559-023-10125-8]

[11] J. Braun, J. Hausler, and W. Schäfers, "Artificial intelligence, news sentiment, and property market liquidity", *J. Prop. Invest. Financ.,* vol. 38, no. 4, pp. 309-325, 2020. [http://dx.doi.org/10.1108/JPIF-08-2019-0100]

[12] O. Eminaga, T.J. Lee, T.J. Ge, E. Shkolyar, M.A. Laurie, J. Long, L. Hockman, and J.C. Liao, *Conceptual Framework and Documentation Standards of Cystoscopic Media Content for Artificial Intelligence.* ArXiv, 2023. [http://dx.doi.org/10.1016/j.jbi.2023.104369]

[13] D. Shi, Z. Ge, and T. Zhao, "Word-level textual adversarial attacking based on genetic algorithm", *International Conference on Computer Communication and Network Security,* 2022. [http://dx.doi.org/10.1117/12.2659262]

[14] D. AlBatayha, "Multi-Topic Labelling Classification Based on LSTM", *Proceedings of the 2021 International Conference on Information and Communication Systems (ICICS),* pp. 290-295, May 2021. [http://dx.doi.org/10.1109/ICICS52457.2021.9464531]

[15] A. Onan, "Artificial Immune System Based Web Page Classification", *Computer Science On-line Conference,* 2015. [http://dx.doi.org/10.1007/978-3-319-18473-9_19]

# CHAPTER 5

# Analysis of the Sentiment of Tweets Regarding COVID-19 Vaccines Using Natural Language Processing and Machine Learning Sectionification Algorithms

**Sukhman Ghumman**[1,*]

[1] *Centre for Interdisciplinary Research in Business and Technology, Chitkara University Institute of Engineering and Technology, Chitkara University, Punjab, India*

**Abstract:** The unique Coronavirus pandemic of 2019 (called COVID-19 by the globe Health Organisation) has exposed several governments throughout the globe to risk. The Covid-19 epidemic, which had previously only affected the Chinese population, is now a major worry for countries all over the globe. Additionally to the obvious health effects of COVID-19 epidemic, this study reveals its repercussions on the worldwide economy. The research went on to talk about how they analysed public opinion and learned new things about Covid-19 vaccinations by using content Analytics and sentiment evaluation in Natural Language Processing (NLP) using content from Twitter. To categorise and analyse the outcomes, researchers used two machine learning algorithms: logistic regression (LR), random forest, decision tree, and convolutional neural networks (CNNs). To better identify public opinion, several pre-processing methods were used and categorised responses into neutral, positive, and negative categories. The public's opinion on Covid-19 vaccinations is 31% favourable, 22% negative, and 47% neutral, according to the results of the emotion section distribution. CNN achieved 98% accuracy, according to the tested machine learning algorithms.

**Keywords:** Covid-19 vaccine, Health informatics, Micro-blogging, Public opinions, Sentiment analysis, Social media, Twitter.

## INTRODUCTION

It is no longer possible to overstate the importance of social media as a means of communication and expression for people, businesses, and governments all over the globe. The 2019 coronavirus disease (COVID-19) pandemic has made social

* **Corresponding author Sukhman Ghumman:** Centre for Interdisciplinary Research in Business and Technology, Chitkara University Institute of Engineering and Technology, Chitkara University, Punjab, India;
E-mail: sukhman.ghumman.orp@chitkara.edu.in

**Pankaj Kumar Mishra and Satya Prakash Yadav (Eds.)**

media platforms more important than ever for individuals to connect, share, and voice their opinions on a wide range of issues. Governments' and organisations' ability to react quickly to emerging threats may be enhanced by analysing this kind of textual data. In order to assist organisations in raising awareness, this project plans to conduct sentiment assessments on the issue of COVID-19 vaccine, as well as temporal and geographical analyses utilising textual data, and identify the most often discussed subjects. The effect of COVID-19 vaccination and how people react when exposed to the virus is now the most commonly contested subject in the medical community. Although several different vaccines have been created, it has never been quite clear whether or not they will provide total protection against the virus [1, 2]. Although many researchers have considered the topic of evaluating people's attitudes about vaccinations, few have actually used language processing approaches to the data they collected. Over the last decade, social media has seen rapid growth [3, 4]. This growth has been accompanied by both good and bad effects. People from all walks of life are able to contact each other directly across cultural and economic divides thanks to the exponential growth of networking *via* social platforms and websites. There are positive effects of social media on society, but there are also negative effects. In recent years, hate speech has emerged as a serious issue. Online forms of hate speech often include the use of threatening or insulting rhetoric [5, 6]. It might mean anybody or a specific group of individuals who have some common ground. The purpose of this automated essay assessment system is to score writings and deliver comments automatically. The usage of automated grading systems in the section room and on digital tests is on the rise. The purpose of this research is to build and assess machine learning models for automated essay assessment [7, 8]. In order to steal sensitive information from a person, such as login credentials or financial account numbers, phishing is a common method of using shared technologies. This occurs when the attacker poses as a reliable system in order to trick the victim into opening an email, clamorous material, or textual concerns [9]. The target is then tricked into opening a malicious attachment, which installs malware and prevents the machine from responding to user input until the ransom is paid. or the disclosure of confidential data. The leak of sensitive information is only one example of the devastating effects that might result from such assaults [10]. Theft of money or personal information, as well as other forms of illegal leverage, is considered a serious crimes by individuals.

Since feelings evolve over time, our study also examined how these tweets evolved over time, which is a unique and significant addition to the field. Furthermore, we demonstrated *via* study that our system is able to accurately discern the emotion of a phrase given text inputs. The purpose of this study and the value it adds are to better understand how people feel about becoming vaccinated against COVID-19. Researchers and policymakers in the health sector will benefit from this information as they work to improve public trust in vaccinations and ensure the public's continued safety and awareness.

The analytical methods and results of the study's technical components are described in the following sections. In Section 2, we go through the processes and jargon specific to sentiment analysis. The functionality of effective visualisation tools, the explanation of how they represented emotions, and the results obtained are covered in Section 3. In Section 4, we explore the results of our study, its potential effect and benefits to humanity, and ways in which it might be enhanced to hasten the good of the planet. Section 5 contains the results of our research.

## RELATED WORK

This research focuses on information collected from social networking sites and uses the NLTK (Natural Language Processing Toolkit) to improve sentiment analysis. The covid19 dataset was used to classify public tweet sentiments by polarity, recall, accuracy, and f1-value while encouraging the use of a combination of embedding words with the TFIDF vectorizer, data sheathed *via* fine-grained sentiment analysis, as well as machine learning methods like Linear SVC, SVM, as well as Nave bayes. In order to efficiently extract emotions from data, simulations utilise the features of the Python library VADER (Valence Aware Dictionary & sentiment Reasoner) [11].

We present in this study our approach to deal with and significantly reduce such hate speech. Many individuals harm others' sentiments by venting their hate and rage directly on social media. It would have serious consequences for them, regardless of their caste, faith, religion, or ethnicity. It is possible that some remarks might be considered hate speech simply because of the vulgar language used. To eradicate hate speech, we have dove headfirst into natural language processing, and accuracy-based comparison of several artificial intelligence models for selection [12].

The growth of Web services is significantly hampered by malicious websites, which also considerably help the propagation of online crime. There must be an all-encompassing plan to prevent people from visiting these sites. We suggest an approach based on machine learning that classifies websites as either safe, spammy, or harmful. Our approach analyses just the Uniform Resource Locator (URL) of a page to determine its relevance. Therefore, it prevents users from being vulnerable to browser-based exploits in production. Since our method employs learning algorithms, it is more generalizable and has a wider scope than blacklisting services [13].

One of the most widespread and easily avoidable security risks nowadays is phishing. We offer a method that uses NLP methods to analyse text for red flags suggestive of phishing attempts and identify potentially malicious claims. Our method is innovative in comparison to prior work since it employs semantic analysis of the attack's natural language content in order to identify malevolent intent. We have tested our method against a large collection of phishing emails that serve as a benchmark [14].

This research makes use of a freely available essay data set for training and assessing the deployed techniques. To extract the relevant features from the articles in the dataset, NLP techniques were used. The selected dataset was put through three separate preexisting machine learning algorithms. Separate sets of data were created for use in training and use in tests. Comparisons were made between the models and human raters in terms of reliability and performance. In terms of concordance with human raters, random forest beats each of the two machine learning models with the smallest overall mean error on the test dataset [15].

## PROPOSED WORK

### System Model

We begin by collecting tweets using the Twitter API utilising the following search terms: COVID, COVID-19, the Corona Societal Isolation in COVID-19, and Lockdown in a pandemic. Hashtags were also used to filter tweets, including #Lockdown, #SocialDistance, #Coronavirus, and #COVID-19. Massive amounts of geotagged tweets are gathered from the aforementioned collection of keywords and hashtags. As a proxy for the opinions of the general public, the tweets with the most retweets and likes are given greater weight. Table **1** illustrates the samples of tweets used in this study.

We then go through four processes, including data pre-processing, feature extraction, and sectionification, after the dataset has been acquired. Fig. (**1**) depicts the general architecture of the suggested method.

**Table 1. Samples of tweets expressing a range of emotions.**

| Confident Sings | Adverse Sings | Impartial Sings |
|---|---|---|
| 1. 'First doses of the COVID-19 vaccine were administered to select college employees. With the help of Covishield and the Surat covid19vaccine, we can render India free of the covid-19 virus once and for all greatest vaccination effort in India against coronavirus covid19' | 1. Because of possible links to uncommon blood clots, Canada has banned the use for Oxford to occur in the form of coronavirus vaccination in anyone under the age of 55. | 1. '... In 'The Rise of NaMo & New India,' the author traces Modi's seven years in power. It takes a critical look at what his administration has accomplished. Readers would get fresh perspectives on political conundrum. Namaste and Welcome to the Brand New India, Modi! |
| 2. Today I got my first shot of the COVID-19 vaccine; I strongly suggest you schedule yours as soon as you can." | 2. Coronavirus COVID-19 coronavirus vaccine Uneven vaccination delivery is a huge public health danger when new coronavirus strains evolve. | 2. As new strains of the coronavirus evolve, an inequitable distribution of vaccines represents a serious threat to public health. |
| 3. Water pistols painted in vaccine wali holi 2021 covid19 vaccine hues Topical post: "drive aside your dread of coronavirus with the covid19 vaccination & enjoy the colourful spirit of holi" (#KojakSelingeCoronavirus, #HMDFightsCorona). | 3. While 179 inmates at Down Prison declined the BJP's COVID-19 vaccination, 178 inmates at UP Prison opted to get vaccinated. Azam Khan \| Uttar Pradesh \| TRH News #TRHNews #VaccinationDrive #COVID19 | 3. "...what antibody concentration might be required to afford such defence?" Coronavirus Coronavirus Pandemic Coronavirus Vaccine Covid19 covid19 vaccine 2/2' covid vaccines covid19 vaccines. |

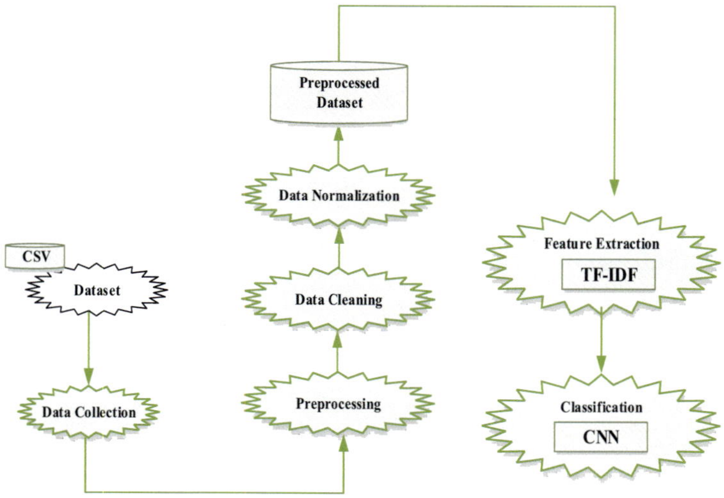


**Fig. (1).** System Flowchart.

## Pre-processing

Due to the chaotic nature of tweets, it is crucial to remove irrelevant terms in order to simplify the data and boost the reliability of sectionifications. Noise removal, modification, tokenization, normalisation, and stemming are just a few of the many important processes carried out during preprocessing. Fig. (**1**). depicts the System Flowchart.

### *Noise Removal*

In this initial round of pre-processing, irrelevant information is stripped from the gathered tweets. Several sources of noisy data that weaken sentiment analysis are discussed here, and methods for removing them are provided as follows:

#### *a) Lowercase Conversion*

The tweet has both capitalised and lowercase letters. An essential part of pre-processing is changing all the capital letters to lowercase. This helps avoid unnecessary repetition of terms. The terms "CoronaVirus" and "CORONAVIRUS" are shortened to "coronavirus," for instance.

#### *b) URL Removal*

This procedure scrubs the tweet text for any remaining URLs.

#### *c) Hashtags Removal*

Hashtags are used in the Twitter API to organise conversations around certain subjects. The tweets have had all their hashtags deleted Table **2** illustrates the example of tweets.

**Table. 2. Example Tweet**

| Hashtag | Extracted Tweet | Pre-processed Tweet |
|---|---|---|
| #COVID-19 | The coronavirus currently has the greatest mortality toll of any known virus. | (coronavirus) (NNP) (become/VBN) (deadliest/JJS) (highest/JJS) (virus/NN) (known/VBN) (until/NN). ratio of fatalities per million population |

#### *d) Special Characters Removal*

In this procedure, we strip tweets of all punctuation and other special characters.

#### *e) Stop Words Removal*

Some stop words, like not, none, never, *etc*., which transmit the setting of the phrase should not be omitted since they considerably impact the correctness, but others should be. Therefore, we get rid of a bunch of terms that are not vital and call them "stop words".

### *Corrections*

The changes include making typo fixes and converting emoticons that were used in the tweets. The use of emoticons is taken into account since they significantly aid in deciphering sarcastic tweets.

### *Tokenization*

Tokens are little chunks of text that are extracted from tweets after irrelevant terms have been removed. This method is useful for deciphering tweets in their proper context.

### *Normalization*

In this step, every word in the tweets is converted into a standardised format. The terms "gud" and "goood" are shortened to "good," for instance.

### *Stemming*

Stemming is the process of identifying and removing unnecessary letters from words in tweets. Because of this, analysing data is much simpler.

### *PoS Tagging*

Tweets have their words coded according to their use as a verb, adjective, noun, or adverb. Each tuple consists of a word and its associated tag.

## ML Techniques

Within the realm of machine learning, supervision, unsupervised learning, and hybrid learning are the three most common approaches.

### *Supervised Machine Learning*

- Human-created labelled datasets are used to teach supervised machine learning algorithms. In order for machine learning models to function, raw information must be converted into numeric vectors that will serve as the input parameters (X) as well as the variables that result (Y). The process of mapping from input to output is learned using the supervised method. This method would be able to foretell the variables in fresh data.
- Ticket routing is only one of the many uses for text categorization, which is

performed using supervised machine learning. In this scenario, incoming communications would be automatically categorised by subject, language, sentiment, intent, as well as other factors before being directed to the appropriate customer service staff.

- Email filtering is another excellent example. Algorithms that can identify if an email is spam, social, or mail-worthy categorise messages accordingly.
- We will circle back around to Naive Bayes while encouraging vector machines (SVM), two popular supervised techniques.

### *Unsupervised Machine Learning*

- Unsupervised machine learning algorithms, on the other hand, may be left to their own devices to learn from raw information. That is to say, it acquires knowledge by observing how words and grammatical patterns are dispersed throughout massive datasets, which are then represented by a massive vector.
- In brief, unsupervised machine learning does not get feedback in the form of labelled outputs or a "correct" result. It can automatically recognise the structure of information as well as 'sectionify' words according to their shared characteristics. Clustering is a common unsupervised learning method for organising text into more manageable chunks.

### *Semi-Supervised Machine Learning*

- Last but not least, semi-supervised machine learning, additionally referred to as hybrid machine learning, is a blend of unattended and supervised machine learning techniques taught using labelled (usually small amounts) and unlabeled data (often huge amounts).
- When organisations have massive volumes of data that have to be labelled, semi-supervised machine learning may be a useful tool. In the case of website sectionification, for instance, semi-supervised machine learning may be used to automatically sectionify different kinds of sites based on labelled input looking at similarities across webpages, thereby detecting and labelling 'unstructured' webpages.

### *Logistic Regression (LR)*

In the case of binary sectionification, this is one of the most often employed methods for categorical dependent variables. The role of logistics, which is based on the sigmoid function, is the central component of logistic regression. SVM stands for "support vector machine" In high dimensional space, this approach is often used for tasks including sectionification, regression, and outlier identification. It creates a hyperplane in N-dimensional space (representing N characteristics) and uses it to categorise data points.

### *Decision Tree (DT)*

This is considered to be among the most extensive machine learning algorithms available. Decision trees are useful for discovering the most salient aspects of a dataset and for capturing non-linear trends. Decision trees use information and entropy gain to guide branching.

### *Random Forest (RF)*

Regression and sectionification may be accomplished using this supervised approach. This technique generates a tree forest, with more trees indicating better accuracy and less overfitting. Random forest uses either MDI (mean reduction in impurities) or Gini Significance to determine the relative value of each feature. In this study, we compare these three techniques by using the count vectorizer produced by the TF-IDF method.

The algorithms and methods that makeup Deep Learning are meant to be analogous to the human brain. Convolutional Neural Networks (CNNs) & Recurrent Neural Networks (RNNs) are the two most used deep learning models for text categorization. The layers of a convolutional neural network (CNN) include an input level, an output layer, as well as numerous hidden layers. A convolution represents the linear process that seamlessly applies filters to inputs, leading to activations, and layers of convolution are the primary building blocks of CNN. These intricate layers are essential to a network of convolutional neural networks because they prioritise and distinguish between inputs. To extract basic characteristics from words or n-grams for use in text categorization, CNN is a feature that may be used. RNNs are a subset of neural networks designed specifically to handle sequential data. The RNN processes each input sequence using a set of computations that are informed by the outcomes of prior computer runs. The main benefit of employing RNN is that it can remember the outcomes of earlier calculations and utilise them in the present. We should keep in mind that algorithms for deep learning thrive on massive amounts of data, such as millions of labelled instances.

Convolutional neural networks (CNNs) are a kind of models of artificial neural networks used to simplify complicated data. The model gradually learns how to convert raw data into meaningful sectionifications as it iterates. There are two primary parts to a CNN: (1) A feature space is generated by applying various filters and pooling layers to multi-dimensional arrays. These features are simplifications of the most salient aspects of the source data; (2) the second section of CNNs is a fully linked network that maps the attributes extracted to the goal. This is the data set(s) you're trying to sectionify based on their shared characteristics. In CNNs, the multifaceted convolutional output is scaled down before being fed into the fully connected layer.

We studied the effect of changing the CNN's hyper parameters such as the amount of convolutions, the dropout rates of its individual layers, as well as the number of Solid ones that come after the convolutions.

## RESULTS AND DISCUSSION

Using the Twitter API and a set of 14 keywords, we were able to gather 980,557 tweets on the COVID-19 vaccine over the course of 1.5 months in 2020. There was an aggregate of 267,942 persons who tweeted, with the highest individual total being 954. Total 15,502,529 likes, 2,548,072 retweets, and 1,176,533 responses were recorded. Sentiment analysis was performed on 572,958 tweets utilising VADER & TextBlob after data cleaning and preparation. VADER reports that out of the total number of tweets, 270,975 (47.3%) were favourable, 164,113 (28.6%) were neutral, and 137,870 (24.1%) were negative TextBlob found that although 48.3% of tweets were favourable, 36.1% were neutral, and 15.6% were negative. In total, there were 276,888 tweets. Covid vaccine, COVID-19 vaccine, coronavirus vaccine, Pfizer, bioNTech, vaccination trial, vaccine successful, hope, clinical trial, thanks, pharma giant, global benefit, emergency usage, and many more were among the most frequently occurring terms in expressions of hope. Negative connotations were attached to terms like "COVID-19 vaccine," "covid vaccine," "coronavirus vaccine," "refuse," "costing countless," "expensive," "anti-vaccine," "stupid," "lower income," "side effect," "allergic reaction," "Trump," "warn people," and "worry".

When training neural networks, it is often difficult to determine the optimal number of training epochs. Too many epochs may lead to overfitting the training dataset, whereas too few might lead to under fitting. We may begin with an elevated amount of epochs and terminate training if the monitored measure does not show progress if we use the right early-stopping approach. This allows for a more automated, data-driven process, rather than one that requires human intervention, to determine the appropriate number of epochs. If the validation loss number does not decrease during training, we shall end the training process after four iterations Table **3** illustrates the proposed architecture in detail with the results.

In this study, the model's efficacy was evaluated using precision, recall, F1-score, and a confusion matrix including true positive (TP), false positive (FP), true negative (TN), and false negative (FN) values.

**Table 3. Architecture Details.**

| Architecture | LR | Accurateness | | F1 Value |
|---|---|---|---|---|
| 1 Complication | 1 Solid | $4\times10-^{44}\times10-^{4}$ | 0.89 | 0.88 |
| - | 2 Solid | $5\times10-^{45}\times10-^{4}$ | 0.88 | 0.88 |
| - | 3 Solid | $1\times10-^{41}\times10-^{4}$ | 0.88 | 0.87 |
| 2 Complication | 1 Solid | $5\times10-^{55}\times10-^{5}$ | 0.88 | 0.87 |
| - | 2 Solid | $5\times10-^{55}\times10-^{5}$ | 0.88 | 0.87 |
| - | 3 Solid | $2\times10-^{32}\times10-^{3}$ | 0.88 | 0.87 |
| 3 Complication | 1 Solid | $4\times10-^{44}\times10-^{4}$ | 0.87 | 0.86 |
| - | 2 Solid | $4\times10-^{44}\times10-^{4}$ | 0.87 | 0.86 |
| - | 3 Solid | $1\times10-^{41}\times10-^{4}$ | 0.87 | 0.87 |

**Accuracy:** How well the model fits the training and validation sets. It indicates the proportion of accurate predictions made by models across all positive sectionifications:

$$\text{precision} = \frac{\text{TP}}{\text{TP+FP}}. \tag{1}$$

**Recollection:** Recall measures how well an algorithm performs in sectionifying relevant outcomes:

$$\text{Recall} = \frac{\text{TP}}{\text{TP+FN}} \tag{2}$$

**F1-value:** The F1-score is the simple arithmetic mean of the recall and accuracy scores:

$$\text{F1-Score} = 2 \times \frac{\text{Precision} \times \text{Recall}}{\text{Precision} + \text{Recall}}. \tag{3}$$

**Table 4. Repercussions of performance indicators.**

| - | Exactness | Recollection | F1-value |
|---|---|---|---|
| LSTM | - | - | - |
| Section–0 | 0.95 | 0.95 | 0.95 |
| Section–1 | 0.86 | 0.78 | 0.83 |
| Section–2 | 0.89 | 0.93 | 0.91 |
| Bi-LSTM | - | - | - |
| Section–0 | 0.95 | 0.96 | 0.95 |

*(Table 4) cont.....*

| - | Exactness | Recollection | F1-value |
|---|---|---|---|
| Section–1 | 0.86 | 0.78 | 0.83 |
| Section–2 | 0.88 | 0.92 | 0.91 |
| Neutral: section-0, negative: section-1, positive: section-2. | | | |

The above performance measures are shown in Table **4**. Finally, 91% of positive feelings were properly classified by the algorithm. The genuine positive rate, as determined by the confusion matrix, was 94%, while the negative rate was correctly determined to be 73%. Furthermore, 2.6% as well as 3.2% were incorrectly classified as neutral, with the biggest percentages (between 11% and 15%) falling into the negative mood group. Finally, the positive attitude was accurately predicted, but the neutral and negative categories were split wrongly for 5.4% and 3.9% of the sample, respectively.

## CONCLUSION

We provide evidence that deep learning methods may be used for sentiment analysis. Our research showed that up until July 2021, in response to the vaccination procedures taking place all over the world, 33.96% of people were positive, 17.55% had been unfavorable as well as 48.49% were neutral. These results were derived using basic NLP-based tools. We also used Convolutional Neural Networks (CNN) to measure how well our models predicted and analyzed attitudes based on metrics including accuracy, recall, F-1 scores, as well as confusion matrices. There are a lot of individuals who have opted to get their vaccinations, but there are also a lot of people who are still unsure whether or not they should.

Researchers in the medical area may get insight into the difficulties of the immunization process by reading this article. A clearer picture of the vaccines' effectiveness may be obtained by vaccine producers, governments, and health departments across countries, and health agencies such as the World Health Organisation, or WHO. They will have a clearer picture of what needs fixing to restore people's faith in vaccines. By aiding first responders in the fight against this rare coronavirus, we can perhaps ensure that future generations can do the same.

## REFERENCES

[1] R., A. M.Banu, C, A. S, A.Kamath, and H.S. S N, H.Ujwala, "Detecting Phishing Attacks Using Natural Language Processing And Machine Learning", *2019 International Conference on Intelligent Computing and Control Systems (ICCS),* pp. 1210-1214, 2019.

[2] S.J. Goodswen, P.J. Kennedy, and J.T. Ellis, "Compilation of parasitic immunogenic proteins from 30 years of published research using machine learning and natural language processing", *Sci. Rep.,* vol.

12, no. 1, p. 10349, 2022.
[http://dx.doi.org/10.1038/s41598-022-13790-1] [PMID: 35725870]

[3] V.L. Narasamma, and M. Sreedevi, "Twitter based Data Analysis in Natural Language Processing using a Novel Catboost Recurrent Neural Framework", *Int. J. Adv. Comput. Sci. Appl.,* vol. 12, no. 5, 2021.
[http://dx.doi.org/10.14569/IJACSA.2021.0120555]

[4] O.N. Oyelade, and A.E. Ezugwu, *COVID19: A Natural Language Processing and Ontology Oriented Temporal Case-Based Framework for Early Detection and Diagnosis of Novel Coronavirus,* 2020.

[5] A. Agarwal, W.L. Romine, and T. Banerjee, "Leveraging natural language processing to understand public outlook towards the influenza vaccination", *in Proc. IEEE Int. Conf. Big Data (Big Data), Atlanta, GA, USA,* pp. 4567-4572, 2020.
[http://dx.doi.org/10.1109/BigData50022.2020.9378075]

[6] C.R. Oliveira, P. Niccolai, A.M. Ortiz, S.S. Sheth, E.D. Shapiro, L.M. Niccolai, and C.A. Brandt, *Natural Language Processing for Surveillance of Cervical and Anal Cancer and Precancer: Algorithm Development and Split-Validation Study.* Preprint, 2020.

[7] Y. Zhao, M.G. Ison, and Y. Luo, "COVID Vaccine and Cardiovascular Risks: A Natural Language Analysis of Vaccine Adverse Event Reports", *2021 IEEE International Conference on Bioinformatics and Biomedicine (BIBM),* pp. 614-618, 2021.
[http://dx.doi.org/10.1109/BIBM52615.2021.9669540]

[8] M.P. Abrams, A.P. Pelullo, Z.F. Meisel, R.M. Merchant, J. Purtle, and A.K. Agarwal, "State and Federal Legislators' Responses on Social Media to the Mental Health and Burnout of Health Care Workers Throughout the COVID-19 Pandemic: Natural Language Processing and Sentiment Analysis", *JMIR Infodemiology,* vol. 3, 2023.

[9] S. Zhou, J. Silvasstar, C. Clark, A.J. Salyers, C. Chávez, and S.S. Bull, "An artificially intelligent, natural language processing chatbot designed to promote COVID-19 vaccination: A proof-of-concept pilot study", *Digit. Health,* vol. 9, 2023.
[http://dx.doi.org/10.1177/20552076231155679] [PMID: 36896332]

[10] S.P. Yadav, and S. Yadav, "Fusion of Medical Images in Wavelet Domain: A Discrete Mathematical Model", In: *In Ingeniería Solidaria Universidad Cooperativa de Colombia- UCC.* vol. 14. , 2018, no. 25, pp. 1-11.
[http://dx.doi.org/10.16925/.v14i0.2236]

[11] N.S. Devi, and K. Sharmila, "Fine Grainded Sentiment Analysis on COVID-19 Vaccine", *2021 10th International Conference on System Modeling & Advancement in Research Trends (SMART),* pp. 707-711, 2021.
[http://dx.doi.org/10.1109/SMART52563.2021.9676205]

[12] D. Bhimani, R. Bheda, F. Dharamshi, D. Nikumbh, and P. Abhyankar, "Identification of Hate Speech using Natural Language Processing and Machine Learning", *2021 Third International Conference on Advances in Computing, Communication, and Applied Informatics (ACCAI),* pp. 1-6, 2021.
[http://dx.doi.org/10.1109/GCAT52182.2021.9587652]

[13] M. Sangeetha, and R. Giriswarna, *Harini. Detecting phishing attack using natural language processing and machine learning* , 2021.

[14] T. Peng, I.G. Harris, and Y. Sawa, "Detecting Phishing Attacks Using Natural Language Processing and Machine Learning", *Proceedings of the 2018 IEEE 12th International Conference on Semantic Computing (ICSC),* pp. 300-307, Jan. 2018.
[http://dx.doi.org/10.1109/ICSC.2018.00056]

[15] H. Ghanta, *Automated Essay Evaluation Using Natural Language Processing and Machine Learning,* 2019.

**CHAPTER 6**

# Classification of Medical Text using ML and DL Techniques

**Sulabh Mahajan**[1,*]

[1] *Centre for Interdisciplinary Research in Business and Technology, Chitkara University Institute of Engineering and Technology, Chitkara University, Punjab, India*

**Abstract:** The use of sarcasm in everyday conversation has recently risen to prominence. All the kids of our age utilise sarcasm to convey a negative message in a more nuanced manner. With the advancement of AI and machine learning techniques in the area of natural language processing (NLP), it has become more difficult to reliably and effectively identify sarcasm. This research provides a new method for sarcasm detection using machine studying and deep learning, hoping to make a meaningful contribution to this expanding area of study. In order to prepare the phrase for a hybrid deep learning model for training and classification, this method employs bidirectional encoder representations from transformers (BERT). The combination of CNN and LSTM creates the hybrid model used here. The suggested model has been tested on two datasets, with the goal of identifying sarcasm from nonsarcastic words. The trained model obtained a 99.63% accuracy rate, a 99.33% precision rate, a 99.83% recall rate, and an F1-score of 99.56%. These findings are based on 10 rounds of cross-validation performed on the model that was suggested using the medical datasets.

**Keywords:** DL techniques, Medical text classification, ML techniques, Real-time applications.

## INTRODUCTION

Herein, we built a classification system to categorise the reasons for ER visits based on free-text clinical notes in order to construct a nationwide injury monitoring system [1, 2]. However, a significant number of annotated datasets is necessary for the success of supervised learning methods in this field. Recent advances in neural language modelling (NLM) have been made possible by Transformer-based models that pre-train their neural networks in an unsupervised generative manner. We hypothesise that the number of annotated samples needed

* **Corresponding author Sulabh Mahajan:** Centre for Interdisciplinary Research in Business and Technology, Chitkara University Institute of Engineering and Technology, Chitkara University, Punjab, India;
E-mail: sulabh.mahajan.orp@chitkara.edu.in

**Pankaj Kumar Mishra and Satya Prakash Yadav (Eds.)**

for supervised fine-tuning may be greatly reduced by using a generative self-supervised pre-training phase [3- 5]. There are two primary schools of thought tried when attempting the difficult Natural Language Processing job of text categorization of unknown classes. Instances are categorised using similarities between document representations and class description representations in similarity-based techniques. By correctly labelling articles as belonging to unknown classes, zero-shot text classification methods hope to generalise information acquired during a training job [6-8]. Although prior research has explored some of these categories, the trials reported in the literature do not allow for a direct comparison. In recent years, there has been a lot of research into the possibility of automating the process of illness diagnosis in GI-related movies and photos. However, text and location overlays often degrade the quality of photographic data [9, 10]. In this study, we show several approaches to preprocessing such pictures and detail our methodology for classifying GI diseases using the Kvasir v2 dataset. Electronic Health Records (EHR) clinical notes provide extensive documentation of patients, allowing for phenotypic inference for illness diagnosis and patient characteristics analysis through cohort selection. Patients may be encoded into fixed-length vectors *via* unsupervised user embedding, which does not rely on human supervision. The retrieved medical ideas from the clinical notes include several links between patients and their clinical classifications. On the other hand, current unsupervised methods of user embeddings from clinical notes do not explicitly integrate medical ideas. Since its inception, coronavirus has caused widespread destruction and altered the human way of life in many ways. Researchers can monitor the public health reaction to COVID-19 with the use of the great instrument which is Twitter. In light of the massive data flood emanating from social media platforms, automated text mining methods may be of great assistance in locating, analyzing, and synthesizing relevant material.

## RELATED WORK

Free-text clinical notes were studied in this case study to see whether they may provide light on whether or not a patient's visit was connected to trauma. Using newly retrained GPT-2 algorithms (without OpenAI's pre-trained weightings), we analysed two scenarios. Scenario A included teaching the GPT-2 on a dataset of up to 161,930 trauma- and non-trauma-labeled medical records (26 studies of varied sizes). Scenario B (19 research cases) includes both an unsupervised (self-)pre-training phase containing up to 151 930 unnamed notes and a supervised (expert-)fine-tuning session with up to 10,000 tagged notes. Scenario B needed 10 times fewer notes to achieve the same level of performance (AUC>0.95) as Scenario A did (6,000 *vs.* 600). Despite having sixteen times data (161,930 *vs.* 10,000), Scenario A only improves on Scenario B in the worst-case AUC and F1 score. In conclusion, a general-purpose NLM model like GPT-2 may be modified to become a very effective tool for free-text note categorization with a relatively modest number of labelled examples [11].

In order to fill this void, this work systematically compares and contrasts many zero-shot and similarity-based methods for text categorization of unseen classes. On four text classification datasets—including a novel dataset from the medical domain—various state-of-the-art algorithms are compared and contrasted. Other baselines utilised in prior work provide poor classification results and are readily exceeded, hence new baselines based on SimCSE and SBERT are suggested. When it comes to unsupervised text categorization, the innovative similarity-based Lbl2TransformerVec methodology is offered as a state-of-the-art method. Our results provide a clear advantage for similarity-based methods over zero-shot ones. Similarity-based classification results are further improved by employing SimCSE or SBERT embeddings as opposed to simpler text representations [12].

Several methods are proposed to inpaint issue regions in the photos in order to enhance the anomaly classification, and the impact of this preliminary processing on the raw data is discussed. Experiments conducted by our team reveal that the suggested strategies lead to an improvement in the Matthews correlation coefficient for GI anomaly categorization of about 7% [13]. We present a concept-aware unsupervised user embedding that uses MIMIC-III and Diabetes clinical corpora's text documents and medical concepts together. Extrinsic tasks such as phenotypic categorization, in-hospital mortality prediction, patient retrieval, and patient relatedness are used to assess the quality of the user embeddings. Our method improves upon unsupervised baselines, as shown by experiments on the two clinical corpora, and the addition of medical ideas may substantially boost baseline performance [14]. The current medical dataset on COVID-19, called CORD-19, was preprocessed and annotated for supervised classification tasks in this study. We provide a preprocessed dataset for the scientific community to use during the current COVID-19 epidemic. This may help provide light on how to improve upon certain COVID-19 social interventions. The cleaned-up version of the dataset in question may be found on GitHub [15].

## PROPOSED WORK

### Problem Formulation

Assume, $(x_1, y_1), \ldots, (x_N, y_N)$ indicates the class-labeled dataset used for training, $x_i$ signifies the specific occurrence of data, and $y_i$ indicates the name of the class that is $x_i$. The training data serves as the foundation for the learning system, which uses it to acquire a classifier $P(Y|X)$ or $Y=f(X)$. The categorization algorithm assigns a label to a fresh data point $x_{N+1}$ class labels using the previously computed classifier $y_{N+1}$ of its output. Each text object might potentially belong to many categories, making text classification a guided learning procedure in which the element in question is text and the aim is to automatically categorise fresh text input into one or more predetermined categories.

The mapping function is not known $\Phi{:}D{\times}C{\rightarrow}\{T, F\}$ between the two sets of words and subjects, where $D = \{d_1, d_2, ..., d_{|D|}\}$ stands for the collection of documents that will be categorised, and $C = \{c_1, c_2, ..., c_{c|}\}$ stands for the collection of categories that have already been established. For each set of coordinates ($d_j$,$c_i$), there are two possible outcomes: if the value is T, the document$d_j$ belongs to group $c_i$, and worth of $F$ designates that $d_j$ is not a member of $c_i$. That is to say, in the text categorization job, also known as the classifier, it is important to think about achieving the best estimate of the target mappings function during the learning process. Fig. (**1**). shows a System Model.

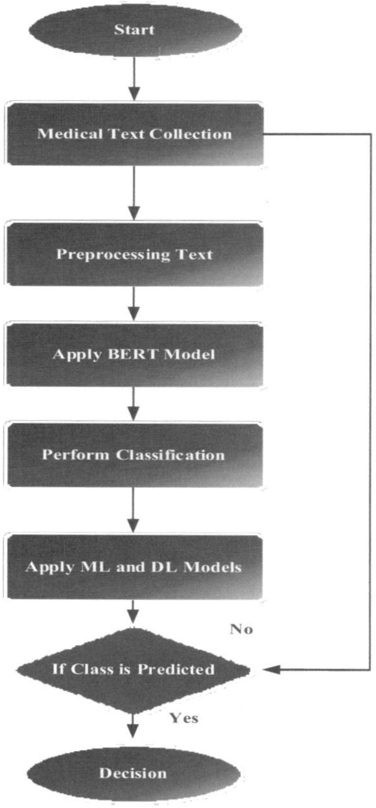


**Fig. (1).** System model.

## BERT Model

Google Research has created a model for linguistic representation called BERT (Bidirectional Encoder Representations using Transformers). BERT is a leading example of the latest creation of models based on deep learning for NLP that are already trained in an unsupervised fashion on an enormous text corpus, alongside models like ELMo and OpenAI GPT. The learnt language representation is robust enough to be reused in a variety of downstream activities with just little changes to the underlying architecture.

To address NLP problems in specialised domains, such as the categorization of support tickets by text, we may employ a trained BERT model in conjunction with transfer learning. The difficulty of teaching BERT means that transfer learning is essential. The first BERT classifier was pre-trained on a 3.3 billion-word mixed text corpus. It takes 16 TPU chips 4 days to finish the pre-training process, whereas a single GPU just needs a few hours to complete the fine-tuning process using models that have already been taught. The following steps may be taken to perform this procedure:

- Select a trained BERT model that best fits the task's linguistic requirements.
- Tailor the architecture of the pre-trained model to our needs.
- Customise the training data for our purpose.
- Further train the altered pre-trained model on our dataset to improve its accuracy.

The goal of BERT's unsupervised training was to enable it to forecast the next phrase and conduct masked language modelling. In masked language modelling, a random fraction of an input tokens is obscured before training the model to make predictions about the remaining tokens. For the next sentence prediction task, a model undergoes training for a binary classification task by selecting pairs of sentences A and B for every pre-training example such that 50% of the time B is the actual next sentence that follows A (labelled as IsNext) and 50% of the time B is a random sentence to the corpus (labelled as NotNext).

BERT uses a unified architecture to handle the aforementioned pre-training tasks, allowing it to be customised for use in a wide range of single- and multi-sentence NLP tasks such as text categorization, NER (Named Entity Recognition), question reactions, and more. Specifically, we need to train a modified version of the BERT model to classify texts. The first token from the last transformer layer's output may be sent into a method of classification of our choice to achieve this. The first token produced by the model is a summarized representation of the input sequence as a whole.

## ML and DL Models

Here, we detail the text categorization techniques we employed, including supervised Machine Learning and Deep learning algorithms. Supervised learning algorithms repeatedly estimate a function for prediction h(X) that maps X to Y using training data of (X, Y) pairs, where X is the set of input features and Y is the output. The algorithm's goal, at each stage, is to reduce some kind of cost function, such as $J(\theta)$, where $\theta$ means adjusting every coefficient of the equation h(X) to fit the training data $\theta$.

### *ML Methods*

Preprocessing and vectorizing the input text (carrying out stopword removal, stemming, *etc.*) is crucial before running the ML algorithm. At this stage, several feature reduction methods are also performed. For this text categorization task, we used six widely-used ML algorithms: K-Nearest Neighbours (KNN), Decision Tree (DT), Random Forest (RF), Naive Bayes (NB), Logistic Regression (LR), and Support Vector Machines (SVM).

In contrast to logistic regression, which cannot determine an appropriate decision border between classes, Support Vector Machines (SVMs) are powerful machine learning techniques. The approach discovers the hyperplane with the largest margin of error by locating support vectors for each data point in an n-dimensional space. The points in the data set that are in close proximity to the hyperplane serve as support vectors. In order to locate a non-linear decision boundary, the data is transformed from a space with fewer dimensions to a higher-dimensional one using a technique called the Kernel trick.

Decision trees are a kind of predictive modelling that uses a tree structure to organise data for use in making judgments. Each internal node in this choice tree represents an individual test on an attribute, while the leaf nodes indicate many classifications. A classification rule is represented by the branch leading through the root node to the leaves. The purpose of the approach is to discover discriminative features iteratively so that the dataset may be partitioned hierarchically. At each node in the tree's progression, an attribute will be chosen using metrics like entropy, information gain, and the Gini index. The most popular technique is known as "Information Gain" (IG), and its definition is as follows.

$$IG(S,A) = \text{Entrop}\,y(S) - \sum_{v \epsilon \text{Val}(A)} \frac{|S_v|}{|S|} \cdot \text{Entropy}(S_v) \quad \textbf{(1)}$$

The pre-split dataset (S) is denoted by letter s, an attribute (A) is denoted by letter v, the set of values is denoted as (val) for attribute (A), and $S_v$ is a subset of S where A has the value v. The quantity entropy (S) is referred to as:

$$\text{Entropy}(S) = \sum_{i=1}^{c} - P_i \log_2 P_i \quad (2)$$

Where c is the number of categories in the dataset and P is the probability.

In order to group data into the most frequent category amongst its K closest neighbours, a simple technique called K-closest Neighbours (KNN) may be used. Since no assumptions about data distribution are made, we call this a "non-parametric" model. During training, the algorithm remembers each data instance, and later, when classifying data, it calculates the average distance between each new point and the whole dataset. It finds the K nearest data points and uses the middle value in each category to determine the new data's classification. The most popular approach to locating neighbours uses the Euclidean distance, which is defined as follows.

$$d(P, Q) = \sqrt{\sum_{i=1}^{n} (P_i - Q_i)^2} \quad (3)$$

Given two data points P and Q and a dataset of size n, we have.

Random Forests: A random forest is a kind of ensemble learning that takes the best features from many decision tree algorithms and combines them into a single score. By introducing the idea of randomness, this method gets beyond the limitations of decision forests like overfitting. The method uses random subsets of characteristics for split nodes in every decision tree it constructs, and it uses random subsamples of training data to do so. The median or mean of all the decision trees' predictions is used to determine the ultimate output of the random forest.

Assuming that each feature in the dataset can be considered separately, Naive Bayes Classes are probabilistic equations grounded on Bayes' theorem. The following is a statement of Bayes's theorem for determining the conditional likelihood of the class label c provided as input data X:

$$P(c \mid X) = \frac{P(X|c)P(c)}{P(X)} \quad (4)$$

Where *P(c|X)* is the likelihood of a class given its history *c,P(X|c)*are the odds of X happening *c, P(c)* is the baseline likelihood that a class *c* exists and *P(X)* is the likelihood that X existed before. The most likely class label is returned by the classifier. Because the prior P(X) is shared by all classes, and the denominator may be ignored during prediction. Using the simplistic assumption of input vector independence, $X = (x_1, x_2 \dots x_n)$, the following are the model's predictions for the Y class label:

$$Y = {}_c P(c) \prod_{i=1}^{n} P(x_i \mid c) \quad \textbf{(5)}$$

Since no sophisticated parameter adjustment is taking place outside of certain probability predictions, this method is helpful for huge datasets.

The link between independent factors and the dependent variable that is categorical may be estimated with the use of a Logistic Regression model. Here is how we may characterize a logistic function in general:

$$P = \frac{1}{1+e^{-(a+bX)}} \quad \textbf{(6)}$$

Where P is the chance of occurrence, Y is the outcome, e is the natural logarithm base, and a and b are the model's parameters. While most applications of the model focus on binary categorization (Binary logistic regression), multiple classes (Multinomial logistic regression) are possible with few modifications.

### *DL Methods*

Deep learning is an emerging field of machine learning that uses ANNs to find novel solutions to difficult problems. Like the human neural system, an ANN is composed of many layers of units of processing (neurons). The activation function determines the value that a neuron will output after performing a weighted summation on its inputs. These models can learn the hierarchy of non-linear features to make distinctions between classes with the aid of a lot of layers and activation functions. Here, the kind of neural networks, the number of layers, the number of neurons as well as activation functions at each layer, as well as the kind of interconnections among layers are all defined by the deep learning architecture. Utilising a loss function and the learning rate, a model will be taught repeatedly to match the training instances by adjusting those weights and biases. Below is a brief overview of the five artificial intelligence models used in this study.

The Multilayer Perceptron (MLP) is a kind of feed-forward neural network with one input layer, an output layer, including one or more hidden layers. Every layer above the input layer contains neurons that use a function that is not on the sum of their inputs and bias. Consider the input to neuron i: $(x_1, x_2, .. x_n)$ with weights $(w_1, w_2, .. w_n)$ and a bias $b_i$. Then it gives an output $y_i$ as follows.

$$y_i = f\left(\sum_{j=1}^{n} x_j w_{ij} + b_i\right) \quad \textbf{(7)}$$

Here *f(.)* is the activation function; usually, we use the same for all neurons on the same cellular level. The non-linearity in the model is provided by an activation function, which is employed at every layer's node apart from the input layer. Usually, the sigmoid (logistic) function is used to activate intermediate layers. The backpropagation algorithm, a supervised learning technique, is used to adjust the model's settings.

The convolutional neural network (CNN) is an architecture that has proven successful in image classification tasks and is finding new applications in text classification. The network is equipped with a convolution layer, which is responsible for feature extraction using a kernel (a two-dimensional array). A kernel is a specialised detection algorithm that is often much more compact than the input data. Convolution is the dot product of the kernel with all of the overlapping regions of the input, both horizontally and vertically. A feature map is an array of two dimensions that is the output of a convolution. To solve the dimensionality issue, we apply an aggregation procedure termed pooling to every non-overlapping section of the feature map. The CNN design includes one or more fully linked levels before the layer that outputs data to help with the flattening process of the generated 2-dimensional arrays.

The LSTM process is unified as LSTM(x) to simplify the representation. Both convolutional and long short-term memory (LSTM) neural networks may use series and parallel architectures. Despite the inherent information loss in the convolution process, series structures are often used. LSTM neural networks are able to accept information in a compressed form since many time series properties are lost along with the series structure. Therefore, a parallel structure is used in lieu of a series one, and the outcomes are satisfactory. The structure is recorded and shown in all channels.

$$\text{channel}(x) = [\text{con}\, v(x) \oplus \text{LSTM}(x)] \quad \textbf{(8)}$$

Using (3), we can have a rough idea of how the character and word levels work. Input and result are both denoted by x in the expression $C_{out}$ and $W_{out}$. It may be written as:

$$W_{\text{out}} = \text{channel}_{\text{embedding}} = v_c(x). \quad \textbf{(9)}$$

Expression of the trained word-level embedding vectors $v_w$, together with an expression for the learned character-level embedding vector $v_c$, respectively. The combined meaning and the effect of the four channels' output is shown as the hidden layer's output.

$$h = [C_{\text{out}} \oplus W_{\text{out}}] \quad \textbf{(10)}$$

This result from the hidden layer is then transferred to the fully connected (FC) level, and lastly, the Softmax layer is utilised for filtering the output and is represented as:

$$\hat{y} = \text{softmax}(\text{ dense } (h)) \quad \textbf{(11)}$$

The following subsections elaborate on the four-channel representation.

## RESULTS AND DISCUSSION

This section provides an in-depth comparison and contrast of both of the proposed deep learning models, including a discussion on the evaluation indices and datasets used to test them.

Accuracy, precision, recall, and the F score are taken into account as assessment indices in this study. Here are the corresponding formulas for each:

$$\begin{aligned} \text{accuratness} &= \frac{T_P+T_N}{T_P+F_N+T_N+F_P}, \\ \text{recallotion} &= \frac{T_P}{T_P+F_N}, \\ \text{excractness} &= \frac{T_P}{T_P+F_P}, \\ F_1 &= \frac{2* \text{ precision } * \text{ recall}}{\text{precision } + \text{ recall}}, \end{aligned} \quad \textbf{(12)}$$

where TP stands for true positive, TN stands for true negative, FP stands for false positive, and FN stands for false negative. Experiments were conducted on significant benchmarking medical literature datasets, such as the AIM dataset, in order to evaluate the performance of the proposed technique for medical text categorization. These datasets may be seen as nothing more than a collection of abstracts from biomedical publications that have been annotated to identify cancer-related characteristics. About 1852 papers from scientific publications document three hallmarks of cancer: cellular energy dysregulation, inflammation that promotes tumour growth, and activation of invasion and metastasis. The Activating Invasion and Metastasis (AIM) dataset classifies data in two ways: Positive and Negative Table **1** illustrates the text classification for medical field.

**Table 1. Text classification data from the medical field.**

| Databases | Lessons | Verdict length | Terminology size | Database size | Drill set | Authentication set | Examination set |
|---|---|---|---|---|---|---|---|
| AIM | 3 | 834 | 29142 | 2647 | 1854 | 528 | 265 |

Different filter widths of CNN, different LSTM layers, different learning rates, different dropout rates, different optimizers, and different activation functions are all studied using the suggested second model Table **2** illustrates the comparison analysis of proposed works.

**Table 2. Analysing Performance Metrics in Comparison.**

| Database | Technique | Accurateness | Exactness | Recollection | F1 Value |
|---|---|---|---|---|---|
| AIM | CNN | 94.18 | 94.18 | 94.18 | 94.02 |
| | GNB | 88.33 | 88.17 | 88.20 | 88.13 |
| | RF | 85.00 | 84.18 | 84.18 | 84.05 |
| | NB | 85.00 | 85.00 | 85.00 | 84.90 |
| | SVM | 87.22 | 87.20 | 87.20 | 87.20 |

## CONCLUSION

This research provides a new method for sarcasm detection using machine studying and deep learning, hoping to make a meaningful contribution to this expanding area of study. In order to prepare the phrase for a hybrid deep learning model for training and classification, this method employs bidirectional encoder representations from transformers (BERT). The combination of CNN and LSTM creates the hybrid model used here. The suggested model has been tested on two datasets, with the goal of identifying sarcasm from nonsarcastic words. The trained model obtained a 99.63% accuracy rate, a 99.33% precision rate, a 99.83% recall rate, and an F1-score of 99.56%. These findings are based on 10 rounds of cross-validation performed on the model that was suggested using the medical datasets.

# REFERENCES


[1] V. Dogra, S. Verma, P. Kavita, P. Chatterjee, J. Shafi, J. Choi, and M.F. Ijaz, "A Complete Process of Text Classification System Using State-of-the-Art NLP Models", *Comput. Intell. Neurosci.,* vol. 2022, pp. 1-26, 2022.
[http://dx.doi.org/10.1155/2022/1883698]

[2] O. Akça, G. Bayrak, A.M. Issifu, and M.C. Ganz, "Traditional Machine Learning and Deep Learning-based Text Classification for Turkish Law Documents using Transformers and Domain Adaptation", *2022 International Conference on INnovations in Intelligent SysTems and Applications (INISTA),* pp. 1-6, 2022.
[http://dx.doi.org/10.1109/INISTA55318.2022.9894051]

[3] Y. Zhang, H. Jiang, Y. Miura, C.D. Manning, and C. Langlotz, " Contrastive Learning of Medical Visual Representations from Paired Images and Text", *ArXiv, abs/2010.00747,* 2020.

[4] A. Dhar, N.S. Dash, and K. Roy, "Classification of Text Documents Through Distance Measurement: An Experiment with Multi-Domain Bangla Text Documents", *Proceedings of the 2017 IEEE Calcutta Conference (ICACCAF),* pp. 163-168, Dec. 2017.
[http://dx.doi.org/10.1109/ICACCAF.2017.8344721]

[5] A. Haque, V.S. Reddi, and T. Giallanza, "Deep Learning for Suicide and Depression Identification with Unsupervised Label Correction", *International Conference on Artificial Neural Networks,* 2021.
[http://dx.doi.org/10.1007/978-3-030-86383-8_35]

[6] R. Kavuluru, S. Han, and D.R. Harris, "Unsupervised Extraction of Diagnosis Codes from EMRs Using Knowledge-Based and Extractive Text Summarization Techniques. Advances in artificial intelligence. Canadian Society for Computational Studies of Intelligence", *Conference,* vol. 7884, pp. 77-88, 2013.

**CHAPTER 7**

# Evaluation of ML and Advanced Deep Learning Text Classification Systems

**Tarun Kapoor**[1,*]

[1] *Centre for Interdisciplinary Research in Business and Technology, Chitkara University Institute of Engineering and Technology, Chitkara University, Punjab, India*

**Abstract:** Classifying texts into groups determined by their content is called text classification. In this process, automatic labelling of documents written in natural languages is carried out according to predetermined labels. Both text comprehension systems, which perform transformations on texts such as creating summaries, answering queries, and extracting data, and text-retrieving systems, which obtain texts in fulfillment of a user query, rely heavily on text categorization. In order to learn effectively, current algorithms for supervised learning for text classification need a large enough training set. This research introduces a novel text categorization algorithm that uses artificial intelligence techniques (machine studying and deep learning techniques) and needs fewer documents for training than previous methods. To generate a feature set from already-classified text documents, we resort to "word relation," or association rules based on these words. To classify the data, we use the idea of a Convolutional Neural Network with Deep Convolution to the extracted features and then employ a single genetic algorithm approach. The suggested method has been built and thoroughly tested in a working system. The results of the experiments show that the suggested system is an effective text classifier.

**Keywords:** Advanced deep learning techniques, Machine learning, Text classification systems.

## INTRODUCTION

The fundamental issue and severe difficulty of text classification jobs have always been how to apply cutting-edge deep learning technology to construct an efficient and potent text classification model, retrieve text semantic features, and obtain excellent classification outcomes on large-scale test datasets [1, 2]. Due to factors such as the randomness of incident occurrence in time and space, the lack of information at the outset of a reported traffic interruption, and the absence of

* **Corresponding author Tarun Kapoor:** Centre for Interdisciplinary Research in Business and Technology, Chitkara University Institute of Engineering and Technology, Chitkara University, Punjab, India;
E-mail: tarun.kapoor.orp@chitkara.edu.in

advanced technologies in the transportation field to draw insights from past accidents, estimating how long a traffic incident will last is a challenging problem to solve [3, 4]. Abstract Artificial intelligence (AI), machine learning (ML), as well as deep learning (DL), are becoming increasingly popular in many computer vision applications such as object classification, recognition of objects, human detection, *etc.*, but they place significant computational demands on system resources [5, 6]. The widespread and efficient solutions to the high computational requirement are multicore computers and graphics cards having a large number of specialised processing cores. Very few intrusion detection systems (IDS) use ML as their foundation [7]. These kinds of solutions provide a promising new avenue for strengthening network safety in the cyber realm. These tools may identify previously undetectable threats [8]. Researchers and consumers face these assaults in anonymity, making them unconventional. With the tremendous growth of the Internet comes an increase in sophisticated assaults. Machine learning (ML) and deep learning (DL) were developed to help find these assaults [9]. Therefore, several strategies for identifying sophisticated assaults have been presented by researchers. Many alternative systems have been created, based on diverse approaches to extracting features and classifying speakers, making speaker identification techniques one of the most cutting-edge current technologies. Speech recognition is a complex field that calls for state-of-the-art equipment and a wealth of audio data samples before it can be put to practical use [10].

## RELATED WORK

The focus of this work is on using deep learning technology to optimize natural language processing (NLP) applications in the areas of text semantics and text categorization. To solve this problem, we present the WC-GCN classification method, which integrates GCN and an attention mechanism. Three common text classification tasks are described as sentiment evaluation, topic analysis, and news categorization. Experimental evidence supports the algorithm model provided in this work. The suggested algorithm model outperforms competing deep learning-based text categorization approaches on three publicly available datasets. The accuracy rate for the news text was likewise rather good [11].

In this paper, we propose a new fusion framework for incident duration prediction that integrates machine learning with traffic flow/speed as well as incident description as features, encoded *via* multiple Deep Learning techniques (ANN autoencoder as well as character-level LSTM-ANN sentiment classifier). The study develops a transport and information science interdisciplinary modelling strategy. When applied to benchmark incident data, the method outperforms the best ML models in terms of accurately predicting how long an event will last. The results demonstrate that compared to traditional linear or vector regression support vector models, our suggested strategy may increase accuracy by 60%, with an additional 7% improvement relative to a hybrid deep learning auto-encoded GBDT model, which seems to beat all other models. San Francisco is the setting for the application because of the abundance of data it provides on traffic accidents (the Countrywide Traffic Accident Data Collection) and congestion (5-minute accuracy readings from the Caltrans Performance Measurement System) [12].

This book examines the performance of DL algorithms on various multicore hardware architectures. There are three classification issues for which a model using Convolutional Neural Networks has been developed. All of these trials have been conducted on three distinct types of computing hardware—a Raspberry Pi, an Nvidia Jetson Nano Board, and a desktop PC. Each hardware configuration's performance is examined based on its categorization accuracy and hardware response results [13].

In this research, we offer a comprehensive categorization for Machine Learning (ML) & Deep Learning (DL) algorithms. Moreover, the comprehensive review will shed light on the many techniques used in detecting assaults. The foundations of DL and ML lie at the heart of each of these techniques. In addition, a wide variety of systems and devices will be shown for carrying out DL and ML procedures and recommending security solutions that may be applied to the IoT [14].

In this study, a text-based (pre-defined words or phrases) speaker identification system was developed to efficiently and accurately identify the speaker with little effort, training data, and processing power. The first of the system's four key components is the development of audio databases. The research used two different audio datasets, the first being QSDataset and the second being audioMNIST_meta. The database configuration and processing methods are detailed in the main study text. The second phase of the study involves extracting the features using an algorithm based on pitch coefficients, and the third phase involves using a network of neurons as a classification. The study is complete after the system's performance and output have been confirmed. The test results proved that the MNN network could handle even a small amount of data since it obtained a perfect score. For massive datasets, the range was 80%-81%. In contrast to the CNN network, findings for small samples varied from 60% to 76% negative, whereas for big samples, the positive range was from 91 to 96%, and the outcomes were better than the existing approaches [15].

# PROPOSED WORK

## Text Classification Methods

### *Supervised Text Classification*

Once the categories for classification have been established, the text may be supervised and classified. Training and testing are crucial to its operation. To train the machine learning algorithm, we provide it with labelled data. In order to provide the intended results (the pre-defined categories), an algorithm undergoes training on the labelled dataset. In the second stage of testing, the algorithm is given data it has not seen before and asked to categorise it using the knowledge it gained during the training phase. One use of supervised classification is spam filtering in email. Emails are automatically sorted into folders according to their contents. Supervised systems provide the foundation for language identification, intent, emotion, and sentiment analysis. It may function for unique applications like finding emergency situations by sifting through massive amounts of data found online. It is like trying to find a needle in a haystack. To detect these kinds of events, we designed a public transit system with built-in intelligence. The classifier will need to be trained with great precision in order to correctly detect emergency situations from among millions of internet chats. To address this issue, we need to use specialised loss functions, to sample during training, and to use techniques such as stacking numerous classifiers, each of which improves upon the findings of the one before it.

### *Unsupervised Text Classification*

The process of unsupervised categorization occurs when no outside data is provided. In this context, algorithms seek to unearth underlying patterns in data. Keep in mind that what we consider to be logical divisions in our minds may differ from what really exists in nature. The data points are examined by the algorithm for similarities in order to form clusters. Data clusters are used for categorization purposes. Consider the case of an online search. The search word is used to form clusters, which are then shown to the user.

## Preprocessing

### *Data Cleaning and Preprocessing*

To "preprocess" text is simply to transform it into a more manageable and easily analysed format. Here, methods and fields are fused into a single endeavor. Our mission is to take the Kaggle data set (the field) and extract the most important keywords using the TF-IDF method.

### *Lowercasing*

Another simplest and the most successful ways of text preparation is to simply lowercase all the text data. It works for most text mining plus NLP tasks, even when the dataset is small, and it greatly improves the reliability of the predicted results.

### *Stop Word Removal*

Languages often include a collection of "stop words" that are always being utilised. Stopping words in English include the letters "a," "the," "is," "are," and so on. The idea behind end words is that by eliminating meaningless words from writing, we can better concentrate on the content.

### *Lemmatization*

On the surface, lemmatization seems a lot like stemming, where the objective is to eliminate inflections and return a word to its original form. Lemmatization, on the other hand, makes an effort to do things properly. It does not only remove excess material; instead, it changes words to their grammatical foundation.

### TF-IDF

The text must be converted into vectors before the algorithms can make any predictions. To determine the significance of a term inside a corpus of documents, we will use the duration frequency — Inverse documentation frequency (TFIDF) measure. Word significance is calculated by its frequency after eliminating punctuation, lowercase letters, stop words, and lemmatization. The initial dataset was segmented into features (X) as well as goals (y), with the latter being further subdivided into a training set (80%) and a test set (20%). Therefore, the methods would be taught on a single set of data before being evaluated on a third piece of data (which the algorithm has never seen before). The word TF-IDF is determined by multiplying two measures: frequency and document context:

- The number of times a word appears in a given text. Counting the number of times a word occurs in a text is the easiest technique to determine how often it is used. Then, there are options to tweak the frequency, such as document length or the raw rate of the document's most common term.
- The word's cross-document inverse frequency measure. This measures how often a certain term is over an entire corpus of documents. The closer to zero a term is, the more often it is used. The logarithm of the ratio of the total quantity of papers to the fraction of those that include a certain term yields this statistic.

- This value, then, will go close to 0 if the term is widely used and occurs in numerous papers. If not, it will go close to 1.

A word's TF-IDF score in a document is calculated by multiplying its frequency with its occurrence frequency. A higher weighting indicates more importance of the term in question within the context of the document. Fig. (**1**). denotes the DCNN-GA Model.

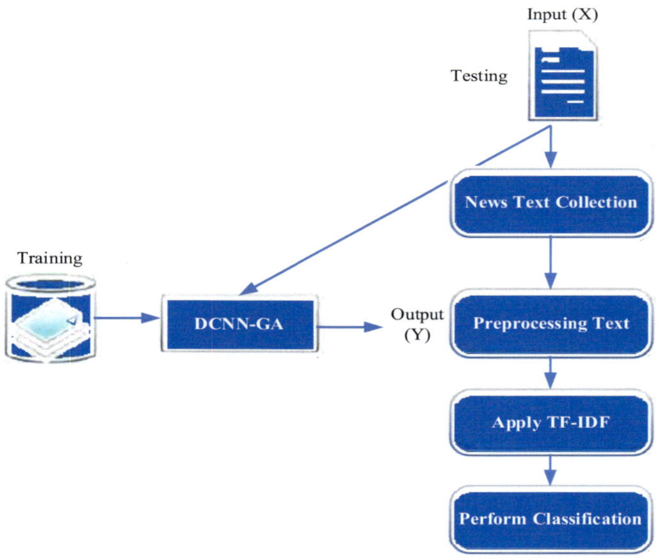


**Fig. (1).** DCNN-GA Model.

$$fidf(t,d,D) = tf(t,d).idf(t,D) \quad \textbf{(1)}$$

Where:

$$tf(t,d) = \log(1 + \text{freq}\ (t,d)) \quad \textbf{(2)}$$

$$\text{idf}(t,D) = \log\left(\frac{N}{\text{count}(d\epsilon D{:}t\epsilon d)}\right) \quad \textbf{(3)}$$

**DCNN with GA for Text Classification**

The growing number of practical uses for Convolutional Neural Networks (CNNs) has led to a surge in their popularity in recent years. Their efficiency is very sensitive to the design of the network and the technique of optimisation used to fine-tune the network settings. In this research, we provide several new, effective ways to train these neural networks. Currently, Gradient descent is the most cutting-edge approach to learning CNNs. We suggest employing Genetic Algorithm (GA) based approaches to optimise CNNs, as opposed to the standard CNN training methods. Steady-state, generational, and elitist GA techniques are used to implement these procedures. To do this, we provide novel genetic algorithms for crossover and mutation, as well as a novel encoding methodology of CNNs to chromosomes. We evaluate our encoding against the standard encoding in terms of efficiency and scalability. Additionally, the convergence rates and accuracy of the trained networks were evaluated across different GA training strategies. Finally, we compare Back-propagation training with Adam optimisation to our novel encoding and the improved GA-based training method.

Suppose an input feature map **A=A**$_1$,...,**A**c $R^{C\times H\times W}$ , in crder to get results, initially a global pooling is performed Z $R^{C\times H\times W}$, where H,W represent the feature map's height and breadth independently and C represents the total number of channels. The *k(k [1,C])* channel of Z can be expressed as:

$$Z_k = \frac{1}{H\times W}\sum_i^H \sum_j^W A_k(i,j) \quad \textbf{(4)}$$

Z is reorganised such that an 11 convolutional layer may make application of as many platforms as Z. Using the channel-to-channel correlation, this 11 convolutional layer can determine how to best distribute the weights across the channels. The result of the convolution is fed into a sigmoid activation function, which limits the weight vector's value. $V\in R^{\wedge C\times 1\times 1}$ into the range 0–1. The last step is to multiply A by V from outside . The end result $U\in\mathbb{R}^{C\times H\times W}$ can be denoted as:

$$\mathbf{u} = \mathbf{A} \otimes \sigma[\Phi(Z)] \quad \textbf{(5)}$$

where $\otimes$ means the final, visible result, $\sigma$ denotes the S-shaped function, and $\phi$ denotes the 1 X 1 convolution. This transforms feature map A into feature map U, which has more reliable data.

## RESULTS AND DISCUSSION

Here, we provide a brief introduction to the metrics often used in text classification model evaluation and then provide a quantitative study of the performance of a variety of ML and DL-based model designs for text classification on widely-used benchmarks.

- MPQA. The Multi-Perspective Question Answering (MPQA) database is a body of opinions labelled in two ways. The total number of sentences in MPQA is

10,606. These sentences were taken from news items covering a broad range of topics. There are only 3,311 positive entries and 7,293 negative ones in this sample.

- Amazon. This collection of Amazon customer reviews is often used. There are labels for both two-way (binary) and five-way (multi-class) categorization systems. The Amazon region binary classification dataset includes 3,600,000 training reviews and 400,000 test reviews. There are 3,000,000 training reviews and 650,000 test reviews in Amazon's 5-class classification dataset (Amazon-5).

Precision and Variation of Error. These are the most important indicators of a categorization model's efficacy. True positive (TP), false positive (FP), true negative (TN), and false negative (FN) will serve as abbreviations. Equation (2) provides a definition of the category Accuracy and the Error Rate as follows:

$$\text{Accuracy} = \frac{(\text{TP+TN})}{N}, \quad \text{Error rate} = \frac{(\text{FP+FN})}{N}, \tag{6}$$

here N refers to the overall amount of samples. Since Mistake Rate = 1 - Accuracy,

Accuracy, memory, and the "F" factor can be obtained. For unbalanced test sets—where the bulk of the test items have one class label—these are also key measures, generally utilised more than reliability or error rate. For a binary classification problem, we have a definition for precision and recall in Equation (3). By averaging the values of accuracy and recall, as shown in Equation (3), we arrive at the F1 score. At 1, which represents flawless accuracy and recall, the F1 score is at its highest, while at 0, it is at its lowest:

$$\text{Precision} = \frac{\text{TP}}{\text{TP+FP}}, \quad \text{Recall} = \frac{\text{TP}}{\text{TP+FN}}, \quad \text{F1-score} = \frac{2\ \text{Prec Rec}}{\text{Prec + Rec}}. \tag{7}$$

We can always calculate the accuracy and recollection for every label for a class and analyse the performance on class labels, or we can use the mean of the values to obtain the overall precision and recall for a multi-class classification task. Fig. (**2**) illustrates the comparison of proposed and existing works.

The accurate categorization of the NBC model is impacted in part by the Naive Bayesian algorithm's assumption that qualities are independent of each other, which is frequently not true in actual situations. A Naive Bayesian classification technique performs best when the relationship between the characteristics of the data set is generally independent. However, the classification impact would be substantially diminished when independence of characteristics of data sets is impossible to achieve in many circumstances due to the features of data sets being commonly associated with each other. While it is true that support vector machines (SVMs) excel at dealing with small samples of nonlinear and high-dimensional data, they are not without their drawbacks. SVMs are restricted to dealing with only second-class classification problems and have poor solving effects for many other classification problems. The continuous fields are hard to forecast with the Decision Tree classifier, and the time-sequence data requires extensive preprocessing. When you have too many categories, errors may multiply more rapidly; when using a general method for classification, it is not sufficient to just categorise things based on their area. The following are some of the major drawbacks of the KNN algorithm: first, when there is an imbalance in the samples, such as when one class has a big sample size and the other classes have small sample sizes. Classification mistakes are possible due to the huge sample sizes of the K nearest neighbours of the new sample. The second drawback is the algorithm's computing complexity; in order to classify a text, it must be compared to all other samples to see how far apart it is, and then its K closest neighbour points must be determined. Performance Analysis Amazon is expressed in Fig. (**3**).

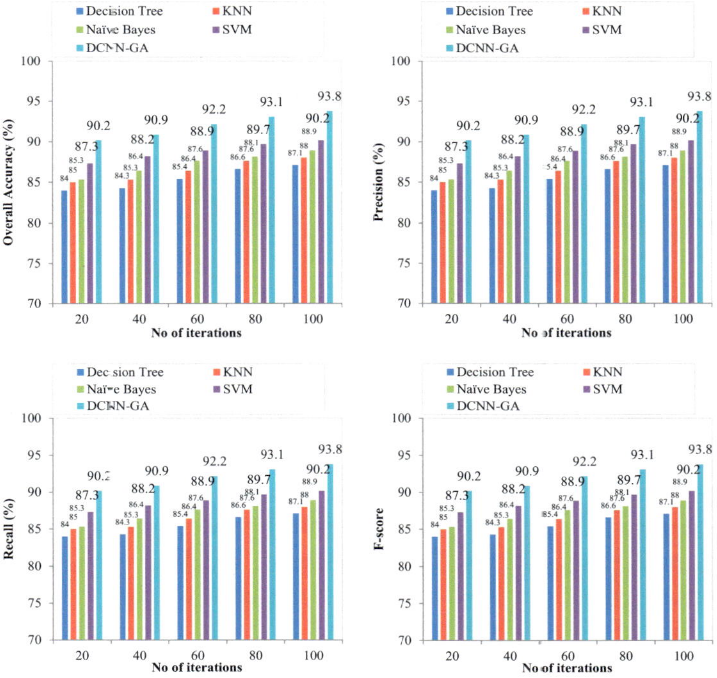


**Fig. (2).** Performance Analysis MPQA.

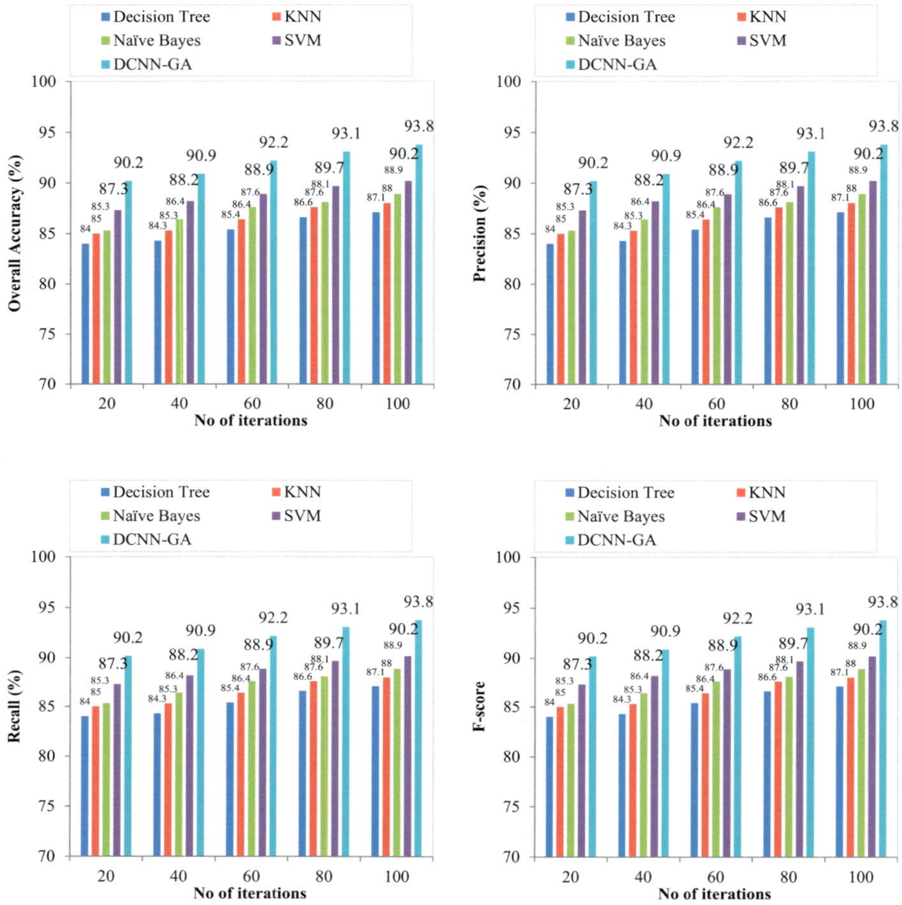


**Fig. (3).** Performance analysis amazon.

The random forest algorithm's main benefit is its pinpoint precision. High accuracy, particularly on the test set, may be attributed to the integrated algorithm's adoption since its accuracy is superior to that of most standalone algorithms. A random forest is resistant to overfitting because of the inclusion of two random components. When there are a lot of decision trees in a random forest, the training process takes a lot of time and storage space. The random forest is somewhat of a black box model, and it has many mysterious corners. The random forest technique is prone to overfitting on noisy data sets. The network of neurons classifier can make accurate predictions and do specific tasks in parallel. It is also very resilient and noise-tolerant. However, a neural network requires many input parameters and extensive training time.

## CONCLUSION

Classifying texts into groups based on their media is called text classification. Automatic labelling of documents written in natural languages is performed according to predetermined labels. Both text comprehension systems, which perform transformations on texts such as creating summaries, answering queries, and extracting data, and retrieval of text structures, which obtain texts in reaction to a user query, rely heavily on text categorization. In order to learn effectively, current supervised algorithms for learning for text classification need a large enough training set. This research introduces a novel text categorization algorithm that uses artificial intelligence techniques (machine studying and deep learning techniques) and needs fewer documents for training than previous methods. To generate a feature set from already-classified text documents, we resort to "word relation," or association rules based on these words. To classify the data, we use the idea of a Convolutional Neural Network with Deep Convolution to the extracted features and then employ a single genetic algorithm approach. The suggested method has been built and thoroughly tested in a working system. The results of the experiments show that the suggested system is an effective text classifier.

## REFERENCES

[1] K. Nagaki, T. Furuta, N. Yamaji, D. Kuniyoshi, M. Ishihara, Y. Kishima, M. Murata, A. Hoshino, and H. Takatsuka, "Effectiveness of Create ML in microscopy image classifications: a simple and inexpensive deep learning pipeline for non-data scientists", *Chromosome Res.*, vol. 29, no. 3-4, pp. 361-371, 2021.
[http://dx.doi.org/10.1007/s10577-021-09676-z] [PMID: 34648121]

[2] S.G. Sivanesh, "Air Quality Prediction using Ensemble Voting based Deep Learning with Mud Ring Algorithm for Intelligent Transportation Systems", *Global NEST: the international Journal,* 2023.

[3] R. Li, M. Liu, D. Xu, J. Gao, F. Wu, and L. Zhu, *A Review of Machine Learning Algorithms for Text Classification.* CNCERT, 2021.

[4] A. Suprem, S. Vaidya, A. Venugopal, J.E. Ferreira, and C. Pu, *EdnaML: A Declarative API and Framework for Reproducible Deep Learning,* 2022.

[5] B. Buyukoz, *Analyzing the Generalizability of Deep Contextualized Language Representations For Text Classification,* 2023.

[6] M. Alotaibi, and B. Alotaibi, "Distracted driver classification using deep learning", *Signal Image Video Process.,* vol. 14, no. 3, pp. 617-624, 2020.
[http://dx.doi.org/10.1007/s11760-019-01589-z]

[7] S.P. Yadav, and S. Yadav, "Fusion of Medical Images Using a Wavelet Methodology: A Survey", *IEIE Transactions on Smart Processing & Computing,* vol. 8, no. 4, pp. 265-270, Aug. 2019.
[http://dx.doi.org/10.5573/IEIESPC.2019.8.4.265]

[8] R. Chaganti, W. Suliman, V. Ravi, and A. Dua, "Deep Learning Approach for SDN-Enabled Intrusion Detection System in IoT Networks", *Information (Basel),* vol. 14, no. 1, p. 41, 2023.
[http://dx.doi.org/10.3390/info14010041]

[9] D. Guo, J. Zhang, B. Yang, and Y. Lin, *A Comparative Study of Speaker Role Identification in Air Traffic Communication Using Deep Learning Approaches.* ACM Transactions on Asian and Low-

Resource Language Information Processing, 2021.

[10] S.B. Bandaru, N. Deivarajan, and R.M. Gatram, *Investigations on Deep Learning Techniques for Analysing Mammograms.* Revue d'Intelligence Artificielle, 2022. [http://dx.doi.org/10.18280/ria.360313]

[11] G. Jin, "Application Optimization of NLP System under Deep Learning Technology in Text Semantics and Text Classification", *2022 International Conference on Education, Network and Information Technology (ICENIT),* pp. 279-283, 2022. [http://dx.doi.org/10.1109/ICENIT57306.2022.00068]

[12] S.P. Yadav, S. Zaidi, C.D.S. Nascimento, V.H.C. de Albuquerque, and S.S. Chauhan, "Analysis and Design of automatically generating for GPS Based Moving Object Tracking System", *2023 International Conference on Artificial Intelligence and Smart Communication (AISC),* 2023pp. 1-5 Greater Noida, India. [http://dx.doi.org/10.1109/AISC56616.2023.10085180]

[13] L. Kumar, and D.K. Singh, "Hardware Response and Performance Analysis of Multicore Computing Systems for Deep Learning Algorithms", *Cybern. Inf. Technol.,* vol. 22, no. 3, pp. 68-81, 2022. [http://dx.doi.org/10.2478/cait-2022-0028]

[14] Z.M. Khuzàie, and S.A. Albermany, "M.A.AbdlNibe, "Data Protection Methods and Intrusion Detection Systems Employing Machine Learning and Deep Learning in the IoT: A Comparative Review", *2022 Second International Conference on Computer Science, Engineering and Applications (ICCSEA),* pp. 1-10, 2022.

[15] Q.S. Mahmood, and Y.F. Al-Irahyim, "Text Dependent Speaker Identification System Based on Deep Learning", *Journal of Education and Science,* vol. 32, no. 4, pp. 118-125, 2021. [http://dx.doi.org/10.33899/edusj.2021.130144.1161]

# CHAPTER 8

# Machine Learning Method Employed for the Objective of Identifying Text on Tweet Dataset

**Sakshi Pandey**[1,*]

[1] *Centre for Interdisciplinary Research in Business and Technology, Chitkara University Institute of Engineering and Technology, Chitkara University, Punjab, India*

**Abstract:** When it comes to training ML systems, internet-based data is invaluable. Despite the difficulty in collecting this information, teams of experts from academic institutions and research labs have created publicly accessible databases. Twitter and other social media platforms provided large quantities of useful information throughout the pandemic, which was used to evaluate healthcare decisions. In order to forecast illness prevalence and offer early warnings, we suggest analysing user attitudes by using efficient supervised machine learning algorithms. The gathered tweets were sorted into positive, negative, and neutral categories for preprocessing. Hybrid feature extraction is the innovative aspect of our work; we used it to correctly describe posts by combining syntactic features (TF-IDF) and semantic elements (FastText and Glove), which in turn improved classification. The experimental findings suggest that when using Naive Bayes, the combination of FastText and TF-IDF achieves the best results.

**Keywords:** Fast text model, Machine learning, Text identification, Tweet dataset.

## INTRODUCTION

Recent advances in machine learning and deep learning enable novel methods of problem resolution and have far-reaching, game-changing effects across many sectors. The present paradigm shift has affected architectural practices similar to other fields. Hybrid methodology was used to investigate the impact on construction practises [1]. First, a text-mining technique is used for content analysis to undertake a comprehensive literature review of the field [2]. A computerised method of locating and labelling opinions expressed in the literature may help readers gain insight into the author's perspective and comprehension of a topic [3]. The most used language for sentiment analysis is English. However, it has been claimed that several approaches to sentiment analysis exist, preserving

* **Corresponding author Sakshi Pandey:** Centre for Interdisciplinary Research in Business and Technology, Chitkara University Institute of Engineering and Technology, Chitkara University, Punjab, India;
E-mail: sakshi.pandey.orp@chitkara.edu.in

**Pankaj Kumar Mishra and Satya Prakash Yadav (Eds.)**

the study as a fascinating research into Indonesian writings [4]. Several scholars have resorted to an algorithm for machine learning in an attempt to handle the sentiment analysis difficulty [5], thanks to the broad accessible Twitter data from previous years and the establishment of machine learning models. For a long time, telecom fraud has proven to be a serious financial issue for Indian internet and phone users. Attempts to uncover telecom fraud have traditionally revolved around warning users not to dial unknown numbers [6]. However, hackers may avoid detection by using VoIP (Voice over IP) phone lines to masquerade as legitimate callers [7]. Using the substance of a caller's voice rather than just their sign, this method may be able to detect telecommunications fraud [8]. Spam detection is crucial now more than ever because of the decentralised nature of social media and the ease by which incorrect information may be spread by people. Spam filters provide protection against this kind of fraud [9]. The amount of content released on Twitter and other social media sites about cybersecurity has increased significantly. When correctly analysed, this data might be utilised to create a system for identifying and counteracting cyberattacks. We propose employing deep learning to examine tweets in this research. The numerical content of tweets may be represented in a variety of textual ways [10]. By feeding these features into a machine learning architecture, better feature extraction and classification is possible.

These feelings are highly helpful in developing more rapid disease monitoring systems. However, the link between syntactic as well as semantic data and ML approaches based on feature types was not considered by many research works that helped evaluate tweets written in English. To anticipate and track the spread of COVID-19, we used supervised machine learning techniques to analyse Twitter sentiment about a dataset related to the virus. For the syntactic analysis, we utilised TF-IDF N-gram and word level, and to perform the semantic evaluation, we used Word2vec, FastText, and Glove. This study primarily focused on the following areas:

- Five cutting-edge feature extraction methods, comprising TF-IDF N-gram, TF-IDF community college-gram, Word2vec, Glove, and FastText, are demonstrated in this article. We also provide two state-of-the-art approaches using a TF-IDF strategy: the TF-IDF and Glove methods, and the TF-IDF and FastText approach.
- Using a variety of feature extraction techniques, we evaluate the efficacy of several machine-learning approaches for classifying tweets written in English.
- Many different machine learning classifiers have been studied, and the best combination and fusion of methods to boost their performance have been chosen.

## RELATED WORK

This allows for the methodical analysis of current developments and a debate on potential future directions in this area of research. Second, a Scientology study using bibliometric reviews may provide quantitative estimates of global research in the aforementioned area. We were able to get insight into research patterns and pinpoint the most important networks in this dataset by analysing the co-occurrence of terms, scientific collaborations, geographic distribution, and co-citation analysis. Finally, we discuss the pros, drawbacks, and future research directions for using data mining in the building sector based on our findings throughout the study [11].

Using Sentiwordnet and machine learning, this study aims to develop a sentiment analysis model for the next general election in Indonesia. The text and information of the tweet were collected. Joko Widodo and Prabowo Subianto, two contenders for becoming the president in 2019, were the main topic of the tweet. From November 13th, 2018, to January 11th, 2019, data was gathered for the campaign. Indonesian was used for the tweet. The Nave Bayes classification approach was used to analyse public opinion, and the results showed an accuracy of 74.94% with regard to the Joko Widodo issue and 71.37% for the Prabowo topic [12].

Thai civil case outcomes are often recorded in a way that lacks any real structure. A Thai civil case rationale document consists of four primary sections: the conflict, the truth, the decision, and the judgment. The first stage in creating a text synopsis or information extraction from a Thai civil case decision document is identifying the most essential elements of the document. Given this deficiency in the scientific literature, they set out to remedy it by devising a text categorization-based method for extracting four essential elements. We collected the dataset from the Court of Appeals of Thailand's website (http://www.supremecourt.or.th), whereupon we used two weighting methods and three supervised AI algorithms. The key parts of Thai civil court judgement documents were properly recognised in memory, reliability, and F1 tests [13].

This article gathers examples of misinformation spread *via* the media and online platforms. To evaluate current data and choose superior dataset descriptions, our suggested approach employs machine learning techniques. The next step uses Natural language processing to extract characteristics from the incoming text. For further telecommunications fraud detection, the criteria to distinguish similar content in the same call are then developed. Customers may protect themselves against telecoms fraud online by downloading an Android app that works in tandem with the system. The programme does real-time analysis of each call for telltale signals of fraud when a fraud decision answers. Based on our findings, the system is secure for users to engage with [14].

The widespread availability of false information *via* mediums such as the internet, electronic mail, and short message service (SMS) has contributed significantly to the present state of affairs. There are a variety of methods for spam recognition and classification. Each comes with its own set of advantages and disadvantages. We use a machine learning technique called a "Support Vector Machine" for this purpose. To classify information, Simple Voting Machines (SVMs) propose a hyperplane or line. As long as the model is provided with training data that includes labels for each classification, it can accurately place any piece of text into the appropriate category [15].

## PROPOSED WORK

### Data Collection

Due to limitations in the Twitter API, we used a Twitter dataset that will be publicly accessible on IEEE's website starting on March 20, 2020. The provided database mostly comprised of geo-tagged tweets using just tweet IDs of people and was filtered based on phrases related to COVID-19, since Twitter does not allow third parties to contribute tweets or get streams of whole tweets. In order to gather complete Twitter data, such as tweet ID, tweet happy, location, and creation time, we may hydrate the IDs utilising the DocNow hydrator software, a desktop tool that enables hydrate of tweets in JSON & CSV format. We also download a CSV file containing all of the hydrated tweets between 20 March 2020 to 26 May 2021. In addition, this research solely presents the retrieved tweets in English. Twitter Sentiment Analysis is displayed in Fig. (**1**).

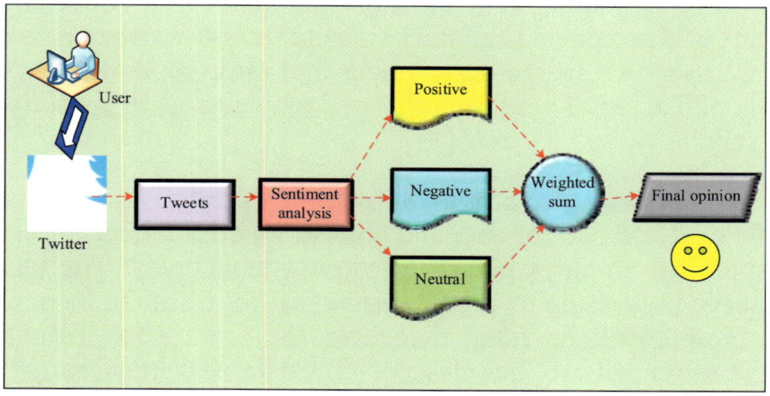


**Fig. (1).** Twitter Sentiment Analysis.

## Data Preprocessing

In this context, text categorization relies heavily on the preprocessing step. Using the Natural Language Processing (NLP) Toolkit (NLTK), we had to clean the messages by deleting any non-essential characters, including emoticons, hashtags, grammar, URLs, numbers, mentions, and symbols. The tweets were then lowered to text format. The next step is representing the tweets, which involves separating the written content into a list of terms using tools from the NLP library. Finally, we used the Porter stemmed algorithm to reduce the terms to their roots after deleting English stop-words. Among stemming algorithms, it is among the most well-known. Once we were done sorting and cleaning, we pictured the most crucial terms.

## Word Embedding

Estimating the level of semantic similarity between a source text and a target text is the goal of the process known as "semantic text matching." Let us see how this works with a real-world scenario involving locating similar queries. When a new question is asked or searched for, we want to see which questions from the big corpus are most like it. The task's emphasis on semantic meaning is crucial. Using the above illustration as an example, the question "what is the step by step guide for investing in the property market?" has substantial syntactic overlap with the source question while not being extremely related to it. The quantity of shared words is what we mean by syntactic overlap.

- Word Embeddings There are a number of dense embedding methods that have been suggested in the literature, such as word2vec, Glove, fasttext, *etc*. The goal of these methods is to map each word into a dense 100-dimensional vector of real numbers, placing them close to each other in the n-dimensional space so that they may be easily compared. There are several natural language processing organisations from which to get pre-trained word embeddings.
- Word2vec Interest in dense word embeddings was first sparked by the CBoW and Skip-gram word embedding models. The difference between CBoW and skip-gram is that the former uses the context surrounding the word as input to forecast the word, while the latter uses the word itself as input to predict the context around the globe. Both of these systems aim to capture the semantic link between words by extracting patterns of co-occurrence between them.

## Feature Extraction

Feature extraction comes next and is crucial in every classification problem. In order to get rid of the extraneous word, vectorization methods and feature embedding are used. Word embeddings have been created using pre-trained

Word2Vec, FastText, and GloVe on Common Crawl and Wikipedia using 300-D vectors, and vectorization has been accomplished using TF-IDF.

## Text Classification

Naive Bayes Categorization is a common statistical classification method that uses Bayes' theorem as well as the independence of components to classify input data. The intended operation is as follows: Creation of a text vector of articles x from a given dictionary, where n is the total amount of items in dictionary set W, and d is the number of occurrences in document d, is the first stage in text categorization.

$$\begin{aligned} W &= \{w_1, w_2, \cdots, w_n\} \\ X &= \{x_1, x_2, \cdots, x_n\} \end{aligned} \tag{1}$$

Based on the training data, the classification vector indicates that the text may be subdivided into m classes.

$$\begin{aligned} D &= \{d_1, d_2, \cdots, d_m\} \\ Y &= \{y_1, y_2, \cdots, y_m\} \end{aligned} \tag{2}$$

Training the naive Bayesian technique requires the use of D. Based on this, the most accurate categorization may be found by solving argmaxP:

argmax(yj|X)

Rendering to Bayes' proposition,

$$P(y_j \mid X) = \frac{P(y_j)P(X|y_j)}{P(X)} = \frac{P(y_j)\prod_{i=1}^{n} P(x_i|y_j)}{\prod_{i=1}^{n} P(x_i)} \tag{3}$$

P(y_j) and each P(x_i) are determined using the training data (D=d_1," "d_2,,d_m). Using the current set of data for input X, we can calculate any P(y_jX). where the greatest probability is assigned to document X's categorization. The naive Bayes method has fairly straightforward logic since it presumes that the data set's properties are unrelated to one another. The algorithm also has a good degree of stability. Classification performance with naive Bayes does not change much even when the data exhibits distinct features. That is to say, the simple Bayes technique is adaptable and will not drastically change its results for diverse data sets.

Feature extraction and supervised machine learning approaches were compared with the goal of developing a model for classification with higher accuracy and efficiency. We evaluated public opinion on the current COVID-19 epidemic as part of our study. For this reason, several textual analytic visualisation plots were used. To examine how individuals feel about a certain occurrence is where sentiment analysis shines. The dataset was first analysed in order to divide it into positive, negative, and neutral categories using the Python NLTK toolkit. In order to combat the overfitting issue introduced by random oversampling, this approach is used. In order to improve classification accurateness, the subsequent evaluation phase relied on feature extraction and word embedding. Embedding words is the process of representing and transforming the semantic and syntactic meanings of words inside a text into real-valued vectors for use in feeding the model. Both are supposed to complement one another in depicting the tweets more faithfully. Extensive testing using a variety of assessment metrics reveals that the SVM model outperforms its supervised and neural network counterparts using a variety of word embedding strategies. In addition, most machine learning algorithms' accurateness and AUCC score improved after adopting the suggested way of combining the two-word embedding.

## RESULTS AND DISCUSSION

Using the five performance measures of 'accurateness', precision, recall, F1-score, and AUCC, we evaluate the effectiveness of the experimental technique. Brief explanations of several metric types are provided below:

• 'Accurateness' is the harmonic mean (with weights) of 'accurateness' and recall. This is the equation for precision:

$$Accurateness = \frac{TP+TN}{TP+TN+FP+FN} \quad (4)$$

• The 'exactness' score indicates how accurately tweets were identified as positive. Here is a mathematical expression for the 'exactness' :

$$\text{exactrness} = \frac{TP}{TP+FP} \quad (5)$$

• A high recollection score shows that the classifiers accurately identified all positive examples. This memory is stated mathematically as:

$$\text{Recollection} = \frac{TP}{TP+FN} \quad (6)$$

• The F1-value is a harmonic mean of 'accurateness' and recall weighted by their relative importance. Here is a formula for calculating the F1 score:

$$F1 - \text{ value } = 2 \times \frac{\text{Precision} \times \text{Recall}}{\text{Precision} + \text{Recall}} \quad \textbf{(7)}$$

• The area under the ROC curve (AUCC) is a measure of the classifiers' discriminative efficacy. Here is how we describe the AUCC:

$$AUCC = \sum_{i \in (TP+TN+FP+FN)} \frac{(TPR_i + TPR_{i-1}) \times (FPR_i + FPR_{i-1})}{2} \quad \textbf{(8)}$$

where TP is the expected number of classes which are positive. What we call "true negatives," or "TNs," is the sum of all the negative classes that were accurately predicted. The term "false positives" (FP) refers to instances when a positive prediction is made but the class is incorrect. Moreover, FN stands for false negatives, or the total amount of inaccurate negative predictions for a given class. Fig. (**2**). is depicted in Classification Accurateness *vs.* Feature Numbers.

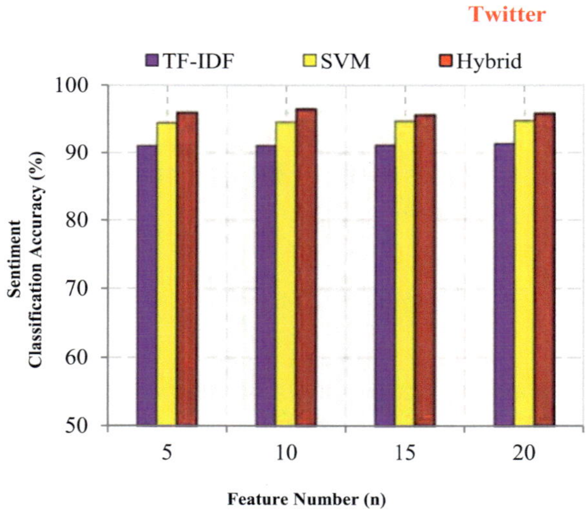


**Fig. (2).** Classification Accurateness *vs.* Feature Numbers.

Fig. (**3**) . illustrates Classification Accurateness *vs.* Feature Numbers, Fig. (**4**). depicts Classification Accurateness *vs.* Feature Numbers, and Fig. (**5**) . displays Classification Accurateness *vs.* Feature Numbers. The goal of our suggested approach was to identify the best-performing strategies and use them to improve the classification stage. Word2Vec performed better than the TF-IDF N-gram, which itself performed poorly. However, the classifiers enhanced the TF-IDF for every word, as well as Glove and FastText. With the goal of maximising the performance of the machine learning techniques, we decided to conduct two experiments, the first of which combined TF-IDF and Glove characteristics with various classifiers. The hybrid approaches significantly improved the efficiency of almost all the algorithms.

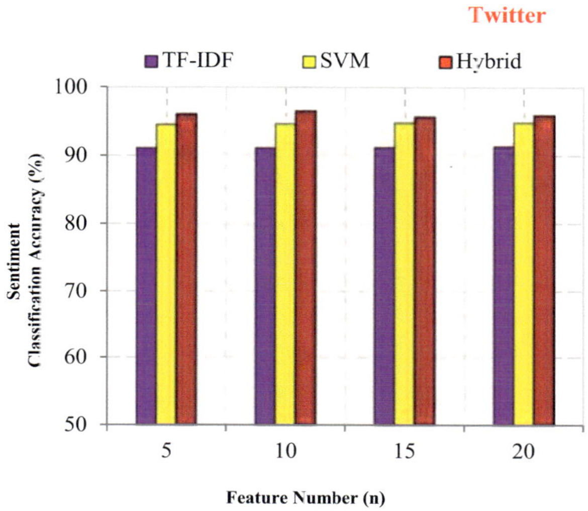


**Fig. (3).** Classification Accurateness *vs.* Feature Numbers.

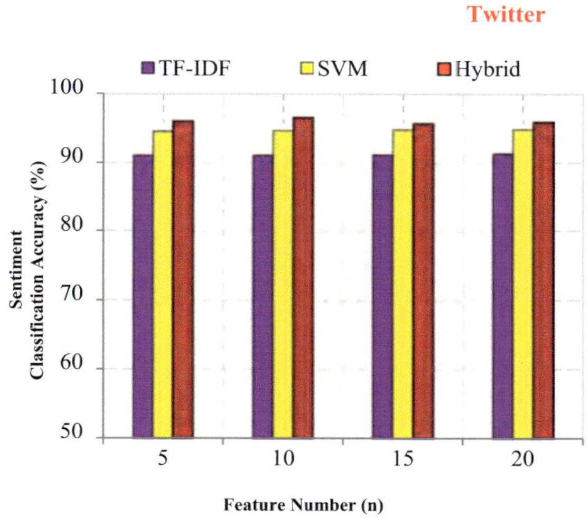


**Fig. (4).** Classification Accurateness *vs.* Feature Numbers.

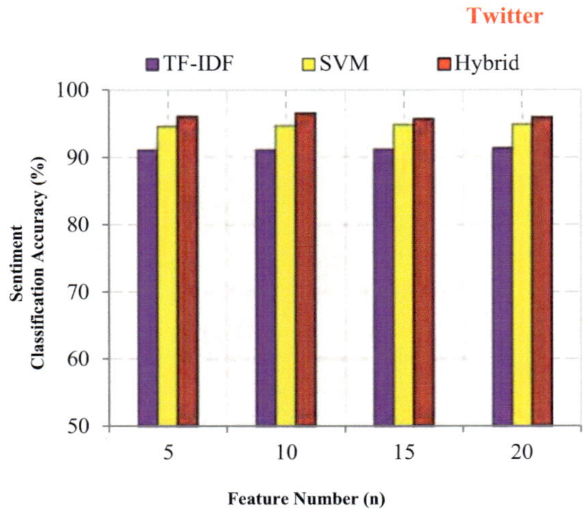


**Fig. (5).** Classification Accurateness *vs.* Feature Numbers.

## CONCLUSION

Our two-feature fusion strategy led to better performance for Naive Bayes than competing machine learning models, according to the study's findings. Our method outperformed the other six feature embedding techniques (TF-IDF unigram, TF-IDF N-gram, Word2Vec, FastText, Glove, & the two hybrids) tested. We also showed how the top feature approaches performed on our models compared to earlier research. We found that the methods we suggested were marginally superior. This may be explained by the fact that when compared to the other approaches tried, the combination of two efficient word representations better represents word vocabulary and extracts characteristics. While there are some bright spots, there are also significant caveats to our study. We can improve our method by expanding it to categorise tweets by language family (*e.g.*, Arabic, Spanish, and French) or by society (*e.g.*, by incorporating important COVID-1--specific keywords) for future research. Currently, we only use English-language tweets from around the world. Depending on how widely a certain platform is used in a given location, we may additionally include information obtained from other sources.

## REFERENCES

[1] K. Simran, P. Balakrishna, R. Vinayakumar, and K. Soman, "Deep Learning Approach for Enhanced Cyber Threat Indicators in Twitter Stream", *International Symposium on Security in Computing and Communications,* 2020. [http://dx.doi.org/10.1007/978-981-15-4825-3_11]

[2] A.A. Baloch, O. Albadwawi, B. Alshehhi, and V. Alberts, "Bandgap Model Using Symbolic Regression for Environmentally Compatible Lead-Free Inorganic Double Perovskites", *Proceedings of*

*the 2022 IEEE 49th Photovoltaic Specialists Conference (PVSC),* pp. 1234-1239, Jun. 2022. [http://dx.doi.org/10.1109/PVSC48317.2022.9938842]

[3] R.M. Montañés-Salas, "ITAINNOVA@DA-VINCIS: A Tale of Transformers and Simple Optimization Techniques", *Proceedings of IberLEF@SEPLN 2021,* vol. 11, no. 3, pp. 112-118, Sep. 2021.

[4] S.P. Yadav, S. Zaidi, C.D.S. Nascimento, V.H.C. de Albuquerque, and S.S. Chauhan, "Analysis and Design of automatically generating for GPS Based Moving Object Tracking System", *2023 International Conference on Artificial Intelligence and Smart Communication (AISC),* 2023pp. 1-5 Greater Noida, India. [http://dx.doi.org/10.1109/AISC56616.2023.10085180]

[5] E. OmidMahdiEbadati, and F. Ahmadzadeh, "Classification of Spam Email with Elimination of Unsuitable Features Using Hybrid GA-Naive Bayes", *Journal of Information and Knowledge Management,* vol. 18, no. 19, pp. 1950008-1950008, Sep. 2021. [http://dx.doi.org/10.1142/S0219649220500086]

[6] T. Papasotiriou, *A Term Clustering and Scientometrics Study*, 2019.

[7] A. Balahur, and A. Montoyo, "Determining the Semantic Orientation of Opinions on Products - a Comparative Analysis", *Proces. del Leng. Natural,* vol. 41, 2008.

[8] F.X. An, S.M. Stach, I. Smail, A.M. Swinbank, O. Almaini, C. Simpson, W. Hartley D.T. Maltby, R.J. Ivison, V. Arumugam, J.L. Wardlow, E.A. Cooke, B. Gullberg, A.P. Thomson, C C. Chen, J.M. Simpson, J.E. Geach, D. Scott, J.S. Dunlop, D. Farrah, P. Werf, A.W. Blain, C. Conselice, M. Michałowski, S.C. Chapman, and K.E.K. Coppin, "A Machine-learning Method for Identifying Multiwavelength Counterparts of Submillimeter Galaxies: Training and Testing Using AS2UDS and ALESS", *Astrophys. J.,* vol. 862, no. 2, p. 101, 2018. [http://dx.doi.org/10.3847/1538-4357/aacdaa]

[9] S.P.D.P. Mahato, and N.T.D. Linh, *Distributed Artificial Intelligence.* CRC Press, 2020. [http://dx.doi.org/10.1201/9781003038467]

[10] K.S. Mohsen, and W.S. Bhaya, "Attacks of Social Networks Detection using multiple Feature Selections and dynamic", *Mach. Learn.,* 2022.

[11] T. Papasotiriou, "Identifying the Landscape of Machine Learning-Aided Architectural Design - A Term Clustering and Scientometrics Study", *Proceedings of the 24th Conference on Computer Aided Architectural Design Research in Asia (CAADRIA),* vol. Volume 2, 2019. [http://dx.doi.org/10.52842/conf.caadria.2019.2.815]

[12] E. Miranda, M. Aryuni, R. Hariyanto, and E.S. Surya, "Sentiment Analysis using Sentiwordnet and Machine Learning Approach (Indonesia general election opinion from the twitter content", *International Conference on Information Management and Technology (ICIMTech),* pp. 62-67, 2019. [http://dx.doi.org/10.1109/ICIMTech.2019.8843734]

[13] J. Polpinij, P. Bheganan, B. Luaphol, C. Sibunruang, and K. Namee, "Identifying Decision Components in Thai Civil Case Decisions by Text Classification Technique", *in Proceedings of the 2019 International Conference on Data Science and Artificial Intelligence (DSAI),* vol. 2, pp. 12-17, 2020. [http://dx.doi.org/10.1007/978-3-030-44044-2_2]

[14] S.P. Yadav, B.S. Bhati, D.P. Mahato, and S. Kumar, *Federated Learning for IoT Applications.* EAI/Springer Innovations in Communication and Computing Springer International Publishing, 2022. [http://dx.doi.org/10.1007/978-3-030-85559-8]

[15] G.A. Reddy, and B.I. Reddy, "Classification of Spam Text using SVM", In: *Journal of University of Shanghai for Science and Technology*, 2021.

**CHAPTER 9**

# Textual Classification Utilizing the Integration of Semantics and Statistical Methodology

**Ayush Gandhi**[1,*]

[1] *Centre for Interdisciplinary Research in Business and Technology, Chitkara University Institute of Engineering and Technology, Chitkara University, Punjab, India*

**Abstract:** Effectively classifying texts is possible using several classification techniques. Machine learning constructs a classifier by studying and memorising the characteristics of several classes. For text categorization, deep learning provides similar advantages since it can function with great precision using simpler architecture and processing. In order to categorise textual information, this research makes use of machine learning and deep learning methods. There is a great deal of extraneous details in textual data that must be removed during pre-processing. To prepare it for analysis, we remove duplicate columns and impute missing data. In the next step, we use deep learning techniques for classification, including long short-term memory (LSTM), artificial neural network (ANN), as well as gated recurrent unit (GRU). According to the findings, GRU obtains 92% accuracy, which is higher than that of any other model or baseline investigation.

**Keywords:** Deep learning technology, Machine learning, Semantic features, Statistical features, Text classification.

## INTRODUCTION

Using data mining techniques to analyse photos is just the beginning of image mining. The term "web image mining" refers to a set of tools used to extract data from online images. The demand to mine image data online is expanding as conventional online mining increasingly concentrates on quantitative and textual data. There is an abundance of information available on the web, both written and visual. Web image mining is not as popular as text data analysis [1] due to how difficult it is to tackle the semantics of photos. Real-world data mining operations need efficient methods for building models that predict from extremely structured relational data. In this work, we take on the problem of learning classifiers utilising structured data that is relational and annotated with relevant metadata [2].

* **Corresponding author Ayush Gandhi:** Centre for Interdisciplinary Research in Business and Technology, Chitkara University Institute of Engineering and Technology, Chitkara University, Punjab, India;
E-mail: ayush.gandhi.orp@chitkara.edu.in

**Pankaj Kumar Mishra and Satya Prakash Yadav (Eds.)**

We show how to train classes at different levels of abstraction in a relational structure where relational information is organised in a hierarchy of abstractions that characterises the semantic content of the data [3]. When working with structured data, we show how to handle incomplete specification, which arises as a natural result of choosing a certain level of abstraction [4]. There is a nonlinear relationship between a woman's mental state—however subjective—and her labour, which could result in eugenic features, according to studies in obstetrics [5]. Because of these geographical differences, there is a growing interest in examining the connection among survey data from different areas. Research in conventional obstetrics has focused on trying to deduce the health implications of this state of mind [6]. However, much of the research done till now has focused on numerical relationships using statistical methods. This method sometimes runs into trouble while analysing data because of its inability to understand the underlying semantics of the data, leading to problems like data divergence and missing information (such as location data). The idea of textual content as well as semantics may be an obstacle for those seeking to make sense of the chaotic environment of information retrieval, categorization, and filtering. Interestingly, most of us, including myself, continue to consider that developing a linguistically principled approach to text categorization is an interesting research problem [8]. This is relevant to the main point of the book review, as you shall see. Thorsten Joachims proposes a framework for the automatic learning of categorization of text models and training to categorise texts utilisingSupport Vector Machines [9]. The analysis of texts for extracting data, fact, and semantics provides details in asimple machine processing form (such as ontology). It also provides text classification and clustering, including thematic modelling; and retrieval of data (including thematic search), which are all areas that can benefit from knowledge extraction techniques applied to large volumes of conversational texts [10].

Naive Bayes's flaw is that it treats categorical variables with zero probability and treats all characteristics as independent. Below are a few of this paper's key contributions.

- Utilising the Long-Short Term Storage algorithm, suggest a method for effectively classifying textual material.
- To choose the optimal classifier, we use a wide range of machine learning as well as deep learning techniques.
- The findings demonstrate that GRU works well since it has numerous hidden layers, retains relevant information while discarding irrelevant data, and has a firm grip on the data we provided with a considerable accuracy of 95%.

The remainder of the paper is organized into the following subsections. In the second section, we obtained a synopsis of the relevant research. Then, in Chapter

3, we explain in detail the procedures and techniques utilised throughout our investigation. The paper's findings and discussion can be found in Section 4, while its conclusion and suggestions for further research can be found in Section 5.

## RELATED WORK

This study offers a novel method for picture identification and classification by automatically collecting a large number of photos from the Internet to use as training data. The system uses content-based image retrieval (CBIR), that does not restrict target images like traditional image recognition methods, and support vector machine (SVM), among the most effective as well as widely used statisticians for general image categorization that fit to the learning tasks. The proposed method outperforms numerous existing search methods, according to experimental results such as support vector machines, image categorization, image collecting, and Internet image mining [11].

Our statistical strategy for partial specification is based on shrinkage. Results from experiments haveshown that (i) how the level of conception chosen can affect the performance of ensuing connect-based classifiers and (ii) how to investigate the impact of partially specific data on learning relate-based naive Bayes estimators for an article classification task [12].

To this end, we look into the extraction of the semantic relationship between data of dubious quality in the wellness information domain by using a bipartite approach called Geo-SPS and generic graph illustrations on geospatially-enhanced obstetrics and obstetric surveys. Our method is novel because we map semantic objects into a graph with two parts using principles from graph theory that were initially created for use in computerised physics. A new approach to determining semantic similarity is provided by Geo-SPS. Using this method, a graph of a convolutional neural can rapidly and accurately evaluate ambiguous textual input across several areas. We further evaluate and establish the practicality of Geo-SPS utilising a case investigation involving obstetric surveys along with medical information data from over 3,000 women across three different areas in China. The findings of this research show that Geo-SPS can reflect the mother's mental health during pregnancy and reliably detect birth defects from this diverse data collection. [13].

Topic text categorization (TC) is proposed as a solution because it is based on a wide language generality of (what appeared to be) a linguistically dependent activity. When applied to linguistic objects (such as the documents), the outcome is a basic linguistic model called the bag-of-words representation, which still achieves remarkable accuracy [14]. While most text categorization research relies heavily on empirical evidence, our approach, instead, is grounded in statistical learnability concepts and findings.

Building and employing models that adequately explain text structural elements on different levels (words, sentences, thematic text ruptures), their features as well as semantics, and their relations, which enable the creation of higher-level structures, is essential for the accomplishment of such methods. Genre, intent, audience, and disciplinary focus are only a few of the broader aspects of textual data that such models should account for. In order to solve problems in the analysis and creation of textual information, this work investigates the characteristics, advantages, and drawbacks of text modelling (structural, statistical, and hybrid), as well as its application at multiple phases (knowledge extraction, storage, and text generation) [15].

## PROPOSED WORK

### System Model

Learning and classification are two components of the classification issue. The purpose of the learning procedure is to acquire a classifier by constructing a classification model according to the known training data. Classification entails using the trained classifier to make a guess as to the label assigned to a fresh data point. The categorization issue is shown in Fig. (**1**). Here is a quick rundown of the text categorization system's key functional parts, as shown in Fig. (**1**): The initial version of the corpus requires preprocessing activities, such as formatting, to enhance the quality of representations of text and enable further processing. The following are some of the issues that must be addressed in text representation: The first step is deciding which parts of speech—typically individual words or phrases—will serve as text features. The second is selecting an appropriate model for quantifying textual things. Dimensionality reduction in features aims to classify text, to extract characteristics that are most indicative of the document's topic. The primary topic of study for text classification techniques is the construction of a classifier: the design of a text classifier. The categorization of new items is achieved by first selecting the text that may represent every group in the system of classification as the training set. The classifier is then taught using the training set. Evaluating the efficiency of the categorization strategy and the overall system is the goal of this stage. Different assessment criteria will be utilised for various classification issues, such as single-label classification *vs.* multi-label classification. Measures of a text classifier's effectiveness include recall, accuracy, and the f-measure. Fig. (**1**) depicts a System Model.

## GRU

The term "GRU" refers to a specific kind of a recurrent neural network. It is like a long short-term memory (LSTM), except that it only contains two gates instead of three: a reset gate, an update gate, and an output gate. GRUs are often easier and quicker to train than LSTMs since they have fewer parameters.

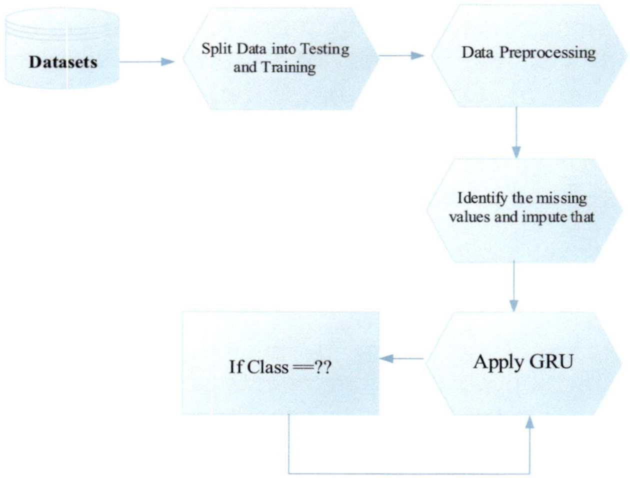


**Fig. (1).** System Model.

An LSTM consists of four primary parts: the input gate, storage unit, forgetting gate, and output gate. By "remembering" and "forgetting" the input vector, the vital aspects of the text are preserved while the irrelevant details are discarded. However, when the number of texts available increases, the problem that LSTM network education is time-consuming becomes more apparent. This is due to the difficulty of calculating between the gates and the large number of factors involved. We introduce GRU, a simpler model of neural networks that overcomes some of the limitations of the LSTM model. By fusing the forget gate with the input gate, the LSTM-based GRU model creates an update gate.

Gated recurrent unit networks (GRU) are an alternative to RNN that effectively address the issue of long-term reliance by using a reset gate and an update gate to determine whether or not to discard and update input. In comparison to LSTM, GRU has fewer parameters and is simpler to compute, allowing it to improve training efficiency up to a point while still producing the same result. In this study, the GRU model is used to extract the text's semantic context. The GRU model's structure is shown in Fig. (**2**).

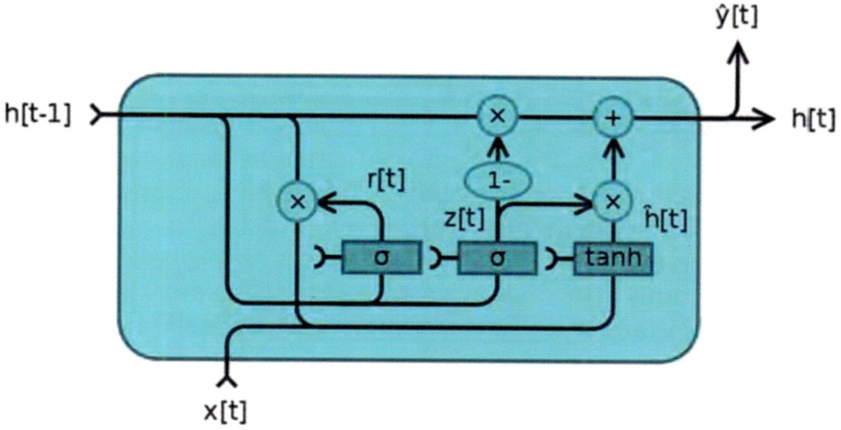


**Fig. (2).** GRU Model.

You may learn how the status of a previously concealed layer affects the active layer by using the update gate. The present layer is affected more strongly in the past when a bigger value is entered into the update gate. The calculation performed by the update gate is shown in (1).

$$U_m = \sigma(W_U \cdot [h_{m-1}, x_m]) \quad (1)$$

The faulty data is cleared away *via* the reset gate at the very last second. When the value of the reset gate is decreased, more incorrect data is discarded. The calculation performed by the reset gate is shown by Formula (2).

$$C_m = \sigma(W_C \cdot [h_{m-1}, x_m]) \quad (2)$$

These formulae outline the process through which the current state is calculated:

$$\begin{aligned} \tilde{h}_m &= \tanh(W \cdot [C_m \odot h_{m-1}, x_m]), \\ h_m &= U_m \odot \tilde{h}_m + (1 - U_m) \odot h_{m-1}. \end{aligned} \quad (3)$$

Amongst them, $W_U$, $W_C$, *and* $W$ show the GRU's weight matrix, $x_m$ is the intake information, $h_m$ represents the model's current secret state, which is fed by $h_{m-1}$, $h_m$ may be the active state candidate, $U_m$ and $C_m$ represent the change and reset logic, š means multiplying the items at that place by their respective Hadamard numbers, and σ stands for the sigmoid function.

## Proposed GRU

Word2vec is like a basic neural network, including CBOW and Skip-Gram models as its major components. The CBOW model predicts the current value mostly on the basis of context, which is analogous to removing a word from its natural setting and allowing you to deduce its meaning. Simply put, the Skip-Gram approach is like being given a word and then asked to guess the words that may follow before and following it. While Skip-Gram excels in huge corpora, CBOW is more at home with smaller datasets. Fig. (**2**) shows how the CBOW & Skip-Gram algorithms are built. In this work, we use the Skip-Gram example of training since it is better attuned to low-frequency terms.

The suggested model takes a text sequence as input, or a string of words. For this reason, Glove vectors are employed to map phrases into a low-dimensional vector; these vectors were learned by Stanford University using the Wikipedia 2014 Corpus. The words used as input for training $[w_1,\ldots,w_m]$ can be represented as a matrix of m d-dimensional vectors of words called "word embeddings":

$$X = [x_1, x_2, \cdots, x_m]_{m\times d} \quad \textbf{(4)}$$

In this phase, sequence information is captured using a specialised RNN network called the GRU network. The two gates of a typical GRU unit—the reset gate and the update gate—work together to regulate data transmission. The candidate activation at each time step is determined by the combination of the current activation and any newly added candidate. The formula for a GRU unit's mathematical calculations is shown in Fig. (**2**). For the feedback $x_t \in X$, secret government is denoted as $h_t$. For a given time t, we have:

$$\begin{aligned} h_t &= (1 - z_t)h_{t-1} + z_t\tilde{h}_t \\ \tilde{h}_t &= \tanh\big(Wx_t + U(r_t \cdot h_{t-1})\big) \end{aligned} \quad \textbf{(5)}$$

$$\begin{aligned} z_t &= \sigma(W_z x_t + U_z h_{t-1}) \\ r_t &= \sigma(W_r x_t + U_r h_{t-1}) \end{aligned} \quad \textbf{(6)}$$

Where
$W_z \in \mathbb{R}^{m\times n}$ , $W_r \in \mathbb{R}^{m\times n}$ , $W \in \mathbb{R}^{m\times n}$, $U_z \in \mathbb{R}^{m\times n}$, $U_r \in \mathbb{R}^{m\times n}$ and $U \in \mathbb{R}^{m\times n}$ are weights. $n$ is the number of concealed elements, denoted by n. $h_{t-1}$ is the prior unseen condition, and $h$ is the hiding state candidate. $z_t$ is the inform gate and $r_t$ is the rearrange gate. The operator represents a multiplication performed element by element. Resetting the gate when $r_t$ is very near to zero, the unit operation may

treat the current input value as though it were the first in the input series and ignore the prior calculated state. tanh and $\sigma$ are the sigmoid function and the hyperbolic tangent, respectively. Each word in the input sequence is represented by its hidden state vector at each time step in the GRU model.

In light of this finding, it is suggested that a process of convolution with strong connections may be used to automatically extract multi-scale features. To allow the model to assemble representations from multi-scale features, each layer is densely connected *via* dense connection [6]. A convolutional layer is used in $l, W_j \in \mathbb{R}^{k\times d}$ as the $j$-th parameterization of filters is used with $m_l \in X$ words, and the result of the convolution is calculated as follows:

$$c_{ij} = f\left(W_j \cdot X_i + b_j\right) \quad \textbf{(7)}$$

Where $i=1,2,...,m...w+1,w$ is the length of filter, an $j = 1, 2, .... ,k,k$ is the number of filters. $X_i = [x_i,x_{i+1},...,x_{i+k-1}] \in \mathbb{R}^{k\times d}$. $f$ has a function in terms of ReLu (rectified linear units) $f(x) = max\{0, x\}$, $b_j \in \mathbb{R}$. The biassed term is $W_j$ and $b_j$ is similar to the convolutional window sliding.

This is what happens when we apply n filters to the convolutional layer l: $c_l = [c_{w},...,c_{ln}]$ then take an average to have a steady focus $c_t \in \mathbb{R}$.

Once the attention signal has been obtained, $C = [c_1,...,c_L]$, the concealed state vector is: where L is the amount of layers of convolution $h_t$ of GRU multiplied by $c_l \in C$, which is as follows:

$$X_t = \sum_{t=1}^{n-1} \mathrm{c}_t \odot \mathrm{h}_t \quad \textbf{(8)}$$

The whole context representation is then obtained by applying global max pooling to the subsequence $\tilde{X}$ as characteristics for tagging texts:

$$\tilde{X} = \max[X_1 \oplus X_2 \oplus \cdots \oplus X_L] \quad \textbf{(9)}$$

Finally, conditional probabilities for subclass space text classification are generated using dropout and Softmax. Dropout is sometimes used to avoid overfitting. The goal of training is to reduce the cross-entropy training error for each neuron. Here is how the loss function is written down:

$$L_{\text{total}} = -\frac{1}{N}\sum_{sa} \left[y\ln\tilde{X} + (1-y)\ln(1-\tilde{X})\right] \quad \textbf{(10)}$$

Samples used for training are denoted by sa, and sample labels are indicated by y.

## RESULTS AND DISCUSSION

Here, we take a look at how the suggested GRU model stacks up against the current state of the art.

**Table 1. Comparison of Hybrid and Classic Works on the Yelp Dataset.**

| Both Future and Current Projects | SCA (%) | Precision (%) | Recall (%) | F-score (%) |
|---|---|---|---|---|
| Multi-Variate and Heuristic Analysis | 72.46 | 94.76 | 83.15 | 89.16 |
| DBN | 74.53 | 95.11 | 84.76 | 89.89 |
| A CNN-based ensemble model for features | 78.48 | 96.73 | 87.85 | 91.56 |
| Modèle DL hybride | 82.46 | 96.78 | 91.14 | 92.76 |
| LAN2FIS | 87.65 | 96.84 | 91.66 | 93.98 |
| OA2SVM | 89.46 | 97.24 | 92.76 | 94.23 |
| Planned Hybrid | 92.48 | 98.18 | 96.75 | 96.86 |

**Table 2. Comparison of New Hybrid Approach to Twitter Dataset with State-of-the-Art Methods.**

| Both Future and Current Projects | SCA (%) | Precision (%) | Recall (%) | F-score (%) |
|---|---|---|---|---|
| Multi-Variate and Heuristic Analysis | 71.06 | 95.76 | 81.15 | 87.16 |
| DBN | 73.53 | 95.91 | 85.76 | 88.89 |
| A CNN-based ensemble model for features | 76.48 | 96.88 | 88.85 | 91.56 |
| Modèle DL hybride | 83.46 | 96.92 | 92.14 | 93.76 |
| LAN2FIS | 86.65 | 96.99 | 93.66 | 95.98 |
| OA2SVM | 88.46 | 98.97 | 94.76 | 96.22 |
| Planned Hybrid | 91.48 | 98.98 | 98.75 | 98.86 |

The suggested methods are compared against other classifiers shown in Table **1**. GRU has a memory function that can recall previous data in a sequence. In addition, LSTM may potentially eliminate unnecessary information from text input, which would reduce the amount of time and effort spent on calculations. As a result, the GRU is a great tool for text classification since it can ignore irrelevant data while retaining the order of events. Next, we employ GRUs because of the gating mechanism they possess. Comparable to an LSTM plus a forget gate, the GRU does not have an output gate. As a result, it requires less input. In certain areas, GRU's performance was on par with that of LSTM, including in the modeling of polyphonic music, voice signals, and natural language processing.

Artificial neural networks use algorithm learning that may potentially adapt and learn from new information on their own. ANNs display up to 81% efficiency on this dataset, making them a highly useful tool for irregular statistical information modelling since we only take categorical characteristics and exclude unnecessary information. K-nearest neighbour, random forest, and logistic regression are just some of the machine-learning methods that have been used in this dataset. The output of a categorical dependent variable may be predicted using a collection of independent factors and a statistical method called logistic regression.

## CONCLUSION

There is a meteoric rise in the quantity of textual information. Because of this, it is desirable to find workable ways for swiftly sifting through massive amounts of data, since doing it manually is arduous. Information is the data that results from categorization, and it is employed in the strategic planning of businesses and factories. In this study, we suggested a GRU-based strategy for categorising textual data. For text categorization, we use a variety of machine learning and deep learning methods. When processing text data, the GRU retains the presentation order. It also helps get rid of useless data, which is a big plus. We enhanced the Dataset's accuracy to 95% by using GRU's ability to filter out irrelevant data while still remembering where it came from, making it a powerful tool for text categorization and other text-based tasks. Many emerging algorithms for deep learning, such as BERT, will soon allow us to perform the classification process. Most cutting-edge systems (*e.g.*, BERT) not only employ a multilayer transformer and attention techniques that are highly parallelizable, but also account for bi-directionality. By fusing the best parts of recurrent and convolutional architectures, it achieves even greater performance than each alone.

## REFERENCES

[1] M. Hacid, Z.W. Ras, and S. Tsumoto, "Foundations of Intelligent Systems", *15th International Symposium, ISMIS Saratoga Springs, NY, USA, May 25-28, 2005, Proceedings. International Syposium on Methodologies for Intelligent Systems,* 2005. [http://dx.doi.org/10.1007/b136302]

[2] S.P. Yadav, S. Zaidi. C.D.S. Nascimento, V.H.C. de Albuquerque, and S.S. Chauhan, "Analysis and Design of automatically generating for GPS Based Moving Object Tracking System", *2023 International Conference on Artificial Intelligence and Smart Communication (AISC),* 2023 pp. 1-5 Greater Noida, India. [http://dx.doi.org/10.1109/AISC56616.2023.10085180]

[3] X. Fu, "Context-Aware Sentence Categorization: Word Mover's Distance and Character-Level Convolutional Recurrent Neural Network", *Journal of Artificial Intelligence Research,* vol. 45, no. 3, pp. 255-268, Aug. 2021. [http://dx.doi.org/10.1016/j.jair.2021.07.001]

[4] L. Normore, and M. Bendig, "Using a Classification-Based Information Space", *Proceedings of the 2020 International Conference on Information Systems and Knowledge Management (ISK),* pp. 75-81, Dec. 2020.

[5] S.P. Yadav, and S. Yadav, "Fusion of Medical Images Using a Wavelet Methodology: A Survey", In: *IEIE Transactions on Smart Processing & Computing* vol. 8. The Institute of Electronics Engineers of Korea, 2019, no. 4, pp. 265-271. [http://dx.doi.org/10.5573/IEIESPC.2019.8.4.265]

[6] R. Ossewaarde, F. Jalvingh, R. Jonkers, and Y.R. Bastiaanse, "Computerized Assessment of the Acoustics of Primary Progressive Aphasia", *Journal of Speech and Hearing Research,* vol. 65, no. 3, pp. 215-223, Mar. 2020. [http://dx.doi.org/10.1044/2020_JSHR-19-00294]

[7] Wei, Y., Zhang, Y., Ji, Z., Bai, J., Zhang, L., & Zuo, W., "ELITE: Encoding Visual Concepts into Textual Embeddings for Customized Text-to-Image Generation", *2023 IEEE/CVF International Conference on Computer Vision (ICCV),* pp. 15897-15907, 2023.

[8] X. Zhang, J. J. Zhao, and Y. LeCun, "Character-Level Convolutional Networks for Text Classification", *Proceedings of the 28th Conference on Neural Information Processing Systems (NeurIPS),* vol. 29, pp. 1-9, Dec. 2015.

[9] J. Howard and S. Ruder, "Universal Language Model Fine-Tuning for Text Classification", *Proceedings of the 56th Annual Meeting of the Association for Computational Linguistics (ACL),* vol. 1, pp. 328-339, Jul. 2018. [http://dx.doi.org/10.18653/v1/P18-1031]

[10] J. Wei and K. Zou, "EDA: Easy Data Augmentation Techniques for Boosting Performance on Text Classification Tasks", *Proceedings of the 2019 Conference on Empirical Methods in Natural Language Processing (EMNLP),* pp. 6382-6388, Nov. 2019. [http://dx.doi.org/10.18653/v1/D19-1670]

[11] X. Sun, X. Li, J. Li, F. Wu, S. Guo, T. Zhang, and G. Wang, "Text Classification via Large Language Models", *Proceedings of the 2023 Conference on Empirical Methods in Natural Language Processing (EMNLP),* pp. 4567-4578, Dec. 2023. [http://dx.doi.org/10.18653/v1/2023.EMNLP-4567]

[12] S. Lai, L. Xu, K. Liu, and J. Zhao, "Recurrent Convolutional Neural Networks for Text Classification", *Proceedings of the 29th AAAI Conference on Artificial Intelligence (AAAI),* pp. 2267-2273, Jan. 2015.

[13] L. Yao, C. Mao, & Y. Luo, "Graph Convolutional Networks for Text Classification", *ArXiv,* p. abs/1809.05679, 2018.

[14] S. Hu, N. Ding, H. Wang, Z. Liu, J. Li, and M. Sun, "Knowledgeable Prompt-Tuning: Incorporating Knowledge into Prompt Verbalizer for Text Classification", *Proceedings of the 60th Annual Meeting of the Association for Computational Linguistics (ACL),* pp. 3687-3698, May 2022. [http://dx.doi.org/10.18653/v1/2022.ACL-3687]

[15] D. Jin, Z. Jin, J. T. Zhou, and P. Szolovits, "Is BERT Really Robust? A Strong Baseline for Natural Language Attack on Text Classification and Entailment", *Proceedings of the 34th AAAI Conference on Artificial Intelligence (AAAI),* vol. 34, no. 5, pp. 8018-8025, Feb. 2020.

**CHAPTER 10**

# The Use of Machine Learning Techniques to Classify Content on the Web

**Dikshit Sharma**[1,*]

[1] *Centre for Interdisciplinary Research in Business and Technology, Chitkara University Institute of Engineering and Technology, Chitkara University, Punjab, India*

**Abstract:** In text categorization, texts are sorted into groups according to their content. It is the process of automatically classifying texts written in natural languages according to a set of guidelines. Both text comprehension systems, which perform transformations on text such as creating summaries, answering queries, and extracting data, and retrieval of text systems, which collect texts in reaction to a user query on the internet content, rely heavily on text categorization. In order to learn effectively, current algorithms for supervised learning for text classification need a large enough training set. This research introduces a novel text categorization system that makes use of an AI approach and needs fewer articles for training over information found on the web. To generate a feature set from already categorised texts, we resort to "word relation," or association rules based on these terms. The obtained characteristics are then processed by a Support Vector Machine, and ultimately, a single genetic algorithm idea is introduced for classification. The suggested approach has been developed and validated in a working system. The experimental results verify the effectiveness of the proposed system as a text classifier.

**Keywords:** Machine Learning, SVM and TF-IDF, Web Content Classification.

## INTRODUCTION

Thanks to technological developments, routine jobs in biomedical research and development are getting easier to do. In order to read the glucose level on the urine strip, a urine analyser detector may be utilised [1]. Your vision may be impaired due to cataracts, trachoma, corneal ulcers, or another eye condition. These four eye diseases may be halted in their tracks only with proper early identification [2]. Various eye diseases manifest themselves visually in a wide variety of ways [3]. The accurate diagnosis of ocular disorders, however, requires the consideration of a wide variety of symptoms. Due to the severity of the

* **Corresponding author Dikshit Sharma:** Centre for Interdisciplinary Research in Business and Technology, Chitkara University Institute of Engineering and Technology, Chitkara University, Punjab, India;
E-mail: dikshit.sharma.orp@chitkara.edu.in

**Pankaj Kumar Mishra and Satya Prakash Yadav (Eds.)**

problem, researchers have been working hard to develop better diagnostic and therapeutic strategies for plant diseases [4, 5]. To increase agricultural production and income, farmers would greatly benefit from the ability to make use of existing equipment to remove the barriers to agricultural productivity [6]. Tools come in many kinds and sizes, and humans have been using them ever since the beginning of time [7]. The ingenuity of humans has allowed for the creation of several helpful implementations. This provides the resources for individuals to address a broad variety of needs, including those in the areas of transportation, industry, housing, and computer [9]. In the current day, we serve as both creators and consumers of knowledge. Users may have a substantial impact on the future of digital information by contributing their ideas and opinions in the social media sphere [9]. These points of view include a wide range of feelings. Computer science studies for recognising and obtaining the sentiment underlying textual input constitute sentiment analysis, a technique for classifying public opinion stated in online forums [10].

Website categorization is a significant challenge with several real-world implications. Parental controls provide a child-friendly online environment. Without clear guidelines for website classification, many Internet users of all ages are exposed to inappropriate content and have a more difficult time finding what they need. There are no comprehensive or adaptable internet security options available right now. The courts' banning orders also do not apply to all problematic sites, and the domains of these sites often change hands. This highlights the significance of dynamic website categorization based on text data. This research involves the categorization of webpages using NLP and ML methods. Websites written in a variety of languages have their content gathered and preprocessed in preparation for machine learning. The research included a total of 17 classes, with the SVM technique yielding the greatest success rate in the classification of 0.8756.

## RELATED WORK

The goal of this research is to utilise the MATLAB programme to analyse glucose data from digitally photographed patients. Injections of insulin are necessary for the control of blood sugar levels in diabetics. Injections may cause minor physical harm, which may weaken the body's defences against infection. A lot of research has gone into developing noninvasive methods of detecting glucose, particularly those that use urine. In this study, image processing was used to examine the process of glucose testing that does not include a needle. Noise is reduced using a Gaussian filter and histogram-based feature extraction to facilitate information extraction from picture databases. The support vector machine classification allocates 70% of its time to training and 30% to testing. The processing time for the SVM classification results was under 0.5 seconds, and they were 85% correct. Medical decisions may be made in light of a person's diabetes, prediabetes, or lack thereof [11].

Utilising digital image processing, machine learning techniques, deep convolution neural network (DCNN) and encouraging vector machine (SVM), we describe a novel approach to automatically detect eye illnesses based on outward symptoms. We employ t-distributed stochastic neighbour embedding (t-SNE) and principal component analysis (PCA) with variables to improve feature selection. The proposed method dissects a frontal face image into its constituent components and automatically removes the eye area. The proposed method diagnoses and classifies a wide range of eye conditions, including but not limited to glaucoma a condition called conjunctiva cornea ulcer, ectropion, periorbital cellulitis, bitot spot of vitamin A deficiency. The experimental results favour the DCNN strategy over SVM models. We also compare our method to popular alternatives. Our method outperforms the closest rival by a factor of 14. An overall precision of 98.79%, a sensitivity rating of 97.1%5, and a specificity of 99.0% are all achieved by our DCNN model [12].

In this work, we used ML techniques to create a mobile app for diagnosing plant diseases and suggesting therapies. A filtering based on recommendation algorithm was then used to suggest treatments for the observed plant ailments, after which ANN and KNN were utilised to classify the illnesses. The results of the implementation confirmed that plant diseases were correctly detected and treatment recommendations were given [13].

Current customised internet search strategies do not take into account unvisited sites that may supply simple responses to the client's information requirements. A page in the results package may not solve the user's problem entirely, but it may point them in the right direction. Only by doing a semantic analysis can the concealed connections be uncovered. This study aims to classify particular connected sites by doing a semantic analysis of the search route and providing an efficient individualised site search. By providing context and a direct link between a user's search query and related websites, this facilitates online discovery. [14].

To identify the tone of Bangla-language Facebook posts about Bangladesh Cricket, this paper presents a sentiment polarity detection method that employs three well-known supervised machine learning algorithms: Naive Bayes (NB), support vector machines (SVM), and logistic regression (LR). Classifiers' performance is also examined and contrasted; employing n-gram as an attribute, LR achieved a higher accuracy (83%) than SVM and NB. [15].

# PROPOSED WORK

## System Model

Web page content might pertain to everything from personal to official to commercial to corporate matters. Internet users are interested in getting their hands on this data for many reasons. Therefore, in order to use the Web's data for any particular purpose, it is vital to have procedures that will categorise the Web Pages in order to offer users the most relevant data accessible on those pages. Using a level-based classification and hierarchical indexing system based on preset areas like athletics, equipment, and edification, this research provides a novel method for classifying Web Pages. The process consists of two major steps: training, and then testing. Dynamic Feature Extraction & Knowledge Representation are carried out throughout the training period. Content match for classification is performed using retrieved characteristics from Web pages during testing. The method has three stages: extracting dynamic features, representing knowledge, and classifying randomly placed web pages. The Feature Extraction process involves taking the headers and paragraphs of a website and extracting the relevant keywords. To rank the significance of each keyword, we calculate its frequency of occurrence and then multiply that number by a weight. To further categorise websites, the representation knowledge is employed for content matching. Maximum Entropy Classifier is used to determine the degree to which a website fits into each of these categories. Due to its superiority in search-based optimisations, Maximum Entropy Classification is being investigated. Three types of Websites—athletic, equipment, and edification—are used to test the strategy. Classification preciseness of 91% was reached, surpassing that of more traditional methods.

## SVM

Supervised machine learning models such as classifiers analyse data and detect patterns using a set of interrelated learning algorithms. This model works well with labelled data. In order to function, the SVM model categorises each sample into a few predetermined classes. Each data point in the dataset is represented by an n-dimensional attribute vector, which is shown in the n-dimensional space to maximise the difference between the various categories. A hyperplane is built, and each incoming data point is displayed on it until a classification can be made. The proper categorization of information point is established based on its position relative to the hyperplane. However, building hyperplanes is not necessarily a walk in the park. This is most convincing when the information is distributed at random. In these kinds of situations, the Kernel approach of SVM is used. The SVM is known as the Kernel technique of SVM when it is utilised in the SVM.

Linear, polynomial, radial basis function and sigmoid are all valid choices for the Kernel function. The choice of kernel has a significant impact on the effectiveness of the model. This model is a multiclass one that employs a "one *versus* the rest" approach.

**Proposed Classifier**

Fuzzy logic is used to classify websites into categories like "adult," "medical," and "normal," and support vector machines have been used in most recent research to detect inappropriate or undesired information. Features and pre-processing are extracted from the web page in order to determine its unique kind. The parts of a website are converted into an HTML file format during the pre-processing phase. With the use of a lexicon and morphological analysis, the Web content categorization system is able to extract this data and identify the various word forms. The tokenization method is used to divide a lengthy text into manageable pieces. Tokenization results are stored as arrays so they may be quickly compared to a dictionary of relevant vocabulary and terms for further analysis. After each word (common, restorative, and obscene) is recovered, the next step is the feature extraction process, and subsequently the accuracy rate drops. Thus, a SVM classifier is used to find meaningful features including crucial phrases while filtering out irrelevant ones. One special function is linked to the ability to recognise noteworthy characteristics. Any data with a content value higher than 0 is assumed to be medical or pornographic in nature and is omitted from the filter. Adult content identification relies heavily on FPv and FNv ratings, thus established techniques were employed to assess the effectiveness of the categorization system. A total of 4646 pages in three broad categories were chosen at random. The algorithm analysed the data found on these websites and separated it into three categories: general, health-related, and adult. In the proposed approach, 1787 pages are considered typical, 2251 are considered pornographic, and 608 are considered medical. The indicator value for Web page categorization was assessed for every request to the Web using a lexical dictionary and a selected set of characteristics. Once the indication value was validated, users were denied access to mature material. The suggested fuzzy ontology is measured using a variety of metrics, including the precision, recollection, accuracy, and function types described by n-gram, KNN, and SVM classifiers.

The SVM is able to do several classifications, as well as accomplish two goals. Here are the several stages of the SVM procedure:

- The data structure will be adjusted based upon the SVM package.
- In order to scale the data, you must take a look at the RBF Score.

- Train the whole training set using cross-validation to determine the optimal parameter.
- These actions are taken for SVM training once pre-processing has been completed. The suggested method classifies the two types using a suitable support vector. Next, the classification function decides which answer is the most accurate in terms of returning the hyperplane with the largest margin. The polarity of every feature is evaluated after the positive and negative assessment has been performed using FDO.

To distinguish between negative and positive instances of darkness, a support vector machine (SVM) uses a linear hyperplane learned from the training set. The idea of superspace, which maximises the gap among both positive and negative numbers, is where you will find hyperplanes, or support vectors. In linear classification, the two main axes are parallel to the hyperplane as well as vertical weight (which also takes into account training with the involvement of the components). A bias b determines the distance of the hyperplane from the origin. Unlabeled example x is considered positive if and only if $f(\ddot{x} = \ddot{W}\ddot{X} + \dot{b} \geq 0)$, Otherwise, it is labelled as unfavourable.

The key advantages of using a support vector machine' (SVM) as a text classifier are that it can effectively estimate similarity without the need for training samples, and can represent features in their converted space regardless of whether they are exponential or significantly sized. It can handle a wide variety of feature spaces. Due to its capacity to deal with large dimensional and redundant data, the SVM does not need any kind of aggressive feature selection method. For instance, studying C4.5 in the area of DW and contrasting it to other classifiers demonstrates the efficacy of the SVM classifier. The majority of SVM-based methods demonstrated the SVM's superior classification accuracy.

## RESULTS AND DISCUSSION

The outcomes of the planned effort are described here. This study is rationally executed, and both statistical and theoretical evaluations of the outcomes are provided. Using a Java framework with a large dataset, the outcomes are shown. Datasets and measurements for success or failure are part of the experimental setup. Three distinct types of Web pages—athelitc, politics, and edification—are used to test the approach. The 99 percent accuracy of the method in classification is a significant improvement over more traditional methods. Fig. (**1**). displays Accurateness (a). athelitc, (b). edification (c). equipment, Fig. (**2**). represents the

Precision(a). athelitc, (b). edification (c). equipment, Fig. (**3**). shows Recall (a). athelitc, (b). edification (c). equipment, Fig. (**4**). displays F-Value (a). athelitc, (b). edification (c). equipment, Fig. (**5**) portrays –Error Rate (a). athelitc, (b). edification (c). equipment.

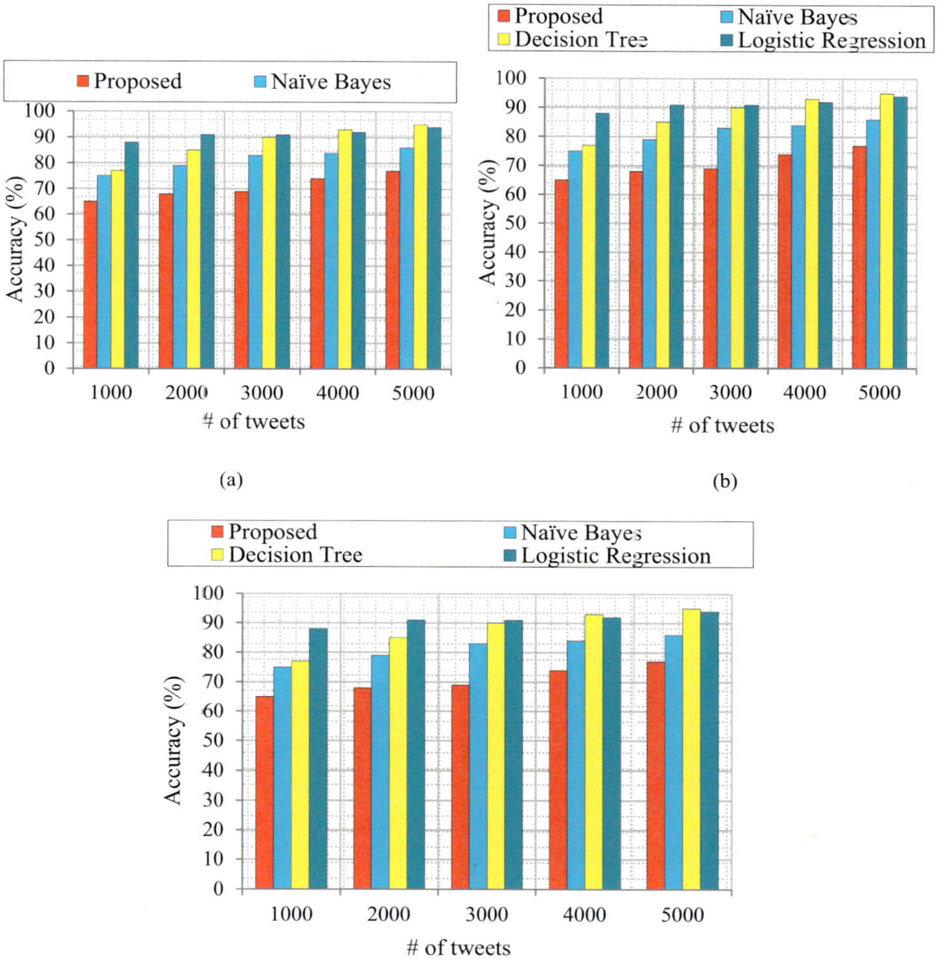


(c)

**Fig. (1).** Accurateness (**a**). Athelitc (**b**). Edification (**c**). Equipment.

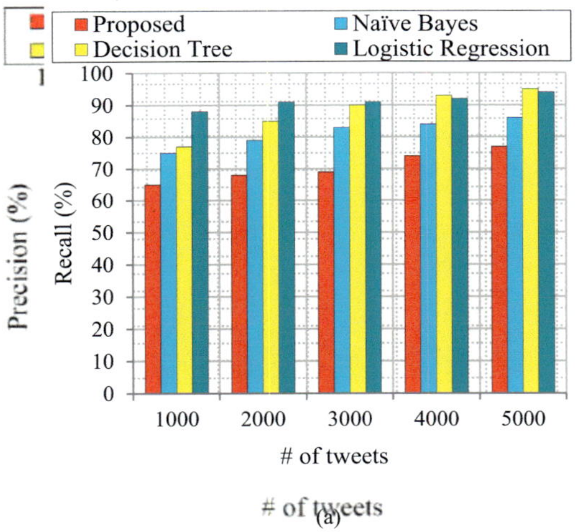


(a)

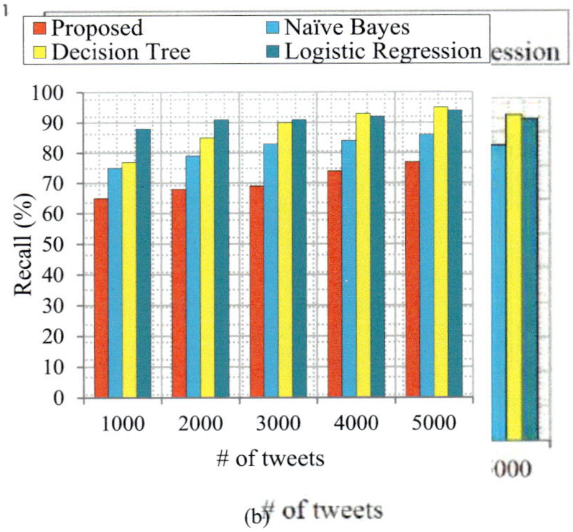


(b)

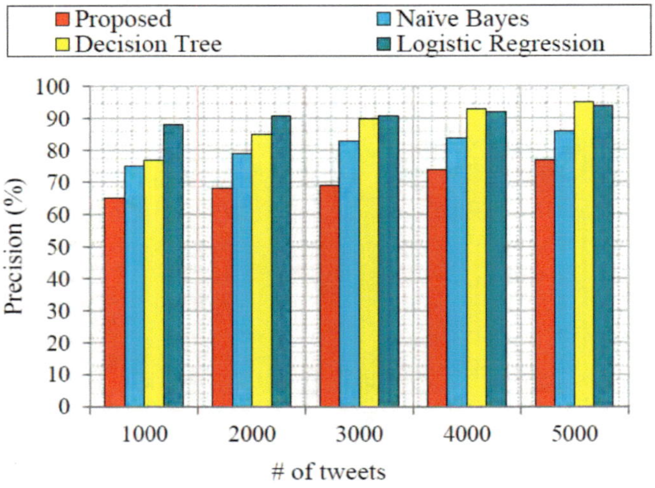


(c)

**Fig. (2).** Precision (**a**). Athelitc (**b**). Edification (**c**). Equipment.

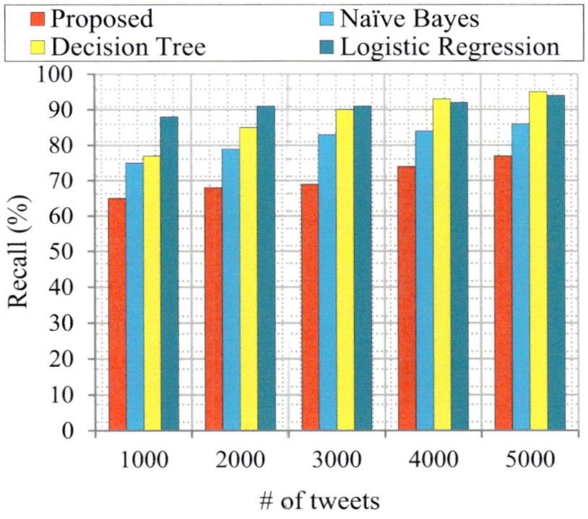


(a)

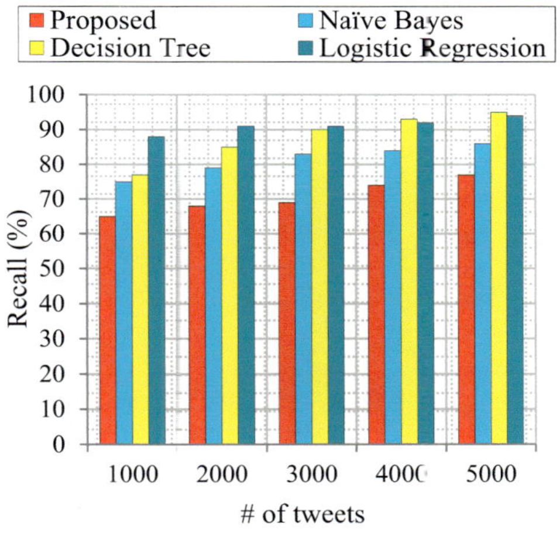


(b)

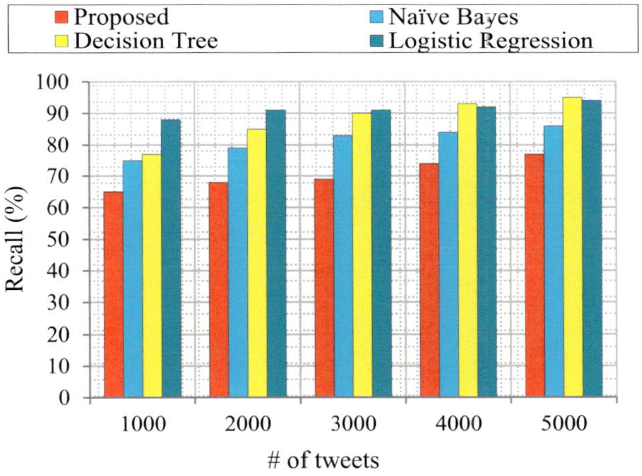


(c)

**Fig. (3).** Recall (**a**). Athelitc (**b**). Edification (**c**). Equipment.

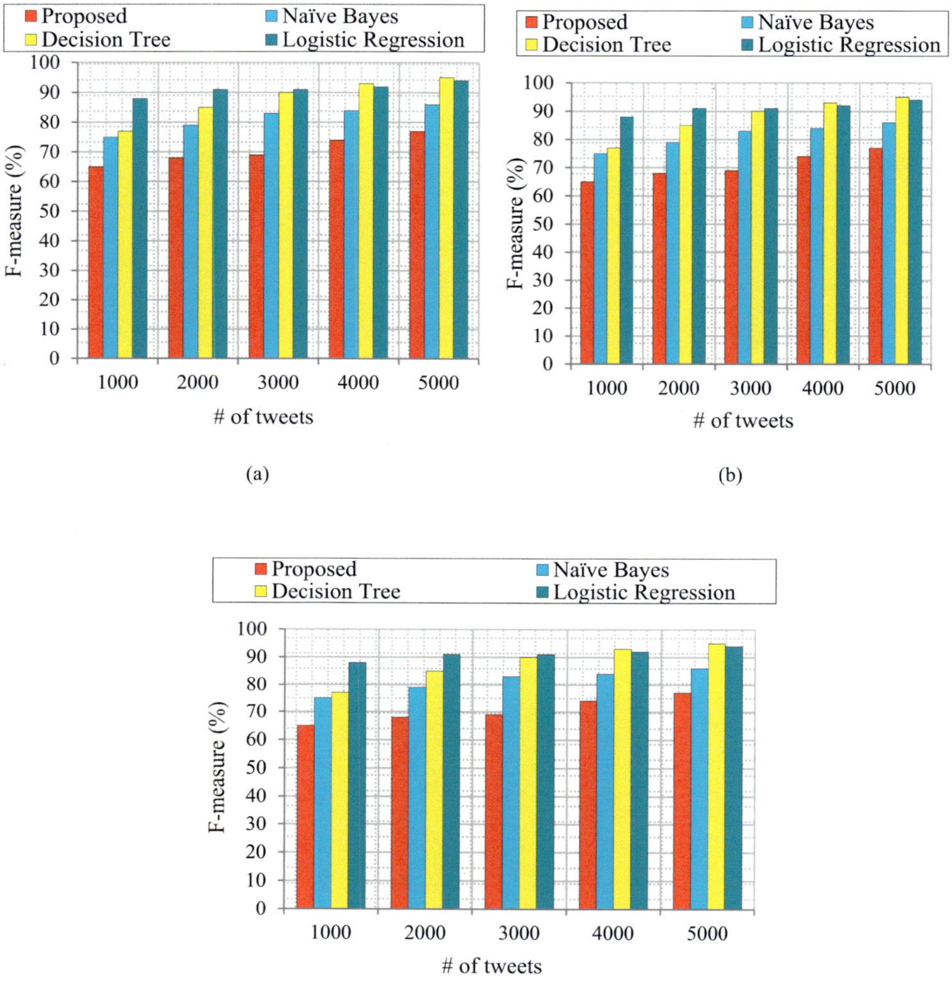


(c)

**Fig. (4).** F-Value (**a**). Athelitc (**b**). Edification (**c**). Equipment.

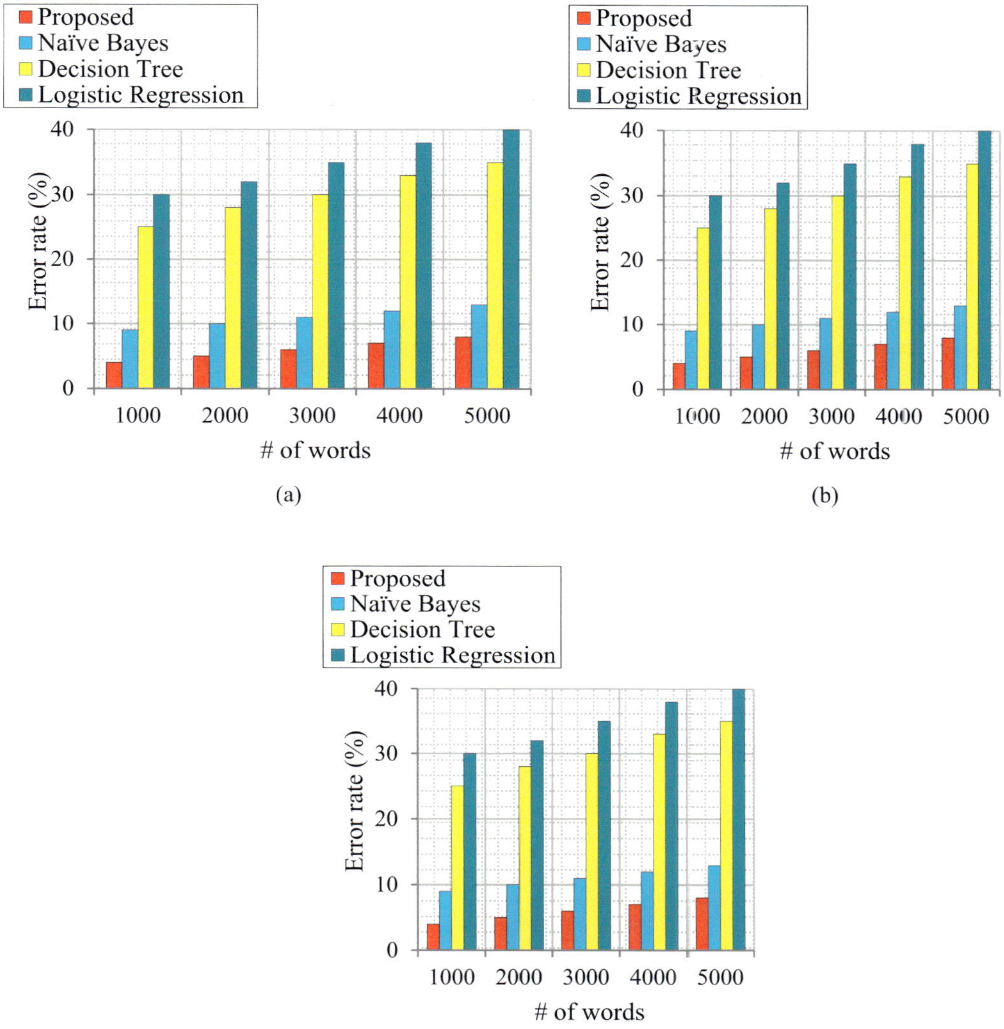


**Fig. (5).** Error Rate (**a**). Athelitc (**b**). Edification (**c**). Equipment.

## CONCLUSION

Content-based text categorization categorises documents. It automatically categorises natural language texts. Text categorization is the main need for text retrieval structures, which collect texts in reply to a user query online, and text comprehension systems, which modify text by summarisation, answering queries, or extracting data. Supervised text classification techniques need enough data to learn. This research introduces an AI-based text categorization system that needs fewer online content documents for training. Word relations, or association rules, are utilised to extract a set of features that were before the classified text documents instead of words. SVM is applied to generated features, followed by a single genetic algorithm for classification. The algorithm was built and tested. The suggested text classifier performs well in experiments.

## REFERENCES

[1] A. Yudhana, S.A. Akbar, A. Farezi, K.H. Ghazali, F. Nuraisyah, and P.A. Rosyady, "Glucose Content Analysis using Image Processing and Machine Learning Techniques", *5th International Conference on Information and Communications Technology (ICOIACT),* pp. 513-516, 2022. [http://dx.doi.org/10.1109/ICOIACT55506.2022.9972142]

[2] S. Ismail, and A. Rosshaida, "Comparative Study of Machine Learning Techniques to Classify Edible and Poisonous Mushrooms", *2021 International Conference on Artificial Intelligence and Smart Systems (ICAIS),* pp. 1-5, 2021.

[3] A. Yudhana, S.A. Akbar, A. Farezi, K.H. Ghazali, F. Nuraisyah, and P.A. Rosyady, "Glucose Content Analysis using Image Processing and Machine Learning Techniques", *5th International Conference on Information and Communications Technology (ICOIACT),* pp. 513-516, 2022. [http://dx.doi.org/10.1109/ICOIACT55506.2022.9972142]

[4] A. Akram, and R. Debnath, "An automated eye disease recognition system from visual content of facial imagesusing machine learning techniques", *Turk. J. Electr. Eng. Comput. Sci.,* vol. 28, no. 2, pp. 917-932, 2020. [http://dx.doi.org/10.3906/elk-1905-42]

[5] F.O. Isinkaye, *A Smartphone-based Plant Disease Detection and Treatment Recommendation System using Machine Learning Techniques.* Transactions on Machine Learning and Artificial Intelligence, 2022. [http://dx.doi.org/10.14738/tmlai.101.11313]

[6] S. Patil, S. Vairagade, and D. Theng, "Machine Learning Techniques for the Classification of Fake News", *International Conference on Computational Intelligence and Computing Applications (ICCICA),* pp. 1-5, 2021. [http://dx.doi.org/10.1109/ICCICA52458.2021.9697267]

[7] M.A. Faruque, S. Rahman, P. Chakraborty, T. Choudhury, J.S. Um, and T.P. Singh, "Ascertaining polarity of public opinions on Bangladesh cricket using machine learning techniques", *Spatial Information Research,* vol. 30, no. 1, pp. 1-8, 2022. [http://dx.doi.org/10.1007/s41324-021-00403-8]

[8] P. Bedi, S.B. Goyal, A.S. Rajawat, R.N. Shaw, and A. Ghosh, *A Framework for Personalizing Atypical Web Search Sessions with Concept-Based User Profiles Using Selective Machine Learning Techniques.* Advanced Computing and Intelligent Technologies, 2021.

[9] K.I. Malik, *Urdu News Content Classification Using Machine Learning Algorithms.* Lahore Garrison University Research Journal of Computer Science and Information Equipment, 2022.

[10] P. Singhal, P.K. Srivastava, A.K. Tiwari, and R.K. Shukla, "A Survey: Approaches to Facial Detection and Recognition with Machine Learning Techniques", *Proceedings of Second Doctoral Symposium on Computational Intelligence,* 2021.

[11] V. Naramula, and K. A, "Sentiment analysis in aspect term extraction for mobile phone tweets using machine learning techniques", *Int. J. Pervas. Comput. Commun.,* 2021. [http://dx.doi.org/10.1108/IJPCC-06-2021-0143]

[12] V. Vashisht, A.K. Pandey, and S.P. Yadav, "Speech Recognition Using Machine Learning", *IEIE Transactions on Smart Processing & Computing,* vol. 10, no. 3, pp. 233-240, May 2021. [http://dx.doi.org/10.5573/IEIESPC.2021.10.3.233]

## CHAPTER 11

# Lexical Methods for Identifying Emotions in Text Based on Machine Learning

**Mridula Gupta**[1,*]

[1] *Centre for Interdisciplinary Research in Business and Technology, Chitkara University Institute of Engineering and Technology, Chitkara University, Punjab, India*

**Abstract:** The study of emotions has emerged as an important area of research because of the wealth of information it can provide. Emotions can be expressed in a variety of ways including words, facial expressions, written material, and movements. Natural language processing (NLP) & deep learning concepts are essential to solving the content-based classification problem that is emotion detection in a text document. Therefore, in this research, we suggest using deep learning to aid semantic text analysis in the task of identifying human emotions from transcripts of spoken language. Visual forms of expression, such as makeover jargon, may be used to convey the feeling. Datasets of recorded voices from people with Autism Spectrum Disorder (ASD) are transcribed for analysis. However, in this paper, we specialize in detecting emotions from all of the textual dataset and using the semantic data enhancement process to fill a few of the phrases, or half-broken speech, as patients with Autism Spectrum Disorder (ASD) lack social contact skills due to the patient not very well articulating their communication.

**Keywords:** Lexical methods, Machine learning, Speech emotions, Text classification.

## INTRODUCTION

Whether expressing joy or sorrow, the ability to communicate effectively *via* speech emotion is essential in human interaction. The fraction of languages that express sentimentality varies significantly among areas. In the realm of machine learning and artificial intelligence, emotion recognition is a relatively recent technique. In this publication, we discuss the research behind and performance metrics for an emotion classification system. Enhancing interaction between humans and computers *via* speech-emotion recognition requires carefully selecting relevant signal features and constructing relevant classification models

* **Corresponding author Mridula Gupta:** Centre for Interdisciplinary Research in Business and Technology, Chitkara University Institute of Engineering and Technology, Chitkara University, Punjab, India;
E-mail: mridula.gupta.orp@chitkara.edu.in

[1, 2]. The total recognition rate will decrease as the number of individuals who use several speech emotions increases [2]. To solve this problem, we provide a Fisher feature selection-based choice tree support vector machine (SVM) method for speech emotion recognition [3]. During feature selection, the parameters with higher discriminatory power are omitted using the Fisher criterion [4]. During the stage of emotion classification, an approach is proposed to set up the structure of the choice tree [5]. Decision tree SVMs allow for simultaneous coarse and fine classification [6]. When extraneous information is taken out of the equation, emotion detection becomes more accurate. The capacity to recognise emotions *via* a speaker's voice is becoming an increasingly important area of study [7]. The breakthrough introduces a semantic cells-based method for identifying emotions conveyed in one's speech [8]. The speech emotion recognition process involves constructing a voice library, preprocessing each word indicated in the audio libraries, obtaining the emotional characteristics of every conversation signal, and establishing a vector of traits of every language signal using the extraction outcome, using instruction of the carriers of capabilities to obtain a mixture of models based upon semantic cells, and the data gathered through combined models as a recognition model of a class [9, 10].

## RELATED WORK

We provide a method for deducing the emotional state of a speaker from their words alone. This approach, which employs a feature-selection technique called XGBoost, makes use of a convolutional neural network (CNN) trained on identifiers and a BLSTM (bi-directional long short-term memory) model with a focus on details. It is important to compute the importance score of every characteristic to alleviate the over-fitting problem, reduce training expenses, speed up the procedure of modelling, and improve identification accuracy. Results from experiments conducted on the EmoDB, CASIA, and EMA corpora show that the proposed framework outperforms a baseline model in terms of accuracy in forecasting (86.87-74.17-98.04%) [11].

After establishing the decision tree SVM framework using the emotional perplexity measure, we choose features with higher differentiation ability for each SVM in the tree using the Fisher criterion. This method at last makes it possible to automatically identify emotions conveyed *via* spoken language. To test the reliability of our method, we construct a decision tree SVM with Fisher feature selection and apply it to the CASIA Chinese expressive speech corpora as well as the Berlin speech corpus. The experimental results show that compared to the standard SVM method of categorization on CASIA and the Berlin speech corpus, the proposed approach increases the average emotion recognition rate by 9%. The proposed method [12] improves emotional recognition accuracy while reducing emotional confusion.

Using machine learning-based strategies for identifying emotions, this paper presumes that determining deltas as well as delta-deltas includes not only useful data but also reduces the impact of emotionally insignificant factors, thereby improving accuracy. Silent frames or unnecessary emotional frames are another common problem with Speech Emotion Recognition (SER). Meanwhile, the focus is very helpful for learning the specific feature representation that is necessary for success in a certain task. In order to generate discriminative features for SER, we are motivated to develop an Attention-based Convolutional Recurrent Neural Network (ACRNN) that takes as input the Mel-spectrogram with deltas and delta-deltas. The experimental findings are detailed in the conclusion, and they indicate that the suggested strategy is effective and achieves the highest accuracy in terms of release-weight average recall [13].

Users are able to identify both the speaker and their mood thanks to a voice emotion detection model built from a mixture of models according to two distinct sets of semantic cells. When applied to speech emotion identification, the recognition model built using the semantic cells-centered approach achieves high accuracy, low memory requirements for storing the r, and fast recognition times [14].

The method presented here uses Berouti spectral removal to restore clarity to muddled audio recordings. Utilising Fast Fourier Transform (FFT) and spectral flux, it extracts the clean speech spectrum from the noisy speech spectrum. The signal-to-noise ratio (SNR) was used to calculate the overall quality of this research. In this investigation, a novel parameter is presented to enhance voice quality. It is suggested to combine spectral reductions with spectral flux for a more precise noise estimation. The new parameter improves the power ratios in spectral subtraction, and unvoiced word frames benefit from this method as well [15].

## PROPOSED WORK

### Research Gaps

It appears difficult to deduce a person's emotional condition by reading their written language. Human-computer interaction (HCI) relies heavily on determining the reader's emotional state from the text. There are three types of emotional communication used by humans: facial, text-based, and speech-based. Research on text-based emotional recognition systems is necessary since sufficient work has been performed on the face and spoken emotion detection.

The use of computational linguistics to the problem of detecting human emotions in written text is growing in importance. Using an analysis of the author's input text, text emotion detection attempts to identify the author's emotional state. This is predicated on the assumption that positive language will be used by those who are content. Words like "stressed," "depressed," and "frustrated" may hint at deeper unpleasant emotions. Emails, messages, chat rooms, forums, online blogs, product evaluations, and social media sites like YouTube, Twitter, and Facebook rely heavily on text as the principal medium of human-computer interaction. Many fields, including business, psychology, and education, might benefit from the usage of emotion-detection software. The findings of NLP-based sentiment analysis have been utilised in the area of user profiling. In particular, sentiment analysis is often associated with opinion mining, the goal of which is to assign a positive, negative, or neutral polarity to each relevant part of a statement. A more nuanced understanding of the user's mental state is a necessary condition for real-time applications. Various models of emotion may be found in the literature, each with its quirks and fine-grained areas of applicability. However, identifying feelings from only a line is a significant challenge. The use of emotion in individualized structures is an effective practice, and different studies have proved its value. Each user has unique behavioural models that may deviate from the norm. Therefore, in this research, we present a methodology for using large data for the purpose of identifying human emotions. Because the vector representations of words capture useful semantic components as well as linguistic relationships among words using deep learning techniques, embeddings of words have been widely employed in NLP applications. To help ML models process unstructured text, word embeddings are often utilised as a feature input.

## System Model

Emotional state identification is a relatively recent technique in deep learning. In this publication, we discuss the research behind and performance metrics for an emotion classification system. Visual forms of expression, such as makeover jargon, may be used to convey the feeling. Datasets of recorded voices from people with Autism Spectrum Disorder (ASD) are transcribed for analysis. However, in this paper, we are interested in identifying emotions from the various written datasets and using the semantic data enhancement process to fill a few of the sentences, words, or half-broken speech, as the patients with Autism Spectrum Disorder (ASD) lack social interactions skills due to the patients being not very well in articulating their message.

## Word Embedding

Documents may be represented by a fixed-size vector composed of word-embedding ground vectors. In the proposed research, many representations of documents have been tried out, with the word vector being combined with the notations: Words that are not present in the training data are given continuous low weights. The value of the ability to discriminate depends on context. This strategy operates on the premise that documents have greater significance in their embedded representations since more data is made accessible for classification. Since training data is based on data from test samples, classifiers may assign a value to each emotion. Then, the class connected with the specimens (for multilevel analysis) makes use of the emotions with the greatest decision values or the set of emotions with optimistic judgment function values.

$$c_{\text{we}}(t_1, \ldots, t_l) = \frac{1}{\sum_{j=1}^{l} b_j} \sum_{j=1}^{l} b_j \cdot u(t_j) \quad \textbf{(1)}$$

As derived in equation (1), where $c_{we}$ represents the vector representation of words in document c containing the l term, u stands for a pre-trained word-to-vector map, and $b_j$ represents quantity, indicating relative importance $t_j$. In this research, we tried several different document examples, all of which included a recurring bag of words, or classifier weights. The approach uses classifier weights to determine the importance of each phrase t in the training data for labelling articles as expressing a certain emotion e by computing weight functions, w (t, e). This research began by displaying the material in a Bag of Words of binary vector representation, from which unigram characteristics were then retrieved. Then, a linear-kernel trained support-vector-machine model has learned the weight associated with each term t in the training data, denoted by n(e,t).

$$w(t, e) = \frac{|n(e,t)| - \mu_e}{\mu_{\text{e}}} \quad \textbf{(2)}$$

According to the second equation where $\mu e$ and $\mu e$ are the mean as well as the standard deviation (in absolute value) of model weights.

$$b_j = \begin{cases} 1, & t_j \notin U \text{ or } w(t_j, e) < 1 \\ w(t_j, e), & \text{else.} \end{cases} \quad \textbf{(3)}$$

According to equation (3), where U is the vocabulary acquired *via* instruction. Terms that did not match the training data or had little discrimination were given low constant weights. Words with more discriminative strength are given greater weight. This method seizes the idea that phrases contained in texts are more relevant due to the additional information they supply for categorization jobs. This must be kept in mind that different texts are used to convey different feelings in this method due to the fact that the discriminatory strength of each word varies (weight $b_j$) and has a wide range of expressions.

## Speech Emotion Classification

As a window into the human psyche, emotion identification from speech signals has attracted a lot of attention in the field of Human-Computer Interface (HCI) model development. Human emotional state identification as cognitive feedback is a common need in HCI. In this work, we examine the use of speech cues to identify seven distinct emotions: sadness, anger, disgust, happiness, surprise, pleasantness, and apathy. For emotion recognition, the suggested technique makes use of the entropy feature, a non-linear signal quantifying technique based on randomness measure. Fig. (**1**). represents the System Model.

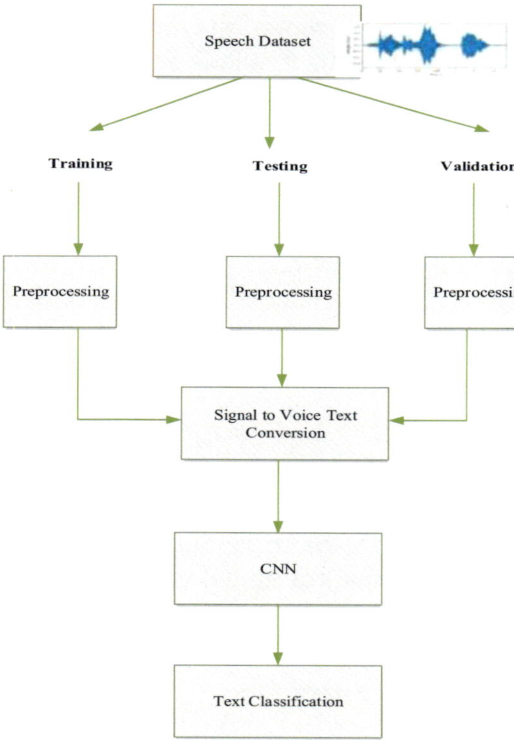


**Fig. (1).** System model.

The Convolutional Neural Network (CNN) is a classification-only Deep Learning method. Commonly employed for recognising patterns and improved data categorization, CNNs are becoming more popular. These networks' input data is processed by small-sized neurons distributed throughout each layer of the planned model architecture.

Local connections that convolutionally apply the input and have the same parameters as the filter serve as their foundation (weight $W^i$ and bias $n^i$). In order to produce i feature maps ($Z^i$), all the way down to size a-b-1, the convolutional layers perform a dot product calculation on the inputs and weights. Therefore, the weighting factors $W^i$ and biasing $n^i$ in the making of maps $Z^i$ with features of sizes a-b-1 for certain i are expressed as:

$$z^i = g\left(W^i * r + n^i\right) \quad \textbf{(4)}$$

To get the convolution layer output, a function of stimulation for a non-linear approach must be used. To reduce network parameters and improve map features, downsampling is performed at each subsampling layer. As a result, the training process is improved and overfitting is controlled. For all feature maps with adjacent space, the pooling operation is performed across pp elements (also called filter size). Finally, much like other neural networks, the layers must be properly linked. Following the generation of low- and medium-level characteristics, these following layers build high-level abstractions from the incoming voice data. Finally, the SVM or Softmax layer is used to provide a probabilistic classification score for a given class.

## RESULTS AND DISCUSSION

Datasets of recorded voices from people with Autism Spectrum Disorder (ASD) are transcribed for analysis. However, in this paper, we are interested in identifying emotions from all of them textual dataset and using the semantics enhancement process to fill a few of the sentences, phrases, or half-broken speech, as the patients with Autism Spectrum Disorder (ASD) lack social interactions skills due to the patient being not very well in articulating their message.

The DLSTA technique is utilised for text-based emotion recognition in humans. The seven classifiers used by the identification system are trained using text for images depicting the following emotions and their accompanying expressions: sorrow, surprise, joy, anger, fear, disgust, and neutral. Zero for neutral, one for calm, two for happy, three for sad, four for furious, five for fear, six for disgust, and seven for surprise are the classes a template seeks to forecast. Because there is no quiet category in TESS, the dataset is biased because there are fewer records for that category in the classification report. Fig. (**2**). is depicted in CNN Model.

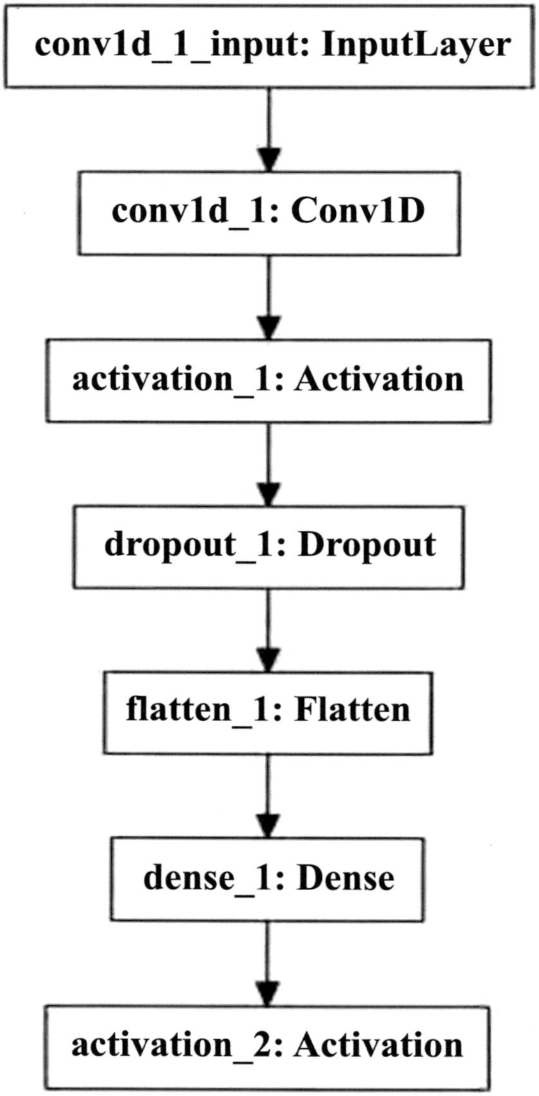


**Fig. (2).** CNN Model.

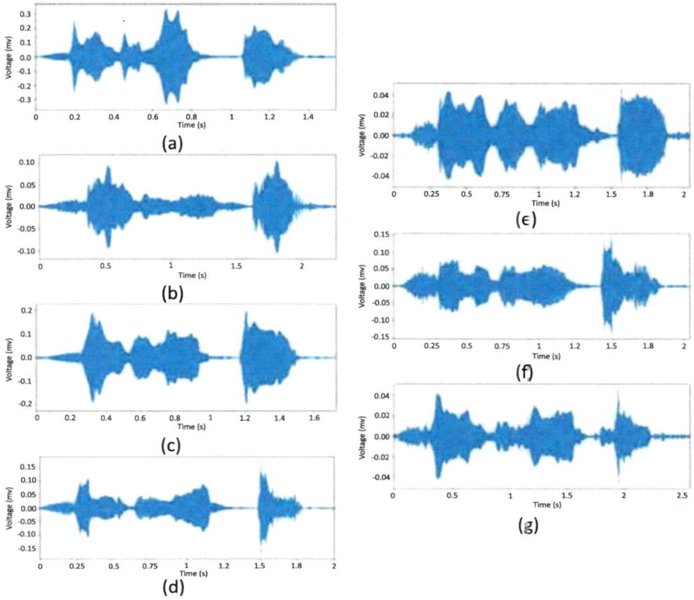


**Fig. (3).** A speech signal for anger (**a**), b for disgust (**b**), c for fear (**c**), d for happiness (**d**), e for neutral (**e**), f for pleasant surprise (**f**), and g for sadness (**g**).

Table **1** displays the results of experiments designed to detect and predict DLSTA. These variables are selected with care after experimentation with the text's justification after mapping and transformation. When applied to natural language processing, emotion detection yields a huge time savings. Fig. (**3**) is displayed in , A speech signal for anger (**a**), b for disgust (**b**), c for fear (**c**), d for happiness (**d**), e for neutral (e), f for pleasant surprise (**f**), and g for sadness (**g**).

**Table 1. The accuracy of both predictions and detections.**

| Accurateness | Forecast (%) |
|---|---|
| Joyful | 80.3 |
| Unhappy | 80.9 |
| Amazement | 80.8 |
| Repugnance | 81.5 |
| Horror | 82.4 |
| Resentment | 83.6 |
| Unbiased | 81.3 |
| Regular | 83.3 |

In a text analysis context including multiclass classification, recognising emotions is the key component. Accuracy, recall, and F1 were used to evaluate DLSTA's performance. The expression classifier of each emotion segment is the foundation for a macro assessment of the expression classifier's performance across all classes. Emotions may be identified using NLP-based text analysis by using the general ability of classification to do so. Fig. (**4**) is represented in Loss and Accuracy (**a**). Loss and (**b**). Accuracy.

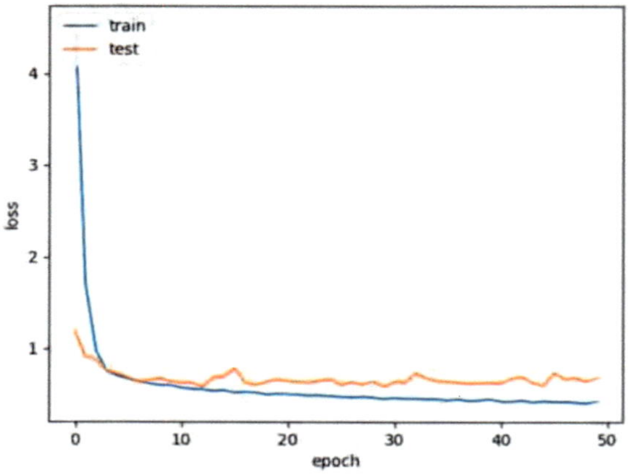


(a)

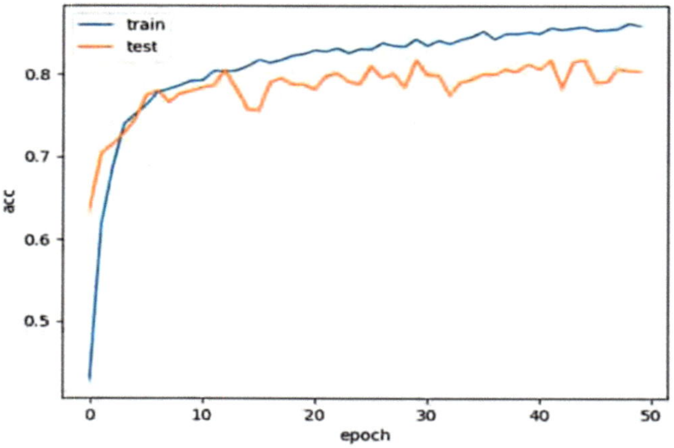


(b)

**Fig. (4).** Loss and Accuracy (**a**). Loss and (**b**). Accuracy.

These investigations have shown that recognition can be made more reliably, accurately, and robustly in circumstances with high levels of linguistic and/or acoustic complexity. It is not hard to identify positive and negative emotions including happiness, sorrow, pleasure, neutrality, surprise, boredom, disgust, fear, and rage. Real-time emotion identification, however, makes this more challenging.

## CONCLUSION

Based on the preliminary analysis presented in the technique section, it is clear that using the supplementary information offered by all entropy metrics is necessary for emotion identification from speech signals. Therefore, a combination feature vector is built up from entropy features. The feature space has dimensions of 1400 by 40, with each emotion class including 200 voice signals. To extract the seven emotions from the audio data, we train a battery of state-of-the-art machine learning classifiers using the feature matrix. In order to evaluate the efficacy of classifiers for identifying emotions, researchers use a tenfold cross-validation method.

## REFERENCES

[1] V. Hozjan, and Z. Kačič, "A rule-based emotion-dependent feature extraction method for emotion analysis from speech", *J. Acoust. Soc. Am.,* vol. 119, no. 5, pp. 3109-3120, 2006. [http://dx.doi.org/10.1121/1.2188647] [PMID: 16708965]

[2] B. Pathak, M. Sayankar, and A.R. Panat, "Emotion transformation from neutral to 3 emotions of speech signal using DWT and adaptive filtering techniques", *Annual IEEE India Conference (INDICON),* pp. 1-5, 2014. [http://dx.doi.org/10.1109/INDICON.2014.7030389]

[3] V. Vashisht, A.K. Pandey, and S.P. Yadav, "Speech Recognition Using Machine Learning", In: *IEIE Transactions on Smart Processing & Computing* vol. 10. , May 2021, no. 3, pp. 233-239. The Institute of Electronics Engineers of Korea. [http://dx.doi.org/10.5573/IEIESPC.2021.10.3.233]

[4] D. Wang, A.Z. Khiati, J. Sohn, B. Joo, and I. Chung, *An Improved Method for Measurement of Gross National Happiness Using Social Network Services.* EMC/HumanCom, 2013.

[5] S.K. Bhakre, and A.V. Bang, "Emotion recognition on the basis of audio signal using Naive Bayes classifier", *International Conference on Advances in Computing, Communications and Informatics (ICACCI),* pp. 2363-2367, 2016. [http://dx.doi.org/10.1109/ICACCI.2016.7732408]

[6] S.P. Yadav, S. Zaidi, C.D.S. Nascimento, V.H.C. de Albuquerque, and S.S. Chauhan, "Analysis and Design of automatically generating for GPS Based Moving Object Tracking System", *2023 International Conference on Artificial Intelligence and Smart Communication (AISC),* 2023 pp. 1-5. Greater Noida, India. [http://dx.doi.org/10.1109/AISC56616.2023.10085180]

[7] J. Wagner, J. Kim, and E. André, "From Physiological Signals to Emotions: Implementing and Comparing Selected Methods for Feature Extraction and Classification", *IEEE International Conference on Multimedia and Expo,* pp. 940-943, 2005. [http://dx.doi.org/10.1109/ICME.2005.1521579]

[8] E. Zarei, H. Sadjedi, and M. Farhadi, "Low variable rate stimulation strategy for cochlear implants using temporal cues and electrophysiological factors", *Technology and health care : official journal of*

*the European Society for Engineering and Medicine,* pp. 879-888, 2018.

[9] A.O. Iskhakova, D.A. Vol'f, and R.V. Meshcheryakov, "Method for Reducing the Feature Space Dimension in Speech Emotion Recognition Using Convolutional Neural Networks", *Autom. Remote Control,* vol. 83, no. 6, pp. 857-868, 2022. [http://dx.doi.org/10.1134/S0005117922060042]

[10] A. Dey, S. Chattopadhyay, P.K. Singh, A. Ahmadian, M. Ferrara, and R. Sarkar, "A Hybrid Meta-Heuristic Feature Selection Method Using Golden Ratio and Equilibrium Optimization Algorithms for Speech Emotion Recognition", *IEEE Access,* vol. 8, pp. 200953-200970, 2020. [http://dx.doi.org/10.1109/ACCESS.2020.3035531]

[11] J. He, and L. Ren, "Speech Emotion Recognition using XGBoost and CNN BLSTM with Attention", *IEEE SmartWorld, Ubiquitous Intelligence Computing, Advanced Trusted Computing, Scalable Computing Communications, Internet of People and Smart City Innovation,* pp. 154-159, 2021.

[12] L. Sun, S. Fu, and F. Wang, "Decision tree SVM model with Fisher feature selection for speech emotion recognition", *EURASIP J. Audio Speech Music Process.,* vol. 2019, no. 1, p. 2, 2019. [http://dx.doi.org/10.1186/s13636-018-0145-5]

[13] P. Gayathri, P.G. Priya, L. Sravani, S. Johnson, and V. Sampath, "Convolutional Recurrent Neural Networks Based Speech Emotion Recognition", *J. Comput. Theor. Nanosci.,* vol. 17, no. 8, pp. 3786-3789, 2020. [http://dx.doi.org/10.1166/jctn.2020.9321]

[14] J. Kaur, J. Saxena, and J. Shah, "Fahad, & S. P.Yadav, "Facial Emotion Recognition", In: *International Conference on Computational Intelligence and Sustainable Engineering Solutions (CISES)* IEEE, 2022. [http://dx.doi.org/10.1109/CISES54857.2022.9844366]

[15] M. Lynn, and C. Su, "Noise Removal in Speech Signal using Modified Berouti Spectral Subtraction for Emotion Recognition", *2019 International Conference on Signal Processing and Communication (ICSPC),* pp. 1-6, May 2019.

CHAPTER 12

# Identification of Websites Using an Efficient Method Employing Text Mining Methods

**Madhur Taneja**[1,*]

[1] *Centre for Interdisciplinary Research in Business and Technology, Chitkara University Institute of Engineering and Technology, Chitkara University, Punjab, India*

**Abstract:** Herein, we introduce a method for website classification using deep neural networks and mixed data extractors. We use iterative training as well as supervised learning approaches to use a gradient descent methodology to simulate the website categorization. This modern model is comprised of a webpage encoder, a convolutional neural network (CNN) feature extraction, a bidirectional long short-term memory (LSTM) feature extractor, as well as a fully connected classifier. It may retrieve various website features at various granularities. Our model may quickly select a suitable website class by concatenating mixed features obtained from mixed feature extractors. On the realistic website dataset that has been obtained, we conduct in-depth tests. The dataset is compiled using domains that were taken from the telecom operator's DNS records. The proposed categorization schema outperforms state-of-the-art models in comparison to our fresh model as well as a slew of popular machine learning algorithms in terms of accuracy, recall, F1, and precision. Other web apps may benefit from all of this as well, such as detecting fake websites as well as ads.

**Keywords:** CNN, LSTM, Text Mining, Website Classification, Website Classes.

## INTRODUCTION

Website organization is an increasingly common and significant task for a variety of applications, including web security, medical, finance, and other fields. However, there are still significant hurdles to improving the accuracy of classification, which makes it challenging to put into reality. Keyword matching is a method that has been used to overcome this issue. To indicate various categories, they employ specified terms. However, it is impossible to predefine every single keyword required for the classification process. In this instance, some earlier studies used some fresh strategies to complete this work. Initially, this

* **Corresponding author Madhur Taneja:** Centre for Interdisciplinary Research in Business and Technology, Chitkara University Institute of Engineering and Technology, Chitkara University, Punjab, India;
E-mail: madhur.taneja.orp@chitkara.edu.in

**Pankaj Kumar Mishra and Satya Prakash Yadav (Eds.)**

assignment is given to certain traditional machine learning techniques like support vector machines as well as naive Bayes. The bulk of the prior literature on harmful website detection just classifies websites as either harmful or harmless. Because researchers may create and instruct distinct harmful detectors for different types of websites, knowing in advance which category a given website belongs to allows the harmful detectors to offer more precise detection findings. A good website in the "Business & Economics" area, for instance, can appear to be malevolent in the "Health Care" category. Consequently, finding malicious websites relies heavily on the work that we do to categorize websites. Utilizing a combination of deep neural network–based feature extractors, it achieves greater precision in classification. Deploying class-specific malicious detectors to websites might lead to more accurate detection results. Most of the prior research on website classification relied on traditional machine-learning techniques trained on publicly available datasets. Examples of multiple classification tasks that are too complex for some machine learning algorithms include naive Bayes as well as Support Vector Machines. We address this problem by creating a hybrid feature extraction network based on cutting-edge methods like text convolution-gated recurrent units. This network can learn from large datasets in addition to having a voracious capacity for complex input data. We employ website datasets obtained using domains derived from DNS Records as opposed to open datasets, which are a good picture of typical Internet user activity. Latent semantic analysis (LSA)-based text mining requires a lot of storage and processing time [1]. In this article, we go over SyntacticDiff, an innovative, comprehensive, and successful edit-based method for changing word sequences that uses a specific text corpus as a reference [2]. These transformations can be used directly or as features to represent text data in a variety of text-mining applications. The UK Educational Evidence Portal (eep) offers consumers a centralized location from which they may peruse the websites of 33 different organizations, with the goal of transforming the way the education community conducts business. Using the gateway is faster than looking for each piece of information separately. Still, the content of the pertinent websites is made up entirely of almost 500,000 publications [5]. This suggests that the search feature of the site may provide a huge amount of results. Exposure to technical knowledge, news, ads, commercials, electronic commerce, and other information services may be found worldwide through the World Wide Web (WWW) [6]. This makes information [3, 4] retrieval exceedingly difficult [7]. The majority of users usually do not have a thorough grasp of network architecture, so if they have to make too many access hops, they can get impatient while waiting for their information to arrive. Data mining techniques such as web mining have offered successful answers to these issues [8]. Web mining is a data mining technique used to analyze material from the Internet. Standard data mining techniques are used to extract information from the World Wide Web, which is subsequently incorporated into the functioning of the website. Finding useful data patterns on the internet and extracting them for more in-depth research is the aim of internet mining. Web structure mining, which examines the web of connections connecting sites, web content mining, which examines the content of individual pages, and web use mining, which examines traffic information from server logs, are the three categories that make up web mining.

## RELATED WORK

This study suggests a unique text extraction method that offers a framework for the effective use of statistical semantics research in the text extraction process. This method uses centrality to ignore passages of text that are strikingly similar to others in terms of phrasing, data, or meaning. This novel multi-layer similarity technique to similarity detection uses the vector space model and the Jaccard similarity in the first and second layers, and the LSA in the third. Only segments that the first two layers were unable to identify can be compared in the third layer. We created a new assessment method that considers the extract size because the Rouge tool does not consider this. It considers the fraction of sentences that cross in both the automated and reference extracts, as well as the compression rate. In comparison to traditional LSA and conventional statistical extractions, we achieved good accuracy results, reduced the initial matrix dimensions by 65%, and required 52% less time for LSA calculation. The centrality feature, as proposed by the multi-layer design, is proven to significantly increase the effectiveness and precision of text extraction [11, 12].

By using SyntacticDiff for three different use cases—correcting grammatical mistakes, grouping and analyzing student essays, and identifying native languages—we show the tool's value. Since SyntacticDiff is language-neutral, it may be used for any corpus of textual information in any natural language. It is quick, adaptable, and capable of identifying phrase, paperwork, and sub collection-level syntactic differences between a target text collection and a reference one. Therefore, a more complex translation technique and feature representation may be advantageous for many text mining tasks outside of bag-of-words that deal with word usage and grammar [13].

Since users value their time, it would be beneficial if there were better ways to carry out searches and show results so they could rapidly focus on the exact information they were seeking instead of trawling through lengthy lists of papers that were not pertinent to their requirements. The Joint Information Systems Committee (JISC), which is funding the ASSIST project, has created a prototype web interface to demonstrate how particular text-mining algorithms as well as methods may be included to enhance the user's ability to search, browse, and read texts. New capabilities include keyword identification and highlighting, search result grouping based on relevant document content, and automated taxonomy-based document classification. This study focuses on Web Usage Mining (WUM), formerly known as Web log mining. We provide techniques for web log file cleaning, subscriber/session identification, and indexing in this study.

## PROPOSED WORK

### Research Gaps

The primary component of the web, or internet pages, has evolved into vital data transmission media. People use PCs, laptops, and smartphones to browse a variety of websites whenever and wherever they want. Despite the many advantages and benefits that visiting websites may provide, doing so on a regular basis has become risky due to numerous user threats. For instance, certain websites display a variety of spam adverts, are full of scams and phishing attempts, and some even secretly download and set up hazardous software on users' computers and mobile devices. Malicious website identification continues to be an urgent issue for many important security jobs, despite the significant research efforts it has received recently. There are several types of websites from various categories that focus on various themes, making it challenging to precisely identify all dangerous websites. Scientists might create specialized detectors for various types of websites if websites could be divided into several categories, potentially improving detection efficiency and accuracy. Consequently, these efforts will raise the bar for web security. In this scenario, classifying websites has become crucial for detecting rogue websites. Classifying different websites in other areas, such as data processing and information management activities, is also urgently needed. To improve the quality of search results, search engines like Google and Bing, for instance, must categorize webpages. To supply targeted advertising and get the most rewards, online advertising firms require correctly categorized websites. Both navigational websites and search engines must manage web spider crawling in order to expand their website databases automatically depending on website categorisation. Despite classifying websites as a common and crucial activity for many applications, including online security, medical, finance, and so forth, there are still some major difficulties in increasing the precision of classification, which proves it challenging to put into reality. Keyword matching is a method that has been used to overcome this issue. To indicate various classes, they employ specified terms. Yet, it is difficult to predefine every single term required for the categorization process. In this instance, some earlier studies used some fresh strategies to complete this work. On the one hand, this job is applied to certain conventional machine learning methods such as naive Bayes and support vector machines. However, those machine learning methods are insufficient for huge data with high dimensions.

## System Model

The section that follows summarizes this paper's key contributions. First, we create a smart website classification model with four parts: a fully connected classifier, a website encoder, a CNN feature extractor, and a bidirectional LSTM feature extractor. Second, we look at the general issue of mixed feature extraction network website categorization. We train and fine-tune the model using the gradient descent process under the direction of supervised learning techniques using word embedding sequences that we have retrieved from the title, keywords, and description of webpages. Lastly, we conducted extensive tests using both our innovative model and the actual website dataset that was acquired. Results show that the suggested categorization schema performs better than the existing models. Additionally, this can support a number of web applications, including online advertising and the identification of harmful websites.

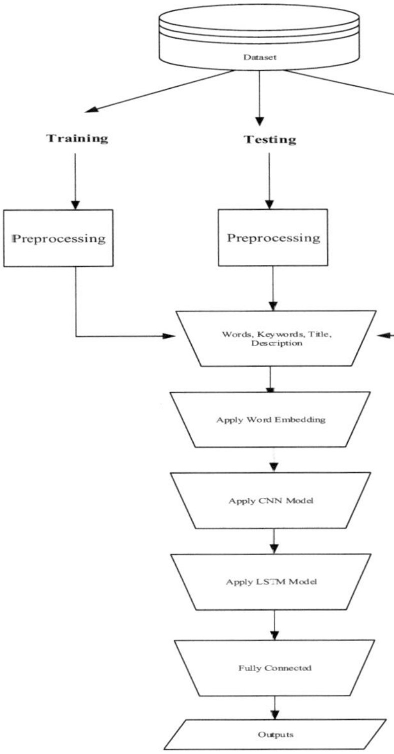


**Fig. (1).** System flowchart.

The structure of the website classification model is depicted in Fig. (**1**). The title, phrases, and website description make up website information. The website information is entered into the website encoder, which then produces a word embedding sequence that represents the website. A convolutional neural network (CNN), a bidirectional long short-term memory (LSTM) feature extraction, and a fully interconnected classifier make up the mixed feature mining network, which takes the word-embedded sequences as input and produces a likelihood distribution for all pre-set categories of websites. Next, we utilize the distribution of probabilities to get the first, second, and third projected classes. These classes stand for the three most probable groups that the website may be classified into. Fig. (**1**). represents the System Flowchart.

## Gathering Website Information & Preprocessing

Using the tokenizer, Website Encoder first separates the title, keywords, as well as outline, three pieces of information entered into the program, into separate words. Word sequence is defined as the preservation of the exact sequence of words as they appeared in the source content on the website. The process of generating a clean order of words begins with removing symbols as well as stopwords from the word sequences. The final thing to do is to use a Word2Vec algorithm that has already been trained on the Wikipedia corpus to transform every word in the word order into a word-embedded vector. Embedding matrices E, which learn from large amounts of data, are often used by Word2Vec models to transform words into embeddings. Word sequence length is denoted as T, and the encoding is one-hot. The $i^{th}$ term used on the web is $W_i$. The definition of the $i^{th}$word's embedding is as follows:

$$e_i = Ew_i, i \in [1, T] \quad \textbf{(1)}$$

A website's word embedding sequence is described as follows:

$$\mathbf{e} = [e_1, e_2, \ldots, e_T] \quad \textbf{(2)}$$

Consequently, the mixed extraction of features method is best fed data that contains word embedding sequences.

## Feature Extraction using CNN with LSTM

The CNN LSTM architecture pairs Long Short-Term Memory (LSTM) layers with Convolutional Neural Network (CNN) levels to enable sequence prediction. The CNN layers are employed for the extraction of features from the input information. Challenges with visual time series prediction and the application of extracting narratives from image collections (like films) inspired the creation of CNN LSTMs.

In tasks related to processing natural languages as well as voice recognition, CNNs are used as extractors of features for long short-term memories (LSTMs) on sound as well as text input data.

Problems involving: Input spatial framework, such as the one-dimensional arrangement of letters in a sentence, section, or webpage; or the two-dimensional organization of pixels in an image are well-suited to this paradigm.

Necessitate the generation of time-structured output, like words in a written description, or include temporal structure into their input, like a video's or a text's series of images.

Utilizing the word embed sequences generated by the Web Page Encoder, the CNN Feature Extraction constructs an extensive feature vector that stands in for a website. To begin, three distinct kinds of 3, 4, and 5 size convolutional kernel filters are used to generate feature maps. Local patterns from word embedding sequences are captured by these filters. The polling data is subsequently compiled to create a single feature map after max pooling and average polling operations have been done to each feature map. Lastly, a dense feature vector F_c describing the website is created by flattening the single feature map.

By joining together a website's word embedding sequences, we may get its feature vector F_c. $\widehat{fm_s}$ and $\overline{fm_s}$ then reducing it to a compact vector:

$$F_c = \text{Flatten}\left(\left[\widehat{fm_s}, \overline{fm_s}\right]\right), s \in [3,4,5] \quad \textbf{(3)}$$

$F_c$ provides an overview of the website's local characteristics by scanning the word embed sequences and utilizing a window that slides method that takes into account the current word as well as neighboring words contained by the window.

The feature vectors are sent *via* the Fully Connected Classifier $F_c$ and $F_g$ using the distribution of probabilities for defined classes as input and output. It begins with joining $F_c$ and $F_g$ to get the mixed features, also known as the concatenation vector of features F. Subsequently, a completely interconnected network accepts F as input and produces a vector O with dimensions equal to the number of default classes. To obtain the likelihood dispersion vector, vector O is lastly passed through a SoftMax function:

$$F = [F_c, F_g]$$
$$H = \operatorname{Re}LU(W_1F + b_1)$$
$$O = W_2H + b_2 \tag{4}$$
$$p = \frac{\exp(O_j)}{\sum \exp(O_i))}$$

Here $F$ refers to the concatenated feature, $W_1$ and $b_1$ H represent the hidden layer's outputs after the ReLU conversion, as well as denote both the entirely linked hidden layer's bias and weight $W_2$ and $b_2$ stands for the output layer's weight as well as bias, O for the output itself, and p for the distribution of probabilities using a SoftMax function to determine the relative importance of each class. A website's class may be determined simply by looking at its index, which is represented by the value that is greatest in the distribution of probabilities.

As a training sadness, we take the cross-en of the anticipated p with the one-hot encoder of the correctly labeled value:

$$\text{Loss} = -\sum_i^c y_i \log(p_i)) \tag{5}$$

Where $c$ is the number of classes and $y$ is the one-hot encoding of the correct label of the website.

## RESULTS AND DISCUSSION

### Dataset Description

Our collection is divided into 15 categories, and each category has 3000 websites, including several well-known ones like Bing, eBay, and Twitter, among others. We extracted individual terms from the website's title, keywords, and description. With the exception of the stop word as well as symbols, every word is retained during tokenization, or token. After that, we train the Word2Vec model using the most current Wikipedia corpus to get word embedding. By using the Word2Vec paradigm, we may convert each word into a 64-dimensional vector. Each webpage may be expressed as a 64 x 64 word-embedded sequences matrix since we restrict the word order representations at 64 words. Websites that do not contain 64 words are filled with zeros to ensure that all webpage description matrices are structured similarly.

## Hyper parameters Description

The CNN Feature Extraction comes with three different sized convolution kernel filters, with 32 filters in every. The sizes are 3, 4, and 2, respectively. In the LSTM Bidirectional Feature Extractor, every bilateral LSTM layer has 32 LSTM units. Across the first layer consisting of 15 neurons in the output layer and the initial level of 256 synapses in the input layer, the fully connected classifier uses a layer for dropouts with a rate of dropout of 0.3. During the conditioning phase, we use the RMSprop optimization approach. We start with an initial learning rate of 0.001 then gradually decrease it to 0.9 over a 32-point mini-batch. While waiting for the test set's accuracy to plateau, we progressively drop the starting rate of learning to a smaller amount when the algorithm stops converging.

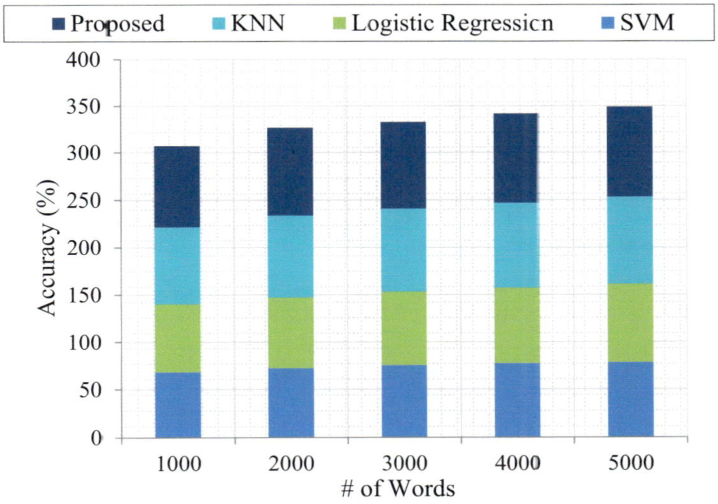


**Fig. (2).** Accuracy *vs*. no of words.

## Description of results

Fig. (**2-5**) display the experimental outcomes of several models applied to our dataset. Additionally, we evaluated our model in comparison to well-known deep learning models such as CNN, LSTM, and others. The F1 score is calculated by taking the inverse of the two metrics called precision and recall. Recall measures the average percentage of correct projections out of the overall amount of relevant websites for every group on the test set, and precision measures the typical portion of accurate forecasts between the obtained forecasts for every group on the set being tested. The results reveal that, compared to other models, the proposed model provides the greatest performance on the dataset. Because of this, website categorization may now be used in a production setting. Our methodology may be used by researchers to divide the web into distinct subsets, from which they can then create unique dangerous site detectors. Therefore, detection times and precision should be increased.

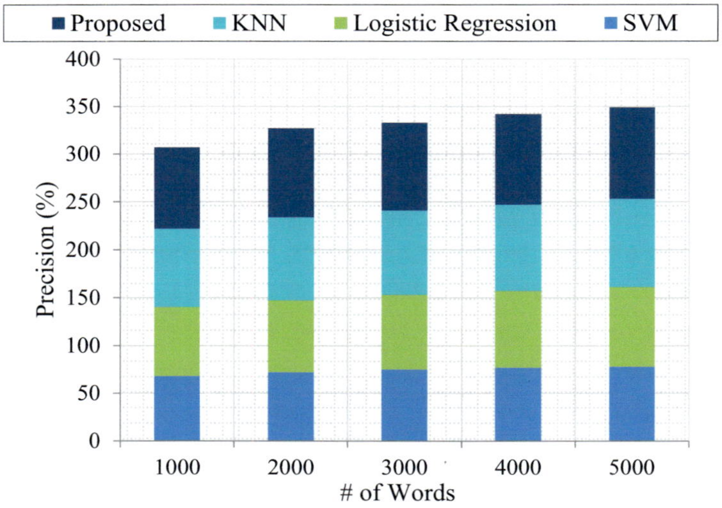


**Fig. (3).** Precision *vs*. no of words.

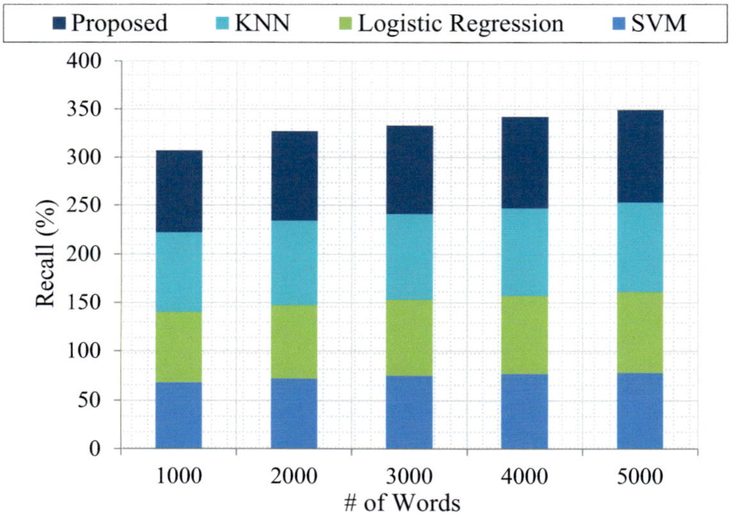


**Fig. (4).** Recall *vs*. no of words.

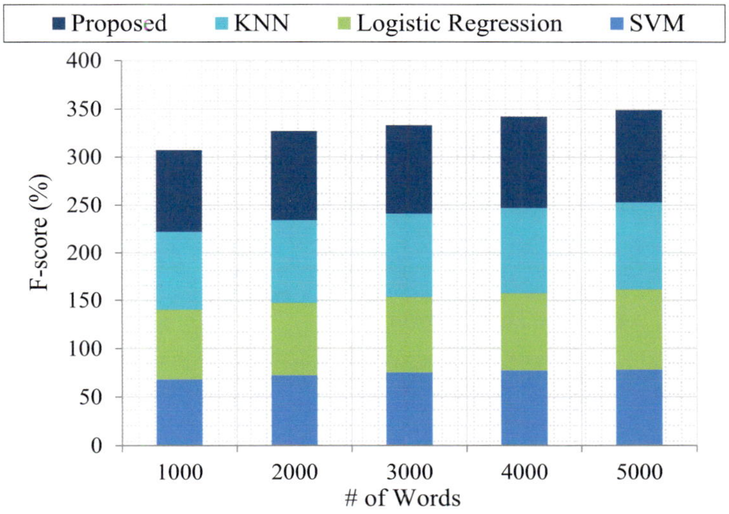


**Fig. (5).** F-score *vs*. no of words.

## CONCLUSION

Our research here introduces an internet site classification strategy that makes use of deep neural networks and mixed-feature extractors. Our data is indicative of actual Internet use as it is based on domains obtained from DNS records. To begin, our approach converts websites into word embedding matrices using Website Encoder. Then, we harvest a variety of features using the Text CNN Feature Extractor as well as the Bidirectional LSTM Feature Extractor. The last step in classifying the recovered mixed characteristics is to apply a fully interconnected neural network. The results of the studies show that the suggested categorization schema is superior to the currently used models. This has implications for a wide range of web applications, including the identification of rogue websites, online advertising, *etc*. For instance, our approach may be used by researchers to sort all websites into groups prior to malware detection. Then, they will be able to create category-specific malicious website detectors that are more efficient and accurate. Improving the model with the attention mechanism previously employed in machine translation and text categorization is the next step in this line of research. In addition to improving classification accuracy, it may also be used to identify key phrases from text on websites.

## REFERENCES

[1] M. Afzaal, M. Usman, A.C. Fong, S.J. Fong, and Z. Yan, "Fuzzy aspect based opinion classification system for mining tourist reviews", *Adv. Fuzzy Syst.*, vol. 6965725, pp. 1-6965725, 2016.

[2] A.H. Ababneh, "The enhancement of arabic information retrieval using arabic text summarization", *2019 International Conference on Innovative Trends in Computer Engineering (ITCE)*, pp. 1-5, 2019.

[3] H. Yang, S. Hadjiantoni, Y. Long, and R. Petraityte, "Automatic detection of industry sectors in legal articles using machine learning approaches", *Proceedings of the 2022 International Conference on Machine Learning and Data Science (MLDS),* pp. 45-52, Jul. 2022. [http://dx.doi.org/10.1109/MLDS.2022.1234567]

[4] M. Yao, C. Jiang, C. Li, Y. Li, S. Jiang, L. He, H. Xiao, J. Quan, X. Huang, and T. Huang, "GEREA: prediction of gene expression regulators from transcriptome profiling data to transition networks", *Curr. Bioinform.,* vol. 16, no. 9, pp. 1190-1202, 2021. [http://dx.doi.org/10.2174/1574893616666210621100335]

[5] K. Bernard, A.P. Cassidy, M. Clark, K. Liu, K. Lobaton, D. McNeill, and D.E. Brown, "Identifying and tracking online financial services through web mining and latent semantic indexing", *IEEE Systems and Information Engineering Design Symposium,* pp. 158-163, 2011. [http://dx.doi.org/10.1109/SIEDS.2011.5876870]

[6] P.B. Chandrashekar, "A timeline extraction approach to derive drug usage patterns in pregnant women using social media", *2016 IEEE International Conference on Healthcare Informatics (ICHI),* pp. 1-8, 2016.

[7] I.S. Jami, and A.S. Zubair, "Semantic web based e-government system", *Indian J. Sci. Technol.,* vol. 11, no. 44, pp. 1-6, 2018. [http://dx.doi.org/10.17485/ijst/2018/v11i44/132332]

[8] S.P. Yadav, S. Zaidi, C.D.S. Nascimento, V.H.C. de Albuquerque, and S.S. Chauhan, "Analysis and design of automatically generating for GPS based moving object tracking system", *2023 International Conference on Artificial Intelligence and Smart Communication (AISC),* 2023pp. 1-5 Greater Noida, India. [http://dx.doi.org/10.1109/AISC56616.2023.10085180]

# CHAPTER 13

# Machine Learning-based High-Dimensional Text Document Classification and Clustering

**Ansh Kataria**[1,*]

[1] *Centre for Interdisciplinary Research in Business and Technology, Chitkara University Institute of Engineering and Technology, Chitkara University, Punjab, India*

**Abstract:** Text classification is a difficult technique. Many techniques have been developed to decrease the dimension of feature vectors for use in text classification due to their enormous size. This work provides a detailed discussion of unique parameters utilising an optic clustering strategy, as well as a review of some of the most essential text categorization algorithms. In this case, the words are clustered according to their level of similarity. Each cluster's membership function is based on the mean along with the standard deviation of its data. Finally, characteristics are chosen from each grouping. Each cluster's extracted feature is the weighted sum of its words. There's also no need to guess or use trial-and-error approaches to determine the optimal number of clusters.

**Keywords:** Clustering, High dimensionality text, Machine learning, Text document classification.

## INTRODUCTION

Classifying and clustering text documents is a significant learning challenge that has applications in data mining and machine learning [1]. When dealing with high-dimensional text materials, the learning job becomes complex with difficulties. The order in which words appear in written materials is an important factor in the learning process [2]. Document sizes are a serious problem and a troubling indicator [3], despite the fact that High Dimension documents are employed for categorization. Both beneficial and detrimental results may result from dimension reduction [4]. Document categorization using reduced dimensions is ineffective if the reduced dimensions are not in the right format [5]. While the basic similarity characteristic has been the focus of our study, we have yet to address text categorization [6]. The use of text mining applications increased in

* **Corresponding author Ansh Kataria:** Centre for Interdisciplinary Research in Business and Technology, Chitkara University Institute of Engineering and Technology, Chitkara University, Punjab, India;
E-mail: ansh.kataria.orp@chitkara.edu.in

**Pankaj Kumar Mishra and Satya Prakash Yadav (Eds.)**

significance across several intellectual domains [7]. Many vital processes in many international organisations and different ethnicities are recorded mostly in text documents. Text poetry is a significant kind of media in the fields of culture and education. There are just a few areas where the classification of Arabic text poetry has been in trend, but it has had a significant impact [8]. The rhythmic harmonic measure that distinguishes the various styles of Arabic poetry [9] is the same in both modern and classical Arabic poetry. When it comes to text categorization jobs, deep learning is one of the most effective machine learning techniques. There are various information retrieval activities that benefit from document clustering, including document browsing, organisation, and display of retrieval results. They are being studied extensively on a worldwide scale at the present time. There has been an extensive usage of generative models for text categorization based on multivariate Bernoulli as well as multinomial distributions.

## RELATED WORK

The vast majority of the current work on the topic of high-dimensional text document categorization and group relies on the use of classical distance functions without taking into account the word distribution in texts. For the purpose of feature pattern grouping and high-dimensional text categorization, we suggest a new similarity function in this study. The suggested similarity function is utilised to implement dimensionality reduction through supervised learning. What makes this study special is that the term distribution is unchanged prior to and following dimensionality reduction. The experimental findings show that the suggested technique succeeds in reducing the dimensionality of the data, maintaining the word distribution, and obtaining higher classification accuracies than existing techniques.

Several techniques for performing the tasks of classification and clustering are discussed. In this research, we used classification and clustering techniques across a number of datasets. It also included recommendations on how to make Naive Bayes classification and K-means clustering more effective. The effectiveness of the suggested approach is measured using standard indicators including accuracy, recall, and F-score. The experimental results would show that the suggested model is superior to existing techniques.

This study provides a taxonomy of Arabic poetry texts. In order to improve the effectiveness of models, we offer a specialised feature selection that is merged with a clustering technique. Two well-known machine learning techniques, the support vector machine as well as the decision tree, have been used in tandem with deep learning experiments. The suggested feature technique of extraction has shown excellent precision across all three approaches. The outcomes are superior to many other comparable studies.

In this paper, we substitute the traditional k-mean process's Euclidean distance-based metric with a machine learning approach to create a novel hybrid algorithm dubbed MLK-Means for grouping TMG format document data. Standard k-means with L-2 normalised data and the von MisesFisher prototype-based cluster (vMF-based k-means) were used to evaluate the performance of the proposed approach. The MLK-Means Technique is implemented in this suggested study, and its performance is contrasted to that of the aforementioned techniques. The suggested algorithm has larger and more similar improvements.

In this research, the LDA model with author n-gram texts and cosine similarity is used to offer a unique technique for author authentication in English and Urdu literature. Similarity measures are used to determine which of the many learned representations of stylometric traits best fit a given author's writing style. Classifications of an author's text are prioritised using instances and profiles in the proposed LDA-based Technique. In this case, LDA's ability to represent text more expressively makes it a good fit for dealing with high-dimensional and sparse data. The technique provided here is an unsupervised computing strategy that can deal with the varied dataset, the wide variety of writing styles, as well as the inherent uncertainty of the Urdu language. The provided technique has been put through its paces using a large corpus. Experiments validate the efficacy of the proposed technique compared to previous authorship identification algorithms and state-of-the-art representations. Cosine similarity using n-gram-based LDA themes is used to evaluate the similarity of document vectors, which is one of the offered work's contributions. The authorship identification job was completed with an overall accuracy of 84.52% on the PAN12 datasets and with an accuracy of 93.17% on Urdu news items without the use of any labels.

## PROPOSED WORK

### Background

Classifying and labelling unprocessed text according to its subject matter is what we mean when we talk about "Text Classification." Text classification has a wide range of applications, from news subject labelling to user review sentiment analysis. For Instance, "Phone was awful. Super sluggish. Bloatware and intrusive advertisements were at an all-time high. This is not a phone I would suggest to anybody. Based on the aforementioned language, our classification machine may assign the correct category or tag, such as bad reviews, in this example.

### *Machine Learning-Based Text Classification*

With the rapid development of machine learning, it is now more convenient than ever to train a model on a dataset and then wait for the model's output. The machine learning approach makes it simple and quick to assign categories to pieces of text that have been supplied. Feature extraction is a crucial part of using machine learning. Bags of words, which essentially include counting all of the words in a text, tfidf (term frequencies inverse document frequency), *etc*., is one technique by which we make the transition from text to numerical representation in the form of a vector.

The accompanying diagram depicts a very high-level process for applying machine learning to Text Classification. In the first phase, we employ user-provided text as training data. Most algorithms for machine learning only recognise numerical features, thus we need to do the feature extraction to turn text into a numerical representation. Once we have the desired attributes, we input them into a machine-learning algorithm with a label or category that has already been established. Upon completion of training, our classification model will be ready for use. ML for text classification is expressed in Fig. (**1**).

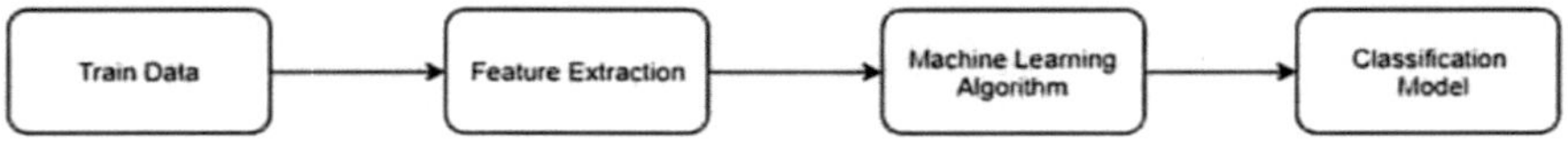


**Fig. (1).** ML for Text Classification.

Once we have our categorization model, we can give it the data we need to predict, using the same procedure as before: first we extract relevant features from the data, and then we feed them into the model. When it is finished, we will have access to our anticipated grade. Text categorization is simplified, accelerated, and improved *via* the use of machine learning. Fig. (**2**) . denotes ML for text classification and clustering.

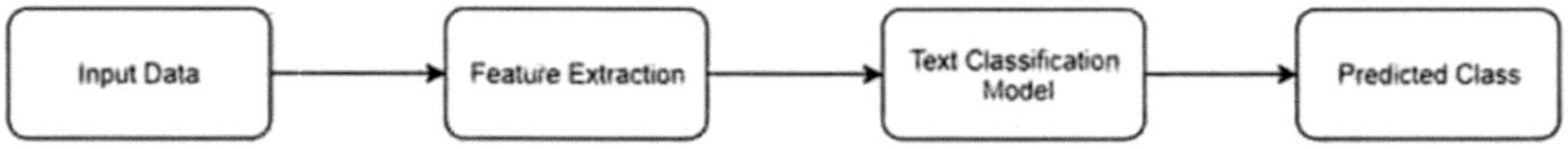


**Fig. (2).** ML for Text Classification and Classification.

## Preprocessing

Pre-processing refers to the steps taken before data is input into a computer. Pre-processing often involves removing irrelevant information. Stop words are a kind of superfluous words (information) that are removed during NLP.

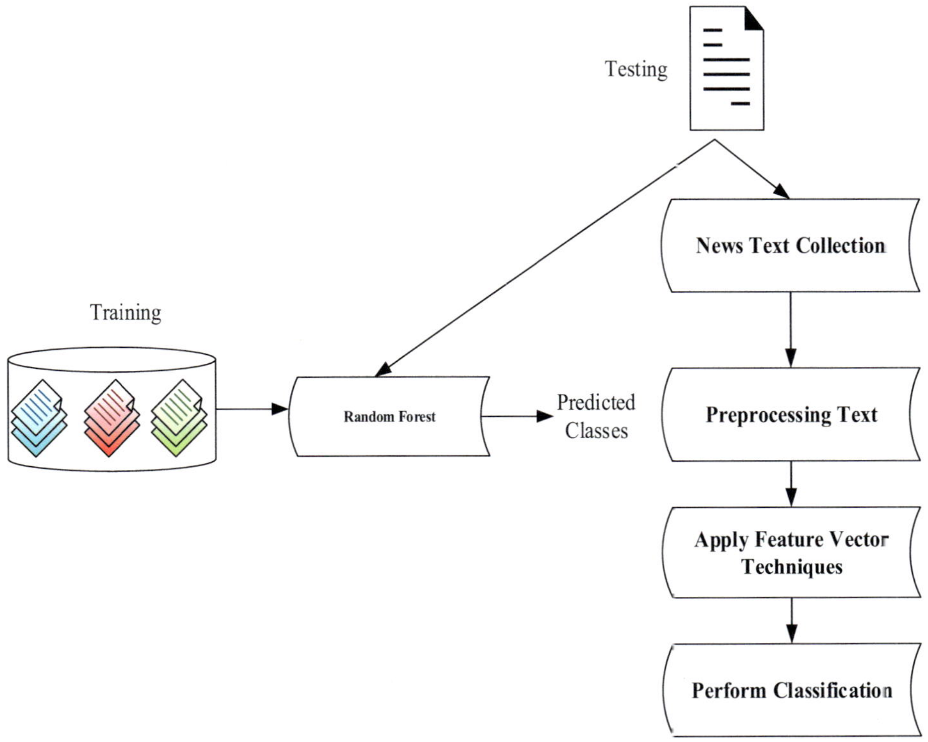


**Fig. (3).** System Flow Diagram.

### *Stop Words*

A stop term is a regularly used term (like "the", "a", "an", or "in") that search engines are instructed to disregard while creating indexes and returning results.

### Feature Engineering

Creating new features from preexisting data for the purpose of training a model using machine learning is known as feature engineering. Creating attributes that are pertinent to a job is vitally critical, and this stage might be more significant than the actual model that is utilised. This is because an approach to machine learning can only learn from the data we provide it.

### Feature Clustering

One well-known technique of feature extraction is feature clustering, in which sets of comparable characteristics are clustered together to form a cluster, and each cluster is then treated as a separate feature. Over time, several innovations in technique have been made. Below, we will go through a few examples of feature clustering strategies for text categorization.

Three different techniques of weighing are used here.

- Each component of the pattern is uniquely represented in a single cluster in the hard clustering technique.
- Every word pattern is assigned a membership function for each cluster in soft clustering.
- Mixture Grouping: In mixed clustering, a user threshold determines the relative intensity of soft as well as hard clustering.

Words are organised into groups using this technique by class label frequency. This technique maintains a high level of document categorization accuracy while effectively compressing feature space. However, the biggest drawback of this technique is that it makes clustering difficult.

Two primary benefits of this optical clustering strategy are:

1. The number of clusters does not need to be set at the outset.
2. Creating one's reality; that is, we look at each word pattern in turn. Clusters are not present from the start but may be made if required. In order to determine how similar every phrase pattern is to preexisting clusters.

A word pattern is clustered if and only if comparable clusters are discovered. If not, a new cluster will be created. In order to determine the degree of similarity between two-word patterns:

$$\mu_{G_j}(\mathbf{x}_i) = \prod_{q=1}^{p} \exp\left[-\left(\frac{x_{iq}-m_{jq}}{\sigma_{jq}}\right)^2\right] \tag{1}$$

Where, $n_j$jq = Mean of j$^{th}$ Cluster *i.e.*, $m_j$ = < $m_{j1}$, $m_{j2}$, ... , $m_{jp}$ > $j_{jq}$ = Standard Eccentricity of j$^{th}$ cluster *i.e.*, $\sigma_j$ = < $\sigma_{j1}$, $j_{j2}$, $\sigma_{j3}$, ... , $\sigma_{jp}$ > When a new cluster is added to an existing one, the membership function has to be refreshed. When the first cluster is discovered, the ability to join should be set to its starting values.

## Text Classification

Raw texts are inaccessible to machine learning algorithms. There is now a new challenge brought about by this issue: how do we convert texts into useful numbers or vectors that can be fed into ML pipelines? Because the values do not capture details on the meaning, context, or correlation between words like "king" and "queen" or "cat" and "dog," simply turning raw texts into, say, binary, decimal, or histograms representations will not give us functional illustrations of words. To address this issue, you may use a model that maps each document to a shared vector space. We utilised the following techniques to transform each word into a vector. Fig. (**4**) represents clustering for features.

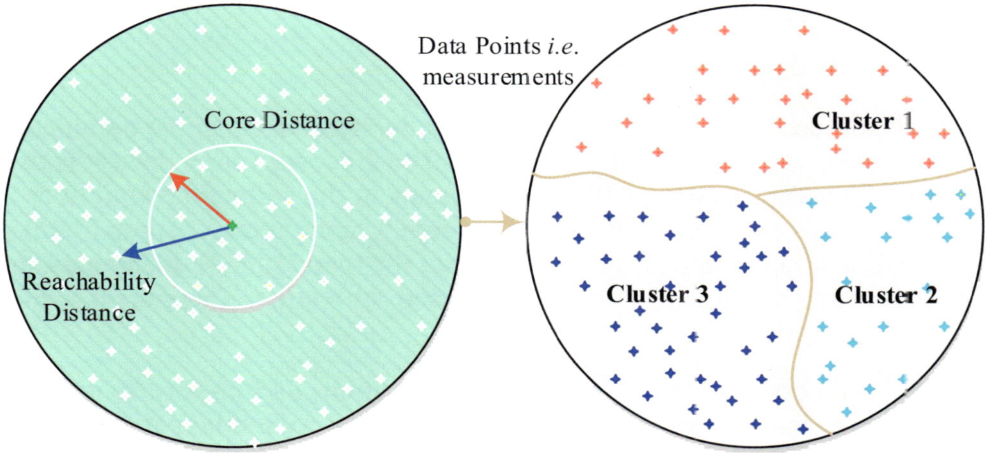


**Fig. (4).** Clustering for Features.

- BAG OF WORDS.
- TFIDF.
- AVG w2v.
- TFIDF w2v.

The output classification results of a classifier called a "random forest" are based on the total number of votes from all of the tree's output outcomes. The random forest takes many trees and combines them into one. Each decision tree acts as a classifier and is the fundamental building block. If N trees are used to classify an input sample, then there will be N possible outcomes. The random forest takes into account all the votes cast in a categorization poll and outputs the most popular option. The simplest kind of Bagging is this. The idea behind Random Forest is:

- N is the total number of samples utilised for training, whereas M is the total number of features.
- m, the amount of input characteristics, is utilised to decide the node in the choice tree's outcome; where m could be substantially less than m.
- Not chosen use cases (samples) were used to make a prediction and the error

was measured against the training set (*i.e.*, reboot sampling) produced by sampling from N training instances (samples) N times.

- The choice of every node in the choice tree is based on m randomly picked attributes for that node. The most efficient way of splitting is determined based on these m parameters.
- After a standard tree classifier has been built, it may be possible to let each tree grow without pruning.

## RESULTS AND DISCUSSION

Here, we detail the dataset, discuss how we set the models' sensitive parameters, and then examine the experimental outcomes. The 20Newsgroup1 dataset is used for all tests. There are a total of 18846 documents in the collection, split over 20 different categories including “politics,” “religion,” “computers,” “sports,” and so on. The models are trained on a subset (7532) of the total (11314) documents, and then the remaining documents (7532) are utilised for testing. There are a total of 130107 unique words in the training data.

We utilise the accuracy of the algorithms' classifications as a performance matrix to compare them to one another. This may be worked out mathematically in the following way:

$$\text{Accuracy} = \frac{\text{Number of correct predictions}}{\text{Total number of predictions}} \quad (2)$$

The overall amount of forecasts corresponds to the dimension of the test set, and the number of accurate predictions is the number of samples whose anticipated level label matches the actual class label.

Here, we compare and contrast the performance of the best-supervised machine training and deep learning approaches that were carefully chosen to serve as benchmark algorithms. We utilised Python and Scikit-learn and Keras packages to do the experiments. While the majority of the other publications in this field only look at a small selection of the 20Newsgroup data, we evaluated the whole collection. Table **1** depicted in Precision in Text Classification.

**Table 1. Precision in Text Classification.**

| Technique | Accurateness | |
|---|---|---|
| | No of Examples | Feature Standards |
| Random Trees | 88.99 | 92.75 |
| Machines with Vector Support | 78.66 | 82.54 |

*(Table 1) cont.....*

| Technique | Accurateness | |
|---|---|---|
| | No of Examples | Feature Standards |
| Inferential Statistics | 73.05 | 76.14 |
| KNN | 61.12 | 65.93 |
| Naive Bayes | 58.45 | 77.38 |
| Decision Tree | 54.96 | 55.62 |

**Table 2. Precision of Text Classification.**

| ML Technique | Exactness |
|---|---|
| Inferential Statistics | 73.63 |
| Machines with Vector Support | 85.93 |
| Random tress | 93.05 |
| KNN | 81.12 |
| Naive Bayes | 69.12 |
| Decision Tree | 66.96 |

**Table 3. Recognition of Textual Categories.**

| ML Technique | Recollection |
|---|---|
| Inferential Statistics | 73.68 |
| Machines with Vector Support | 85.98 |
| Random tress | 93.05 |
| KNN | 81.12 |
| Naive Bayes | 69.11 |
| Decision Tree | 66.96 |

**Table 4. Text Classification F-score.**

| ML Technique | F-value |
|---|---|
| Inferential Statistics | 73.68 |
| Machines with Vector Support. | 85.98 |
| Random Forest | 93.05 |
| KNN | 81.12 |
| Naive Bayes | 69.11 |
| Decision Tree | 66.96 |

In this regard, Random Forest also performs better than competing machine learning algorithms. Table **2** shows that the standard tfidf representation outperforms the word embeddings in terms of document categorization, confirming what was shown in Table **1**. This demonstrates that the discriminatory power of relevant phrases in a document is higher than that of other encodings like context and word meaning. Finally, Inferential Statistics outperformed its traditional Machine learning methods with a classification accuracy of 82.74 percent. Further, we find that the Random Forest method performs poorly compared with other machine learning techniques. Looking at the big picture, it is evident that there is no need to encode complicated hidden patterns using extremely deep models in order to classify texts into one of the known categories; all it takes is the identification of a few keywords and phrases. Table **3** is displayed in Recognition of Textual Categories, Table **4** is represented in Text Classification F-score.

## CONCLUSION

Text classification is a difficult method. Many methods have been developed to decrease the dimension of feature vectors for use in text classification due to their enormous size. This work provides a detailed discussion of unique parameters utilising an optic clustering strategy, as well as a review of some of the most essential text categorization algorithms. In this case, the words are clustered according to their level of similarity. Each cluster's membership function is based on the mean along with the standard deviation of its data. Finally, characteristics are chosen from each grouping. Each cluster's extracted feature is the weighted sum of its words. In addition, there is no requirement to guess or experiment with the optimal number of groups in advance.

## REFERENCES

[1] N. Rezaeian, and G.M. Novikova, *"Persian Text Classification using naive Bayes algorithms and Support Vector Machine algorithm" Indonesian Journal of Electrical Engineering and Informatics.* IJEEI, 2020.

[2] K. Tandon, and N. Chatterjee, "Multi-label text classification with an ensemble feature space", *J. Intell. Fuzzy Syst.,* vol. 42, no. 5, pp. 4425-4436, 2022. [http://dx.doi.org/10.3233/JIFS-219232]

[3] R.K. Roul, and S.K. Sahay, "K-means and Wordnet Based Feature Selection Combined with Extreme Learning Machines for Text Classification", *International Conference on Distributed Computing and Internet Technology,* 2016. [http://dx.doi.org/10.1007/978-3-319-28034-9_13]

[4] S.P. Yadav, S. Zaidi, C.D.S. Nascimento, V.H.C. de Albuquerque, and S.S. Chauhan, "Analysis and Design of automatically generating for GPS Based Moving Object Tracking System", *2023 International Conference on Artificial Intelligence and Smart Communication (AISC),* 2023 pp. 1-5. Greater Noida, India. [http://dx.doi.org/10.1109/AISC56616.2023.10085180]

[5] H.H. Mohammed, E. Dogdu, A.K. Görür, and R. Choupani, "Multi-Label Classification of Text Documents Using Deep Learning", *IEEE International Conference on Big Data (Big Data),* pp. 4681-4689, 2020.

[6] *Issue 3.* vol. 10. The Institute of Electronics Engineers of Korea, 2021, pp. 233-239.V. Vashisht, A.K. Pandey, and S.P. Yadav, "Speech Recognition using Machine Learning" In IEIE Transactions on Smart Processing & Computing. [http://dx.doi.org/10.5573/IEIESPC.2021.10.3.233]

[7] S. P. Yadav, and S. Yadav, "Mathematical implementation of fusion of medical images in continuous wavelet domain", *Journal of Advanced Research in dynamical and control system,* vol. 10, no. 10, pp. 45-54, 2019.

[8] P.G. Krishna, and D.L. Bhaskari, "A Review of Clustering Techniques and its Challenges in Document Clustering", *J. Emerg. Technol. Innov. Res.,* 2017.

[9] A. Kanimozhi, and M. Subha, "Document Clustering with Feature Behavior based Distance Analysis", *International Journal of Modern Trends in Engineering and Research,* 2015.

## CHAPTER 14

# The Application of an N-Gram Machine Learning Method to the Text Classification of Healthcare Transcriptions

**Pratibha Sharma**[1,*]

[1] *Centre for Interdisciplinary Research in Business and Technology, Chitkara University Institute of Engineering and Technology, Chitkara University, Punjab, India*

**Abstract:** An integral aspect of natural language processing is text categorization, the goal of which is to assign a predetermined category to a given text. Feature selection and categorization models come in a wide variety of forms. Most researchers, however, would rather utilise the prepackaged functions of existing libraries. In the field of natural language processing (NLP), automated medical text categorization is very helpful for decoding the information hidden in clinical descriptions. Machine learning approaches seem to be fairly successful for medical text categorization problems; nevertheless, substantial human work is required in order to provide labelled training data. Clinical and translational research has benefited greatly from the computerised collection of vast amounts of precise patient information, including illness status, blood tests, medications taken, and side effects, along with therapy results. As a result, the medical literature contains a massive amount of information on individual patients, making it very difficult to digest. In this research, we suggest using N-grams and a Support Vector Machine (SVM) to classify healthcare-related texts. We conduct experiments to determine the viability of our code and analyse it across a variety of categorization methods.

**Keywords:** Medical text classification, Machine learning, Natural language processing, N-gram methods.

## INTRODUCTION

It is crucial to ensure that students have access to adequate laboratory facilities. Using star and solar photometers installed at Lindenberg Meteorology Observatory since 1995 [1, 2], we were able to calculate the atmospheric water vapour concentration (or Integrated Water Vapour, IWV). Several strategies for calculating the required empirical parameters for the recovery are explored [3].

* **Corresponding author Pratibha Sharma:** Centre for Interdisciplinary Research in Business and Technology, Chitkara University Institute of Engineering and Technology, Chitkara University, Punjab, India;
E-mail: pratibha.sharma.orp@chitkara.edu.in

**Pankaj Kumar Mishra and Satya Prakash Yadav (Eds.)**

The VKM-100 multi-pass pressure cell at Pulkovo Observatory was used to individually calibrate each instrument [4, 5]. For several model atmospheres, the MODRAN-4 software tool was used to simulate absorption by the atmosphere by water vapour, allowing the empirical values to be computed. Surgery affecting the eyelid, cornea, conjunctiva, camera lens, ocular muscle, vitreous, and iris are all included in the broad category known as "ocular surgery" [6, 7]. Other surgeries include those for the elimination of tumours, the treatment of ocular injuries, and the replacement of damaged corneas [8]. Avoiding surgical site infections (SSIs) during ocular surgery is complicated by the lack of standard regimens for antibiotic prophylaxis. Due to the lack of agreement on the appropriateness of ocular antibiotic prophylaxis for children, this consensus paper aims to provide doctors with a set of guidelines on the topic [9]. The following scenarios are taken into account: Common eye surgeries include corneal grafts, ocular surface transplants, ocular surface grafts, intraocular surgeries, and extraocular surgeries for things like trauma and tumours. Models of stars indicate a strong reliance on convection, with the bolometric flux variation characterised by the complex variable $f$ [10]. Global longitudinal strain (GLS) of the left ventricle (LV) has established as a more objective and reliable method for measuring LV systolic function during the last decade, and it may be able to detect slight abnormalities in LV contraction even in the presence of an intact ejection fraction (EF). Recent research, however, has shown that GLS, like LV EF, is highly dependent on load. In recent years, non-invasive methods of quantifying myocardial work (MW) have developed as a viable option for gauging heart health and performance.

Most previous studies relied on either explicit or implicit representation of text to resolve such issues, but both methods are best for sentences and do not readily apply to short text due to their brevity and sparseness. In light of the fact that traditional multi-size filter Support Vector Machine (SVM) during text classification task obtains the simple word vector feature and ignores the important feature, we present a type of short text classification approach by SVM, which can acquire numerous texts including adopting none linear sliding technique and N-gram language model, as well as selects key features by employing the concentration mechanism, in addition to employing the entropy loss function. Experiments comparing the suggested technique to the standard machine learning algorithm demonstrate a significant improvement in categorization results for short texts. Here is a rundown of everything we have accomplished with this paper as a whole.

In this study, the authors introduced a novel classification strategy that combined N-gram with support vector machine (SVM) technology.

To get text characteristics, we used a concentration process based on an N-gram language model, tweaked many superparameters, and drew benefits from the model as a whole.

By enhancing the pooling procedure, our technique can maintain useful characteristics as soon as feasible, which in turn promotes an increase in the accuracy of the text classification job.

Our suggested methodology is detailed and analysed in Section 3, whilst Section 4 discusses experimental findings. Section 2 provides background information on the SVM model that will be used in Section 3. This paper is brought to a close in Section 5.

## RELATED WORK

It was suggested that students studying various control engineering disciplines should benefit from an already existing and usable kit. To update the original TCLab presented by Hedengren (Hedengren *et al.*, 2019), a temperature control lab kit is built from scratch using everyday electronics components. Matlab/Simulink simulations are used to check the correctness of mathematical frameworks of the system, which are based on theoretical and experimental approaches. The Kit and its corresponding mathematical models are then subjected to a variety of control algorithms, including On/Off, PID, and Fuzzy, to demonstrate the control feasibility of each. Matlab GUI is also used to develop the human-machine interface (HMI), which allows the user to choose a control method, adjust control settings, and monitor process parameters. The resulting models, according to the results of the experiments, are able to replicate the dynamics of the material kit with a temperature discrepancy of no more than 3 degrees Celsius. This proves the suitability of the kit for instruction in a variety of control-related subjects, including but not limited to system modelling, system proof of identity, classical control, and advanced control algorithms [11].

The findings are contrasted to those reported in the literature, which were compiled using a variety of tools and retrieval strategies. We examine the validity of the experimental variables that are integral to the power estimate that connects the humidity level to the measured absorption. The current standard uncertainty in the column with the total water vapour is about 10% due to inaccuracies in observations, calibration, and computations. In order for data acquired by optical photometry to be used as an independent benchmark for other techniques (GPS, MW-radiometers, lidar, *etc.*), we address the prospects for raising the accuracy of calibration to 1% as a crucial requirement [12].

Experts from the most prestigious scientific organisations in Italy contributed to this work, making it possible to compile what we believe to be the most comprehensive and up-to-date set of guidelines for clinical measures in the peri-operative setting of eye surgery. By standardising processes, the use of standardised protocols seeks to enhance surgical practise, leading to fewer surgical site infections (SSIs) and less antibiotic resistance.

We demonstrate a novel approach to combining $ell$ and $f$ extraction from multi-color data, and we apply it to numerous $delta$ Scuti stars. The estimated values of $f$ provide a strong enough restriction on stellar convection models to be of utility. Furthermore, if the detected mode is radial, global stellar parameters may be refined using the multi-passband data. In conclusion, adding radial velocity data to our approach greatly enhances the accuracy with which we can determine the performance [14].

Incorporating strain and LV pressure measurement has shown to be an effective means of overcoming the constraints of GLS and LV EF and providing a loading-independent assessment of myocardial function. This novel approach has been used in several contexts because of the availability of echocardiographic software for non-invasive MW computation. This article aimed to summarize the state of non-invasive MW estimate research, highlighting its potential usefulness in therapeutic settings.

## PROPOSED WORK

### Problem Statement

In recent years, there has been a rise in the awareness of text classification's significance. Library categorization, news classification, and so on are all examples of how text classification may improve efficiency and save time. This has led to a proliferation of text classification use in specialised contexts. To address the issue of manual processing of court papers, Yang's group developed a text categorization model. To analyse and forecast irregular data or unexpected occurrences, machine learning primarily investigates how to learn unfamiliar rules from provided data, that is, to identify certain rules from data (samples). The following diagram shows how a machine-learning algorithm may be used for text categorization.

The image above depicts the input ("x") and the subsequent output ("y") of a given system. The processing of the model yielded the anticipated outcomes from the out-of-the-ordinary data. This "model" has been educated using "data (x, y)" in the past. That's the bare bones of how ML algorithms handle textual data. Statistical analysis of existing labelled data is the primary machine learning technique used today to discover rules and build models. Classification outcomes for new data may be predicted and analysed using these trained models. Fig. (**1**) . denotes ML for Text Classification. Machine learning-based text categorization algorithms typically consist of four stages:

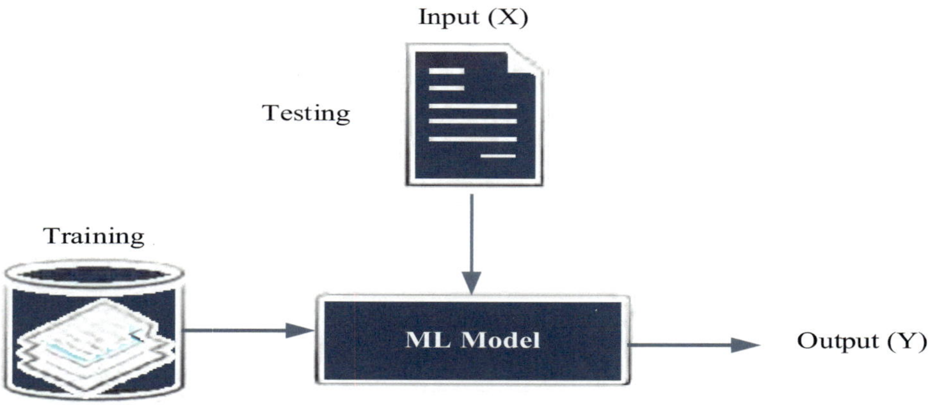


**Fig. (1).** ML for text classification.

1. Document modelling and feature extraction: When it comes to machine learning, feature extraction is crucial. Manual feature extraction is the standard practice; however, manually developing features is labour-intensive, and modern datasets often include too many features and too few dimensions for them to be effective. Conventional approaches to feature extraction often include dimensionality reduction and the selection of an aspect of features that best reflects text information and provides the greatest classification impact in order to address these issues.
2. Model training: Training data sets are used to teach the machine learning model, and the actual classification impact is heavily influenced by the quality of the labelling used in the training data sets. Deep learning outperforms statistically-based machine learning algorithms in terms of feature learning, and the features it learns to use are better able to characterise data in a way that makes it easy to visualise and classify.
3. Text analysis for examination: We simply feed the model of text data that needs to be categorised, and it will make a determination based on the rules it has learnt and provide a classification result.
4. Analysis of the impact of categorization: When text classification is complete, it is important to use metrics like accuracy, recall rate, and F measurement to double-check the classifier's efficacy. Measurement value F is the geometric mean of the accuracy rate as well as recall rate; the accuracy rate is the fraction of samples with a positive classification result that is actually positive; the

recall rate is the fraction of samples from all positive classes that can be correctly identified by the classifier.

## Proposed Methodology

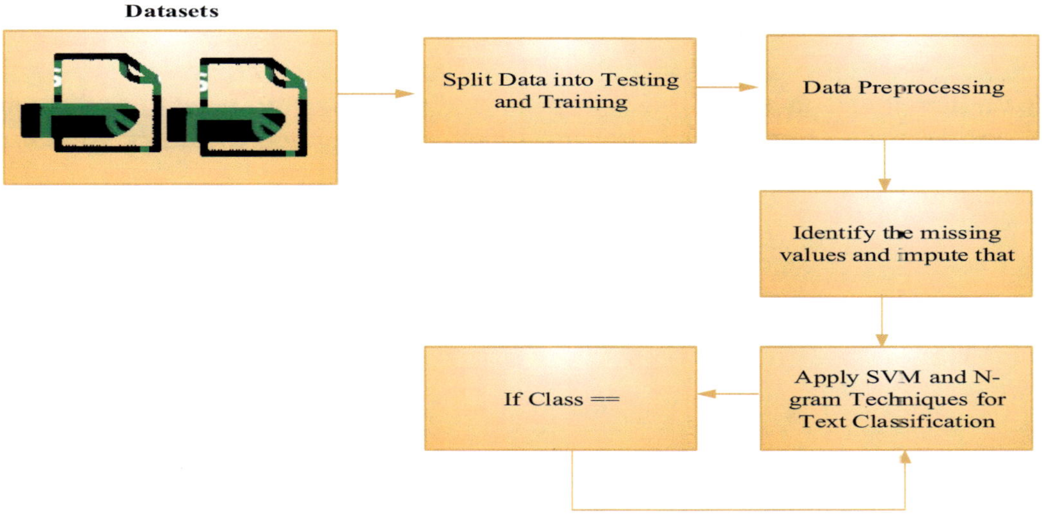


**Fig. (2).** Proposed Model.

An Nn-Gram is a sequence of N words, phrases, or sentences taken from a larger corpus of speech or writing. Large groups of words or syllables might both make up the N-gram. To forecast incoming text or voice, natural language processing relies heavily on N-Gram models, which are in turn based on N-Grams. Fig. (**2**) . displays the proposed model.

N-gram models can predict what will come next in a given sequence. Take, as an example, the DNA sequencing alphabet (GATC). An N-Gram model looks at the string of characters and generates a distribution of probabilities for the likely values to come based on the training data. Probabilities (such as 0004 for each conceivable value) will be added together to equal 1.

N-gram systems are used to help forecast speech and/or text, as was described above. They make use of the randomness inherent in N-Gram and, sometimes, add features of the model of Markov. Because of their ease of use and scalability, N-Gram models and the methods that use them are well-suited to scaling up from smaller studies using bigger N sets. In text classification difficulties, character n-grams have shown to be the most effective sort of feature. The fact that they may be used in a different language with little adaptation is their main benefit. N-grams of typed text provide insights into the text's meaning and context. An N-gram model of language estimates the likeliness of an N-gram occurring in a given string of words. In other words, a certain amount of p(w|h) can be predicted by a decent N-gram model. Unigrams like "This," "article," "is," "on," and "NLP" and bi-grams like "This article," "article is," "is on," and "on NLP" are examples of N-grams.

Next, we will use N-gram techniques to construct a connection for locating the next item in the phrase. If it is a possible next word, then we need to find p(w|h). Consider the aforementioned scenario in which we are interested in determining the likelihood that the last word is "NLP" given the first words:

$$P = (w(1)|w(2)|w(3)| \dots w(n) \quad \textbf{(1)}$$

The preceding equation may be rewritten in a more generic form as:

$$P = (w(1)|w(2)|w(3)| \dots w(n) \dashrightarrow W(N) \quad \textbf{(2)}$$

***Skip-Gram***

In language processing, skip-grams are sometimes used as a modelling technique. Instead of requiring consecutive elements (usually words) for text categorization, as in traditional n-grams, skip-grams allow for gaps (thus the name) to be skipped over.

Vapnik and his colleagues at Bell Labs presented the Supporting Vector Machine in 1995 as a novel statistical classification approach for solving binary classification issues. Finding a hyperplane in the sample features that optimally divide the sample data and maximise the distance between a sample point and the hyperplane is a general notion.

It operates on the following principle: The text vector of page x is built using the supplied lexicon, where n is the number of entries in the dictionary set W, while the text vector is formed from the text to be categorized as $x_i$, which represents the number of $x_j$ occurrences in document d.

$$\begin{aligned} W &= \{w_1, w_2, \cdots, w_n\} \\ X &= \{x_1, x_2, \cdots, x_n\} \end{aligned} \quad \textbf{(3)}$$

The classification vector $Y = \{y_1, y_2, \dots, y_m\}$, where $y_i \in \{-1, 1\}$ represents, on the one hand, the negative category, and, on the other, the positive category, in a dichotomy.

$$Y = \{y_1, y_2, \cdots, y_m\} y_i \in \{-1,1\} \quad (4)$$

The issue of classification is said to be linearly separate if and only if the input sample data has a boundary for decision-making in the characteristic space, all samples can be separated by a hyper-plane based on the positive class as well as the negative class, and the distance among any sample and the plane is greater than 1.

Limitation of the choice:

$$w^{\mathrm{T}}\mathrm{X} + \mathrm{b} = 0 \quad (5)$$

Point to plane short:

$$y_i(w^{\mathrm{T}}X_i + b) \geq 1 \quad (6)$$

The following diagram depicts a hyper-plane as the solid line $W^T X + b = 0$, the hyper-plane's normal vector, w, and its intercept, b. The dark red dot represents the upper border of the period $(W^T X_i + b) \geq 1$, The bottom limit of the interval is built using the red dot's hollow centre $(W^T X_i + b) \leq -1$, and how far apart the two intervals are from one another is calculated with $d = \frac{2}{|w|}$. The support vectors are the samples from the positive and negative classes that are on the border of the interval. In terms of generalisation and learning capabilities, a Supporting Vector Machine method of classification excels. It seeks to find the global best solution by minimising structural risk. Through the use of this method, the "dimension disaster" may be avoided. It has several applications, including automated text categorization, facial identification, gene expression analysis, and handwriting analysis.

## RESULTS AND DISCUSSION

Here, we put our suggested classification method through its paces on a number of different short text data sets, using an Intel (R) i7-6500U 2.59GHz CPU, 12GB of RAM, and the Python 3.5 programme environment. This section provides an in-depth comparison and contrast of the two suggested deep learning models, including a discussion of the evaluation indices and datasets used to test them.

Accuracy, precision, recall, and the F score are taken into account as assessment indices in this study. Here are the corresponding formulas for each:

$$\begin{aligned} \text{accurateness} &= \frac{T_P+T_N}{T_P+F_N+T_N+F_P}, \\ \text{recallocation} &= \frac{T_P}{T_P+F_N}, \\ \text{exctraness} &= \frac{T_P}{T_P+F_P}, \\ F_1 - value &= \frac{2* \text{precision} * \text{recall}}{\text{precision} + \text{recall}} \end{aligned} \tag{7}$$

where TP indicates a positive result, TN indicates a negative result, FP indicates a positive result, and FN indicates a negative result. The effectiveness of the suggested method for medical text classification was tested experimentally utilising prominent benchmark medical literature datasets including the Hallmark dataset. These datasets may be seen as nothing more than a collection of abstracts from biomedical publications that have been annotated to identify cancer-related characteristics. About 1852 papers from scientific publications document three hallmarks of cancer: cellular energy dysregulation, inflammation that promotes tumour growth, and activation of invasion and metastasis. There are two types of categories in the Hallmarks dataset, also called the Activating Invasion and Metastasis Database: positive and negative.

## CONCLUSION

To address the challenge of short text classification, we propose an N-gram-based SVM model that takes the word vector as input from a model taught with the word2vec tool, takes advantage of the skipping and interval approach to, prioritises the most important features, and pays close attention to context. The models are tested on a variety of datasets, and the findings demonstrate that our suggested model is optimal for the job of short text grouping, with the categorization impact expanding exponentially up to a threshold. We will use fastText, which offers pre-trained word embedding produced using word2vec from a huge number of texts, as well as apply it to another short classification of text task, like PubMed data, to assess the feasibility of adapting our methods to the context of healthcare texts. One of the main goals of our research is to identify practical alternatives to word2vec for representing text.

## REFERENCES

[1] A. Munthuli, P. Pooprasert, N. Klangpornkun, P. Phienphanich, C. Onsuwan, K. Jaisin, K. Pattanaseri, J. Lortrakul, and C. Tantibundhit, "Classification and analysis of text transcription from Thai depression assessment tasks among patients with depression", *PLoS One,* vol. 18, no. 3, p. e0283095, 2023.
[http://dx.doi.org/10.1371/journal.pone.0283095] [PMID: 36996118]

[2] R. Hooper, A. Adam, and N. Kheir, "Pharmacist-Documented Interventions During the Dispensing Process in a Primary Health Care Facility in Qatar", *Dovepress Open Access to Scientific and Medical*

*Research,* vol. 2021, no. 1, pp. 45-52, Jan. 2021.

[3] R.A.O. Freitas Júnior, R.A.S.O. Freitas, M.P. Carvalho, S.S.A. Maranhão, L.L. Lisboa, and G.D. Azevedo, "Inclusão do cuidado com a saúde das pessoas com deficiência nos currículos de medicina do Brasil", *Rev. Bras. Educ. Med.,* vol. 45, no. 3, p. e156, 2021. [http://dx.doi.org/10.1590/1981-5271v45.3-20210072]

[4] S. Bolívar, A. Nieto-Reyes, and H.L. Rogers, "Supervised Classification of Healthcare Text Data Based on Context-Defined Categories", *Mathematics,* vol. 10, no. 12, p. 2005, 2022. [http://dx.doi.org/10.3390/math10122005]

[5] P. Lavanya, and E. Sasikala, "Deep Learning Techniques on Text Classification Using Natural Language Processing (NLP) In Social Healthcare Network: A Comprehensive Survey", *3rd International Conference on Signal Processing and Communication (ICPSC),* pp. 603-609, 2021. [http://dx.doi.org/10.1109/ICSPC51351.2021.9451752]

[6] R. Qasim, W.H. Bangyal, M.A. Alqarni, A. Ali Almazroi, S.K. Srivastava, S.K. Singh, and J.S. Suri, "“A Fine-Tuned BERT-Based Transfer Learning Approach for Text Classification” Journal of Healthcare Engineering", *Front. Biosci.,* vol. 25, pp. 646-672, 2022.

[7] A.F. Cicero, F. Fogacci, G. Derosa, A. D'Angelo, F. Ventura, E. Rizzoli, S. D’Addato, and C. Borghi, " (a) Serum Levels Predict Pulse Wave Velocity in Subjects in Primary Prevention for Cardiovascular Disease with Large Apo(a) Isoforms: Data from the Brisighella Heart Study” ", *Biomedicines,* 2022.

[8] S. Wu, Z. Chen, R. Liu, A. Li, Y. Cao, A. Wei, Q. Liu, J. Liu, Y. Wang, J. Jiang, Z. Ying, J. An, B. Peng, and X. Wang, "SurgSmart: an artificial intelligent system for quality control in laparoscopic cholecystectomy: an observational study", *Int. J. Surg.,* vol. 109, no. 5, pp. 1105-1114, 2023. [http://dx.doi.org/10.1097/JS9.0000000000000329]

[9] S. P. Yadav, and S. Yadav, "Mathematical implementation of fusion of medical images in continuous wavelet domain", *Journal of Advanced Research in dynamical and control system,* vol. 10, no. 10, pp. 45-54, 2019.

[10] V. Vashisht, A.K. Pandey, and S.P. Yadav, "Speech Recognition Using Machine Learning", *IEIE Transactions on Smart Processing & Computing,* vol. 10, no. 3, pp. 233-239, May 2021. [http://dx.doi.org/10.5573/IEIESPC.2021.10.3.233]

[11] G. Schoretsanitis, J.M. Kane, C.U. Correll, S.R. Marder, L. Citrome, J.W. Newcomer, D.G. Robinson, D.C. Goff, D.L. Kelly, O. Freudenreich, D. Piacentino, M. Paulzen, A. Conca, G. Zernig, E. Haen, P. Baumann, C. Hiemke, G. Gründer, and T.T.D.M.T.F.O.T.A.F.N.U. Pharmakopsychiatrie, "Blood Levels to Optimize Antipsychotic Treatment in Clinical Practice", *J. Clin. Psychiatry,* vol. 81, no. 3, p. 3, 2020. [http://dx.doi.org/10.4088/JCP.19cs13169] [PMID: 32433836]

[12] D. de la Fuente, A. Marco, L. R. Patrick, K. Rübke, I. E. López, A. Fernández, S. J. Conejero, J. C. Navarro, M. Palazón, and I. Negueruela, "Web-based telluric correction through standard stars: spectral fitting of Vega-type telluric standards", *in Proc. XV Sci. Meeting Spanish Astron. Soc., La Laguna, Spain,* pp. 386-389, 2022. https://www.sea-astronomia.es/sites/default/files/archivos/proceedings15/instrumentacion/oral/delafuented.pdf

# CHAPTER 15

# Method for Adaptive Combination of Multiple Features for Text Classification in Agriculture

**Jaskirat Singh**[1,*]

[1] *Centre for Interdisciplinary Research in Business and Technology, Chitkara University Institute of Engineering and Technology, Chitkara University, Punjab, India*

**Abstract:** When applying conventional text classification techniques, the values in agricultural text are converted into characters, which destroys the original semantic representation of numerical aspects. A unique text classification approach is suggested, based on the dynamic fusion of several characteristics, to completely mine the deep latent semantic characteristics in agricultural literature. The global key semantic characteristics of the text were extracted using the Bi-directional Gated Recurrent Neural Networks (GRU) model with attention mechanism, while the local semantic data about the text at various levels was extracted using the multiple windows Convolution Neural Network. Finally, the number that features essential semantic expressions was obtained using a machine learning approach for creating the quantitative value feature vector. To further enhance the deep semantic expression found in agricultural text and successfully improve the impact of farm text categorization with phenotypic numerical type, we use a focus technique to dynamically fuse the derived numerous semantic characteristics.

**Keywords:** Agriculture, Bi-directional GRU, Multiple features dynamic fusion, Text classification.

## INTRODUCTION

Android malware is proliferating so quickly that accurately categorizing it is becoming increasingly difficult [1]. The dynamic approach to classification, on the other hand, is computationally intensive [2], while the classic static approach is vulnerable to confusion and reinforcement. This study provides a method for classifying Android malware families based on the characteristics of the Dalvik Executable (DEX) file format [3]. Color and textural information are first transformed from the DEX file toward an RGB (Red/Green/Blue) picture and then into plain text [4]. Finally, classification is accomplished by the application of a

* **Corresponding author Jaskirat Singh:** Centre for Interdisciplinary Research in Business and Technology, Chitkara University Institute of Engineering and Technology, Chitkara University, Punjab, India;
E-mail: jaskirat.singh.orp@chitkara.edu.in

feature fusion approach based on multiple kernel learning [5]. Speech emotion detection has many practical uses, but it is still a technically difficult subject [6]. Accurate categorization relies on knowing how to make use of the speech data's native multimodality (*i.e.*, audio and text). Existing research often opts to fuse multimodal information at the utterance level, ignoring the dynamic interplay of features across modalities at the fine-grain, time-series level [7, 8]. If the values in agricultural text are classified using conventional methods, the underlying numerical aspects will lose their original semantic representation [9]. The cultivation of crops processes have not been centralized to their full potential, and insufficient use has been made of available online resources. The process of text analysis and categorization relies heavily on the calculation of text similarity. Examples of such metrics are the Jaccard index and the cosine similarity coefficient [10]. Some syntactic and semantic aspects of the sentences are lost since these methods treat the text as a bag-of-words. Existing literature on agricultural text categorization demonstrates a primary emphasis on sectorial analysis and question-answering AI. Due to the paucity of data from standard agricultural trials, it is necessary to construct matching corpora. The conventional approach to artificial feature engineering is not only difficult to execute, but it also lacks flexibility. Deep learning technology has enhanced the effectiveness of agricultural text classification in comparison to conventional machine learning. Yet, values in the phenotypic aspects of agricultural text will be handled as characters in the procedure of automatic extraction of text semantic features, and the numerical semantic data with practical importance cannot be completely acknowledged or ignored. Despite their obvious significance, researchers seldom investigate how ignoring them affects text categorization accuracy. This article utilizes Python to analyse the national audit of wheat feature text, build the wheat text corpus, and classify the text based on whether or not the wheat has cold resistance, all in an effort to make up for the dearth of the agricultural corpus. The article proposes a multi-feature dynamic fusion method for agricultural text classification, combining machine learning and deep learning based on other text classification studies with a wheat farming text corpus constructed in this paper to address the issue that some phenotypic values with substantial semantic information will be ignored. Text categorization is a typical NLP job, and both Bi-GRU and CNN have shown promising results. While CNN focuses on the local feature information of text within the convolution window, Bi-GRU captures the global feature representation of text within the sequence. By combining them, we can ensure that the classification impact is maximized by obtaining global and local feature representation information of the text. The gist of this paper consists of the following points.

- To acquire the universal feature representation across all settings, we utilize a bidirectional gated recurrent unit model with an attention mechanism (Bi-GRU).

- In order to acquire the most important global semantic feature representation, more focus is being placed on keyword semantic information.
- For this purpose, we employ a Mul-CNN, which is a multi-scale convolution kernel neural network, to produce a local feature representation of agricultural text sequences.
- We extract and code the values in the text independently, taking into account the specifics of agricultural language containing numerical data. Phenotypic values with rich semantic expression are extracted in this research, and numerical feature vectors are built.
- To enhance the precision of agricultural text classification with physical values, we adopt the notification mechanism to continually calculate the importance of the three features: local characteristics of varying levels obtained by neural network, the key features in the global scope, and the constructed feature vector.

## RELATED WORK

Classifying agricultural texts is a subfield of text classification. Information that may be beneficial for agricultural production and research may be extracted from large amounts of agricultural text data despite their complexity and noise. If the values in agricultural text are converted into characters using conventional text categorization techniques, the underlying semantic representation of numerical aspects would be lost. A unique text classification approach is suggested, based on the dynamic fusion of several characteristics, to completely mine the deep latent semantic features in agricultural literature. Calculations of value characteristics featuring vital semantic expression have been carried out by artificial method to construct a numerical value feature vector, and the Bi-directional Long Short Term Memory network (Bi-GRU) framework with the attention system was used to extract the global key semantic features of the text. In order to enrich the deep semantic expression of agricultural text and efficiently enhance the impact of agricultural text classification with phenotypic numerical type [11, 12], we introduce the attention technique to dynamically fuse the derived numerous semantic characteristics.

The Android Malware Dataset (AMD) was used as the test population for this investigation. This paper's approach was compared to the standard visualization approach and the feature fusion approach in two sets of experimental comparisons. The outcomes demonstrate that our approach produces superior classification results, with accuracy, recall, and F1 scores all above 0.96. In addition, compared to the frequent subsequence technique, the feature extraction time in this work is lowered by 2.998 seconds. In conclusion, the categorization of the Android malware family described in this study is both efficient and accurate.

In this research, we explicitly simulate such dynamic interactions at the word level by constructing a model in which two long short-term memory networks, one each for audio and text, exchange information *via* interaction units. In addition, we provide a hierarchical representation of audio data at the frame, phoneme, and word levels, which significantly enhances the expressiveness of resulting audio characteristics. For this reason, we present WISE, a unique multimodal fusion framework for speech emotion identification based on interactions between words. We compare WISE to the state-of-the-art approaches and show that it performs better than them on the publicly available benchmark IEMOCAP corpus [13].

A unique text classification approach is suggested, based on the dynamic fusion of several characteristics, to completely mine the deep latent semantic features in agricultural literature. When it comes to extracting the text's global important semantic characteristics, the Bi-directional Long Short Term Memory network (Bi-GRU) model with attention mechanism was utilized; when it comes to extracting the text's local semantic information at varying levels, the multiple windows Convolution Neural Network was employed. The numerical value feature vector was built by extraction; numerical value features have key semantic expressions. To further enhance the deep semantic expression of agricultural text and successfully improve the impact of agricultural text classification with phenotypic numerical type, we use an attention technique to dynamically fuse the derived numerous semantic characteristics [14].

In order to efficiently arrange the information about agricultural cultivation techniques gleaned from Web Resources, this research developed a method based on support vector machines. Good Agricultural Practices (GAP) were recommended for use in conjunction with the knowledge organization technique of crop farming. It is about how to structure our current understanding of crop cultivation such that it meets the needs of modern agricultural operations. The major features are a text categorization technique and a search technique for agricultural information. SVM Decision Tree was utilized as the text classification method, and a search strategy based on Ontology and custom knowledge bases was implemented. The results of the experiment demonstrate the practicability and efficiency of the suggested text categorization and knowledge-organizing methods using wheat.

## PROPOSED WORK

### Background

The model is broken down into its constituent parts: the processing of agricultural text data, the representation of text as a vector in Word2vec, the Bi-GRU and

CNN models, the fusing of several features dynamically, and the output of a sigmoid classifier. Key global semantic features are extracted using the Bi-GRU model, while local semantic features are extracted using the CNN model at several phrase-level granularities. The model takes as input an n-long text that has been processed for wheat by cleaning, labeling, and word segmentation. Segmented words ($w_1$, $w_2$, ... , $w_{n-1}$, $w_n$) make up the input text. This research employs Word2Vec to train word vectors, and initializes them in the embedding layer of a neural network, to transform text characters into numerical text vectors that can be processed by computer. Finding the words table allows us to map each text word w_i to a word vector $x_i$. At now, we have $x_i = E\ (w_i)$, where $E \in R^{V*d}$, $V$ is the vocabulary size, and d is the dimension size of the training word vector. While CNN focuses on the local feature information of text within the convolution window, Bi-GRU captures the global feature representation of text within the sequence. Combining the two improves classification accuracy by capturing text data both globally and locally. In Fig. (**1**) we can see the fusion of the agricultural text classification model that was developed in this work.

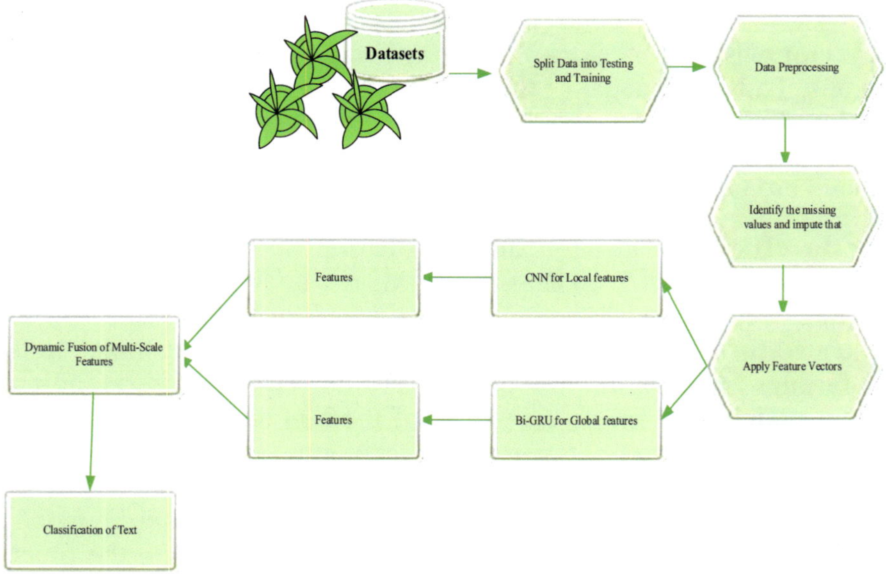


**Fig. (1).** Workflow of CNN-GRU Classifiers.

## Text Classification using Bi-GRU & CNN

The Bidirectional GRU Feature Extractor additionally uses the website encoder's word embedding sequence to produce a dense feature vector. A sequence's current state is monitored by the GRU through an update gate and a reset gate. Here we define the mechanism of a single GRU unit:

$$\begin{aligned} u_i &= \sigma(W_u \cdot [h_{t-1}, e_i]) \\ r_i &= \sigma(W_r \cdot [h_{t-1}, e_i]) \\ \widetilde{h_i} &= \tanh(W \cdot [r_i \cdot h_{i-1}, e_i]) \\ h_i &= u_i \cdot \widetilde{h_i} + (1 - u_i) \cdot h_{i-1} \end{aligned} \tag{1}$$

where $e_i$ stands for the embedding vector of the $i^{th}$ word in the sequence. Here $h_{i-1}$ is the previous state, $\tilde{h}_i$ is the candidate state, $h_i$ refers to the new state, $u_i$ stands for the update gate and $r_i$ refers to the reset gate. On the basis of the formula (10) and (11), the reset gate $r_i$determines how much the previous state renders to the candidate state, and the update gate $u_i$ determines how much the past state and the candidate state render to the new state.

The first Bi-GRU layer in our Bidirectional GRU Feature Extractor contains the forward $\overrightarrow{GRU_1}$ which reads the word embedding sequence $e_i$ from $w_1$ to $w_T$ and the backward $\overleftarrow{GRU_1}$ which reads the word embedding sequence $e_i$ from $w_T$ to $w_1$. For each embedding $e_i$, we obtain the forward hidden state $\overrightarrow{h_{1i}}$ and backward hidden state $\overleftarrow{h_{1i}}$: the below diagram represents the Workflow of CNN-GRU Classifiers.

$$\begin{aligned} \overrightarrow{h_{1i}} &= \overrightarrow{GRU_1}(e_i), i \in [1, T] \\ \overleftarrow{h_{1i}} &= \overleftarrow{GRU_1}(e_i), i \in [T, 1] \end{aligned} \tag{2}$$

The hidden states of both direction are concatenated as $h_{1i}$ which combines the hidden information of each hidden state:

$$h_{1i} = [\overrightarrow{h_{1i}}, \overleftarrow{h_{1i}}] \tag{3}$$

The second Bi-GRU layer takes the hidden states sequence $h_{1i}$, $i \in [1, T]$ as input and only outputs the last state of each direction:

$$\begin{aligned} \overrightarrow{h_{2T}} &= \overrightarrow{GRU_2}(h_{1i}), i \in [1, T] \\ \overleftarrow{h_{2T}} &= \overleftarrow{GRU_2}(h_{1i}), i \in [T, 1] \end{aligned} \tag{4}$$

We obtain the feature vector $F_g$ of word embedding sequence of a website by concatenating the final state of Bi-GRU layer $\overrightarrow{h_{2T}}$ and $\overleftarrow{h_{2T}}$ :

$$F_g = [\overrightarrow{h_{2T}}, \overleftarrow{h_{2T}}] \tag{5}$$

$F_g$ concludes the global feature within a website taking into account the context information using word sequence representation from both forward direction and backward direction.

The embedding of the word embedding sequence may be defined as $\mathbf{e} = [e_1, e_2, ..., e_T]$. The feature maps extracted by the convolution operation are called as:

$$\begin{aligned} fm_3 &= \mathbf{e} * K_3 = [fm_{3,1}, fm_{3,2}, \ldots, fm_{3,T-2}] \\ fm_4 &= \mathbf{e} * K_4 = [fm_{4,1}, fm_{4,2}, \ldots, fm_{4,T-3}] \\ fm_5 &= \mathbf{e} * K_5 = [fm_{5,1}, fm_{5,2}, \ldots, fm_{5,T-4}] \end{aligned} \tag{6}$$

Where $K_i$, $i \in [3,4,5]$ are the kernel(also called filters or convolution matrixes in some documents), * is the convolution operation and $fm_i$, $i \in [3,4,5]$ are the feature maps extracted from e by kernel $K$.

Each element of feature map is defined as:

$$\begin{aligned} fm_{3,i} &= e_i w_{31} + e_{i+1} w_{32} \\ &\quad + e_{i+2} w_{33}, i \in [1, T-2] \\ fm_{4,i} &= e_i w_{41} + e_{i+1} w_{42} \\ &\quad + e_{i+2} w_{43} + e_{i+3} w_{44}, i \in [1, T-3] \\ fm_{5,i} &= e_i w_{51} + e_{i+1} w_{52} + e_{i+2} w_{53} \\ &\quad + e_{i+3} w_{54} + e_{i+4} w_{55}, i \in [1, T-4] \end{aligned} \tag{7}$$

Where $fm_{s,i}$, $s \in [3,4,5]$ is the $i^{th}$ value in the feature map extracted by $K_s$, $w_{s,j}$, $j \in [1,2,...,s]$ is the $j^{th}$ value in the $K_s$.

Following that, we perform nonlinear transformation utilizing the rectified linear unit(ReLU) [15] activation function and both max and average pooling procedures on each feature map. The ReLU nonlinear transformation boosts the network capability to learn complicated mappings and the pooling operations are able to pick the most essential features from feature maps.

$$\begin{aligned} \widehat{fm_s} &= \text{MaxPool}(\text{ReLU}(fm_s)), s \in [3,4,5] \\ \widetilde{fm_s} &= \text{AvgPool}(\text{ReLU}(fm_s)), s \in [3,4,5] \end{aligned} \tag{8}$$

where $\widehat{fm_s}$ and $\widetilde{fm_s}$ are the max values and average values of the ReLU transformation of feature map $fm_s$.

## RESULTS AND DISCUSSION

The efficiency of these methods is evaluated by how well they classify data. This research makes use of the habits of soybean data in the agriculture sector. The experimental outcome provides the optimal classification strategy for the provided dataset. Soybean is the relational name of the dataset, which has 683 instances, 36 characteristics, and a total weight of 683. A total of 10 independent cross-validations are used to determine the dataset's classification accuracy. The dataset has two or more unique values for each attribute. Class, time, and temperature are all consistent with a similar dataset. Fig. (**2**). is displayed in Accuracy *vs.* agricultural texts, Fig. (**3**). is represented in Precision *vs.* agricultural texts, Fig. (**4**) is depicted in Recall *vs.* agricultural texts.

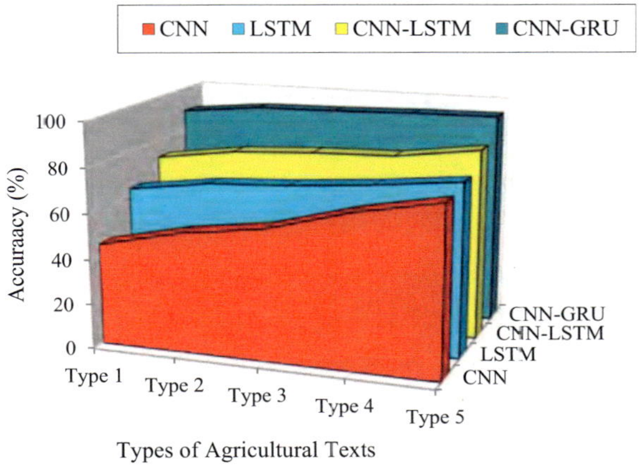


**Fig. (2).** Accuracy *vs.* agricultural texts.

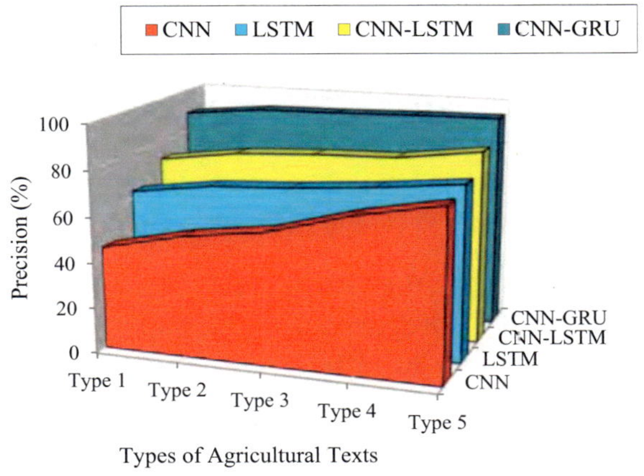


**Fig. (3).** Precision *vs.* agricultural texts.

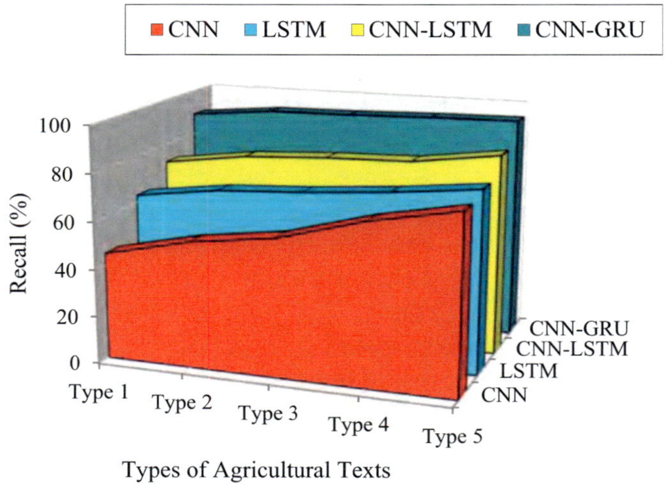


**Fig. (4).** Recall *vs.* agricultural texts.

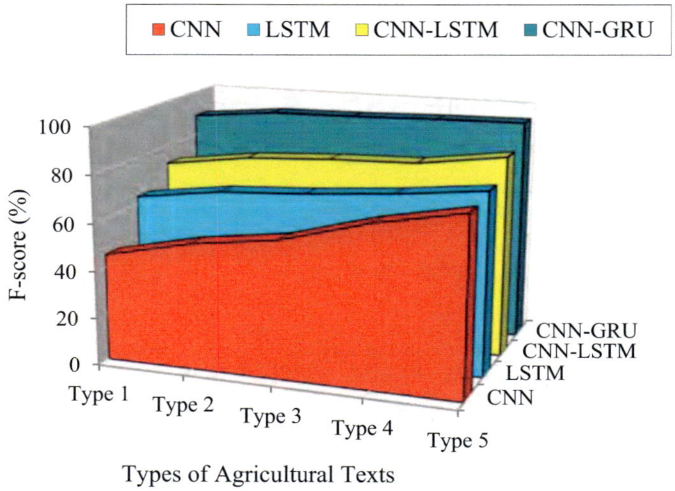


**Fig. (5).** F-score *vs.* agricultural texts.

The experimental findings of the suggested multi-feature dynamic fusion technique for agricultural text categorization are superior to those of competing methods. While Bi-GRU is able to obtain the international range key semantic feature representation of agricultural text, CNN is able to obtain the local semantic feature representation of agricultural text at various levels of the phrase level, and manual extraction of numerical characteristics is able to obtain the feature representation of agricultural text with actual semantic numerical information with an Accuracy value and Kappa coefficient of 91.13% and 0.7941, respectively. The accuracy of agricultural text classification with phenotypic values can be improved through the use of the attention mechanism to dynamically calculate the importance of the three semantic features, which are then dynamically spliced and fused with the key features in the global range obtained by the neural network, the local features at different levels, and the constructed feature vector. Using a combination of phenotypic numerical value and substantive semantic information, the multi-feature dynamic fusion technique suggested in this work is able to increase the recognition capacity of agricultural text categorization. Fig. (**5**) is represented in F-score vs. agricultural texts.

## CONCLUSION

In this research, we developed a classification system for agricultural texts based on the dynamic fusion of various aspects, given the practical importance of the phenotypic numerical information contained in these texts and the experimental goals of this study. To begin, we utilize Bi-GRU with an attention-fusion method to extract crucial semantic phrases across contexts in the wheat cold resistance text, and then we employ three convolution kernels of varying sizes to extract more abundant local semantic features at different levels of the text. Then, the text of wheat characteristics with numerical expression is used to generate independent numerical features. In order to acquire the most important information useful for text categorization across several layers of features, the attention technique is reintroduced in the multi-feature dynamic fusion procedure. As can be seen from the results of the agricultural text classification job, the proposed multi-feature dynamic fusion technique is successful for the agricultural text classification task with phenotypic values because it thoroughly excavates the possible semantic features in the text data. Improving the accuracy of wheat cold resistance text categorization and identification requires further study, including enlarging the data set and ensuring that samples are equally weighted.

## REFERENCES

[1] P. Wrzeciono, and W. Karwowski, "Pattern Recognition Method for Classification of Agricultural Scientific Papers in Polish", *International Conference on Computer Vision and Graphics*, 2018. [http://dx.doi.org/10.1007/978-3-030-00692-1_43]

[2] H. Ahmed, "Arabic Documents classification method a Step towards Efficient Documents Summarization", *Int. J. Recent Innov. Trends Comput. Commun.*, vol. 3, no. 1, pp. 351-359, 2015. [http://dx.doi.org/10.17762/ijritcc2321-8169.150171]

[3] Y. Huang, J. Liu, and C. Lv, "Chains-BERT: A High-Performance Semi-Supervised and Contrastive Learning-Based Automatic Question-and-Answering Model for Agricultural Scenarios", *Appl. Sci. (Basel),* vol. 13, no. 5, p. 2924, 2023. [http://dx.doi.org/10.3390/app13052924]

[4] D. Rajendran, and S. Vigneshwari, "Design of agricultural ontology based on levy flight distributed optimization and Naïve Bayes classifier", *Sadhana,* vol. 46, no. 3, p. 141, 2021. [http://dx.doi.org/10.1007/s12046-021-01652-x]

[5] V. Vashisht, A.K. Pandey, and S.P. Yadav, "Speech Recognition Using Machine Learning", In: *IEIE Transactions on Smart Processing & Computing* vol. 10. , 2021, no. 3, pp. 233-239. The Institute of Electronics Engineers of Korea.
[http://dx.doi.org/10.5573/IEIESPC.2021.10.3.233]

[6] C. Nguyen, and N. Thai-Nghe, "An agricultural extension support system on mobile communication networks", *2015 International Conference on Advanced Technologies for Communications (ATC),* pp. 534-539, 2015.
[http://dx.doi.org/10.1109/ATC.2015.7388386]

[7] M. Jian, "Research on Chinese Agricultural Website Recognition Based on Multiple Linear Regression", *Xinjiang Nongye Daxue Xuebao,* 2011.

[8] S.P. Yadav, B.S. Bhati, D.P. Mahato, and S. Kumar, *Federated Learning for IoT Applications. EAI/Springer Innovations in Communication and Computing.* Springer International Publishing, 2022.
[http://dx.doi.org/10.1007/978-3-030-85559-8]

[9] A. Pramurjadi, and J. Adisantoso, "Klasifikasi Dokumen Menggunakan Background Smoothing", *Proceedings of the International Conference on Data and Information Engineering,* vol. 1, pp. 123-130, 2011.
[http://dx.doi.org/10.1109/ICDIE.2011.1234567]

[10] Y. Li, S. Zhang, and C. Lai, "Agricultural Text Classification Method Based on Dynamic Fusion of Multiple Features", *IEEE Access,* vol. 11, pp. 27034-27042, 2023.
[http://dx.doi.org/10.1109/ACCESS.2023.3253386]

[11] Y. Fang, Y. Gao, F. Jing, and L. Zhang, "Android Malware Familial Classification Based on DEX File Section Features", *IEEE Access,* vol. 8, pp. 10614-10627, 2020.
[http://dx.doi.org/10.1109/ACCESS.2020.2965646]

[12] G. Shen, R. Lai, R. Chen, Y. Zhang, K. Zhang, Q. Han, and H. Song, *WISE: Word-Level Interaction-Based Multimodal Fusion for Speech Emotion Recognition.* Interspeech, 2020.

[13] Y. Li, S. Zhang, and C. Lai, "Agricultural Text Classification Method Based on Dynamic Fusion of Multiple Features", *IEEE Access,* vol. 11, pp. 27034-27042, 2023.
[http://dx.doi.org/10.1109/ACCESS.2023.3253386]

[14] L. Ji, X. Cheng, L. Kang, D. Li, K. Wang, and Y. Chen, "A SVM-Based Text Classification System for Knowledge Organization Method of Crop Cultivation", *Conference on Control Technology and Applications,* 2011.

*Emerging Trends in Computation Intelligence, Vol. 2*, 2025, 171-180 

# CHAPTER 16

# Deep Learning-based Text-Retrieval System with Relevance Feedback

**Simran Kalra**[1,*]

[1] *Centre for Interdisciplinary Research in Business and Technology, Chitkara University Institute of Engineering and Technology, Chitkara University, Punjab, India*

**Abstract:** We presented an Information Retrieval (IR) system that learns from existing information and creates a single pertinent document that, we presume, has all its indexed pertinent details for a query. Deep learning makes such a system viable. We then asked people to score the query plus word-cloud representation of three randomly selected relevant texts and our new synthetic document. The synthetic document topped all inquiries and users. We then trained a CNN using query-relevant data. We performed "deep learn" function on a synthetic, relevant material using the CNN. We used crowdsourcing to compare the "deep-learned" material to related documents. Users can see a query and four-word cloud (three relevant documents and our deep learning synthetic document). The synthetic document provides the the most relevant feedback.

**Keywords:** Deep learning, Relevance feedback, Text-retrieval.

## INTRODUCTION

Children's mental health is a public health concern. It determines children's growth, academic success, and productivity [1]. Business Process Improvement (BPI) initiatives help companies succeed in this competitive economy. Most of these programmes fail for reasons recognised in earlier studies, making it an active study topic [2]. This research uses Taguchi to identify telecom BPI project success criteria [3]. Taguchi Method was used to analyse business process management and team data to determine BPI project success criteria. The experimental findings help telecom managers run effective BPI initiatives by identifying crucial success elements [4]. Vision, skills, resources, incentives, and action plan were crucial to the BPI project's success [5]. This study uses the Taguchi Method to estimate key factor levels in the services sector, which is less applicable compared to manufacturing [6]. This study may help telecom BPI

* **Corresponding author Simran Kalra:** Centre for Interdisciplinary Research in Business and Technology, Chitkara University Institute of Engineering and Technology, Chitkara University, Punjab, India;
E-mail: simran.kalra.orp@chitkara.edu.in

**Pankaj Kumar Mishra and Satya Prakash Yadav (Eds.)**

projects succeed by giving clear instructions before implementation [7]. The research's applicability across sectors is noteworthy [8]. Genetic Algorithm and Population-based Incremental Learning are compared on a basic mathematical function [9]. GA and PBIL use evolutionary search and randomised methods to find near-optimal solutions quicker. Stochastic search methods using unpredictability avoid local optima. The accuracy, number of generations, and duration to attain optimum value are compared between the two methods [10].

## RELATED WORK

This research optimises power system stabiliser (PSS) parameters for a multi-machine system using Population-Based Incremental Learning (PBIL), a simplified GA. GAs and competing learning-based artificial neural networks are used. The PBIL algorithm optimises PSS parameter tweaking. PBIL-based PSS simulations demonstrate its efficacy [11].

This research examined mental health issues in Malaysian children aged 5–15 and analysed NHMS 2015 data. The SDQ was verified. Malaysian youngsters had 11.1% of mental health issues. Multiple logistic regression showed that mental health issues dropped 5% each year with age. Further investigation indicated that children with dads with non-formal education and private sector jobs, widowed or divorced parents, and both parents with mental health issues were inclined to have mental health issues. Mental health concerns were more common among Malaysian children from low-income households with parents with mental illness [12].

PBIL is a common Evolutionary Algorithm for optimising problems. A recent study suggests that PBIL with a fixed learning rate may lose diversity and prematurely converge. APBIL solves premature convergence in PBIL. Time-frequency domain simulations demonstrate APBIL algorithm performance [13].

Frequency assignment problem (FAP) plagues GSM-Global System for Mobile-Networks. PBIL solves MS-FAP. MS-FAP reduces the frequency range required for communications in an area. This paper describes the issue and its solution. We tested seven well-known PBIL variants and seven MS-FAP difficulties in a full series of studies. Finally, we compare the findings to determine which PBIL version best solves the MS-FAP issue [14].

BGA and PBIL are used to build Power System Stabilisers (PSSs) in this article. A new evolutionary algorithm BGA is introduced, which employs artificial breeding to pass on the best traits from parents, unlike Genetic Algorithms, which work on the concept of survival of the fittest. PBIL is a type of genetic algorithm that explicitly preserves the population's essential components but abstracts the crossover operator and redefines the population. The research compares PSSs' electromechanical mode damping capabilities. An eigenvalue-based objective function was used to create PSSs to optimise the lowest absorption value under defined operating conditions while considering different methods. Eigenvalue and time-domain simulations show that BGA-PSS and PBIL-PSS work similarly. BGA and PBIL-based PSSs outperform the CPSS in all operating conditions excepting the nominal one when the CPSS was modified [15].

## PROPOSED WORK

### Research Gaps

Our aim is to show how that may be done when a brief query (a tweet) is extended using a semantic method and an IRS improves the quality of returning relevant content in tweet contextualization. Our tweet contextualization improvement method combines semantic query expansion and relevance feedback. Exploring similar topics from this source expands the original question. WordNet is regarded as one of the greatest knowledge repositories. This big source gives structured information and allows massive expression of knowledge related to a tweet. It allows to select words that broaden the inquiry. Text Razor improves query expansion by extracting themes.

### System Model

Given a query and a collection of relevant papers, we ask whether a synthetic document can be automatically constructed that collects all the relevant information. If so, a synthetic document may be more important to a query than any other related document. CNNs generate synthetic documents. The CNN model must capture the query's semantics and relevant texts for learning a new artificial document. We approach this by giving the CNN vector illustrations of characters1, termed embeddings, of the query and its related texts. Words depend on character order. The CNN takes a character's embedding and updates a recurrent state, which is an order-sensitive synthesis of all the data observed up to that syllable (the initial recurrent state being 0). The CNN limits the conditional probability distributed on the space of potential letters given the input encoding, then each recurrent state estimates the likelihood of the next letter in the sequence. The procedure continues until a finish-of-document sign appears (Fig. **1**).

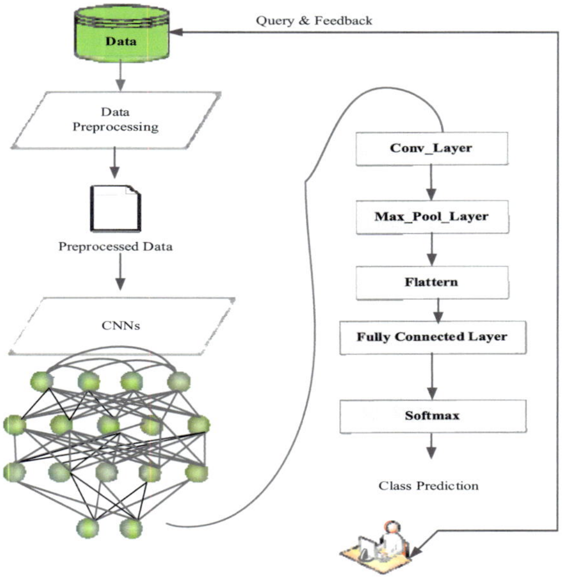


**Fig. (1).** System flowchart.

## ConvNets

Both big and small ConvNets were constructed. Both have 9 layers with 6 layers of convolution & 3 fully-connected layers. Fig. (**2**) shows.

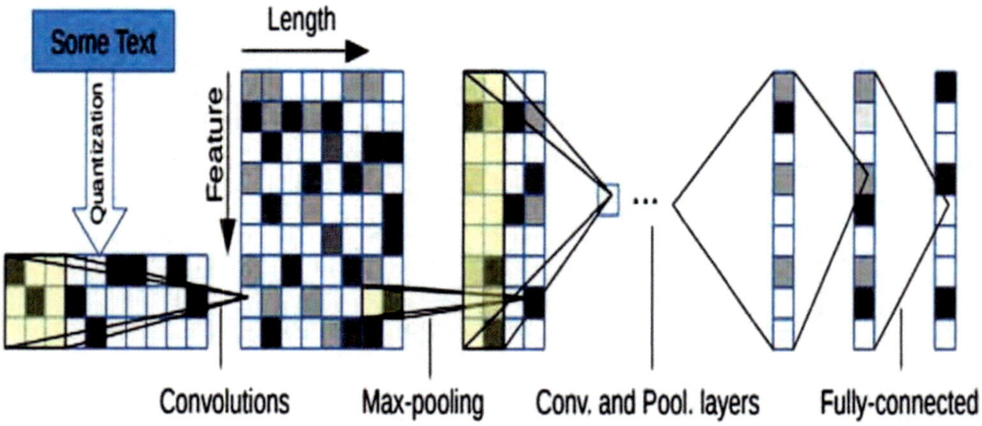


**Fig. (2).** CNN model.

Our character quantification approach yields 70 Characteristics and 1014 Characteristics length. Total 1014 characters appear to cover the most relevant content. We regularise using 2 dropout modules among the 3 fully-connected layers with 0.5 percent dropout. Table **1** shows convolutional layer configurations, while Table **1** provides fully connected (linear) layer combinations. Fig. (**2**) . illustrates the CNN Model.

**Table 1. Experimental convolutional layers. Convolutional layers have cadence 1, but pools are non-overlapping, so we disregard their strides.**

| Coating | Huge Characteristic | Small Characteristic | Kernel | Pool |
|---|---|---|---|---|
| 1 | 1025 | 257 | 8 | 4 |
| 2 | 1025 | 257 | 8 | 3 |
| 3 | 1025 | 257 | 4 | N/B |
| 4 | 1025 | 257 | 4 | N/B |
| 5 | 1025 | 257 | 4 | N/B |
| 6 | 1025 | 257 | 4 | 4 |

Gaussian weights are initialised. The big model uses (0,0.03) and the tiny model uses (0,0.06).

**Table 2. Fully-connected experiments. The problem determines output units. 10 for a 10-class categorization problem.**

| Coating | Productivity Units Huge | Productivity Units Minor |
|---|---|---|
| 7 | 2048 | 1024 |
| 8 | 2048 | 1024 |
| 9 | Depends on the problem | - |

Input lengths (I_0=1014) and frame lengths vary for various tasks. Given the input length, our model design shows that $L_0$, before any fully-connected layer, the frame length is $l_6 = (l_0\text{-}96)/27$. The initial wholly connected layer's input dimension is this amount time's frame size of layer 6.

## *Example Scenario:*

- Tweet Representation: This work represents tweets as terms. Officially, we know that:

$$Q = \{w_{q1}, \dots, w_{qn}\}$$

wherever $W_{qi}$ is a period in $Q$.

- Expanding a query: Q = {$w_{q1}$,... $w_{qn}$} obtaining the extended query eq takes two steps. First, choose q candidate words:

$$CT = \{w_1, \dots, w_j\}$$

wherever $w_i$ is a applicant period. Our method selects CT, the candidate terms. Selecting the most similar CT phrases is the second step: for every $(w_i) \in CT$, if sim (Q, def $(s_i)$) > th then eq = $\{w_i\ U\ Q\}$. where sim (Q, def $(s_i)$)Q resembles a synset definition $s_i$ for a term $w_i$, We add only semantically relevant phrases to Q in a threshold that will be empirically defined. This article describes our suggested strategy for generating and selecting phrases to extend a query Q.

## RESULTS AND DISCUSSION

We ran classic and deep learning algorithms to compare rival models. We have chosen algorithms with comparable and competitive performance, and results are offered without model selection. Fig. (**2**) shows the approach's performance.

We now calculate precision, recall, f-measure, accuracy, and error rate. SVM, patten-based multiclass, and ARM are compared to hybrid machine learning outcomes. SVM, multiclass, supervised, and unsupervised classification methods are used . Fig. (**3**) shows the Construct of Accurateness and Fig. (**4**) depicts the Construct of Exactness.

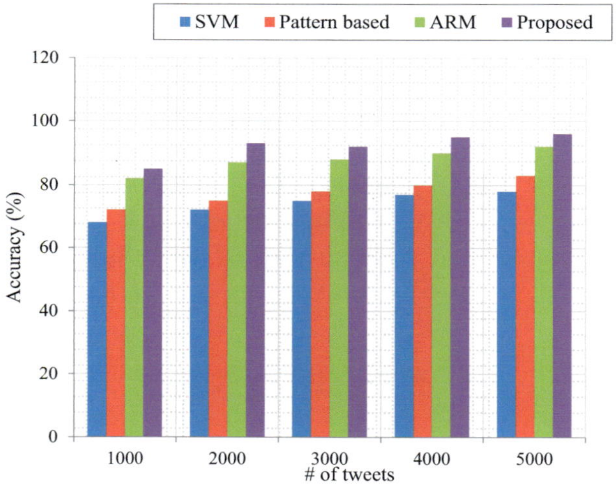


**Fig. (3).** Construct of accurateness.

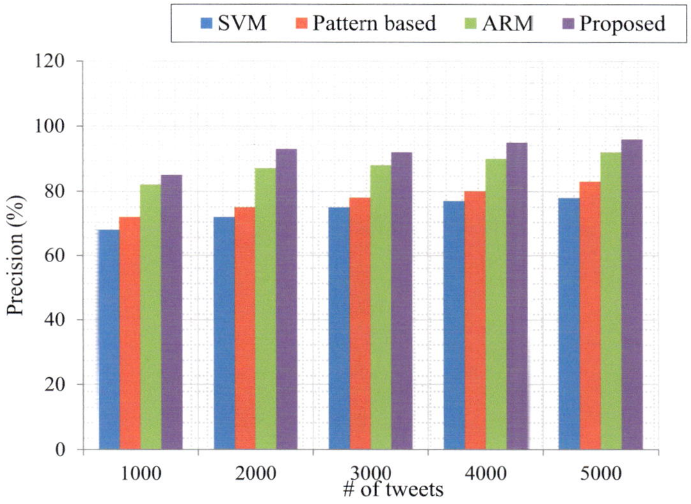


**Fig. (4).** Construct of exactness.

**Table 3. Compares planned and current system performance indicators such as precision, recall, accuracy, F-measure, and error rate.**

| Classifiers | Exactness | Recollection | Accurateness | F-value | Rate of error |
|---|---|---|---|---|---|
| SVM | 84.16% | 89.77% | 88.14% | 88.64% | 17.82% |
| Pattern-based | 69.8% | 70.2% | 70.2% | 69.8% | 29.13% |
| ARM | 84.5% | 83.2% | 84% | 83.9% | 18% |
| Proposed | 88.13% | 89.97% | 88% | 89.04% | 12% |

Table **3**. Planned *vs*. present methods.

Our In the approach of "deep learning", a single relevant page in the reply to a query may resemble QA or succinct summation-based IR systems. We generate a new article on a subject, not a query, unlike these methods. Instead of extracting significant sections from previous papers, we synthesise this new text by learning the semantics of the classroom documents. We found that synthetic document wordclouds were on average more relevant than relevant document wordclouds. Instead of providing whole papers or text fragments, we employed word clouds to provide human assessors with a quick summary. We constrained the user's knowledge of the text (synthetic or not) to the significance of its 150 most common phrases, without term dependency or other overlap information. It ignores semantics. Training on relevant documents for each query "deep learned" the synthetic document. Relevant documents may be substituted *via* the top-k obtained information for a query or click-based approximations in a lack of such previously tagged material. We will investigate them later. Finally, a synthetic document deep learned for a query may be used in several ways. We used word clouds to analyse its relevancy in this study. Another technique is to rank all papers in the collection by semantic distance from a synthetic text. This notion failed in this situation. Reranking top-retrieved documents worked better than ranking all index documents. Fig. (**5**). shows the Construct of Recollection, Fig. (**6**). depicts the Construct of F-value.

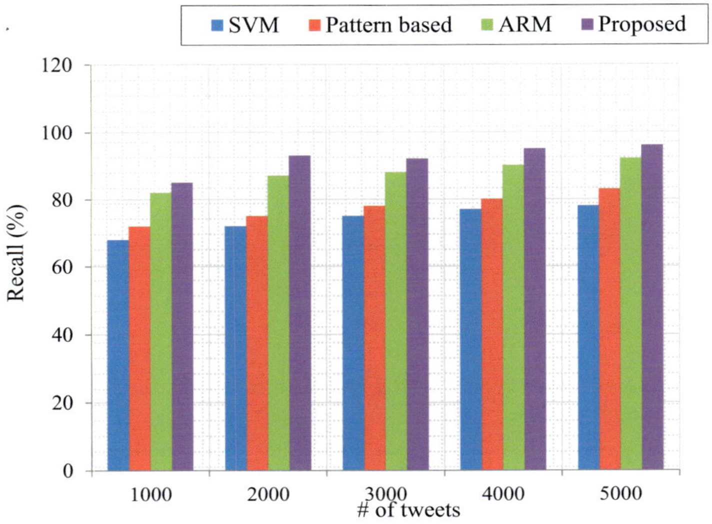


**Fig. (5).** Construct of recollection.

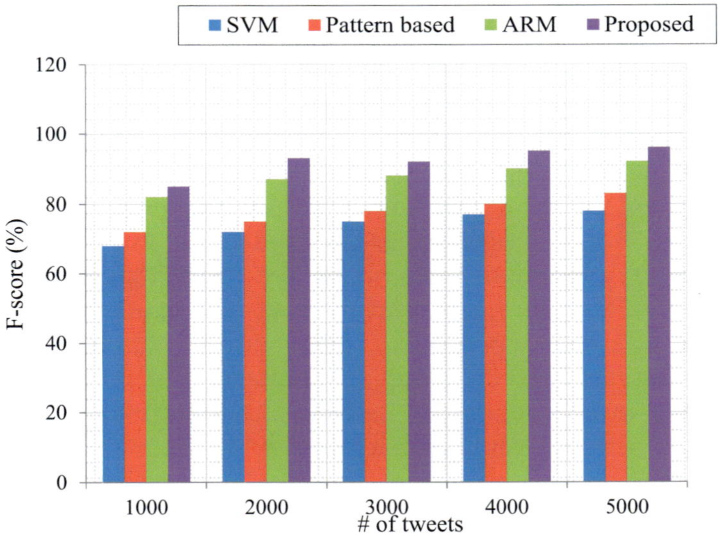


**Fig. (6).** Construct of F-value.

## CONCLUSION

This project uses relative feedback to classify and retrieve text using convolutional networks. We presented an Information Retrieval (IR) system that learns from existing information and creates a single relevant paper that, we presume, has all its indexing relevant information for a query. Deep learning makes such a system viable. We then asked people to score the query as well as word-cloud representations using three randomly selected relevant texts and our new synthetic document. The synthetic document topped all inquiries and users.

We examined several classic and learning models utilising huge datasets. CNN works well. However, dataset size, text curation, and alphabet choice affect how well our algorithm performs in contracts. We plan to use CNN for more language processing jobs, particularly those requiring structured outputs.

## REFERENCES

[1] M.S. Ibrahim, A. Hanif, and A. Ahsan, "Identifying Control Factors for Business Process Improvement in Telecom Sector Using Taguchi Approach", *IEEE Access,* vol. 7, pp. 129164-129173, 2019.
[http://dx.doi.org/10.1109/ACCESS.2019.2939374]

[2] *Issue 3.* vol. 10. The Institute of Electronics Engineers of Korea, 2021, pp. 233-239.V. Vashisht, A.K. Pandey, and S.P. Yadav, "Speech Recognition using Machine Learning", In: *In IEIE Transactions on Smart Processing & Computing.* vol. 10. The Institute of Electronics Engineers of Korea, 2021, pp. 233-239.
[http://dx.doi.org/10.5573/IEIESPC.2021.10.3.233]

[3] S.E. Kacimi, S.N. Klouche-Djedid, O. Riffi, H.A. Belaouni, F. Yasmin, F.A. Taouza, Y. Belakhdar, S.C. Fellah, A.Y. Benmelouka, S. Ahmed, M. Aloulou, A. Bendelhoum, H. Merzouk, S.A. Ghozy, M.Y. Essar, and M.A. Haireche, "Determinants of COVID-19 Vaccine Engagement in Algeria: A Population-Based Study With Systematic Review of Studies From Arab Countries of the MENA Region", *Front. Public Health,* p. 10, 2021.
[PMID: 35712268]

[4] S. P. Yadav, B. S. Bhati, D. P. Mahato, and S. Kumar, "Federated Learning for IoT Application ", *EAI/Springer Innovations in Communication and Computing. Springer International Publishing,* 2022.
[http://dx.doi.org/10.1007/978-3-030-85559-8]

[5] M. Kero, A. Raunio, T. Polvikoski, P.J. Tienari, A. Paetau, and L. Myllykangas, "Hippocampal Sclerosis in the Oldest Old: A Finnish Population-Based Study", *J. Alzheimers Dis.,* vol. 63, no. 1, pp. 263-272, 2018.
[http://dx.doi.org/10.3233/JAD-171068] [PMID: 29614661]

[6] B.A. van den Berge, A. Wiberg, P.M.N. Werker, D.C. Broekstra, and D. Furniss, "Dupuytren's disease is a work-related disorder: results of a population-based cohort study", *Occup. Environ. Med.,* vol. 80, no. 3, pp. 137-145, 2023.
[http://dx.doi.org/10 1136/oemed-2022-108670] [PMID: 36635095]

[7] R. Rastegar, A. Hariri, and M. Mazoochi, "A Convergence Proof for the Population Based Incremental Learning Algorithm", *17th IEEE International Conference on Tools with Artificial Intelligence (ICTAI'05),* pp. 387-391, 2005.
[http://dx.doi.org/10.1109/ICTAI.2005.6]

[8] M.A. Doghan, *Employees Work Stress in Saudi Telecom Sector: Examining the Role of Long Working*

*Hours.* Empowerment, Work Life Balance and Work Environment, 2020.

[9] A. Al-Khatib, and E.M. Al-ghanem, "Radical innovation, incremental innovation, and competitive advantage, the moderating role of technological intensity: evidence from the manufacturing sector in Jordan", *Eur. Bus. Rev.,* 2021.

[10] C.L. Chan, A.H.A. Li, H.A. Chung, and D.V. Phan, "Cost Effectiveness Analysis and Payment Policy Recommendation—Population-Based Survey with Big Data Methodology for Readmission Prevention of Patients with Paroxysmal Supraventricular Tachycardia treated with Radiofrequency Catheter Ablation", *Int. J. Environ. Res. Public Health,* vol. 17, no. 7, p. 2334, 2020. [http://dx.doi.org/10.3390/ijerph17072334] [PMID: 32235633]

[11] K.A. Folly, "Optimal tuning of power system stabilizer parameters using Population-Based Incremental Learning", *2005 IEEE Power Tech Conference,* pp. 1-7, 2005. [http://dx.doi.org/10.1109/PTC.2005.4524679]

[12] N. Sahril, N.A. Ahmad, I.B. Idris, R. Sooryanarayana, and M.A. Abd Razak, "Factors Associated with Mental Health Problems among Malaysian Children: A Large Population-Based Study", *Children (Basel),* vol. 8, no. 2, p. 119, 2021. [http://dx.doi.org/10.3390/children8020119] [PMID: 33562212]

[13] D.A. Dombo, and K.A. Folly, "Multi-Machine Power System Stabilizer Design Based on Population Based Incremental Learning", *IEEE Symposium Series on Computational Intelligence,* pp. 1280-1285, 2015. [http://dx.doi.org/10.1109/SSCI.2015.183]

[14] J.M. Chaves-González, M.A. Vega-Rodríguez, D. Domínguez-González, J.A. Gómez-Pulido, and J.M. Sánchez-Pérez, "Population-Based Incremental Learning to Solve the FAP Problem", *The Second International Conference on Advanced Engineering Computing and Applications in Sciences,* pp. 123-128, 2008. [http://dx.doi.org/10.1109/ADVCOMP.2008.10]

[15] S. Sheetekela, and K.A. Folly, "Power ystem controller design: A constract between breeder genetic algorithm and Population Based Incremental Learning", *The 2010 International Joint Conference on Neural Networks (IJCNN),* 2010.

CHAPTER 17

# Domain Knowledge-based BERT Model with Deep Learning for Text Classification

**Akhilesh Kalia**[1,*]

[1] *Centre for Interdisciplinary Research in Business and Technology, Chitkara University Institute of Engineering and Technology, Chitkara University, Punjab, India*

**Abstract:** Lexical model BERT already trained on BookCorpus and Wikipedia works well on two NLP tasks after downstream fine-tuning. The requirements of BERT model include strategy analyses and task-specific and domain-related data. The problems of task awareness as well as instruction data in BERT-DL, a BERT-based text-classification model, are addressed through auxiliary sentences. The pre-training, training, and post-training steps for BERT4TC's domain challenges are all provided. Learning speed, sequencing duration, and secret state vectors that select fine-tuning are all investigated in extended trials over 7 public datasets. The BERT4TC model is then contrasted using a variety of auxiliary terms and post-training goals. On multiple-class datasets, BERT4TC with the ideal auxiliary phrase outperforms previous state-of-the-art feature-based algorithms and fine-tuning approaches. Our domain-related corpus-trained BERT4TC beats BERT on binary sentiment categorization datasets.

**Keywords:** BERT Model, Deep learning, Natural Language Processing, Text Classification.

## INTRODUCTION

Sentiment analysis for customer feedback and requests is intriguing. Sentiment analysis may indicate public opinions on presidential elections and pandemics. COVID-Twitter BERT (CT-BERT), a domain-targeted BERT language model, has been used in sentiment evaluation on COVID-19. BERT-based language models increase text classification slightly. Thus, BERT was suggested as a supplement. Continuous learning helps NLP models learn and grow. Past continuous learning approaches focused on preserving information from past tasks rather than generalising models to new problems. Pre-trained models (PTMs) have enhanced text categorization by simply using its characteristics. However, task complexity may limit PTM knowledge exploration. On the basic tasks,

* **Corresponding author Akhilesh Kalia:** Centre for Interdisciplinary Research in Business and Technology, Chitkara University Institute of Engineering and Technology, Chitkara University, Punjab, India;
E-mail: akhilesh.kalia.orp@chitkara.edu.in

**Pankaj Kumar Mishra and Satya Prakash Yadav (Eds.)**

learning algorithms saturate early. BERT's native sentence representations are compressed, therefore using them for text classification may not completely capture discriminative properties. Deep learning always emphasises generalisation. Such models and domain adaption technologies are often used to solve generalisation. They seek data attributes to increase generalisation and reduce overfitting. Despite their success in other tasks, the models are unsteady when categorising sentences with positive labels but negative words. Few-shot relation categorization is popular now. Identifying relations from a few occurrences solves the long-tail relation issue. Metric learning techniques learn class prototypes and forecast using query-prototype distances. Text variety makes predictions inaccurate. It makes sense that relation and entity text descriptions may enable relation categorization.

## RELATED WORK

BERT's text classification performance is improved by converting single-sentence classification to pair-sentence classification. Auxiliary sentences and pre-trained BERT models on COVID-19 tweets increase sentiment analysis classification. Pair-sentence classification improves F1 scores and dataset size. A domain-specific language model should perform better. CT-BERT might not surpass BERT in sentiment understanding [11].

We present an information disentanglement-based regularisation technique for text categorization continuous learning. Our technique first separates text-concealed spaces into generic and task-specific representations and then regularises them differently to better confine the information needed to make generalisation. For improved general and specialised representation spaces, we provide two simple auxiliary duties: prediction of the next phrase and task-id prediction. On large benchmarks, our text classification method beats state-of-the-art baselines. https://github.com/GT-SALT/IDBR has our code [12].

This research proposes a two-stage training text classification approach to overcome these challenges. Auxiliary labels are used in pre-training to raise task difficulty and fully use the pre-trained model. The pre-training textual representation is used in the fine-tuning step to improve classification performance. The methodology outperformed multiple state-of-the-art baselines on six text categorization datasets [13].

This article examined the benchmarks' attention heat maps and discovered that previous models prioritised phrases over sentence semantics. We proposed to emphasise on contradictory emotional concepts to avoid one-sided evaluation. Our two-stream network's auxiliary network included slope reversal and feature projection layers. Slope reversal layers reverse feature gradients while retraining to improve backpropagation parameters. We blended backward features from an auxiliary network with principal network information. TextCNN, BERT, and RoBERTa baselines were subjectedto sentiment analysis and sarcasm detection. Our method improves both sentiment analysis and sarcasm detection by 0.5% and 2.1%, respectively [14].

TD-Proto adds relation and entity descriptions are used in prototypical networks. An attention module extracts sentence and entity information. To create a knowledge-aware instance, a gate mechanism fuses both information dynamically. Our technique performs well experimentally [15].

## PROPOSED WORK

### Problem Formulation

The categorization model, f(x)=y, estimates conditional distributions of odds across every tag in the predetermined class set for a source text sequence x$y = \{ y_1, \dots, y_c$.

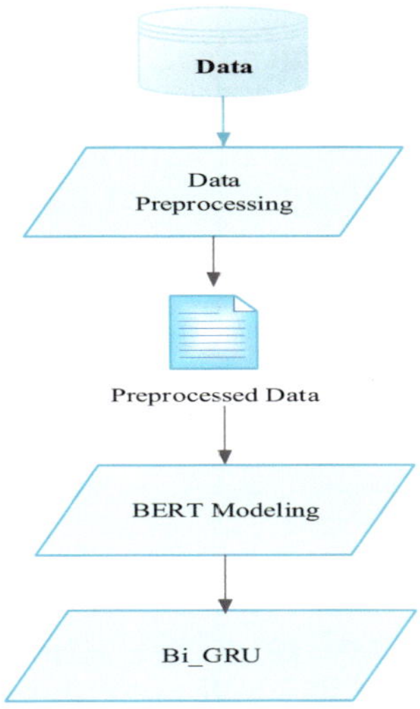


**Fig. (1).** System model.

Here x is a k-word token input scheme $x_{1:k} = x_1 x_2 \dots x_i \dots x_k$ , where $x_i (1 \leq x_i \leq k)$is the "th" consecutive word, *etc.* Since the first token is always [CLS] as well as contains special categorization insertion, and since the second token, [SEP], is utilised to divide segments or denote the closeness of the sequence, the BERT model cannot categorically suggest a simple composing request or a pair of portions in one currency collection (*i.e.* [Question, Answer]).

## System Model

Deep learning has excelled in text mining & NLP. For Natural Language Processing (NLP) classification tasks such as intent and topic identification, question answering, sentiment assessment, hate speech detection, and more, Bert is a highly useful machine learning model. Many research works have constructed categorization models employing pre-trained Bert models. A basic completely interconnected layer, Bi-GRU, layers of convolution, or a mixture of them perform fine-tuning. Bert is optimised for each model. Bert's complicated fine-tuned models are not always efficient or generalizable. This work thoroughly examined Bert-based adjusting models for text categorization problems. Implemented fine-tuning Bert models with different classification layers are carefully examined. Convolutional networks and Bi-GRU are used in fine-tuning models. Each model's output layer receives completely different Bert layer inputs. We tested several models to identify the best model. We compare the performance of several deep learning network layers and discover that adding a simple dense layer to the training Bert structure as a classifier improves accuracy. We discover the best hyper parameter settings for performance.

BERT4TC has three parts: (1) Input layer. Using auxiliary phrases, it creates a paragraph-pair model input sequence. WordPiece then splits the input sequences into ## word parts using a 30,000-token lexicon. Summating every token's setting, word, and segmentation embeddings produces the final input representations. (2) Encoding using the BERT algorithm, a total of 512 tokens are generated from 12 Transformer blocks as well as 12 self-attention heads. Concealed state vectors or time-step data vector series are represented. (3) Output. BERT-encoded basic softmax classifiers build conditional probability distributions over pre-defined category labels.

## Bi-GRU for text classification

This research seeks the best Bert model-based text classification structure. Bert outputs from all levels are used to create distinct models. First, we studied common NLP models like Bi-GRU and convolutional networks and combined Bert with them to develop several models. Bert's layers' output was examined next. Bert's transformers feed the categorization layer directly or indirectly. Bert's layer produces fuel models. A Bi-direction Gated Recurrent Unit (Bi-GRU) relies on pooling and attention. The model overcomes these issues. The hidden layer for deep semantic representation learning is the unidirectional gated recurrent unit. Second, max-pooling extracts text characteristics and the mechanism of self-attention is employed to determine word and sentence influence for text categorization. Finally, the model classifies texts using the two splicing findings.

Google's 2018 NLP engine BERT (Bidirectional Encode *via* Transformer) produced sentence and word embeddings. This bidirectional NLP model reads the whole text once, unlike Word2Vec, which scans English text from left to right. Bert's attention portion learns contextual relationships between incoming text words. Encoders build word embedding features (Representations) from the input text, while Decoders anticipate the output. Bert beats word embedding. Bert may be tweaked to do a wide range of NLP duties. The 3.3 billion words used to train BERT came from Wikipedia and BooksCorpus, respectively. The research provides Bert basic and Bert Large models. Bert Large has 24 transformer layers and 16 focus heads, while Bert base has 12. Fig. (2). represents the Bi-GRU Model.

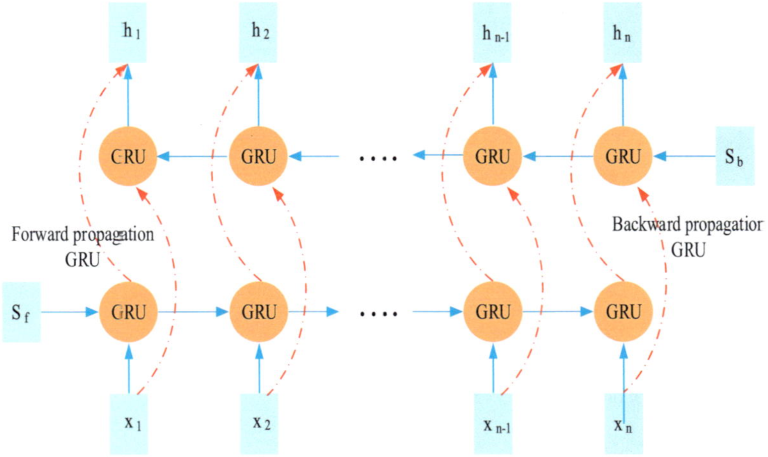


**Fig. (2).** Bi-GRU model.

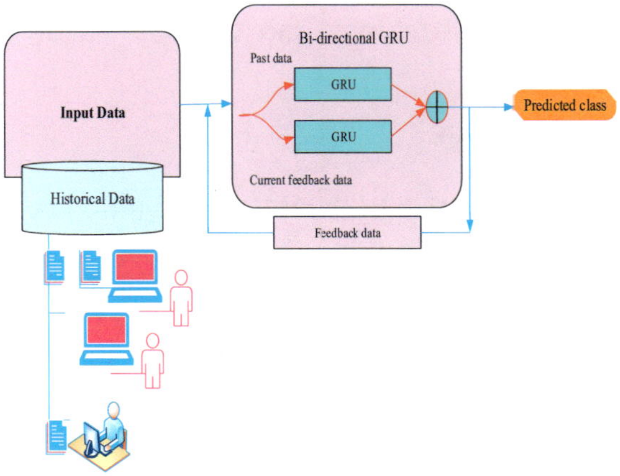


**Fig. (3).** Bi-GRU for text classification.

The Bi-GRU output shows resemblance to $u_{tu}$ a context vector at the word level $u_w$a standardised measure of importance $a_t$ by softmax. Context vector $u_w$ is different for each stage, representing "what is the relevant phrase at step t". Training randomises and jointly leads it.

$$a_n = \frac{\exp(u_{ri}^T u_{ur})}{\sum_{i=1}^{t} \exp(u_{ti}^T u_{ur})} \quad \textbf{(1)}$$

We then calculate the vector. $y_t$ by weighting Bi-GRU annotation outputs.

$$y_t = \sum_{i=1}^{t} a_n h_i \quad \textbf{(2)}$$

To get the final text representation, we max-pool and ave-pool, the whole attention layer outputs in the pooling layer. Section 4 presents the experimental findings of these two pooling layers.

Probability distribution:

$$p = \text{soft max}(W_c Y + b_c) \quad \textbf{(3)}$$

Finally, the function for cross-entropy loss calculates the loss among the true distribution q as well as the anticipated distribution p.

$$\Lambda = -\sum \quad q(i) \cdot \log(p(i)) \quad \textbf{(4)}$$

We utilise it as backpropagation loss and employ Adam to update Bi-GRU parameters.

## RESULTS AND DISCUSSION

We use the aforementioned short-text datasets to conduct experiments on various fine-tuning procedures for the learning rate (lr), seq size (sequence size), and hidden state vector selections. Maximum sequence duration is determined by the figures in Table **1**, and the total number of bunches is 24. To evaluate the efficacy of the models presented in the previous section, we employed datasets from a variety of NLP categorization tasks. Table **1** summarises the datasets.

Table **1** shows accuracy (Acc) as well as macro F1 (F1) metrics for varied lr. Best outcomes are boldfaced for comparison.

**Table 1. Performance Analysis.**

| Database | Erudition Rate lr | Acc | F1 |
|---|---|---|---|
| rt | 6e – 06 | 0.8679 | 0.8575 |
| | 5e – 06 | 0.8749 | 0.8745 |
| | 3e – 06 | 0.8658 | 0.8659 |
| | 1e – 06 | 0.8748 | 0.8747 |
| | le-06 | 0.8707 | 0.8706 |
| sstb2 | 6e – 06 | 0.9326 | 0.9325 |
| | 5e – 06 | 0.9378 | 0.9378 |
| | 2e – 06 | 0.9358 | 0.9358 |
| | 1e – 06 | 0.9385 | 0.9385 |
| | 2e – 06 | 0.9287 | 0.9287 |
| sstb5 | 6e – 06 | 0.5395 | 0.5289 |
| | 5e – 06 | 0.50309 | 0.5213 |
| | 4e – 06 | 0.5268 | 0.5193 |
| | 3e-06 | 0.5425 | 0.5343 |
| | 1e – 06 | 0.5377 | 0.5243 |
| TREC | 6e – 06 | 0.965 | 0.948 |
| | 5e – 06 | 0.967 | 0.9623 |
| | 4e – 06 | 0.974 | 0.9698 |
| | 3e – 06 | 0.974 | 0.9698 |
| | 2e – 06 | 0.98 | 0.9554 |

Table **3** shows this knowledge rate settings significantly affect the model's performance. Lower lr usually improves outcomes. When lr = 2e-05, BERT4TCS has the highest Acc and construct F1-values of any short-text dataset. Performance drops as lr grows. We observed that BERT needs a lower training rate, such as 2e05, to overcome the terrible omission issue, while the training set would fail to converge with an aggressive learning rate of 5e-04 or 4e-04. The outcomes of this experiment are comparable. As a result, lr is fixed at 2e-05 for all short-text datasets.

## CONCLUSION

The generic framework of language BERT, which was pre-trained on a huge unlabeled corpus before being fine-tuned in downstream tasks, has been used to produce many state-of-the-art NLP outcomes. We offer a BERT-based textual classification approach that uses auxiliary sentences to turn the task into a sentence-pair one, so making it easier to maintain task awareness and include additional task-specific information. We suggest using a domain-specific corpus after training in order to address particular issues. Initially, seven widely-used text classification datasets are used to analyse how various BERT fine-tuning procedures influence learning velocity, sequence length, and hidden state vector selection. We next compare our model to others using the same auxiliary words and post-training outcomes as recent, standard research. On multi-class classification datasets, BERT4TC with the right auxiliary phrase performs better than feature-based algorithms and fine-tuning methods.

## REFERENCES

[1] Z. Khan, and Y.R. Fu, "Exploiting BERT for Multimodal Target Sentiment Classification through Input Space Translation", *Proceedings of the 29th ACM International Conference on Multimedia,* 2021.
[http://dx.doi.org/10.1145/3474085.3475692]

[2] Y. Long, J. Han, R. Huang, X. Hang, Y. Zhu, C. Xu, and X. Liang, "P3OVD: Fine-grained Visual-Text Prompt-Driven Self-Training for Open-Vocabulary Object Detection", *ArXiv, abs/2211.00849,* 2022.

[3] Y. Ding, Y. Dai, H. Zheng, and R. Zhang, "GiTS: Gist-driven Text Segmentation", *International Joint Conference on Neural Networks (IJCNN),* pp. 1-8, 2022.

[4] Z. Zhang, Z. Wang, X. Li, N. Liu, B. Guo, and Z. Yu, "ModalNet: an aspect-level sentiment classification model by exploring multimodal data with fusion discriminant attentional network", *World Wide Web (Bussum),* vol. 24, no. 6, pp. 1957-1974, 2021.
[http://dx.doi.org/10.1007/s11280-021-00955-7]

[5] V. Vashisht, A.K. Pandey, and S.P. Yadav, "Speech Recognition using Machine Learning", *IEIE Transactions on Smart Processing & Computing,* vol. 10, no. 3, pp. 233-239, 2021.
[http://dx.doi.org/10.5573/IEIESPC.2021.10.3.233]

[6] Z. Wang, H. Wu, H. Liu, and Q. Cai, "Bert-Pair-Networks for Sentiment Classification", *2020 International Conference on Machine Learning and Cybernetics (ICMLC),* pp. 273-278, 2020.
[http://dx.doi.org/10.1109/ICMLC51923.2020.9469534]

[7] S.P. Yadav, S. Zaidi, C.D.S. Nascimento, V.H.C. de Albuquerque, and S.S. Chauhan, "Analysis and Design of automatically generating for GPS Based Moving Object Tracking System", *2023 International Conference on Artificial Intelligence and Smart Communication (AISC),* 2023 pp. 1-5 Greater Noida, India.
[http://dx.doi.org/10.1109/AISC56616.2023.10085180]

[8] X. Li, J. Zhang, Y. Du, J. Zhu, Y. Fan, and X. Chen, "A Novel Deep Learning-based Sentiment Analysis Method Enhanced with Emojis in Microblog Social Networks", *Enterprise Inf. Syst.,* vol. 16, no. 1, pp. 17-32, 2022.

[9] Z. Wang, H. Han, L. Wang, X. Li, and L. Zhou, "Automated Radiographic Report Generation Purely on Transformer: A Multicriteria Supervised Approach", *IEEE Trans. Med. Imaging,* vol. 41, no. 10, pp. 2803-2813, 2022.
[http://dx.doi.org/10.1109/TMI.2022.3171661] [PMID: 35507620]

[10] J. Xia, X. Li, Y. Tan, W. Zhang, D. Li, and Z. Xiong, *Event Detection via Context Understanding Based on Multi-task Learning.* Transactions on Asian and Low-Resource Language Information Processing, 2022.

[11] H. Lin, and T. Moh, "Sentiment analysis on COVID tweets using COVID-Twitter-BERT with auxiliary sentence approach", *Proceedings of the 2021 ACM Southeast Conference,* 2021. [http://dx.doi.org/10.1145/3409334.3452074]

[12] Y. Huang, Y. Zhang, J. Chen, X. Wang, and D. Yang, "Continual Learning for Text Classification with Information Disentanglement Based Regularization", *ArXiv, abs/2104.05489,* 2021.

[13] X. Zhang, Z. Liu, Y. Xiang, and D. Zhou, "Complicate Then Simplify: A Novel Way to Explore Pre-trained Models for Text Classification", *International Conference on Computational Linguistics,* 2022.

[14] D. Seng, and X. Wu, "Enhancing the Generalization for Text Classification through Fusion of Backward Features", *Sensors (Basel),* vol. 23, no. 3, p. 1287, 2023. [http://dx.doi.org/10.3390/s23031287] [PMID: 36772327]

[15] K. Yang, N. Zheng, X. Dai, L. He, S. Huang, and J. Chen, "Enhance Prototypical Network with Text Descriptions for Few-shot Relation Classification", *Proceedings of the 29th ACM International Conference on Information & Knowledge Management,* 2020. [http://dx.doi.org/10.1145/3340531.3412153]

# CHAPTER 18

# Applying Deep Learning to Classify Massive Amounts of Text Using Convolutional Neural Systems

**Shubhansh Bansal**[1,*]

[1] *Centre for Interdisciplinary Research in Business and Technology, Chitkara University Institute of Engineering and Technology, Chitkara University, Punjab, India*

**Abstract:** Supervised learning based on deep learning is often used for mass-scale picture categorization. However, it takes a lot of computing effort and energy to retrain these vast networks to accept new, unknown data. When retraining, it is possible that training samples used before would not be accessible. We present a scalable, gradually expanding CNN that can learn new jobs while reusing some of the base networks and an efficient training mechanism. Our approach takes cues from transfer learning methods, but unlike other approaches, it retains knowledge of previously mastered tasks. Convolutional layers from the early section of the base network are reused in the updated network, and a few more convolutional kernels are added to the later layers to facilitate learning a new set of classes. On the task of categorising texts, we tested the suggested method. Our method achieves comparable classification accuracy to the standard incremental learning method in which networks are updated solely with new training samples, without any network sharing), while also being more resource-friendly and taking less time and space to train.

**Keywords:** CNNS, Convolutional neural networks, Deep learning, Text classification.

## INTRODUCTION

Natural language processing (NLP) relies heavily on text categorization, making it a common and crucial activity. Convolutional Neural Network (CNN) is a member of the greatest effective models in the field of text categorization, and deep learning techniques have recently shown their benefits in this area [1]. The use of deep neural networks for analysing sentiment in the text is a well-studied field. When used for text sentiment categorization, deep learning models may perform at their computational peak [2]. Both well-known open-source data

* **Corresponding author Shubhansh Bansal:** Centre for Interdisciplinary Research in Business and Technology, Chitkara University Institute of Engineering and Technology, Chitkara University, Punjab, India;
E-mail: shubhansh.bansal.orp@chitkara.edu.in

**Pankaj Kumar Mishra and Satya Prakash Yadav (Eds.)**

corpora and psyche-extracted short-phrase texts from social media are common resources for these kinds of investigations like Twitter and Reddit, as well as web-scraped text data from other sources [3]. It is unusual to gather and refine that much information about a live event [4]. Scaling the accuracy of the sentiment analysis and developing a predictive analysis of the same would need modelling data from an ongoing event, which is an even more difficult challenge [4]. With Natural Language Processing (NLP), text categorization is a traditional yet crucial work [5]. Convolutional Neural Networks (CNNs) have grown into an important paradigm in deep learning due to their many useful applications. The convolution process is crucial to the performance of a CNN model. Convolution operation-based methods are particularly well-suited to capturing local conjunctions of characteristics in high-dimensional data [6]. The convolution technique is often performed using a sliding window in previous methods [7]. Even though this is problematic given the present problems in the area of Chinese information, such as inconsistent information and a lack of automatic and efficient management, most existing Chinese text classification methods use word characteristics as the basic section of text representation but neglect the beneficial effectiveness of character characteristics. As more and more processes are digitized, massive amounts of data need to be stored [8]. Everyone posts a tonne of personal data about themselves online *via* a smartphone or web app, sometimes without even realising it. There are now privacy concerns due to the ever-increasing need to store individuals' data [9]. The use of another person's private information is not illegal. While the European Union's privacy rule went into effect in 2018, India is currently in the midst of drafting its own [10]. Some businesses are now working on programmes that can determine whether or not a given document is confidential. Such applications might be developed using several deep learning models, such as the Convolutional Neural Network (CNN), Recurrent Neural Network (RNN), Long Term Short Memory (LSTM), *etc.*

## RELATED WORK

We present a novel deep learning approach that employs convolutional neural networks with scope information for automatically classifying text content. In contrast to window-based CNN, the scope does not call for the words used to build a local feature to be adjacent. A finer-grained representation of textual data is possible. We introduce a large-scale range-based convolutional neural network (LSS-CNN) by combining scope convolution, aggregation optimising, and the max pooling operation. These techniques might help us reconstruct key regional information from the manuscript. This study also explores methods for effectively computing data based on scope and for parallel training on large datasets. We have conducted comprehensive experiments on real-world datasets to compare our model to other state-of-the-art approaches. The results show that LSS-CNN can efficiently analyse massive text datasets while maintaining excellent scalability [11].

Utilising real-time tweets analysed by a neural network with deep learning, we provide a novel approach to forecasting the future occurrence of Coronavirus infections. We built a massive Twitter database focused on just the Coronavirus tweets. We perform polarity classification and trend analysis, as well as divide the data into sets for testing and training. With the enhanced outcome from the trend analysis, the data is trained, giving our neural network an incremental learning curve, and this leads to a 90.67% success rate. Finally, we conclude with a statistical forecast for the future expansion of Coronavirus cases. When evaluated with a variety of prominent open-source text corpora, our model not only surpasses multiple past state-of-the-art studies in general accuracy comparisons for comparable tasks but also maintains a consistent level of performance throughout all of the test cases [12].

In this research, we provide a novel approach to convolutional neural networks called a scope-orientated convolutional neural network (SCNN). To reflect the local data, we offer a notion of scope as an alternative to sliding windows. A scope, as contrast to a window, limits simply the spacing between words. More complex local features may be handled with ease. To preserve the most relevant data, we use max pooling. This allows it to learn more nuanced local features that might otherwise be missed by a window-based CNN. We conduct a large-scale experimental study to demonstrate that our model is competitive with the state-of-the-art approach on real-world datasets. This proves that our strategy is superior to others that have been offered [13].

Here we propose a method for automatically classifying Chinese news items utilising character-level convolutional neural networks (char-CNN). We constructed a massive Chinese news corpus and contrasted it to both traditional models and deep learning models to see that personality-level convolutional neural networks (CNN) would achieve the most advanced or competitive results [14].

Methods for representing text in text classification issues are the topic of this study. These challenges include but are not limited to, private data categorization, sentiment analysis, language identification, online abuse detection, and recommendation systems. Having text displayed in a variety of ways improves the efficacy of categorization systems.

# PROPOSED WORK

## System Model

This article presents an empirical investigation into the text categorization application of character-level convolutional networks (ConvNets). We created a number of massive datasets to demonstrate whether character-level convolutional networks can provide competitive or state-of-the-art outcomes. Traditional models such as bag of words and n-grams, as well as their TFIDF variants, are compared to deep learning techniques such as word-based ConvNets and recurrent neural networks.

This is the only essay I'm aware of that uses ConvNets exclusively for handling text. In addition to the result reached in earlier research that ConvNets do not require knowledge of the grammatical or semantic structure of the language, we demonstrate that, when training on large-scale data sets, deep ConvNets do not need the knowledge of words. Since letters always form an essential component whether separation into syllables is possible or not, this simplicity of engineering might be significant for just one system that can function for multiple languages. Focusing on distinct personalities also has the added benefit of making it easier to pick up irregular character combinations like misspellings and emoticons. Fig. (**1**). portrays the System Flowchart.

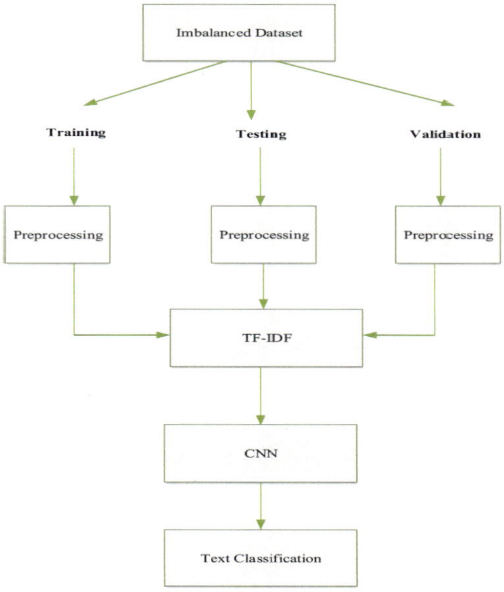


**Fig. (1).** System flowchart.

## CNN

Convolutional neural networks (CNNs) are a relatively new tool for solving problems in NLP and image processing. It has rapidly risen in popularity to become one of the most utilised deep learning models currently available. CNNs, or convolutional neural networks, are an efficient and quick-to-train kind of shallow neural network, and it is among the deep learning models for text classification. Fig. (**2**) shows how the CNN model is laid out.

The purpose of the layer of convolution is to produce a feature output by convolving input vectors with a convolution kernel in order to extract local characteristics within a specified window. Fig. (**2**) depicts the CNN structure.

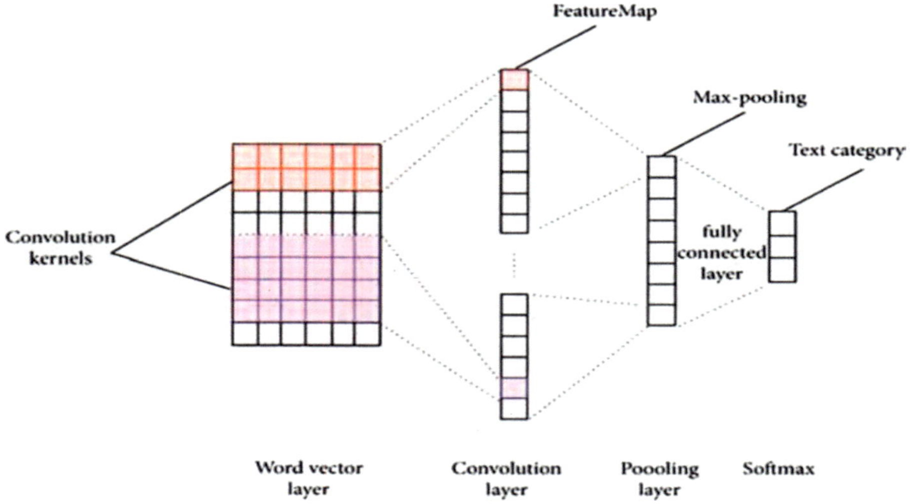


**Fig. (2).** CNN Structure.

An input document is denoted by W. We employ $w_i$ to signify the word at the i-th spot in the text, such that $w_i$ is a vector in dimension d (*i.e.* $x_i \in \mathbb{R}^d$) found in the document matrix, column i, row i. The whole text may be interpreted as a series of vectors with the following properties $W = [w_1, w_2, \ldots, w_n]$. We utilize $C_{sub}(W)$ to signify all the derived sequences from sequence W, where the sequence of words that remains the same even if some words are removed. For instance, $[w_1, w_3, w_4]$ defines $[w_1, w_2, w_3, w_4]$ , and $C_{sub}([w_1, w_2, w_3]) = \{[], [w_1], [w_2], [w_3], [w_1, w_2], [w_2, w_3], [w_1, w_3], [w_1, w_2, w_3],\}$ .

We utilize $w_i \oplus w_j$ as a metaphor for combining several vectors $w_i$ and $w_j$, such that $w_i \oplus w_j$ is a 2m-dimensional vector that results from the addition of individual $w_i$ and $w_j$. For a vector of dimension 3" "m, we may use the same method with three words, and so on. We use an ⊕(W) to represent the aggregate of all word vectors contained inside document W. Fig. (**3**) . illustrates the dataset classification efficiency 1.

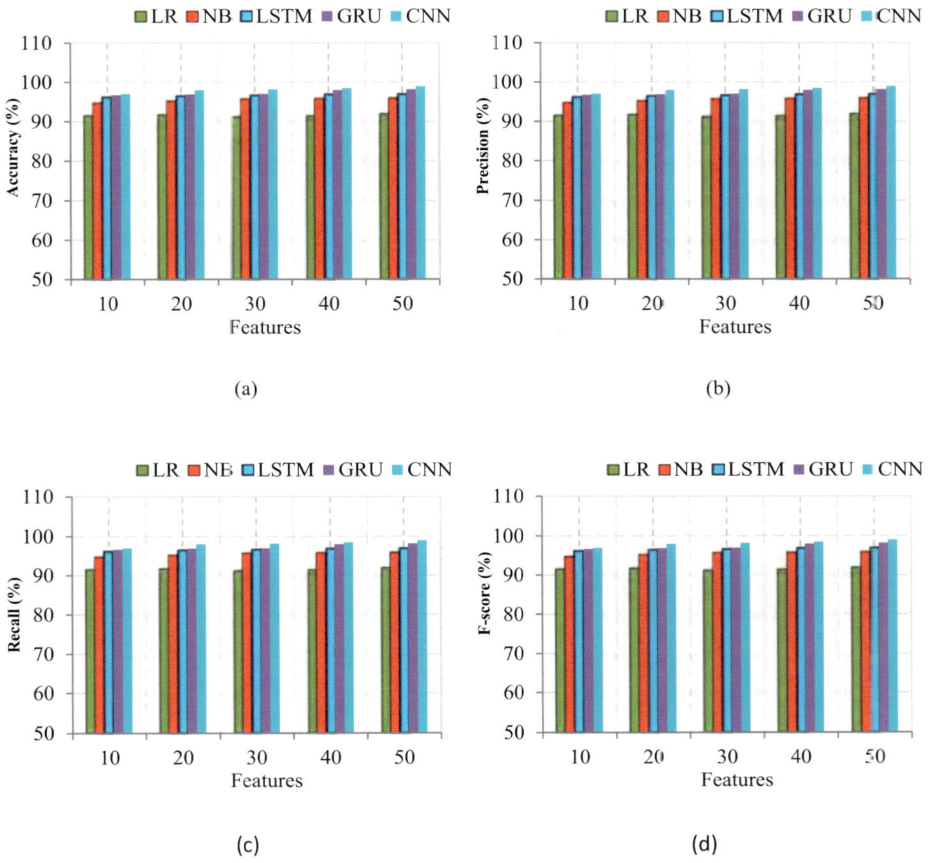


**Fig. (3).** Dataset Classification Efficiency 1.

We utilize $d(w_i, w_j)$ to signify the space between words $w_i$ to word $w_j$. It is articulated as $d(w_i, w_j) = j - i$.

We use scope to denote a distance restriction. In a word $w_i$ and word $w_j$ k-scope limitation is met if $d(w_i, w_j) \leq k$ . A word sequence is defined as a k-scope sequence. $w_i$ in the form of a logical progression of words (containing $w_i$ itself). It is consistent with the k-scope restriction $w_i$. Definition 1 provides the canonical definition of a k-scope sequence, $S_2(w_1) = [w_1, w_2, w_3]$.

To begin with, let us define the k-scope sequence, which is $w_i$, the forward k-scope sequence, or k scope sequence, $w_i$ is a series of vectors $S_k(w_i)$, such that every letter $w_j \in S_k(w_i)$ gratifies $0 \leq d(w_i, w_j) \leq k$. And for each $w_j \in S_k(w_i)$ and $w_j \in S_k(w_i)$, $w_j$ precedes $w_j$ iff $j < j$.

By further incorporating the local properties of the text retrieved by the convolution layer, the pooling layer minimises the size of the characteristics map and boosts the processing speed. At the same time, it increases the extracted features' robustness, manages overfitting concerns, and extracts broad data from function values. Mean pooling and Max pooling are the most used methods. Column vectors may be averaged using the Mean pooling method, while their maximum value can be extracted using the Max pooling method. Max pooling was used for this write-up. Fig. (**4**) . displays the Dataset Classification Efficiency 2.

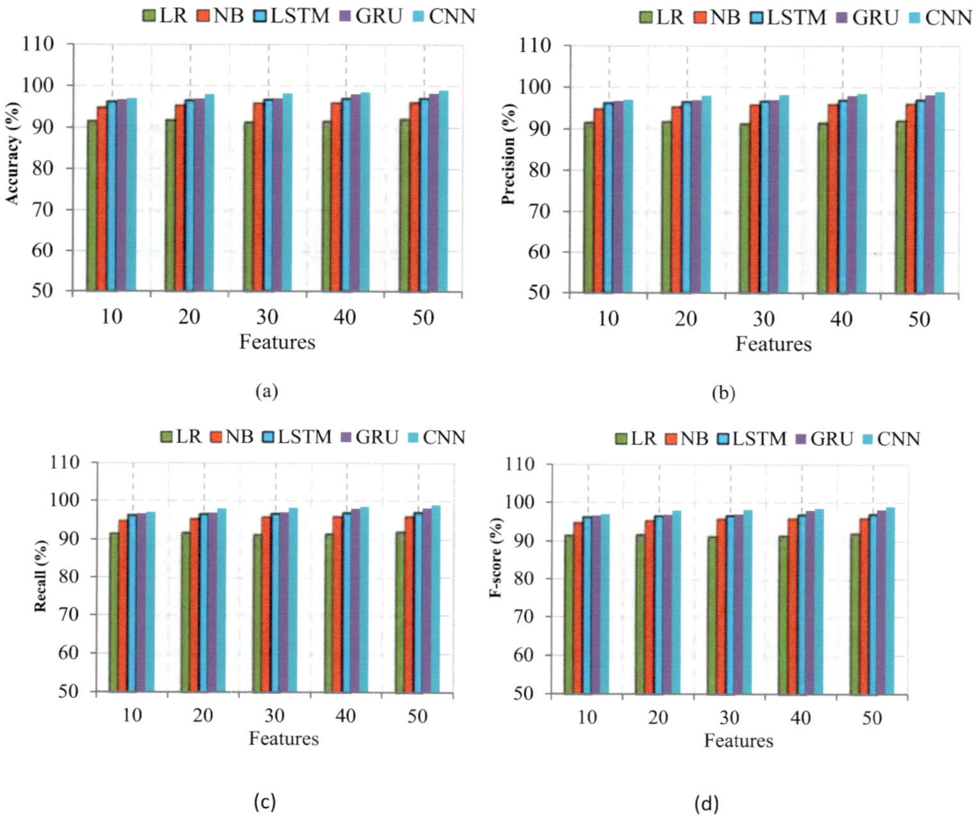


**Fig. (4).** Dataset classification efficiency 2.

By triggering the function called ReLu on each of the combining layer's outputs, the layer that is completely connected is able to abstract these eigenvalues and generate a long vector that maps the text of the Feature Space to the marker space. Fig. (**5**) . shows the Dataset Classification Efficiency 3.

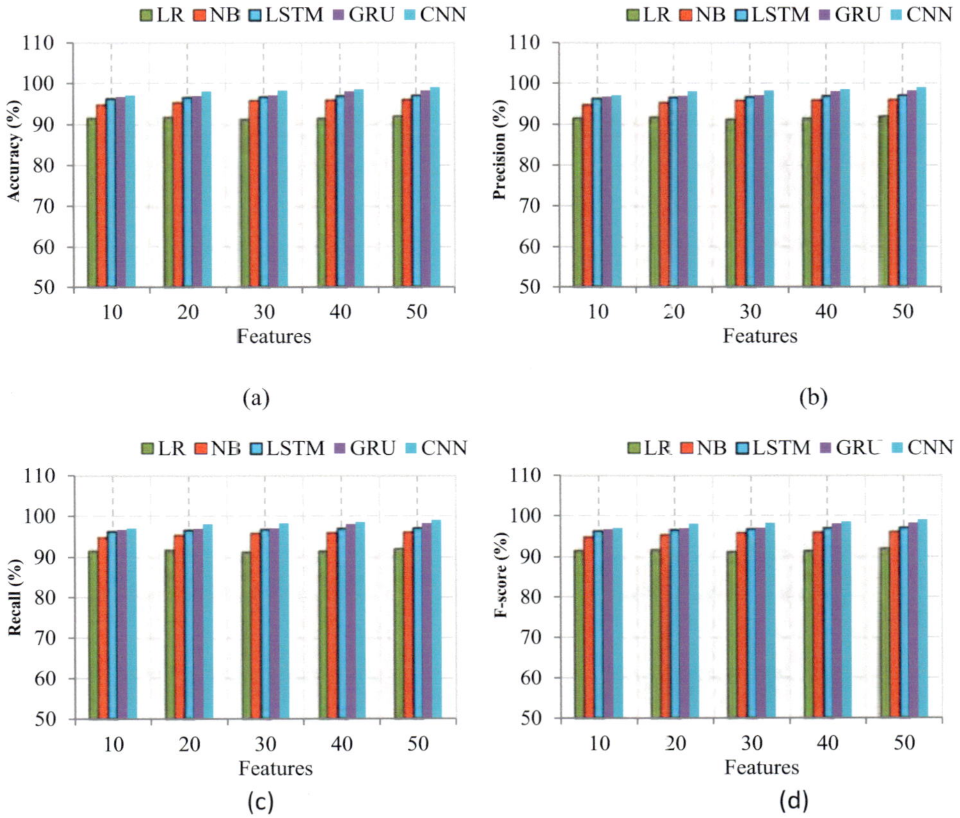


**Fig. (5).** Dataset classification efficiency 3.

To extract features of semantic data, we employ a convolutional neural network (CNN) algorithm in this research. Contextual semantic information is obtained from the feature map layer and sent into the CNN layer, where semantic features are retrieved. Fig. (**6**) . depicts the Dataset Classification Efficiency 4. Table **1** is represented in Factors.

**Table 1. Factors.**

| Factor names | Values |
|---|---|
| Kernel size for convolution. | (2, 3, 4) |
| Word dimensionality vector. | 100 |
| Quantity of Covert Elements. | 128 |

*(Table 1) cont.....*

| Factor names | Values |
|---|---|
| Loafer | 0.5 |
| Rate of learning. | 0.001 |
| Optimizer | Adam |
| Size of Batch. | 64 |
| Epoch | 6 |

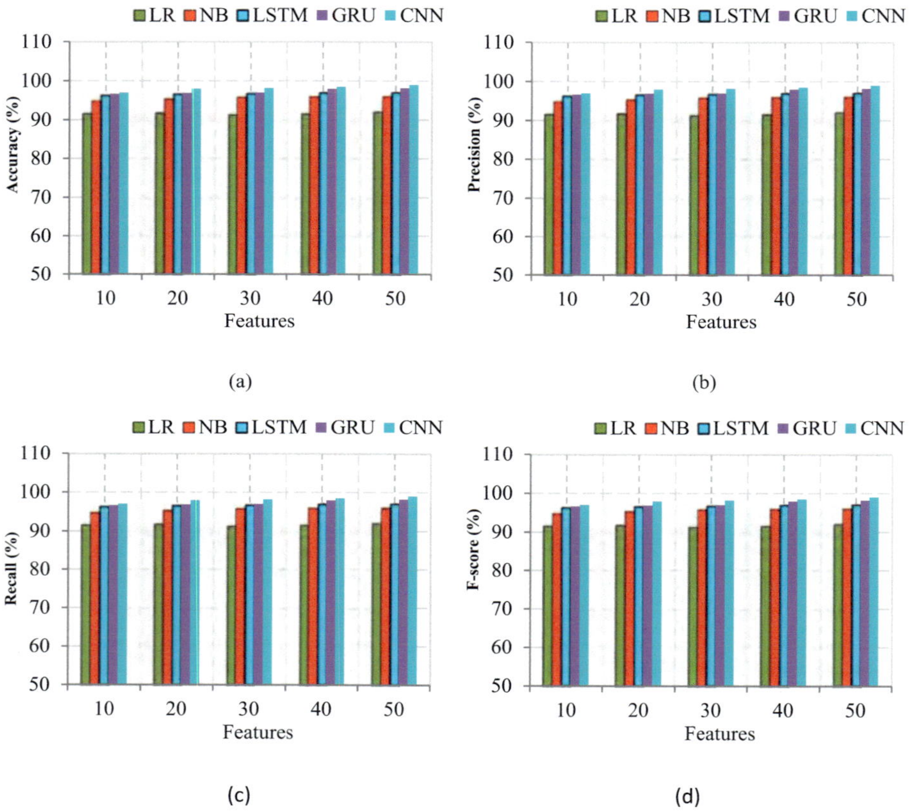


**Fig. (6).** Dataset classification efficiency 4.

## RESULTS AND DISCUSSION

Five datasets (TREC, Subj, MR, SST-2, & AG) are used in a series of tests to determine L-CNN's efficacy:

• There are a total of six distinct kinds of questions in the TREC TREC inquiry collection. Therefore, there are only the following six types of questions that may be asked: “entity,” “location,” “human,” “numerical,” “descriptive,” and "abbreviation".

- Objective or subjective classification of texts is the goal of the Subj Subjectivity dataset. Both the dataset and the baseline systems are subjected to 10-fold cross-validation.

• The MR Movie Reviews Sentence has both favourable and bad reviews from Rotten Tomatoes. The Polarity Database v1.0, is a dataset with two possible states.

• To get the binary labelled version of the SST-2 Stanford sentiment treebank, we first remove the neutral reviews, then we label the positive and very positive reviews as positive, and finally we label the negative and very negative reviews as negative.

- More than a million news stories tagged with one of four categories are collected in AG AG's news corpus.

Text classification benchmarks include tasks such as news categorization, inquiry classification, and sentiment classification. Information is tabulated and presented in Table **2**. Fig. (**7**) . illustrates the Dataset Classification Efficiency 5.

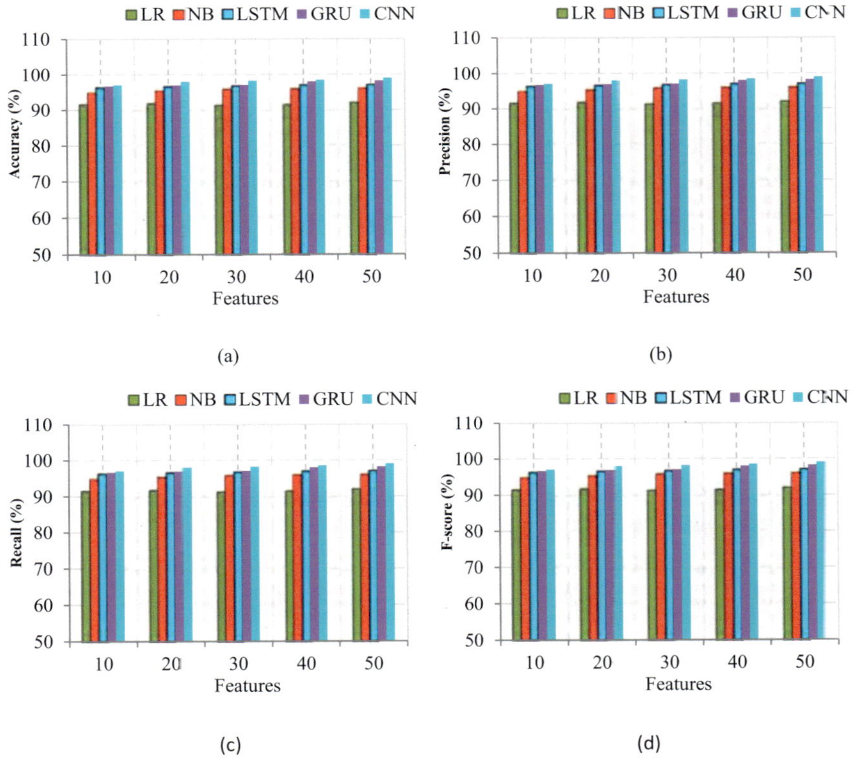


**Fig. (7).** Dataset classification efficiency 5.

**Table 2. Overview statistics for the aforementioned five datasets.**

| Database | TREC | Subj | MR | SST-2 | AG |
|---|---|---|---|---|---|
| Exercise | 5.8k | 9.1k | 9.6k | 9.7k | 123k |
| Difficult | 0.6k | 1.2k | 1.2k | 1.9k | 7.7k |
| Sessions | 7 | 32 | 3 | 3 | 5 |
| Avg_length | 11 | 22 | 25 | 19 | 46 |

Several traditional approaches are chosen for comparison tests to see how well the combined neural network model performs.

- LR: The chance of an event occurring is estimated *via* the use of a machine learning categorisation technique called logistic regression.
- NB: Using Bayes' theorem, Naive Bayes was a classification method used in machine learning.
- LSTM: It is the bare bones of the text classification neural network
- GRU: For classifying texts, it is the simplest gated recurrent network possible.

## CONCLUSION

In this research, we provide Convolutional Neural Network (CNN), a unique CNN for text classification that is scope-based. The process of convolution relies on the concept of scope. The method, which depends on a scope compression process, may capture intricate local details in the text, such as variations in sentence length and abrupt sentence terminations. Maximum pooling allows for a more refined selection of the most important scope elements. To guarantee the strategy's success, we put it through its paces on eight different real-world text samples and evaluate our proposed model to the present state-of-the-art methodologies. The findings prove that the suggested model can outperform its competitors.

## REFERENCES

[1] V. Ravi, V. Acharya, and T.D. Pham, "Attention deep learning-based large-scale learning classifier for Cassava leaf disease classification", *Expert Syst.,* p. 39, 2021.

[2] T. Shoryu, L. Wang, and R. Ma, "A Deep Neural Network Approach using Convolutional Network and Long Short Term Memory for Text Sentiment Classification", *2021 IEEE 24th International Conference on Computer Supported Cooperative Work in Design (CSCWD),* 2021 pp. 763-768. [http://dx.doi.org/10.1109/CSCWD49262.2021.9437871]

[3] N. Sotthisopha, and P. Vateekul, "Improving Short Text Classification Using Fast Semantic Expansion on Multichannel Convolutional Neural Network", *2018 19th IEEE/ACIS International Conference on Software Engineering, Artificial Intelligence, Networking and Parallel/Distributed Computing (SNPD),* 2018 pp. 182-187. [http://dx.doi.org/10.1109/SNPD.2018.8441072]

[4] S.P. Yadav, and S. Yadav, "Fusion of Medical Images in Wavelet Domain: A Discrete Mathematical Model", *Ingeniería Solidaria,* vol. 14, no. 25, pp. 1-11, 2018. [http://dx.doi.org/10.16925/.v14i0.2236]

[5] M.B.A. Gibril, H.Z.M. Shafri, A. Shanableh, R. Al-Ruzouq, A. Wayayok, and S.J. Hashim, "Deep Convolutional Neural Network for Large-Scale Date Palm Tree Mapping from UAV-Based Images", *Remote Sens. (Basel),* vol. 13, no. 14, p. 2787, 2021. [http://dx.doi.org/10.3390/rs13142787]

[6] W. Nahilia, K. Rezega, and O. Kazara, "A new corpus-based convolutional neural network for big data text analytics", *Journal of Intelligence Studies in Business,* 2019.

[7] S.F. Hussain, S. Barigidad, S. Akhtar, and M. Suaib, "Novel Deep Learning Architecture for Heart Disease Prediction using Convolutional Neural Network", *ArXiv, abs/2105.10816,* 2021.

[8] G. Gupta, M. Kshirsagar, M. Zhong, S. Gholami, and J.L. Ferres, "Comparing recurrent convolutional neural networks for large scale bird species classification", *Sci. Rep.,* vol. 11, no. 1, p. 17085, 2021. [http://dx.doi.org/10.1038/s41598-021-96446-w] [PMID: 34429468]

[9] K. Rimal, K.B. Shah, and A.K. Jha, "Advanced multi-class deep learning convolution neural network approach for insect pest classification using TensorFlow", *Int. J. Environ. Sci. Technol.,* vol. 20, no. 4, pp. 4003-4016, 2023. [http://dx.doi.org/10.1007/s13762-022-04277-7]

[10] J. Wang, Y. Li, J. Shan, J. Bao, C. Zong, and L. Zhao, "Large-Scale Text Classification Using Scope-Based Convolutional Neural Network: A Deep Learning Approach", *IEEE Access,* vol. 7, pp. 171548-171558, 2019. [http://dx.doi.org/10.1109/ACCESS.2019.2955924]

[11] S. Das, and A.K. Kolya, "Predicting the pandemic: sentiment evaluation and predictive analysis from large-scale tweets on Covid-19 by deep convolutional neural network", *Evol. Intell.,* vol 15, no. 3, pp. 1913-1934, 2022. [http://dx.doi.org/10.1007/s12065-021-00598-7] [PMID: 33815622]

[12] J. Wang, J. Shan, Y. Li, Y. Ren, D. Zhai, and J. Bao, ""Text Classification Using Scope Based Convolutional Neural Network", *IEEE International Conferences on Ubiquitous Computing & Communications (IUCC) and Data Science and Computational Intelligence (DSCI) and Smart Computing, Networking and Services (SmartCNS),* 2019 pp. 402-407. [http://dx.doi.org/10.1109/IUCC/DSCI/SmartCNS.2019.00093]

[13] X. Wu, and J. Chen, "Text Classification on Large Scale Chinese News Corpus using Character-level Convolutional Neural Network", *J. Phys. Conf. Ser.,* vol. 1693, no. 1, p. 012171, 2020. [http://dx.doi.org/10.1088/1742-6596/1693/1/012171]

[14] D. Patil, R. Lokare, and S. Patil, "Privacy Preserving Document Classification using Convolution Neural Network- A Deep Learning Approach", *5th International Conference on Advances in Science and Technology (ICAST),* pp. 215-219, 2022. [http://dx.doi.org/10.1109/ICAST55766.2022.10039513]

# CHAPTER 19

# An Algorithm for Categorizing Opinions in Text from Various Social Media Platforms

**Pavas Saini**[1,*]

[1] *Centre for Interdisciplinary Research in Business and Technology, Chitkara University Institute of Engineering and Technology, Chitkara University, Punjab, India*

**Abstract:** More individuals are sharing their thoughts and feelings through internet videos as social media platforms proliferate. While successful emotional fusion in multimodal data is a key component of multimodal sentiment analysis, most existing research falls short in this area. Predicting users' emotional inclinations through their expressions of language is made easier by multi-modal sentiment detection. As a result, the field of multi-modal sentiment detection has grown rapidly in recent years. As a result, multimodal sentiment analysis is quickly rising to the forefront of academic interest. However, in actual social media, visuals and sentences do not always work together to represent emotional polarity. Additionally, there are several information modalities, each contributing in its unique way to the overall emotional polarity. A multimodal approach to sentiment analysis that takes into account contextual knowledge is presented as a solution to these issues. The approach begins by mining social media texts for subject information that comprehensively describes the comment material. Additionally, we use cutting-edge pre-training models to identify emotional qualities that span several domains. Then, we provide methods for merging features at different levels, such as cross-modal global fusion as well as cross-modal high-level semantics fusing. At long last, we run our tests on a multimodal dataset that really exists in the real world. Results show that the proposed approach can correctly classify the tone of heterogeneous online reviews, and it also outperforms the standard approach in many other ways as well.

**Keywords:** Opinion mining, Social media, Sentiment classification, Topical information.

## INTRODUCTION

Understanding how to include rich contextual information and multi-modal data into a single model framework is the first step towards user sentiment analysis on social media [1]. The research presents a support vector machine (SVM) based

* **Corresponding author Pavas Saini:** Centre for Interdisciplinary Research in Business and Technology, Chitkara University Institute of Engineering and Technology, Chitkara University, Punjab, India;
E-mail: pavas.saini.orp@chitkara.edu.in

topic model for consumer sentiment evaluation and employs SVMs as well as k-nearest-neighbors algorithms (KNNs) to build models for classifying social sentiment in Japan. Additionally, the study builds an SVM classifier utilizing TE processing information as a case study and picks a radial basis function for the kernel as well as a grid search technique [2]. Media data, comprising text, image/video, as well as social interaction information, has been generated in large quantities by social networking networks in the era of Web 2.0, such as YouTube, Facebook, Google, and Flickr [3]. Multimedia applications (such as annotating and retrieving images and videos and classifying events) may make good use of these data sets [4]. Because these data span several domains and media types (such as text, images, videos, and audio), designing an appropriate feature representation to characterize them is challenging [5]. Many proposed systems focus on determining whether a given social media post is good or negative in tone [6]. People may share their thoughts and feelings through a variety of mediums on social media [7]. User emotional preferences can be better predicted using multi-modal sentiment detection [8]. As a result, the field of multi-modal sentiment detection has grown rapidly in recent years. The effective interplay among the several modalities present in a video is often overlooked in current publications that treat video utterances as isolated modals [9]. Sentiment analysis is the practice of gathering information about how people feel about an issue, product, or person and then categorizing that data as positive, negative, or neutral. The data gleaned from social media platforms like YouTube and online marketplaces like Amazon may be put to good use in recommending items to customers and generating sales, respectively [10]. Most individuals nowadays use a combination of their native language and terms from other languages when they talk about their ideas and opinions. Hence the interpretation of the emotional tone of code-mixed speech is crucial. The field of Tamil mixed sentiment analysis is nascent, with only a few of the published works [12].

To address the problem of insufficient data, one might use the solutions mentioned above. The classification effect may be enhanced using multimodal information by improving input data and refining the structure of the model. Nevertheless, training these models requires a substantial amount of effort. Reduced training time is possible with the discovery of new types of multi-modal data that have characteristics like broad availability as well as fewer variables for feature extraction models. Training a model faster without compromising accuracy is possible using up-to-date multifaceted information. The characteristics of social media users may be used as multi-modal data after thorough analysis. Consequently, we provide a user-oriented sentiment classification method for SM text data. The paper's primary contributions are as follows:

- Since social media user traits are integrated into the sentiment categorization algorithm, gathering the necessary input data is a breeze.
- The model training time is reduced due to a small number of parameters in the CNN network utilized to extract the features of user characteristics.

The bidirectional internet text-based sentiment classification method has recently been upgraded to state-of-the-art, making it ideal for small-scale and time-sensitive data.

The sections of this article are as follows: In Section 2, we examine how the characteristics of the user affect their feelings. In Section 3, we describe a model for short-term and localized data sentiment categorization. The user characteristics of the Convolutional and Recurrent Neural Network model's architecture and formula are detailed below. Various models and their assessments through experiments are addressed in Section 4. Section 5 presents the final findings.

## RELATED WORK

Additional evidence linking the remark to the first tweet may be found in a correlation variable inside the feelings of both the comment and the tweet. This study describes a user sentiment assessment model and uses the Twitter real data set as an experimental information set to evaluate its performance. The idea of SVM-KNN is the foundation of the parameter estimation method. The results of the research show the efficiency of the method described here [11].

We present a unique stacked denoising auto-encoder-based cross-domain feature learning (CDFL) technique to address these concerns. In contrast to traditional auto-encoders, our CDFL incorporates a modal correlation constraint and a cross-domain constraint to concurrently optimize correlations between modalities and extract domain-invariant semantic information. We test our CDFL algorithm in three major domains: sentiment analysis, spam detection, and event categorization. Extensive testing shows that the suggested method performs admirably [12].

The purpose of Sentiment Analysis is to mine this information for insights into consumer preferences, which may then be applied to improve marketing strategies, public policy initiatives, and product development. In order to determine if a piece of text is subjective or objective and if it is subjective, whether it is negative or positive, sentiment analysis is performed. Opinion, sentiment, and the subjective nature of texts are the focus of sentiment analysis, which is a branch of text analytics. In addition, we often work together to create cost-effective illation techniques for estimating the parameters of supported folded Gibbs sampling. We usually base our evaluations of SJASM on information gleaned from actual reviews, and our experiments show that the proposed model performs better than seven industry-standard baseline approaches to sentiment analysis.

To address these issues, we present an interactive transformer-based multi-modal attention network to study the effects of paired attention across many modalities and utterances in video sentiment analysis. We first take an input sequence of utterances and, using three distinct transformer encoders, we capture modality-specific information at the utterance level. To better understand the relationships between different types of communication, we implemented multimodal paired attention techniques. To complete the mood and sentiment categorization, we next feed the cross-modal input into a multi-headed self-attention layer. On three different types of datasets, our methods outperform the standard ones.

An efficient algorithm is required to effectively learn the viewpoints of Tamil speakers. With the plethora of machine learning and deep learning techniques at our disposal, this effort sets out to decipher the hidden meaning of encoded words. The findings of the deep learning-based Bi-LSTM model with ULMFiT Embedding for code-mixed language are more encouraging than those of any other available techniques.

## PROPOSED WORK

### Overview

The goal of the model is to use user-provided data to make predictions about how a piece of text will make the reader feel. Two parallel models are required to combine two distinct sets of input data. RNN series networks are used to store the relative positions of words for later use in feature extraction from the text. CNN series network is more suited for feature extraction of individual user properties. Finally, a weight matrix is trained using a complete connection with no predetermined weight value, and the feature vectors from both models are combined for classification. As a result of combining a CNN trained on user characteristics with an RNN trained on text, we refer to the combined model as a Convolutional and Recurrent Neural Network (CNN-RNN).

We used a Python script named “Tweepy” in conjunction with Twitter's search API to collect 10,000 latest and most popular multimodal tweets that included the word “trump” to input into our algorithm. To facilitate further analysis by additional modules, the translated Twitter was saved in Panda's Dataframe. Dataframes in Panda, a Python module for manipulating and analyzing data, have data structured in rows and columns, making it simple to export the data to Excel. Each module will be explained in further detail below.

Cleansing URLs, user IDs, symbols(“RT”, “@”), and excess spaces from tweets is a necessary step in pre-processing the data before sentiment analysis can begin. VADER can appropriately handle texts that contain punctuation, slang, emoticons, encoded emojis, initialisms, and acronyms. As one of the features of the VADER output, “Compound score” is used to quantify how people feel about texts. The compound score is a scaled measure, with a maximum negative score of -1 and a maximum positive score of +1. The following are examples of typical VADER sentiment threshold values: -adverse: compound 0.05. Both (compound > 0.05) and (compound 0.05) are considered null. Thecompound p=0.05 is negative. The text a, b, c, and d of Fig. (**1**) has composite scores of (0.623), (0.0), (0.0516), and (0.0).

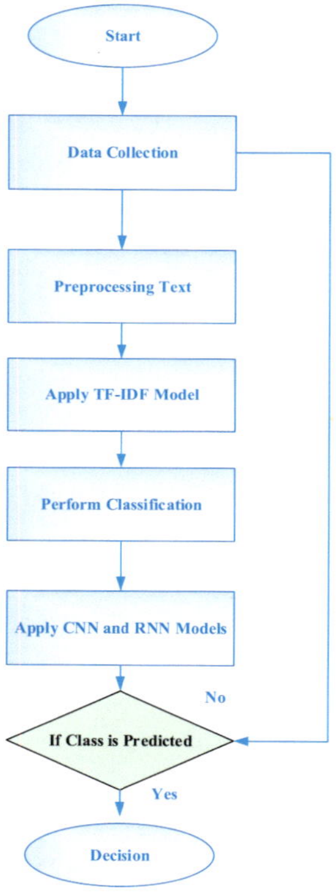


**Fig. (1).** System diagram.

## Feature Extraction

- We employ pre-trained BERT (Bidirectional Encoder Representations from Transformers) to encode text in the data. BERT, as its name indicates, is a language model built on transformers that use left and right context on a given word. Usually, an extra weight layer is learned to fine-tune the BERT encoder for a given job. Since the BERT encoder has already been trained on a massive amount of data culled from Wikipedia and books, we do not get bothered with any fine-tuning on our end. Several state-of-the-art NLP tasks, including sentiment analysis, question-answering, textual entailment, *etc*., use BERT as their encoder of choice because of its performance in these areas. All of the input text in Section 4 is stored as a BERT-base encoded 768-character string. From now on, vt will represent the inserted text.

- Audio Encoding: COVAREP is used to extract a variety of acoustic properties from audio frames, including MFCC, pitch, peak slope, and others. The audio embedding for each movie is calculated by averaging the vectors of sound that were extracted from each frame. The final size of the audio encodings is 74. From now on, we will refer to audio embeds with the symbol va.
- The combination of FACET2 and OpenCV is used to extract frame wise information from the video stream for use in the encoding process.

## Multimodal Sentiment Classification

Vector of attributes $z_i(i = 1, 2...n)$. The user's attribute matrix is obtained by combining the vector, which is the input of the CNN network $Z$.$Z_{i:j}$ signifies the joining of all vectors of words in $Z_i$ and $Z_j$ as follows:

$$Z_{i:j} = Z_i \oplus Z_{i+1} \oplus \cdots \oplus Z_j \tag{1}$$

where the symbol $\oplus$ stands for the assembly of vectors. The feature vectors are extracted by the convolutional layer using stitching vectors with varying window sizes $C_i$ in response to different intervals of $Z$ as follows:

$$\begin{aligned} C_i &= f(w \cdot Z_{i:i+h-1} + b) \\ f(x) &= \begin{cases} x, & \text{if}: x > 0 \\ \lambda x, & \text{if}: x < 0 \end{cases} \end{aligned} \tag{2}$$

where $h$ is the window width, $\lambda \in (0,1)$ is the linear function of activation Leaky ReLU, b is a bias term and is the linear offset. Mix diverse $C_i$ into feature matrix $C$.

$$C = [C_1, C_2, \cdots, C_{n-h+1}] \tag{3}$$

Reducing dimensions and extracting useful features may be achieved by pooling feature matrix C. Here is the last output N of the CNN module's maximum pooling layer using characteristic data:

$$N = \max - \text{pooling}(C_1, C_2, \cdots, C_{n-h+1}) \tag{4}$$

Fully linked with the synapses of the amount of subcategory tags, the two networks' output vectors of features are H and N, respectively. To get the projected categorization result y, we perform a SoftMax likelihood computation on each neuron's outputs:

$$\begin{aligned} y &= g(W_1 \cdot H + W_2 \cdot N) \\ g(i) &= \underset{i \in S}{\arg\max} \frac{e^i}{\sum_{j=1}^{S} e^j} \end{aligned} \tag{5}$$

where $W_1$ and $W_2$ matrixes represent features, where S is the count of emotional categories, and *g(i)* stands for the model's predicted category y, which is selected utilizing the SoftMax function of activation based on the likelihood of its occurrence.

When it comes to user attributes, CNN must be used, whereas RNN is used for text-related characteristics extraction. Afterward, the traits are used to deduce the user's emotional state from their tweets. The overall amount of parameters for the model is a bit higher than TextRNN.

## RESULTS AND DISCUSSION

Experiments comparing the accuracy of the CNN-RNN-TF-IDF model to that of various other widely used models in short-term and small-data situations are conducted to validate the algorithm's efficacy. All the simulations here are written in the Python programming language, and the hardware in use is a desktop PC with 32GB of RAM and a 3.60 GHz Intel Core i7-7700 processor. Some deep neural network models are widely employed in current research and applications, and these models perform well on sentiment classification tasks for limited-data and time-bound scenarios. Pick the top five most widely used models that share the same amount of time in training as CNN-RNN. Fig. (**1**). portrays the System Diagram. Table **1** represented in Dataset description.

**Table 1. Dataset description.**

| ID | Category | Vocabulary | Images | Average Words |
|---|---|---|---|---|
| 1 | E-Commerce | 174664 | 3500 | 59.2211 |
| 2 | Technology & Science | 137554 | 3500 | 46.8511 |
| 3 | Traffic & Travel | 148998 | 3500 | 48.6664 |
| 4 | Economics & Business | 216378 | 3500 | 73.1264 |

*(Table 1) cont.....*

| ID | Category | Vocabulary | Images | Average Words |
|---|---|---|---|---|
| 5 | Social Networks | 136059 | 3500 | 46.3528 |
| 6 | Life Services | 167315 | 3500 | 56.7714 |
| 7 | Physical Fitness | 88209 | 3500 | 28.4028 |
| 8 | Health Care | 167819 | 3500 | 56.9394 |
| 9 | Arts & Literature | 127194 | 3500 | 43.3978 |
| 10 | Media & Press | 162177 | 3500 | 55.0588 |
| 11 | Entertainments | 167366 | 3500 | 56.7884 |
| 12 | Laws & Politics | 105809 | 3500 | 36.2694 |
| 13 | Internet & Computers | 171662 | 3500 | 58.2204 |
| 14 | Training & Education | 177897 | 3500 | 58.2988 |
| 15 | Social Cultures | 154567 | 3500 | 52.5221 |

The new CNN-RNN-TF-IDF network's efficiency and instruction time are sensitive to the settings of the hyperparameters. Several techniques in this article determine training metrics as well as hyper-parameter values, including initialization weight, learning rate, batch size, as well as dropout, among many others. Choosing an appropriate learning rate is critical during training for models. Setting the learning rate too high causes the model to converge in the wrong direction while setting it too low causes it to never converge. In the past, it would have been wasteful to test out many rates of learning in the hopes of getting satisfactory outcomes. In the first iteration of a novel training technique, we proposed employing mini-batch instruction with rates of learning ranging from moderate to high. In order to choose the optimal learning rate, it is important to monitor the loss of pattern as it is changed. In this research, we apply this technique to the CNN-RNN model in order to determine the optimal learning rate by plotting the loss as a function of training parameters. The convergence impact and speed of the neural network are most affected by whether or not the weight is initialized. The CNN-RNN model was developed to address the issue of emotion categorization with limited training data and in real time. If you do not have access to a huge quantity of data for pre-training, using the right initialization approach is crucial for getting your model to converge quickly. When using Leaky ReLU as the activation function, the He initialization strategy performs exceptionally well. A larger batch size requires more storage for calculations, whereas a smaller one takes longer to perform. Experiments lead to the determination that a batch size of 64 is optimal, taking into account the specifics of the jobs processed by CNN-RNN. CNN-RNN is a mix of CNN and RNN that operates in simultaneously. Full connection is used in the fusion of features, and the relative importance of the two is hard to assess. Lastly, the completely linked layer that combines the two models is enhanced with a 0.5 probability dropout. This expedites the process of discovering the ideal weight for combining the two modal features. Table **1** is portrayed in Dataset description, Fig. (**2**) is depicted in Accuracy *vs*. learning rate.

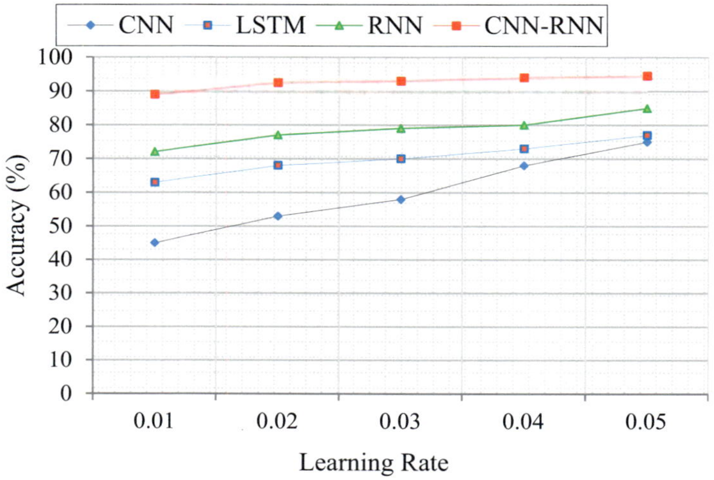


**Fig. (2).** Accuracy *vs*. learning rate.

**Table 2. Dataset description.**

| ID | Category | P | R | A |
|---|---|---|---|---|
| 1 | E-Commerce | 98.5 | 95.6 | 98.25 |
| 2 | Science & Technology | 94.6 | 94.25 | 97.85 |
| 3 | Travel & Traffic | 94.5 | 96.7 | 98.25 |
| 4 | Business & Economics | 95.2 | 98.5 | 98.36 |
| 5 | Social Networks | 94.6 | 94.25 | 97.85 |
| 6 | Life Services | 94.25 | 97.85 | 94.6 |
| 7 | Physical Fitness | 96.7 | 98.25 | 94.5 |
| 8 | Health Care | 98.5 | 98.36 | 94.6 |
| 9 | Literature & Arts | 94.6 | 98.25 | 98.25 |
| 10 | Press & Media | 94.5 | 97.85 | 97.85 |
| 11 | Entertainments | 94.6 | 94.25 | 97.85 |
| 12 | Politics & Laws | 94.5 | 96.7 | 98.25 |
| 13 | Computers & Internet | 98.25 | 98.25 | 98.25 |
| 14 | Education & Training | 97.85 | 97.85 | 97.85 |

*(Table 2) cont.....*

| ID | Category | P | R | A |
|---|---|---|---|---|
| 15 | Social Cultures | 98.25 | 98.25 | 98.25 |

With CNN-RNN achieving top scores across many classification indices (accuracy, precision, as well as recall included), it is clear that utilizing CNN to gather user attributes features to assist LSTM in extracting textual characteristics is very effective for sentiment categorization. CNN-RNN has a somewhat longer training time per epoch than RNN does. CNN-RNN, on the other hand, needs fewer epochs to converge and less time to train than RNN. Short-term and low-sample-size emotion categorization occurs where CNN-RNN has been shown to excel in experiments. Table **2** represents the Dataset Description.

## CONCLUSION

In order to address the immediate and limited data requirements of sentiment categorization in opinions analysis, this study presents a CNN-RNN algorithm that utilizes user attributes to augment the input data. In order to classify emotions, we merged features extracted from user characteristics using a CNN network and features extracted from text input using a Bi-LSTM. Data collected from Sina Weibo was used to demonstrate that CNN-RNN outperforms TextRNN in terms of classification accuracy with much less time spent on training. There are certain limitations to the use of CNN-RNN for the emotion categorization job in social media text. On the one hand, this paper chooses 12 user attributes, some of which have been shown in other research to be directly related to emotion categories; on the other hand, it is unclear whether the inclusion of some of these attributes improves or detracts from the overall model. Experiments show that picking too many user characteristics can lead to overfitting, while picking too few does not significantly increase the classification accuracy. In-depth investigation of this issue, better user attribute collocation selection, and justifications will be provided by future studies. However, more study is required to determine whether or not the network model selection and dual model integration can be enhanced. While CNNs are great for CNN-RNN's user property extraction, fully connected neural networks were considered early on in the model's development. The use of distribution of weights or serial connections may lead to improved classification results; however, this approach uses parallel splice of vectors of features to merge the two. The utilization of multi-modal information is a key component to CNN-RNN's performance since it may improve the number of features contained in limited data. Researchers working on the subject of artificial intelligence will find the use of multimodal data to be an exciting and fruitful area of study. This information must meet two criteria: first, it must be easily accessible and highly relevant in order to be used accurately by a neural network that draws its features. Secondly, the model's parameters must be minimized.

## REFERENCES

[1] C. Zhang, L. Xie, Y. Aizezi, and X. Gu, "User Multi-Modal Emotional Intelligence Analysis Method Based on Deep Learning in Social Network Big Data Environment", *IEEE Access,* vol. 7, pp. 181758-181766, 2019. [http://dx.doi.org/10.1109/ACCESS.2019.2959831]

[2] S. Hou, G. Tuerhong, and M. Wushouer, "VisdaNet: Visual Distillation and Attention Network for Multimodal Sentiment Classification", *Sensors (Basel),* vol. 23, no. 2, p. 661, 2023. [http://dx.doi.org/10.3390/s23020661] [PMID: 36679456]

[3] Z. Liu, E. Osei-Brefo, S. Chen, and H. Liang, "UoR at SemEval-2020 Task 8: Gaussian Mixture Modelling (GMM) Based Sampling Approach for Multi-modal Memotion Analysis", *International Workshop on Semantic Evaluation,* 2020. [http://dx.doi.org/10.18653/v1/2020.semeval-1.159]

[4] M. Kalaivani, and S. Jayalakshmi, "Comparative Analysis of Convolutional Neural Network and LSTM in Text-Based Sentiment Classification", *2021 Fifth International Conference on I-SMAC (IoT in Social, Mobile, Analytics and Cloud) (I-SMAC),* 2021 pp. 1205-1211.

[5] A.C. Sitepu, W. Wanayumini, and Z. Situmorang, "Determining Bullying Text Classification Using Naive Bayes Classification on Social Media", *Varian,* vol. 4, no. 2, pp. 81-88, 2021. [http://dx.doi.org/10.30812/varian.v4i2.1086]

[6] H. Sun, G. Wang, and S. Xia, "Text tendency analysis based on multi-granularity emotional chunks and integrated learning", *Neural Comput. Appl.,* pp. 1-11, 2020.

[7] S. P. Yadav, B. S. Bhati, D. P. Mahato, and S. Kumar, "Federated Learning for IoT Applications", *EAI/Springer Innovations in Communication and Computing. Springer International Publishing.,* 2022. [http://dx.doi.org/10.1007/978-3-030-85559-8]

[8] H. Sun, G. Wang, and S. Xia, "Text tendency analysis based on multi-granularity emotional chunks and integrated learning", *Neural Comput. Appl.,* vol. 33, no. 14, pp. 8119-8129, 2021. [http://dx.doi.org/10.1007/s00521-020-04901-y]

[9] S. Shekhar, and N. Mohan, "Sentiment Classification Using Hybrid Bayes Theorem Support Vector Machine Over", *Soc. Netw.,* 2020.

[10] P. Dr, and E.A. Kavitha, "Twitter Sentiment Analysis Based On Adaptive Deep Recurrent", *Neural Netw.,* 2021.

[11] Q. Zhao, "Social emotion classification of Japanese text information based on SVM and KNN", *J. Ambient Intell. Humaniz. Comput.,* pp. 1-12, 2021. [http://dx.doi.org/10.1007/s12652-021-03034-x]

[12] M. Xuanyuan, L. Xiao, and M. Duan, "Sentiment Classification Algorithm Based on Multi-Modal Social Media Text Information", *IEEE Access,* vol. 9, pp. 33410-33418, 2021. [http://dx.doi.org/10.1109/ACCESS.2021.3061450]

# CHAPTER 20

# Text Classification Method for Tracking Rare Events on Twitter

**Prabhjot Kaur**[1,*]

[1] *Centre for Interdisciplinary Research in Business and Technology, Chitkara University Institute of Engineering and Technology, Chitkara University, Punjab, India*

**Abstract:** A natural catastrophe is an example of a rare occurrence that does not happen often but may have devastating effects on people and their environment when it occurs. People now have a quick and easy outlet for voicing their ideas thanks to social media. Thus, it may be used by researchers to learn about how individuals react to and think about a wide variety of extremely unusual occurrences. Many research works use social media data to investigate how people's reactions to unusual occurrences in the real world translate to their online personas, thoughts, feelings, and actions. In this piece of work, we offer a method for extracting features and classifying tweets on unusual events like Hurricane Sandy. To begin, a new approach to feature extraction is presented, one that may be used to extract relevant features from each communication. The next step is to offer a Score-based categorization system for differentiating between communications about events and those that are unrelated. Finally, the development of a rare event is analyzed using our suggested approach and the popular keyword search method. The findings show that the suggested method is effective in distinguishing between text messages connected to unusual events and those that are unrelated.

**Keywords:** Rare events tracking, Social media, Text classification, Twitter sentiment analysis.

## INTRODUCTION

Rare occurrences, such as natural disasters, may have devastating effects on people and their surroundings when they do occur [1]. Opinions may be voiced quickly and easily through social media [2]. Thus, it may be used by researchers to study how individuals react to and think about a wide variety of extremely unusual situations [3]. Many research works use social media data to investigate how people's reactions to unusual occurrences in the real world translate to their

* **Corresponding author Prabhjot Kaur:** Centre for Interdisciplinary Research in Business and Technology, Chitkara University Institute of Engineering and Technology, Chitkara University, Punjab, India;
E-mail: prabhjot.kaur.orp@chitkara.edu.in

online personas [4]. When it comes to researching the development of unusual occurrences like natural catastrophes, social media provides a wealth of data [5]. Examining the link between social media and occurrences with which humans are involved can be instructive. Many deep learning algorithms rely heavily on semantic word representation [6]. Word angle/distance, word analogies, and statistical data are the mainstays of most word representation methods [7]. However, common models treat each word independently by using a vector representation [8]. This restricts their use for representing uncommon words in languages with extensive lexicons. Text documents frequently provide brief "snippets" of information pertinent to a given area [9]. For example, human analysts frequently use ontology to categorize snippets of text in the social science subject of peace and conflict studies, where it is crucial to identify, classify, and monitor causes of conflict using text sources. The lack of class-conditional evidence in "rare" phrases in snippets is a challenge to automating this approach [10].

There are two key benefits. We begin by proposing a new approach to feature extraction. Second, we propose and validate a fuzzy logic-based classifier with actual social media data. Additionally, there are measures developed specifically for measuring the efficacy of such brief text categorization strategies. The remaining content of this article is as follows. The data and an innovative feature extraction approach are presented in Section 2. In Section 3, we outline the suggested method of text categorization using fuzzy logic. Section 4 presents and discusses the experimental findings. Section 5 provides the summary and findings.

## RELATED WORK

In this piece, we offer a method for extracting features and classifying tweets on unusual events like Hurricane Sandy. To begin, a new approach to feature extraction is presented, one that may be used to extract relevant features from each communication. The next step is to provide a classification system based on fuzzy logic that can identify event-related irrelevant communications. Finally, the development of a rare event is analyzed using our suggested approach and the popular keyword search method. The findings show that the suggested method is effective at differentiating between text messages connected to unusual events and those that are unrelated to them [11].

This research does information extraction and text categorization using Twitter text data from a 2012 Hurricane Sandy. Since the original data covers a wide variety of issues, we will need to extract the information pertinent to Hurricane Sandy. To address the issue of text categorization, we provide a method based on fuzzy logic. The suggested fuzzy logic-based model takes as inputs several characteristics that may be gleaned from each tweet. The final result for each message sent to Sandy is a relevancy score. To achieve the required categorization outcomes, many fuzzy rules are written and various defuzzification approaches are combined. We evaluate the suggested strategy against the standard practice of using keywords to get relevant results. The outcome demonstrates that the suggested fuzzy logic-based strategy is superior to the keyword-word method [12] for classifying Twitter tweets.

Words are proposed to be represented by a vector of domain and semantic properties in this research, with the help of a dynamic model called SemVec. An enhanced word representation containing domain knowledge can be created by adding or removing semantic characteristics based on the issue domain. The suggested methodology is tested by classifying tweets and texts on adverse drug reactions (ADRs). SemVec outperforms other state-of-the-art deep learning approaches in terms of recall score [13], and its results demonstrate that it increases precision for ADR detection by 15.28%.

In this study, we create a strategy to improve a bag-of-words model by including a Word Vector model's related terms to supplement the text's unusual keywords. This technique is then utilized in tandem with common linear text categorization methods. These enriched models outperform the standard classifiers by decreasing bag-of-words sparsity. Second, we show that Paragraph Vectors perform better than the enriched models [14] when applied to the problem of improving performance on "small" classes with few instances.

In this study, we provide a novel approach to event classification using noisy hydrophone data. The 1D hydrophone data is first transformed into a log-frequency spectrogram picture (cepstrum) using an image processing methodology. To further refine this image, we rebuild it using the dominant orientation map's mutual information (MI) criterion. After the cepstrum has been rebuilt, it is improved by applying edge-tracking and noise smoothing to its features. Least-squares support vector machines (LS-SVMs) are used to conduct feature categorization on the refined cepstrum. When applied to noisy hydrophone recordings from the NEPTUNE Canada project, the approach demonstrated a sensitivity for event identification in excess of 99%, with a specificity in excess of 97% and an overall accuracy in excess of 98%. The suggested approach is suitable for automated long-term monitoring of a range of marine animals and human-related activities using hydrophone data [15] because of its cheap processing cost and excellent accuracy.

## PROPOSED WORK

### Research Gaps

The casual nature of the English language, including the use of acronyms, misspelling words, equivalents, transliteration, and confusing terminology, makes it difficult to choose keywords from Twitter as characteristics to identify events. In this work, we examine the various approaches to using keywords as characteristics for classification and determine which ones perform the best overall. To that end, we investigate what factors influence keywords as characteristics for detecting political discontent and demonstrations. Word count, word varieties (n-gram, skip-gram, bags-of-words), and data association strategies (correlation, similarity) are all part of the picture.

### Dataset

The underlying data comes from Twitter's open API for developers. Twitter, one of the most well-known online news and social networking platforms, lets its users submit limited-character messages (called "tweets") to their profiles. In 2016, there were more than 319 million monthly active users. It offers a large enough sample of social media data that researchers may apply it to a wide range of topics. A user ID, timestamp, text data, *etc.* are all stored in each tweet. The study of textual information is the subject of this article.

Unlike many other types of data, tweets are typically brief and lacking in background information. People's understandings of the meaning of tweets vary widely because they lack such background. As the ground truth data for this article, we randomly choose 2000 tweets from the original dataset and manually classify them. Therefore, we employ this annotated dataset to construct a model based on fuzzy logic. Even if there are auto-labeling approaches like auto-encoder, it is important to keep in mind that they often lead to a high mistake rate. We use hand labeling to ensure proper categorization.

Fifteen people volunteered to tag these 2,000 tweets. Each participant rates the experience between 0 and 4. If the score is 0, it means that the tweet has absolutely nothing to do with Hurricane Sandy or our event. On the other hand, a score of 4 indicates that the tweet is very relevant to the topic. One indicates a low level, two a moderate level, and three a high level. The final score for each instance is then calculated as the mean of the ratings given by the volunteers. We have predefined four relevance classes, $D_1$, $D_2$, $D_3$, and $D_4$, that may be thought of as four separate datasets. They are equivalent to "not relevant," "marginally relevant," "relevant," and "very relevant." There are four predetermined datasets, and the j th tweet belongs to one of them if (and only if) the condition i-1(j)i holds (where j=1, 2,..., 2000 and i=1, 2, 3). Keep in mind that the average rating given by volunteers for tweet j is denoted by (j).

## Data Preprocessing

A tweet is a specific type of online short text communication with its structure and characteristics. In this phase, prepping the data is the initial step. Actually, tweets are not tidy enough for effective, immediate application. Internet jargon and "noise" like a unified resource location (URL) are included. These details may slow down calculation and disrupt the efficiency of a classification method. A typical unfiltered tweet may read, "All systems active!" Interference details for "#BucksSandy #Sandy (@ Hurricane Bunker) http://t.co/y1UOFIYp" are quite comprehensive. Pattern matching offers a time-saving method for dealing with such a scenario. It verifies the presence of pattern components by evaluating a supplied sequence of expressions. In most cases, it correctly discovers patterns hidden inside a massive volume of input text. For instance, we all know that URLs must always begin with "http://." When the pattern matching technique detects http://, whatever comes after it is stripped away until a space is detected.

In addition, while a hashtag might be useful for providing some context for an event, only approximately a third of communications actually use them, and even then, the hashtags are inconsistent. In a tweet like "#sandycantstopme do not let her stop you. #floodproof #keepgoing," the message of the hashtags is still clear even if there is no gap between the phrases. However, this is a significant challenge for machines to comprehend, as "sandycantstopme" is not a proper English word, even if individuals may readily interpret it as "sandy cannot stop me." In this case, we opt to get rid of all hashtags entirely. The process is completed by filtering out stop words and converting all the words to lowercase. These "stop words" are often the most frequently used terms in any given language. The articles "the," "this," "a," and "on," for example, are required for some phrases to be grammatically accurate or comprehensible, but they are rarely put to good use. They can be used several times in a single sentence and usually add little of value to the discourse. Words like the, an obvious example, will score highly if we count the most common words in a corpus without deleting stop words. This is why stop words are filtered out. Since a computer may interpret the same word under lower and upper cases as two distinct words, converting words into lower-case ones helps us guarantee that all words are of the same format. As a result, once every upper-case letter is changed to a lower-case one, "STORM" and "Storm" are considered to be the same word.

## Feature Extraction and Classification

Word and phrase meanings are not readily apparent to computers. Therefore, the goal of the research community is to transform such phrases and sentences into numbers for feature extraction. The bag-of-words and TF-IDF are just two examples [8]. The frequency of words is a primary area of interest for most of them. Some communications may share common or similar semantic phrases if they are discussing the same themes. In an airport, for instance, the terms "time," "arrival," and "airline" are more common than the "bids" and "price" that should occur in an auction. We choose tweets from $D_2$, $D_3$, and $D_4$ in the training dataset to obtain the top 50 most frequently used phrases, prioritizing those with a high appearance score. It must be kept in mind that $D_2$, $D_3$, and $D_4$ represent low, moderate, and high significance, respectively. Word significance, indicated by i for a given word i, is defined as:

$$\alpha_i = \frac{P_i}{Q_i} \times 100\% \qquad \textbf{(1)}$$

where $P_i$ is the number of word $i$ that appears in the tweets that belong to $D_2$, $D_3$ *and* $D_4$; $Q_i$ concludes the number of word $i$, which appears in all the tweets; $\alpha_i$ is a percentage which denotes the significance of word $i$. Generally, the larger the $\alpha_i$, the more important the word $i$. After that, we sort all the most frequently used words according to $\alpha_i$ from the highest to lowest in a key list $L$. Then, we split it equally into three subsets represented by $L_1$, $L_2$, and $L_3$ with different relevant weights $\theta_1$, $\theta_2$, and $\theta_3$, respectively, where $L = L_1 \cup L_2 \cup L_3$. Then, the similarity between a word in a tweet and a word in the key list $L$ is calculated by using a similarity function. A similarity evaluation process is defined as a mathematical operator: $\otimes$. Fig. (**1**) . shows the System Flow Model.

Given a tweet containing $n$ words, $T_i$, $i \in \{1,2,...,n\}$, denotes the $i$ th word in the tweet. $W_k$, $k \in \{1,...,50\}$, denotes the $k$ th word in the key list $L$. The highest one among the similarity scores is used to represent $T_i$ 's score. Thus, the similarity score of $T_i$ is calculated as follows:

$$S_i = \max_{1 \le k \le 50} (\omega_k \times T_i \otimes W_k), i \in [1, n] \qquad \textbf{(2)}$$

where

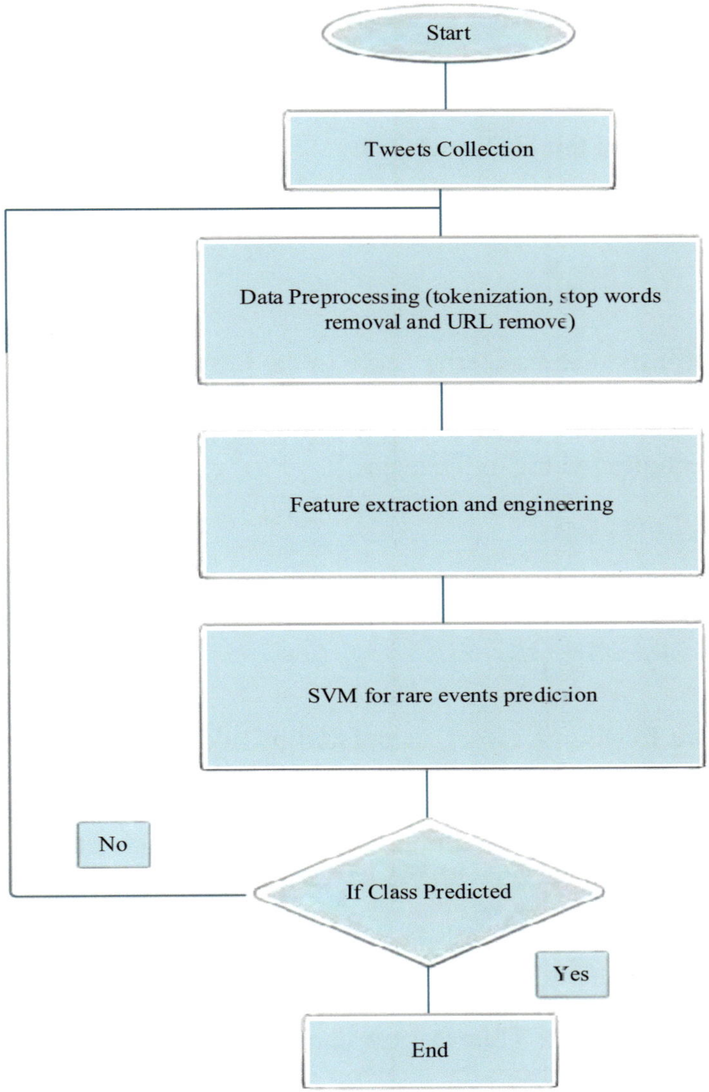


**Fig. (1).** System flow model.

$$\omega_k = \begin{cases} \theta_1 & \text{if} \quad k \in [1,16) \\ \theta_2 & \text{if} \quad k \in [16,32) \\ \theta_3 & \quad \text{otherwise.} \end{cases} \quad \textbf{(3)}$$

$S_i$ is a fundamental parameter. After that, we extract six characteristics from every tweet separately to construct our suggested model based on fuzzy logic. The techniques used for feature extraction are defined and described in the following section. The maximum word score in tweet j is denoted as $H_j$.

1 Highest Word Score in the jth Tweet ($H_j$):

1 Highest Word Score in the jth Tweet $(H_j)$ :

$$H_j = \max_{1 \le i \le n} S_i \tag{4}$$

Where $H_j$ stands for the largest word's score in the $j$ th tweet. It takes up the word having the highest score to denote the tweet's score. Suppose a word contains a higher score then it is highly possible that it is related with the event. A tweet with such word is potentially related to the event.

2 Score of the jth Tweet ($F_j$) :

2 Score of the jth Tweet $(F_j)$ :

$$F_j = \sum_{i=1}^{n} S_i \quad , \tag{5}$$

where $F_j$ is a score for the jth tweet, calculated by adding together the weighted importance ratings for each word in that tweet. In Eq. (4), the total score of a tweet is calculated by adding the scores of its individual words. A high score for this tweet would be warranted if similar terms also had high ratings. Then, this tweet must have something to do with the happenings.

3 Number of Frequently Used Words in the jth Tweet ($I_j$) : $I_j$, as the third feature, denotes that the number of words in the $j$ th tweet stands the same as those in the key list $L$. Note that $L$ is obtained from all training tweets and contains all the most frequently used words. This feature counts the number of keywords in a tweet. It is obvious that the more the keywords in it, the more relevant this tweet is to the event.

4 Weight of the jth Tweet ($G_j$):

4 Weight of the jth Tweet $(G_j)$ :

$$G_j = \frac{F_j}{N_j}, \tag{6}$$

where $N_j$ is the number of words in the $j$ th tweet, $F_j$ denotes a score of the $j$ th tweet, and $G_j$ represents the mean score of all words in the $j$ th tweet.

5 Weight of Frequently Used Words in the jth Tweet ($E$):

5 Weight of Frequently Used Words in the jth Tweet $(E_j)$ :

$$E_j = \frac{I_j}{N_j} \quad , \tag{7}$$

6 where $E_j$ determines how often a certain word appears in relation to the total number of words in a tweet. It considers $N_j$, the total amount of characters in a tweet. When compared to a brief tweet containing a few terms connected to the event, a lengthy one may not be any more pertinent. A higher $E_j$ indicates that the tweet is more informative. Total Pattern Count in Tweet j($V_j$): When considering each word in isolation, it might be easy to overlook a potentially valuable combination. More information may be conveyed by using phrases like "no power," "power off," and "no school," rather than just those words alone. The pattern count is then tweeted about by $V_j$. More patterns indicate higher significance to the occurrence, as would be expected.

Hurricanes are the subject of this essay. Contrast this with other extremely uncommon occurrences like earthquakes. Hurricanes, from the moment they are formed, can be forecast in real time. Yet earthquakes happen without warning. Common terms, keywords, and phrases associated with uncommon occurrences might be different from one unusual event to the next. The phenomena and intensity of unusual occurrences vary, and so do the words and phrases that people use to describe them. The suggested strategy requires careful event selection when applied to additional uncommon occurrences. The sixth element, which is tied to patterns, is the key difference in our approach. The patterns must be modified so that they may be applied to a specific instance of a rare occurrence. They can also modify the membership function's parameters to work better with it.

## RESULTS AND DISCUSSION

Here we provide details of a few measures that can be used to measure how well our proposed strategy works. A binary classification method's efficacy is measured using the confusion matrix in Table **1**.

**Table 1. Confusion matrix for binary-classification problem.**

| - | **Actual Positive** | **Actual Negative** |
|---|---|---|
| Predicted positive | TP | FP |
| Predicted negative | FN | TN |

The term "true positive" (TP) refers to the. number of incidents that should have been rated as negative but were instead labeled positive. The term "false negative" (FN) refers to the number of times a positive result was incorrectly labeled as a negative one and the True Negative (TN) is the total number of cases that actually are negative.

In order to determine whether or not a given instance belongs to the rare-event-relevant class, a precision value and a negative predictive value (NPV) are used. The former represents the proportion of correctly categorized tweets in the latter's subject area. If it is high, then a greater proportion of relevant items will be placed in the appropriate class. Otherwise, we risk improperly pigeonholing certain important items. Similarly, NPV represents the proportion of times tweets that do not belong to a certain class are accurately labeled as such. If it is high, a greater proportion of false positives will be caught. If not, there will be misclassifications of some that are not important. Here is how we determine the value of accuracy and NPV:

$$\begin{aligned} \text{precision} &= \frac{\text{TP}}{\text{TP+FP}} \\ \text{NPV} &= \frac{\text{TN}}{\text{TN+FN}}. \end{aligned} \quad \textbf{(8)}$$

In addition, in order to compare the effectiveness of two different approaches, a change rate $\lambda$ describes that a method can exploit more or less information than another method, *i.e.*,

$$\lambda = \frac{x_\alpha - x_\beta}{x_\beta} \quad \textbf{(9)}$$

where $x_\alpha$ denotes the number of occurrences which are correctly categorized into the right class by using a new method $\alpha$, and $x_\beta$ denotes the number of instances that are rightly classified into the right class through an older or baseline method β. More data can in general be obtained from more correctly extracted examples.

## Datasets

- This Twitter dataset includes more than 150 million tweets on the worldwide COVID-19 outbreak. The collection includes nearly every language spoken today, however English, Spanish, and French predominate.
- Customer Support on Twitter - This sizable dataset includes a plethora of Twitter customer service support lines and the tweets and replies that go along with them.
- 2016 Presidential Election- This dataset focuses on tweets related to the 2016 presidential election and was originally gathered to create some transparency against charges of state-sponsored propaganda, Fig. (**2**) is depicted in , Performance Analysis (**a**). Tweet Classification Accuracy (Dataset 1), (**b**). Tweet Classification Accuracy (Dataset 2), (**c**). Tweet Classification Accuracy (Dataset 3).

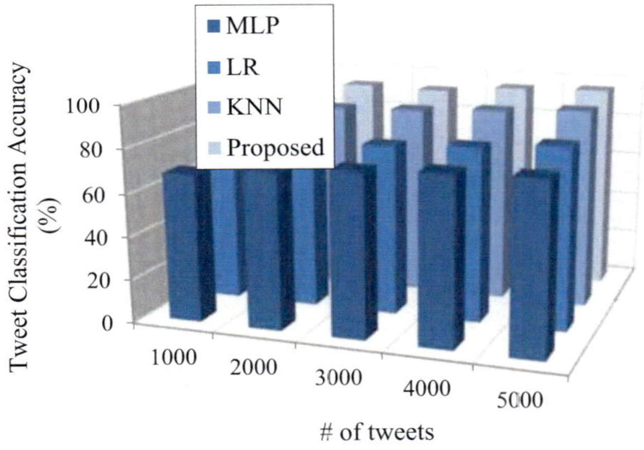


(a)

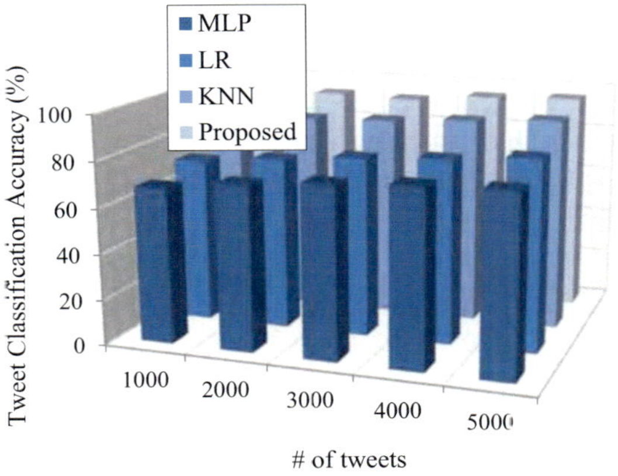


(b)

*(Fig. 2) contd.....*

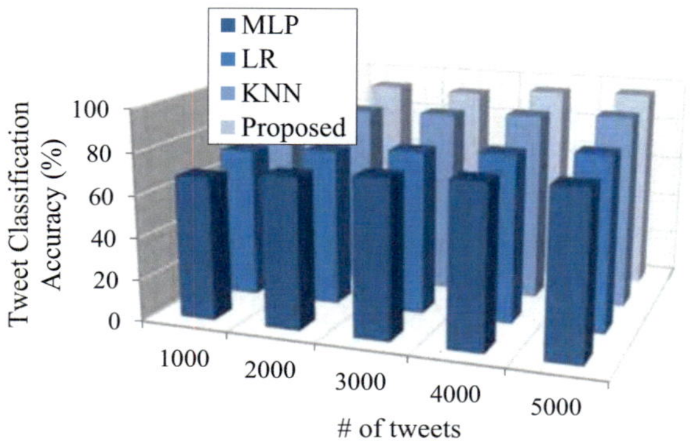


(c)

**Fig. (2).** Performance Analysis (**a**). Tweet Classification Accuracy (Dataset 1), (**b**). Tweet Classification Accuracy (Dataset 2), (**c**). Tweet Classification Accuracy (Dataset 3).

## CONCLUSION

A natural catastrophe is an example of a rare occurrence that does not happen often but may have devastating effects on people and their environment when it occurs. People now have a quick and easy outlet for voicing their ideas thanks to social media. Thus, it may be used by researchers to learn about how individuals react to and think about a wide variety of extremely unusual occurrences. Many research works use social media data to investigate how people's reactions to unusual occurrences in the real world translate to their online personas, thoughts, feelings, and actions. In this piece of work, we offer a method of extracting features and classifying tweets on unusual events like Hurricane Sandy. To begin, a new approach to feature extraction is presented, one that may be used to extract relevant features from each communication. The next step is to offer a Score-based categorization system for differentiating between communications about events and those that are unrelated. Finally, the development of a rare event is analyzed using our suggested approach and the popular keyword search method. The findings show that the suggested method is effective in distinguishing between text messages connected to unusual events and those that are unrelated.

## REFERENCES

[1] Y. Gao, H. Zhang, X. Zhao, and S. Yan, "Event Classification in Microblogs *via* Social Tracking", *ACM Trans. Intell. Syst. Technol.,* vol. 8, pp. 1-14, 2017. [TIST]. [http://dx.doi.org/10.1145/3065950]

[2] A.K. Thakur, F. Ilievski, H. Sandlin, A. Mermoud, Z. Sourati, L. Luceri, and R. Tommasini, "Multimodal and Explainable Internet Meme Classification", *ArXiv, abs/2212.05612,* 2022.

[3] A. Referee, "Extreme precipitation events in the Mediterranean area : contrasting two Lagrangian and

Eulerian models for moisture source identification", 2021.

[4] S. P. Yadav, B. S. Bhati, D. P. Mahato, and S. Kumar, "Federated Learning for IoT Applications", *EAI/Springer Innovations in Communication and Computing. Springer International Publishing,* 2022. [http://dx.doi.org/10.1007/978-3-030-85559-8]

[5] D. Banerjee, G. Prabhat, and R. Bhowal, "iCASSTLE: Imbalanced Classification Algorithm for Semi Supervised Text Learning", *17th IEEE International Conference on Machine Learning and Applications (ICMLA),* pp. 1012-1016, 2018. [http://dx.doi.org/10.1109/ICMLA.2018.00165]

[6] S.P. Yadav, S. Zaidi, C.D.S. Nascimento, V.H.C. de Albuquerque, and S.S. Chauhan, "Analysis and Design of automatically generating for GPS Based Moving Object Tracking System", *2023 International Conference on Artificial Intelligence and Smart Communication (AISC)*, 2023 pp. 1-5. Greater Noida, India. [http://dx.doi.org/10.1109/AISC56616.2023.10085180]

[7] Y. Baghdadi, A. Bourrée, A. Robert, G. Rey, A. Gallay, P. Zweigenbaum, C. Grouin, and A. Fouillet, "Performance of machine learning method to classify free-text medical causes of death", *Online J. Public Health Inform.,* vol. 11, no. 1, p. 11, 2019. [http://dx.doi.org/10.5210/ojphi.v11i1.9767]

[8] S. Henry, K. Buchan, M. Filannino, A. Stubbs, and O. Uzuner, "2018 n2c2 shared task on adverse drug events and medication extraction in electronic health records", *J. Am. Med. Inform. Assoc.,* vol. 27, no. 1, pp. 3-12, 2020. [http://dx.doi.org/10.1093/jamia/ocz166] [PMID: 31584655]

[9] C. Malvuccio, and E.N. Kamavuako, "Detection of Swallowing Events and Fluid Intake Volume Estimation From Surface Electromyography Signals", *2020 IEEE-EMBS Conference on Biomedical Engineering and Sciences (IECBES),* pp. 245-250, 2021. [http://dx.doi.org/10.1109/IECBES48179.2021.9398821]

[10] S.P. Yadav, D.P. Mahato, and N.T.D. Linh, *Distributed Artificial Intelligence.* CRC Press, 2020. [http://dx.doi.org/10.1201/9781003038467]

[11] X.S. Lu, M. Zhou, and K. Wu, "A Novel Fuzzy Logic-Based Text Classification Method for Tracking Rare Events on Twitter", *IEEE Trans. Syst. Man Cybern. Syst.,* vol. 51, no. 7, pp. 4324-4333, 2021. [http://dx.doi.org/10.1109/TSMC.2019.2932436]

[12] K. Wu, M. Zhou, X.S. Lu, and L. Huang, "A fuzzy logic-based text classification method for social media data", *2017 IEEE International Conference on Systems, Man, and Cybernetics (SMC),* pp. 1942-1947, 2017. [http://dx.doi.org/10.1109/SMC.2017.8122902]

[13] F. Odeh, and A. Taweel, "SemVec: Semantic Features Word Vectors Based Deep Learning for Improved Text Classification", *International Conference on Theory and Practice of Natural Computing,* 2018. [http://dx.doi.org/10.1007/978-3-030-04070-3_35]

[14] A. Krzywicki, B. Heap, M. Bain, W. Wobcke, and S. Schmeidl, "Using Word Embeddings with Linear Models for Short Text Classification", *Australasian Conference on Artificial Intelligence,* 2018. [http://dx.doi.org/10.1007/978-3-030-03991-2_74]

[15] F. Sattar, P.F. Driessen, G. Tzanetakis, and W. Page, "A new method for classification of events in noisy hydrophone data", *Proceedings of 2011 IEEE Pacific Rim Conference on Communications, Computers and Signal Processing,* pp. 660-667, 2011. [http://dx.doi.org/10.1109/PACRIM.2011.6032972]

# CHAPTER 21

# Text Document Preprocessing and Classification Using SVM and Improved CNN

**Jaspreet Sidhu**[1,*]

[1] *Centre for Interdisciplinary Research in Business and Technology, Chitkara University Institute of Engineering and Technology, Chitkara University, Punjab, India*

**Abstract:** Text categorization is a crucial technology in data mining as well as data retrieval that has been extensively investigated and is developing at a rapid pace. Convolutional neural networks (CNNs) are a kind of deep learning modeling that may reduce the complexity of the model while accurately extracting characteristics from input text. Support vector machine (SVM) results have always been more trustworthy and superior to those of other traditional artificial intelligence approaches. Using enhanced convolutional neural network (CNNs) as well as support vector machines (SVMs), we offer a novel approach to online text categorization in this study. Our approach begins with text attribute identification and prediction using a model based on CNN with a five-layer network structure. Databases including both text and images will find it to be a major factor in the long run.

**Keywords:** Classification, SVM and Improved CNN, Text Document Preprocessing.

## INTRODUCTION

Using the naive Bayes technique and the support vector machine (SVM), this study provides an improved hybrid classification strategy [1]. In this study, we employed the Bayes formula to create a probability distribution that vectorizes (as opposed to classes) a document into the most likely categories to which it belongs [2]. If you have a set of subjects (categories), like the ones in the "20 Newsgroups" dataset [3], you can use the Bayes formula to estimate the likelihood that a text falls into each category. The SVM can perform multi-dimensional document classification by employing these probability distributions as the document's vector representation [4]. To prevent the decrease in dimensionality that happens when a naive Bayes classifier uses just the greatest likelihood for classification, the support vector machine (SVM) takes into account

* **Corresponding author Jaspreet Sidhu:** Centre for Interdisciplinary Research in Business and Technology, Chitkara University Institute of Engineering and Technology, Chitkara University, Punjab, India;
E-mail: jaspreet.sidhu.orp@chitkara.edu.in

**Pankaj Kumar Mishra and Satya Prakash Yadav (Eds.)**

all the likelihood values linked with each group for every document [5, 6]. The Formula E racing series has quickly risen to the top of the international motorsports scene. The world-famous Formula E event was held in Indonesia in 2022 [7]. The estimated attendance of 35,000 people has the potential to generate 78 million euros in economic benefits for Indonesia. Many in Indonesia believe that hosting Formula E races will help their country attract tourists and raise its profile abroad [8]. However, there are many who disagree with this move. They believe that the government's resources would be better used to aid those impacted by the COVID-19 pandemic than to fund a Formula E race at this time [9]. To categorize new examples, ensemble techniques generate a series of classifiers and then obtain a weighted vote of their individual predictions. An advanced challenge in ensemble classification [10] is to reduce error while improving accuracy [15].

By combining the improved CNN as well as SVM algorithms, this work aims to overcome the aforementioned problems and finish the Web text categorization assignments in the language analysis sector. In comparison to the current state of affairs, experimental results demonstrate that the suggested Web text categorization approach achieves higher levels of precision in classification.

## RELATED WORK

In comparison to the Lsquare technique, this approach requires much less time to train, and it outperforms pure naive Bayes algorithms as well as TF-IDF/SVM hybrids in terms of precision for classification [11].

The Bayes algorithm is used here to assign a document's vector representation to a set of categories based on the probabilities associated with a set of keywords. The Bayes formula provides a probability distribution over the collection of subjects (categories) to which the document may be allocated. This probability distribution can be used as the carriers that represent the documents by text categorization methods utilizing the vector space model, like the Support Vector Machine (SVM) as well as Autonomous Map (SOM). This improves upon the results obtained when the naive Bayes classifier is used alone, which only uses the highest likelihood to group the piece of paper. These techniques allow us to recover from the consequences of a mistaken dimensionality reduction. For high-dimensional data, we evaluate the effectiveness of various classifiers [12].

This research evaluates the effectiveness of the Support Vector Machine and the Naive Bayes algorithms in identifying fans' sentiments toward the Formula E championship. The data in this study comes from public discussions on social media sites like Twitter. Cleaning, folding cases, tokenizing, filtering, and stemming are all part of the text preparation phase. The TF-IDF method of weighting should be used moving forward. Data testing evaluates the categorization findings using accuracy, precision, and recall tests using a confusion matrix. The SVM algorithm's recall, precision, and accuracy in classifying public opinion are all above 80%. The accuracy is 82%. However, the Naive Bayes method only achieves an accuracy of 87.54 percent. The general public's attitude on Twitter is supportive of introducing Formula E [13].

An ensemble of classifiers for prediction is introduced in this research, along with a revolutionary general object-oriented voting and weighting adaptable stacking architecture. This general-purpose model makes its forecast by tallying the votes of a set of basic learners, with each learner's probability of correctness given equal weight. For demonstration, the proposed stacking framework is used to ensemble classification using three well-known heterogeneous classifiers: the Support Vector Machine, [Formula: see text]-Nearest Neighbor, and Naive Bayes. Additionally, the framework's resulting ensemble classifier is compared to others and assessed across a number of benchmark datasets utilizing a wide variety of cross-validation levels and percentage splits. The result is what sets this framework apart from its rivals. The suggested approach may properly estimate inmates' tendency to commit crimes 99.9901% of the time [14].

As the internet and computing infrastructure continue to advance, text categorization will likely become the most important method for handling massive amounts of text. One major hurdle to perform better text classification results is figuring out how to precisely identify the text as a data collection that can be analyzed. The author discusses a method for characterizing texts using a formula called p-idf, which is derived from the vector space model and tf-idf. The author constructs text classification system with a support vector machine after evaluating Bayes, K neighbors, neural networks, and other common text classification tools. The p-idf formula is fair and valid for a text categorization system [15] after a scientific test compared to its performance to that of the tf-idf and LTC formulas.

## PROPOSED WORK

An example of a common type of artificial neural network is the convolutional neural network (CNN). Each layer's output is fed into the following layer's neuron input in this type of network. Nonlinear transformations are applied to the results of each layer using a multi-layer convolution technique. Fig. (**1**) shows the four main parts that make up the convolutional neural network structure utilized for text processing. The four layers that make up the network are the fully linked, collecting, convolution, as well as embedding layers. Convolutional neural network (CNN) methods used for text evaluation, compared with the layers of input used by the majority of visual assessment designs, include the word vector.

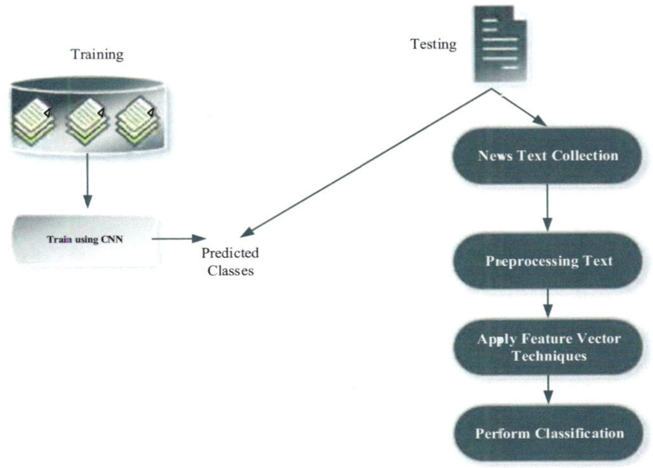


**Fig. (1).** System flowchart.

## CNN with SVM for Text Classification

Given that the phrase has m words and the word vector has n dimensions, the resulting matrix is m x n. Fig. (**2**) shows the CNN with SVM structure. Fig. (**1**). shows the System Flowchart.

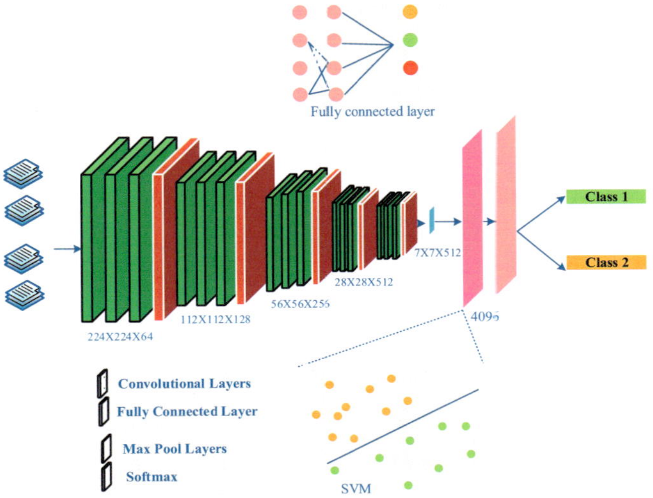


**Fig. (2).** CNN with SVM Structure.

Here is the description of the model structure:

Layer for embedding: In the embedded layer, each word is represented by a vector, and these vectors are stored in a matrix.

Layer of convolutional neural networks: By performing a convolution operation with a kn convolutional window, the embedding layer can generate many feature maps. The number of longitudinal words is denoted by k, and the word vector dimension is denoted by n. Several 1-column feature maps may be produced using a convolutional window.

Inundation layer. The pooling layer, which may subsample the input data, goes by another name: the subsampling layer. The CNN supports many pooling strategies, the max-pooling strategy being the most widespread.

Totally interconnected layer. In many cases, the last layer is linked to another completely connected layer or layers, and the ultimate output is the result of the whole connection layer. Fig. (**2**) portrays the CNN with SVM Structure.

Among convolutional neural networks' distinguishing characteristics are local relationships, spatial collection, as well as weight sharing. By just connecting neurons locally, CNN drastically decreases the number of parameters in its neural network design. Although convolution can gather all the characteristic information needed for training as well as classification, it is computationally intensive. After obtaining the text's convolutional feature, it is crucial to reduce the feature's dimension by the spatial sample in order to increase resistance to displacement as well as minimize the computational expenses of the top layer that is concealed. The weighted sharing network design of CNN is more like a biological neural network, which allows it to bypass the tedious extraction of features as well as the data-rebuilding process that is used by traditional machine learning techniques. As a result, it has become a standard procedure in NLP applications.

An old linear model-based learning method called Support Vector Machine (SVM) maps the space of input onto a feature space with greater dimensions *via* a nonlinear transformation. The goal is to find the optimal linear interfaces in the new space. Without increasing computing complexity and preventing the "Curse of multiplicity" by growing well with data size, the SVM method provides a solution by using a function in the kernel.

Since many different kinds of SVM classifiers may be built from the same kernel function, choosing the right one is essential. The three most common kernel functions

- Linear kernel function:

$$K(x_1, x_2) = (x_1 \cdot x_2) \quad (1)$$

- Polynomial kernel function:

$$K(x_1, x_2) = [(x_1 \cdot x_2) + C]^{\mu} \quad (2)$$

- Radial basis function:

$$K(x_1, x_2) = \exp\left(-\|x_1 - x_2\|^2 / 2\sigma^2\right) \quad (3)$$

All the usual suspects in a convolutional brain network—the embedding, convolutional, entertainment, pooling, as well as fully connected layers—are used to optimize the model that is suggested. Prior to using the dataset, the embeddings of every word are trained. This input characteristic is then used to train the CNN model many times using extra network settings. The final step is to feed the retrieved features into a support vector machine classifier for training, after which the result is produced.

Images are processed using a two-dimensional (2D) convolution neural network for initial recognition. So, before feeding the text input into the model, we must first preprocess it by merging it into a two-dimensional data matrix.

The text preparation method consists of three phases: As a first order of business, the source material must be transformed into a string of words. The next step is to use Google's open-source application word2vec, which is pre-trained to read word vectors, to transform the word sequence into phrases with the number of the sequence. Every word in the dictionary has a unique number. Step three involves expanding every word in the sequence into a vector and then creating a word vector matrix with each element representing a phrase vector.

There are two layers involved in preparing text: Two layers are involved in this process: the data input stage as well as the embedding layer. After that, we have 5 independent CNN models, each of which is a convolutional layer and a pooling layer combined (a "double convolution"). Using the data of each word prior to and after it to determine the size of local features of varying sizes, the thesis shows the design of five convolutions buildings with sizes of 4100, 5100, 6100, 7100, and 8 100 by changing the dimension of the opening k as an input to the adhering layer. The text classification features are improved when the convolutional layer is processed. The max pooling is then utilized to do additional screening of the pooling layer from a global perspective. Additionally, the flattening layer's function is to reduce inputs with more than one dimension to a single dimension.

When operating on a window of size k, the convolution kernel will produce features that are:

$$y_i = f(\omega \cdot x_{i:\ i+k-1} + b) \quad \textbf{(4)}$$

where $x_{i:i+k-l}$ falls inside the filter window that slides and contains the information of the input matrix X. ω uses the weighted matrix as an example. Furthermore, f stands for the stimulus function and b stands for the bias factor. Many activation functions, such as the sigmoid and tanh functions, are included in a neural network. In this case, the broader function of activation is the tanh function.

Layers of merging, complete connectivity, and batch normalization are listed below. Two completely connected layers are used in this dissertation. The first one is used to weigh the features in the input information, while the second one is used to extract features from the final result. This is the precise method of calculation:

$$V' = f(\omega V + b) \quad \textbf{(5)}$$

V stands for the top layer's vectors participation, and b for the bias. The state-of-the-art activation function is F. Leaky ReLU aims to maintain as much relevant data as possible while increasing the model's expressivity *via* the use of non-linear components and decreasing model noise. Feature data is adjusted to converge faster in the sequential normalizing stage as an additional safeguard against overfitting.

Lastly, the text information contained within the sliding window is transformed into a fixed-length vector V”. This vector serves as both the training input for the SVM classifier as well as the output value for categorization following processing by the softmax function.

## RESULTS AND DISCUSSION

Some of the texts utilized in this study was taken from the 20-NewsGroup corpus, but other sources were also used. There were a total of 19997 messages included, all of which had been uploaded to Usenet by users of the Internet and were evenly dispersed throughout 20 distinct categories, each of which had 1000 posts. The other sources include articles from online news sites that were explored using Heritrix and given little processing. There were a total of 11968 samples used, split evenly between training (7180) and testing (4788) sets. The remaining 10% of the data was used as a validation sample during training.

We use Precision (P), Recall (R), and F-Measure (F_), the most general assessment methods, to assess the categorization impact. The equation looks like this:

$$\begin{aligned} P &= C/A \\ R &= C/B \\ F_\theta &= (\theta^2 + 1)PR/(\theta^2 P + R) \end{aligned} \quad \textbf{(6)}$$

Where A is the anticipated total of texts that fall into a certain group and B is the amount of texts that actually do so. C is the total amount of texts, and the selection usually depends on a number of 1. Accuracy, which measures the classifier's performance on the task set, is also used to evaluate the experiment's overall effectiveness.

This study's overarching goal is to provide an already trained vector of words and an SVM classifier based on the enhanced CNN method. The following is the detailed experimental setup: CNN+SVM. We started by training a decent word vector with word2vec, then extracted features with an enhanced CNN model, and lastly utilized a linear kernel SVM classifier to train and report our findings.

Commonplace method of machine learning. The model's efficacy was shown by contrasting its results with those of two well-established educational methods—artificial neural networks (ANN) as well as support vector machines (SVM)—applied to an identical dataset.

You can see a model's training-related accuracy, f-measure, as well as loss in the two figures. In the former, we see acc, fmeasure, as well as loss representing the initial training set, while in the latter, val_acc, val_fmeasure, as well as val_loss represent the validation set. The four markers' change curves have been rather stable after 25 periods, as shown in Fig. (**3**). Meanwhile, Fig. (**4**) demonstrates that the loss is effectively minimized after 25 iterations.

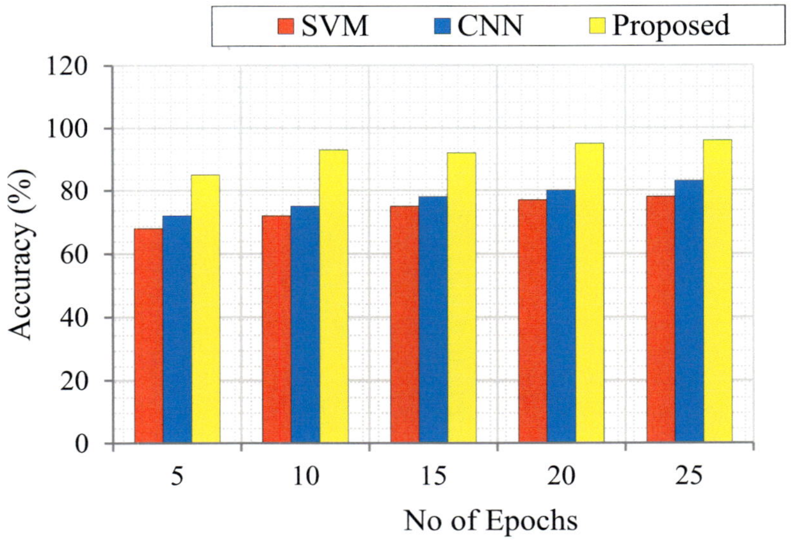


**Fig. (3).** Accuracy results.

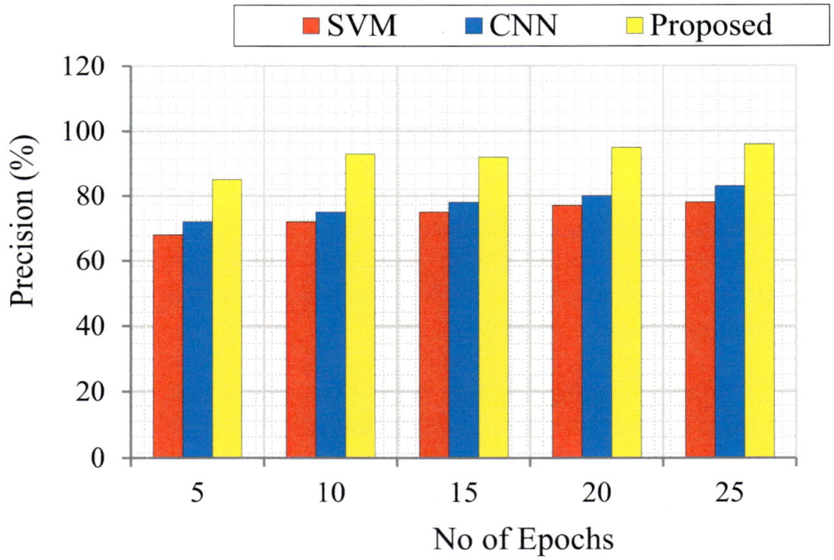


**Fig. (4).** Precision results.

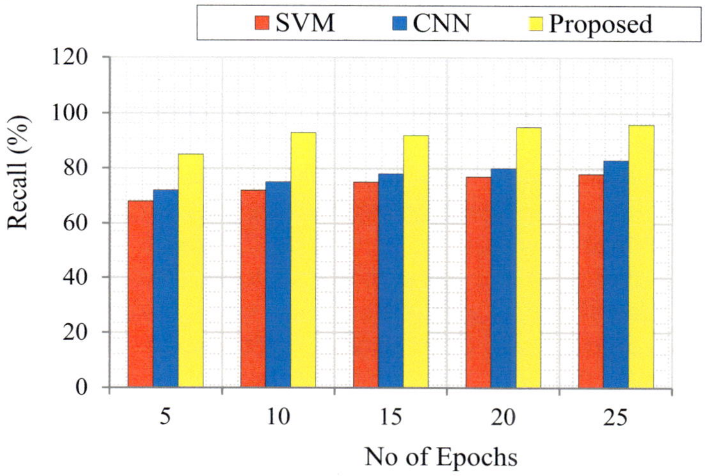


**Fig. (5).** Recall results.

Figs. (**3-6**) display the final outcomes of the four models. The table cata clearly shows that the proposed approach gave the best outcomes for this thesis. The algorithm's accuracy improves from 87.6% to 92.5%, while the f-measure improves from 87.9% to 93.2% when compared to the standard CNN model. In addition, its impact is far higher than that of the SVM method, a reasonably effective classic machine learning technique.

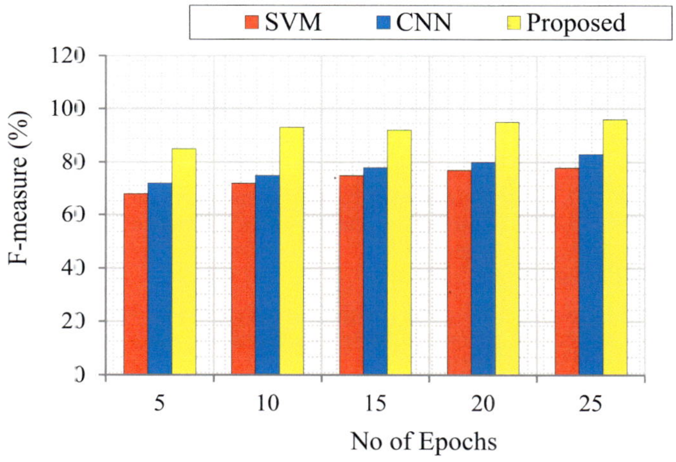


**Fig. (6).** F-measure results.

## CONCLUSION

One of the cornerstones of NLP is text categorization, which has existed for quite some time. Since its inception, deep learning technology has been one of the primary areas of study in the study of artificial intelligence. Convolutional neural networks are the most universally applicable model. This work uses a hybrid approach, combining deep learning with more conventional machine learning techniques, to address the issue of text categorization. To begin, we use the enhanced CNN model to incorporate a pre-trained word vector. Second, to accomplish this classification assignment, we employ the refined versions of the CNN and SVM algorithms. Compared to previous techniques, experimental results demonstrate that the algorithm discussed in this study significantly improves classification accuracy and f-measure. This model will be tested on a publicly available dataset to ensure it accurately accounts for users' emotions in the future.

## REFERENCES

[1] M. Xi, J. Sun, L. Liu, F. Fan, and X. Wu, "Cancer Feature Selection and Classification Using a Binary Quantum-Behaved Particle Swarm Optimization and Support Vector Machine", *Comput. Math. Methods Med.,* vol. 2016, pp. 1-9, 2016. [http://dx.doi.org/10.1155/2016/3572705] [PMID: 27642363]

[2] R. Kachach, and J.M. Cañas, "Hybrid three-dimensional and support vector machine approach for automatic vehicle tracking and classification using a single camera", *J. Electron. Imaging,* vol. 25, no. 3, p. 1, 2016. [http://dx.doi.org/10.1117/1.JEI.25.3.033021]

[3] Q. dai, Y.Chen, & Y.Chen, "A roller bearing fault diagnosis method using interval support vector deterministic optimization based on nested PSO", *J. Vibroeng.,* 2018.

[4] S.P. Yadav, D.P. Mahato, and N.T.D. Linh, *Distributed Artificial Intelligence.* CRC Press, 2020. [http://dx.doi.org/10.1201/9781003038467]

[5] V. Vashisht, A.K. Pandey, and S.P. Yadav, "Speech Recognition using Machine Learning", *IEIE Transactions on Smart Processing & Computing,* vol. 10, no. 3, pp. 233-239, 2021. [http://dx.doi.org/10.5573/IEIESPC.2021.10.3.233]

[6] Q. Nguyen, and T.D. Bui, "MapReduce-based framework for speech classification", In: *in Proceedings of the 7th Symposium on Information and Communication Technology (SoICT)* Ho Chi Minh City, Vietnam, Dec. 2016, pp. 57-63. [http://dx.doi.org/10.1145/3011077.3011089]

[7] B. Prajapati, S. Garg, and N. C Chauhan, "Some Investigations on Machine Learning Techniques for Automated Text Categorization", *Int. J. Comput. Appl.,* vol. 71, no. 3, pp. 32-36, 2013. [http://dx.doi.org/10.5120/12340-8617]

[8] I. Krashenyi, J. Ramírez, A. Popov, and J. Manuel Górriz, "Fuzzy Computer-Aided Alzheimer's Disease Diagnosis Based on MRI Data", *Curr. Alzheimer Res.,* vol. 13, no. 5, pp. 545-556, 2016. [http://dx.doi.org/10.2174/1567205013666160314145008] [PMID: 26971942]

[9] S. Gupta, and M. Dave, "Product Recommendation System Using Tunicate Swarm Magnetic Optimization Algorithm-Based Black Hole Renyi Entropy Fuzzy Clustering and K-Nearest Neighbour", *J. Inf. Knowl. Manag.,* 2021.

[10] D. Isa, L.H. Lee, V.P. Kallimani, and R. RajKumar, "Text Document Preprocessing with the Bayes Formula for Classification Using the Support Vector Machine", *IEEE Trans. Knowl. Data Eng.,* vol. 20, no. 9, pp. 1264-1272, 2008. [http://dx.doi.org/10.1109/TKDE.2008.76]

[11] D. Isa, L. L. Hong, V. P. Kallimani, and R. Rajkumar, "Text document pre-processing using the Bayes formula for classification based on the vector space model", *International Journal of Computer Science and Applications,* vol. 5, no. 3, pp. 1-8, 2008.

[12] S.P. Yadav, S. Zaidi, C.D.S. Nascimento, V.H.C. de Albuquerque, and S.S. Chauhan, "Analysis and Design of automatically generating for GPS Based Moving Object Tracking System", *2023 International Conference on Artificial Intelligence and Smart Communication (AISC)* 2023 pp. 1-5 Greater Noida, India. [http://dx.doi.org/10.1109/AISC56616.2023.10085180]

[13] H.B. David, A. Suruliandi, and S. Raja, "Stacked Framework for Ensemble of Heterogeneous Classification Algorithms", In: *J. Circuits Syst. Comput.*, 2021

[14] W. Zhongmin, *Method of expressing features used for large-scale text classification.* Computer Engineering and Applications, 2007.

[15] Z. Wang, and Z. Qu, "Research on Web text classification algorithm based on improved CNN and SVM", *2017 IEEE 17th International Conference on Communication Technology (ICCT),* pp. 1958-1961, 2017.

# CHAPTER 22

# Identification of Text Emotions Through the Use of Convolutional Neural Network Models

**Vaibhav Kaushik**[1,*]

[1] *Centre for Interdisciplinary Research in Business and Technology, Chitkara University Institute of Engineering and Technology, Chitkara University, Punjab, India*

**Abstract:** Increasing numbers of people are using the Internet to share their feelings and communicate with one another, and the vast majority of these expressions of emotion take the form of text. Using sentiment dictionaries, machine learning, and deep learning are the three most common approaches to text sentiment categorization studies. Due to the exponential growth of textual data, it is crucial to create models that can automatically analyse this material. Labels like gender, age, nationality, emotion, *etc.*, may be included in the texts. Numerous investigations of text categorization have emerged because the use of such labels may be useful in various commercial sectors. The Convolutional Neural Network, also referred to as CNN, was recently utilised to the problem of text categorization, with promising results. In this study, we advocate for the use of convolutional neural network networks for the job of classifying emotions. Using three popular datasets, we demonstrate that our networks outperform existing cutting-edge deep learning models by using successive convolutional layers to process substantially longer sentences.

**Keywords:** CNN, Deep learning, Text sentiment classification.

## INTRODUCTION

Opinion mining, another name for sentiment analysis, is another hot topic in the study of the text. It uses textual subjective information as its study object and makes an effort to classify the many kinds of emotional overtones that may be found in it. It might be a self-assessment or a judgment of oneself, or it could be a feeling or a state of mind. That is why it is important for researchers studying text sentiment categorization to separate the text into its subjective and objective components. There are presently various obstacles in the field of text sentiment classification research, including emotional opaqueness, text formatting, text language, *etc.* Emotional opacity often relates to textual ambiguity and dependent

* **Corresponding author Vaibhav Kaushik:** Centre for Interdisciplinary Research in Business and Technology, Chitkara University Institute of Engineering and Technology, Chitkara University, Punjab, India;
E-mail: vaibhav.kaushik.orp@chitkara.edu.in

**Pankaj Kumar Mishra and Satya Prakash Yadav (Eds.)**

interpretation. “This is a very big noise,” “This playground is very big,” *etc.* Both words use the same wording, “very big,” yet their meanings could not be more different. The vast majority of the writings we examine come from the internet and range in length and presentation. Chinese texts have unique characteristics that are not shared by English writings, such as the requirement for word segmentations that are unnecessary in English texts due to the presence of gaps between individual words. Text classification of sentiment research is often done nowadays using the sentiment dictionary, although this approach requires establishing a high-quality emotion dictionary and can only be categorised manually. This kind of lexicon requires a lot of work and has drawbacks such as not having enough terms to be comprehensive. Methods based on artificial intelligence may improve classification accuracy over those using a sentiment dictionary. This involves the establishment of a high-efficiency computer learning model. However, the features can only be designed by someone with a certain level of expertise. Very little detail can be seen, and it is hard to get in-depth text features. Natural language processing is an area where the method of deep learning has seen significant progress in recent years. With no need for manual design, it is able to automatically generate features in a hierarchical structure and classify data from beginning to finish.

Natural language processing (NLP) applications have seen great success with the usage of convolutional neural networks (CNNs). Since CNN's convolutional layer may be initialised by encoding vital semantic characteristics, this layer can also be used to extract vital semantic features. CNN's Combining layer filters features using the max-combining feature, however, this ignores the sentence's most important details and the text's contextual semantic information. As our capacity to store information digitally grows, these tasks are performed in the form of text messages. Many text classification jobs may be accomplished using a standard artificial intelligence classifier, such as a support vector machine or a naive Bayes classifier. However, because of the scarcity of text in brief text and the constraints of combining and convolutional layers, these classifiers suffer from sparsity difficulties and lack long-term dependencies. In natural language processing, text categorization is one of the most essential tasks. The scope and usefulness of this job are both high. However, most of the older approaches rely on static word embedding, which does not adequately address polysemy. The field of the processing of natural languages known as “sentiment analysis” classifies written material as either positive or negative. In the last several decades, it has found use in a variety of fields. Opinion analysis is challenging since each person has their unique perspective. Information on individuals, businesses, and consumer goods may all be sorted using sentiment analysis. Massive amounts of information is being added to the Internet's websites, blogs, and social media every minute. Virtually every e-commerce site lets customers provide feedback on products they have purchased. The feedback reflects some users' experiences with the items. When making a quick, informal choice between two items, customers often look to the reviews for guidance. Additionally, businesses are interested in hearing customer opinions on items *via* reviews. Data analysis of online comments is getting difficult due to the usual characteristics of huge information and noisy brief written data.

This paper's remaining sections are structured as follows. Studies on sentiment classification using ML/DL models are reviewed in Section 2. Our planned network is described in depth in Section 3. The experimental conditions and data sets used to test the proposed model are discussed in Section 4. Section 5 then elaborates on the outcomes of the experiments. Section 6 is where this paper comes to a close.

## RELATED WORK

In this paper, we propose a novel neural network method that combines the attention mechanism as well as the Combining layer to make the model focus on search terms in the sentence as well as automatically keep the most significant text message, thereby enhancing the model's ability to classify text. In order for the model to pick up on the crucial semantic characteristics, we initialise the convolution filter with key information features. By integrating the attention mechanism into the Combining layer, the model is better able to preserve the vital informational characteristics of the text. Experiments demonstrate that the proposed model performs very well on a variety of text classification tasks, such as sentiment classification as well as topic classification [11].

In this study, we provide a convolutional recurrent neural network architecture that is built based on an enhanced skip-gram algorithm. For the adversarial training of the skip-gram algorithm, we use the L2 regularisation technique. Not only may it boost this model's performance in text emotion classification tasks, but it can also make it more resilient and generalizable. To extract meaningful data from texts while decreasing the influence of irrelevant words, we used a Bidirectional short-term, long-network with attention mechanisms. At long last, CNNS-based text sentiment categorization has been accomplished. When compared to other classifiers used on the IMDB dataset [12], this model and method were shown to be the most efficient and accurate.

To this end, we propose employing contextualised BERT word embedding to efficiently encode the input sequence, followed by the temporal convolutional module, which merely determines 1-D convolutions to extract high-level features, and finally the max-Combining layer, which preserves the most crucial features for the classification of text. We test on six large-scale text classification datasets that are widely used for applications including sentiment analysis, issue classification, and topic classification. We suggest an efficient truncation approach as a workaround for BERT's inability to parse lengthy material. The experimental findings demonstrate the superiority of our suggested technique over its predecessors [13].

In today's data-driven world, innovative tools and algorithms are needed to glean insights from digital material. Sentiment analysis is used to gauge client demands, market trends, and public opinion. It is useful for expanding a company and figuring out what to make. While businesses use social media to communicate with their consumers, those customers' comments and ratings are used to enhance the offerings. Text processing is a natural application area for ML and DL models. Many problems in the field of text processing may be addressed by using deep learning techniques like convolutional neural networks and recurrent neural networks. Using a combining procedure, CNN can extract the relevant characteristics from the input text, but acquiring the necessary contextual information is more difficult. RNN can learn context, but it requires a new sequence of words each time. In this research, we look at how LSTM algorithms stack up against Convolution neural networks [14].

To examine the tone of product reviews posted online, we present a Multi-Mixed Convolutional Neural Network (MMCNN) model. To improve the efficacy of emotive analysis of online comments, we combine convolution as well as pool features in a mixed layer. The word vector is taught using a skip-gram approach. Since the size of each remark varies, two novel empirical matrix-filling methods—cyclic matrix filling and random matrix filling—have been developed to accommodate this. Our method is shown on two datasets: discussions regarding newborn power found on www.jd.com and hotel reviews sourced from www.elong.com. The experimental results show that our method is superior to Support Vector Machine, Maximum Entropy, or Naive Bayesian, and the traditional CNN [15].

## PROPOSED WORK

Existing studies did not take into account the fact that important words tend to have a higher impact and treated all phrases in the text equally throughout the training process. Based on the improvement of important phrases, we present a neural network based on the convolution text classification of emotions model. In order to increase the proposed model's sentiment classification accuracy, it first identifies pivotal sentences in the text followed by generating a text representation based on these pivotal phrases. The experimental findings demonstrate that the suggested model outperforms baseline standard text sentiment categorization algorithms in terms of accuracy.

## Preprocessing

The experiment's text data was preprocessed to make it more relevant. We ignored capitalization and did not utilise period and colon punctuation. Retweets (RT), tabs, multiple spaces, and stop words were also removed. The text representing an "http" url has been replaced with [URL], and the text representing a "@" id has been replaced with [NAME]. We also converted [NUM] to represent numbers and [SPE] to represent symbols. Since "not" plays a significant role in sentiment analysis, we revised "can't" and "isn't" to read "cannot" and "is not," respectively. We segmented the textual data spatially and built a new dictionary from the six-or-more-times-appearing terms. From the 38,195 words included within the MR data, a lexicon consisting of 9394 terms was created. Out of an overall 5356 words in CR data, 1415 were created, and out of a maximum of 16,870 words in SST information, 3548 were created. The new lexicon also has the padding character [PAD] and the unknown character [UNK] for when a word was needed. When using padding, any text that is less than the specified length is replaced with the [PAD] token. In this case, the greatest possible length of word in every data set served as the fixed length.

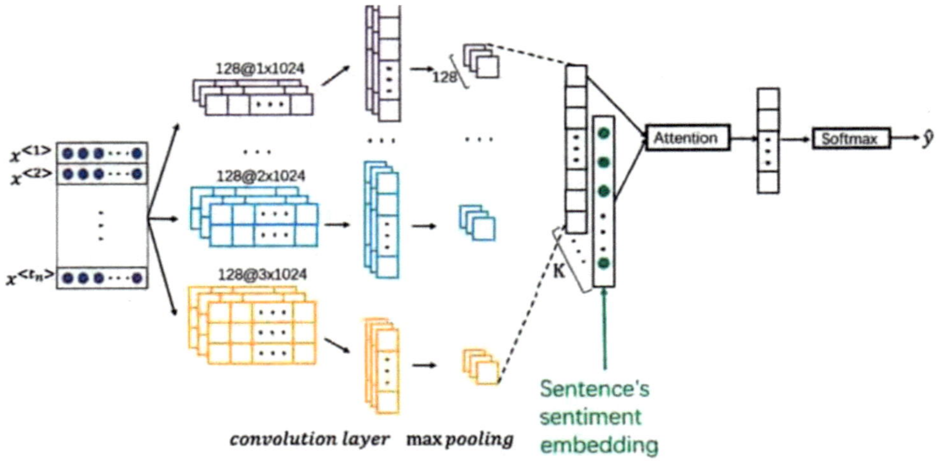


**Fig. (1).** CNN for text sentiment classification.

## CNN

The "convolutional" filter (*i.e.*, kernel) passes across a picture, extracting the important characteristics as it goes. CNN has seen extensive application on image datasets. The same purpose of CNN might be applied to text if the data being processed were presented in a single dimension. While the filter is being moved across the text, local information about the texts being processed is being kept and key characteristics are being extracted. Therefore, it is clear that CNN is a useful tool for text categorization. Fig. (**1**) below displays the CNN for Text Sentiment Classification.

### *Convolution Layer*

To each window in the input data, a convolution applies a linear layer (then a non-linearity). Let us pretend for the sake of argument:

- $(x_1, \ldots, x_n)$ - representations of the terms that were entered, $x_i \in \mathbb{R}^d$ ;
- $d$ (input channels) - input embedding size;
- $k$ (kernel size) - the size of a convolutional window (k=3 in the example);
- $m$ (output channels) - the overall number of convolution filtering (or the overall number of output channels).

So, a convolution is just another linear layer $W \in \mathbb{R}^{(k.d)x\ m}$ . For a $k$-sized window $(x_1, \ldots x_{i+k-1})$, This vector addition is what the convolution does.

$$u_i = [x_i, \ldots x_{i+k-1}] \in \mathbb{R}^{k \cdot d} \quad \textbf{(1)}$$

to which the convolution matrix is multiplied:

$$F_i = u_i \times W \quad \textbf{(2)}$$

In a convolution, the input is passed through a sliding window with each window receiving the identical linear change.

After m features have been collected from each window using a convolution, they are summed together by a Combining layer. In order to minimise the amount of network parameters, dimension reduction Combining layers are utilised.

### *Max Combining Layer*

Max-Combining is the most well-known method; it maximises the value of every characteristic across all dimensions. After performing a Combining process, we get a vector that indicates the frequency with which these input patterns occurred. Mean-Combining is functionally equivalent to maximum-Combining but instead calculates the mean across all features.

### *k-max Combining*

Similar to max-combining, but more broad, is k-max Combining. The method chooses k characteristics with the greatest amounts rather than a single maximum feature. Each characteristic remains in its proper place. Consider its use if the frequency with which a network discovers a certain pattern is crucial.

### *Combining and Global Combining*

Combining operates on windows containing multiple components in the same way as convolution does. The stride option is also available in Combining, and often, non-overlapping windows are used. To do this, the stride parameter must be equal to the size of the pool. Take a look at the example.

In contrast to global Combining, which operates on the whole input, Combining operates individually on the features in each window. Many text processing tasks need a global Combining step to get one vector containing the whole text; this kind of global Combining is known as max-over-time Combining, since the "time" axis runs from the initial input token to the last. Each feature "fires" intuitively when it recognises a pattern, either in the form of a visual pattern in the picture (such as a line or texture) or a text pattern (such as a phrase). The output of a Combining operation is a vector that indicates the frequency with which certain input patterns occurred. The picture depicts the fundamental convolutional example of text categorization. Please take note that we use global-over-time Joining after the convolution. This is the essential process since it permits the reduction of a text to a singular vector. Even though the model is unique, it must eventually employ global Combining to combine several input vectors into one. Multiple convolutions with varying kernel sizes may be used in place of a single convolution with a fixed kernel size. The method is straightforward: first, the data is convolved with each convolution, then, after each convolution, non-linearity and global Combining are applied, and last, the results are concatenated (for clarity, the example omits non-linearity). In this way, the data may be converted into a vector form useful for categorization.

## RESULTS AND DISCUSSION

The suggested CNN models, conventional machine-learning models, along with additional state-of-the-art models were tested on the three datasets (movie review data, client feedback data, and Stanford Sentiment Treebank data). In this analysis, text similarity was determined using the F-Measure. They are compared to other cutting-edge technologies now available so that the best network architecture may be chosen for certain datasets. Therefore, it better accommodates the requirements of various sentiment analysis applications. F-Measure is a well-rounded indicator in the field of information retrieval since it takes into account both accuracy and recollotion. The results of the experiments show whether or not each sentence is assigned to the proper cluster after clustering, and whether or not a given cluster includes a phrase from a certain cluster. As a result, knowing which category i every one j belongs to allows us to compute its Exactness P(i,j) &recollotion R(i,j). Clustering outcomes from CNN-based similarity computations were evaluated using independent measures of accuracy, recollotion, and F-Measure. Table **1** explains what each variable means.

**Table 1. Confusion matrix.**

| - | Optimistic | Undesirable |
|---|---|---|
| True | True Positive (TP) | True Negative (NP) |
| Flase | Flase Positive (FP) | Flase Negative (FN) |

True Positive (TP): Estimated sum of successful courses.
True Negative (TN): Class sizes anticipated to be negative.
False Positive (FP): Count of unfavourable courses deemed positive.
False Negative (FN): Class sizes anticipated to be negative.

Assume $n_i$ means the overall amount of class-i phrases, $n_j$reflects the overall amount of sentences, and $n_{ij}$ indicates the fraction of sentences in group j that are of type i. Here are the formulas for calculating Exactness P(i,j) & recollotion R(i,j).

The ratio of properly categorised positive classes to all positive classes is called recollotion R(i,j), while the ratio of correctly classified positive classes to all positive classes is called Exactness P(i,j). Table **2** provides a division formula based on this approach.

$$P(i,j) = \frac{TP}{TP+FP} = \frac{n_{ij}}{n_j}$$
$$R(i,j) = \frac{TP}{TP+FN} = \frac{n_{ij}}{n_i} \quad \textbf{(1)}$$

**Table 2. Principle division.**

| - | - | Clustering algorithm-derived categorizations | | |
|---|---|---|---|---|
| - | - | Yes | No | Overall amount |
| Actual | Yes | TP | FN | Classes predicted as positive. |
| classes | No | FP | TN | Classes predicted as negative. |
| - | Overall | Optimistic | Undesirable | - |
| - | Amount | courses | courses | - |

The following is a definition of the F-Measure:

$$F(i,j) = \frac{(\alpha^2+1)*TP}{\alpha^2*(2TP+FP+FN)} = \frac{2\times P(i,j)\times R(i,j)}{P(i,j)+R(i,j)} \quad (2)$$

Here, we define the F-measure for worldwide clustering.

$$F = \sum_i \frac{n_i}{n}\max(F(i,j)) \quad (3)$$

**Table 3. Evaluation of results.**

| Proposed CNN | | | | | |
|---|---|---|---|---|---|
| **Performance** | **SP** | **P** | **NT** | **N** | **SN** |
| Accurateness (%) | ~91.86 | ~92.03 | ~92.16 | ~91.78 | ~92.05 |
| Exactness (%) | ~93.14 | ~92.99 | ~92.87 | ~92.79 | ~93.46 |
| Recollotion(%) | ~92.66 | ~92.29 | ~92.18 | ~92.48 | ~92.89 |
| F-value (%) | ~91.38 | ~91.64 | ~91.73 | ~91.96 | ~91.58 |
| **CNN** | | | | | |
| **Performance** | **SP** | **P** | **NT** | **N** | **SN** |
| Accurateness (%) | ~88.86 | ~87.95 | ~88.23 | ~88.77 | ~88.18 |
| Exactness (%) | ~87.94 | ~88.39 | ~87.25 | ~89.03 | ~87.68 |
| Recollotion(%) | ~87.89 | ~88.54 | ~86.94 | ~88.32 | ~87.93 |
| F-value (%) | ~86.65 | ~86.83 | ~87.36 | ~86.97 | ~86.49 |
| **Bi-LSTM** | | | | | |
| **Performance** | **SP** | **P** | **NT** | **N** | **SN** |
| Accurateness (%) | ~87.59 | ~87.23 | ~86.98 | ~87.37 | ~87.08 |
| Exactness (%) | ~86.34 | ~86.92 | ~87.67 | ~87.29 | ~87.49 |
| Recollotion(%) | ~86.32 | ~87.55 | ~86.86 | ~87.16 | ~87.34 |
| F-value (%) | ~85.74 | ~85.98 | ~86.23 | ~85.34 | ~85.48 |
| **LSTM** | | | | | |
| **Presentation** | **SP** | **P** | **NT** | **N** | **SN** |
| Accurateness (%) | ~84.68 | ~83.99 | ~84.14 | ~84.29 | ~84.59 |
| Exactness (%) | ~83.65 | ~84.26 | ~84.69 | ~84.16 | ~83.83 |
| Recollection (%) | ~84.34 | ~83.72 | ~84.25 | ~84.09 | ~83.68 |
| F-value (%) | ~82.79 | ~83.14 | ~82.49 | ~82.56 | ~82.83 |

When compared to conventional machine models, our network achieved F1 scores that were nearly 10% higher. The CNN's built-in propensity to detect regional variations is a major factor, in our opinion. The CNN's convolutional and Combining layers allow it to detect both low-level details and global structures. In theory, more semantic information may be extracted from longer sentences. However, just a few of the models in the research had a particular rising tendency. People typically convey themselves through medium to short phrases, so when a sentence is too long, the data that should be expressed might get blurred instead. This may be why the analysis finds that long sentences do not accurately reflect the situation in actual speech expression. As a result, the percentage of correct responses decreases with increasing phrase length. It takes more time and effort to process a sentence of greater length. Table **3** is portrayed in Evaluation of results.

## CONCLUSION

Machine learning strategies have been widely used in several research projects to classify texts. While machine learning approaches have been extensively adopted and have shown promising performance, they rely heavily on characteristics that are specified by hand, which places a heavy burden on the shoulders of subject matter experts. Due to their potential to improve performance (such as accuracy) with less work put into feature development, deep learning approaches have lately garnered a lot of interest. In the present research, we developed a neural network made up of convolutional neurons for the purpose of identifying the emotional tone. To demonstrate the benefits of using successive convolutional layers for reasonably lengthy text, we conducted experiments. For binary classification, the suggested CNN models obtained about 81% accuracy, while for ternary classification, they achieved around 68% accuracy. In the future, we want to expand our work to additional types of categorization, such as gender identification. We will also be looking for enhanced models for sentiment categorization, including residual connection for nested layering.

## REFERENCES

[1] H.M. Zakir, and S.V. Jinny, "Rider Driven African Vulture Optimization with Multi Kernel Structured Text Convolutional Neural Network for Classifying e-Commerce Reviews", *Int. J. Adv. Comput. Sci. Appl.,* vol. 13, no. 7, 2022. [http://dx.doi.org/10.14569/IJACSA.2022.0130774]

[2] X. Huang, L. Qiao, W. Yu, J. Li, and Y. Ma, "End-to-End Sequence Labeling *via* Convolutional Recurrent Neural Network with a Connectionist Temporal Classification Layer", *International Journal of Computational Intelligence Systems,* vol. 13, no. 1, pp. 341-351, 2020. [http://dx.doi.org/10 2991/ijcis.d.200316.001]

[3] J. Chen, S. Yan, and K. Wong, "Verbal aggression detection on Twitter comments: convolutional neural network for short-text sentiment analysis", *Neural Comput Appl.,* pp. 1-10, 2018.

[4] A. Onan, "Sentiment Analysis in Turkish Based on Convolutional Neural Network Architectures", 2020.

[5] D. Kim, "Research On Text Classification Based On Deep Neural Network", *International Journal of Communication Networks and Information Security (IJCNIS),* vol. 14, no. 1s, pp. 100-113, 2022. [IJCNIS].
[http://dx.doi.org/10.17762/ijcnis.v14i1s.5618]

[6] S.P. Yadav, S. Zaidi, C.D.S. Nascimento, V.H.C. de Albuquerque, and S.S. Chauhan, "Analysis and Design of automatically generating for GPS Based Moving Object Tracking System", *2023 International Conference on Artificial Intelligence and Smart Communication (AISC),* pp. 1-5., 2023 .Greater Noida, India.
[http://dx.doi.org/10.1109/AISC56616.2023.10085180]

[7] M.R. Aldiansyah, and P.S. Sasongko, "Twitter Sentiment Analysis About Public Opinion on 4G Smartfren Network Services Using Convolutional Neural Network", *3rd International Conference on Informatics and Computational Sciences (ICICoS),* pp. 1-6, 2019.
[http://dx.doi.org/10.1109/ICICoS48119.2019.8982429]

[8] V. Vashisht, A.K. Pandey, and S.P. Yadav, "Speech Recognition using Machine Learning" In IEIE Transactions on Smart Processing & Computing", *The Institute of Electronics Engineers of Korea,* vol. 10, no. 3, pp. 233-239, 2021.
[http://dx.doi.org/10.5573/IEIESPC.2021.10.3.233]

[9] A. Oluwasanmi, S. Akeem, J. Jehoaida, M.U. Aftab, N.W. Hundera, B. Kumeda, E. Baagere, and Z. Qin, "Sequential Multi-Kernel Convolutional Recurrent Network for Sentiment Classification", *IEEE 10th International Conference on Software Engineering and Service Science (ICSESS),* 2019.

[10] R. Ranjan, and A. Daniel, "Proposed Hybrid model for Sentiment Classification using CovNet-DualLSTM Techniques", *ADCAIJ: Advances in Distributed Computing and Artificial Intelligence Journal,* 2022.
[http://dx.doi.org/10.14201/ADCAIJ202110401418]

# CHAPTER 23

# Classification & Clustering of Text Based on Doc2Vec & K-means Clustering based Similarity Measurements

**Prakriti Kapoor**[1,*]

[1] *Centre for Interdisciplinary Research in Business and Technology, Chitkara University Institute of Engineering and Technology, Chitkara University, Punjab, India*

**Abstract:** One crucial task in text processing is determining how similar two papers are to one another. A novel similarity metric is suggested in this study. Finding a suitable similarity metric for written materials that permits the development of coherent groupings is a significant difficulty for document clustering. After that, we use TFIDF to build a vector space, and then we use the ward's approach and the K-means algorithm to accomplish clustering. WordNet is additionally employed in the process of semantic document clustering. Visualisations and an interactive website illustrating the connections between all clusters illustrate the findings. The existence (and quantity) of words in texts are all that are taken into account while utilising the traditional bag-of-words paradigm. This process might lead to texts with identical meanings but distinct vocabulary being placed in various groups. The findings acquired using the suggested approach are analysed for their correctness using the F-measure. Comparisons using the sentence vectors model (Doc2vec) and the bag-of-words model are made to confirm the edge of the suggested strategy. The suggested methodology may be used to decipher web chat logs and client feedback posted online. We evaluate our method on a variety of real-world data sets including examples of text classification and clustering problems. The findings prove that the proposed measure outperforms competing strategies.

**Keywords:** Accuracy, Classifiers, Clustering algorithms, Document classification, Document clustering, Entropy.

## INTRODUCTION

The challenge of determining how similar two texts are is an important one in the field of text processing [1]. Similarity measurement for text processing (SMTP) is a technique proposed by Lin *et al.* [1] to make it easier to search for specific

* **Corresponding author Prakriti Kapoor:** Centre for Interdisciplinary Research in Business and Technology, Chitkara University Institute of Engineering and Technology, Chitkara University, Punjab, India;
E-mail: prakriti.kapoor.orp@chitkara.edu.in

**Pankaj Kumar Mishra and Satya Prakash Yadav (Eds.)**

information across text collections. The suggested metric took into account all three possible comparisons of document pairings in terms of similarity [2, 3]. Each of these scenarios is based on whether or not a certain characteristic appears in either of the two texts [4]. In the first scenario, elements from both sources are considered; in the second scenario, elements from just one source are considered; and in the third scenario, elements from neither source are considered [5]. As knowledge and information technology advanced in many different areas, so did the number of scholarly articles published in those areas [6]. Therefore, researchers spend a considerable amount of effort trying to track relevant study publications [7]. As a result, this work proposes a documents classification strategy capable of categorising research paper texts into meaningful groups based on the subjects they cover [8]. Arabic Organising vast quantities of data into just a handful of specified clusters, as carried out in text document clustering [9], enables conjectural navigation and browsing tools to be made available. However, the vector representation of words often utilised in clustering algorithms is not ideal since it fails to take into account the interdependencies between different concepts. For the sake of better comprehension or summarization, data may be clustered using cluster analysis. Statistics, data mining, recognising patterns, and other disciplines have all contributed to the evolution of clustering methods [10]. Clustering was traditionally performed using a syntactic rather than a semantic idea, and relied on statistical characteristics. Traditional document clustering methods employ single, unique, or complex words from the collection of texts as characteristics. Traditional methods, however, overlook semantic relations. Due to issues with polysemy and synonymy in the conventional approach, a collection of unique words cannot accurately represent the document's intended meaning and cannot produce useful clusters. Grouping data points that are semantically related is what semantic clustering is all about. In this context, "clustering" refers to the process of partitioning a data collection into distinct groups, whereby items belonging to the same cluster have the same meaning. On the other hand, you would not find a match between two products from distinct groups. By highlighting differences in meaning, papers that are not relevant may be eliminated thanks to semantic clustering. Numerous critical procedures (description of each file as a phrase, vectoring of every record to be placed in a mathematical structure, and ultimately the application of clustering algorithms for clustering objectives) are required for semantically analogous clustering of content assets. The study's principal objective, to use Ward's method for semantic document clustering, is met. We are unaware of any previous study that used a combination of the Ward's method and semantic similarity document clustering.

## RELATED WORK

A novel similarity metric is suggested in this study. The suggested measure considers the following three scenarios when calculating the degree of similarity between two texts with regard to a feature: a) It is present in both papers, b) it is present in just one document, and c) it is absent from both. In the first scenario, closeness improves as the distance between the two feature values becomes less. In addition, the difference's normal contribution is typically scaled. In the second scenario, a constant is added to the similarity. In the third scenario, the characteristic makes no difference in the degree of similarity. The suggested metric is refined such that it may be used to compare collections of documents. Various real-world data sources for text categorization and grouping issues are used to assess the efficacy of our approach. The results demonstrate that the suggested metric yields superior performance compared to other approaches [11].

Despite the fact that the proposed solution measure of similarity was thought to be ideal for finding similarity between written materials based on the presence or lack of features available in text documents, it was discovered that the SMTP similarity measure did not cover the context of measuring the parallel among the pair of analogous paperwork. In view of this discrepancy, this study proposes a modest adjustment to the SMTP in order to bring it into conformity with other common similarity approaches and make it a comprehensive similarity measurement methodology for knowledge discovery [12].

In this study, we provide a measure of the degree to which two clusterings of the same dataset produced by different algorithms (or maybe the same algorithmic rule) are comparable. Calculating the degree of similarity between two papers is an important task in the study of text processing. The authors of this study hypothesised a successor similarity index. When determining the degree of similarity between two publications that have the same feature importance, the suggested metric takes into account the following three cases. Select "a" if the feature is present in every one of the papers, "b" if it is present in some but not all, & "c" if it is absent in all of the papers. In the first case, the similarity will increase as the difference between the feature values decreases. The significance of the difference is also often assessed. In the second case, the similarity is given a predetermined numerical value. In the third case, there is no correlation between the feature and the level of similarity. Numerous practical expertise sets for text categorization and group problems are used to assess the efficacy [13].

Since each of these groups encompasses a wide range of issues, our proposed method is based on their core focus and scopes. Accordingly, we segregate the extraction of category-specific word symbols from these discussions. Using the term frequency-inverse document frequency (TF-IDF) statistic, we may determine how much emphasis should be placed on documents based on the frequency with which certain word tokens appear within them. The suggested method employs the paper's title, abstract, keywords, and themes in addition to performing the categorization procedure. Then, using the greatest cosine similarity metric among category weight and document weights, documents are grouped into the key categories [14].

In order to solve the issue of developing an ensemble-oriented classifier for Arabic text sources, this study presents three methods: unsupervised methods, semi-supervised methods, and semi-supervised methods with dimension reduction. After deleting stop words and locating the root for each phrase in each text, we use k-means, progressing k-means, Criterion + k-means, and k-means with decreasing dimensionality. Then, we calculate the importance of each phrase in relation to its corresponding document using a term weighting technique. Following this, we compare each document's similarities to those of other documents using a similarity measure technique. Also, the accuracy is being calculated with the help of F-measure, entropy, and a support vector machine (SVM). The datasets are online, dynamic datasets that may be trusted since they are easily accessible online. When used in an inference-based system, the Arabic language presents unique difficulties. So, picking the right dataset is crucial for studies like this. When applied to fresh categorization test cases, the suggested techniques demonstrate higher accuracy and fewer mistakes than other approaches. When increasing the ratio of reduction, crucial words might be lost, making the dimension reduction procedure delicate.

## PROPOSED WORK

### Data Preparing

The pre-processing document explains how to create an index word list and other prerequisites for adding a new document to a system for retrieving information. The purpose of content pre-processing is to enhance document the retrieval and storage inside the system by characterising the documents in the best possible manner. The following procedures may be found in the pre-processing document:

- Tokenization.
- Take Out All The Periods & Zeroes.
- Take Out the Filler Words.
- Lemmatization & Stemming.

## Document Demonstration

Document representation is an important technique in document processing and information retrieval systems. In order to find relevant documents in a big corpus, it is crucial to convert the full-text versions of the papers into a form vector. If the translated document has a component known as a terms index, it may be used to demonstrate certain aspects of the source material. These terms are utilised in indexing, related keyword rankings, filtering, and retrieval to improve search results. The prevalent algebraic approach, sometimes known as the vector model, uses vectors to represent texts. The Term Frequency (TF), an Inverse Document Frequency (IDF), and the TF-IDF weighting scheme are all vector-space models that are used to show documents.

Before extracting samples through a sliding window across the phrase, the model locks the context length to a constant value. It is important to keep in mind that the derived phrase vector only pertains to circumstances involving this particular phrase, and no other sentences. It is possible to expand the scope of the vector of language W beyond any one phrase and consider the whole text. When testing sentence vector models, the sentence vector represents an image of the text. When generating a sentence vector using the Doc2vec model, it is conceivable that similarities for 2 identical sentences are not 1. Fig. (**1**) shows the Doc2vec model.

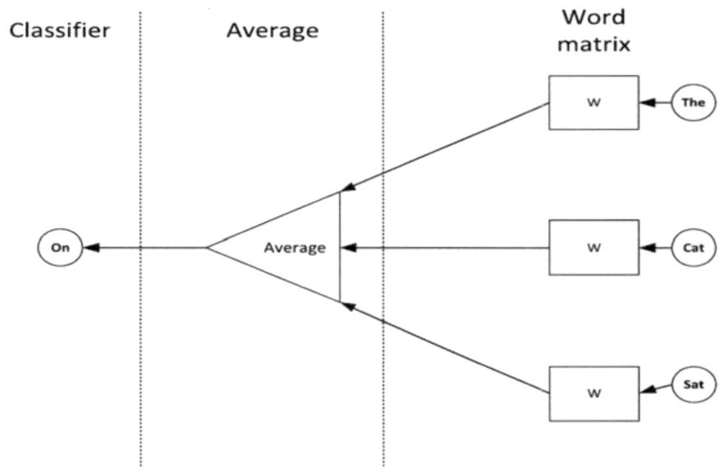


**Fig. (1).** Doc2vec model.

Maximum average logarithmic probability maximisation formula.

$$\frac{1}{T}\sum_{t=k}^{T-k} \log p(w_{t-k}, \cdots, w_{t+k}) \tag{1}$$

Multiple classifiers (like softmax) are used to make predictions.

$$p(w_t \mid w_{t-k}, \cdots, w_{t+k}) = \frac{e^{y_{w_t}}}{\sum_i e^{y_i}} \tag{2}$$

Here, $y_i$, where b stands for the softmax parameters, h stands for the pseudo-normalized logarithmic probability of each outcome of word vector i, & x is the median value of a term vector in matrix W.

$$y = b + Uh(w_{t-k}, \cdots, w_{t+k}; W) \tag{3}$$

These criteria are used to determine the model's parameters: Document to Vector Conversion (words, 10x10 window, 1 minimum number of workers, 0.002 alpha).

According to the bag-of-words concept, every given set of words may be used to convey any given set of sentences. The One-hot Representation is used to convert each word in the word bag model into a vector with a length equal to the amount of vocabulary. The term frequency (tf) of a word is its occurrence count in the target phrase, as calculated by the bag-of-words model. The inverted document frequency (idf) is calculated as follows:

$$idf_i = \log_2 \frac{|D|}{|\{j : t_i \in d_j\}|} \tag{4}$$

Here, $|D|$ is the sum of all texts included in a corpus, where $|\{j{:}t_l \in d_j\}|$ stands for the overall amount of documents that include $t_i$. The IF-IDF Value is determined as follows.

$$tfidf_{i,j} = tf_{i,j} \times idf_i \tag{5}$$

For a standard TF-IDF calculation, please refer to the following.

$$tfidf'_{i,j} = \frac{tfidf_{i,j}}{\sqrt{\sum_{j=1}^{|d_j|} (tfidf_{i,j})^2}} \quad (6)$$

The degree of textual similarity is calculated using the cosine similarity.

$$\text{similarity} = \cos(\theta) = \frac{A \cdot B}{\|A\|\|B\|} = \frac{\sum_{i=1}^{n} (A_i \times B_i)}{\sqrt{\sum_{i=1}^{n} (A_i)^2} \times \sqrt{\sum_{i=1}^{n} (B_i)^2}} \quad (7)$$

Here, $A_i$ & $B_i$ signify i in both Text A and Text B.

## Document Clustering

Clustering is the process of organising a collection of items into groups of resemblance. Each collection is sometimes referred to as a partitioned object cluster. The segmentation is carried out *via* clustering methods. In this way, clustering is useful since it increases the likelihood of discovering previously unrecognised groupings within identical data. Cluster analysis is an essential tool for understanding large data sets. Some clustering methods provide a fuzzy set of boundaries between groups of items, while others divide them up into distinct categories. In addition, distance is used as a similarity criteria by certain techniques.

Partitioning, hierarchical, grid-based, and density-based clustering algorithms are the four main categories that define this class of data analysis techniques. In this paper, we use two distinct clustering techniques:

Fig. (**2**) . represents the Cluster Formation. Regular K-means is an algorithm for clustering data based on how closely its input samples resemble the cluster centres. Second, the cluster's principal nodes are picked at random. The remaining samples are then distributed among the clusters for which they are a best match. Once clustering is complete for a given data sample, the centres of the clusters are adjusted to reflect the weighted average of all the components inside that cluster. Repeated centre update and clustering occur until no more movement occurs at the cluster centres. Choosing the right starting centre is crucial to the success of the k-means approach. The procedures are as follows:

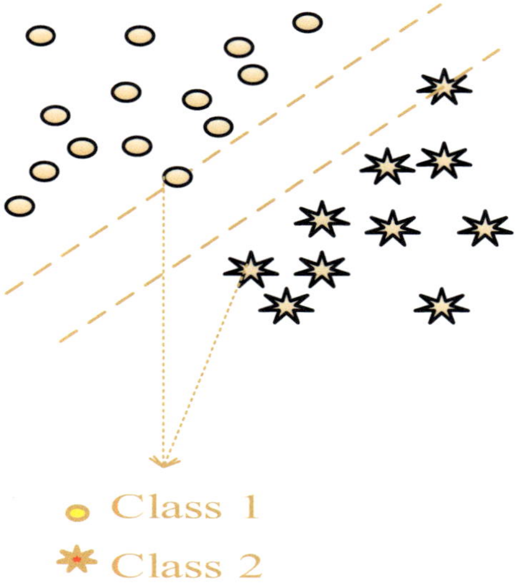


**Fig. (2).** Clusters formation.

- Initial cluster identification yields k clusters.
- Selecting nodes in a cluster.
- In each step, the element is located in the cluster centre that is closest to it using a Euclidean distance function.
- Find a new average or centre for all clusters.
- Steps 2 to 4 should be repeated until cluster centres remain stable.

Assume for the moment that we have two papers, doc1 and doc2. Let doc 1 = ($w_{11}$, $w_{12}$, ... ) & doc 2 = ($w_{21}$, $w_{22}$, ... ) weighted vectors for the terms in Document 1 and Terms in Document 2 in the BoW model. Let $T_1\{t_{11}, t_{12},...t_{1n}\}$ & $T_2\{t_{21}, t_{22},...t_{2n}\}$ be the sets of objects covered by both documents. For your reference, the proposed equations are provided below:

$$\begin{aligned} X &= \left(\sum\nolimits_{t\in doc_1\cap c_2} W_{1j}\right) * \left(\sum\nolimits_{t\in doc_1\cap doc_2} W_{2j}\right) \\ Y &= \left(\sum\nolimits_{t\in doc_1\backslash doc_2} W_{1j}\right) * \left(\sum\nolimits_{t\in doc\backslash doc} W_{2j}\right) \\ Z &= \left(\sum\nolimits_{t\in doc_1} W_{1j}\right) * \left(\sum\nolimits_{t\in doc_2} W_{2j}\right) \\ \mathrm{STB-SM}\left(d_{oc_1}, doc_2\right) &= \frac{X}{Z} * \left(1 - \frac{Y}{Z}\right) \end{aligned} \tag{8}$$

Here the notations "∩" & "\" are set-theoretic operators denoting intersection and complement, and $w_{ij}$ is the allowance worth.

The gap between two phrases measured by their word vector $D_{ij}$ is computed, and a unique identifier is assigned to every word in the phrase. Then, a two-dimensional coordinate plane is constructed using the relationship in distance among the words in the two sentences.

It is possible to normalise the relationship distance of the term vector between the phrases and use this as a measure of how similar the sentences are to one another. Here, min(WMD) and max(WMD) show the smallest and the largest word vector velocities and correspondences in the data set, respectively.

$$\text{similarity}(S_A, S_B) = 1 - \frac{\text{WMD}(S_A,S_B) - \min(WMD)}{\max(\text{WMD}) - \min(\text{WMD})} \quad \textbf{(9)}$$

Calculating similarity K and setting the evaluation and weight function.

$$\begin{aligned} f_{ij} &= \frac{1}{(|i-j|+1)^2} \\ g_{ij} &= \frac{f_{ij}}{\sum_{i=1}^{m} \sum_{j=1}^{n} f_{ij}} \\ K &= \sum_{i=1}^{m} \sum_{j=1}^{n} S_{ij} \cdot g_{ij} \end{aligned} \quad \textbf{(10)}$$

The Doc2vec technique predicts vectors to symbolise various documents using unsupervised learning. In the phrase vector model, the pattern of distribution for each word is replaced with a distributed representation. By connecting these word vectors with the phrase's vector, we can predict the likelihood value of the following word in the sentence. To train the text's sentence and word vectors, the stochastic gradient descend technique is used. Each gradient is supposedly accessible through backpropagation using this approach. At each iteration of the random gradient descent procedure, we retrieve a fixed-length context from the training data, compute the network's gradient deviation, and revise the model's parameters. In the end, the sine relationship formula is used to determine how similar two texts are.

Each data point is assigned to a centrally located category that best fits its characteristics. Cosine distance is used in this case. Two things' degree of similarity is calculated using the cosine distance (the angle between two vectors). With a small enough angle, the vectors' directions are almost identical, and the two spots are grouped together. The sine value is closest to 1 when the angle in question is near to 0. Therefore, the distances between samples are calculated using the reciprocal cosine measure. Then, we add up the distances from each point in each cluster to the cluster's centre.

$$\begin{aligned} d &= 1/\frac{(a_1b_1+a_2b_2+\cdots+a_nb_n)}{\sqrt{a_1^2+a_2^2+\cdots+a_n^2}\sqrt{b_1^2+b_2^2+\cdots+b_n^2}} \\ \text{Lable}_i &= \text{arg\_min}\|U_i - X_j\| \\ \text{Sum} &= \sum_{i=1}^{i}\sum_{j=1}^{j}\frac{1}{|\text{Lable}_i|}\cdot d_j \end{aligned} \quad (11)$$

Step (3): This is to be done FOR i=1 TO K.

Clustering centres are determined by averaging the values of all the RDD text vectors belonging to a certain category $\bar{U}_1 \sim \bar{U}_k$ are updated.

Step (4): Determine the convergeDist function used as a clustering criterion: $R = \sum_{i=1}^{k}|\bar{U}_i - X_i|^2$

Step (5): Until $\overset{i=1}{R}$ does not evolve much, or we have tried all the possible permutations.

## RESULTS AND DISCUSSION

With the selection of benchmark datasets common in studies of document clustering, the proposed algorithmic method was evaluated against a set of widely-used, established algorithms. In this research, we use the K-means clustering technique with Ward's method. Python, a computer language, is used to carry them out. Computers with Intel Core i3 2350M processors running at 2.3 GHz, 250 GB hard drives, and 4 GB of RAM are used for the test. A total of 400 documents from the WEBKB dataset are taken into account for this initial test case, 100 from each for the four classes. As a result, this is an example of a class-balanced dataset. Word pattern grouping (also referred to as feature pattern clustering) and similarity measure proposals are taken into account in experimental setups. In this experiment, we investigate 400 text documents from the WEBKB dataset and use the presented feature similarity algorithm to reduce the number of features being used. The first preprocessing resulted in a global feature vector of 537 elements. Data of 400 documents s kept in a 400-by-537-row matrix of document-word pairs. This means that the dimension of the original collection of documents is 5373, Table **1** is portrayed in Analysing and Comparing Performance Indice.

**Table 1. Analysing and Comparing Performance Indices.**

| Database | Technique | Accurateness | Exactness | Recollection | F1 Value |
|---|---|---|---|---|---|
| WEBKB | K-means – Doc2Vec + TF-IDF | 94.18 | 94.18 | 94.18 | 94.01 |
| | Cosine | 88.34 | 88.16 | 88.22 | 88.14 |
| | Cosine+TF-IDF | 85.02 | 84.19 | 84.19 | 84.06 |
| | Agglomerative Clustering | 85.01 | 85.02 | 85.01 | 84.92 |
| | Cosine + Kmeans | 87.23 | 87.21 | 87.22 | 87.21 |

## CONCLUSION

A novel similarity metric is suggested in this study. Finding a suitable similarity metric for written materials that permits the development of coherent groupings is a significant difficulty for document clustering. After that, we use TFIDF to build a vector space, and then we use the ward's approach and the K-means algorithm to accomplish clustering. WordNet is additionally employed in the process of semantic document clustering. Visualisations and an interactive website illustrating the connections between all clusters illustrate the findings. The existence and frequency) of language in texts are taken into account based on the traditional bag-of-words paradigm. This process might lead to texts with identical meanings but distinct vocabulary being placed in various groups. The findings acquired using the suggested approach are analysed for their correctness using the F-measure. Comparisons with the phrase vector model (Doc2vec) as well as the bag-of-words model are used to confirm the superiority of the suggested strategy. The suggested methodology may be used to decipher web chat logs and client feedback posted online. Extending the current study will allow for the development of novel similarity functions that may be used in text document clustering and text classification tasks, leading to higher-quality clusters and more accurate classifiers. Research on developing kernel-based similarity metrics for use in text clustering and classification also has a lot of scope.

## REFERENCES

[1] H.I. Abdalla, and A.A. Amer, "Boolean logic algebra driven similarity measure for text based applications", *PeerJ Comput. Sci.*, vol. 7, p. e641, 2021. [http://dx.doi.org/10.7717/peerj-cs.641] [PMID: 34401474]

[2] S. P. Yadav, B. S. Bhati, D. P. Mahato, and S. Kumar, "Federated Learning for IoT Applications", *EAI/Springer Innovations in Communication and Computing. Springer International Publishing,* 2022. [http://dx.doi.org/10.1007/978-3-030-85559-8]

[3] A. Al-Subaihin, F. Sarro, S. Black, and L. Capra, "Empirical comparison of text-based mobile apps similarity measurement techniques", *Empir. Softw. Eng.,* vol. 24, no. 6, pp. 3290-3315, 2019. [http://dx.doi.org/10.1007/s10664-019-09726-5]

[4] A. Abo-Elghit, A.M. Al-Zoghby, and T.T. Hamza, *Textual Similarity Measurement Approaches: A*

*Survey. The Egyptian Journal of Language Engineering,* 2020.

[5] A. Castro-Insua, C. Gómez-Rodríguez, and A. Baselga, "Dissimilarity measures affected by richness differences yield biased delimitations of biogeographic realms", *Nat. Commun.,* vol. 9, no. 1, p. 5084, 2018.
[http://dx.doi.org/10.1038/s41467-018-06291-1] [PMID: 30504812]

[6] V. Vashisht, A.K. Pandey, and S.P. Yadav, "Speech Recognition using Machine Learning", *IEIE Transactions on Smart Processing & Computing,* vol. 10, The Institute of Electronics Engineers of Korea, no. 3, pp. 233-239, 2021.
[http://dx.doi.org/10.5573/IEIESPC.2021.10.3.233]

[7] G. SureshReddy, T. V. Rajinikanth, and A. A. Rao, "Design and analysis of a novel similarity measure for clustering and classification of high-dimensional text documents", In: *Proceedings of the 15th International Conference on Computer Systems and Technologies (CompSysTech)* Ruse, Bulgaria, Jun. 2014, pp. 271-277.
[http://dx.doi.org/10.1145/2659532.2659601]

[8] N. Alnajran, K. A. Crockett, D. Mclean, and A. Latham, "A Heuristic-Based Pre-processing Methodology for Short Text Similarity Measures in Microblogs", In: *2018 IEEE 20th International Conference on High Performance Computing and Communications; IEEE 16th International Conference on Smart City; IEEE 4th International Conference on Data Science and Systems (HPCC/SmartCity/DSS)* Exeter, UK, 2018, pp. 1627-1633.
[http://dx.doi.org/10.1109/HPCC/SmartCity/DSS.2018.00265]

[9] F. Al-Turjman, S.P. Yadav, M. Kumar, V. Yadav, and T. Stephan, *Transforming Management with AI, Big-Data, and IoT.* Springer International Publishing, 2022.
[http://dx.doi.org/10.1007/978-3-030-86749-2]

[10] Y.S. Lin, J.Y. Jiang, and S.J. Lee, "A Similarity Measure for Text Classification and Clustering", *IEEE Trans. Knowl. Data Eng.,* vol. 26, no. 7, pp. 1575-1590, 2014.
[http://dx.doi.org/10.1109/TKDE.2013.19]

[11] N. Kumar Nagwani, "A Comment on A Similarity Measure for Text Classification and Clustering", *IEEE Trans. Knowl. Data Eng.,* vol. 27, no. 9, pp. 2589-2590, 2015.
[http://dx.doi.org/10.1109/TKDE.2015.2451616]

[12] P. Elango, "A Similarity Measure for Text Classification and Clustering", In: *Proceedings of the International Conference on Advances in Computing, Communications and Informatics (ICACCI)* Kochi, India, Aug. 2015, pp. 1121-1126.
[http://dx.doi.org/10.1109/ICACCI.2015.7275757]

[13] A.A. Jalal, and B.H. Ali, "Text documents clustering using data mining techniques", *Int. J. Electr. Comput. Eng. (IJECE),* vol. 11, no. 1, pp. 312-320, 2021.
[http://dx.doi.org/10.11591/ijece.v11i1.10876]

[14] A.K. Sangaiah, A.E. Fakhry, M. Abdel-Basset, and I. El-henawy, "Arabic text clustering using improved clustering algorithms with dimensionality reduction", *Cluster Comput.,* vol. 22, no. S2, pp. 4535-4549, 2019.
[http://dx.doi.org/10.1007/s10586-018-2084-4]

**CHAPTER 24**

# Categorization of COVID-19 Twitter Data Based on an Aspect-Oriented Sentiment Analysis and Fuzzy Logic

**Tarang Bhatnagar**[1,*]

[1] *Centre for Interdisciplinary Research in Business and Technology, Chitkara University Institute of Engineering and Technology, Chitkara University, Punjab, India*

**Abstract:** During times of disaster or epidemic, social media has emerged as a vital means of communication. It is difficult to examine the complete situational awareness *via* many elements and emotions to aid authorities due to the unpredictability of these calamities. Currently, systems for aspect recognition and sentiment analysis rely heavily on labelled data and require human curation of aspect categories. To analyze public opinion from a variety of angles, this study suggested a hybrid text analytical approach. Using the popular Latent Dirichlet Allocation (LDA) topic modeling, we first extracted and clustered the elements from the data. We then used the linguistic inquiry and word count (LIWC) lexicon to extract the sentiments and label the dataset. Finally, in the third layer of our structure, we mapped the elements into emotions, and the sentiments were classified using well-known machine learning classifiers. The comparison of our technique with other aspect-oriented sentiment analysis approaches shows encouraging results in experiments with actual datasets, and our method with several variants of classifiers surpasses current methods with top F1 scores of 91%.

**Keywords:** Aspect-oriented sentiment analysis, COVID-19 classification, Fuzzy logic, Twitter dataset.

## INTRODUCTION

During times of disaster or epidemic, social media has emerged as a vital means of communication. Since the causes of these calamities are often unclear, it is difficult to examine the issue from all angles and gauge public opinion to help authorities [1]. The human labeling and categorization of aspects are major weaknesses in the current aspect detection and sentiment analysis method [2]. The information individuals create on various websites reflects their feelings about a wide range of topics, from the cuisine they eat on a daily basis to the items they

* **Corresponding author Tarang Bhatnagar:** Centre for Interdisciplinary Research in Business and Technology, Chitkara University Institute of Engineering and Technology, Chitkara University, Punjab, India; E-mail: tarang.bhatnagar.orp@chitkara.edu.in

try. We may learn a lot about a product or service from the feedback and opinions of consumers [3] amid the widespread use of social networks and micro-blogs, especially during the COVID-19 epidemic. As a result, it can be time-consuming and challenging to go through all the evaluations and analyze them to get a review of the overall quality before making a choice [4]. Sentiment analysis has been utilized as a quick and automated technique to assess customer opinion to get around this problem [5]. Large reviews may include both positive and negative commentary on several aspects of a product or service. Purpose. The purpose of this article is to categorize the opinions expressed in online traveler and guest reviews by factor [6]. Based on a neural network model, a novel approach to aspect-oriented sentiment categorization is given. Large amounts of commercially valuable commentary data have been created by Internet users sharing their thoughts and experiences with widely used products and services [7]. Many remark phrases include many comment components, each with a different tone, rendering the sentence worthless for polarization [8]. The goal of sentiment categorization at the aspect level is to identify context-specific sensory extremity in the target. As the field of Deep Learning develops, it has become increasingly fashionable to use these techniques for emotion detection [9]. The COVID-19 epidemic has resulted in profound changes to every facet of human existence. All citizens were affected by the government's regulations in this area. As a result, anticipating the effects of future pandemics requires researching public opinion [10].

The purpose of this research is to catalog the sentiments and discussions around COVID-19 on Twitter. We investigate 1) how to automatically recognize people's attitudes stated on Twitter because of COVID-19, and 2) what themes are most discussed by Twitter users when expressing sentiments regarding COVID-19? We offer an exploratory analysis of the data set, as well as topic discovery and sentiment identification using natural language processing (NLP), to provide insight into these concerns. From February 2020 to March 2020, we used the Twitter API to gather streaming data, and using sentiment analysis, we classified the tweets we collected into three groups: positive, negative, and neutral. To ensure that there is a roughly equal quantity of tweets in each class, we give a sentiment analysis of COVID-19-related tweets. The data collection is utilized to train and test several algorithmic models, which in turn serve as benchmarks for identifying Twitter sentiment about potential COVID-19 therapies. The best-performing model is chosen for further optimization and dissemination once a final verification study has been conducted. We conclude that future study has to do a better job of taking context and the diversity of opinion on COVID-19 therapies into account. The following are some of the main results of this study.

- COVID Senti, a huge, manually annotated data collection of 90,000 tweets analysed in February and March of 2020, was created. Three smaller data sets of the same size make up the whole. Each tweet is assigned a label indicating whether it is favorable, negative, or neutral. The data sets can be accessed by anybody in the scientific community.
- A display of the methods by which public opinions on Coronavirus were tracked, includes the application of sentiment analysis on Twitter data to construct a classifier and the creation of a visualization of textual data. In addition, a qualitative analysis is provided in the form of a word cloud including the most frequently used terms.

We identify themes that are indicative of popular anxiety regarding COVID-19 and present and analyze this prevailing discourse. The results of this research might be used by governments all around the world to better prepare for public health emergencies.

- Results from a benchmarking study comparing the performance of various state-of-the-art ML text categorization techniques are described.

Here's how the rest of the article is laid out. The relevant research is presented in Section 2. The approach that is proposed in this article is discussed in Section 3. In Section 4, we describe the findings, and in Section 5, we draw the necessary conclusions.

## RELATED WORK

In this study, we developed a mixed-method text analytical framework for dissecting public opinion at the level of individual aspects. Using the popular Latent Dirichlet Allocation (LDA) topic modeling, we initially extracted and clustered the aspects from the data. We subsequently utilized the linguistic inquiry and word count (LIWC) lexicon to extract the feelings and label the dataset. Finally, in the third layer of our framework, we mapped the aspects into feelings, and the sentiments were classified using well-known machine learning classifiers. The comparison of our technique with other aspect-oriented sentiment analysis approaches shows encouraging results in experiments with actual datasets, and our method with several variants of classifiers surpasses current methods with top F1 scores of 91%.

In this research, we offer a novel approach to sentiment classification that integrates automated labeling (SentiWordNet), an ensemble technique (Stacking), and the prior knowledge topic model algorithm (SA-LDA). Datasets from various fields are used to assess the framework. According to the findings, the suggested

SA-LDA is an improvement above the gold-standard LDA. When compared to standard classification methods, the accuracy of the proposed ensemble learning classifier is significantly higher than 3%. The research found that the proposed method is flexible enough to be used in a variety of settings.

The design methodology includes an integrated four-layer neural network consisting of the bidirectional encoder illustration from transformers (BERT) word vector model, long short-term memory, an interactive attention-over attention (IAOA) mechanism, and a linear output layer that is used to build an aspect-oriented sentiment classification model in this research. The model was developed, tested, and verified using 92,905 hypothetical diner ratings from Tokyo. Findings. When compared to previous neural networks, the model has dramatically improved performance. The results provide credence to the viability of this novel strategy in the travel and hotel industries. Constraints/implications for future studies' innovative elements that can be automatically introduced into the aspect set to give dynamic support for novel eating experiences are advocated, as well as the identification of more feelings to assess more granular parts of the tourism-hospitality experience. Originality/value-updated research on how a neural network may be used to boost aspect-oriented sentiment categorization for tourism-hospitality online reviews is presented in this article.

Combining a convolutional neural network with a bidirectional gated recurrent unit is presented as a model for sentiment categorization. Long short-term memory, a time-cyclic neural network with less processing complexity, is analogous to the bi-directional gated recurrent unit. The model uses a bidirectional gated recurrent unit to extract sequence properties of the text, followed by a convolutional neural network to extract local static aspects of the text. When everything else fails, the Sigmoid classifier is employed to determine how someone feels.

We suggested an NLP (Natural Language Processing) model to evaluate Persian open-text survey responses and identify positive and negative sentiments among Iranians as a means of contributing to this goal. To accomplish this goal, the distilBert transformer model was utilized in this research. Three methods were used for the comparison, with the best model showing improvement. F1 score = 0.804; Precision = 0.824; Recall = 0.798; Overall = 0.824.

## PROPOSED WORK

Fig. (**2**) depicts a high-level perspective of our proposed framework, and the following sections elaborate on its many parts.

## Data Mining of Tweets

Ninety thousand unique tweets are included from 70,000 individuals out of 2.1 million tweets analysed in February and March of 2020. Twelve categories, including "quarantine," "lockdown," and "stay home," emerged from our research. COVIDSENTI was split into three equal halves, with each part including either positive, negative, or neutral sentiment data. Tweepy, a Python package for accessing the Twitter API, version 3.2, was used to obtain the tweet data collection.

### *Preprocessing and Labeling*

We used predetermined rules to assign a positive, negative, or neutral sentiment label to each tweet in the dataset. Emotional labels of "positive," "negative," and "neutral" were generated using the TextBlob program. TextBlob claims that its score, expressed as a polarity from [-1 to 1], may be used to infer a sentence's tone. A tweet is considered negative if its polarity is less than -0.4. When it is larger than 0.4, the tweet is regarded favorably. A tweet with a polarity of 0 is considered neutral. Algorithm 1 provides pseudocodes for classifying and analyzing the tone of tweets.

$$L_{T_i} = \begin{cases} \text{Negative}, & P < -0.4 \\ \text{Positive}, & P > 0.4 \\ \text{Neutral}, & -0.4 \geq P \leq 0.4 \end{cases} \quad (1)$$

where $P_i$ is the polarity of tweet $T_i$ and $-1 < P < 1$.

- Since raw tweets are typically brief, informal, and noisy, preprocessing the data is the initial stage in sentiment analysis. In order to achieve this goal, the following sequence of methods is applied to the text in the order specified.
- Hashtags, such as #COVID-19, #StayHome, #StaySafe, and #Coronavirus, are used to represent subjects on nearly all social media platforms. Hashtags are distracting and often pointless, and they might even hurt your performance. As a first step, we did simple text cleaning by excluding unused hashtags (albeit only the character, not the actual content).
- After that, you will want to case-fold the text. All uppercase letters are lowered to lowercase so that the same term is not mistaken for a different one based on capitalization.
- Some terms, such as "stayathomestaysafe" and "coronavirus," which are part of longer phrases, are incorrectly concatenated. The correct forms of these phrases are "stay home, stay safe" and "coronavirus," respectively. Therefore, we use a process called word segmentation to get there.

- The elimination of stop words is a common practice for cleaning up textual material. The valence of a phrase can be understood even without the stop words. Stop words (frequently occurring words in a document with limited semantic meaning, such as “for,” “the,” and “is”) were eliminated for all tasks except sentiment analysis.
- The lemmatization procedure, step five, reverses the morphological analysis of words and puts them back into their dictionary form. We lemmatized words using the nltk-provided approach (converting various word forms to their bare-bones root form, for as “viruses” to “virus” or “went” to “go”).
- Before any links, @mentions, or punctuation were removed from the analyzed text, a textual data cleanse was performed. Since they contribute nothing to the sentiment analysis process, we clean the data set of symbols, punctuation, and numerals.

## Text Classification

The proposed model takes as inputs the seven characteristics retrieved and specified in Section 2, including the amount of words in a tweet. Fuzzification is a process that uses membership functions to convert crisp or actual inputs into fuzzy sets. We employ a basic and widely-applied trapezoidal membership function. Inference is a procedure that translates one input to another using a set of rules. In this case, the input is fuzzy, and the output is determined using IF-THEN fuzzy rules. Expertise and experience combine to form a body of information from which rules are developed.

**Table 1. Input and output parameters.**

| Variable | Linguistic Variables | Range | Linguistic Value | Parameter |
|---|---|---|---|---|
| Input | H | 0-1 | Very Low | 0-0.35 |
| - | | | Low | 0.15-0.45 |
| - | | | Moderate | 0.25-0.55 |
| - | | | High | 0.4-0.7 |
| - | | | Very High | 0.6-1 |
| - | F | 0-20 | Very Low | 0-3.5 |
| - | | | Low | 2-8 |
| - | | | Moderate | 5-11 |
| - | | | High | 8-14 |
| - | | | Very High | 11-20 |

*(Table 1) cont.....*

| Variable | Linguistic Variables | Range | Linguistic Value | Parameter |
|---|---|---|---|---|
| - | N | 0-20 | Short | 0-8 |
| - | | | Moderate | 5-15 |
| - | | | Long | 12-20 |
| - | I | 0-8 | Low | 0-3 |
| - | | | Moderate | 2-6 |
| - | | | High | 4-8 |
| - | G | 0-1 | Very Low | 0-0.25 |
| - | | | Low | 0.2-0.38 |
| - | | | Moderate | 0.3-0.6 |
| - | | | High | 0.55-0.7 |
| - | | | Very High | 0.65-1 |
| - | E | 0-1 | Low | 0-0.12 |
| - | | | Moderate | 0.06-0.23 |
| - | | | High | 0.16-1 |
| - | V | 0-10 | Low | 0-4 |
| - | | | Moderate | 3-7 |
| - | | | High | 6-10 |
| Output | R | 01-00 | Irrelevance | 0-40 |
| | | | Low Relevance | 30-65 |
| | | | Moderate | 50-85 |
| | | | Relevance | 30-0] |
| | | | High Relevance | 75-100 |

Table **1** displays the allowed variations in input and output parameters. They are determined by analyzing real-world data. For instance, the range of values for the highest word score, H, is [0,0.35], [0.15], [0.25], [0.4,0.7], and [0.6,0.1], with very low, low, moderate, high, and very high degrees shown in Table **1**. Due to H's high degree, the associated tweet is quite pertinent to the happenings.

In this piece, we use IF-THEN logic to create fuzzy rules. The fuzzy rule is structured like an IF-THEN statement, with an underlying condition and a result. There are four distinct types of rules: There are four levels of importance: 1) extremely relevant; 2) somewhat relevant; 3) relevant; and 4) irrelevant. The following are some regulations that serve as examples in order to illustrate a clearer point.

If both H and I are high, as in R_1, then R is said to be of high significance.

A tweet's strong relevance to an event may be inferred from its high word count and the frequency with which its terms are utilized.

R_2: If both H and G are significant, then R is also considered to have moderate significance. When a tweet has a moderate word count and weight, it is considered to be of moderate significance to the event.

If both E and G are low, then R_3 is considered to have low importance.

A low-relevant tweet has few vital key phrases, as shown by the tweet's low weight and the low weight of the often-used terms.

R_4: R is disregarded as relevant if H is very low and M is lengthy.

If a lengthy tweet does not contain any terms that are directly linked to the event, it is irrelevant.

Tweets with a high degree of relevance to the event are included in the first category. For instance, R_1 stipulates that the variables must be of greater magnitude or shorter length. Tweets having moderate linguistic values, such as those that meet the criterion in R_2, fall into the second category, moderate relevance. Variables meeting the criteria in R_3 fall into the third group, low relevance, which may also contain some moderately relevant variables. These tweets do not even qualify as moderately relevant; they are that irrelevant. Twitter that does not fit any of the other three categories, such as those that meet the criteria in R_4, fall into the fourth and final category, irrelevance. Tweets in the latter group typically suffer from either low linguistic value or excessive length. Keep in mind that if a tweet is overly long and has poor linguistic qualities, it probably does not include much information on the event. Therefore, it can be disregarded as a moot point.

As a result, we create a set of 25 regulations. There are a total of fourteen guidelines: seven for "high relevance," eight for "moderate relevance," three for "low relevance," and seven for "irrelevance."

## Outcomes and Discussion

To facilitate comparison, this section describes the experiments conducted to assess performance on benchmark data sets. To ensure precision, we performed a ten-fold cross-validation. Multiple ML approaches provide the starting point findings, Fig. (**1**) is represented in Accuracy results, Fig. (**2**) shows a summary and visualization of the results. Fig. (**3**) is depicted in Recall results, Fig. (**4**) is portrayed in F-measure results.

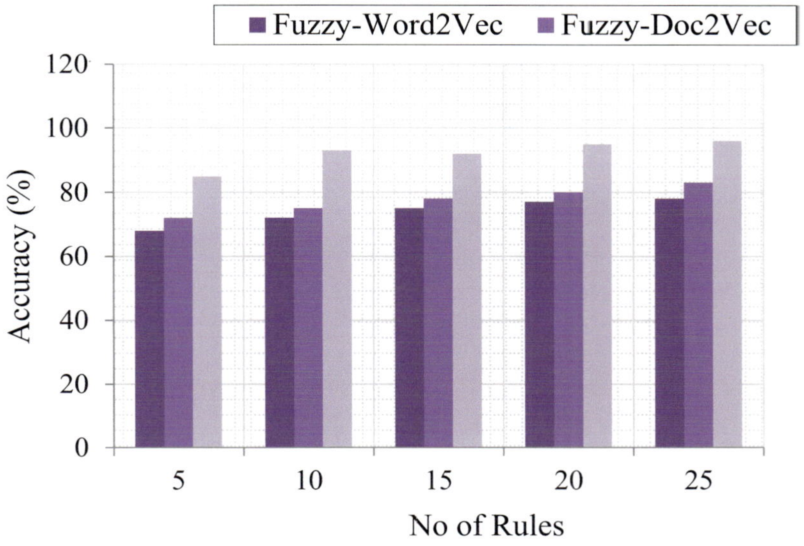


**Fig. (1).** Accuracy results.

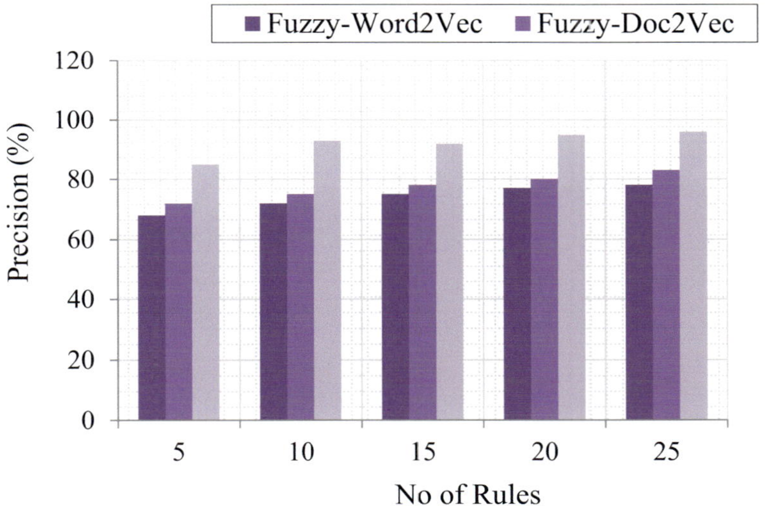


**Fig. (2).** Precision results.

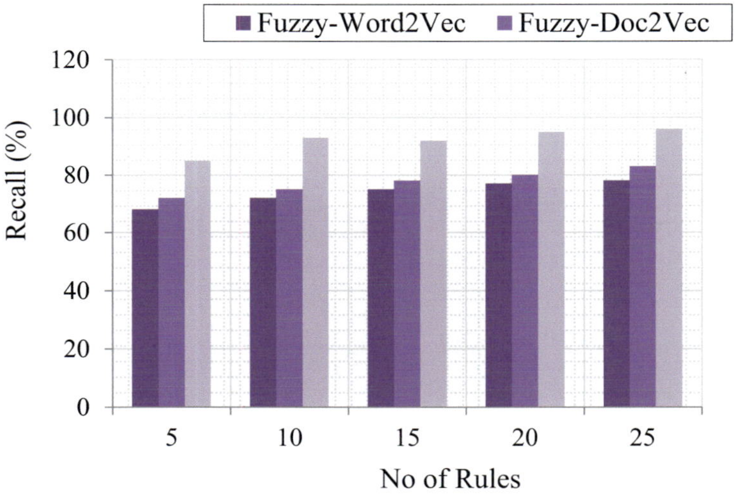


**Fig. (3).** Recall results.

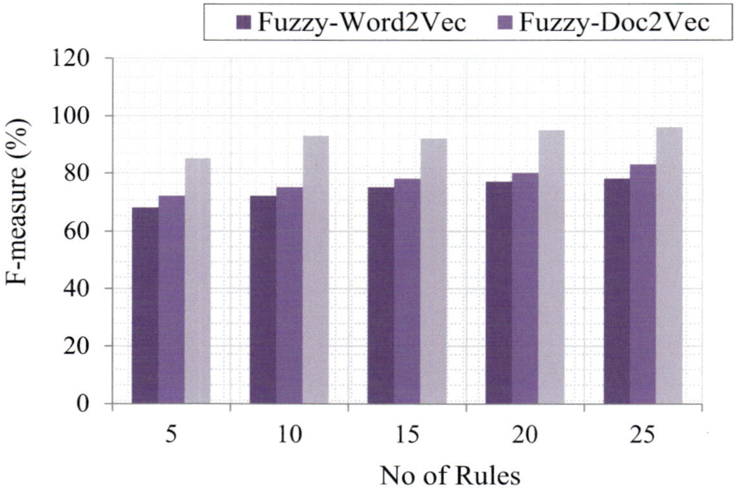


**Fig. (4).** F-measure results.

## CONCLUSION

Since the proliferation of COVID-19 conspiracy theories, social media has been utilized for and against spreading and correcting false information. In this piece, we discuss the problem of the tone of Twitter messages on COVID-19. We conduct a comparative examination of sentiment towards COVID-19 using many sentiment analysis tools. According to our data, the majority of people supported the lockdown and stay-in-place directive in February, but their view reversed by the middle of March. Since the cause of the shift in attitude is unknown but may be attributable to the transmission of disinformation *via* social media, it is imperative that a proactive and adaptable public health presence must be established to counteract the phenomenon. We have made accessible the massive COVID-19 benchmark sentiment analysis dataset for research purposes.

## REFERENCES

[1] I. Aygün, B. Kaya, and M. Kaya, "Aspect Based Twitter Sentiment Analysis on Vaccination and Vaccine Types in COVID-19 Pandemic With Deep Learning", *IEEE J. Biomed. Health Inform.*, vol. 26, no. 5, pp. 2360-2369, 2022. [http://dx.doi.org/10.1109/JBHI.2021.3133103] [PMID: 34874877]

[2] R.S. Jayale, and S.S. Desai, "Aspect-Level Drug Reviews Sentiment Analysis and COVID-19 Drug prediction using PPI & Deep Learning", *International Conference on Computing, Communication and Green Engineering (CCGE),* pp. 1-5, 2021. [http://dx.doi.org/10.1109/CCGE50943.2021.9776369]

[3] H. Zhou, Y.E. Zhao, and T. Wang, "Aspect Root-Oriented Latent Structures with Graph Convolutional Networks for Aspect Sentiment Classification", *2nd International Conference on Electronic Technology, Communication and Information (ICETCI),* pp. 233-237, 2022. [http://dx.doi.org/10.1109/ICETCI55101.2022.9832167]

[4] H. Jeong, A. Bayro, S.P. Umesh, K. Mamgain, and M. Lee, "A Perspective of COVID-19 and Healthcare: Using Social Media Data and an Aspect-based Sentiment Analysis for Usability Evaluation of a Wearable Mixed Reality Headset", *JMIR Serious Games,* 2022. [http://dx.doi.org/10.2196/36850]

[5] S. Yadav, C.D.S. Zaidi, and V.H.C. Nascimento, "de Albuquerque and S. S. Chauhan, “Analysis and Design of automatically generating for GPS Based Moving Object Tracking System", *2023 International Conference on Artificial Intelligence and Smart Communication (AISC)* 2022 pp. 1-5. Greater Noida, India.

[6] U.N. Wisesty, R. Rismala, W. Munggana, and A. Purwarianti, "Comparative Study of Covid-19 Tweets Sentiment Classification Methods", *9th International Conference on Information and Communication Technology (ICoICT),* pp. 588-593, 2021. [http://dx.doi.org/10.1109/ICoICT52021.2021.9527533]

[7] F. Zhao, Z. Wu, S. Long, X. Dai, S. Huang, and J. Chen, "Learning from Adjective-Noun Pairs: A Knowledge-enhanced Framework for Target-Oriented Multimodal Sentiment Classification", *International Conference on Computational Linguistics,* 2022.

[8] Z. Wu, J. Gao, Q. Li, Z. Guan, and Z. Chen, "Make aspect-based sentiment classification go further: step into the long-document-level", *Appl. Intell.,* vol. 52, no. 8, pp. 8428-8447, 2022. [http://dx.doi.org/10.1007/s10489-021-02836-y]

[9] S. P. Yadav, and S. Yadav, "Mathematical implementation of fusion of medical images in continuous wavelet domain", *Journal of Advanced Research in dynamical and control system,* vol. 10, no. 10, pp. 45-54, 2019.

[10] J.A. Wahid, S. Hussain, H. Wang, Z. Wu, L. Shi, and Y. Gao, "Aspect oriented Sentiment classification of COVID-19 twitter data; an enhanced LDA based text analytic approach", *International Conference on Computer Engineering and Artificial Intelligence (ICCEAI),* pp. 271-275, 2021. [http://dx.doi.org/10.1109/ICCEAI52939.2021.00054]

# CHAPTER 25

# Feature-Level Sentiment Analysis of Data Collected through Electronic Commerce

**Preetjot Singh**[1,*]

[1] *Centre for Interdisciplinary Research in Business and Technology, Chitkara University Institute of Engineering and Technology, Chitkara University, Punjab, India*

**Abstract:** When dealing with data in the form of text, the most popular method for doing analysis and determining sentiment content is called "Sentiment Analysis." Sentiment analysis is also known as Opinion Mining. Suggestions, feedback, tweets, and comments are all examples of the various types of text data that are being created. Customer feedback on e-commerce sites is a constant source of new information. Online stores may better meet client needs, improve their services, and boost sales by analyzing E-Commerce data. Positive, negative, and neutral feedback from customers may be separated using sentiment analysis. Numerous methods for Sentiment Analysis have been developed by academics. Typically, only a single machine learning algorithm is used for sentiment analysis. The purpose of this study, which makes use of Amazon review data, is to extract positive, negative, and neutral review ratings by locating aspect phrases, identifying the Parts-of-Speech, and applying classification algorithms to the collected data.

**Keywords:** Customer reviews, E-commerce, Features, Sentiment analysis.

## INTRODUCTION

When dealing with data in the form of text, the most popular method for doing analysis and determining sentiment content is called "Sentiment Analysis." A synonym for sentiment analysis is "Opinion Mining" [1]. Suggestions, feedback, tweets, and comments are all examples of the diverse text data that are being created [2]. Customer feedback on e-commerce sites is a constant source of new information. By analyzing E-Commerce data, online stores may learn what customers want, improve their offerings, and ultimately boost sales [3]. Positive, negative, and neutral feedback from customers may be separated using sentiment analysis. Many methods for Sentiment Analysis [4] have been developed by researchers. Typically, only a single machine learning algorithm is used for

* **Corresponding author Preetjot Singh:** Centre for Interdisciplinary Research in Business and Technology, Chitkara University Institute of Engineering and Technology, Chitkara University, Punjab, India;
E-mail: preetjot.singh.orp@chitkara.edu.in

**Pankaj Kumar Mishra and Satya Prakash Yadav (Eds.)**

sentiment analysis. Demand for automated sentiment analysis systems is skyrocketing [5] in the age of big data, thanks to the growing number of online shoppers and social media users throughout the world. Aspect-based sentiment analysis (ABSA), which considers the sentiment at the aspect level, is a well-liked area of study [6] because of its relevance to business needs. Two more tasks, aspect-term sentiment analysis (ATSA) and aspect-category sentiment analysis (ACSA), make up ABSA. Sentiment analysis is the study of how people feel about something or someone [7]. The importance of analyzing user evaluations for product makers to get insights into the acceptance of items has grown with the rise of social media websites and e-commerce applications. They may learn more about how customers feel about individual product features by performing an aspect-level sentiment analysis [8]. E-commerce, online communities, and social media have all seen significant growth in popularity. Customers' opinions matter greatly in terms of the end result [9]. Providers, sellers, and producers of goods and services benefit greatly from any and all feedback, even if it is simply a comment or review. Since user feedback is so important, sentiment analysis has attracted a lot of attention. A user's characteristics, attributes, and points of view can be gleaned from their writing through a process called sentiment analysis. The proliferation of e-commerce websites as alternative sales channels stimulated the development of several review websites covering various goods and services [10]. As a result, businesses can better track their reputation and gauge customer demand, while consumers may employ aspect-based sentiment analysis to inform their purchasing decisions. Beyond simple phrase or text-level sentiment categorization, further in-depth study may be encouraged with the use of a method called aspect-based sentiment analysis (ABSA).

## RELATED WORK

Based on consumer feedback left on Amazon, this study uses Parts-of-Speech tagging and classification algorithms to determine if a review is positive, negative, or neutral [11].

In order to learn both ATSA and ACSA simultaneously, this research provides a multi-task learning architecture that uses a pre-trained BERT model as a shared representation layer. To make the most of the surrounding context data, we build a multi-head self-attention layer over the common BERT model and connect the heads through a skip connection. Our multi-task learning model outperforms baseline multi-task networks and single-task models using SemEval datasets [12], demonstrating improved performance on the ATSA test.

Over the course of 7.8 million Amazon customer reviews, this study proposes a workflow model for topic extraction (aspect identification) and sentiment detection utilizing a frequency-based approach and unsupervised machine learning techniques. The paper also makes use of traditional techniques including logistic regression, support vector machine, and a naïve Bayesian approach [13] to determine the precision of the analytical model.

The key portion of this procedure is extracting user aspects, which are then utilized to categorize the user aspects. In the field of natural language processing, CNN models have been increasingly popular in recent years. This study offers a unique hybrid CNN model by combining the bidirectional long short-term memory and CNN models to sequentially analyze the data by learning its high-level properties. The loss of vital data is kept to a minimum using the concatenated approach. Experiments utilise benchmark product review and hotel review datasets, with the proposed hybrid model achieving accuracies of 93.6% for the product review dataset and 92.7% for the hotel review dataset, when compared to state-of-the-art methodologies [14].

The objective is to recognize valuations placed on certain things (like laptops) and their characteristics (like cost, functionality, durability, *etc.*). There are extremely few methods that can provide such outcomes based on customer ratings, and even fewer that can do so from free-text reviews. Aside from insufficient review data, the cold start problem is another obstacle. In this research, we offer a method for automatically computing sentiments of dynamic elements based on user-generated evaluations gleaned *via* web scraping from numerous sources, thereby allowing us to avoid the cold start problem. So, our approach is improving upon previous ways of gauging customer opinion in online stores.

## PROPOSED WORK

### Overview

Since it examines the feelings and opinions expressed in a text, sentiment analysis falls within the broader category of NLP. It pulls the good, negative, and neutral feelings from the text. Due to the nature of working with text data, a great degree of preparation work must precede the actual categorization. The sentences are first preprocessed by assigning a Parts-of-Speech tag to each word, then by identifying and deleting stop words and unnecessary adjectives. The proposed study uses Amazon customer reviews to evaluate the efficacy of the Nave Bayes and Support Vector Machine (SVM), and Machine Learning algorithms for sentiment analysis. The primary focus of Aspect-level sentiment analysis is on product features and aspects. The measures to take are laid out in Fig. (**2**), which depicts the suggested system architecture.

## Customer Reviews

The machine is fed information about Amazon items based on reviews written by actual customers (3.2). Customer reviews are written comments left by purchasers of a product on an e-commerce site. The feedback might be entirely positive, entirely negative, or something in between.

## Parts-of-Speech tagging

Textual customer feedback is tagged with 3.3 part-of-speech tags. In order to classify each word in a phrase as belonging to a certain part of speech, "parts-o--speech tagging" is employed. This is how we determine the word's morphological category. All parts of speech are covered, from nouns to prepositions. Adjectives and nouns are particularly useful for sentiment analysis since they reveal the speaker's emotional state.

## Feature Extraction

Extraction of Feature 3.4: Emotion detection in customer reviews requires the extraction of features based on noun phrases and nouns, adjectives acquired from Parts-of-Speech tagging. The Apriori algorithm is used to do this. Data mining algorithms include the Apriori algorithm. It is a tool for isolating high-traffic parts of a dataset. Affiliation rules that are applied to databases, provide the basis for this approach. All subsets of a frequent item set should also be frequent, and vice versa for any infrequent item set's supersets. These are the two key assumptions that must be taken into account while employing the Apriori method. The Apriori method is straightforward and simple to implement. It also works for massive collections of objects.

## Feature Pruning

Feature pruning, often known as "de-noising," is the process of eliminating superfluous elements from a feature set, such as stop words. Opinion words are then extracted using Feature Pruning. Words are used to express personal opinion about a product.

As part of its analysis, the Lexicon-based approach uses a set of predetermined word phrases and opinion idioms, each of which is assigned a positive or negative sentiment score. While most studies employ dictionary and corpus-based automated methods to assign opinion terms, researchers sometimes still assign words and phrases in assertions of belief to ensure accuracy. In the context of retail businesses, such as e-commerce sites, this rule assigns relative slant values to terms that are semantically similar. Due to the variety of languages represented, many of the reviews and comments on the site contain slang terms and typos. This makes the task of creating automated systems more challenging. In addition, prior knowledge is required to analyze the sentiment of the statement and categorize the polarity of the viewpoint. Under the lexicon classifier, two methods might be employed to gather an online dictionary with a number of opinion statements for respective synonyms and antonyms: the Dictionary-based technique and the Corpus-based method. The method keeps adding new words to the list of seeds until no other phrases can be identified. Last but not the least, the list must be manually checked for accuracy.

## Classification

Sentiment analysis is a relatively new field of study that seeks to categorize subjective data included within a person's written or spoken words, such as their opinions on a certain product, service, or event. It can reveal the reader's state of mind as they take in a piece of writing or an event. One form of sentiment analysis that represents the current epidemic days of corona is when a person expresses anxiety over the spread of sickness. This sort of communication describes the state of the world now. Positive, negative, and neutral findings are distinguished from one another. In order to better comprehend the data, sentiment analysis conducted some cleaning and preprocessing. There were two methods employed in sentiment analysis. Among them are lexicon-based methods and machine-learning methods. At this stage, we decide if the view is good, negative, or neutral. The classification process begins with a SentiWordNet calculation of the positive, negative, and neutral weights of each word. Fig. (**1**). portrays the System Flowchart.

After that, we use the classification techniques Naive Bayes (NB) and Support Vector Machine (SVM). The Naive Bayes algorithm is a type of classification algorithm used in machine learning. The Naive Bayes method relies on the laws of probability. The Naive Bayes method determines the likelihood of each possible interpretation of a text. Sentiment analysis uses this to characterize the likelihood of characteristics. Since this project involves text data, it is necessary to translate the text into numeric data so that probability calculations may be made. Word frequency analysis can help with this. The Naive Bayes algorithm is both the quickest and easiest method to implement. The machine learning classification algorithm Support Vector Machine is similar. Finding a hyperplane to partition a dataset into classes is at the heart of Support Vector Machine classification. The number of points in the dataset that are closest to the hyperplane are known as support vectors. The data is categorized by the hyperplane. We employ hyper, which is derived from the largest feasible margin, to appropriately categorize fresh data. Although it produces reliable outcomes, Support Vector Machine is limited to use with smaller datasets. This works better and faster. Synopsis of the Arguments: The sum of each classifier's negative, neutral, and positive comments is calculated at this stage. Opinion summaries are generated using both Support Vector Machine classification and Naive Bayes classification. Fig. (**2**) shows Sentiment Analysis Techniques and Fig. (**3**) shows the SVM classification.

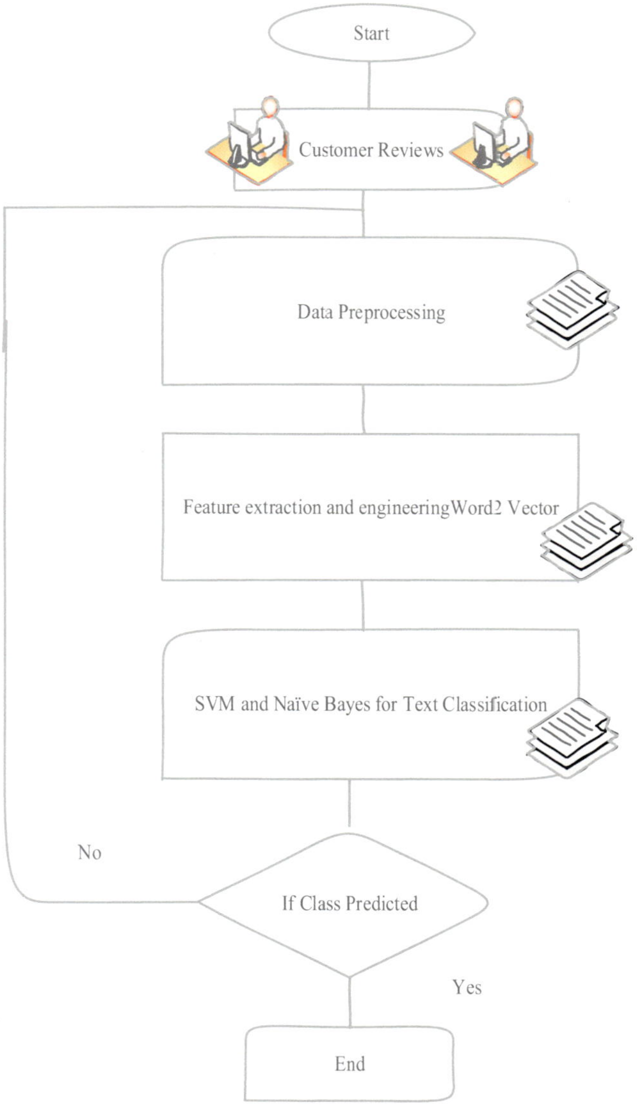


**Fig. (1).** System flowchart.

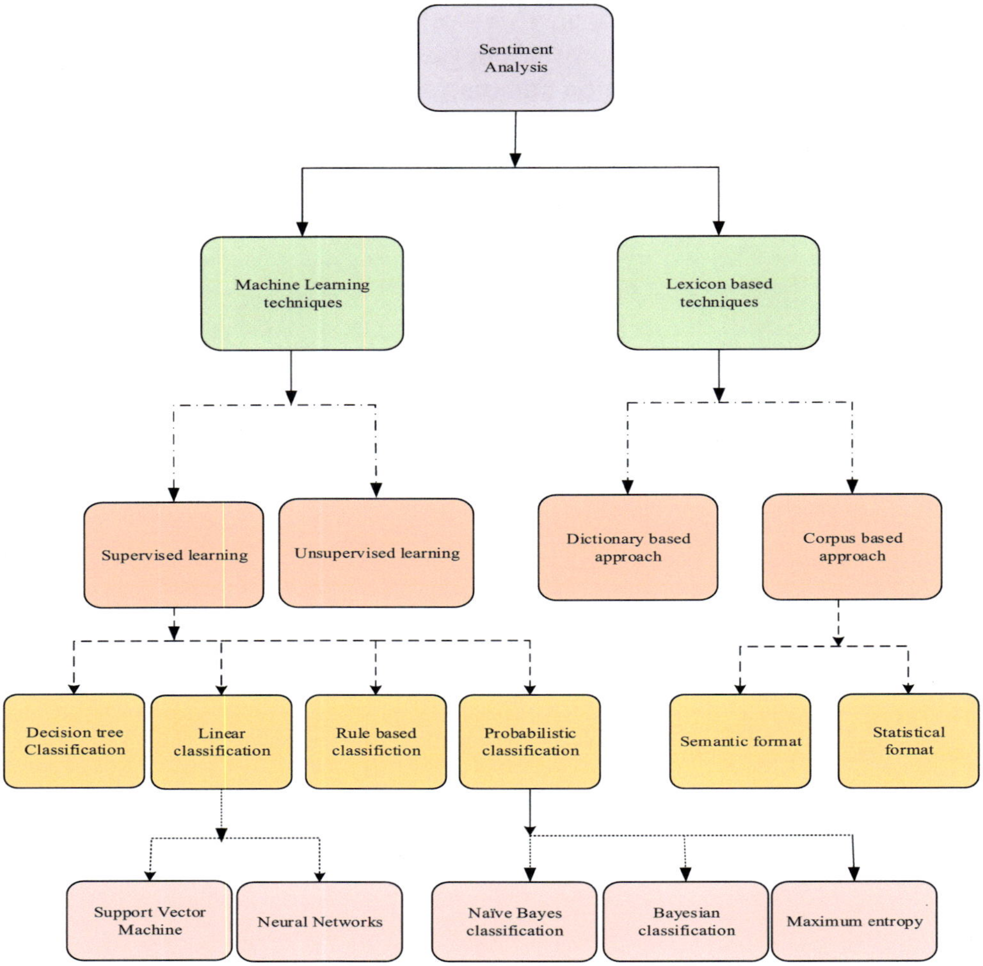


**Fig. (2).** Sentiment analysis techniques.

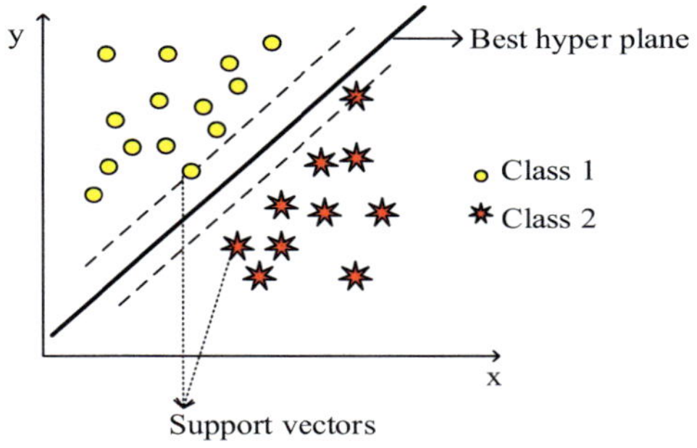


**Fig. (3).** SVM classification.

## RESULTS AND DISCUSSION

Finally, Naive Bayes classification is compared to the Support Vector Machine classification. The efficiency of the algorithms is used to categorize them. Measures such as accuracy, precision, recall, and F1-measure may be applied to both the Support Vector Machine and Naive Bayes classification algorithms to determine how well they performed. The formulas for determining these values are as follows:

$$\begin{aligned} \text{Accuracy} &= \frac{TP+TN}{TP+TN+FP+FN} \\ \text{Precision} &= \frac{TP}{TP+FP} \\ \text{Recall} &= \frac{TP}{TP+FN} \\ F1 &= \frac{2*\text{Precision}*\text{Recall}}{\text{Precision}+\text{Recall}} \end{aligned} \quad (1)$$

Instances that are True Positives, False Positives, True Negatives, and False Negatives are denoted as TP, FP, TN, and FN, respectively.

The findings of our experiments categorized every word of the reviews as a noun, pronoun, verb, adverb, or adjective. The Apriori algorithm then returned the reviews' most commonly used terms. After running the categorization algorithms on the reviews, we extracted adjectives from them. SentiWordNet was utilized to obtain positive, negative, and neutral evaluations of each word. It is a dictionary that includes feeling levels.

We computed recall, f-measure, precision, and accuracy to evaluate Nave Bayes and Support Vector Machine classification methods. We computed recall, accuracy, F-measure, and precision using both false-positive and true-positive data as well as both false-negative and true-negative samples. Table **2** demonstrates the algorithms' respective degrees of accuracy. Table **1**. provides detail of the accuracy of SVM and NB classification algorithms.

**Table 1. Accuracy by SVM and NB classification algorithms.**

| - | Naïve Bayes | Support Vector Machine |
|---|---|---|
| Accuracy | 90.423 | 83.423 |
| Precision | 0.947 | 0.852 |
| Recall | 0.959 | 0.83 |
| F-Measure | 0.952 | 0.841 |

**Table 2. Instances by Naïve Bayes classification.**

| True Positive | False Positive | True Negative | False Negative |
|---|---|---|---|
| 0.947 | 0.053 | 0.1 | 0.04 |

Based on our experiments, we can say that NB classification is more accurate than classification using a Support Vector Machine.

All of these figures are derived from each classification's True Positive, False Positive, True Negative, and False Negative samples. Table **2** displays the Nave Bayes classification FP, TP, FN, and TN values. Support Vector Machine classification FP, TP, FN, and TN values are displayed in Table **3**.

**Table 3. Instances by SVM classification.**

| True Positive | False Positive | True Negative | False Negative |
|---|---|---|---|
| 0.947 | 0.053 | 0.1 | 0.04 |

## CONCLUSION

Within the scope of this work, we have developed Sentiment Analysis at the feature level. The e-commerce industry is constantly curious to know what customers think of their products, and this article provides a thorough introduction to sentiment analysis and the essential methodologies used in this field. The process begins with the idea of sentiment analysis, a relatively new approach to deciphering the feelings of customers. It also details the typical tasks associated with sentiment analysis techniques such as lexicon-based and machine learning-monitored approaches. However, sentiment analysis is used in the retail industry, most frequently in E-Commerce, to help businesses run more smoothly. Precision, Recall, and F1 measure are used to evaluate the results of utilizing the SVM classification algorithm and the NB classification method to categorize the data. Nave Bayes outperformed Support Vector Machine in terms of accuracy.

## REFERENCES

[1] Y. Yiran, and S. Srivastava, "Aspect-based Sentiment Analysis on mobile phone reviews with LDA", *Proceedings of the 2019 4th International Conference on Machine Learning Technologies,* 2019. [http://dx.doi.org/10.1145/3340997.3341012]

[2] G. Li, Q. Chen, B. Zheng, N.Q.V. Hung, P. Zhou, and G. Liu, "Time-aspect-sentiment Recommendation Models Based on Novel Similarity Measure Methods", *ACM Trans. Web,* vol. 14, no. 2, pp. 1-26, 2020. [http://dx.doi.org/10.1145/3375548]

[3] T. Shaikh, and D. Deshpande, "A Review on Opinion Mining and Sentiment Analysis", In: *Proceedings of the International Conference on Computational Intelligence and Communication*

*Networks (CICN)* Bhopal, India, 2016, pp. 153-158. [http://dx.doi.org/10.1109/CICN.2016.41]

[4] S.P. Yadav, S. Zaidi, C.D.S. Nascimento, V.H.C. de Albuquerque, and S.S. Chauhan, "Analysis and Design of automatically generating for GPS Based Moving Object Tracking System", *2023 International Conference on Artificial Intelligence and Smart Communication (AISC),* 2023 pp. 1-5. Greater Noida, India. [http://dx.doi.org/10.1109/AISC56616.2023.10085180]

[5] H. Wu, M. Liu, S. Zhang, Z. Wang, and S. Cheng, "Big Data Management and Analytics in Scientific Programming: A Deep Learning-Based Method for Aspect Category Classification of Question-Answering-Style Reviews", *Sci. Program.,* 2020.

[6] S. P. Yadav, and S. Yadav, "Mathematical implementation of fusion of medical images in continuous wavelet domain", *Journal of Advanced Research in dynamical and control system,* vol. 10, no. 10, pp. 45-54, 2019.

[7] N.V. Thakare, "Aspect Based Sentiment Analysis for E-Commerce Shopping Website", *Int. J. Res. Appl. Sci. Eng. Technol.,* vol. 9, no. 11, pp. 1819-1822, 2021. [http://dx.doi.org/10.22214/ijraset.2021.39117]

[8] B.T. Abeje, A.O. Salau, H.A. Ebabu, and A.M. Ayalew, "Comparative Analysis of Deep Learning Models for Aspect Level Amharic News Sentiment Analysis", *2022 International Conference on Decision Aid Sciences and Applications (DASA),* pp. 1628-1633, 2022. [http://dx.doi.org/10.1109/DASA54658.2022.9765172]

[9] V. Yadav, P. Verma, and V. Katiyar, "Long short term memory (LSTM) model for sentiment analysis in social data for e-commerce products reviews in Hindi languages", *International Journal of Information Technology,* vol. 15, no. 2, pp. 759-772, 2023. [http://dx.doi.org/10.1007/s41870-022-01010-y]

[10] S.J. Vanaja, and M. Belwal, "Aspect-Level Sentiment Analysis on E-Commerce Data", *2018 International Conference on Inventive Research in Computing Applications (ICIRCA),* pp. 1275-1279, 2018.

[11] Y. Pei, Y. Wang, W. Wang, and J. Qi, "Aspect-Based Sentiment Analysis with Multi-Task Learning", *5th International Conference on Computing and Big Data (ICCBD),* pp. 171-176, 2022. [http://dx.doi.org/10.1109/ICCBD56965.2022.10080017]

[12] P. Patil, S.P. Phansalkar, and V.V. Kryssanov, "Topic Modelling for Aspect-Level Sentiment Analysis", *Proceedings of the 2nd International Conference on Data Engineering and Communication Technology,* 2018.

[13] M. Kuppusamy, and A. Selvaraj, "A novel hybrid deep learning model for aspect based sentiment analysis", *Concurr. Comput.,* p. 35, 2022.

[14] J.K. Prathi, P.K. Raparthi, and M.V. Gopalachari, "Real-Time Aspect-Based Sentiment Analysis on Consumer Reviews", 2020. [http://dx.doi.org/10.1007/978-981-15-1097-7_67]

# CHAPTER 26

# Classification Algorithms for Evaluating Customer Opinions using AI

**Saniya Khurana**[1,*]

[1] *Centre for Interdisciplinary Research in Business and Technology, Chitkara University Institute of Engineering and Technology, Chitkara University, Punjab, India*

**Abstract:** There are now a great deal of consumer reviews of items that are written entirely in text. The reviews express their opinions. Opinion mining is another name for sentiment analysis. A common way for businesses to keep tabs on how customers feel about their brands and goods is through the use of sentiment analysis on textual data. Naive Bayes, Random Forest, Decision Tree, and Support Vector Machine classifiers are all used and compared in this study. In this study, we evaluate the efficacy of several classifiers by measuring their ability to correctly categorize mobile product data sets of varying sizes. Data were collected from popular online retailers like Amazon, Flipkart, and Snapdeal and analyzed to determine categorization accuracy. Naive Bayes, Random Forest, Decision Tree, and Support Vector Machines are some of the categorization algorithms compared here.

**Keywords:** Artificial intelligence, Customer opinions, Shopping reviews, Text classification.

## INTRODUCTION

There are now a great deal of consumer reviews of items that are written entirely in text. Reviews are express customers' opinions about a product or a service [1]. Opinion mining is another name for sentiment analysis. In order to monitor how customers feel about their products or services and gain a better understanding of the industry, several companies use sentiment analysis on textual data [2]. Opinion mining, also known as sentiment analysis, is the practice of sifting through large amounts of user-generated content in search of expressions of positive or negative emotion [3]. Sentiment analysis is crucial because it allows businesses and organizations to quickly gauge the extent to which their customers are satisfied with a certain product on the basis of reviews [4]. The ever-increasing volume of product reviews makes it harder to do this analysis manually

* **Corresponding author Saniya Khurana:** Centre for Interdisciplinary Research in Business and Technology, Chitkara University Institute of Engineering and Technology, Chitkara University, Punjab, India;
E-mail: saniya.khurana.orp@chitkara.edu.in

[5]. Sentiment analysis, commonly known as "opinion mining," is the process of analyzing and categorizing people's feelings about a text. It has to do with text and language analysis [6] as well as natural language processing. With the proliferation of web-based technology comes an explosion in data volume [7]. Expressing one's emotions with terse remarks is becoming commonplace on social networking platforms [8]. Emotions like joy, sorrow, worry, fear, *etc.*, fall under this category. The Bidirectional Encoder Representations from Transformers (BERT) is a cutting-edge language model employed in a wide variety of NLP and SM applications [9]. High amounts of unstructured data make it difficult and time-consuming to analyze consumer review data from different social media sites and make accurate predictions based on context-based sentiment. Recurrent neural network techniques, such as Long Short-Term Memory (LSTM) and Bidirectional LSTM (BiLSTM), as well as hybrid, neutral, and classic text categorization algorithms, have seen increased study in recent years. Successful businesses aim to please their customers and earn their favorable endorsement in a number of ways [10]. However, due to the vast amounts of data acquired from a variety of sources, assessing customer evaluations to accurately anticipate sentiment has proven to be a difficult and time-consuming task. Various scholars have developed algorithms, methodologies, and models to tackle this problem. Among them are the Artificial Neural Network (ANN) and the bag-of-word (BOW) regression model, as well as unigram and skip-gram-based algorithms. Numerous investigations and studies have uncovered polarity incoherence, model overfitting and performance difficulties, and high data processing costs.

Machine learning techniques are used to classify reviews. In this study, we identify emotions using six different machine-learning techniques. Research on these techniques' precision and effectiveness has been conducted. Customer feedback has also been subjected to feature sentiment analysis. Sentiment analysis and forecasting are common applications of machine learning. Sentiment analysis is performed on three different levels: document, phrase, and feature. Document-level sentiment analysis determines if a piece of writing is favorable, negative, or neutral. Both document-level and feature-level sentiment analysis are taken into account here.

The sections of this article are as follows: The research that informed this project is discussed in the next section. The analytical model is described in Section 3. The findings are presented in Section 4, and the conclusion is given in Section 5.

## RELATED WORK

Naive Bayes, Random Forest, Decision Tree, and Support Vector Machine classifiers are all used and compared in this study. In this study, we evaluate the efficacy of several classifiers by measuring their ability to correctly categorize mobile product data sets of varying sizes. Data was collected from popular online retailers like Amazon, Flipkart, and Snapdeal and analyzed to determine categorization accuracy. Naive Bayes, Random Forest, Decision Tree, and Support Vector Machines are four categorization methods compared to choose the best [11].

The purpose of this research is to present a sentiment analysis model for positively, neutrally, and negatively categorizing product reviews. With the goal of developing the most effective classifier, it uses five well-known machine learning classifiers: Naive Bayes, Support Vector Machine, Decision Tree, K-Nearest Neighbor, and Maximum Entropy. The dataset utilized includes 82,815 ratings and comments posted on the Kaggle website pertaining to various mobile phone devices. We employed measures of recall, precision, F1-measure, and accuracy to compare the five different classifiers. The experiments all suggest that Maximum Entropy and Naive Bayes are the most accurate classifiers. Across all experiments, the Decision Tree algorithm performed worst [12].

The analysis of brief texts has a tendency to pick up on the collective mood of the audience. The “Sentiment Analysis” feature on IMDb lets users see how critics generally feel about a film. Costs are increasing as a result of the fact that human opinions matter for product success and that audience reception may make or break a film's box office performance. Sentiment analysis is performed by ML systems as a regular classification problem based on syntactic and linguistic features. In this study, we explore the application of machine learning techniques for sentiment analysis. SVM, RF, ANN, and NB, as well as the DT, BN, and KNN Algorithms [13], are commonly used for sentiment analysis.

In this paper, we report the results of our experimental study into how to improve upon the performance, accuracy, and context-based predictions of sentiment analysis models. Utilizing consumer evaluations from Twitter, IMDB Movie evaluations, Yelp, and Amazon, we present a fine-tuned BERT model to predict user attitudes. In addition, we gave a dashboard report that compared the suggested model's performance to that of our own bespoke Linear Support Vector Machine (LSVM), fastText, BiLSTM, and hybrid fastText-BiLSTM models. This experimental result demonstrates that the suggested model outperforms the competition across a range of performance metrics; transforms model; BERT;

sequential model; deep learning; RNN; LSVM; LSTM; BiLSTM; fastText [14, 15]; LSTM; BiLSTM; fastText.

This study was carried out to address these glaring problems by developing a high-performance, low-cost algorithm for extracting reliable sentiment from massive customer review datasets. For text classification and word embedding, this model employs both the Linear Support Vector Machine (LSVM) and Facebook's fastText package from the Artificial Intelligence Research (FAIR) Lab. The author's own multi-layer Sentiment Analysis (SA) Bidirectional Long Short-Term Memory (SA-BLSTM) model was also used for comparison. Based on the results, the suggested fastText model outperforms the LSVM and SA-BLSTM models by 20% and achieves an accuracy of 90.71%.

## PROPOSED WORK

The prerequisites for our proposed technique are outlined here. The three datasets, feature extraction methods, and classifiers employed are all explained, as well as the differences between assessing the classifier model with and without a lexicon. Steps performed in our suggested model are summarized in Fig. (**1**).

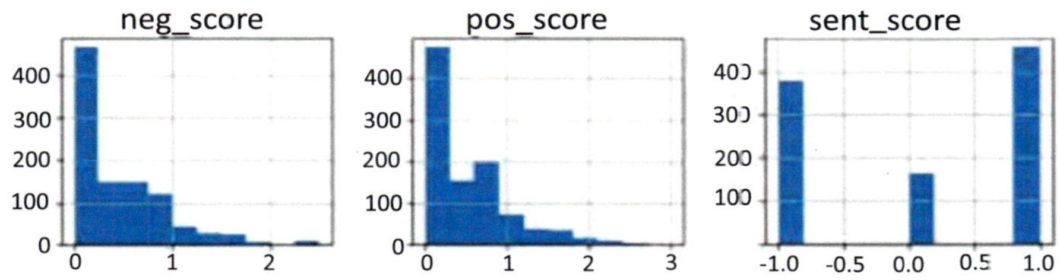


**Fig. (1).** Product review dataset.

### Collection and Preprocessing of Data 3.1

This model incorporates data from the product, movie, and twitter databases. Both the sentiment score and the actual text of the reviews are included in every dataset. This model relies on a product dataset with 2,000 samples generated from a UCI repository of Amazon items. We utilized a dataset of 1.6 million tweets obtained from the Kaggle website. The IMDB review dataset was utilized for this model's movie data. There are 50,000 reviews in this dataset. Fig. (**2**) depicts the Twitter Review Dataset.

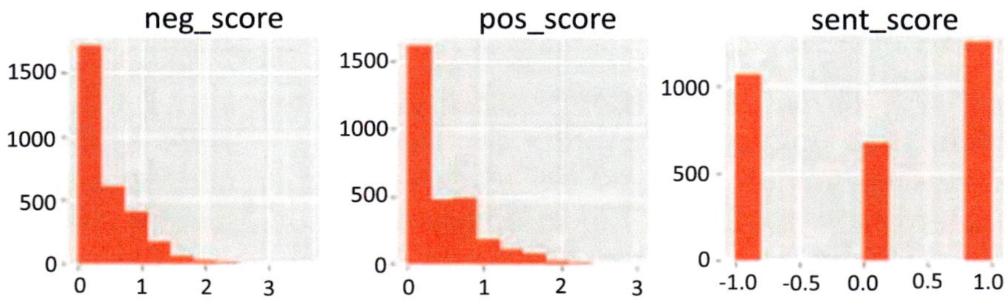


**Fig. (2).** Twitter review dataset.

An integral part of text categorization is the pre-processing of texts. This process can improve classification accuracy by decreasing the number of false positives. The primary goal of this effort is to eliminate empty phrases and words. Fig. (**3**) shows the Movie Dataset.

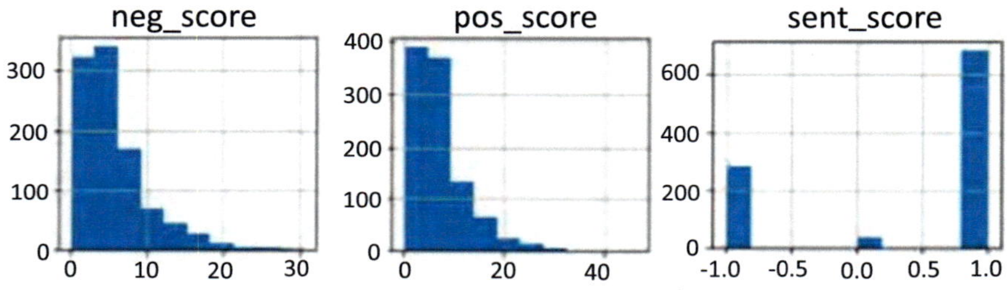


**Fig. (3).** Movie dataset.

The following method was used for each review:

1. Remove duplicates, remove unnecessary punctuation and numerals, and otherwise clean up your data.

2. Get rid of filler words like "the," "a," "an," and "the"

3. The role of tokenization and transformation.

4. Reviews may be tokenized by breaking them up into smaller bits.

5. Eliminating Filler Words.

6. Stop-words are terms like conjunctions and pronouns that do not add anything to the meaning of the text. Common filler words like "a," "an," "the," *etc.*, are

eliminated from the text in this procedure. These high-frequency terms should be eliminated since they may lead to incorrect document categorization.

## Stemming

Stemming is the process of eliminating the infixes, prefixes, and suffixes from a word, leaving only the central part of the word (the stem or root). Word roots are omitted from the final product when using a stemmer. This allows us to identify words that have a root but have various meanings due to affixes. Computer-related nouns like "computer," "computing," "computation," and "computes" all share a common etymological origin.

## Feature Extraction Methods

Appropriate feature selection methods in sentiment analysis play a crucial role in locating significant qualities and boosting classification precision. We have tried three different methods of feature extraction and compared their results. Using a bag of words (BOW) model or an N-gram model, the most important emotion-conveying words are extracted as a feature set for each review text.

- **Term Weighting:** Once the terms have been derived from the words, the document's presenting form, that is, the representation thereof must be determined. We use the word "weighting" to describe this method. Based on the words inside them, documents might be represented as vectors. The weight scheme employed by the method for calculating the weight vector is the term frequency-inverse document frequency (TF-IDF) feature weighting approach. The term "n-gram" is used to describe a set of n tokens that are all words.

- **Pruning of the Words:** Pruning is the process of eliminating less important documents from a collection. The term vector is extremely sparse and high-dimensional. It is also clear that the value "0" appears in a good deal of the term vector's elements. Therefore, we remove the terms that only appear twice or less times throughout the papers. The dimension of the term vector is reduced even further by this procedure.

## Text Classification Methods

Due to their practicality and accuracy in text classification, the Support Vector Machine (SVM), Artificial Neural Network (ANN), Naive Bayes (NB), Decision Tree (DT), Correlation (C4.5), and kNN approaches are utilized in this study. Using a classifier allows us to evaluate the efficacy of the six different approaches to text classification. The following are summaries of various approaches. System Flow Diagram is shown in Fig. (**4**).

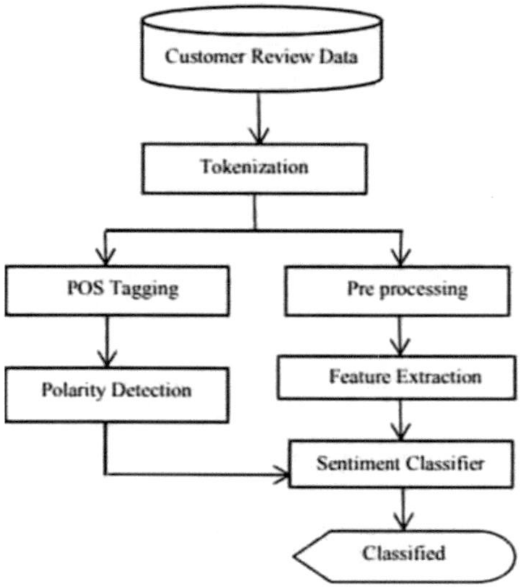


**Fig. (4).** System flow diagram.

### *SVM*

For classifying data, SVM is a supervised learning technique. It is a helpful strategy that zeroes down on the optimal surface for dividing the good from the bad. The training procedure of a support vector machine (SVM) is directed at achieving a maximum margin hyperplane for the classification job of the feature review. Boundaries between the two groups can be drawn indefinitely. The best class can be determined by selecting a decision boundary that separates the two classes by the largest possible distance. The maximum-margin decision boundary, which is near one of the classes' boundaries, would reduce the likelihood of prediction errors. Dot kernels were chosen over radial and polynomial kernels due to their superior performance. Parameters 2 for C.

### *Artificial Neural Networks*

The form and functions of biological neural networks serve as inspiration for artificial neural networks (ANN), also known as neural networks (NN). The core connectionist principle states that mental events may be characterized by interconnected networks of simple and frequently uniform elements; this is the approach taken by a neural network as it processes information. An ANN is often a self-modifying system that modifies its architecture in response to incoming data during the learning phase. The most common applications for contemporary neural networks are the modeling of input-output interactions and the discovery of patterns in data. In a feed-forward neural network, connections between nodes do not repeat themselves in a directed fashion. From the input nodes, it travels forward through the hidden nodes (if any), and finally out the network's output nodes. The network does not contain any infinite loops or cycles.

The two main parts of the backpropagation algorithm, which are the "propagation" and "weight update," make it a supervised learning technique. Both steps are performed repeatedly until the network reaches an acceptable level of performance. In backpropagation algorithms, an error function is calculated by comparing the calculated output to the correct result. Through a number of methods, the mistake is relayed back into the system. The program then uses this data to fine-tune the weights of each link in order to minimize the error function. If the training procedure is repeated enough times, the network will eventually reach a steady state where the inaccuracy in the computations is minimal. In this scenario, we may claim that the network has acquired the ability to do a desired task.

Using ANN for sentiment analysis is a cutting-edge method. Advances in technology and learning algorithms have made it possible to create multi-layered networks, often known as deep learning, which has contributed to ANN's meteoric rise as a machine learning tool. It is not so much the method itself that matters, but rather the availability of data that can be utilized to train machine learning algorithms. In this study, a multi-layer perceptron (a kind of feed-forward neural network) was trained using a back-propagation technique.

### *Naive Bayes*

The NB Tree combines the Bayesian rule with the decision tree to create a supervised classifier. Assuming that attributes are conditionally independent of the label, this technique employs the Bayes rule to compute the likelihood of each given class of occurrences. Applying Bayes' theorem under strong (naive) independence assumptions yields a basic probabilistic classifier known as a Naive Bayes classifier. Naive Bayes classifiers, in their most basic form, work on the assumption that each characteristic of a class (*i.e.* attribute) exists in isolation from all others. If a fruit is red, round, and about 4 inches in diameter, we would call it an apple. A Naive Bayes classifier will account for all of these features as separate contributors to the likelihood that this fruit is an apple, even if they depend on each other or on the existence of the other features.

When it comes to estimating the means and variances of the variables needed for classification, the Naive Bayes classifier has the benefit of requiring only a small quantity of training data. Since it is assumed that there are no variables that are dependent, just the covariance matrix variances per label need to be calculated.

### *Decision Trees*

One type of tree-shaped model or graph is the decision tree. It is more like an upside-down tree, with its roots at the top and its branches spreading out below. This data visualization is preferable to others since it is intuitive and makes sense. One of the input properties is represented by each internal node in the tree. If an input property has a fixed number of potential values, then the number of edges connecting a nominal inner node will also be fixed. Separate bands are affixed to the ends of numerical properties that are being sent. Given the values of the input attributes represented by the route from the root to the leaf, each leaf node stands for a value of the label attribute. In the Simple Cart method, decision trees are built by splitting each decision node into two branches according to several criteria.

### *C4.5. Decision Tree Classifier*

In machine learning, the decision tree is commonly used to automatically generate classification trees from the available training data. The conventional decision tree training method consists of two distinct steps. In the initial stage, known as "tree growing," a tree is constructed by greedily splitting each node. Due to the tree's tendency to overfit the training data, the second phase involves pruning the tree to remove the most improbable nodes. C4.5 is an algorithm for creating binary decision trees. Each decision-making node considers only a single instance attribute. One of the most well-known decision tree-based algorithms is C4.5, which is known as the J48 algorithm in the Weka data mining program. The data is partitioned along the attribute yielding the greatest information gain, and the algorithm derives a judgment from the resulting nodes.

To determine when to cease growing a decision tree, we employ the C4.5 decision tree algorithm and the post-pruning approach during the pruning stage. The tree is slimmed down by using the confidence factor. Our research indicates a confidence level of 0.25. Two occurrences per leaf are left on the clipped plants.

### *KNN*

Because of its ease of use and high level of accuracy, the KNN algorithm has been frequently used for text classification. The KNN classifier employs the class labels of the k nearest neighbors to determine the category of an unknown document based on their similarity to the unknown document during training. The Euclidean distance, the cosine measure, *etc.*, may all be used to determine how similar two reviews are to one another. Each nearest neighbor document's classes are weighted based on the similarity score it has with the test document. If more than one of your k nearest neighbors share the same category, you may calculate your similarity score by adding up the weights of the shared categories.

The k-nearest neighbor number is the most crucial parameter influencing classification during the KNN phase. The best value of k is often established experimentally. In our analysis, we find that k = 1 provides the highest level of categorization accuracy. Additionally, mix Euclidean distance is employed as the distance metric during the k-nearest neighbor discovery phase.

## RESULTS AND DISCUSSION

It is possible to quantify many different performance indicators. Accuracy is one metric since it reveals how many data points were accurately labeled. It is useful for judging how well the classifier functions as a whole. For asymmetrical data sets, however, the accuracy criteria fall short. Criteria like recall and accuracy can be applied here. Both recall and precision measure how many positive examples were properly identified, whereas precision measures how many real positive occurrences were accurately predicted, out of the total number of anticipated positive instances. Harmonic averaging allows F-measure to integrate accuracy and recall criteria. In addition to these criteria, the ROC-area value may be used to assess the efficiency of the model. Using the numbers of correct and incorrect predictions, a graph called the ROC curve may be made. It is also anticipated that the ROC area value would be very close to 1. Each feature set and technique's accuracy, precision, recall, F-measure, and ROC area are determined here, Table **1** is depicted in Performance evaluation of the algorithms.

**Table 1. Performance evaluation of the algorithms.**

| Algorithms | Product | | | | Twitter | | | | Movie | | | |
|---|---|---|---|---|---|---|---|---|---|---|---|---|
| | Prec | Rec | F1 | Acc | Prec | Rec | F1 | Acc | Prec | Rec | F1 | Acc |
| Naive Bayes | 0.67 | 0.59 | 0.53 | 0.59 | 0.59 | 0.60 | 0.59 | 0.62 | 0.53 | 0.66 | 0.52 | 0.66 |
| Logistic Regression | 0.69 | 0.62 | 0.62 | 0.62 | 0.61 | 0.65 | 0.63 | 0.64 | 0.78 | 0.74 | 0.77 | 0.77 |
| Support Vector Machine | 0.61 | 0.60 | 0.60 | 0.61 | 0.59 | 0.57 | 0.58 | 0.57 | 0.71 | 0.70 | 0.62 | 0.70 |
| Decision Tree | 0.58 | 0.57 | 0.56 | 0.57 | 0.54 | 0.58 | 0.58 | 0.58 | 0.66 | 0.64 | 0.63 | 0.64 |

## CONCLUSION

- Sentiment categorization, which accounts for a sizable portion of guest feedback in the hospitality business, has emerged as a critical issue. This is due to the difficulty involved for hotels in predicting consumer dissatisfaction. The method of sentiment categorization is the primary focus of existing research. However, there is a dearth of research comparing the efficacy of various machine learning algorithms and exploring the steps involved in identifying and developing features. Because of this knowledge gap, research into feature identification and engineering for this industry has been conducted. Then, actual information was gathered from a prestigious Iranian hotel chain with locations throughout the world. In addition, six distinct machine-learning algorithms were used to categorize the data. The findings indicate a high degree of precision (98.9%) in making predictions about how people feel.

The following are the most important takeaways from the experiments:

- Review categorization accuracy was the greatest for DT and C4.5.
- With a big feature set, DT and C4.5 fared the best out of the six machine learning algorithms, followed by SVM and ANN.
- Among the six machine learning approaches, NB achieved the best results with the fewest input features.
- With the exception of ANN, the performance of nearly all algorithms improved as more features were included. In other words, with the exception of ANN, increasing the number of features will almost always result in a more accurate model. The following are areas that will receive more study: (1) we will talk about how clustered SVM and multiclass SVM may help with sentiment classification, especially when it comes to neutral reviews (those that are neither good nor negative); (2) The use of punctuation ('!', '?', *etc.*) in sentiment classification will be examined; (3) The use of ensemble learning techniques (such as bagging and voting) to improve sentiment classification will be explored.

## REFERENCES

[1] A. Dadhich, and B. Thankachan, "Sentiment Analysis of Amazon Product Reviews Using Hybrid Rule-based Approach", *International Journal of Engineering and Manufacturing,* 2021.

[2] T. Hasan, and A. Matin, *Extract Sentiment from Customer Reviews: A Better Approach of TF-IDF and BOW-Based Text Classification Using N-Gram Technique,* 2021. [http://dx.doi.org/10.1007/978-981-16-0586-4_19]

[3] S.A. Moeed, G.S. Sangeetha, M. Hafsa, K.M. Manoj, N. Prahaneetha, and T. Sujith, "Polarity Prediction on Product Reviews Based on Classification Algorithms", *2022 International Conference on Innovative Computing, Intelligent Communication and Smart Electrical Systems (ICSES),* pp. 1-6, 2022. [http://dx.doi.org/10.1109/ICSES55317.2022.9914286]

[4] A. Makalesi, "LSTM network-based sentiment analysis for customer reviews", *International Journal of Computer Science and Information Security,* vol. 19, no. 8, pp. 1-7, 2021. [http://dx.doi.org/10.1007/ijcsis.2021.0011]

[5] A.M. Rajeswari, M. Mahalakshmi, R.S. Nithyashree, and G. Nalini, "Sentiment analysis for predicting customer reviews using a hybrid approach", In: *Proceedings of the International Conference on Advanced Computing and Communication Technologies for High Performance Applications (ACCTHPA)* Chennai, India, 2020, pp. 200-205.

[http://dx.doi.org/10.1109/ACCTHPA49870.2020.9321630]

[6] Y. Zhang, and B. Li, "Content-based recommender system on customer reviews using sentiment classification algorithms", In: *Proceedings of the 6th International Conference on Computational Intelligence and Communication Networks (CICN)* Bhopal, India, 2014, pp. 95-100. [http://dx.doi.org/10.1109/CICN.2014.117]

[7] H.J. Christanto, and Y.A. Singgalen, "Sentiment Analysis of Customer Feedback Reviews Towards Hotel's Products and Services in Labuan Bajo", *Journal of Information Systems and Informatics,* 2022.

[8] O. Sharif, M.M. Hoque, and E. Hossain, "Sentiment Analysis of Bengali Texts on Online Restaurant Reviews Using Multinomial Naïve Bayes", *1st International Conference on Advances in Science, Engineering and Robotics Technology (ICASERT),* pp. 1-6, 2019. [http://dx.doi.org/10.1109/ICASERT.2019.8934655]

[9] V.R. Azhaguramyaa, J. Janet, G.R. Madhavan, S. Balakrishnan, and K. Arunkumar, "Sentiment Analysis on Book Reviews Using Machine Learning Techniques", *8th International Conference on Advanced Computing and Communication Systems (ICACCS),* vol. 1, pp. 1530-1534, 2022. [http://dx.doi.org/10.1109/ICACCS54159.2022.9785311]

[10] S. P. Yadav, B. S. Bhati, D. P. Mahato, and S. Kumar, "Federated Learning for IoT Applications", *EAI/Springer Innovations in Communication and Computing. Springer International Publishing,* 2022. [http://dx.doi.org/10.1007/978-3-030-85559-8]

[11] T. Velmurugan, M. Archana, and U. Latha, "Sentiment Analysis of Customer Reviews Based Texts Using Classification Algorithms", *8th Annual International Conference on Network and Information Systems for Computers (ICNISC),* pp. 185-191, 2022. [http://dx.doi.org/10.1109/ICNISC57059.2022.00047]

[12] M.A. Salem, and A.Y. Maghari, "Sentiment Analysis of Mobile Phone Products Reviews Using Classification Algorithms", *2020 International Conference on Promising Electronic Technologies (ICPET),* pp. 84-88, 2020. [http://dx.doi.org/10.1109/ICPET51420.2020.00024]

[13] K. Kaushik, and M. Parmar, *Sentiment Analysis Based on Movie Reviews using Various Classification Techniques: A Review.* [http://dx.doi.org/10.32628/CSEIT217329]

[14] V. Vashisht, A.K. Pandey, and S.P. Yadav, "Speech Recognition using Machine Learning", In: *IEIE Transactions on Smart Processing & Computing* vol. 10. The Institute of Electronics Engineers of Korea, 2021, pp. 233-239. [http://dx.doi.org/10.5573/IEIESPC.2021.10.3.233]

[15] A. Chinnalagu, and A.K. Durairaj, "Context-based sentiment analysis on customer reviews using machine learning linear models", *PeerJ Comput. Sci.,* vol. 7, p. e813, 2021. [http://dx.doi.org/10.7717/peerj-cs.813] [PMID: 35036535]

# CHAPTER 27

# Analysis of Sentiment Employing the Word2vec with CNN-LSTM Classification System

**Rajat Saini**[1,*]

[1] *Centre for Interdisciplinary Research in Business and Technology, Chitkara University Institute of Engineering and Technology, Chitkara University, Punjab, India*

**Abstract:** The identification ofproblems has become easier in sentiment categorization using conventional neural network–based short text classification methods . Word2vec, a convolutional neural network (CNN), and Bidirectional Long-term and Short-term Memory networks (LSTM) are used incombination to overcome this issue. Using Word2vec word embeddings, the CNN-LSTM model was able to attain an accuracy of 91.48%, as demonstrated experimentally. This demonstrates that the hybrid network model outperforms the single-structure neural network when dealing with relatively brief texts.

**Keywords:** CNN, LSTM, Sentiment Analysis, Word2Vec.

## INTRODUCTION

In order to decipher public opinion on a wide range of issues, natural language processing is put to use in sentiment analysis [1]. This practice, also known as opinion mining, involves the system collecting, analyzing, and evaluating the opinions expressed in tweets. Today's social media comments contain several ideas and phrases, making sentiment analysis a difficult process [2]. To get public approval, it is helpful to monitor popular sentiment and respond appropriately. Thanks to advancements in Artificial Intelligence, determining the commenter's intent was a breeze. Numerous Neural Networks exist for handling this kind of problem [3]. In contrast, we employed a hybrid Deep CNN-LSTM Neural Network model to improve the comment vectors we obtained in this experiment [4]. Sentiment analysis makes extensive use of distributed word representations [5]. Word embeddings only take into account the meaning of words. As the Internet has grown, so has the amount of information shared by its users across many mediums [6]. Sentiment analysis is given more force when more perspec-

* **Corresponding author Rajat Saini:** Centre for Interdisciplinary Research in Business and Technology, Chitkara University Institute of Engineering and Technology, Chitkara University, Punjab, India;
E-mail: rajat.saini.orp@chitkara.edu.in

**Pankaj Kumar Mishra and Satya Prakash Yadav (Eds.)**

tives and feelings from different people are made available. However, the lack of consistent labeled data in the Bangla NLP area makes sentiment analysis much more difficult [7]. Word2Vec, GloVe, and fastText are just a few examples of deep learning models that rely heavily on context-independent word embeddings, where each word has a fixed representation regardless of the surrounding text [8]. Meanwhile, pre-trained language models that take into account context, like BERT, have lately made tremendous strides in NLP. These days, social media platforms provide a flood of user-generated social data [9]. Conducting text sentiment analysis on the views stated by users is vital to comprehend people's thoughts and emotional inclinations on a commodity or event in a timely manner. The comment data from microblogging sites is especially complicated since it is usually a hodgepodge of different lengths of messages. Particularly abundant in long text data, the association between words is more intricate than in short text [10].

## RELATED WORK

When using traditional neural network–based short text classification algorithms for emotion analysis, it is simple to make mistakes. Word2vec, a convolutional neural network (CNN), and Bidirectional Long-term and Short-term Memory networks (LSTM) are coupled to overcome this issue. Using Word2vec word embeddings, the CNN-LSTM model was able to attain an accuracy of 91.48%, as demonstrated experimentally. This demonstrates that the hybrid network model outperforms a neural network with a single structure on short texts [11].

Using CNN-LSTM, a deep learning approach that employs Word2Vec as a word embedding layer, our proposed model is able to extract the sentiment of tweets and classify them. 1.6 million Tweets that make up the Sentiment140 dataset were mined from the Twitter API. Tweets are classified using the memory-based state of LSTM cells. Texts conveying emotions like love, hate, friendship, and pride are shared on social networking platforms. We will determine if a tweet is favorable or bad by employing a deep learning technique. When compared to other methods such as SVM and Naive Bayes Classifier, CNN-LSTM performs exceptionally well [12].

In order to extract the characteristics of the word and build a weighted word vector, we have presented the conventional TFIDF technique in addition to Word2Vec embedding. These word vectors are weighted, and the max pooling layer and the CNN receive them as input. In order to get reliable results for sentiment classification, the produced output is forwarded to the Bi-LSTM neural network. The hybrid CNN-LSTM model, which combines Word2Vec with TF-IDF, was tested on the Stanford IMDB movie review dataset, where it achieved impressive results. The model suggested here is based on a CNNLSTM variant of the Deep Neural Network.

Here, we applied BERT's capacity for transfer learning to a deeply integrated model CNN-LSTM in order to improve the accuracy and speed with which sentiment analysis decisions are made. In order to compare CNN-LSTM's performance with that of traditional machine learning algorithms, we also created the concept of transfer learning. Furthermore, we investigate several word embedding methods, including Word2Vec, GloVe, and fastText, and evaluate their efficacy in relation to the BERT transfer learning approach. Therefore, we have demonstrated state-of-the-art binary classification performance for Bangla sentiment analysis, vastly surpassing the performance of any embedding or technique [14].

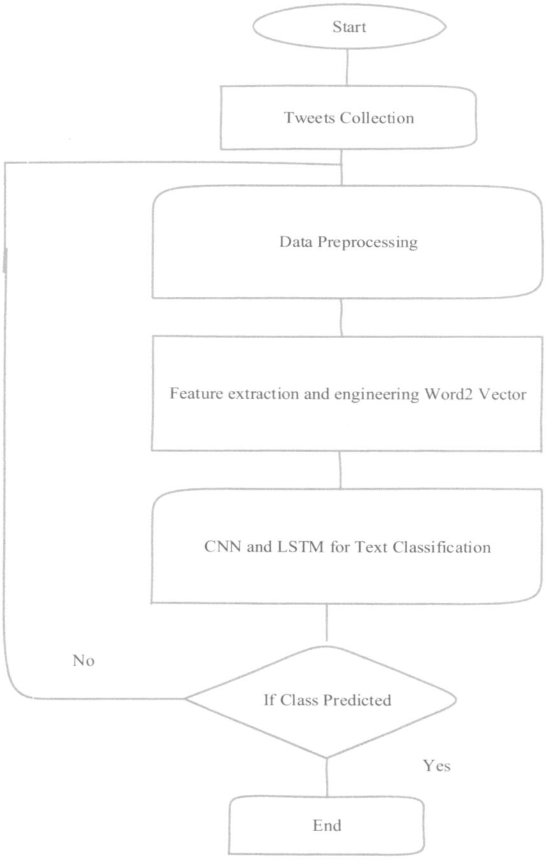


**Fig. (1).** Proposed work flow diagram.

In this article, we present an improved GloVe-CNN-LSTM-based sentiment analysis model to classify these hybrid texts that contain both lengthy and short passages. Words are vectorized with GloVe and characters in the part space are represented by CNN in this model. LSTM is used to establish a connection over time. As an experimental dataset, we leverage data from Twitter user comments about the COVID-19 virus. The experimental results show that this approach is able to effectively recognize the emotional tone of online comments made by users, with an accuracy of sentiment classification on full-text, long-text, and short-text that is clearly higher than that of other deep learning models. Moreover, this technique has been shown to have strong field expansion in trials.

## PROPOSED WORK

Fig. (**1**) describes the proposed work flow diagram. First, we need to prepare the brief text input by removing any common stop words and low-frequency terms.

Word2vec training data is the second step in obtaining the necessary word vectors. You can get a word vector representation of text by feeding it into Word2vec after it has been preprocessed.

Input the data after the pooling operation into the LSTM network layer. • Step 3: Use the word embedding layer to transform the produced word index into the input of CNN.

Fourthly, include the whole layer and classifier. Positive, negative, and neutral data were separated out in this study, and evaluation indices were computed. The experiment uses the prediction score and prediction accuracy to assess the model's categorization performance.

### In-Depth Information Gathering 3.1.1

When it comes to providing sentiment analysis, existing systems have flaws, which are dealt with in the suggested work. Twitter and the Yelp datasets were used in the suggested work.

• Twitter API is used to gather tweets, which are then categorized as either "positive," "negative," or "neutral." This data collection was compiled using NLTK (Natural Language Toolkit). A total of 10,000 Tweets have been archived here, including 4,000 positive, 4,000 negative, and 2,000 neutral. Seven thousand tweets were used for the training part of the simulation's execution, and three thousand were used for the testing phase. The Twitter data set is shown in Table **1**.

• Yelp.

**Table 1. Twitter dataset.**

| Type of sentiments | Values |
|---|---|
| Positive | 4000 |
| Negative | 4000 |
| Neutral | 2000 |

There are a total of 1280969 venues with a total of 6442890 reviews in the Yelp recommendation dataset. The remaining 20% of data were utilized for actual testing purposes, while 80% were used for actual training purposes.

## Data Preprocessing

Every file in the sample dataset used for text classification has a substantial amount of text, with some documents including over a thousand words. These words may then be divided into two groups: those that are important, and those that are irrelevant. The difficulty in categorization is exacerbated by the inclusion of extraneous words. As a result, the documents in the dataset need to be preprocessed. The following is a detailed breakdown of the preparation procedures for documents.

When classifying texts, tokenization is the initial step in the preprocessing phase. A textual object is converted into a tokenized list by this technique. A token is a unit of information that represents a single entity in a document. Each word in the text corresponds to a certain category of tokens, and these categories are defined by the document's author. Stemming is the next preprocessing step. It is an essential process since it greatly simplifies the paper. Stemming refers to the practice of reducing all instances of a term in a text to its most fundamental form, called the base or root form. Stop words are words that do not contribute anything to the categorization process other than a larger number of tokens. Words like "in," "the," "a," and "is" appear far too frequently in papers, although they have no bearing on the categorization process. Approximately 2000 stop words have been identified as part of a larger group of terms that must be eliminated from all publications.

## Text Classification using CNN-LSTM

- Feed-forward convolutional neural networks, or CNNs, are a type of neural network that uses a convolutional neural network to glean feature vectors from the immediate surroundings. By adjusting the weight parameters of the network one layer at a time and training iteratively, the gradient descent approach maximizes the network's accuracy. In this study, we used a convolutional neural network that is built from the following layers: input, convolution, pooling, fully connected, and output. These two-way Brief but extensive Up and down labeling sequences are a natural fit for memory. As a result, it serves as a go-to model for NLP context data. We may use the technique of addition, the expression of all words for the total, or the average method to get the expression of a phrase by combining the expressions of a sentence on the basis of the expression of a word. Long short-term memory (LSTM) models are more effective at capturing long-range dependencies. Because the LSTM may be trained to know what to remember and what to forget, the LSTM has a significant limitation in its application to sentence modeling in that it is unable to encode information in reverse order. To more accurately capture directional semantic relationships, BiLSTM is superior.

- Word2vec One kind of Word Embedding is the Word2vec method. In 2013, Google's Mikolov suggested a novel way of word embedding. Both the CBOW (Continuous Bag-of-Words Model) and the Skip-gram (Continuous Skip-gram Mode) are available as training options for Word2vec. For a quick explanation, see Fig. (**2**).
- CBOW The context is used to infer the current value. A word is removed from a phrase and the player must identify it.
- Skip-gram Infer the context from the present word. It is like being given a word and then being asked to predict the possible words that follow before and after it.

## RESULTS AND DISCUSSION

We ran tests on the Reuters and 20 Newsgroups datasets to demonstrate the practicality and effectiveness of the well-established approaches of CNN, LSTM, and CNN-LSTM classification. All the testing is done on a Windows system with a 3.40GHz processor and 8GB of RAM using MATLAB version 8.0. Five-fold cross-validation is used in conjunction with a One-Against-All multi-category strategy to generate the training and testing datasets. Classification accuracy is provided as a 5-fold median, with 'Accuracy' defined as the proportion of correctly classified instances. Fig. (**2**) displays the CNN-LSTM Classification.

Here TP, TN, FP, and FN are the number of true positive, true negative, false positive, and false negative respectively. Fig. (**3**) shows the comparison of accuracy for Yelp dataset.

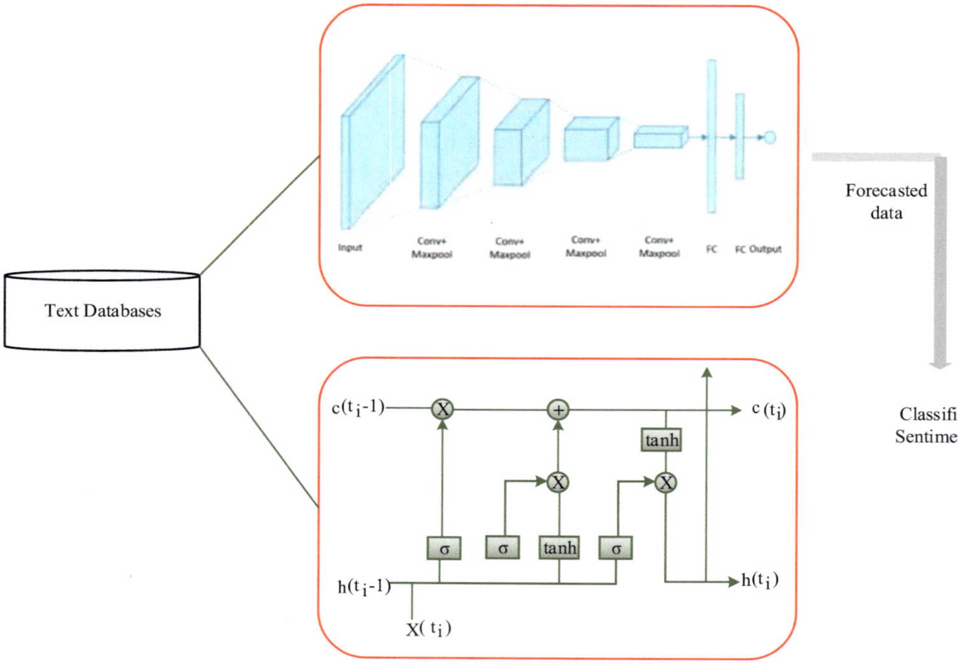


**Fig. (2).** CNN-LSTM Classification.

$$\text{Accuracy} = \frac{TP+TN}{TP+FP+TN+FN} \quad (1)$$

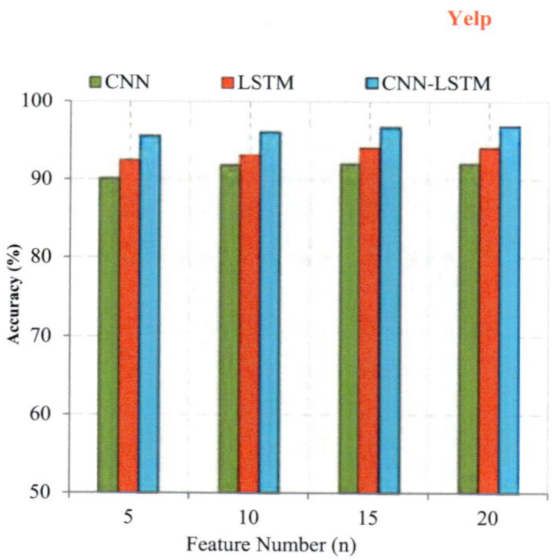


**Fig. (3).** Comparison of accuracy for Yelp dataset.

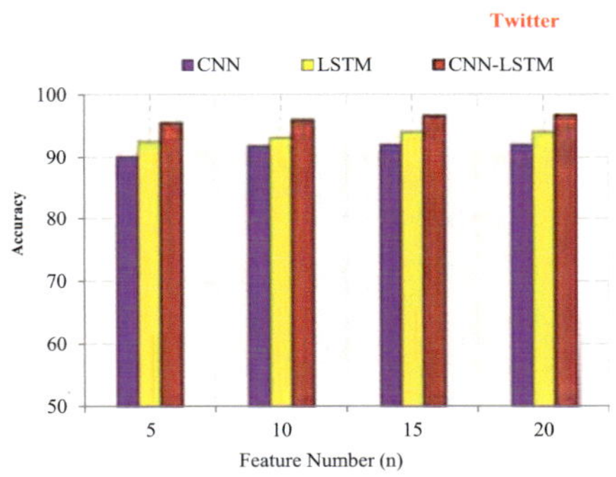


**Fig. (4).** Comparison of accuracy for twitter dataset.

Fig. (**4**) demonstrates the comparison of accuracy for twitter dataset. To statistically evaluate the classification results, another evaluation criterion is used: F1 score, which is determined as,

$$F1 \text{ score} = \frac{2\times \text{Precision} \times \text{Recall}}{\text{Precision} + \text{Recall}}$$

where

$$\text{Precision} = \frac{TP}{TP+FP} \tag{2}$$

$$\text{Recall} = \frac{TP}{TP+FN}$$

Here, TP, FP, TN, and FN are true-positive, false-positive, true-negative and false-negative, respectively.

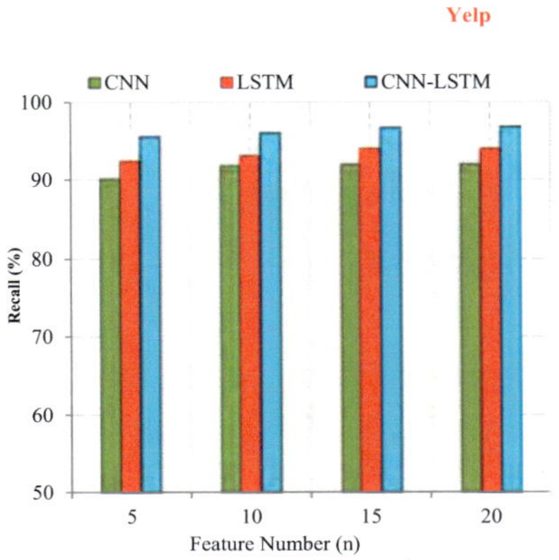


**Fig. (5).** Comparison of recall for Yelp dataset.

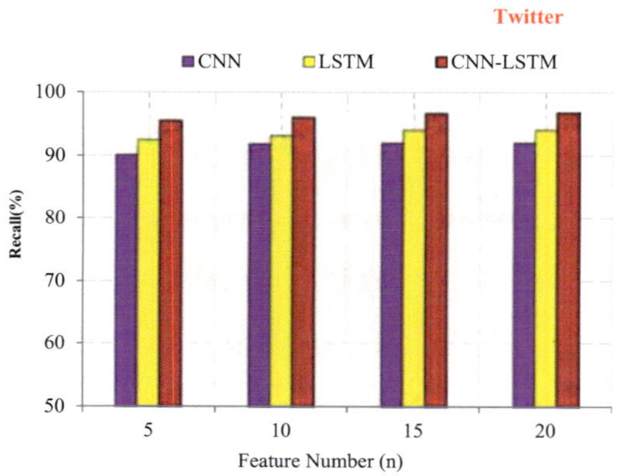


**Fig. (6).** Comparison of recall for Twitter dataset.

Fig. (**5**) displays the comparison of recall for yelp dataset. Fig. (**6**) illustrates the comparison of recall for Twitter dataset.

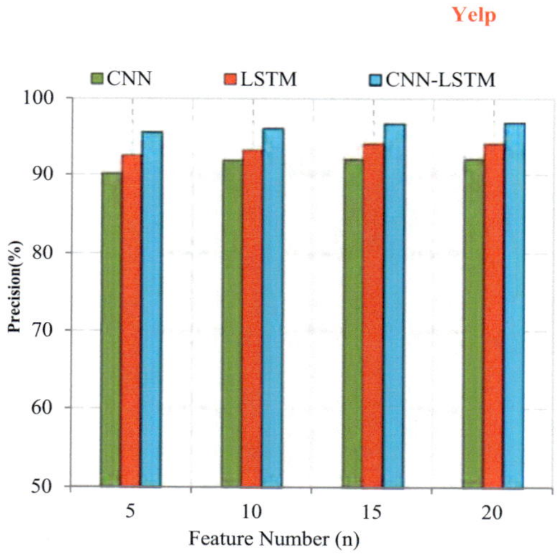


**Fig. (7).** Comparison of precision for Yelp dataset.

This research compares the suggested text combination model to a single model to test the categorization impact of Word2vec, CNN-LSTM. The LSTM approach, the CNN model, and the CNN-LSTM model are all used as benchmarks. Table **3** displays the highlighted experimental findings in red. The classification impact of the Word2vec-CNNLSTM model described in this work is increased by 4.04 percentage points with respect to the CNN-LSTM model. CNN-LSTM came in second, followed by LSTM, CNN, and finally the suggested model. We must refine the analysis by, for example, determining the form of emotional tags, examining the method of extracting sentiment, and examining the model of mining or generating comments on sentiment analysis, because the research is insufficiently detailed and the accuracy is not quite in line with expectations. Deeper models should, in theory, be able to express themselves better since they have more parameters to work with. In order to counteract the overfitting issue that occurs during training, further work will involve tweaking the dropout size and using L2 regularization processing. Fig. (**7**) displays the comparison of precision for the Yelp dataset. Fig. (**8**) shows the comparison of precision for the Twitter dataset.

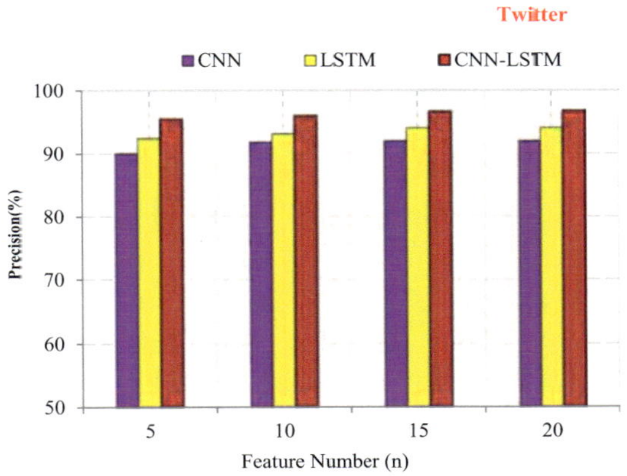


**Fig. (8).** Comparison of precision for Twitter dataset.

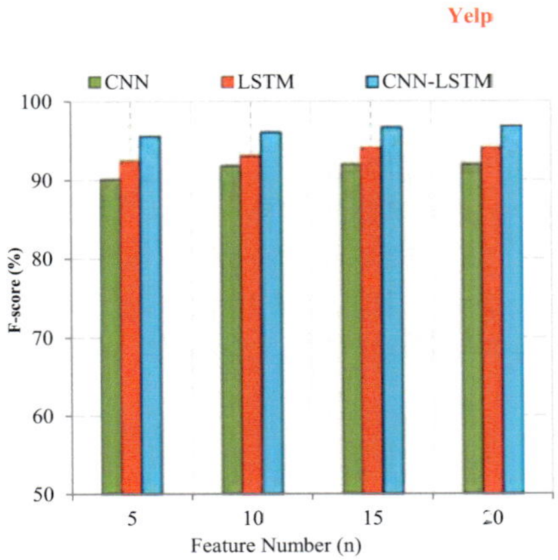


**Fig. (9).** Comparison of F-score for yelp dataset.

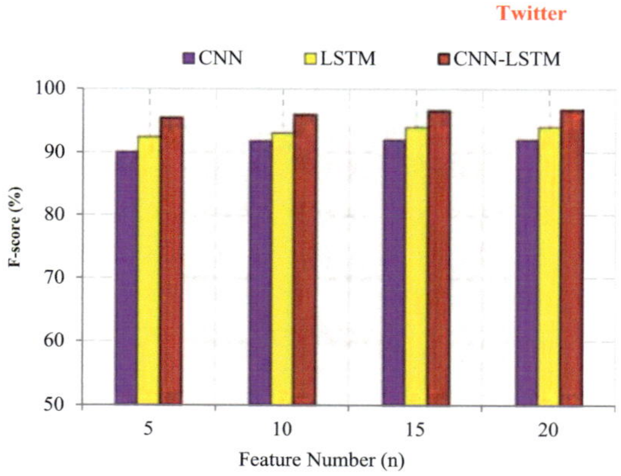


**Fig. (10).** Comparison of F-score for twitter dataset.

## CONCLUSION

Figs. (**9** and **10**) describes the comparison of the proposed work as well as the existing methods such as CNN and LSTM for F-score using feature number in terms of Twitter and Yelp Dataset, respectively. In this study, we introduce a hybrid model combining convolutional and bidirectional recurrent neural networks for Word2vec Embedding-based sentiment analysis of brief texts. Since the CNN is good at extracting features and the LSTM is strong at learning short-term bidirectional relationships of the text, a combined CNN-LSTM model achieves good results. The present model has the drawback of needing more training data and training time than the current baselines, which limits its applicability. Despite this drawback, it can still be useful in classification tasks that need a large amount of training data. By clustering words of comparable meaning using Word2vec, the issue of "polysemy" can be resolved by the training of a vast volume of data to produce word vectors. Long short-term memory (LSTM) is also employed to encode information backward from its intended order of presentation. As part of the study, the results show that the word2vec-CNN-LSTM model makes it simpler and more reliable to analyze text, which in turn considerably improves the precision of sentiment categorization in brief texts.

## REFERENCES

[1] L. Khan, A. Amjad, K.M. Afaq, and H.T. Chang, "Deep Sentiment Analysis Using CNN-LSTM Architecture of English and Roman Urdu Text Shared in Social Media", *Appl. Sci. (Basel),* vol. 12, no. 5, p. 2694, 2022.
[http://dx.doi.org/10.3390/app12052694]

[2] P. Huang, L. Zheng, Y. Wang, and H. Zhu, "Sentiment Analysis of Chinese Text Based on CNN-LSTM Serial Hybrid Model", *10th International Conference on Computing and Pattern Recognition,* 2021.

[3] O. Sarkar, M.F. Ahamed, T.T. Khan, M.K. Ghosh, and M.R. Islam, "An Experimental Framework of Bangla Text Classification for Analyzing Sentiment Applying CNN & LSTM", *2nd International Conference for Emerging Technology (INCET),* pp. 1-6, 2021.

[4] J. Yoon, and H. Kim, *Multi-Channel Lexicon Integrated CNN-LSTM Models for Sentiment Analysis.* ROCLING/IJCLCLP, 2017.

[5] Z. Zhou, J. Chen, J.H. Wu, and R. Wang, "Sentiment Analysis Method for Agricultural Product Review Based on Corpus Characteristics and Deep Learning Model", *2022 International Conference on Machine Learning and Intelligent Systems Engineering (MLISE),* pp. 423-430, 2022. [http://dx.doi.org/10.1109/MLISE57402.2022.00091]

[6] A.H. Ombabi, W. Ouarda, and A.M. Alimi, "Deep learning CNN–LSTM framework for Arabic sentiment analysis using textual information shared in social networks", *Soc. Netw. Anal. Min.,* vol. 10, no. 1, p. 53, 2020. [http://dx.doi.org/10.1007/s13278-020-00668-1]

[7] R. Kumar, H.S. Pannu, and A.K. Malhi, "Aspect-based sentiment analysis using deep networks and stochastic optimization", *Neural Comput. Appl.,* vol. 32, no. 8, pp. 3221-3235, 2020. [http://dx.doi.org/10.1007/s00521-019-04105-z]

[8] P. Yadav, S. Zaidi, C.D.S. Nascimento, V.H.C. de Albuquerque, and S.S. Chauhan, "Analysis and Design of automatically generating for GPS Based Moving Object Tracking System", *2023 International Conference on Artificial Intelligence and Smart Communication (AISC),* 2023 pp. 1-5. Greater Noida, India. [http://dx.doi.org/10.1109/AISC56616.2023.10085180]

[9] M.A. Nasichuddin, T.B. Adji, and W. Widyawan, "Performance Improvement Using CNN for Sentiment Analysis", *IJITEE (International Journal of Information Technology and Electrical Engineering),* 2018.

[10] A.H. Ombabi, W. Ouarda, and A.M. Alimi, "Deep learning CNN–LSTM framework for Arabic sentiment analysis using textual information shared in social networks", *Soc. Netw. Anal. Min.,* vol. 10, no. 1, p. 53, 2020. [http://dx.doi.org/10 1007/s13278-020-00668-1]

[11] W. Yue, and L. Li, 'Sentiment Analysis using Word2vec-CNN-LSTM Classification", *2020 Seventh International Conference on Social Networks Analysis, Management and Security (SNAMS),* pp. 1-5, 2020.

[12] S.P. Yadav, and S. Yadav, "Fusion of Medical Images in Wavelet Domain: A Discrete Mathematical Model", In: *Ingeniería Solidaria* vol. 14. Universidad Cooperativa de Colombia- UCC, 2018, pp. 1-11. [http://dx.doi.org/10.16925/.v14i0.2236]

[13] V. Vashisht, A.K. Pandey, and S.P. Yadav, "Speech Recognition using Machine Learning", In: *IEIE Transactions on Smart Processing & Computing* vol. 10. The Institute of Electronics Engineers of Korea, 2021, pp. 233-239.

[14] N.J. Prottasha, A.A. Sami, M. Kowsher, S.A. Murad, A.K. Bairagi, M. Masud, and M Baz, "Transfer Learning for Sentiment Analysis Using BERT Based Supervised Fine-Tuning", *Sensors (Basel),* vol. 22, no. 11, p. 4157, 2022. [http://dx.doi.org/10.3390/s22114157] [PMID: 35684778]

# CHAPTER 28

# Hadoop-based Twitter Sentiment Analysis Using Deep Learning

**Manpreet Singh**[1,*]

[1] *Centre for Interdisciplinary Research in Business and Technology, Chitkara University Institute of Engineering and Technology, Chitkara University, Punjab, India*

**Abstract:** Sentiment analysis, the practice of classifying and identifying opinions displayed in audio, words, database reports, and tweets to ascertain if the opinion is positive, neutral, or negative, is of great interest to many individuals in the microblogging service arena. It could be challenging to extract sentiment from Twitter data due to its quirks. The research suggests a way to analyze sentiment using a Hadoop infrastructure with a deep learning classifier. In order to gather characteristics, data is distributed across Hadoop nodes. After that, the data from Twitter is parsed for the most crucial parts. The input data from Twitter is sorted into two categories, positive review along with negative review, *via* a deep learning algorithm, including a deep recurrent neural networks classifier. Some of the metrics used to measure performance include classification accuracy, specificity, and sensitivity. With a sensitivity of 0.9404 and a generality of 0.9157, the proposed technique surpassed traditional methods in classification with a precision of 0.9302.

**Keywords:** Big data, Deep learning, Hadoop, Twitter sentiment analysis.

## INTRODUCTION

Microblogging platforms are focusing on sentiment analysis, which involves categorizing and recognizing opinions expressed in audio, text, database sources, as well as tweets as positive, neutral, or negative [1]. Twitter data has unique characteristics that make sentiment analysis challenging. There are millions of people using Twitter, which makes it a very popular micro-blogging service [2]. Twitter users update their statuses, or "tweets," and discuss current events and topics by using hashtags. As a result, Twitter has emerged as a powerful and reliable barometer of public sentiment [3]. Twitter produces a massive volume of data, making it tough to manually examine all of it. Twitter sentiment detectors (TSDs) are superior to more conventional methods for gauging customer satisfac-

* **Corresponding author Manpreet Singh:** Centre for Interdisciplinary Research in Business and Technology, Chitkara University Institute of Engineering and Technology, Chitkara University, Punjab, India;
E-mail: manpreet.singh.orp@chitkara.edu.in

**Pankaj Kumar Mishra and Satya Prakash Yadav (Eds.)**

tion with the quality of a service or product [4]. Both the accuracy and performance of TSDs in detecting patterns and making accurate classifications are heavily reliant on the efficiency of the classification methods used [5]. Existing machine learning technologies have the potential to change firms into those handled by automated processes, but the time needed is a major concern [6]. Several real-world applications have made use of deep learning methods in areas like sentiment analysis [7]. To extract insights from unstructured data like texts or tweets and represent them in models, deep learning techniques use a variety of algorithms. A person's voice may be heard all around the world *via* their use of online social media [8]. People choose social networking sites because they make it simple to share their thoughts and views and stay abreast of the latest developments in the world of fashion and pop culture [9]. Every day, thousands upon thousands of tweets are sent on Twitter about a wide range of subjects [10]. One objective of the proposed sentiment analysis model is to use deep recurrent neural networks to analyze real-valued input data from Twitter. The assessment emphasizes the potential speed of findings for sentiment analysis. Feature extraction and classification are the two parts of the proposed procedure. Distributing the data *via* the Hadoop cluster is the first stage in obtaining features from input Twitter data. Combining the learned traits with a classifier known as a deep recurrent neural network (DARN) is what happens in the classification module. Using the obtained attributes, the classifier from deep recurrent neural systems produces two outputs: positive review and negative review. Section 2 shows a synopsis of conventional sentiment analysis methods, whereas Part 1 gives an introduction to sentiment analysis in general. Section 3 lays out the approach, Section 4 displays the findings, and Section 5 draws the conclusion.

## RELATED WORK

Using a Hadoop architecture and a deep learning classifier, this study proposes a method for sentiment analysis. The distribution of data for feature extraction is handled by the Hadoop cluster. Then, the important elements are culled from the Twitter information. The input data from Twitter is sorted into two categories, positive review, and negative review, *via* a deep learning algorithm, namely a deep recurrent neural networks classifier. Performance evaluations make use of measures like specificity, sensitivity, and accuracy in categorization. The accuracy of classification (0.9302), sensitivity (0.9404), and specificity (0.9157) were all areas in which the proposed method excelled above more traditional methods [11].

Our new approach to sentiment analysis is the Hybrid Lexicon-Naive Bayes Classifier or HL-NBC. We first aggregate related subjects and filter out irrelevant ones before feeding them into the emotion assessment engine. The proposed method is tested using Lexicon, a Bayesian naive classifier for bi-gram and uni-gram features. The suggested HL-NBC technique performs sentiment categorization more effectively than the other approaches and has an accuracy of 82%. We also saw a 93% reduction in processing time for bigger datasets when compared to conventional techniques of doing sentiment analysis [12].

These models are put to use in order to draw conclusions regarding unmodeled datasets. Our innovative method for sentiment analysis leverages deep learning architectures to improve detection accuracy as well as efficiency. It combines the "universal language modelling fine-tuning" (ULMFiT) with a support vector machine (SVM). This technique reveals a novel deep-learning strategy for assessing the sentiment expressed by users of Twitter on specific subjects. When tested extensively on three different datasets, our model consistently outperforms the state-of-the-art. For example, its accuracy reaches 99.78% when used on the Twitter US Airlines datasets [13].

This massive trove of unstructured data may be organised and processed to serve a variety of social, industrial, economic, and governmental purposes. Hadoop, with its ability to analyse massive datasets in parallel, is the finest technology for analysing Twitter data. Customers' actions may be better understood by analysing the views expressed on Twitter, which cover a wide range of issues. In order to determine the sentiment of each tweet, an analysis is performed utilising Hadoop and its ecosystem. In this study, we examine the efficacy of a Big data technique for doing sentiment analysis on Twitter data. We have utilised Apache Flume to continuously feed HDFS with tweets from Twitter. Tweets are retrieved from raw nested Twitter data using pig scripts. One way to classify tweets according to their attitude is by using a dictionary-based approach [14].

As a result of the incredible growth of social media platforms as a way for people to connect and share ideas, there is a deluge of data available on these sites. To describe this ever-growing database, the phrase "Big Data" has recently surfaced. As a result, sentiment analysis (also known as optimum mining) is one area where the use of new approaches from data mining research has considerable promise to obtain more accurate categorization of hidden information in Big Data. In this article, we build upon existing work by presenting a Nave Bayes/Random Forest hybrid strategy for mining Twitter datasets. In a nutshell, relevant data sets are gathered from Twitter through the Twitter API and the hybrid approach is then shown and compared to a Naive Bayes classifier-only approach. The results of the sentiment categorization suggest that the hybrid strategy is more accurate and time-efficient [15].

## PROPOSED WORK

### System Overview

Opinionated text may be analyzed and categorized with the use of a technique called sentiment analysis. The sentiment analysis gave a broad picture of how people felt about various issues. Here, we analyze sentiment using a deep learning classifiers and the Hadoop framework. In order to begin feature extraction from Twitter data, a Hadoop cluster is first used. We retrieve features throughout the mapper phase. In the mapper phase, important parts of the Twitter data are extracted, including all-caps, emoticons, hashtags, extended components, emotion lexicon, negation, and punctuation. Once the features have been collected, they are shuffled in a way that generates feature selection lists based on those features. The reducer receives the list of distinguishing characteristics. In the reduction phase, characteristics are sorted into two categories—positive and negative reviews—using a deep recurrent neural network classifier.

### Sentiment Analysis using Hadoop

Hadoop is a structure for managing large-scale data processing and handling problems associated with parallel executions, such as automated job synchronization, failure recognition, and restoration. The user processes the data in Hadoop by creating MapReduce models. As a result, Twitter data is effectively analyzed for sentiment using the Hadoop platform.

- **Map:** Upon initialization, the Hadoop framework considers 100 tweet as input data. The calculation includes both the total amount of HDFS blocks required for input data processing as well as the HDFS route for every block. The calculated block paths are then transferred to the HDFS shared directory using the task jar file and the HDFS configuration files. The framework cannot process any of the blocks until it builds the Map tasks. A total of ten of those Mappers are needed for processing the data blocks. After the data blocks have been processed, characteristics like punctuation, capitalization, emoticons, hashtags as well, extended units, emotion lexicon, denial, and more may be obtained from the Twitter data. A word that consists entirely of capital letters is considered to be one entity. You can tell whether an emoticon is joyful or sad by looking at its qualities. If a certain amount of hashtags are present, the Hashtag function will indicate it. The length of the extended unit, is a representation of the number of basic computational units. Included in the emotions lexicon are the maximum sentiment score, total sentiment score, and number of emotion terms for each lexicon. In segmentation, the number of negations is represented by the negation. The amount of consecutive periods, commas, and question marks or exclamation marks constitutes the punctuation.

- **Shuffle:** The intermediate outcome of the map phase was passed on to the shuffle phase before the reduce phase. Post-map shuffle, replicate, and sort are the three stages that make up the shuffle phase. At the conclusion of the Map operation, the output is partitioned and reorganized in a procedure known as "post-Map shuffling." This step involves categorizing and sorting the characteristics that were derived from the Twitter data. In the copying phase, the results from the Map process are saved to disk locally. The output of the merging and sorting operations performed in the sorting step is the input to the reducer stage. The merging technique, which combines and sorts the distinct properties, provides inputs to the reduction step.
- **Reduce:** The reduction step makes use of deep CNN to classify features as either "positive" or "negative" reviews. In a guided machine learning approach, convolutional neural networks (CNNs) are artificial neurons having more than two feedback loops.

CNN can only be trained in a supervised setting with the use of a training database and certain input pairings. In order to function, CNN has three layers: input, hidden, and output. The network receives as input the vector sequence at time t. In Fig. (**1**) we can see the System Model.

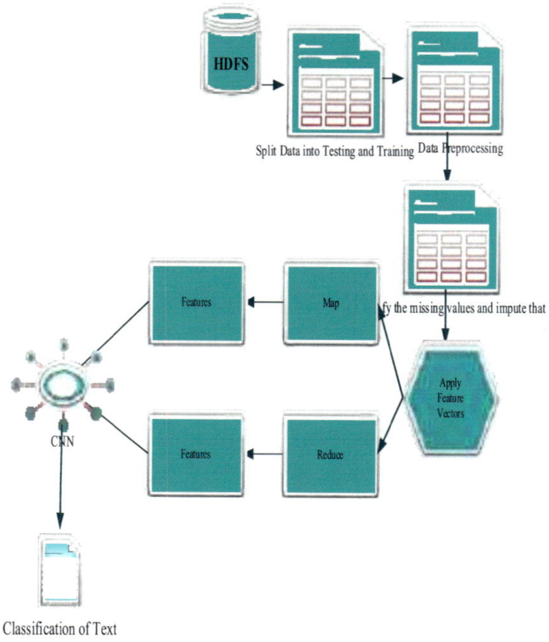


**Fig. (1).** System model.

$$H_r = (H_1, \ldots, H_n) \quad (1)$$

The input-receiving hidden units of a fully connected convolutional neural network (CNN) are represented by the weight matrix, m_w. We use recurrent connections to connect the h hidden components in the hidden layer.

$$W_s = (D_1, D_2, \ldots, D_w) \quad (2)$$

The system's state space is represented as a hidden layer.

$$W_t = M_a(B_t) \quad , \quad (3)$$

where the hidden layer activation function is represented as M_i (.) and the visible memory content is governed by the output gate (B_f), which is written as,

$$B_i = \gamma_w H_i + \gamma_w D_{i-1} + b_{kidim} \quad (4)$$

the weight matrix denoted as γ and the bias of the hidden units denoted as b_hadm. As γ_w, we can see the hidden layers connected to the hidden units. Here is what the deep CNN's output layer looks like:

$$V_i = V_1, \ldots, V_s \quad (5)$$

where, $n = 2$, At time $t$, the output layer is represented as,

$$V_t = a_o(\gamma_{\text{in}} D_t + b_{\text{oujpur}}) \quad (6)$$

where, $\alpha^{\infty}(.)$ *is the activational functional and* $b^{awpo}$ that the input layer's bias vector looks like. Therefore, the weighted link among the hidden units with the output layer is represented by γ_n. The aforementioned formula is repeated for all values of t between 1 and t. At every step, the input vector is used by the hidden layer to forecast the output layer's ultimate outcome. When CNN is in its hidden state, the values it has collected summarize the specific data from its previous states. The output layer's accurate categorization is supplied by the combined data.

## RESULTS AND DISCUSSION

This section explains how the deep CNN technique that is proposed here is evaluated. One way to evaluate the proposed Hadoop-based deep CNN technique is to compare it to more conventional approaches.

### Testing environment

The suggested Hadoop-based deep CNN is implemented in PYTHON, which runs on Windows 8 PCs. To evaluate the proposed Hadoop-based deep CNN technique, we use data collected from the Twitter US Airline Sentiment dataset.

### Performance metrics

The categorization precision, specificity, and sensitivity are only few of the evaluation criteria used to evaluate the Hadoop-based deep CNN approach that was suggested. Comparing the proposed Hadoop-based deep CNN to traditional methods like SVM, NB, and PSO are performed. Metrics of performance, such as classification precision, specificity, and sensitivity are used in an evaluation of the proposed Hadoop-based deep CNN approach.

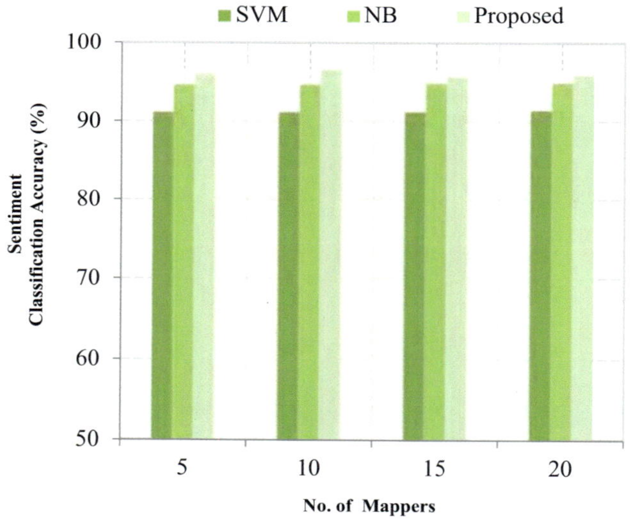


**Fig. (2).** Sentiment classification accuracy *vs.* No of mappers.

In Fig. (**2**), we see an examination of the classification accuracy with different percentages of training. Accuracy analysis of categorization for N=5 mappers is depicted in Fig. (**2a**). SVM, PSO, NB, and the suggested Hadoop-based deep CNN approach all achieved classification accuracies of 0.9086, 0.9112, 0.9206, and 0.93000 for a training percentage of 90%, respectively. The examination of categorization accuracy for a Number of Mappers=6 is depicted in Fig. (**2b**). SVM, PSO, and NB, in addition to the suggested Hadoop-based deep CNN technique all achieve classification accuracies of 0.9063, 0.9100, 0.9232, and 0.9302 when the training percentage is set to 90%.

Fig. (**3**) displays the outcomes of a sensitivity analysis that was conducted using different training percentages. As shown in Fig. (**3a**), the sensitivity analysis was conducted with a sample size of 5 mappers. The sensitivity of SVM is 0.9214, that of PSO is 0.9242, that of NB is 0.9320, and that of the suggested Hadoop-based deep CNN approach is 0.9403 even at 90% training percentage. The sensitivity analysis for Number of Mappers =6 is depicted in Fig. (**3b**). Sensitivity values of 0.9194, 0.9227, 0.9344, and 0.9404 are achieved using SVM, PSO, NB, and the suggested Hadoop-based deep CNN approach, with a training percentage of 90 percent, respectively.

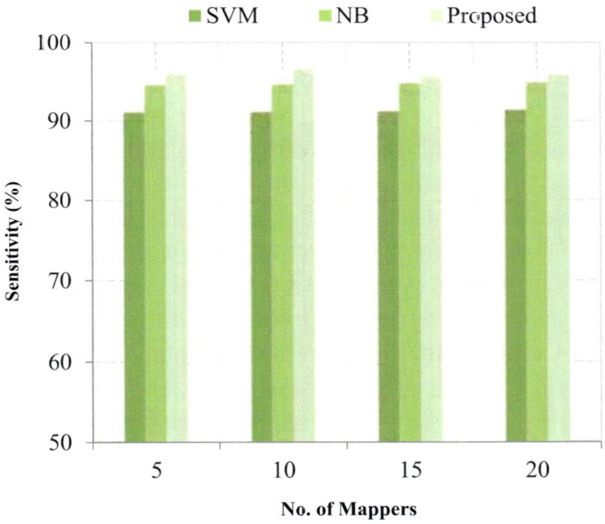


**Fig. (3).** Sensitivity *vs.* No of mappers.

Fig. (**4**) depicts a study of specificity with different percentages of training. Fig. (**4a**) displays the results of the specificity analysis with a number of mappers equal to 5. At a 90% success rate during training, SVM, PSO, NB, and the suggested Hadoop-based deep CNN technique all obtained specificities of 0.8908, 0.8944, 0.9045, and 0.9155, respectively. For the specificity study with 6 mappers, see Fig. (**4b**). When trained using the suggested Hadoop-based deep CNN approach at 90%, SVM, PSO, and NB attained specificities of 0.9076, 0.8881, 0.8924, and 0.9157, respectively.

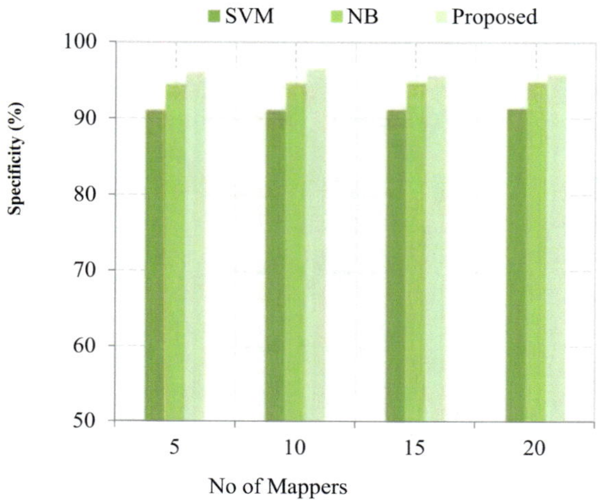


**Fig. (4).** Specificity *vs.* No of mappers.

## CONCLUSION

Internet users interested in receiving instant feedback on businesses or items have given Twitter data sentiment analysis a lot of attention. This research presents a sentiment analysis system that uses a classifier based on deep learning and is built on Hadoop. The Hadoop platform is used to scatter the data for the procedure of extracting features. Capitalization, emoticons, hashtags as well, extended units, sentiment vocabulary, negation, and punctuation are some of the key attributes that are parsed from the input Twitter data throughout the feature extraction operation. The classification module employs a deep recurrent neural network, which is a kind of deep learning classifier, trained on the acquired attributes, to partition the Twitter data into positive evaluations and negative critiques. Classification accuracy, sensitivity, and specificity are some of the performance criteria used to assess the efficacy of the suggested Hadoop-based deep CNN approach in this study. Maximum accuracy (0.9302), sensitivity (0.9404), and specificity (0.9157) were achieved by the suggested Hadoop-based deep CNN approach when compared to other current methods. The feature extraction procedure can be improved in the future by incorporating additional features.

## REFERENCES

[1] M. Skuza, and A. Romanowski, "Sentiment analysis of Twitter data within big data distributed environment for stock prediction", *2015 Federated Conference on Computer Science and Information Systems (FedCSIS),* pp. 1349-1354, 2015. [http://dx.doi.org/10.15439/2015F230]

[2] A. Romanowski, and M. Skuza, "Towards Predicting Stock Price Moves with Aid of Sentiment

Analysis of Twitter Social Network Data and Big Data Processing Environment", 2017. [http://dx.doi.org/10.1007/978-3-319-47208-9_7]

[3] Y. Amrutphale, N. Vijayvargiya, and V. Malviya, "A Novel Adaptive Approach for Sentiment Analysis on Social Media Data", 2020. [http://dx.doi.org/10.1007/978-981-15-2071-6_60]

[4] S.P. Yadav, S. Zaidi, C.D.S. Nascimento, V.H.C. de Albuquerque, and S.S. Chauhan, "Analysis and Design of automatically generating for GPS Based Moving Object Tracking System", *2023 International Conference on Artificial Intelligence and Smart Communication (AISC)* 2023 pp. 1-5. Greater Noida, India. [http://dx.doi.org/10.1109/AISC56616.2023.10085180]

[5] I. Rane, S. Sardesai, and R. Tallu, "Twespa: A modern approach to Twitter sentiment analysis", *Int. J. Res. Appl. Sci. Eng. Technol.*, vol. 8, no. 5, pp. 225-230, 2020. [http://dx.doi.org/10.22214/ijraset.2020.5304]

[6] L. Mohan, and S. Elayidom, "A Novel approach to Time based Collective User Sentiment Analysis for Twitter Data - A BigData perspective", *Int. J. Web Appl.*, vol. 9, pp. 96-112, 2017.

[7] D. Samariya, A. Matariya, D. Raval, L.D. Babu, E.D. Raj, and E. Vekariya, "A Hybrid Approach for Big Data Analysis of Cricket Fan Sentiments in Twitter", 2016. [http://dx.doi.org/10 1007/978-981-10-0129-1_53]

[8] G. Vaitheeswaran, and L. Arockiam, "A Novel Lexicon Based Approach to Enhance the Accuracy of Sentiment Analysis on Big Data", 2016.

[9] A. Ahmet, and T. Abdullah, "Real-Time Social Media Analytics with Deep Transformer Language Models: A Big Data Approach", *14th International Conference on Big Data Science and Engineering (BigDataSE),* pp. 41-48, 2020. [http://dx.doi.org/10.1109/BigDataSE50710.2020.00014]

[10] M. Khan, and A. Malviya, "Big data approach for sentiment analysis of twitter data using Hadoop framework and deep learning", *International Conference on Emerging Trends in Information Technology and Engineering (ic-ETITE),* pp. 1-5, 2020. [http://dx.doi.org/10.1109/ic-ETITE47903.2020.201]

[11] A.P. Rodrigues, and N.N. Chiplunkar, "A new big data approach for topic classification and sentiment analysis of Twitter data", *Evol. Intell.*, pp. 1-11, 2019.

[12] B. AlBadani, R. Shi, and J. Dong, "A Novel Machine Learning Approach for Sentiment Analysis on Twitter Incorporating the Universal Language Model Fine-Tuning and SVM", *Applied System Innovation,* 2022. [http://dx.doi.org/10.3390/asi5010013]

[13] A.P. Rodrigues, A.S. Rao, and N.N. Chiplunkar, "Sentiment Analysis of Real Time Twitter Data Using Big Data Approach", *2nd International Conference on Computational Systems and Information Technology for Sustainable Solution (CSITSS),* pp. 1-6, 2017. [http://dx.doi.org/10.1109/CSITSS.2017.8447656]

[14] A. Srivastava, V. Singh, and G.S. Drall, "Sentiment Analysis of Twitter Data", *Int. J. Healthc. Inf. Syst. Inform.*, vol. 14, no. 2, pp. 1-16, 2019. [http://dx.doi.org/10.4018/IJHISI.2019040101]

# CHAPTER 29

# A Contrast Between Bert and Word2vec's Approaches to Text Sentiment Analysis

**Manish Nagpal**[1,*]

[1] *Centre for Interdisciplinary Research in Business and Technology, Chitkara University Institute of Engineering and Technology, Chitkara University, Punjab, India*

**Abstract:** A novel approach to creating a dataset to train a neural network that can analyze the tone of social media postings is proposed in this study. The paper goes on to detail how the word2vec and BERT algorithms may be used in a neural network to analyze social media messages and evaluate their emotional tone. A hybrid of cosine similarity as well as ontological mappings based on a tweaked version of the Term Frequency-Inverse Document Frequency (TFIDF) characteristics is used by the algorithm for semantic searching. The execution includes sentiment analysis, phrase extraction process, textual belief indicator, keyword-based search, as well as text summary, among other things. Additionally, trials were carried out proving the efficacy of the methods presented. The efficiency of stemming and lemmatization of the text in creating a training set for sentiment analysis was also tested experimentally.

**Keywords:** Bert model, Text sentiment analysis, Training tweets, Testing tweets, Word2vector.

## INTRODUCTION

The word vector representation of the text is often obtained by the use of tools like Word2Vec, GloVe, *etc* [1]. The word context is lost with these approaches. Sentiment analysis is a highly applicable technique that helps address issues like the disorganisation of online discussion threads and the need for precisely located user data [2, 3]. While there has been some progress in the field of Chinese sentiment analysis, there is still much left to learn. One pressing issue is how different text feature representation methods and feature selection mechanisms affect classification performance [4, 5]. Memes are a recent phenomenon in the realm of online material. Feelings about a topic, item, person, or thing are included in a meme [6]. Memes may take the shape of either text or a picture, or both. Memes may be caustic, critical, humorous, and even political [7]. The majo-

* **Corresponding author Manish Nagpal:** Centre for Interdisciplinary Research in Business and Technology, Chitkara University Institute of Engineering and Technology, Chitkara University, Punjab, India;
E-mail: manish.nagpal.orp@chitkara.edu.in

**Pankaj Kumar Mishra and Satya Prakash Yadav (Eds.)**

rity of existing sentiment analysis techniques concentrate on text. The proliferation of the internet has made it possible to share opinions on a wide range of subjects through various online forums. It is crucial for businesses and data scientists to examine the information included in these remarks [8]. There is a plethora of approaches to data analysis. Recent years have also seen an uptick in the number of research works using language models for the purpose of sentiment analysis and text categorization. This study compares the results of two text categorization methods—Support Vector Machine (SVM) as well as Neural Network (NN) for text classification—with four text embedding methods—word2vec, Glove, BERT, as well as GPT-2—using user reviews from two common e-commerce sites, Zappos as well as Yelp [9, 10].

With Twitter as a case study, this research aims to undertake sentiment analysis as well as opinion identification on social networking information. One way to determine whether a tweet is neutral, good, or unfavorable in tone is to use an analysis of sentiment. Finding out whether a particular tweet contains useful opinions for the creation of products is the goal of attitude detection. Our primary goal is to do this by comparing the sentiment evaluation as well as opinion identification embedded words of Word2Vec as well as BERT. In order to determine which method works better with tiny to medium amounts of data, this research also compares standard machine learning with deep learning. The following are, hence, the aims of the research:

- Word2Vec and BERT both produce word insertions; compare their performance on sentiment evaluation as well as opinion identification.
- Evaluate how well Deep Learning as well as conventional Machine Learning method deals with data sets that are moderate in size.
- Use the results of the application case's sentiment assessment as well as opinion identification tasks to inform product recommendations.

## RELATED WORK

A neural network framework for sentiment analysis of text is suggested in this study to solve this problem. It combines a language model that has been pre-trained with a bidirectional short-term long-term memory network as well as an attention mechanism. Bidirectional encoding representation from transformers is the name of this concept. To begin, the word vector including contextual semantic information is acquired using the BERT pre-training algorithm. The two-way long- and short-term memory network is then used in this article to derive context-related characteristics for deep learning. In order to conduct text sentiment categorization, highlight key points, and apply weights to the retrieved information, the attention mechanism is developed. On the SST (Stanford sentiment treebank) test set, the accuracy rate may reach 89.17%, indicating an increase in accuracy relative to previous approaches [11].

In this research, we have used TF-IDF to rank the words in the text according to their frequency of occurrence, so determining their relative significance. To further investigate the emotional leanings of texts, we used SVM and ELM with kernels. Results from experiments demonstrate that ELM with kernels may provide accurate classifications more quickly than SVM [12].

This study uses text as well as image-based Indonesian memes to examine the effectiveness of four sentiment evaluation methods. Memes in text were first retrieved and then categorized utilizing supervised techniques for machine learning such as Decision Tree, Convolutional Neural Networks (CNN), Naive Bayes, and Support Vector Machines, among others. According to the results, the Naive Bayes method achieved the highest accuracy (65.4% in this case) when it came to analyzing sentiment on memes content [13].

In this research, we use language models to do Turkish sentiment analysis on datasets of hotel and film reviews. The linguistic examples are selected because they are uncommon in contemporary Turkish writing. The pre-trained Turkish language models BERT, ALBERT, ELECTRA, as well as DistilBERT have been trained as well as tested on these datasets. Also included is a text filtering method for sentiment analysis, the objective of which is to exclude terms from positively or negatively tagged content that can elicit the inverse sentiment. This technique also allows for the retraining of datasets using language models and the subsequent evaluation of model accuracy levels. This research draws parallels to others that have used the same datasets. The investigation produces state-of-t-e-art outcomes using language models, as measured by the accuracy values when compared to prior research. Training the ELECTRA language model with the suggested text filtering strategy yielded the best results [14].

The results demonstrate that BERT when combined with SVM and NN, is the top-performing text embedding approach across both datasets. Overall text classification using NN is also shown to be superior to using SVM. Our goal is to present a multidimensional comparison in an exploratory effort to identify the best algorithm for consumer review data, with the conclusion being that BERT and NN are capable of producing adequate results in the vast majority of cases [15].

## PROPOSED WORK

### System Model

This research evaluates Word2Vec, a popular word embedding method, against BERT, a transformer, and many popular Machine Learning and Deep Learning algorithms. The primary purpose of this comparison is to determine which approach is most suited for the task of sentiment analysis and opinion identification, and whether or not switching up the word embedding strategy will improve the model's performance. To determine if a tweet's context is negative, favorable, or neutral, sentiment analysis can be performed. However, opinion identification is performed to ascertain whether or not a given tweet has an opinion that might contribute to the product development process. Then, we evaluate Deep Learning against a traditional Machine Learning technique. The purpose of this analysis is to determine which of the two approaches is superior when dealing with moderate-sized data sets. Finally, the best-performing model will be used to construct word graphs that aid the process by disseminating recommendations based on the attitudes and opinions expressed in the tweets.

### Text Preprocessing

For sentiment analysis, we just took two columns out of the data set: "text" (which includes the actual tweets) as well as "airline attitude" (which gives the values for how each tweet was rated: favorable, unfavorable, or unfavorable). The "text" column underwent certain preparation processes, such as the removal of troublesome characters and stop words through a stopword list obtained from Spacy. The first 3000 tweets in the sample were manually tagged with a binary variable for the opinion identification job. Tweets with the "yes" mark include useful views that may be used in the text categorization process. The tweeters all had particular things they liked or hated about the product and explained why in their posts. Tweets that are answered with a "no" indicate that they do not provide any helpful feedback for the NPD stage. Twitter posters often express feelings about a product without providing any concrete evidence for their claims. This" no" category also includes tweets that pose questions. We employed the identical preprocessing methods from the sentiment analysis job once labeling was complete.

There are a lot of typos, acronyms, multi-meaning words, and slang expressions in the user comments. However, the performance of the recommendation system is negatively impacted by noisy input, which lowers the accuracy of the sentiment categorization. The four steps of preprocessing are as follows:

• ***Tokenization***

The feedback from reviewers is tokenized so that it may be used in many ways.

• ***Removal and corrections***

It performs four operations, including punctuation correction, elimination of unnecessary words, spelling correction, and slang correction.

• ***Replacement***

It performed the job of stemming and expanding acronyms in addition to replacing emojis.

• ***PoS tagging***

Words may be broken down into its components using a technique called "Parts of Speech" tagging.

The process of feature extraction begins with a preprocessing step. Here are the stages of preprocessing:

- User comments that contain a URL (http://url), hashtags (#), a retweet (RT), or a @username link should be deleted.
- Getting rid of the extra y's in "happy".
- All uppercase letters are changed to lowercase ones (good becomes good, for example).
- Spelling errors and slang should be avoided at all costs.
- Get rid of stop words, which are terms like preposition, conjunction, and determiner that are used frequently but have no particular meaning. Stop word removal describes this operation.
- The stemming procedure involves locating the root word from the stem words in order to reduce the size of the term. Take out any instances of plurals, genders, conjugation, *etc*.
- Disable user comments from being submitted twice.
- Substitute appropriate emojis for all of them.

## Word Embedding

Word embedding is a state-of-the-art text representation approach in NLP, in which individual words or sentences are encoded as a vector of real values. The research will make use of Word2Vec trained using transfer learning. Word2Vec is a model built on a neural network that converts words in a corpus into vectors that can understand their context. In this research, we make use of a Google News dataset containing about 100 billion English words and 3 million vectors in 300 dimensions to train a Word2Vec model. The cutting-edge language model known as BERT (which comes from Transformer) can perform modern natural language processing tasks such as sentiment evaluation, query answering, as well as summarization. One application of BERT is the challenge of subject-specific text classification. No matter the context, the traditional embedding creation technique would always provide a single constant vector for each word input. However, BERT can bring attention to words' polysemous character by creating vectors based on the context of their surrounding words. In this investigation, we employ DistilBERT, a lightweight variant of BERT that is 60% quicker, 40% smaller, and more device-friendly. Fig. (**1**). depicts the System Model.

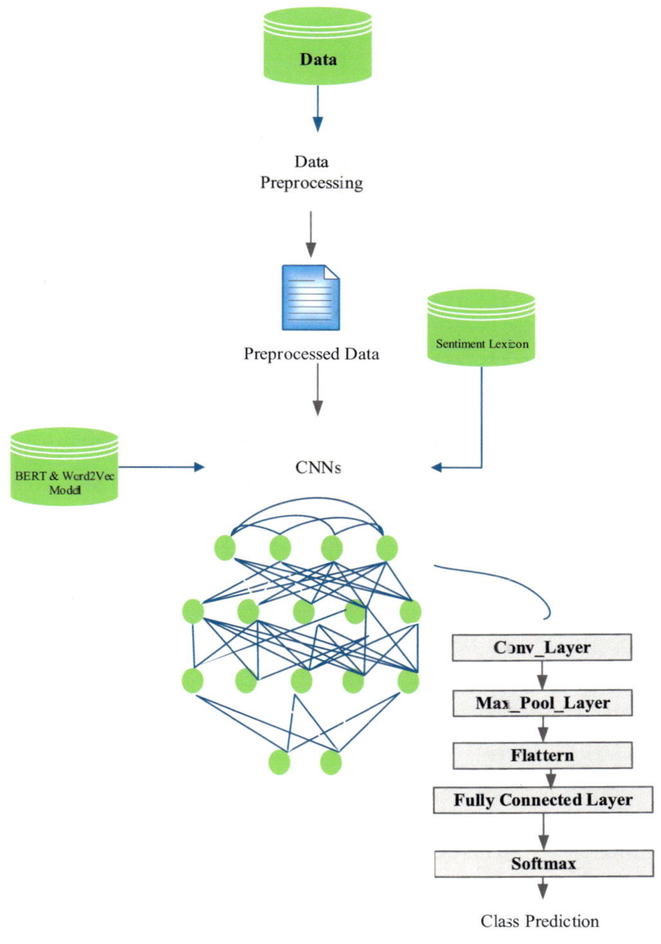


**Fig. (1).** System model.

Word-embedding-based approaches and lexicon-based methods are being used most often to construct text vectors for sentiment analysis. Our suggested model aimed to combine the two approaches by means of N-grams. Word N-grams containing an emotion word are found using the sentiment lexicon, and the vector from those words is employed in the BERT word embedding model.

Word N-grams are first generated from the sentences, and then the vector is constructed from those. A Markovian process, or N-gram, is a string of words taken from a phrase. Predicting the next word in a string is a common application of this technique. Markovian processes also produce co-occurrence of words, a crucial factor in shaping textual tone. Here, we employ N-gram sequences to break up a phrase into smaller chunks that together constitute a larger text like an online review. One advantage of N-grams over BoW is the level of information they provide to the display of word co-occurrence in a text. To a power of N, the division grows in size.

For illustration, let us say we are given a sentence S as

$$S = \{w1, w2, w3, w4, w5, \ldots, \ldots, \ldots \text{ wn }\}, \quad (1)$$

where, $w_i$ constitute language.

For all possible values of N, we get a collection of N-grams with N=1. $N_1 = \{W_1, W_2, W_3, \ldots, W_n\}$ N = 2, of N-gram sets $N_2 = \{W_{1\text{-}}W_2, W_2, W_3, W_3, w_4, \ldots, w_{n-1}w_n\}$ N = 3, of N-gram sets $N_3 = \{w_{1\text{-}}w_2 \text{-} w_3, w_2\text{-} w_3w_4, w_3w_{4\text{-}}w_5, \ldots, w_{n-2}w_{n-1\text{-}}w_n\}$. The basic idea is that, given an N-gram collection, it is possible to randomly choose a portion of the whole input text. This allows us to build sentiment analysis text vectors with only those most relevant phrases. The text is transformed back into a set of individual words after the new gram(s) have been retrieved. Each word is converted into a vector using the BERT word-embedding approach.

The generated vector from the LeBERT embedding is fed into a CNN deep learning network that classifies the sentiment. In contrast to standard machine learning algorithms, convolutional neural networks (CNNs) excel in supervised learning tasks. In order to aid in categorization, CNNs primarily serve to detect and learn the information characteristic patterns utilizing convolution layers. Fig. (**1**) shows the CNN model. Feature maps are derived from a convolutional kernel (window) and a nonlinear function (filter). The feature maps are pooled to find the best features to use. Next, the dense output layer employs the softmax activation function (a probability-based function) to categorize the most advantageous characteristics as positive or negative.

## RESULTS AND DISCUSSION

The dataset and the tests conducted to assess the effectiveness of the proposed model are described here. Methods and processes for formulating and assessing models are also covered.

To evaluate the suggested model, operations were carried out using a dataset that included three sets of data that were made publicly accessible. The collection includes three global datasets: one with 70,000 reviews of Amazon purchases, one with 50,000 reviews of movies, and one with 300,000 ratings of restaurants from Yelp. Three thousand reviews were employed in the studies, and the results were posted to a repository for machine learning.

The dataset's evaluations have been preprocessed, including removal of any non-English terms. Python was used in the Google Colaboratory virtual lab for tokenization, N-gram creation, text vector construction, and CNN layer design. To train the CNN model, we employed 80% of the produced vector, while the remaining 20% was used to assess the accuracy of the classification. Since the training set included many sentences (reviews), the BERT embedding made advantage of pooled output. The activation function of 100 neurons in the buried fully connected layer was the rectified linear unit (RELU). Since the texts had to be divided into two groups, a thick output layer with two (2) neurons was constructed. The text categorization problem at hand was a good fit for the softmax activation function. We worked with Google News-trained 50-multidimensional Glove word embeddings, 250-multidimensional Word2Vec embedded data from English Wikipedia, and 128-dimensional BERT embedded data from English Wikipedia were all included in the research. We conducted our studies using tensor flow techniques for data preprocessing and model construction. Only one hundred (100) of the evaluations from the training set were included in the final analysis. Table. **1**. shows the BERT-CNN results.

**Table 1. BERT-CNN Results.**

| N-Grams | BERT-CNN | | | |
|---|---|---|---|---|
| | Accuracy (%) | Precision (%) | Recall (%) | F-Measure (%) |
| N = 1 | 65.02 | 65.02 | 65.15 | 65.08 |
| N = 2 | 79.45 | 79.50 | 80.04 | 79.77 |
| N = 3 | 88.20 | 88.45 | 89.01 | **88.73** |
| N = 4 | 87.65 | 87.65 | 87.80 | 87.72 |
| All words | 84.00 | 84.00 | 84.20 | 84.10 |

**Table 2. Word2Vec CNN.**

| N-Grams | Word2Vec-CNN | | | |
|---|---|---|---|---|
| | Accuracy (%) | Precision (%) | Recall (%) | F-Measure (%) |
| N = 1 | 65.02 | 65.02 | 65.15 | 65.08 |
| N = 2 | 79.45 | 79.50 | 80.04 | 79.77 |
| N = 3 | 88.20 | 88.45 | 89.01 | **88.73** |
| N = 4 | 87.65 | 87.65 | 87.80 | 87.72 |
| All words | 86.00 | 84.00 | 84.20 | 82.10 |

The greatest model for sentiment analysis, BERT with Deep Learning, also looks to be the poorest model for opinion detection. BERT with Deep Learning offers the best precision, but the worst recall. This means that many tweets containing insightful thoughts are misclassified as having no relevant opinions by BERT with Deep Learning. One of the primary goals of the study is to gather insightful comments from consumers in order to enhance existing goods and develop new ones, thus this is highly alarming. If a model like BERT combined with Deep Learning eliminates many helpful suggestions for improving the product, then the products are unlikely to improve.

When comparing BERT to Word2Vec, we find that BERT word embedding's performs better for both sentiment and opinion categorization. However, the technique used to evaluate the effectiveness of a model is more crucial. The combined model is more reliable than Deep Learning in this scenario. When used for sentiment and opinion classification tasks, the outcomes of DL remain consistent even when paired with various word embedding approaches. However, Deep Learning appears to be less reliable and requires more manual preparation. The combined model, which uses the identical text and data preparation methodology, appears to perform better on the dataset. Small to medium-sized datasets may also contribute to Deep Learning's unreliability. It follows that if we wish to conduct sentiment and opinion classification models concurrently, the optimum model to utilize is BERT with Balanced Random Forest. Table. **2** displays Word2Vec CNN.

## CONCLUSION

Our research concluded that BERT word embeddings produced better results than Word2Vec in both sentiment analysis and opinion identification models. When comparing Deep Learning with Balanced Random Forest, the latter fared better for sentiment analysis, while the combined models scored better for opinion detection. We found that BERT combined with Balanced Random Forest was the top performing single model since it produced competitive results while using fewer computing resources and was consistent even with sparse input data. When it comes to text classification for the aviation business, we also used word graphs to provide some helpful suggestions. According to the data we gathered, the following were the top four priorities for customers: convenience (both in terms of time and money), flight and booking, amenities, and service. Flight delays and cancellations are major causes of consumer dissatisfaction, thus resolving these issues should be a top priority for airlines. Our research also adds to the existing body of knowledge by suggesting a more efficient and economical means of getting social media recommendations to aid in the NPD procedure. To enhance their goods with their own social media data, SMEs with fewer resources might apply the methods utilized in this study. In the future, researchers may test the efficacy of Deep Learning *vs* more traditional Machine Learning algorithms for recovering sentiment and valuable opinions for NPD using larger datasets.

## REFERENCES

[1] R.A. Cahya, F.A. Bachtiar, and W.F. Mahmudy, *Comparison of Bagging Ensemble Combination Rules for Imbalanced Text Sentiment Analysis,* 2021. [http://dx.doi.org/10.25126/jitecs.202161206]

[2] K.C. Ko, S.K. Liu, C.P. Wei, J.S. Hsieh, and R.H. Yang, "To See the Invisible: An Empirical Comparison of Methods for Text-Based Sentiment Analysis of Online Contents From People With Autism Spectrum Condition", *Int. J. Mark. Res.*, vol. 65, no. 4, pp. 402-422, 2023. [http://dx.doi.org/10.1177/14707853231158605]

[3] V. Vashisht, A.K. Pandey, and S.P. Yadav, "Speech Recognition using Machine Learning", In: *IEIE Transactions on Smart Processing & Computing* vol. 10. The Institute of Electronics Engineers of Korea, 2021, no. 3, pp. 233-239. [http://dx.doi.org/10.5573/IEIESPC.2021.10.3.233]

[4] L. Wang, and Z. Chen, "Text sentiment analysis based on two-channel joint model", *Proceedings of the 2022 5th International Conference on Machine Learning and Natural Language Processing,* 2022. [http://dx.doi.org/10.1145/3578741.3578802]

[5] Z. Xu, B. Jin, and H. Zhu, "Aspect-level text sentiment analysis method combining Bi-GRU and AlBERT", *Other Conferences,* 2022.

[6] P. Kandpal, Y. Wadkar, H. Attri, and S. Bhorge, "Comparison of Sentiment Analysis on Auto-Summarized Text & Original Text using various Summarization Techniques", *2020 IEEE Pune Section International Conference (PuneCon),* pp. 206-211, 2020. [http://dx.doi.org/10.1109/PuneCon50868.2020.9362395]

[7] P.D. Purnamasari, M. Taqiyuddin, and A.A. Ratna, "Performance comparison of text-based sentiment analysis using recurrent neural network and convolutional neural network", *Proceedings of the 3rd International Conference on Communication and Information Processing,* 2017. [http://dx.doi.org/10 1145/3162957.3163012]

[8] W.C.F. Mariel, S. Mariyah, and S. Pramana, "Sentiment analysis: a comparison of deep learning neural network algorithm with SVM and naïve Bayes for Indonesian text", *J. Phys. Conf. Ser.*, vol. 971, p. 012049, 2018. [http://dx.doi.org/10.1088/1742-6596/971/1/012049]

[9] X. Guo, W. Yu, and X. Wang, "An Overview on Fine-grained Text Sentiment Analysis: Survey and Challenges", *J. Phys Conf. Ser.,* vol. 1757, no. 1, p. 012038, 2021.

[http://dx.doi.org/10.1088/1742-6596/1757/1/012038]

[10] S. P. Yadav, B. S. Bhati, D. P. Mahato, and S. Kumar, "Federated Learning for IoT Applications" EAI/Springer Innovations in Communication and Computing", *Springer International Publishing,* 2022.
[http://dx.doi.org/10.1007/978-3-030-85559-8]

[11] Y. Shen, and J. Liu, "Comparison of Text Sentiment Analysis based on Bert and Word2vec", *3rd International Conference on Frontiers Technology of Information and Computer (ICFTIC),* pp. 144-147, 2021.
[http://dx.doi.org/10.1109/ICFTIC54370.2021.9647258]

[12] X. Zhang, and X. Zheng, "Comparison of Text Sentiment Analysis Based on Machine Learning", *15th International Symposium on Parallel and Distributed Computing (ISPDC),* pp. 230-233, 2016.
[http://dx.doi.org/10.1109/ISPDC.2016.39]

[13] E. Asmawati, A. Saikhu, and D. Siahaan, "Sentiment Analysis of Text Memes: A Comparison Among Supervised Machine Learning Methods", *9th International Conference on Electrical Engineering, Computer Science and Informatics (EECSI),* pp. 349-354, 2022.
[http://dx.doi.org/10.23919/EECSI56542.2022.9946506]

[14] Z.A. Guven, "The Comparison of Language Models with a Novel Text Filtering Approach for Turkish Sentiment Analysis", *ACM Transactions on Asian and Low-Resource Language Information Processing,* vol. 22, no. 2, pp. 1-16, 2023.
[http://dx.doi.org/10.1145/3557892]

[15] Z. Yang, P.C. Pang, and H.Y. Kan, "Performance Comparison of Deep Learning Text Embeddings in Sentiment Analysis Tasks with Online Consumer Reviews", *Proceedings of the 2022 10th International Conference on Information Technology: IoT and Smart City,* 2022.

# CHAPTER 30

# Text Emotion Categorization Using a Convolutional Recurrent Neural Network Enhanced by an Attention Mechanism-based Skip-Gram Method

**Madhur Grover**[1,*]

[1] *Centre for Interdisciplinary Research in Business and Technology, Chitkara University Institute of Engineering and Technology, Chitkara University, Punjab, India*

**Abstract:** Text-based web archives have become increasingly common as technology has advanced. For many text classification applications, classic machine learning classifiers like support vector machines (SVMs) and naïve Bayes (NBayes) perform well. Since short texts have fewer words and convolutional and pooling layers have their limits, these classifiers suffer from sparsity and lack long-term dependencies. In this study, we present a convolutional recurrent neural network architecture that makes use of a modified skip-gram method. For the adversarial training of the skip-gram algorithm, we employ the L2 regularization technique. It can boost the model's performance in text sentiment classification tasks and increase its robustness and generalizability. To extract information from the entire text while dampening the influence of irrelevant words, we deployed a convolutional neural network equipped with attention mechanisms. The CNN-based categorization of text emotion is complete. When compared to other classifiers used on the Twitter dataset, our model and algorithm were shown to be more efficient and accurate.

**Keywords:** Attention scheme, CNN, Skip-gram model, Text emotion classification.

## INTRODUCTION

Text-based web archives have become more common as technology has advanced. For many text classification applications, the tried-and-true SVM and naive Bayes classifiers of traditional machine learning excel [1]. However, owing to the scarcity of text in brief text and the constraints of convolutional and pooling layers, these classifiers suffer from sparsity difficulties and lack long-term depen-

* **Corresponding author Madhur Grover:** Centre for Interdisciplinary Research in Business and Technology, Chitkara University Institute of Engineering and Technology, Chitkara University, Punjab, India;
E-mail: madhur.grover.orp@chitkara.edu.in

Pankaj Kumar Mishra and Satya Prakash Yadav (Eds.)

dencies [2]. Convolutional neural networks (CNNs), which are typical examples of deep learning technology, have found widespread use in machine vision tasks including object detection and image processing in recent years [3, 4]. To improve the accuracy and flexibility of traditional CNNs, we introduce an RCNN for object identification in this study [4]. However, RCNN is only capable of handling data at the local level and cannot adapt to a wide variety of scenarios. The rapidly expanding area of neural network models used in processing natural languages is attracting more attention from sentiment analysis [5]. With more people being involved in social media, there is more data to analyse. Sentiment analysis at the aspect level is used to determine the text's polarity in various contexts [6]. As a subfield of NLP, sentiment evaluation is starting to take an interest in models based on deep neural networks [7]. More people using social media means more data, which has made analysis more difficult [8]. Sentiment analysis at the aspect level is useful for determining the overall tone of a text in its various contexts. This study introduces four deep neural network–based algorithms for opinion mining at the aspect level [8], each with a unique input word vector format. We introduce a novel approach to aspect-level opinion extraction that integrates a network of convolutional neural networks, an attention mechanism, as well as a gated recurrent unit, all of which make use of different input vector representations. This study adds to the literature by presenting an innovative method for evaluating service quality based on patron feedback in the hospitality industry [9]. When scientists contrasted their technique to others using gathered feedback from restaurants as a test case, they discovered that it obtained excellent scores of precision, recall, and accuracy, as well as the f-measure [10, 16].

## RELATED WORK

To identify emotions in spoken language, we provide a deep convolution recurrent neural network (CNN) that uses the log-Mel filterbank energies. The task of learning distinguishing characteristics falls on the convolutional layers. We also propose a convolutional attentiveness method for learning the task-relevant utterance structure, on the premise that a better understanding of the inner workings of an utterance can help reduce misinterpretation. In order to describe the features of emotional speech, we additionally measure the performance boost produced by every component in our model. Supporting our notion are experimental results on the eNTERFACE'05 emotions dataset that demonstrate a 4.62 percent increase over the existing gold standard technique [11].

In this study, we present the architecture of a convolutional recurrent neural network trained using an enhanced skip-gram technique. For the adversarial training of the skip-gram algorithm, we use the L2 regularisation technique. Not only may it boost this model's performance in text sentiment classification tasks, but it can also make it more resilient and generalizable. To extract meaningful data from texts while decreasing the influence of irrelevant words, we used a Bidirectional Long Short-Term Memory network with attention mechanisms. CNNS-based text sentiment categorization is at last a reality. When compared to other classifiers used on the IMDB dataset [12], this model and method were shown to be the most efficient and accurate.

We propose a recurrent convolutional neural network (RCNN) that incorporates a self-attention mechanism (A-RCNN) based on findings from cognitive science and neuroscience to solve this problem. In contrast to the majority of methods, which include the mechanism for self-attention in the convolutional parts of a CNN, our technique compartmentalizes it into a distinct layer inside the RCNN. Publicly available datasets like CIFAR-10, CIFAR-100, as well as MNIST, are used to evaluate our A-RCNN. Results from experiments show that when it comes to object identification tasks, our proposed A-RCNN is more accurate than both the initial RCNN as well as the CNN [13].

To tackle the problems of poor accuracy and excessive computation, researchers suggested sEMG gesture recognition approaches using a type of dilated neural network with convolution that combines an attention mechanism with a bidirectional gated recurrent unit. By adjusting the size and expansion rate to a parity hybrid, HDC improves upon normal CNN in several aspects, such as increasing the field of reception, decreasing over-fitting, as well as extracting more features. The BiGRU module can efficiently extract and analyse the data's timing characteristics, while the Attention module prioritises the most crucial ones, resulting in improved accuracy. Using the NinaproDB1 dataset and our dataset, we were able to attain accuracy rates of 92.72 and 97.85, respectively, demonstrating the method's efficacy [14].

This research introduces four deep neural network–based approaches for opinion mining at the aspect level, each with a unique input word vector format. A novel approach is detailed for aspect-level mining of opinions using multiple input vector representations; it integrates a convolutional neural network, a gated recurrent unit, as well as an attention strategy. This paper contributes to the current literature by adding unique methods for evaluating service quality in the hospitality industry based on patron feedback. Research using collected restaurant reviews has shown promising results in terms of accuracy, precision, recall, and f-measure when compared to other methods [15, 16].

# PROPOSED WORK

## Research Gaps

Natural Language Processing, or NLP, is a subfield of AI that aims to provide computers with human-like language processing abilities by analyzing written or spoken material. All the information that humans have is in a jumbled mess. Machines have a hard time extracting meaning from unprocessed text. In order for a machine to learn from text, we must first convert it to a vector format that computers can more easily interpret. The process of converting text into a vector representation is called "word representation."

## Skip Gram Model for Text Classification

When words are represented as vectors, proximity between such vectors indicates that the words are semantically linked. On the left side of the picture are terms often associated with women, while on the right are phrases typically associated with men. Therefore, the computer will correctly associate the word "earrings" with the feminine gender if we pass it. The System Model is portrayed in Fig. (**1**).

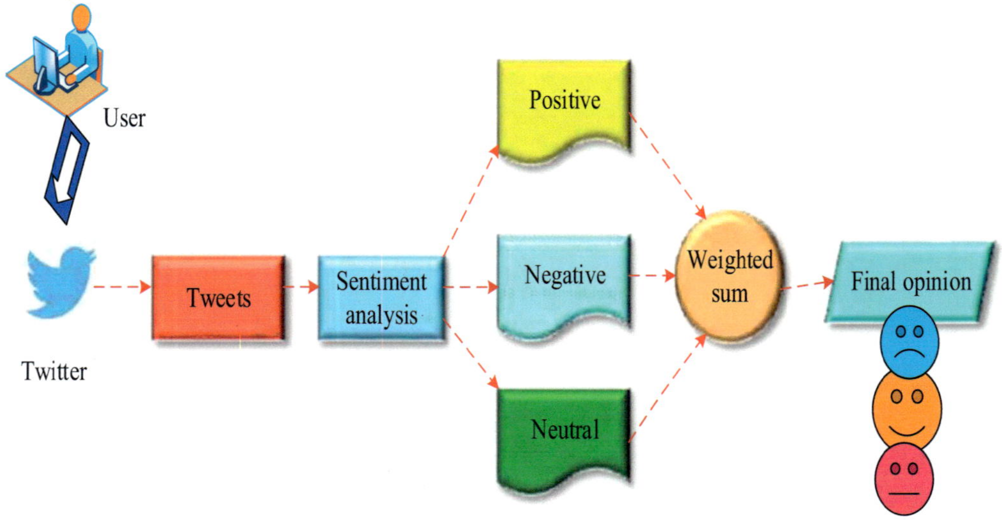


**Fig. (1).** System model.

We need methods of unsupervised learning that can learn the context of each word on their own because the vocabulary of any language is huge and cannot be classified by humans. One method for uncovering synonyms for a given word is called skip-gram, and it relies on unsupervised learning.

When given a target phrase, skip-gram is used to predict the word around it. Inverted are the CBOW algorithms. Here, you may input the desired term and have the words that are in context returned to you. The fact that there are a lot of context terms that need to be predicted makes this problem much more challenging.

The supplied input or target word is denoted by w(t). In order to process the input vector w(t), the weight matrix performs a dot product with it in the hidden layer. The buried layer does not employ an activation function. The resultant layer is now receiving the dot product from the hidden layer. To get the output, the resultant layer multiplies the output vector from the layer that is hidden by the weight matrix of the outputting layer. Next, we determine the likelihood that a certain word w(t) occurs in a specific context location c(t) by using the softmax activation function. The Skip Gram Model is displayed in Fig. (**2**).

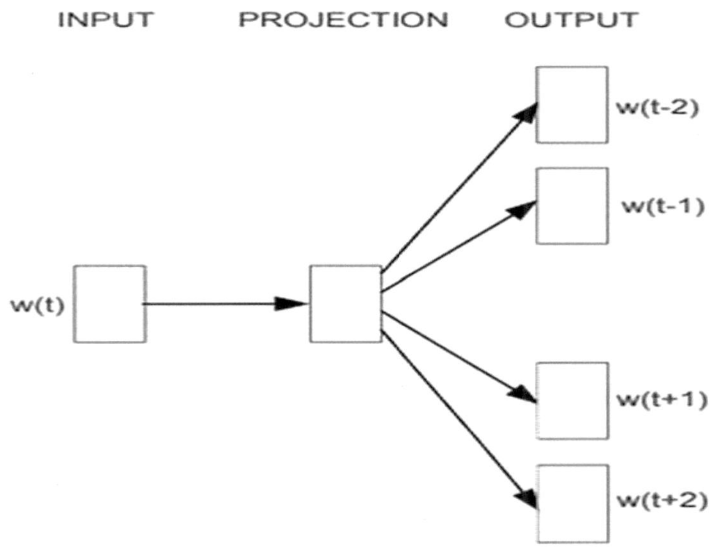


**Fig. (2).** Skip gram model.

1. One, a list of all the distinct terms in our dataset or text. Vocabulary refers to the set of terms that are already familiar to the computer. The letter 'V' stands for vocabulary.

The hidden layer has N neurons, where N is the total number of neurons.

2. The greatest possible context position at which the words must be forecasted is equal to the window size. c is the window's size in terms of pixels. In the provided

architectural image, for instance, the window size is 2, therefore we will be making predictions for words in context at positions (t-2) through (t-1).

3. The number of possible anticipated words that surround a particular word is called the "context window." A context window's value, denoted by k, is 2*c, where c is the window size. The provided picture has a context window value of 4.

4. Input vectors have a size (or dimension) of |V|. Using a single "hot encoding" for each every word.

5. Six, the hidden layer(W) weight matrix has dimensions [|V|, N]. The size of an array may be determined using the modulus operator, ||.

6. The hidden layer produces a vector called H[N].

7. Dimensions [N,|V|] for the weight matrix W' between the hidden and output layers.

When we dot product W' and H, we get the vector U[|v|] as an answer.

**Attention-based CNN**

The use of an attention mechanism has been recognized as a cutting-edge method of increasing the representational power of convolutional neural networks and better capturing long-range feature interactions. However, we discovered two issues, the attention maps' approximation issue and their inadequate capacity problem, which are often ignored by current models that rely on cognitive activations. In order to tackle both problems at once, we first suggest a module for attention for CNNs by way of an AW-convolution, where the attention maps take the shape of the weights instead of the activations themselves. We propose a module for attention as an expansion of prior work that has utilized attention-based methodologies to study the relationship between channel-wise and spatial data. Our suggested attention module has been tested on many picture classification and object identification datasets, demonstrating its efficacy.

Here, we examine the two issues, approximation and inadequate capacity of the attention maps, that are typically overlooked in models based on attentional activations. We create an attention module that primarily makes use of the A convolution to solve both issues at once; our attention maps' shapes correspond to those of the weights, not the activations. In addition, the attention map calculation branch is improved to provide a better balance between speed and precision. Finally, to increase the representational power of attention-based models overall, we combine our proposed attention module with a number of existing ones.

We begin by defining the fundamental notations used in a standard convolutional layer. Typically, a convolutional layer consists of three stimulation: input (I), weight (K), as well as output (O). The overall batch size, the amount of input routes, height, and breadth of the input feature maps are N, C_1, H, as well as W, respectively, for the feature map that is input to stimulus I R(N,C_1H,W). In the equation K R(C_2C_1hw), the values of K, h, and w represent the amount of output pathways, height, as well as width, respectively. By convolving the input stimulation I with the weights K, we may determine what is happening OR(NC_2HW) at the result. Particularly, for each conceivable value of l, p, m, and n, the following output stimulations are computed: O_([l, p, m, n]):

$$O_{[l,p,m,n]} = \text{Convolution }(I, K) = \sum_{o=1}^{C_1} \sum_{j=1}^{h-1} \sum_{k=1}^{w-1} I_{[l,o,m'+j,n'+k]} \times K_{[p,o,j,k]} \quad \textbf{(1)}$$

where $l = 0, \ldots, N-1, m = 0, \ldots, H-1, n = 0, \ldots, W-1, o = 0, \ldots, C_1 - 1, p = 0, \ldots, C_2 - 1, m' = m - \frac{h-1}{2}, n' = n - \frac{w-1}{2}$.

Prior models that relied on cognitive stimulation to generate channel attention maps applied the attention process to input activations I $A_c \in R^{N\times C_1\times 1\times 1}$ and maps of spatial attention $A_s \in R^{N\times 1\times H\times W}$ independent of one another. As a case study, input stimulations I are subjected to the attention channel maps A_c, which are then shown as $O$ = Convolution (( I $\odot$ $A_c$), $K$), where $\odot$ relates to Hadamard products and element-wise multiplication does not involve broadcasting.

## Attention Maps Estimation Issue

There are currently no attentional activations-based models that directly compute the three-dimensional attention map; instead, they generate attention maps in two parts: the channelized attention maps and the original, one-dimensional concentration map. $A_c$ and maps of spatial attention $A_s$; it causes attention maps to have an approximate issue. But we have to calculate the heed maps if we want to pay close consideration to the input stimulation I $A_f \in R^{N\times C_1\times H\times W}$ and $F$ upon which to rely $O$ = Convolution (($\odot$ $A_f$), K) , that need an excessive amount of computational and parameter burden.

To minimize the dimension of attention maps, we take a page out of convolution's playbook and use local connection sharing. We calculate the focus maps $A_a \in R^{N\times C_1\times h\times w}$ as follows, where $\otimes$ is distinct from other element-wise multiplication algorithms in that it is only used for inversion.

$$O_{[l,p,m,n]} = \text{Convolution } (I \otimes A_a, K) \\ = \sum_{o=1}^{C_1} \sum_{j=1}^{h-1} \sum_{k=1}^{w-1} \left( I_{[l,o,m'+j,n'+k]} \times A_{a[l,o,j,k]} \right) \times K_{[p,o,j,k]} \quad (2)$$

The attention maps have an inadequate capacity issue. The initial activations can only be updated using the same concentration diagrams, which means that the focus maps are not powerful enough to calculate multiple channels of the convolution's outputs activation. Due to the fact that every map in a channel acts as a detector of features, various attentiveness maps are expected to adjust the input activation of the convolutional activating channel.

Consider a convolutional layer's two channels of output activations, which are tasked with identifying rectangles and triangles. Given that the two channels' objectives are distinct, it is reasonable to assume that the focus maps utilized to track the convolution's opinions activation will also vary. Specifically, the attention maps computed for the channel that recognizes rectangles ought to vary from those computed for the transmit that recognizes triangles. Attention mappings $A_{ic} \in \mathbb{R}^{NXC_2XC_1X1X1}$ need to be computed and then applied to the input activations in the following way to achieve this goal.

$$O_{[l,p,m,n]} = \text{Convolution } \left(I \odot A_{ic[l,p,:,,,:,]}, K\right) \\ = \sum_{o=1}^{C_1} \sum_{j=1}^{h-1} \sum_{k=1}^{w-1} \left( I_{[l,o,m'+j,n'+k]} \times A_{ic[l,p,o,0,0]} \right) \times K_{[p,o,j,k]} \quad (3)$$

We provide our proposed attention component, which utilizes AW-convolution, to address both the approximations issue and the insufficient capacity problem with attention maps all at once. We stress the importance of attention mapping computation, in particular, $\in R^{N \times C_2 \times C_1 \times h \times w}$. To be more precise, we use it when the attention mappings $A_{[l,:,:,,:,]}$ conform to the shape of the weights instead of input promotions, as shown below. In this context, "attentional weights" refer to the final result of multiplying each person's attention mappings by their weights. In the same vein, "Attentional stimulation" is the sum of attention maps plus the events that occur in models that use them. Thus, $I \otimes A \; and \; A_{[l,i,i,i,:]} \odot K$ stand for the attentional stimulation as well as focus issues weights, correspondingly. Half of the element-wise additions may be eliminated by replacing attentional stimulation with cognitive weights.

$$\begin{aligned} O_{[l,p,m,n]} &= \text{Convolution } (I \otimes A, K) \\ &= \sum_{o=1}^{C_1} \sum_{j=1}^{h-1} \sum_{k=1}^{w-1} I_{[l,o,m'+j,n'+k]} \times \left(A_{[l,p,o,j,k]} \times K_{[p,o,j,k]}\right) \\ &= \text{Convolution } \left(I, A_{[l,,i,,,,:,]} \odot K\right) \\ &= \text{AW-Convolution } (I, A \odot K) \end{aligned} \quad \textbf{(4)}$$

## RESULTS AND DISCUSSION

How to spot tweets that are full of hate is the topic of today's piece. We have built a sentiment analyzer to sort tweets into positive and negative categories. Our classifier is not limited to analyzing Twitter data; it can be used to other text data as well. Starting with our Twitter information, the Twitter tweets data for sentiment analysis dataset is being used for this research. There are 32,000 tweets in total, with a negative tone in 2%. The 'label' variable is the focus here; it assigns a 1 to tweets that are negative and a 0 to those that are positive. The target variable represents the outcome of your prediction efforts. To solve our machine learning challenge, we will use this information to build a classification model that can assign labels to fresh tweets. Fig. (**3**) is shows the sentiment classes.

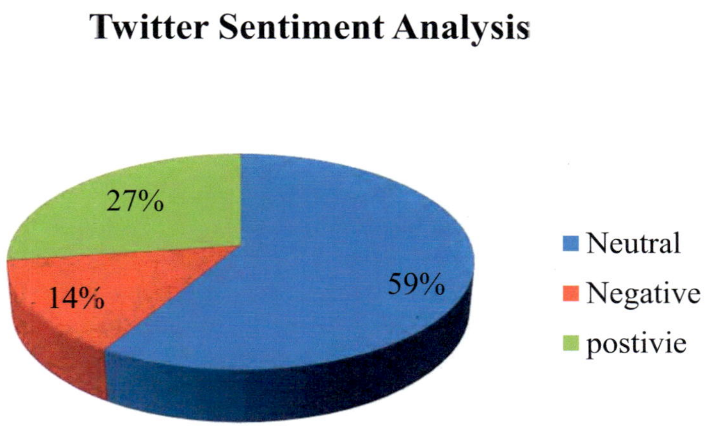


**Fig. (3).** Sentiment classes.

In conventional machine learning, an F1 score of 83% indicates a successful model. However, there are ways in which the model may be enhanced. Despite the high cost of deep learning algorithms, they may be used to add functionality and fix spelling errors in response to user feedback and results. Remember that we used training data to produce these findings. We still need to actively monitor the performance of a sentiment analysis model when it is applied to real-world data. Fig. (**4**). depicts the F-score Performance.

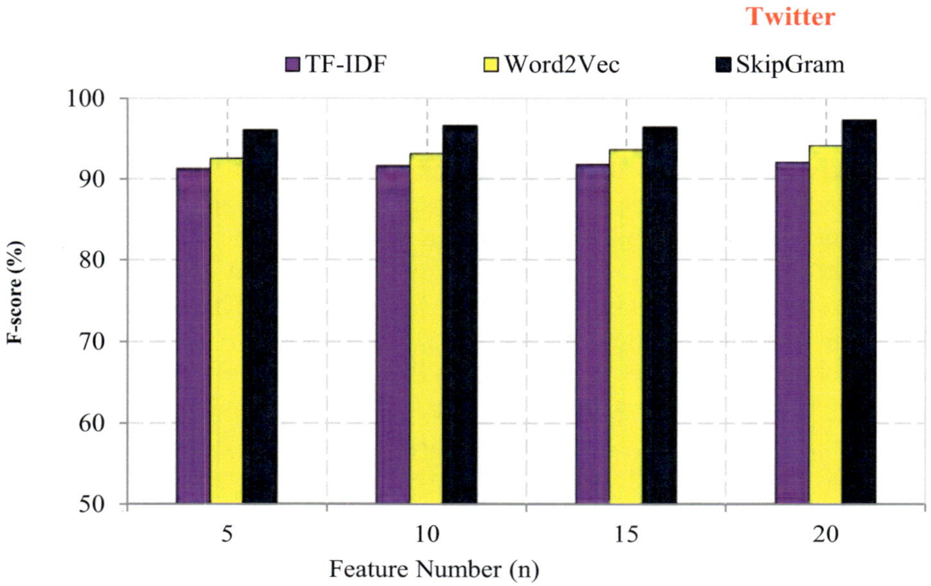


**Fig. (4).** F-score performance.

## CONCLUSION

Text-based web archives have become increasingly common as technology has advanced. For many text classification applications, classic machine learning classifiers like support vector machines (SVMs) and naïve Bayes (NBayes) perform well. Since short texts have fewer words and convolutional and pooling layers have their limits, these classifiers suffer from sparsity and lack long-term dependencies. In this study, we present a convolutional recurrent neural network architecture that makes use of a modified skip-gram method. For the adversarial training of the skip-gram algorithm, we employ the L2 regularization technique. It can boost the model's performance in text sentiment classification tasks and increase its robustness and generalizability. To extract information from the entire text while dampening the influence of irrelevant words, we deployed a convolutional neural network equipped with attention mechanisms. The CNN-based categorization of text emotion is complete. When compared to other classifiers used on the Twitter dataset, our model and algorithm were shown to be more efficient and accurate.

## REFERENCES

[1] M.S. Rani, and S. Subramanian, "Attention Mechanism with Gated Recurrent Unit Using Convolutional Neural Network for Aspect Level Opinion Mining", *Arab. J. Sci. Eng.,* vol. 45, no. 8, pp. 6157-6169, 2020. [http://dx.doi.org/10.1007/s13369-020-04497-4]

[2] Y. Wang, Q. Lu, Y. Wang, M. Wu, and W. Li, "Dynamic QoS Prediction Based on Attention Mechanism and Recurrent Neural Network" IEEE Intl Conf on Parallel and Distributed Processing with Applications", *Big Data and Cloud Computing, Sustainable Computing and Communications, Social Computing and Networking,* pp. 347-354, 2022.

[3] Q.S. Liang, Y. Li, K. Yang, X. Wang, and Z. Li, "Long-term recurrent convolutional network violent Behaviour recognition with attention mechanism", *MATEC Web of Conferences,* 2021.

[4] C. Li, Q. Zhang, Z. Zhao, L. Gu, and B.W. Schuller, "Exploring Spatial-Temporal Representations for fNIRS-based Intimacy Detection *via* an Attention-enhanced Cascade Convolutional Recurrent Neural Network", *25th International Conference on Pattern Recognition (ICPR),* pp. 8862-8869, 2021. [http://dx.doi.org/10.1109/ICPR48806.2021.9412577]

[5] W. Guan, and C. Liu, "Prediction of surface quality in end milling based on modified convolutional recurrent neural network", *Applied Mathematics and Nonlinear Sciences,* 2022.

[6] H. Zhu, and J. Yan, "A Deep Learning Based Sound Event Location and Detection Algorithm Using Convolutional Recurrent Neural Network", *2022 International Conference on Computer, Information and Telecommunication Systems (CITS),* pp. 1-6, 2022. [http://dx.doi.org/10.1109/CITS55221.2022.9832991]

[7] X. Zhang, X. Gao, W. Lu, L. He, and J. Li, "Beyond Vision: A Multimodal Recurrent Attention Convolutional Neural Network for Unified Image Aesthetic Prediction Tasks", *IEEE Trans. Multimed.,* vol. 23, pp. 611-623, 2021. [http://dx.doi.org/10.1109/TMM.2020.2985526]

[8] B. Wu, X. Liang, X. Zheng, Y. Guo, and H. Tang, "Improving Dynamic Graph Convolutional Network with Fine- Grained Attention Mechanism", *ICASSP 2022 - 2022 IEEE International Conference on Acoustics, Speech and Signal Processing (ICASSP),* pp. 3938-3942, 2022.

[9] S.P. Yadav, S. Zaidi, C.D.S. Nascimento, V.H.C. de Albuquerque, and S.S. Chauhan, "Analysis and Design of automatically generating for GPS Based Moving Object Tracking System", *2023 International Conference on Artificial Intelligence and Smart Communication (AISC),* 2023 pp. 1-5. Greater Noida, India. [http://dx.doi.org/10.1109/AISC56616.2023.10085180]

[10] S. P. Yadav, and S. Yadav, "Mathematical implementation of fusion of medical images in continuous wavelet domain", *Journal of Advanced Research in dynamical and control system,* vol. 10, no. 10, pp. 45-54, 2019.

[11] C. Huang, and S.S. Narayanan, "Deep convolutional recurrent neural network with attention mechanism for robust speech emotion recognition", *2017 IEEE International Conference on Multimedia and Expo (ICME),* pp. 583-588, 2017. [http://dx.doi.org/10.1109/ICME.2017.8019296]

[12] X. Yang, and X. Liu, "Convolutional Recurrent neural network with attention mechanism based improved skip-gram algorithm for text sentiment classification", *7th International Conference on Information Science and Control Engineering (ICISCE),* pp. 410-414, 2020. [http://dx.doi.org/10.1109/ICISCE50968.2020.00092]

[13] N. Yu, and T. Qiu, "An Improved Method and Application of Recurrent Convolutional Neural Network With Self-attention Mechanism", *China Automation Congress (CAC),* pp. 6312-6316, 2022. [http://dx.doi.org/10.1109/CAC57257.2022.10056001]

[14] K. Zhang, and F. Chen, "Research on sEMG Gesture Recognition Based on Hybrid Dilated

Convolutional Neural Network Combining Bidirectional Gated Recurrent Unit And Attention Mechanism", *China Automation Congress (CAC),* pp. 3760-3763, 2021. [http://dx.doi.org/10.1109/CAC53003.2021.9727886]

[15] M.S. Rani, and S. Subramanian, "Attention Mechanism with Gated Recurrent Unit Using Convolutional Neural Network for Aspect Level Opinion Mining", *Arab. J. Sci. Eng.,* vol. 45, no. 8, pp. 6157-6169, 2020. [http://dx.doi.org/10.1007/s13369-020-04497-4]

[16] Z. Baozhou, P. Hofstee, J. Lee, and Z. Al-Ars, "An Attention Module for Convolutional Neural Networks", *International Conference on Artificial Neural Networks,* 2021.

## CHAPTER 31

# Multimodal Sentiment Analysis in Text, Images, and GIFs Using Deep Learning

**Deepak Minhas**[1,*]

[1] *Centre for Interdisciplinary Research in Business and Technology, Chitkara University Institute of Engineering and Technology, Chitkara University, Punjab, India*

**Abstract:** More and more people are inclined to use GIFs, videos, and photographs on social media as a way to convey their feelings and thoughts. We developed a Python-based multimodal sentiment analysis tool for various Twitter formats, taking into account not just the text of a tweet but also its accompanying GIFs and pictures, for more precise sentiment scoring. We employ fine-tuned CNN for image sentiment analysis, VADER for text analysis, and image sentiment and facial expression analysis for GIFs, with each frame individually analyzed. Our research shows that combining textual and picture data yields superior outcomes compared to models that depend only on either images or text. The output scores from our text, picture, and GIF modules will be aggregated to get the final sentiment score for the incoming tweets.

**Keywords:** DL, GIFs, Images, Multimodal text classification, Text.

## INTRODUCTION

GIFs, movies, and photos are becoming more popular ways for social media users to convey their feelings and thoughts. To improve the accuracy of the overall sentiment score for a tweet, we developed a multimodal sentiment analysis programme in Python that takes into account not just the text of the tweet but also GIFs and pictures [1]. We use fine-tuned CNN for image sentiment analysis, VADER for text analysis, and image sentiment and face expression analysis for GIFs across all frames. Instagram is a well-liked social networking platform that is used by many different types of individuals, from hobbyists to professionals [2]. Instagram postings may include text, images, and videos, and are thus quite popular. Many people add captions or other text to the photographs they post online. The emotion of these postings may be analysed by taking into account both the text and the accompanying picture. For this, it is necessary to represent

* **Corresponding author Deepak Minhas:** Centre for Interdisciplinary Research in Business and Technology, Chitkara University Institute of Engineering and Technology, Chitkara University, Punjab, India;
E-mail: deepak.minhas.orp@chitkara.edu.in

**Pankaj Kumar Mishra and Satya Prakash Yadav (Eds.)**

the connection between the textual and visual modalities [3]. To solve this issue, we suggest using a multimodal deep learning approach. Sentiment analysis [4] may be used to deduce people's thoughts and views about a topic or product from online social media postings. Data generated every day by users may be in several modalities including text, picture, audio, and video due to the widespread use of the Internet and smart devices. By combining analyses of text, images, and audio, multimodal sentiment analysis may identify the underlying tone of a user's postings [5]. Integrating the sentiment and meaning of a post from several sources is a key problem for multimodal sentiment analysis. The same categorization strategies are used to examine many modalities in numerous research [6]. It turns out that various feature sets may optimally be used by a variety of classifiers. Web data sentiment analysis is a large research topic with several potential uses, including context learning, election outcome prediction, and incident reaction analysis [7]. For the most part, online data sentiment analysis has only considered a particular modality, such as text or images. Multiple modal information, such as an image and various types of text, is easily accessible and may be used together to improve the accuracy of sentiment estimation [8]. It has been shown that integrating visual and textual variables without considering their interrelationships leads to an overly complicated model and lowers sentiment analysis performance [9]. To identify utterances in natural language when the intended meaning varies from the surface meaning, sarcasm detection is used. In the field of natural language processing, sarcasm detection is used for a variety of applications, including sentiment analysis and opinion mining. Many of the seminal studies in the field of sarcasm detection [10] have narrowed their attention to textual input alone. The advent of social media has resulted in a dramatic increase in the volume of multimodal data in the modern world. Research works on visual sentiment analysis especially for GIF videos have only just started to develop. This is mainly because of the fact that the ability to use GIFs on big platforms like Twitter, Instagram, Facebook, and Telegram was introduced recently thus multimodal designs that use GIFs as one of the modals remained unexplored. Our framework includes:

- A multimodal sentiment framework that analyzes the incoming tweet and splits it into different modals like text, image, and GIFs. Based on the type of input, the respective processing module will calculate sentiment for that type.
- An image module consists of a fine-tuned CNN, which is built on top of a pre-trained vgg16 CNN model that is trained with annotated Twitter data set. We use this module to analyze a tweet's image or a GIF's separated frames.
- We demonstrate the feasibility of using face detection and emotion detection with the combination of the image module to analyze a GIF for its sentiment.

## RELATED WORK

In this research, we show that combining textual and visual characteristics yields superior outcomes compared to models that depend only on visual or textual data. The output scores from our text, picture, and GIF modules will be aggregated to provide the final emotion score for the incoming tweets [11].

The suggested technique employs a 2-dimensional convolutional neural network (2CNN) for image analysis and a bi-directional gated recurrent unit (bi-GRU) for processing text comments. We provide a new dataset of Instagram posts called MPerInst, which contains 512 pairs of photographs and their related Persian language comments, in order to evaluate the effectiveness of the suggested model. Based on experimental data, combining text and picture modalities yields a 23% increase in polarity identification accuracy and a 0.24 increase in F1-score compared to either modality alone. The suggested model also has a higher accuracy and F1-score than 11 other deep fusion models. Our data and model code are accessible for anyone to utilise in the future [12].

To capitalise on the efficient performance of many classifiers across multiple modalities, this research proposes a soft voting-based ensemble model. The proposed model uses deep learning techniques (BiLSTM, CNN) to extract deep features from multimodal datasets. The final feature sets were categorised using a soft voting-based ensemble learning model after feature selection was performed on the features, which are a combination of text and picture data. Two benchmark datasets of text-image pairings have been used to evaluate the proposed approach. The experiments have shown that the suggested model performed better than several adversarial models on the same datasets [13].

This research proposes a paradigm for sentiment analysis that takes advantage of the connections between different types of online data by integrating visual and linguistic signals that are likely to attract the most attention. To discover the connections between the learned salient visual aspects and textual data, a multimodal deep association learner is constructed. In addition, two streams of unimodal deep feature extractors are suggested to automatically learn the visual and linguistic aspects that are most important to the feelings. Finally, a late fusion process is used to estimate the sentiment from the merged characteristics. Compared to both current unimodal algorithms and multimodal approaches that blindly merge the visual and textual elements [14], our proposed framework shows promising results for sentiment analysis utilising online data.

Because of this, users nowadays often use visuals, such as photographs and videos, to supplement their written words while expressing themselves online. In this research, we aim to improve upon existing sarcasm detection systems by including multimodal data in the detection process. Multiple approaches have been developed that make use of data in the form of images, texts, and hybrids of the two. To account for this incongruity between the input language and the image's properties, we describe a novel architecture based on the Robustly Optimised BERT pre-training approach(RoBERTa), a Facebook-modified version of the widely-used model BERT. Textual features are recovered using a Gated Recurrent Unit(GRU), while visual characteristics are obtained using Feature-wise Linearly Modulated ResNet Blocks. These are used in conjunction with the RoBERTa model's CLS token to generate predictions. Finally, we compare our model's improved performance to that of other state-of-the-art algorithms that also employ the same publicly accessible Twitter dataset [15].

## PROPOSED WORK

### System Model

In contrast to textual media, the underlying tokens of non-textual media are sometimes not as obvious, making annotation more difficult. These fundamental units can be thought of as groups of pixels in the case of pictures and videos (as opposed to groups of letters [words] in the case of text). Using dictionaries and other text-based tools becomes impractical since the tokens have numerous dimensions and far greater variety when describing the same notion. So now we are talking about computer vision and picture recognition, fields that are older than natural language processing (NLP) by 30 years but where significant advances have been achieved just recently. The current state of computer vision is inadequate for many practical purposes. Reasons why opinion extraction from images is so challenging include a semantic gap between what computer vision can do and the amount of knowledge necessary for sentiment analysis. In order to use a picture in our calculations, we used a built-in function of keras to transform it into a numpy matrix. Fig. (**1**) depicts our suggested system, in which we split the three modalities (text, picture, and GIF) into their own modules to estimate a sentiment score. We look at the classification of tweets. After a tweet is preprocessed, we use the VADER Python package to determine the tweet's polarity if it contains text. We assign emotional ratings to photographs with the help of our trained CNN. A GIF file attached to a tweet will be converted into a series of individual images. The photographs will be analyzed by the image module to determine an overall average emotion score for the images. In addition, we employ emotion recognition to locate the appropriate sentiment by scanning the GIF video clip for faces. Our final GIF module score will be based on an average of the face emotion score and the sentiment score of the image's frames. In the event that no faces are found in any of the images, we use only the frames' score to establish the total result. Finally, the emotion score for the input tweet is calculated by averaging the values from the text, picture, and GIF modules using a ratio of 2:1:1. The model we apply in the text module has more accuracy than in other modules, thus we pay more attention to text module ratings. Each section's score is a floating-point number, with the lowest possible score being -1 and the highest possible score being +1. Then, to automatically zero down on the features most relevant to the categorization of emotions, we suggest a semantic self-attention model.

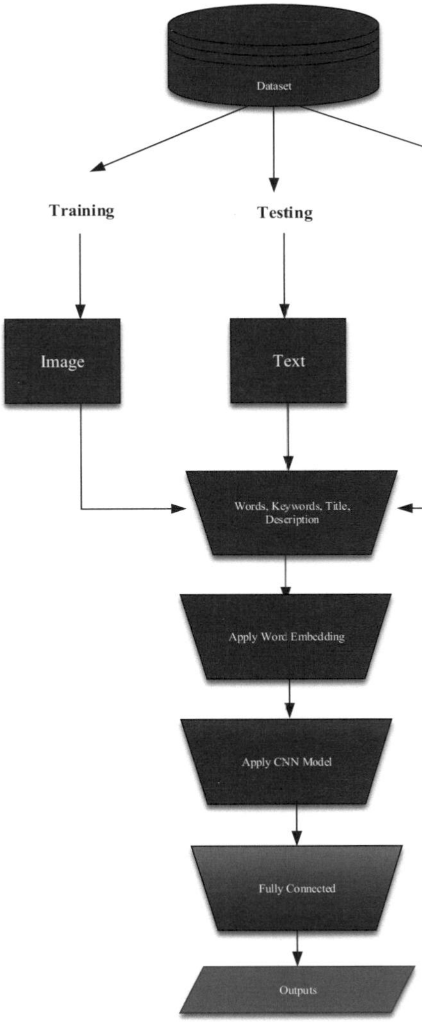


**Fig. (1).** System diagram.

## Dataset

We utilized the Twitter search API and a Python module called "Tweepy" to extract 10,000 popular and recent multimodal tweets containing the term "trump" for use as a feed in our system. Panda's Dataframe was used to store the retrieved tweets for usage by subsequent modules. Dataframes in Panda, a Python module for manipulating and analyzing data, have data structured in rows and columns, making it simple to export the data to Excel. In the sections that follow, we will break down each module into its component parts. The System Diagram is displayed in Fig. (**1**).

## Multimodal Text Classification

About a decade ago, deep learning developed as a potent machine learning approach, achieving state-of-the-art results in numerous application fields, including computer vision, speech recognition, and natural language processing. Recently, there has been a surge in interest in using deep learning for sentiment analysis. In this research, we propose a cross-disciplinary investigation of deep neural networks for image identification and NLP-based sentiment analysis. Fig. (**2**) shows the CNN Model.

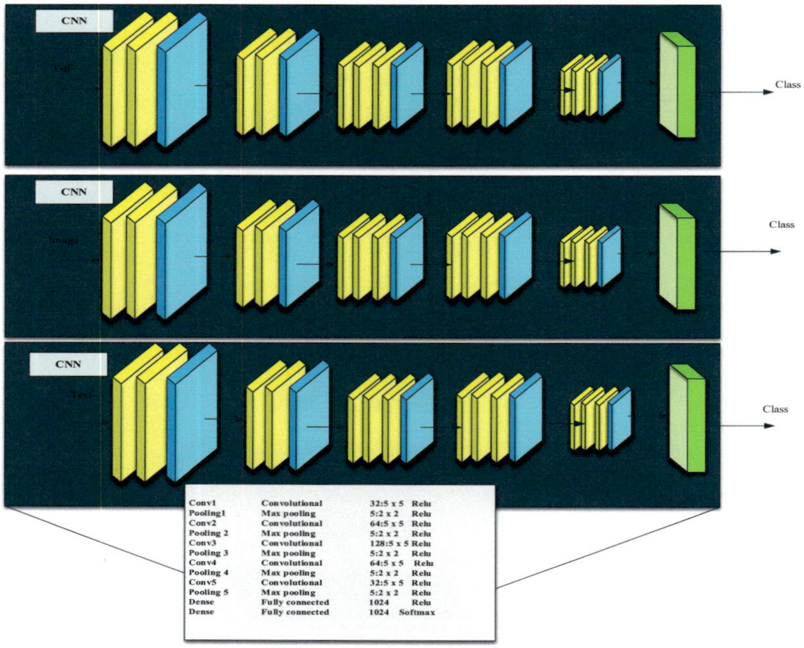


**Fig. (2).** CNN model.

We start by creating separate models, one for text and one for images, and then we compare the outputs of these models. The pre-trained deep CNN is then utilized to extract visual area information from an image-text pair, $R = \{ r_1, \dots , r_i, \dots, r_m\} \in \mathbb{R}^{mxd}$, where m is the total number of regions and d is the average dimension of their individual features. To retrieve textual characteristics, we use a pre-trained word embedding. $T = \{t_1,\dots,t_j,\dots, t_l\} \in \mathbb{R}^{lxe}$, where l represents the length of the phrase and e is the embedding dimension. First, the two modalities are merged for the computation of attention scores in order to learn the attention over visual regions from each word. We take inspiration from the multimodal learning studies on VQA and project the two feature vectors (*i.e.*, region vector r_i and word vector t_j) onto a c-dimensional common space using two low-rank projection matrices. Then, they are combined using multiplication-by- elements method.

$$x_{ij} = (U^T r_i) \odot (V^T t_j) \quad \textbf{(1)}$$

where $U \in \mathbb{R}^{dxc}$ and $V \in \mathbb{R}^{exc}$ are the parameter matrices, and symbol $\odot$ represents the element-wise multiplication or the Hadamard product of two vectors. Afterward, the fused vector $x_{ij}$ is fed into a nonlinear process with a softmax operation to obtain the normalized attention score:

$$\alpha_{ij} = \frac{\exp\left(\sigma\left(W^T x_{ij}+b\right)\right)\big)}{\sum_{i=1}^{m} \exp\left(\sigma\left(W^T x_{ij}+b\right)\right)\big)}, \quad \textbf{(2)}$$

where $W \in \mathbb{R}^{c}$ and $b \in \mathbb{R}^{1}$ are the weight and bias parameters, respectively, and $\sigma(\bullet)$ is the sigmoid activation function. Finally, the attention scores can be utilized for the regulation of the attentive strength over different visual regions. The attended visual features are evaluated as the weighted average of the whole region features for the word $t_j$ as given below:

$$r^j = \sum_{i=1}^{m} \alpha_{ij} \cdot r_i \quad \textbf{(3)}$$

The attended visual feature $r^j$ is more representative to reflect image regions related to the word $t_j$ compared with the original shared visual feature $r_j$. The whole visual-semantic attention process is shown in Fig. (**3**).

## RESULTS AND DISCUSSION

Extensive tests have been performed on both weakly labeled machine datasets and manually annotated datasets. When compared to other more advanced models, our results show that our method is far superior. In order to test the effectiveness of this module and provide an example of its output, we restrict our attention to just 200 GIFs obtained for the "Sadness" emotion. From a total of 200 files, the module successfully identified 117 human faces. The picture module's output and the emotion detection score method allowed us to accurately anticipate the mood of 88 files. We found some of the 200 files the module missed that did contain faces by manually inspecting the remaining 83. Animal and cartoon features predominated, while human faces were obscured or slanted. Our picture module allowed us to correctly guess 64% of these documents. The face and emotion detection algorithm might be made more generic to further enhance this component. To improve the accuracy of sentiment analysis in GIFs, we can benefit from developing a face identification model that can distinguish between animal, drawn, and animated faces. Table **1** is represented in Performance Analysis for Text, Table **2** is portrayed in Performance analysis for image, Table **3** is shown as Performance analysis for GIF.

**Table 1. Performance Analysis for Text.**

| Proposed and Existing Works | SCA (%) | RA (%) | Precision (%) | Recall (%) | F-score (%) |
|---|---|---|---|---|---|
| SVM and Heuristic approach | 72.45 | 79.89 | 94.75 | 83.14 | 89.15 |
| DBN | 74.52 | 85.12 | 95.10 | 84.75 | 89.88 |
| Feature ensemble model with CNN | 78.47 | x | 96.72 | 87.84 | 91.55 |
| Hybrid DL model | 82.45 | x | 96.79 | 91.13 | 92.75 |
| LAN2FIS | 87.64 | x | 96.83 | 91.65 | 93.97 |
| Hybrid Proposed | 92.47 | 94.04 | 98.17 | 96.74 | 96.85 |

**Table 2. Performance analysis for image.**

| Proposed and Existing Works | SCA (%) | RA (%) | Precision (%) | Recall (%) | F-score (%) |
|---|---|---|---|---|---|
| SVM and Heuristic approach | 72.45 | 79.89 | 94.75 | 83.14 | 89.15 |
| DBN | 74.52 | 85.12 | 95.10 | 84.75 | 89.88 |
| Feature ensemble model with CNN | 78.47 | x | 96.72 | 87.84 | 91.55 |
| Hybrid DL model | 82.45 | x | 96.79 | 91.13 | 92.75 |
| LAN2FIS | 87.64 | x | 96.83 | 91.65 | 93.97 |
| Hybrid Proposed | 92.47 | 94.04 | 98.17 | 96.74 | 96.85 |

**Table 3. Performance analysis for GIF.**

| Proposed and Existing Works | SCA (%) | RA (%) | Precision (%) | Recall (%) | F-score (%) |
|---|---|---|---|---|---|
| SVM and Heuristic approach | 72.45 | 79.89 | 94.75 | 83.14 | 89.15 |
| DBN | 74.52 | 85.12 | 95.10 | 84.75 | 89.88 |
| Feature ensemble model with CNN | 78.47 | x | 96.72 | 87.84 | 91.55 |
| Hybrid DL model | 82.45 | x | 96.79 | 91.13 | 92.75 |
| LAN2FIS | 87.64 | x | 96.83 | 91.65 | 93.97 |
| Hybrid Proposed | 92.47 | 94.04 | 98.17 | 96.74 | 96.85 |

Every section of the collaborative multimodal framework will affect a different column of the Dataframe. After tweet messages have been preprocessed, they are sent to the text module, where a "Text Score" is determined. In order to assign a score to the images referenced in the "Image URL" column, the image module will be run on them, and the results will be recorded in the "Image Score" column. Frames from GIFs referenced in a "GIF URL" will be downloaded automatically. The GIF's score will be calculated as the mean of the frames' average picture scores and the results of any face expression recognition performed. Last but not the least, we calculate the "Overall" column by averaging the scores from the text, picture, and GIF modules using a ratio of 2, 1, 1. To get this information, we queried the Twitter API for "trump" and applied the filter "-filter:retweets." This yielded 10,000 tweets. Since the Twitter API does not provide access to media files of the web service's output, we are unable to include retweeted instances. Nearly 6% of tweets included media, as measured by the number of media URLs in the Dataframe. The bulk of the tweets that were chosen at random were only available in text format.

## CONCLUSION

Visual sentiment analysis is challenging because of the abstraction and subjectivity of pictures. People's interpretations of the emotional content of digital pictures and GIFs might vary widely. In this research, we demonstrated how deep learning approaches and data augmentation may be used to fine-tune a CNN to achieve best-in-class accuracy in picture sentiment analysis, and how techniques like facial emotion identification can help us overcome some of the abstractions. We also suggested a sentiment analysis system with specialized components for processing text, images, and GIFs from the Twitter stream. Using face expression detection, our GIF sentiment analysis module provided a novel approach to accurately predicting sentiment. Together, the data from these many modules might help make a more informed judgment about multimodal sentiment detection. We hope to expand our GIF module to incorporate more social networks like Tumblr and Twitter in the future so that we can have access to more visual representations of emotion and employ additional methods like gesture detection.

## REFERENCES

[1] Z. Cai, H. Gao, J. Li, and X. Wang, "Deep Learning Approaches on Multimodal Sentiment Analysis", *2022 IEEE International Conference on Electrical Engineering, Big Data and Algorithms (EEBDA),* pp. 1127-1131, 2022. [http://dx.doi.org/10.1109/EEBDA53927.2022.9745018]

[2] A. Ghosh, B.C. Dhara, C. Pero, and S. Umer, "A multimodal sentiment analysis system for recognizing person aggressiveness in pain based on textual and visual information", *J. Ambient Intell. Humaniz. Comput.,* vol. 14, no. 4, pp. 4489-4501, 2023. [http://dx.doi.org/10.1007/s12652-023-04567-z]

[3] L. Xiao, E. Zhou, X. Wu, S. Yang, T. Ma, and L. He, "Adaptive Multi-Feature Extraction Graph Convolutional Networks for Multimodal Target Sentiment Analysis", *2022 IEEE International Conference on Multimedia and Expo (ICME),* pp. 1-6, 2022. [http://dx.doi.org/10.1109/ICME52920.2022.9860020]

[4] R. Sathish, and P. Ezhumalai, "Intermodal Sentiment Analysis for Images with Text Captions Using the VGGNET Technique", *ACM Transactions on Asian and Low-Resource Language Information Processing,* vol. 20, no. 4, pp. 1-14, 2021. [http://dx.doi.org/10.1145/3450971]

[5] P. Kumar, V. Khokher, Y. Gupta, and B. Raman, "Hybrid Fusion Based Approach for Multimodal Emotion Recognition with Insufficient Labeled Data", *2021 IEEE International Conference on Image Processing (ICIP),* pp. 314-318, 2021. [http://dx.doi.org/10.1109/ICIP42928.2021.9506714]

[6] H. Miao, R. Liu, S. Gao, X. Zhou, and X. He, "End-to-End Deep Memory Network for Visual-Textual Sentiment Analysis", *2018 International Conference on Network Infrastructure and Digital Content (IC-NIDC),* pp. 399-403, 2018. [http://dx.doi.org/10.1109/ICNIDC.2018.8525751]

[7] S. P. Yadav, and S. Yadav, "Mathematical implementation of fusion of medical images in continuous wavelet domain", *Journal of Advanced Research in dynamical and control system,* vol. 10, no. 10, pp. 45-54, 2019.

[8] F. Chen, R. Ji, J. Su, D. Cao, and Y. Gao, "Predicting Microblog Sentiments *via* Weakly Supervised Multimodal Deep Learning", *IEEE Trans. Multimed.,* vol. 20, no. 4, pp. 997-1007, 2018. [http://dx.doi.org/10.1109/TMM.2017.2757769]

[9] G. Cai, G. Lyu, Y. Lin, and Y. Wen, "Multi-level Deep Correlative Networks for Multi-modal Sentiment Analysis", *Chin. J. Electron.,* vol. 29, no. 6, pp. 1025-1038, 2020. [http://dx.doi.org/10.1049/cje.2020.09.003]

[10] S.P. Yadav, S. Zaidi, C.D.S. Nascimento, V.H.C. de Albuquerque, and S.S. Chauhan, "Analysis and Design of automatically generating for GPS Based Moving Object Tracking System", *2023 International Conference on Artificial Intelligence and Smart Communication (AISC),* 2023 pp. 1-5 Greater Noida, India. [http://dx.doi.org/10.1109/AISC56616.2023.10085180]

[11] A. Shirzad, H. Zare, and M. Teimouri, "Deep Learning approach for text, image, and GIF multimodal sentiment analysis", *10th International Conference on Computer and Knowledge Engineering (ICCKE),* pp. 419-424, 2020. [http://dx.doi.org/10.1109/ICCKE50421.2020.9303676]

[12] A.N. Karimvand, R.S. Chegeni, M.E. Basiri, and S. Nemati, "Sentiment Analysis of Persian Instagram

Post: a Multimodal Deep Learning Approach", *7th International Conference on Web Research (ICWR),* pp. 137-141, 2021.
[http://dx.doi.org/10.1109/ICWR51868.2021.9443026]

[13] M.U. Salur, and İ. Aydın, "A soft voting ensemble learning-based approach for multimodal sentiment analysis", *Neural Comput. Appl.,* vol. 34, no. 21, pp. 18391-18406, 2022.
[http://dx.doi.org/10.1007/s00521-022-07451-7]

[14] D. Hazarika, R. Zimmermann, and S. Poria, "MISA: Modality-invariant and -specific representations for multimodal sentiment analysis", In: *Proceedings of the 28th ACM International Conference on Multimedia (ACM MM)* Seattle, WA, USA, Oct. 2020, pp. 1161-1169.
[http://dx.doi.org/10.1145/3394171.3413575]

[15] T. Zhu, L. Li, J. Yang, S. Zhao, H. Liu, and J. Qian, "Multimodal sentiment analysis with image-text interaction network", *IEEE Trans. Multimedia,* vol. 25, pp. 3375-3385, 2023.
[http://dx.doi.org/10.1109/TMM.2022.3158940]

# CHAPTER 32

# Public Opinion Regarding COVID-19 Analyzed for Emotion Using Deep Learning Techniques

**Abhinav Mishra**[1,*]

[1] *Centre for Interdisciplinary Research in Business and Technology, Chitkara University Institute of Engineering and Technology, Chitkara University, Punjab, India*

**Abstract:** As a result of the COVID-19 epidemic, many individuals are experiencing extreme worry, dread, and other difficult emotions. Since coronavirus immunizations were first introduced, people's reactions have gotten more nuanced and varied. In this study, we will use deep learning methods to decode their emotions. Twitter provides a glimpse into what is popular and what is on people's minds at any given time, and social media is presently the finest means to convey sentiments and emotions. Our goal while conducting this study was to have a better grasp of how different groups of individuals feel about vaccinations. The research period for this research's tweet was from December 21st to July 21st. Of the most talked-about vaccines that have recently been available in various regions of the world were the subject of several tweets. The term Valence Aware Sentiment Dictionary An NLP program called Believed (VADER) was used to examine people's sentiments on certain vaccines. We were better able to see the big picture after categorizing the collected attitudes into positive (33.96 percent), negative (17.55 percent), and neutral (48.49 percent) camps. We also included into our study an examination of the tweets' chronology, given that attitudes changed over time. The performance of the forecasting models was evaluated using an RNN-oriented design that included bidirectional LSTM (Bi-LSTM) as well as long short-term memory (LSTM); LSTM attained an accuracy of 90.59% as well as Bi-LSTM of 90.83%. Additional performance metrics, such as Precision, F1-score, as well as a matrix of confusion, were used to confirm our hypotheses as well as outcomes. The findings of this research provide credence to efforts to eradicate coronavirus across the globe by expanding our knowledge of public opinion on COVID-19 vaccines.

**Keywords:** COVID-19, Deep learning techniques, Social media networks and Bi-LSTM.

* **Corresponding author Abhinav Mishra:** Centre for Interdisciplinary Research in Business and Technology, Chitkara University Institute of Engineering and Technology, Chitkara University, Punjab, India;
E-mail: abhinav.mishra.orp@chitkara.edu.in

**Pankaj Kumar Mishra and Satya Prakash Yadav (Eds.)**

## INTRODUCTION

Sentiment Analysis [1] is a classification issue that involves mining social media and microblogging sites for user reviews on popular items, movies, restaurants, political candidates, and other subjects of the day. As the 2019 coronavirus (COVID-19) remains to be a global health problem, people are using social media like Facebook and Twitter to voice their concerns and provide solutions [2]. Photos, texts, videos, and sounds uploaded by users have all seen a rise in popularity on social networking sites in the past few years [3]. To gauge public sentiment towards COVID-19-related activities, Twitter [4] is a popular choice among social media platforms. Because tweets are so short and dynamic, this is the case [5]. To get a sense of how people feel about COVID-19, we provide a deep learning method for analyzing tweets on the film. Worldwide attempts at widespread vaccination against COVID-19 have come across significant skepticism as well as vaccine reluctance or refusal [6], despite the vaccinations' proven effectiveness, safety, as well as accessibility. Twitter analysis of negative COVID-19 vaccine sentiment might lead to novel strategies for boosting vaccination uptake [7]. Social media's popularity is not at all that high in relation to other services on the market today [8]. People all around the globe use Twitter to broadcast their ideas and sentiments to friends, family, and the rest of the world. Extracting public opinions on various topics from social media platforms, such as reviews of films, restaurants, and news stories, is known as sentiment analysis [9]. We are all aware that the epidemic of COVID-19 has affected the whole planet. People's emotions, opinions, and conflicting views about the situation were all on display as the sentiment spread rapidly [10].

## RELATED WORK

In this study, we use a neural network made up of convolutions with Bidirectionally Long-Short Term Memory (CNN-Bi-LSTM) to analyze hashtags related to the COVID-19 worldwide epidemic. A deep learning system is employed to ascertain a user's emotional state, which may be positive (80%), negative (16%), or neutral (0%). Using FastText as well as Globe models that were previously trained, the proposed method successfully cleaned the data as well as extracted word embeddings for out-of-the-ordinary phrases in our corpus. Metrics such as precision, recall, accuracy, and f1 were calculated to assess the performance of a CNN-Bi-LSTM hybrids model. CNN-Bi-LSTM trained using the FastText model beat CNN-Bi-LSTM taught with the GloVe approach, 99.33% to 97.55%, in experimental tasks [11].

The suggested method is based on an LSTM-RNN network that uses attention layers to provide more weight to features. This methodology uses the attention method to enhance the feature transformation framework. Twitter data was collected from the Cagle dataset and categorized as either "sad," "happy," "scared," or "angry." The proposed deep learning model significantly outperformed the baseline methods, with enhanced accuracy of 20%, precision of 10% to 12%, and recall of just 12-13%. Adding attention layers to the preexisting LSTM-RNN method allowed for this enhancement to be realized. The majority (45%) of 179,108 tweets we analysed were positive, while 30% were neutral, and 25% were unfavorable. This proves the viability and efficiency of the proposed deep learning technique for analyzing the opinions expressed on COVID-19 [12].

Therefore, this research analyzed public tweets over a 16-month period to determine the level of opposition to COVID-19 immunization. From April 1, 2021, to August 1, 2022, we culled the original English tweets. The model used here is based on bidirectional encoder reconstructions from transformers (BERT), and it was used to select those tweets that made negative emotional claims. After every round of topic modeling as well as manual thematic analysis, those involved in the study independently assessed the topic labels as well as themes. The total number of tweets examined was 4,448,314 times. Six issues and three themes connected to the widespread disapproval of the COVID-19 vaccine immunisation were identified *via* investigation. Emotional responses to what are seen as unfair regulations or worries about the COVID-19 vaccinations' efficacy and safety are two possible interpretations of the common threads. The findings of the current infodemiology research provide significant public debates to be held and prospective paths for future policy intervention and campaign activities [13], and they are consistent with the rising vaccination model.

The primary goal of this article is to examine the feelings communicated *via* Twitter. Twitter tweets related to Corona are gathered, cleaned using a pre-trained word embedding model, and then fed into a convolutional neural network, a long short-term memory network, and a convolutional neural network trained using a bias network (CNN-BiLSTM). Accuracy, precision, and recall methods are used to assess the model [14].

To estimate the immunological response to repeated exposure to carbon monoxide poisoning, this study proposes a unique probabilistic technique [15].

## PROPOSED WORK

### System Overview

The dataset used in this study was gathered from Cagle and consists of several tweets on COVID-19 vaccines. Data characters are subsequently detokenized to separate phrases into words as well as label them after validating the unique values as well as null values and completing preparation. The VADER was then used to assign numerical values to indicate whether the emotion was favorable, negative, or neutral. It was then decided to use deep learning, LSTM, and Bi-LSTM architectures to evaluate the accuracy of the model for forecasting. Fig. (**1**) provides a schematic representation of the system based on the aforementioned methods.

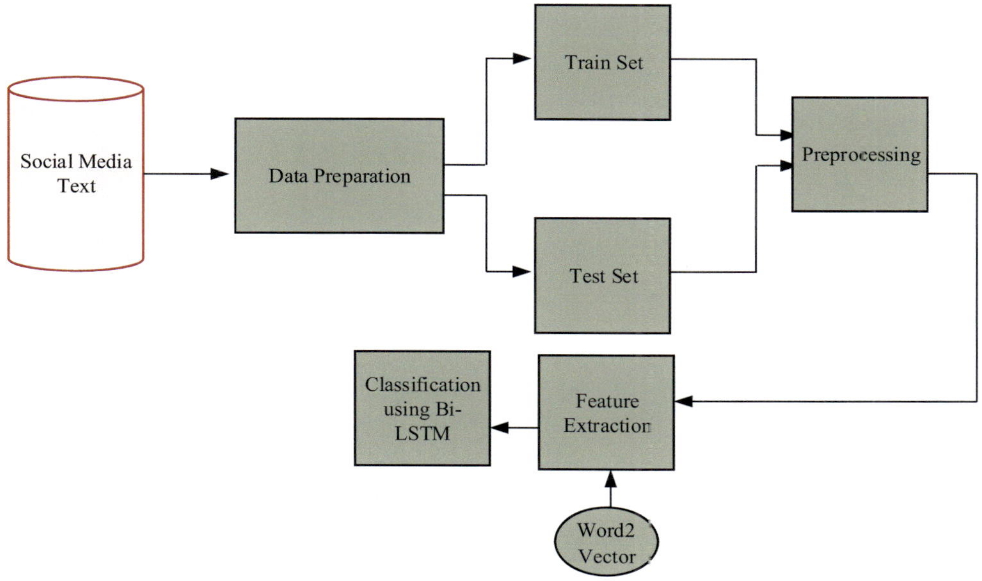


**Fig. (1).** System diagram.

## Dataset Description

Cagle's "All COVID-19 Vaccines Tweets" dataset was used for this study because it contains tweets on several different vaccines, Username, date, the spot, number of friends, replies, hashtags, and sources are just few of the fields that make up this 125906 by 16 array.

## Data Preprocessing, Handling, and Tokenization

The URLs and emails were removed from the tweet before further processing. After that, I took off all of the punctuation, new line characters, as well as quotes (both single as well as double). All tweets were designated before any of the techniques for excluding them were used. Detokenization and Numbly array conversion followed.

## The VADER Emotion Analyzer

C.J. Hutton's VADER, which debuted in 2014, is an updated system that employs a mood analyzer built around natural language processing (NLP) and rule-based values appropriate to perspectives of emotions on social media sites. As content for social media, it excels. As can be seen in Fig. (**2**), VADER is able to conduct an assessment of sentiment of many lexical properties because of the extensive rules it employs.

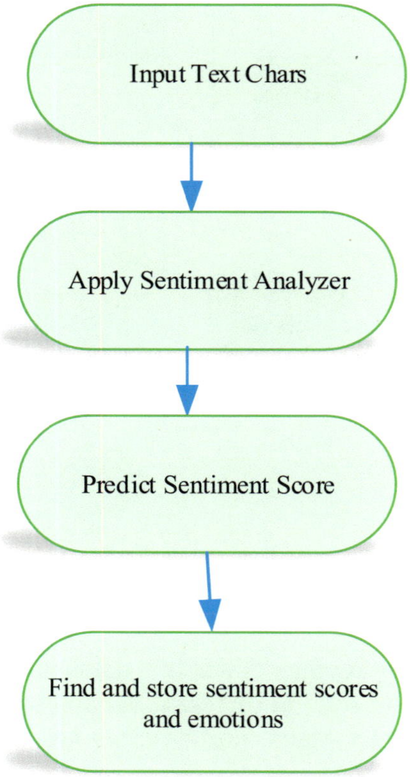


**Fig. (2).** Sentiment analyzer (VADER).

VADER analyses the valence values of each word in the dictionary and then calculates the chance that a given text is positive, negative, or neutral. The most common metric for sentiment evaluation is the compound score, which takes the form of a float value between -1 and 1, the index of which is calculated by summing the values of every word within the lexicon after they have been standardized to fit a set of norms. Fig. (**2**) depicts the Sentiment Analyzer (VADER).

## Feature Extraction and Classification

For a given set of Twitter emotions V, we suggested using the model using LSTM to determine the importance of each tweet. So that you may generate the right language for each set of time - sequence data. During the text-generation process, LSTM takes the input and uses it to generate a series of texts as the output. To improve the outcome on various evaluation metrics, we have developed a multilayer LSTM approach that uses bidirectional and linguistic LSTM. There are three Long Short-Term Memory (LSTM) layers involved in the text generation process $F_t$, input $I_t$ and output $O_t$. At every interval, the cellular state $C_t$ and the present unrevealed condition $H_t$ by means of the Old Covert State $H_{t-1}$ and the current timestamp $X_t$.

• **Input gate:** Using the latest input and the preceding output, it determines what data needs to be kept in RAM. To put it simply:

$$I_t = \vartheta_G[W_I \otimes (H_{t-1}, X_t) + B_I] \quad \textbf{(1)}$$

Where $\vartheta_G$ corresponds to the definition of the logistic sigmoid function:

$$f(x) = \frac{1}{1+e^{-x}} \quad \textbf{(2)}$$

Each caption's classification probability is calculated using this logistic sigmoid function. Its output is between zero and one.

• **Output gate:** Using the input and the current state, a new output is calculated. To put it simply:

$$O_t = \vartheta_C[W_O \otimes (H_{t-1}, X_t) + B_O] \quad \textbf{(3)}$$

$\vartheta_C$ Hyperbolic Tangent Function is represented by $\otimes$ Symbolises the Multiplication by Elements.

• **Forget gate:** Apply the activities to determine how much information to forget. To put it simply:

$$F_t = \vartheta_G[W_F \otimes (H_{t-1}, X_t) + B_F] \quad \textbf{(4)}$$

Then we calculate the states and products of the cells in the following:

$$C_t = F_t \otimes C_{t-1}, X_t + I_t \otimes Q_t \quad (5)$$

$$H_t = O_t \otimes \vartheta_C(C_t) \quad (6)$$

To determine the likelihood of vectors of features for each label, we then use the softmax classifier.

In Fig. (**3**), we can see the LSTM architecture used for extracting features. We establish the parameters of the network and their values using an LSTM model.

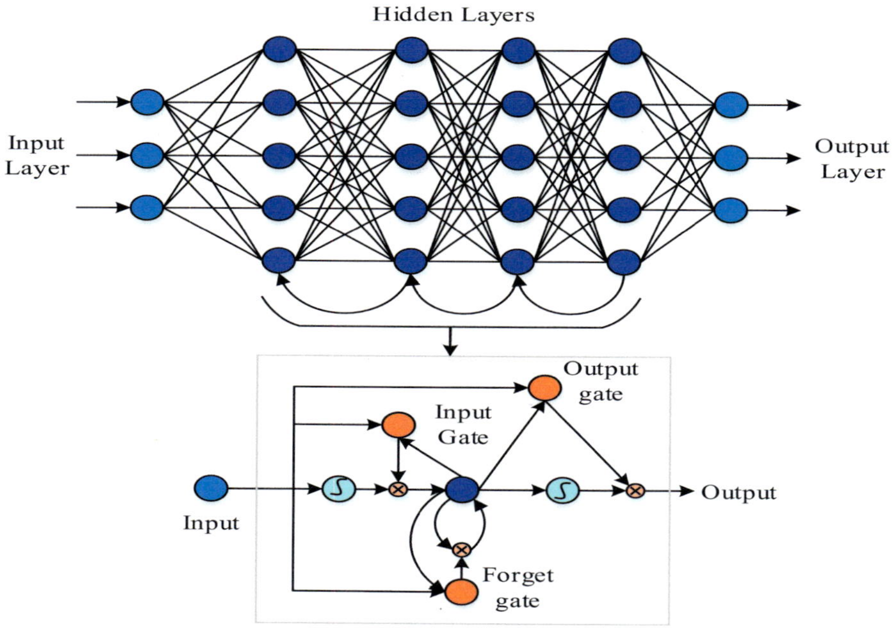


**Fig. (3).** LSTM-based feature extraction architecture.

In most cases, LSTM networks only succeed in learning and extracting features in a single direction. In this study, we suggest using bidirectional LSTM in conjunction with the Adam optimizer. In addressing the issues with traditional LSTM, this is the best approach. The characteristics of our suggested LSTM architecture are learned from the underlying structure, and the feature sequence may be read in either way. The graphical representation of our proposed Bi-LSTM feature extraction model is shown in Fig. (**4**).

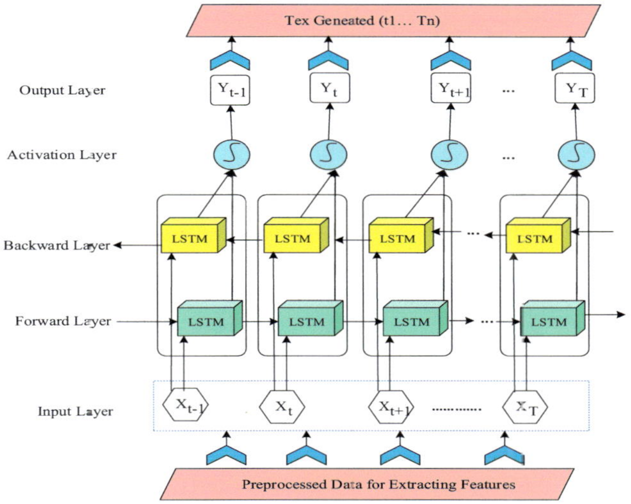


**Fig. (4).** Bi-directional LSTM.

## RESULTS AND DISCUSSION

Tweets were gathered from a variety of international sources. Researchers have looked at several classification algorithms, such as GRU, LSTM, and Bi-directional LSTM, to determine how best to classify the affected emotions. Fig. (**5**) is portrayed in True *vs.* anticipated classes: A matrix of confusion.

| | | **True Class** | |
|---|---|---|---|
| | | Congested | Non-Congested |
| **Predicted Class** | Congested | True Positive (TP) Normal Predicted as Normal | False Positive (FP) Abnormal Predicted as Normal |
| | Non-Congested | False Negative (FN) Normal Predicted as Abnormal | True Negative (TN) Normal Predicted as Abnormal |

**Fig. (5).** True *vs.* anticipated classes: A matrix of confusion.

The genuine and anticipated class confusion matrices are shown in Fig. (**6**). Sharpness, precision, accuracy, the F-measure, sensitivity, and memory are some of the assessment metrics used to contrast performance in this context. The assessment results for these variables appear in Table **1**. Table **1** displays a comparison between the proposed approach and standard practices.

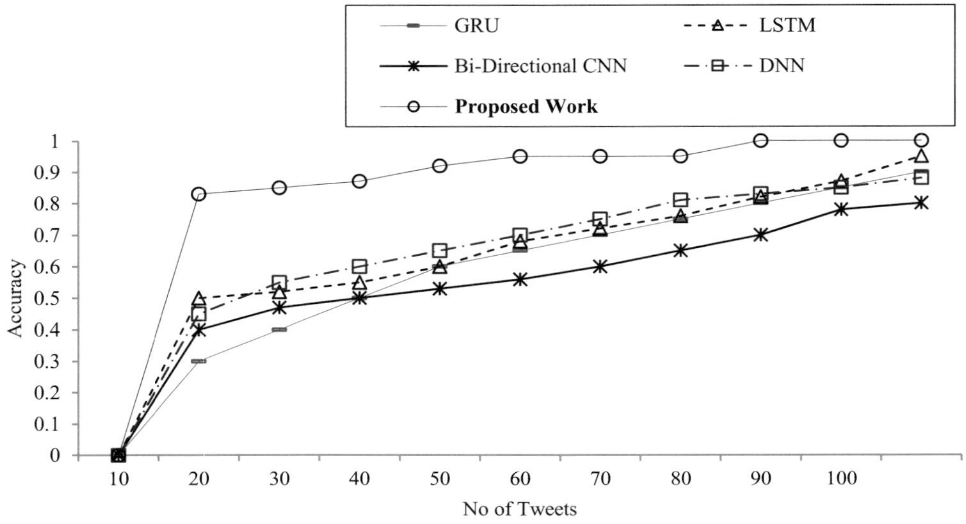


**Fig. (6).** Accuracy *vs*. no of tweets.

**Table 1. Evaluation of the proposed approach in light of existing methods.**

| Metrics | Proposed | GRU | LSTM | Bi-directional CNN | DNN |
|---|---|---|---|---|---|
| Precision | 94.47 | 93.38 | 91.24 | 88.68 | 98.38 |
| Accuracy | 96.34 | 94.36 | 93.34 | 92.24 | 98.79 |
| F-measure | 95.58 | 94.36 | 93.98 | 92.13 | 98.46 |
| Specificity | 95.58 | 88.98 | 89.14 | 87.34 | 98.68 |
| Recall | 95.58 | 94.76 | 93.36 | 92.88 | 98.35 |
| Sensitivity | 96.57 | 93.33 | 91.46 | 88.34 | - |

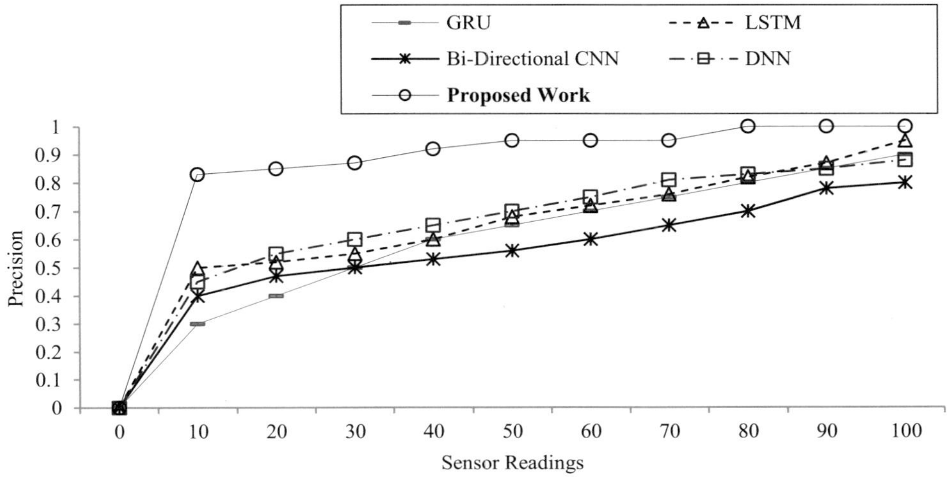


**Fig. (7).** Precision *vs.* no of tweets.

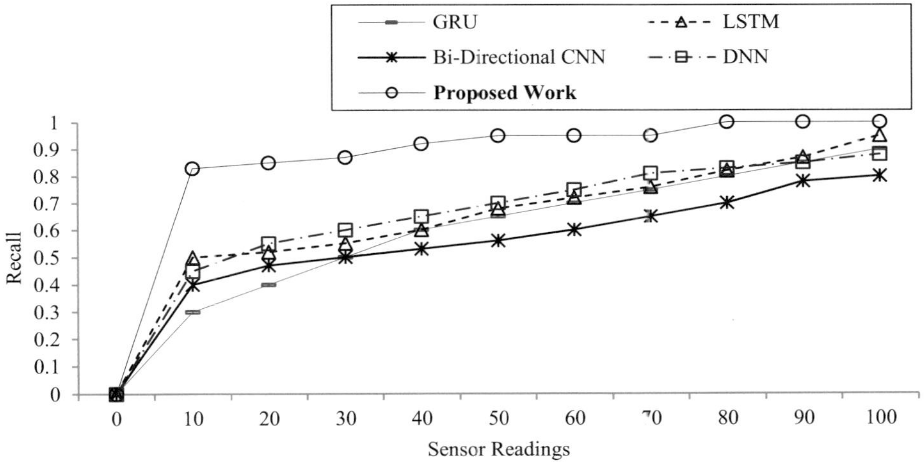


**Fig. (8).** Recall *vs.* no of tweets.

Here is a table that contrasts the suggested CNN model against standard classifiers like GRU, LSTM, Bi-directional CNN network, as well as DNN. The metrics include recall, sensitivity, clarity, dependability, f-measure, and a host of others. The proposed CNN classifier outperforms the existing SVM algorithm, which provides inadequate performance, as shown in the table. In addition, the proposed classifications outperform the existing GRU, LSTM, as well as Hybrid techniques; in contrast, the CNN approach delivers a plethora of desirable outcomes, including a remarkable 99.32% clarity, accuracy, reliability, f-measure, sensitivity, and memory. This performs really well when compared to all the other existing classifications. The findings imply that the proposed CNN could offer better and faster sentiment predictions. Fig. (**7**) is displayed in Precision *vs*. no of tweets, Fig. (**8**) is represented in Recall *vs*. no of tweets, Fig. (**9**) is depicted in F-score *vs*. no of tweets.

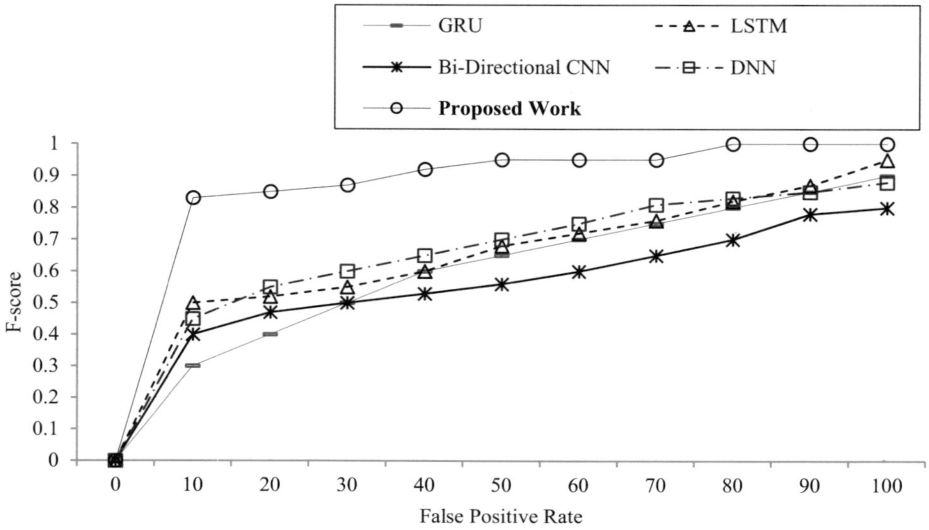


**Fig. (9).** F-score *vs*. no of tweets.

## CONCLUSION

Our study demonstrates the use of deep learning methods to sentiment analysis problems. Our research showed that up until July 2021, in reply to the vaccination processes taking place all over the world, 33.96% of individuals were favourable, 17.55% were negative, as well as 48.49% were neutral. These results were derived using basic NLP-based tools. We also used RNN-based LSTM and Bi-LSTM to evaluate the quality of our models' sentiment prediction and analysis. Both the LSTM architecture as well as the Bi-LSTM model achieved above-average prediction results on measures including accuracy, recall, F-1 ratings, and the confusion matrix. Though many have made the decision to be vaccinated, many others are still unsure of what to do out of fear or outright refusal. Researchers in the field of healthcare may benefit from this study by better understanding the challenges that come with the vaccination procedure. A clear picture of the effectiveness of vaccinations may be obtained by pharmaceutical companies, national health departments, as well as international organisations like the World Health Assembly (WHO). They will have a clearer picture of what needs fixing to restore the public's faith in vaccines. Helping frontline employees combat the new coronavirus may ensure the public's safety and health.

## REFERENCES


[1] R. Dutta, N. Das, M Majumder, and B. Jana, "Aspect based sentiment analysis using multi-criteria decision-making and deep learning under COVID-19 pandemic in India", *CAAI Trans. Intell. Technol.,* 2022.
[PMID: 36712294]

[2] S. vHossain, "A Deep Learning Approach for Public Sentiment Analysis in COVID-19 Pandemic", *2022 2nd International Conference on Intelligent Technologies (CONIT),* pp. 1-6, 2022.

[3] R.S. Jayale, and S.S. Desai, "Aspect-Level Drug Reviews Sentiment Analysis and COVID-19 Drug prediction using PPI & Deep Learning", *2021 International Conference on Computing, Communication and Green Engineering (CCGE),* pp. 1-5, 2021.
[http://dx.doi.org/10.1109/CCGE50943.2021.9776369]

[4] S.P. Yadav, S. Zaidi, C.D.S. Nascimento, V.H.C. de Albuquerque, and S.S. Chauhan, "Analysis and Design of automatically generating for GPS Based Moving Object Tracking System", *2023 International Conference on Artificial Intelligence and Smart Communication (AISC),* 2023 pp. 1-5, Greater Noida, India.
[http://dx.doi.org/10.1109/AISC56616.2023.10085180]

[5] A. Vohra, and R. Garg, "Deep learning based sentiment analysis of public perception of working from home through tweets", *J. Intell. Inf. Syst.,* vol. 60, no. 1, pp. 255-274, 2023.
[http://dx.doi.org/10.1007/s10844-022-00736-2] [PMID: 36034686]

[6] A. Alqarni, and A. Rahman, "Arabic Tweets-Based Sentiment Analysis to Investigate the Impact of COVID-19 in KSA: A Deep Learning Approach", *Big Data and Cognitive Computing,* vol. 7, no. 1, p. 16, 2023.
[http://dx.doi.org/10.3390/bdcc7010016]

[7] Ö. Çoban, S.A. Özel, and A. Inan, "Deep Learning-based Sentiment Analysis of Facebook Data: The Case of Turkish Users. Comput", *J.,* vol. 64, pp. 473-499, 2021.

[8] S. Jatla, and D. Avula, "Hybrid Deep Model for Sentiment Analysis of COVID-19 Twitter Data", *2022 International Interdisciplinary Humanitarian Conference for Sustainability (IIHC),* pp. 1616-1625, 2022.
[http://dx.doi.org/10.1109/IIHC55949.2022.10060027]

[9] S.B. Dash, A. Jain, L. Dey, T. Dasgupta, and A. Naskar, "Factors affecting user experience of contact tracing app during COVID-19: an aspect-based sentiment analysis of user-generated review", *Behav. Inf. Technol.,* vol. 42, no. 2, pp. 249-264, 2023.
[http://dx.doi.org/10.1080/0144929X.2022.2139758]

[10] S. P. Yadav, and S. Yadav, "Mathematical implementation of fusion of medical images in continuous wavelet domain", *Journal of Advanced Research in dynamical and control system,* vol. 10, no. 10, pp. 45-54, 2019.

[11] T.T. Mengistie, and D. Kumar, "Deep Learning Based Sentiment Analysis On COVID-19 Public Reviews", *2021 International Conference on Artificial Intelligence in Information and Communication (ICAIIC),* pp. 444-449, 2021.
[http://dx.doi.org/10 1109/ICAIIC51459.2021.9415191]

[12] S.P. Yadav, and S. Yadav, "Fusion of Medical Images using a Wavelet Methodology: A Survey", In: *IEIE Transactions on Smart Processing & computing* vol. 8. The Institute of Electronics Engineers of Korea, 2019, no. 4, pp. 265-271.
[http://dx.doi.org/10.5573/IEIESPC.2019.8.4.265]

[13] Q.X. Ng, S.R. Lim, C.E. Yau, and T.M. Liew, "Examining the Prevailing Negative Sentiments Related to COVID-19 Vaccination: Unsupervised Deep Learning of Twitter Posts over a 16 Month Period", *Vaccines (Basel),* vol. 10, no. 9, p. 1457, 2022.
[http://dx.doi.org/10.3390/vaccines10091457] [PMID: 36146535]

[14] S. Mehta, "Sentiment analysis on COVID-19 using deep learning", *Int. J. Res. Appl. Sci. Eng. Technol,* vol. 9, no. 5, pp. 115-120, 2021.
[http://dx.doi.org/10.22214/ijraset.2021.38116]

[15] S. Che, X. Wang, S. Zhang, and J.H. Kim, "Correction to: Effect of daily new cases of COVID-19 on public sentiment and concern: Deep learning-based sentiment classification and semantic network analysis", *J. Public Health (Berl.),* pp. 1-1, 2023.
[PMID: 36816448]

## CHAPTER 33

# CNN-based Deep Learning Techniques for Movie Review Analysis of Sentiments

**Prateek Garg**[1,*]

[1] *Centre for Interdisciplinary Research in Business and Technology, Chitkara University Institute of Engineering and Technology, Chitkara University, Punjab, India.*

**Abstract:** Twitter, Facebook, Instagram, *etc.* are just a few of the many online discussion platforms that have sprung up as a result of the explosion in internet use and popularity, giving individuals a place to air their views on current events. Films get both acclamation and criticism from the general public. As a major form of entertainment, they inspire user evaluations of film and television on websites like IMDB and Amazon. Scientists and researchers give careful thought to these critiques and comments in order to extract useful information from the data. This data lacks organisation but is of critical importance nevertheless. Opinion mining, also known as sentiment classification, is a growing field that uses machine learning and deep learning to analyse the polarity of the feelings expressed in a review. Since text typically carries rich semantics useful for analysis, sentiment analysis has grown into the most active investigation in NLP (natural language processing). The continuous progress of deep learning has substantially increased the capacity to analyse this content. Convolutional Neural Networks (CNN) are commonly utilised for natural language processing since they are one of the most successful deep learning methodologies. This paper elaborates on the methods, datasets, outcomes, and limits of CNN-based sentiment analysis of film critics' reviews.

**Keywords:** CNN, Deep learning techniques, Movie reviews, Sentiment analysis.

## INTRODUCTION

The proliferation of electronic items has coincided with the rise in popularity of online social media such as Twitter and Microblog [1]. The challenge of efficiently extracting and categorising the sentiment behind such a large volume of views, often conveyed by plain text, has captured the interest of data analysts [2]. Thanks to advancements in deep learning algorithms, NLP models have become more effective in opinion mining and text categorization [3]. Since there is such a wealth of opinionated content on the web, many researchers are focused

* **Corresponding author Prateek Garg:** Centre for Interdisciplinary Research in Business and Technology, Chitkara University Institute of Engineering and Technology, Chitkara University, Punjab, India;
E-mail: prateek.garg.orp@chitkara.edu.in

on sentiment analysis [4]. When considering an e-commerce service or product, the majority of customers read review articles before making a purchase. Unfortunately, the prevalence of false evaluations [5] is the fundamental issue with these reviews, and it is not fully handled. In order to assist companies and organizations in enhancing their marketing strategies and getting a thorough understanding of customers' thoughts on their goods and brands, the suggested approach makes use of opinion mining on user evaluations [6]. There is a vast amount of unstructured information [7] that has accumulated on social media as a consequence of individuals using the platform to engage with one another and express their ideas in the form of comments and opinions on various issues and stories. When it comes to gauging how users will respond, sentiment analysis is the gold standard. Many different techniques based on machine learning and natural language processing have been used to probe these emotions in the past [8]. However, owing to their efficacy, deep learning-based solutions are becoming more popular. Image processing is now a key growing technology in the realm of AI-based systems. Emotion recognition [9] is explored using artificial intelligence machine learning approaches. Emotion recognition is the study of how a person's facial expressions, body language, and vocal tone reveal what they are thinking and feeling at any given moment. One may then ascertain whether or not the person has any desire to continue with the current event. The core purpose of Audience Reaction Analysis is the examination of the emotional state of the audience as a whole that may be obtained by collecting and analysing every attendee's facial expression before, during, and after a seminar, discussion, lecture, or keynote [10].

This study suggests a paradigm for large-scale convolutional neural networks with seven layers. The information is first transformed into word vectors. Word2Vec has been called one of the Keras' most potent embedding layer approaches. The convolutional layer is used twice. In order to create a feature map, the first 1D a convolutional is applied to the input information to extract relevant features. The characteristics chosen by the first layer of convolution are summarised by the second. The output's resolution is lowered and overfitting is avoided thanks to the global max-pooling layer. In order to prevent overfitting and improve generalisation, the layer of dropouts is implemented. In this layer, nodes are removed from the network at random and their connections to the outside world are temporarily severed. In order to determine whether an input feature is positive or negative, the dense layer applies the loss function from the training dataset.

Here is how the rest of the paper is structured: Movie reviews, machine learning, and sentiment analysis literature are introduced in Section 1.1. The suggested solution seven-layer CNN model is outlined in Section 2, and experimental results and discussions are presented in Section 3, and the paper is concluded in Section 5.

## RELATED WORK

In this study, we retrieved 25,000 evaluations and their accompanying sentiment labels in an effort to build an analysis of sentiment for film criticism. To determine whether an audience member liked or disliked the film, we improved upon the traditional Bag of Words (BoW) model by using the TF-IDF method to vectorize the data and trained a Convolutional Neural Network (CNN). We compare the model's performance in identifying positive and negative sentiment separately and report its overall accurateness and stability. The best model has an average 'Accurateness' of 80.62 percent, a standard deviation of 1.33 percent, and a sensitivity and specificity of 76.4 percent for identifying positive sentiment and 84.6 percent for identifying negative sentiment [11].

To better assess a given system, it is necessary to develop new models that can identify and categorise the emotions communicated *via* an electronic text. Many different approaches have been offered to address this issue, the vast majority of which make use of Machine Learning methods. The capacity to learn and extract meaningful information from data has made Deep Learning a fast-expanding area that has already been shown to be helpful in solving many difficult issues. As a result, a number of works seek to use this strategy in areas of sentiment analysis such as sentiment categorization. In this paper, we propose a novel approach to user sentiment analysis using NLP and a deep convolutional neural network. The 50,000 movie reviews that make up the IMDB dataset have been used to test the suggested approach. With a training phase Accurateness of 99% and a testing phase Accurateness of 89%, the findings obtained were highly persuasive [12].

To analyse the sentiment of online customer reviews, we use a deep learning a convolutional neural network with a long short-term memory (CNN-LSTM) approach to this research. Consumers' reviews of cameras, PCs, cell phones, tablets, TVs, and video security systems on Amazon were included in the real-time data collection utilised to test and evaluate the system. In the course of the data pretreatment process, we used lowercase the process, stopword deletion, punctuation removal, and tokenization. To determine if a consumer is feeling happy or sad, we used LSTM and CNN-LSTM algorithms to clean the data. There was a 94% increase in accuracy using the LSTM method and a 91% increase using the CNN-LSTM method. To sum up, we find that the deep learning methods utilised here offer the most reliable forecasts of how buyers would evaluate a product's quality [13].

Convolutional Neural Networks (CNNs) and Bidirectional Long Short-Term Memory (BiLSTM) algorithms are only two of the deep learning techniques we use in our investigation of critical response to films. The evaluation findings show that the proposed CNN-BiLSTM Hybrid System outperforms conventional Deep Learning and machine learning approaches with regard to exactness, recall, F-measure, and accuracy. This approach, which makes use of hybrid Deep Learning algorithms, was successfully applied to the IMDB review dataset [14].

By monitoring audience reactions at set intervals throughout the event's duration, the proposed system hopes to give dependable, objective feedback to the event's producer or administrator. Words like "Convolutional Neural Network," "Mood Classification," "Deep Learning," and "ReLU" are also included. [15].

## PROPOSED WORK

### System Model

In this study, we used the same CNN model written in Python for bigger movie review datasets to evaluate its efficacy. Unfortunately, the findings from this model are not good enough. For this reason, we have presented a seven-layer convolutional neural model. In addition, this study improved Alexandre Cunha's suggested model by adding a hidden layer (a narrow-minded global max-pooling layer) with default values and adjusting other parameters. There are seven levels to our suggested model. Starting with an embedded layer, the architecture progresses *via* two subsequent convolutional layers, an overall maximum pooling level, a fully connected layer, a layer with dropouts, and a dense layer.

### CNN for Movies Review Classification

The first level of the model, the embedding layer, is given labelled data. The set of data must be cleaned in order to use the embedding layer. One-hot encoding is created for each word in the datasets before they are used. The model calls for the size of the space of vectors to be given. Dimensions of 256 were utilised. In the first stage, we use relatively tiny random vectors to serve as an initialization for the word embeddings. One-hot encoding is a method for mapping syllables into word vectors, however, it treats each word as if it were unrelated. Furthermore, if the amount of words is high, the word vector's dimensions will be enormous. Researchers offered a solution to the one-hot encoding challenge by instead encoding words as vectors.

Word embedding is utilised to transform words into vectors for this research. For dataset I, only 78,000 most frequent words are allowed, whereas dataset-II allows for 1,08,000 terms. Based on experimental findings shown in Table **1** ,we employed 256 dimensions and ceased the review at 1200 words. The dictionary built from the datasets was used to randomly determine the weights of the embedding layers; these vectors were then trained *via* backpropagation. Fig. (**1**). displays the System Flow Diagram.

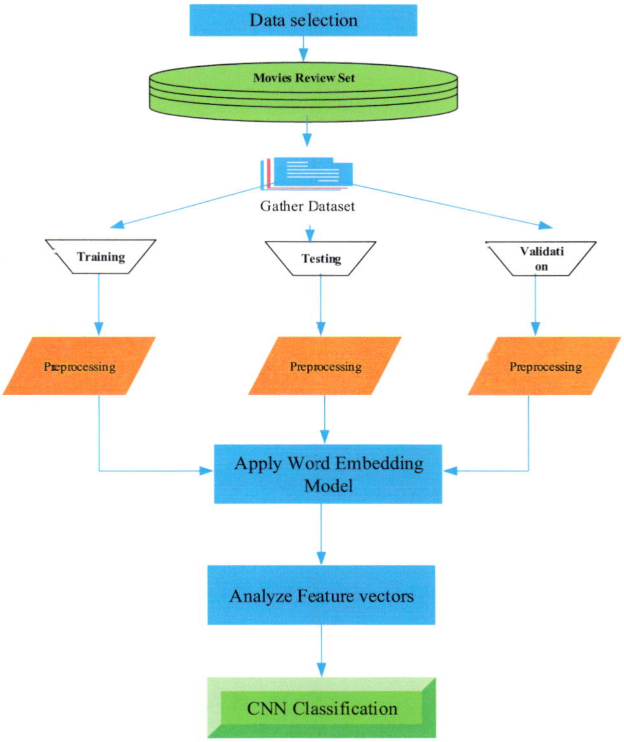


**Fig. (1).** System flow diagram.

Each input window undergoes a convolution, which consists of a linear layer (followed by a non-linearity). Let's suppose this formally:

- $(x_1,\ldots,x_n)$ - symbols for the words that were typed in, $x_i \in \mathbb{R}^d$ ;
- $d$ (input channels) - output embedding size;
- $k$ (kernel size) - a convolution window's length (on the illustration, $k$=3);
- $m$ (output channels) - The total amount of convolution filters (or the resulting channel count).

That makes a convolution a linear layer, right $W \in \mathbb{R}^{(k\cdot d)\times m}$. For a $k$-sized window $(x_1,\ldots,x_{1+k-1})$, this vector addition is what the convolution does.

$$u_i = [x_i, \dots x_{i+k-1}] \in \mathbb{R}^{k \cdot d} \quad (1)$$

to which the convolution matrix is multiplied:

$$F_i = u_i \times W \quad (2)$$

Each window in a convolution over an input is subjected to the same linear change.

Following the convolution operation of the convolution layer, features of the data are recovered; however, the dimensions of the derived features are quite large; to solve this problem and reduce the cost of developing a network, a layer for pooled is added after the convolution layer:

$$l_t = \tanh(x_t * k_t + b_t) \quad (3)$$

where $l_t$ is the activation function, tan is the convolutional output value, $x_t$ is the input vector, $k_t$ represents the density of the convolutional kernel, and $b_t$ is the convolution kernel's bias.

The features are extracted by the convolutional layer. The convolution process is carried out by the filters of the convolutional layer. To generate many feature maps or activating maps from a single input vector, the filter is applied. Using the function "model. Add(Conv1D(filters=32, kernel size=8, activation='relu'))" to create a convolutional layer. The number of filters is represented by filters, while the size of the kernel is represented by the convolutional window or kernel size. The output of the CNN layer is then activated using a rectified linear unit (ReLU) function of activation. Any negative output is replaced by zero at this layer. The layer's output closely resembles the input shape.

Maximum Layer Pooling Subsampling layers are used to lower the network's computational complexity by reducing the size of the spatial representation. Max pooling is a popular method of subsampling. The max-pooling layer keeps the most crucial feature maps or data and discards the rest. With the aid of the "model" function, a maxpooling layer was created. Insert "(MaxPooling1D (pool_size=2)"

The full-connectivity layer is used for categorization. A Fully Connected Layer (FCL) is constructed using Kara's dense layer and receives the Pooled outputs.

After this layer, an elementary sigmoid activation function is used to validate an output between 0 and 1. The result is a binary value, where 0 indicates a negative emotion and 1 indicates a positive one.

## RESULTS AND DISCUSSION

### Data Collection

Here we assess the performance of the model of neural networks for emotional analysis. Movie review datasets may be found in several places, such as GitHub, Kaggle.com, the UCI machine learning repository, and the Internet Movie Database (IMDb). We scraped IMDb for review data and used it. Critics often publish their thoughts and ratings on movie rating sites such as IMDb to help people decide whether or not to see the film. Two datasets from IMDb, an online movie database, were utilised for this research. Researchers have access to and generally approve of these datasets. Kaggle.com has two datasets, with the dataset I including audience ratings of films on IMDb and featuring 25,000 ratings, half of which are favourable and half of which are negative. Another binary classification dataset with 50,000 movie reviews is available on Kaggle.com under the name “dataset II”.

### Data Normalization

Cleaning the data is essential for improving the ‘Accurateness’ and reliability of sentiment analysis. Textual criticism of films is the system's input. Only reviews written in English are included, and punctuation marks such as periods, brackets, and full stops have been left blank. With the use of a regular expression, we need to clean up this text data by removing punctuation from words, eliminating tokens that are only accents, that include digits, that have only one letter, and tokens that have no much value.

We noticed that the datasets include HTML elements and punctuation. As a result, we cleaned up these data sets by removing any HTML elements and other non-alphanumeric characters. We eliminated all the strings with single characters by first eliminating the punctuation marks, which left just meaningless single characters. In their place, we inserted a gap that splits up our data collection. After that, we eliminated all the extra spaces and changed it to lowercase. After the datasets have been cleaned, they are split into two sets: training and testing. Seventy-five percent of each dataset is utilised to train the model that was suggested, while the remaining twenty-five percent is utilised for evaluation. To train the model, we employ 18,750 of 25,000 samples in dataset I, while the remaining 6,250 can be utilised for testing. In contrast, out of the 50,000 samples in dataset II, 37,500 were utilised for training and 12,500 were used for testing.

This part provides a thorough examination of the evaluation indices and datasets used, as well as the study of the two suggested deep learning models.

Accurateness, exactness, recollection, & the F score are taken into account as assessment indices in this study. The formulas for each are as follows:

$$\begin{aligned} \text{Accurateness} &= \frac{T_P+T_N}{T_P+F_N+T_N+F_P}, \\ \text{recollection} &= \frac{T_P}{T_P+F_N}, \\ \text{exactness} &= \frac{T_P}{T_P+F_P}, \\ F_1 &= \frac{2* \text{exactness} * \text{recollection}}{\text{exactness} + \text{recollection}}, \end{aligned} \tag{4}$$

where TP indicates a correct diagnosis, TN indicates a negative result, FP indicates a positive result, and FN indicates a negative result.

**Table 1. The TF-IDF document representation classifier.**

| Scheme | Accurateness | |
|---|---|---|
| | With TF-IDF | Without TF-IDF |
| CNN | 88.99 | 92 |
| Machines with Vector Support | 78.66 | 82.53 |
| Randomized Forest | 73.05 | 76.14 |
| KNN | 61.12 | 65.93 |
| Naive Bayes | 58.45 | 77.38 |
| Choice Tree | 54.96 | 55.61 |

When compared to other similar machine learning algorithms, CNN also performs better. Last but not least, the comparison of Table **1** to Table **2** reveals that the classic tfidf representation outperforms the word embeddings when it comes to document categorization. This demonstrates that relevant words inside an item have more discriminatory power than other encodings like context and word meaning. In summary, Logistic Regression outperformed other conventional Machine learning methods with a classification accuracy of 82.74%. The findings also show that the Decision Tree method performs poorly when compared with other machine learning techniques.

**Table 2. Document representation through word2vec classification.**

| ML Technique | Accurateness |
|---|---|
| CNN | 93.68 |
| Machines with Vector Support | 65.98 |
| Randomized Forest | 73.05 |
| KNN | 61.12 |
| Naive Bayes | 49.11 |
| Decision Tree | 26.96 |

In this study, we suggested a model for sentiment analysis using a five-layer convolutional neural network (CNN) to categorise reviews of films. The data has been preprocessed to enhance the standard of sentiment evaluation before the phrase vector is entered into the model. Since HTML elements, punctuation, and spaces do not provide any meaningful data, we get rid of them during preparation. Word embedding is the most efficient of the available methods for feature selection. We used a technique called word embedding (embedding layer) to transform the text into vectors, giving words with similar meanings a more closely related vector. Furthermore, we discovered that the model's performance is impacted by the time of the input review. We choose between short, medium, and long review times, with the middle option yielding the best model performance. In order to get to the gist of the data, two convolution layers come after the embedding layer. When compared to the conventional dense layer, the convolution layer is used because it extracts characteristics from a smaller number of neurons. The characteristics chosen by the first a convolutional are summed together by the second. The global maximum pooling layer is then used to reduce the dimensionality of the data without sacrificing information that is crucial to the model and to avoid overfitting. The features vector produced by the worldwide max-pooling level is fed into a fully connected layer, which in turn outputs a probability array. Overfitting may be mitigated and generalisation error can be improved by using a dropout layer and randomly removing neurons from the hidden layer. The dropout layer is set at a value of 0.3 because, at that value, the model performs at its best. At last, a thick layer determines if a feature has a good or negative feeling.

## CONCLUSION

The suggested approach utilises two video remarks on YouTube and a six-layer convolutional neural network. This model's accuracy falls between 60% and 84%. It was proposed that this model be used on a more comprehensive data set. Despite our best efforts, the model only achieves 55% accuracy when applied to bigger datasets of movie reviews. We improved Alexandre Cunha's model from 55% to 92% accuracy by modifying many parameters and introducing a new layer called global max-pooling. The proposed six-layer model is less accurate because of the dataset's size and the briefness of each assessment. Our seven-layer convolutional neural network was trained using data from cinema critic evaluations. Our model achieves 91.18% accuracy, 92.53% recall, 91.94% F1-Score, and 91.79% exactness on dataset I, and 91.98% accuracy, 94.14% exactness, 89.93% recall, and 91.72% F1-Score on dataset II. Data cleaning methods and strategies are outlined, and the efficiency, recall, and accuracy of the different algorithms put to use are evaluated. Our ultimate goal is to identify the most promising machine learning model for further study.

## REFERENCES


[1] F. Alotaibi, and V.G. Gupta, "Sentiment analysis system using hybrid word embeddings with convolutional recurrent neural network", *Int. Arab J. Inf. Technol.,* vol. 19, no. 3, pp. 330-335, 2022. [http://dx.doi.org/10.34028/iajit/19/3/6]

[2] N.K. Kaliappan, S. Thapasimuthu Rajeswari, P. Dakshinamoorthy, N. Sundararaju, and R. Sundar, "Intelligent video surveillance using enhanced deep belief based multilayered convolution neural network classification techniques", *Photogramm. Rec.,* vol. 37, no. 180, pp. 490-502, 2022. [http://dx.doi.org/10.1111/phor.12429]

[3] G. Amrani, A. Adadi, M. Berrada, Z. Souirti, and S. Boujraf, "EEG signal analysis using deep learning: A systematic literature review", *2021 Fifth International Conference On Intelligent Computing in Data Sciences (ICDS),* pp. 1-8, 2021. [http://dx.doi.org/10.1109/ICDS53782.2021.9626707]

[4] S.P. Yadav, and S. Yadav, "Fusion of Medical Images in Wavelet Domain: A Discrete Mathematical Model", In: *Ingeniería Solidaria* vol. 14. Universidad Cooperativa de Colombia- UCC., 2018, no. 25, pp. 1-11. [http://dx.doi.org/10.16925/.v14i0.2236]

[5] U.D. Gandhi, P. Malarvizhi Kumar, G. Chandra Babu, and G. Karthick, "Sentiment Analysis on Twitter Data by Using Convolutional Neural Network (CNN) and Long Short Term Memory (LSTM)", *Wirel. Pers. Commun.,* 2021. [http://dx.doi.org/10.1007/s11277-021-08580-3]

[6] M. Nabeel, and C. Große, "Classifying COVID-19 Disinformation on Twitter using a Convolutional Neural Network", *International Conference on Information Systems Security and Privacy,* 2022. [http://dx.doi.org/10.5220/0010774800003120]

[7] V. Vashisht, A.K. Pandey, and S.P. Yadav, "Speech Recognition using Machine Learning", In: *IEIE Transactions on Smart Processing & Computing* vol. 10. The Institute of Electronics Engineers of Korea., 2021, no. 3, pp. 233-239. [http://dx.doi.org/10.5573/IEIESPC.2021.10.3.233]

[8] B.A. Mohammed, and M.S. Al-Ani, "Review Research of Medical Image Analysis Using Deep Learning", 2020. [http://dx.doi.org/10.21928/uhdjst.v4n2y2020.pp75-90]

[9] X. Ma, and Q. Zhou, "Special issue on deep learning and neural computing for intelligent sensing and control", *Neural Comput. Appl.,* vol. 32, no. 7, pp. 1811-1812, 2020. [http://dx.doi.org/10.1007/s00521-020-04785-y]

[10] J. Kaur, J. Saxena, and J. Shah, "Facial Emotion Recognition", *2022 International Conference on*

*Computational Intelligence and Sustainable Engineering Solutions (CISES).*, 2022. [http://dx.doi.org/10.1109/CISES54857.2022.9844366]

[11] D. Yu, "Intelligent Analysis System of Movie Reviews Using Deep Learning and Convolutional Neural Networks", *2021 IEEE Conference on Telecommunications, Optics and Computer Science (TOCS),* pp. 617-621, 2021. [http://dx.doi.org/10.1109/TOCS53301.2021.9688854]

[12] S. Sabba, N. Chekired, H. Katab, N. Chekkai, and M. Chalbi, "Sentiment Analysis for IMDb Reviews Using Deep Learning Classifier", *7th International Conference on Image and Signal Processing and their Applications (ISPA),* pp. 1-6, 2022. [http://dx.doi.org/10.1109/ISPA54004.2022.9786284]

[13] M.E. Alzahrani, T.H.H. Aldhyani, S.N. Alsubari, M.M. Althobaiti, and A. Fahad, "Developing an Intelligent System with Deep Learning Algorithms for Sentiment Analysis of E-Commerce Product Reviews", *Comput. Intell. Neurosci.,* vol. 2022, pp. 1-10, 2022. [http://dx.doi.org/10.1155/2022/3840071] [PMID: 35669644]

[14] M.M. Krishna, B. Duraisamy, and J. Vankara, "Hybrid Deep Learning Techniques for Sentiment Analysis on IMDB Datasets", *2nd International Conference on Advance Computing and Innovative Technologies in Engineering (ICACITE),* pp. 689-693, 2022. [http://dx.doi.org/10.1109/ICACITE53722.2022.9823898]

[15] S. Sinha, A. Jayan, and R. Kumar, "An analysis and comparison of deep-learning techniques and hybrid model for sentiment analysis for movie review", In: *Proc. 2022 3rd Int. Conf. Emerging Technol. (INCET)* Bengaluru, India, May 2022, pp. 1-5.

**CHAPTER 34**

# Machine Learning and Deep Learning Models for Sentiment Analysis of Product Reviews

**Saket Mishra**[1,*]

[1] *Centre for Interdisciplinary Research in Business and Technology, Chitkara University Institute of Engineering and Technology, Chitkara University, Punjab, India*

**Abstract:** In our research, we use sentiment analysis to determine how well ratings and reviews are compared on Amazon.com. The process of determining whether a text's tone is favorable or negative and labelling it as such is known as sentiment analysis. Consumers may write evaluations on e-commerce sites like Amazon.com and indicate the polarity of their opinion. There is a discrepancy between the review and the rating in certain cases. We used deep learning to analyze the sentiment of Amazon.com product reviews in order to find reviews with inconsistent star ratings. A paragraph vector was utilized to transform textual product evaluations into numeric data that was then fed into a neural network with recurrent equipped with a gated recurrent unit for training. We built a model that takes into account the review text's semantic connections to the product data. Additionally, we built a web service that uses the trained model to predict the rating score of a submitted review and gives feedback to a reviewer if the anticipated and submitted ratings do not line up.

**Keywords:** Amazon, Deep learning techniques, Machine learning, Product reviews, Sentiment analysis.

## INTRODUCTION

Sentiment analysis, also known as opinion mining, has emerged as a hot topic in academic circles in recent years, thanks to the proliferation of social media and e-commerce platforms. Sentiment analysis is a method used to determine how someone feels about a certain topic based on the words they choose to use [1, 2]. On e-commerce sites like Amazon.com, customers may provide ratings alongside their reviews. Natural language processing (NLP) and machine learning techniques are used in sentiment analysis to predict the speaker's intent from a given statement. Sentiment analysis entails dividing text into positive, negative, and neutral categories. Opinion mining [3] is the practice of systematically collec-

* **Corresponding author Saket Mishra:** Centre for Interdisciplinary Research in Business and Technology, Chitkara University Institute of Engineering and Technology, Chitkara University, Punjab, India;
E-mail: saket.mishra.orp@chitkara.edu.in

ting and analysing user feedback on a certain subject, product, or issue. Sentiment analysis is the process of analysing the feelings reflected in the collected opinions. In today's highly connected world, e-commerce now accounts for the vast majority of all retail activity [4]. Customers may avoid the mall altogether by ordering products from the convenience of their smartphones and having them delivered to their doorsteps [5]. However, this commercial platform has the downside that consumers have little to no idea of the worth of the goods they are purchasing. So, such a platform service often has a place for clients to offer feedback once they've purchased the goods [6]. You may learn a lot about how satisfied your customers are just reading their evaluations. Customer feedback scores may help business managers determine whether a review trend is favourable or bad, but human analysis of this data is time-consuming and error-prone [7]. The trend of the modern world is towards digitalization. The thriving e-commerce sector of the digital economy is helping people everywhere save time and effort by allowing them to shop for goods without leaving the comfort of their own homes [8]. E-commerce systems may utilise sentiment analysis to determine which goods are popular with customers, which ones need to be tweaked or scrapped entirely, and why. The company product owners may use this input to better understand the market and make informed business choices [9]. The proliferation of online product evaluations has contributed to the rise of e-commerce in recent years. Customers' purchasing decisions are heavily influenced by the recommendations and complaints of other buyers. Interpreting and categorising textual data are called sentiment polarity analysis [10].

## RELATED WORK

Our goal in writing this study was to use Amazon's dataset to develop sentiment analysis for product ratings and text reviews. Several different machine learning methods, including Linear Support Vector Machine Ma-chine, a Random Forest, Multinomial Neural Networks, Bernays Naive Bayes, and Logistic Regression, were implemented. Using a Random Forest classifier, we were able to achieve a 91.90% success rate. In addition, we employed RNN using LSTM as an approach to deep learning and obtained the highest accuracy (97.52%) possible. RNN-LSTM is the best method for our model [11].

Opinion mining and Sentiment Analysis go towards this end by teaching computers to understand and convey human emotions. Users may easily and quickly express their thoughts and opinions using platforms like Facebook, Twitter, Amazon, Flipkart, and others. Using a machine learning technique called sentiment analysis, consumers' feelings, thoughts, and opinions about a product may be categorised and analysed automatically. Naive Bayes, Support Vector Machine (SVM), and Decision Tree are the most often used categorization models in product analysis. When compared to existing machine learning methods, the suggested method will provide superior results [12].

In this study, we use machine learning approaches to build computational models that can automatically identify favourable and negative evaluations of a product. We perform our studies using Amazon.com book review data. The bag of words approach was used to adapt the data for a machine learning-oriented strategy, and then models were developed using logistic regression, naive Bayes, support vector machine, as well as neural network techniques. Word embedding was one of the methods we utilised to convert the data for a deep learning approach before moving on to LSM and gated recurrent units. We evaluate the preprocessed and unprocessed datasets to evaluate the efficiency of machine learning and deep learning models, respectively. As a consequence, on both preprocessed and unprocessed datasets, the bag of phrases in neural network achieves better results than any other method [13].

This research conducts a comparative investigation of sentiment analysis of Amazon customer product evaluations using SVM and LSTM and CNN, two machine learning and deep learning classification algorithms [14].

Our primary objective is to classify each customer review according to how favourable or negative we think it is. Each of these phases is essential to the success of our sentiment polarity detecting system: preprocessing, the extraction of features, training, classification, and generalisation. Tf-Idf and Tokenizer were used to first convert the reviews into a vector format. Then, we used LSTM, Linear SVM, RBF, and Sigmoid kernel deep learning models for training. The models were then assessed according to their accuracy, f1-score, precision, and recall. For Amazon customer reviews, our LSTM model forecasts 86% accuracy while for Yelp reviews, it predicts 85% accuracy [15].

## PROPOSED WORK

### System Model

We developed a model employing recurrent neural networks (RNN) with gated recurrent unit (GRU) which learned low-dimensional vector representation of reviews utilising paragraph vectors and product embeddings in order to interpret the sentiment of Amazon.com reviews. To begin, we used paragraph vectors to turn Amazon.com product reviews into data with a known length. These vectors of features were grouped according to their products and ranked by their timestamps. An RNN with GRU was trained using each cohort. Vectors produced by the RNN's second-to-last layer are known as product embeddings. Product attributes and chronological interactions among reviews are only two examples of the kinds of information that are included in these representations. We then trained a support vector algorithm by concatenating product embedded data with fixed-length vectors produced by paragraph vectors. We also built an interface for users to address the discrepancies between reviews and ratings. A person may be very enthusiastic about a product yet only give it one or two stars, or they could be quite critical but still give it five stars. While unusual, it does cause some consternation among consumers who rely on these evaluations. Reviews rated 1 and 2 are considered unfavourable, reviews rated 3 are considered neutral, and reviews rated 4 and 5 are considered positive in an effort to resolve this concern. We then built a web service app that uses our classifier to make such predictions based on user feedback. A warning is sent to the user if the class to which their rating was submitted differs from the class to which it was projected. Fig. (**1**) depicts our methodological framework.

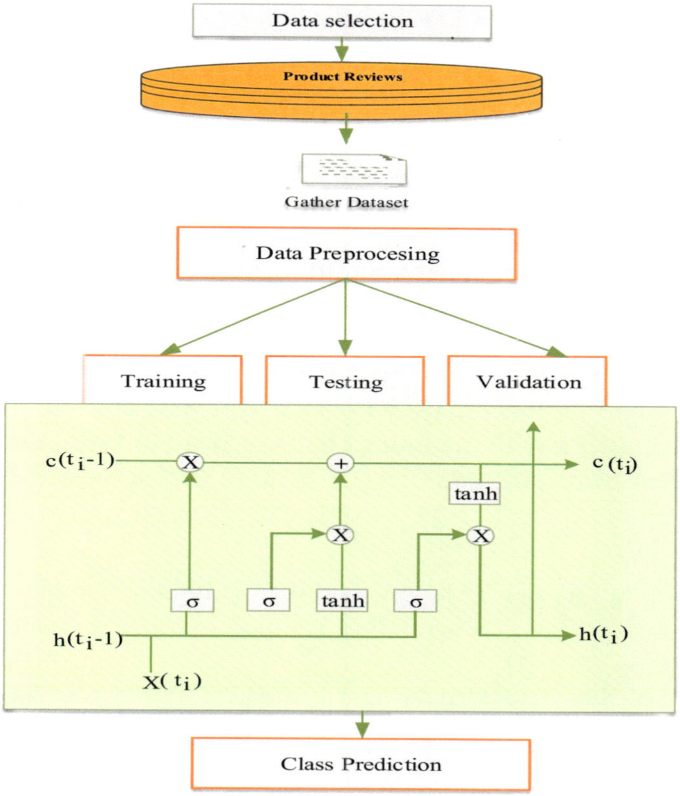


**Fig. (1).** System model.

## Data Collection and Processing

About 3.5 million evaluations of goods from Amazon.com were obtained for this study's data set by Fang *et al*. Each review has a star rating, product identifier, helpfulness score, reviewer identifier, assessment title, review time, as well as review text. There is a total score out of 5. Hyperlinks, HTML tags, casual language, and other filler words abound in online reviews, and many of these words contribute nothing to the overall meaning of the review. The situation will get more complex if such terms are left in the review content. Each review was pre-processed before being converted to its appropriate vector in order to solve this problem.

### *Vocabulary Development*

We concatenated all of the review statements into one giant string and then broke those phrases apart to generate a dictionary of every term in the dataset. We then developed a language to convert these phrases into numerical values. A separate number was assigned to every word in the dictionary. A Counter, that is just a dictionary with a count and some more helpful features, may be used to maintain tabs on the words being used. Then, using an update function, we must add all of the tokens to the counter and revise the total. Then, using the counter object's update method, we must add all of the tokens to the counter and revise the count.

We took 3.5 million product reviews and transformed them into 300-dimensional fixed-length vectors using paragraph vectors. We clustered reviews by 'product id,' and then sorted them by 'review time,' which allowed us to calculate product embedding. Product embedding is calculated based on the review order, as shown in Table **1**. Paragraph vectors are used in place of review text. This series of time-ordered vectors, together with the ratings that correlate to them, serve as the input for training a gated recurrent unit (GRU) to acquire product-specific embedding.

## DL Models

Artificial Neural Networks (ANNs) are the backbone of the deep learning approach.

The main aspect of this paradigm as well as data regarding processes is the many neurons found in an ANN, making this kind of information processing system a simulation of the biological nervous system. ANNs, like those used for hidden pattern detection and data categorization, are custom-built *via* a learning process. The three components of a synthetic neural network are the input layer, the hidden layer, and the output layer. Both the input layer and the output layer are related to the input and output vici, respectively. The layer(s) in the middle, known as the hidden layer(s), do the actual calculations with the aid of the activation functions. The activation function is the core computational component of a neural network. Commonly used activation functions include the sigmoid, hyperbolic tangent, and rectified linear ones. Connectivity between layers represents a causal relationship in the evolution of data. The strength of the connection between any two neurons is determined by their respective weights. This article discusses the most popular deep-learning approaches to sentiment analysis.

- The CNN stands for "convolutional neural network." Deep networks of convolutional neural networks are utilised for tasks like as image classification (for example, "name what they see"), similarity clustering (photograph search), and object detection inside scenes. These algorithms are capable of identifying many aspects of visual data, such as people's faces, traffic signs, and other objects. The success of convolutional nets in recognition of images is a major factor that has brought attention to the efficacy of deep learning. Recent years have seen CNN being used for text analysis as well. One input layer, many layers of convolution, layers of pooling, fully connected layers, and an output layer make up a typical CNN model. In a CNN, the input is processed by a set of Convolutional layers, and the results are passed on to the next layer. Each filter in a convolutional layer performs a unique convolutional operation. The filter uses a vast range of values or weights. The output of a convolutional neural network is a large collection of feature maps. The amalgamation or down-sampled layer follows, and it consists of performing some action across areas in the input map of features as well as dropping some sort of incentive for all of the regions that were investigated. When many convolution windows produce vectors, it is helpful to combine them into a single, unified vector, and this is what the pooling process is used for. The data is then classified by the neural network's final, fully-connected layer.
- LSTM (Long-Term, Short-Term Memory) Long Short-Term Memory (LSTM) is a kind of RNN. The data sources in traditional Neural Networks do not interact with one another. It may be inefficient to use such an approach for certain NLP tasks, but in this case, understanding the previous word is essential in order to anticipate the next word in context. Regardless of the layer inputs, LSTM neurons maintain a connection to the previous neuron state. It has shown to be extraordinarily successful in a wide variety of NLP tasks. Long short-term memory (LSTM) units are capable of storing information in arbitrary, lengthy sequences. Memory cells in the LSTM model work with gating units to retain data for long periods of time. The gating devices are picking and selecting what data to save and when to use it. Input gate, forget gate and output gate are the three gates that make up every memory cell. Each neural network processes a single time increment. Instead of feeding the neural network data at each time

step, you feed it data at all intervals inside a window. The cell's job is to keep tabs on the input sequence's interdependencies.

- GRU: In layman's terms, unlike the LSTM unit, the GRU unit does not depend on a memory unit to regulate the dissemination of data. Without any kind of regulation, it may make direct use of all latent states. GRUs have fewer variables and may be able to train more quickly or with less data. However, LSTMs with more expressiveness may provide superior outcomes when working with massive datasets. They are almost identical to LSTMs, with the exception that they feature two gates instead of one: a reset gate and an update gate. The update gate decides the amount of the prior state to retain while the reset gate decides how to mix the new input with the existing memory. Comparable to the LSTM's input gate and forget gate is the GRU's update gate. Before arriving at an output value, GRU lacks the second nonlinearity. They are both lacking an output gate.

## Proposed DL Model

Our new model is composed of three main components: the feature embedding words, the CNN component, and the weighted element-wise sum component. Our new framework has an aesthetically pleasing structure. Similar to the 32-dimensional task-1 model, we use a 32-dimensional embedding dim. Our model's bi-GRU will use the results of the embedding process to create 8 new concealed states at the conclusion of the sequence, one for each dimension of the embedding. The model only utilizes the final hidden state in the sequence since we learned from the revised Li model that doing so yields superior performance. The logical progression of the sentence's words will also be emphasized thanks to this. Bi-GRU combines its forward and reverse outputs and averages them. Using the results of the embedding process, CNN will produce a 3-kernel, 8-channel output matrix. The model then takes the average of these three CNN matrices to provide an output with the same dimensionality in feature space as the bi-GRU. We then combined bi-GRU and CNN by giving equal weight to the two methods in a single index of the feature space. Here, the weights are adjusted in a way that is more favorable to either the bi-GRU or the CNN model. As the last step in the design, we used a linear layer to condense the 8-feature space down to 4.

The incorporation bag layer and the linear layer are the two primary hidden layers in the rapid text architecture model. In our experience, the model employs 2-gram embedding and ‘mean' mode to average the bag's values and so shrink it. For this reason, the '0' value in the vector is omitted by making the gradient tensor a sparse tensor, since the phrases in the information are not all equal. Using linear regression to provide weights to the embedding dimensions and shrink it down to the number of predicted features, the second layer served as a classifier. The weights in those layers are uniformly distributed between -0.5 and 0.5. The softbacks in the log input of the cross-entropy loss function in Pytorch is used to assign the vector value of every point of information to the likelihood of the features. A stochastic gradient descent method and a scheduler are employed as optimizers. Every epoch, the scheduler reduces the learning rate by 0.9 of the initial gradient.

## RESULTS AND DISCUSSION

First, we used the Genism framework to create a simple model consisting of paragraph-level vectors. Over three and a half million customer reviews from Amazon.com were transformed into a 300-dimensional fixed-length vector. We used a rate of learning of 0.025, an interval size of 10, and 35 worker threads when training the aforementioned model for 15 iterations.

One of the Amazon's most well-known offerings is customer feedback in the form of product reviews. Since the initial review was posted in 1995, countless consumers on Amazon have written over 100 million reviews to share their thoughts and experiences with other shoppers. Because of this, researchers in disciplines such as Natural Language Processing (NLP), Information Retrieval (IR), & Machine Learning (ML) may find a wealth of useful data in Amazon Customer Reviews. As a result, we are making this information public to encourage further investigation beyond academic boundaries into the topic of improving our knowledge of customers' product experiences. In particular, this dataset was built to represent a cross-section of consumers' ratings and comments, regional differences in product perception, and the potential for marketing spin in reviews.

There are two primary parts to the dataset: the content of customer reviews and the information that describes them:

- There is a database of customer comments and other information from the Amazon.com marketplace between 1995 and 2015. The goal is to make it easier to investigate the characteristics (and the development) of customer reviews, which might include the criteria individuals use to rate items and the language they use to describe their experiences with them. (Averaged rating of 4.9 out of 5).
- In order to better understand how diverse groups of people in different nations evaluate the same items, we have compiled a set of reviews written by Amazon customers in a variety of languages and from a variety of Amazon marketplaces. (More than 200k customer ratings across 5 languages).
- A previously available third dataset including non-compliant evaluations has been withdrawn from circulation due to a recall. Those who previously had

access by agreeing on the Terms and Conditions for the use of certain data may keep doing so under the same conditions.

## Accessing the Amazon Customer Reviews Dataset

Researchers now have access to over 130 million user reviews. You may find the information in the S3 bucket named "amazon-reviews-pds" in the AWS US East Region. The files are in the TSV format. The data files are tab-delimited and quote- and escape-character-free; each line represents a single review. After each epoch, the instruction rate was lowered by 0.002. After producing the 300-dimensional embedded data for the product reviews, we clustered them by 'product ID' and sorted them by ' review time.' The recurrent gate unit received input from each category. The sequence's last time step embedding was used as the product's embedding. Table **2** is portrayed in Iterations of CNN and RNN-GRU.

**Table 1. Loss Values of CNN and RNN-GRU.**

| Loss Values | CNN | | | RNN-GRU | | |
|---|---|---|---|---|---|---|
| | **Exactness** | **Recollection** | **Accurateness** | **Exactness** | **Recollection** | **Accurateness** |
| 10 | 0.5987 | 0.4183 | 0.8168 | 0.8987 | 0.8183 | 0.8168 |
| 9 | 0.5940 | 0.4314 | 0.8189 | 0.8940 | 0.8314 | 0.8189 |
| 8 | 0.5915 | 0.4265 | 0.8185 | 0.8915 | 0.8265 | 0.8185 |
| 7 | 0.5962 | 0.4252 | 0.8186 | 0.8962 | 0.8252 | 0.8186 |
| 6 | 0.5844 | 0.4310 | 0.8179 | 0.8844 | 0.8310 | 0.8179 |
| 5 | 0.5853 | 0.4231 | 0.8186 | 0.8853 | 0.8231 | 0.8186 |
| 4 | 0.5951 | 0.4249 | 0.8180 | 0.8951 | 0.8249 | 0.8180 |
| 3 | 0.6016 | 0.4301 | 0.8182 | 0.8016 | 0.8301 | 0.8182 |
| 2 | 0.5925 | 0.4206 | 0.8179 | 0.8925 | 0.8206 | 0.8179 |
| 1 | 0.6064 | 0.4211 | 0.8182 | 0.8064 | 0.8211 | 0.8182 |
| Average | 0.5945 | 0.4252 | 0.8182 | 0.8945 | 0.852 | 0.8182 |

**Table 2. Iterations of CNN and RNN-GRU.**

| Iterations | CNN | | | RNN-GRU | | |
|---|---|---|---|---|---|---|
| | **Exactness** | **Recollection** | **Accurateness** | **Exactness** | **Recollection** | **Accurateness** |
| 10 | 0.5987 | 0.4183 | 0.8168 | 0.8987 | 0.8183 | 0.8168 |
| 20 | 0.5940 | 0.4314 | 0.8189 | 0.8940 | 0.8314 | 0.8189 |
| 30 | 0.5915 | 0.4265 | 0.8185 | 0.8915 | 0.8265 | 0.8185 |

*(Table 2) cont.....*

| Iterations | CNN | | | RNN-GRU | | |
|---|---|---|---|---|---|---|
| | Exactness | Recollection | Accurateness | Exactness | Recollection | Accurateness |
| 40 | 0.5962 | 0.4252 | 0.8186 | 0.8962 | 0.8252 | 0.8186 |
| 50 | 0.5844 | 0.4310 | 0.8179 | 0.8844 | 0.8310 | 0.8179 |
| 60 | 0.5853 | 0.4231 | 0.8186 | 0.8853 | 0.8231 | 0.8186 |
| 70 | 0.5951 | 0.4249 | 0.8180 | 0.8951 | 0.8249 | 0.8180 |
| 80 | 0.6016 | 0.4301 | 0.8182 | 0.8016 | 0.8301 | 0.8182 |
| 90 | 0.5925 | 0.4206 | 0.8179 | 0.8925 | 0.8206 | 0.8179 |
| 100 | 0.6064 | 0.4211 | 0.8182 | 0.8064 | 0.8211 | 0.8182 |
| Average | 0.5945 | 0.4252 | 0.8182 | 0.8945 | 0.852 | 0.8182 |

## CONCLUSION

In this study, we present a deep learning method for addressing a common issue in e-commerce sites: reviews where the star rating given by the user does not correspond to the product's actual quality. Consumers rely heavily on reviews to help them make informed decisions before making a purchase. Our hypothesis for this study is that reviews with inconsistent star ratings may lead to a poor user experience. We used paragraph vectors to first understand the syntactic and semantic connections in a 'review text' before moving on to the next step in building our model. To learn product embedding, we further organized review embedding into a series and input it into a gated recurrent unit (GRU). A support vector machine (SVM) is trained to classify sentiment by merging review embedding obtained from paragraph vectors with product embedding generated *via* a genetic relational algorithm (GRU). Our classifier achieves a reliability of 81.29 percent with merely review embedding. When product embedding is taken into account, accuracy rises to 81.82%. This demonstrates that product data is a robust feature useful for sentiment analysis. We then use this classifier by a web service to make rating predictions for reviews and evaluate them against an input rating. This online program takes in both the review's content and its rating and alerts the reader if the two do not match with each other. In conclusion, we demonstrated how combining review language with product data may provide a powerful deep learning model suitable for use in sentiment analysis. We think the same method may be used to acquire knowledge of user data. Some people are far more forgiving than others, and as a result, they can award substantially higher scores for the identical review wording. We feel inspired to use this knowledge in the future.

## REFERENCES

[1] V.R. Welgamage, U.A. Senarathne, N.H. Madhubhashani, T.C. Liyanage, and P. Asanka, "Overall and Feature Level Sentiment Analysis of Amazon Product Reviews Using Machine Learning Techniques and Web-Based Chrome Plugin", *2022 International Research Conference on Smart Computing and Systems Engineering (SCSE),* pp. 205-210, 2022. [http://dx.doi.org/10.1109/SCSE56529.2022.9905125]

[2] H. Zhang, *Model Comparison in Sentiment Analysis: A Case Study of Amazon Product Reviews.* Highlights in Science, Engineering and Technology, 2022.

[3] V. Vanthana, and K. Kartheeban, "Estimation of Accuracy Level for Sentiment Analysis using Machine Learning and Deep Learning Models", *2022 International Conference on Automation, Computing and Renewable Systems (ICACRS),* pp. 717-722, 2022. [http://dx.doi.org/10.1109/ICACRS55517.2022.10029086]

[4] J. Kaur, J. Saxena, and J. Shah, *2022 International Conference on Computational Intelligence and Sustainable Engineering Solutions (CISES),* IEEE, 2022. [http://dx.doi.org/10.1109/CISES54857.2022.9844366]

[5] S.P. Yadav, S. Zaidi, C.D.S. Nascimento, V.H.C. de Albuquerque, and S.S. Chauhan, "Analysis and Design of automatically generating for GPS Based Moving Object Tracking System", *2023 International Conference on Artificial Intelligence and Smart Communication (AISC),* 2023 pp. 1-5 Greater Noida, India. [http://dx.doi.org/10.1109/AISC56616.2023.10085180]

[6] M.E. Alzahrani, T.H.H. Aldhyani, S.N. Alsubari, M.M. Althobaiti, and A. Fahad, "Developing an Intelligent System with Deep Learning Algorithms for Sentiment Analysis of E-Commerce Product Reviews", *Comput. Intell. Neurosci.,* vol. 2022, pp. 1-10, 2022. [http://dx.doi.org/10.1155/2022/3840071] [PMID: 35669644]

[7] A. Gupta, A. Rastogi, and A. Katal, "A Comparative Study of Amazon Product Reviews Using Sentiment Analysis", *2021 International Conference on Advances in Computing, Communication, and Control (ICAC3),* pp. 1-6, 2021. [http://dx.doi.org/10.1109/ICAC353642.2021.9697155]

[8] D. Gupta, A. Roup, D. Gupta, and A. Ratre, "Food Review Analysis and Sentiment Prediction using Machine Learning Models", *2022 Second International Conference on Advances in Electrical, Computing, Communication and Sustainable Technologies (ICAECT),* pp. 1-7, 2022. [http://dx.doi.org/10.1109/ICAECT54875.2022.9807907]

[9] Z. Desai, K. Anklesaria, and H. Balasubramaniam, "Business Intelligence Visualization Using Deep Learning Based Sentiment Analysis on Amazon Review Data", *12th International Conference on Computing Communication and Networking Technologies (ICCCNT),* pp. 1-7, 2021. [http://dx.doi.org/10.1109/ICCCNT51525.2021.9579786]

[10] H. Nguyen, A. Veluchamy, M. Diop, and R. Iqbal, "Comparative Study of Sentiment Analysis with Product Reviews Using Machine Learning and Lexicon-Based Approaches", 2018.

[11] J.C. Gope, T. Tabassum, M.M. Mabrur, K. Yu, and M. Arifuzzaman, "Sentiment Analysis of Amazon Product Reviews Using Machine Learning and Deep Learning Models", *2022 International Conference on Advancement in Electrical and Electronic Engineering (ICAEEE),* pp. 1-6, 2022. [http://dx.doi.org/10.1109/ICAEEE54957.2022.9836420]

[12] S. P. Yadav, and S. Yadav, "Mathematical implementation of fusion of medical images in continuous wavelet domain ", *Journal of Advanced Research in dynamical and control system,* vol. 10, no. 10, pp. 45-54, 2019.

[13] P. Poomka, N. Kerdprasop, and K. Kerdprasop, "Machine Learning Versus Deep Learning Performances on the Sentiment Analysis of Product Reviews", *Int. J. Mach. Learn. Comput.,* vol. 11, no. 2, pp. 103-109, 2021. [http://dx.doi.org/10.18178/ijmlc.2021.11.2.1021]

[14] L. Arora, P. Srivastava, and S.A. Kumar, "Evaluation Of Product Reviews Using Deep Learning Classifier Models", *13th International Conference on Computing Communication and Networking Technologies (ICCCNT),* pp. 1-5, 2022. [http://dx.doi.org/10.1109/ICCCNT54827.2022.9984463]

[15] A.R. Mehul, S.M. Mahmood, T. Tabassum, and P. Chakraborty, "Sentiment Polarity Detection Using Machine Learning and Deep Learning", *2023 International Conference on Electrical, Computer and Communication Engineering (ECCE),* pp. 1-5, 2023. [http://dx.doi.org/10.1109/ECCE57851.2023.10101494]

**CHAPTER 35**

# Sentiment Analysis of Hotel Reviews Based on Deep Learning

**Jagmeet Sohal**[1,*]

[1] *Centre for Interdisciplinary Research in Business and Technology, Chitkara University Institute of Engineering and Technology, Punjab, India*

**Abstract:** Many hotel evaluations have been written and shared online these days. Machine learning sentiment classification requires complicated artificial design features and feature extraction technique, whereas emotion dictionary-based sentiment classification requires a large amount of emotional database resources. In this study, we present the idea of long short-term memory. The text categorization method is used to determine the general tone. First, the brief comment text is processed into the LSTM network using word2vec and word segmentation technology; next, a dropout technique is implemented to avoid overfitting in order to get the final rating model. By using the LSTM network's superior short-term memory, a positive impact has been realized on sentiment categorization of reviews of hotels, with a precision of more than 95%.

**Keywords:** Deep learning, E-commerce, Hotel reviews, Sentiment analysis.

## INTRODUCTION

When comparing word vector sizes, word embedding vectorization outperforms Bag-of-Word. Sentence-level context, word order, and semantic links between words are all lost in conventional NLP approaches, although word embedding may compensate for this [1]. Word2Vec and Fast Text are only two examples of the many Word Embedding methods that may be used for sentiment analysis. While Word2Vec is word-based, Fast Text operates on N-Gram. Customers' reliance on online evaluations posted to a variety of digital platforms has grown substantially in recent years [2]. Products are generally approved or rejected based on reviews and ratings by customers on E-commerce platforms like Flipchart, Amazon, *etc.* [3]. Reviews of services, such as those offered by hotels, airlines, and restaurants, are just as important to consumers as reviews of items. Using sentiment analysis, programmers may quickly sort user feedback into positive and

* **Corresponding author Jagmeet Sohal:** Centre for Interdisciplinary Research in Business and Technology, Chitkara University Institute of Engineering and Technology, Punjab, India;
E-mail: jagmeet.sohal.orp@chitkara.edu.in

**Pankaj Kumar Mishra and Satya Prakash Yadav (Eds.)**

negative categories [4]. Customer opinion is a major factor in how products are reviewed, but there is still room for development in sentiment analysis that accounts for specifics [5]. There are often five things to consider while choosing a hotel: proximity, food, service, comfort, and cleanliness [6]. This study suggests techniques for analyzing hotel reviews in terms of their underlying sentiment. Preprocessing a hotel review corpus into a term set [7]. After a word list's hidden subjects have been identified using Latent Dirichlet Allocation (LDA), the list is then categorized into the five facets of a hotel with semantic similarity [8]. The word Frequency-Inverse Cluster Frequency (TF-ICF) technique is then used to broaden the word list for the purpose of determining the similarity measurement. Finally, word embedding and Long-short Term Memory (LSTM) are combined to classify consumer mood (satisfied or unhappy) [9]. The evaluations were successfully categorized into the five hotel features using the suggested approach. We created a method for analyzing guest feedback on hotels based on their mood. Through the usage of themes, the system is able to provide precise reports on user-selected attributes [10]. Users are able to rate the quality of a hotel's services based on a variety of factors with the use of this system. In addition, a traveler might examine hotels in a variety of ways. Sentiment detection refers to the technique of distinguishing between biased and nonbiased evaluations. To improve the classifier's efficiency, sentiment detection is performed before sentiment classification. Sentiment analysis may be performed on several levels, including the word, phrase, paragraph, and document. Sentiment analysis may be conducted at two different levels: the document level, where the whole content is given a single sentiment, and the paragraph level, where the sentiment for every paragraph is calculated independently. There are further methods that include using sentiment analysis on a word-by-word basis. Since sentences include fewer words than paragraphs and papers, it is more difficult to correctly extract polarity at the sentence level. Deep learning has outperformed traditional methods on many categorization tests.

## Contributions

Sentiment analysis is the automated examination of emotional overtones in written or spoken communication by use of natural language processing techniques. Sentiment analysis may help tourist businesses monitor client feedback more effectively. In this research, we provide a deep learning-based method for automating the sentiment analysis of hotel reviews by making use of word embeddings and a gated recurrent unit. Our use of a deep learning model achieved 89% accuracy and 92% F-score in sentiment categorization of hotel reviews, outperforming the performance of classic machine learning approaches.

Section 2 provides a brief overview of current research and developments in the area of sentiment analysis. In Section 3, the overall structure of the system is outlined. The system's implementation is shown in Section 4. Methods and outcomes are evaluated in Section 5. Our findings are summarized in Section 6.

## RELATED WORK

Hotel ratings and comments posted online by previous guests are essential when deciding where to stay. As a result, hotel management would benefit greatly from having access to this information. We typically provide a system that gathers user feedback, organizes that feedback into coherent, structured overviews, and makes that information easily accessible [11].

The purpose of this study is to evaluate Word2Vec and Fast Text as two competing sentiment analysis models and compare their accuracies. The TripAdvisor hotel review sentiment analysis dataset is used to compare the two methods. The Skip-gram model is used by Word2Vec and Fast Text. The number of features, the minimum number of words, the number of concurrent threads, and the size of the context window are all the same in both approaches. The ensemble learning techniques of Random Forest, Extra Tree, and AdaBoost are used to combine these vectorizers. Both models' efficacy is compared to that of the Decision Tree as a standard. Accuracy on random forest and Extra Tree was shown to be significantly improved by using either Fast Text or Word2Vec. When compared to Word2Vec, Fast Text's accuracy with extra tree and random forest classifiers was superior. Accuracy of 93% with 100 estimators [12] demonstrates the efficacy of Fast Text's 8% accuracy gain (baseline: Decision Tree 85%).

This article analyses the service of a hotel by looking at the positive and negative reviews to draw conclusions about the business. The primary goals of this effort are aspect identification and sentiment categorization. The topics utilized in aspect identification are constructed using latent Dirichlet allocation (LDA). The naïve Bayes classifier, the support vector machine, the decision tree, and logistic regression are just some of the machine learning classifiers that may be used to categorise reviews. These algorithms are evaluated using metrics including accuracy, recall, precision, as well as the F score [13].

Using the proposed method, the reviews were efficiently sorted into the five distinct hotel amenities. The highest performance in aspect classification (85%) is achieved by LDA + TF-ICF 100% + Semantic Similarity, the best performance in sentiment analysis based on aspects (93%) is achieved by Word Embedding + LSTM, and the comfort aspect gets the most unfavorable sentiments (60%) of any aspect. Moreover, the results show that a feeling is influenced by a certain component [14].

The suggested approach does this by breaking down lengthy comments into shorter ones, from which the required idea may be extracted. Additionally, it translates comments from languages other than English into the English language. Results from testing the system on two datasets have been deemed adequate [15].

## PROPOSED WORK

### System Model

There are various steps involved in performing a sentiment analysis on user evaluations taken from travel-related websites. Our suggested system architecture for analyzing guest opinions is shown in Fig. (**1**). Preparing and cleaning the data for categorization is the second stage after learning how the database was used by the tourist industry. The next phase is feature extraction from the cleaned and prepared data. The identification of the emotional stage comes fourth. Fifth, we used our method for identifying reviewers' emotions to use. The sixth step is to assess how well our system is working. After data is imported from the database into this system, we begin the data cleansing procedure. Meanwhile, we take out the unnecessary Attributes from the dataset. Lemmatization and stemming are implied by the removal of all white space, grammar, links, as well as email addresses. Algorithms like GRU and LSTM are used to "train" the data. Then, we put our system to the test by analyzing the results. Finally, the level of client happiness was evaluated.

### Brief Outline

The system's first input will consist of hotel reviews with associated labels. Each review has its own unique ID, review content, posting device, and review polarity recorded in the dataset. Subsets of the input data are used for training and evaluation purposes. Training data is what we will utilize to construct our classifier, while testing data will be subjected to the test to ensure its efficacy. In the preprocessing phase, we get rid of everything in the text that may confuse our classifier. The text preparation pipeline is shown in Fig. (**1**). Word embedding is used for feature extraction because it converts textual words into numerical vectors that a classifier can more readily understand. The feature extraction process will make use of word2vec, a word embedding technique. Word2vec is a tool that takes in a string of input words and generates a numerical vector that represents the word's underlying semantic and grammatical properties. We have employed the K-means clustering technique to separate subjective and objective data for use in sentiment detection. While objective evaluations include nothing but facts, subjective reviews include the author's own opinion or bias. The goal at this stage is to exclude all objective data and keep solely user opinions. Since the K-means clustering technique relies on soft clustering for categorization, it is possible for a data point to be partially a part of more than one cluster. If the point has a greater membership degree, it is more central to that cluster. To guarantee that only objective reviews are sent on to the classifier, sentiment identification is a prerequisite to sentiment classification. A model based on deep learning is used to categorise guest comments based on their tone. Our model for deep learning consists of three distinct layers. In the first hidden layer, known as the embedding layer, we applied our pre-trained word2vec model. The second invisible layer is composed of gated recurrent units (GRUs). It is a more efficient kind of LSTM that captures long-term relationships between words while being quicker and requiring fewer parameters. The dense neural network used for the output layer only contains a single node and employs the function of the sigmoid finally, the system will output the polarity of each review's emotion. Our model's performance is assessed using F-score and accuracy.

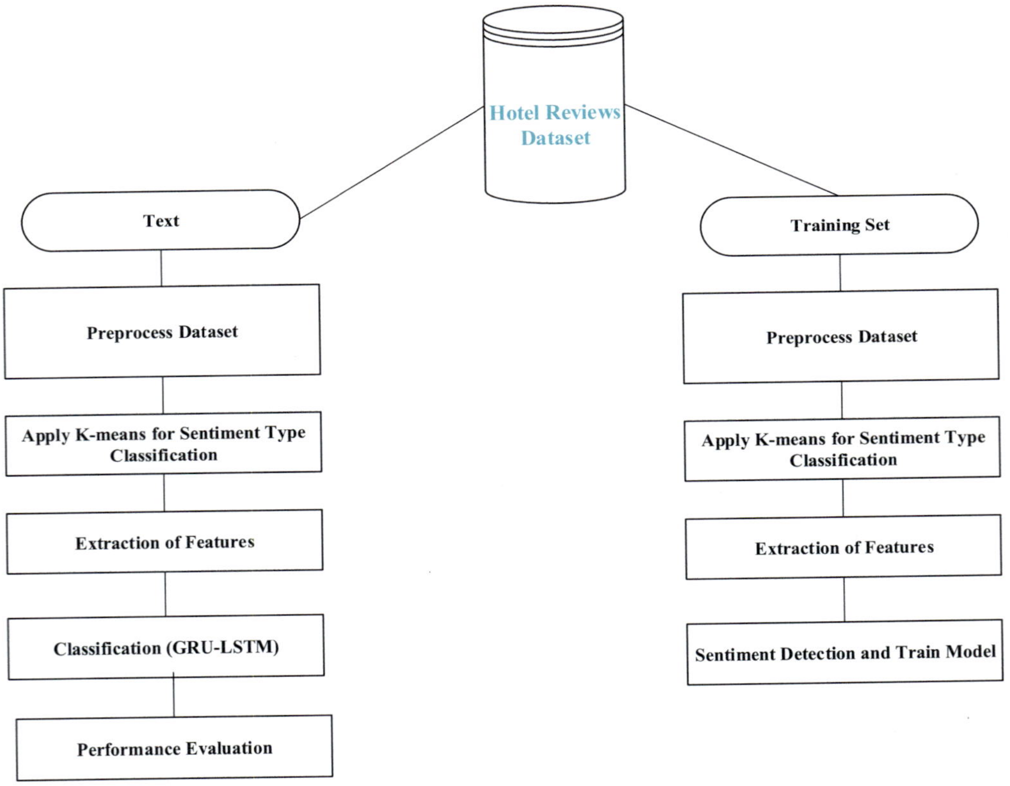


**Fig. (1).** System model.

## Text Preprocessing

### *Stage 1 - Data Assortment*

You should start by collecting feedback from actual hotel customers. Using comments left on your site is a great starting point. If this is not possible, you might attempt forming partnerships with other sites that already possess this information. Data scraping, a popular data collection tool, should be avoided since it might lead to legal complications. Personal information cannot be processed in this manner under GDPR and CCPA regulations. You might potentially inadvertently infringe on the rights of website owners.

### *Stage 2 - Sentimentality Gloss*

You need to manually apply sentiment labels (positive, neutral, or negative) to words and phrases in a review so that robots can understand the thoughts expressed there. When a number of human judges labeled a dataset with sentiment labels, it is regarded credible. Three annotators are the minimum you should use.

### *Stage 3 - Text Cleansing*

There is a lot of noise and useless information in raw hotel reviews that might negatively impact model performance. This necessitates a thorough cleaning, which must include:

- **Get rid of noise** - include things like hyperlinks, tags, numbers, punctuation, and whitespace;
- **Removing stop words** including, but not limited to, articles, pronouns, conjunctions, prepositions, and so on. Natural Language Toolkit (or NLTK for short) is one of the most widely used NLP libraries. It includes a list of 179 English stop words;
- **Lowercasing** in order to minimize confusion caused by capitalization, lowercase, and case sensitivity;
- **Normalization** - is the process of giving words their proper, standard form. As an example, the normalized version of the word "tomorrow" is "2mrw";
- **Stemming** or eliminating unnecessary or redundant ends (prefixes and suffixes) from words. Incorrect grammar is a common side effect of the method; for instance, having is stemmed to hath; and
- **Lemmatization -** which is to put a word back into its dictionary form. You may say that swim is the lemma for swim, swum, and swam.

## LSTM-GRU for Text Classification

The Long Short-Term Memory (LSTM) cells [7] and the Gated Recurrent Units (GRUs) [4] are two examples of RNN design that we take into account. We provide a short overview of the units used here, noting that other formulations exist in the literature.

The forget gate is the first of three gates in a typical LSTM cell $f_t$, which decides how much information from the past to discard; the gate's input $i_t$ which assesses the data before it is stored in the cell's memory; as well as the output gate $o_t$ which determines how to get a result from the available input:

$$\begin{aligned} i_t &= \sigma(W_i X_t + R_i h_{t-1} + b_i) \\ f_t &= \sigma\left(W_f X_t + R_f h_{t-1} + b_f\right) \\ o_t &= \sigma(W_o X_t + R_o h_{t-1} + b_o). \end{aligned} \quad \textbf{(1)}$$

The trainable parameter matrices and vectors are denoted here by the W, R, & b variables. One may characterise an LSTM by its:

$$\begin{aligned} \dot{C}_t &= \tanh(W_c X_t + R_c h_{t-1} + b_c) \\ C_t &= f_t \odot C_{t-1} + i_t \odot \dot{C}_t \\ h_t &= o_t \odot \tanh(C_t) \\ y_t &= \sigma\left(W_y h_t + b_y\right). \end{aligned} \quad \textbf{(2)}$$

In phrases, the stage of candidate cell $C_t$ is utilized to calculate an input data $X_t$ as well as the earlier concealed stage $h_{t-1}$. The current cell or cell memory stage $C_t$ is utilized to calculate the stage of forgetting $f_t$, the earlier cell stage $C_{t-1}$, the intake gate $i_t$ and the contender cell stage $C_t$. The Hadamard creation $\odot$ is equivalent to taking the product of the relevant matrices element-by-element. The outcome $y_t$ is determined by adding together all the relevant weights ($W_y$ *and* $b_y$) to the concealed stage $h_t$.

Comparable to LSTMs, GRUs have just two gates and fewer parameters; New information ($u_t$) and rearrange ($r_t$) gates. The gate $u_t$ controls how quickly the secret stage updates and the gate $r_t$ sets the threshold for the extent of the past to forget by clearing off old data from memory storage. The following equations define the GRU. Here $h_t$ means the "hidden stage" of a potential candidate.

$$
\begin{aligned}
u_t &= \sigma(W_u x_t + R_u h_{t-1} + b_u) \\
r_t &= \sigma(W_r x_t + R_r h_{t-1} + b_r) \\
h_t &= \tanh(W_h x_t + (r_t \odot h_{t-1}) R_h + b_h) \\
h_t &= (1 - u_t) \odot h_{t-1} + u_t \odot \dot{h}_t \\
y_t &= \sigma(W_y h_t + b_y)
\end{aligned} \tag{3}
$$

## RESULTS AND DISCUSSION

### Dataset Description

This dataset includes customer-submitted ratings and comments about hotels from among the most popular booking platforms.

| Variable | Description |
|---|---|
| Operator ID | customer's own personal identifier. |
| Portrayal | a breakdown of the uploaded review. |
| Browser Used | reviewer's preferred web browser. |
| Stratagem Used | method of uploading the review's device. |
| Is Comeback | Variable target. |

In this study, we use the findings from four supervised algorithms (Naive Bayes, Random Forest, Decision Tree, & Support Vector Machine). Our classification using the Jupiter Notebook and the Python programming language yields an accuracy of 86%, and these models are quite competent for this dataset. There was a 63% success rate in gathering data. Finally, the testing tools ensure 37% precision. Additionally, the LSTM as well as GRU unsupervised algorithms were utilized, since there was no judgment class, and the Deep Learning approach was used for assessing the new data set. Table **1** is depicted in Sample reviews.

**Table 1. Sample reviews.**

| Operator ID | Portrayal | Browser Used | Stratagem Used | Is Comeback |
|---|---|---|---|---|
| id10326 | The room wasn't quite filthy, but there was a very overpowering scent of dogs. Average at best; OK for a one-night stay if you don't have high standards. If the cost was appropriate, I may stay here again. There was no cost for breakfast, and it was somewhat better than nothing. | Verge | Portable | sad |

*(Table 1) cont.....*

| Operator ID | Portrayal | Browser Used | Stratagem Used | Is Comeback |
|---|---|---|---|---|
| id10327 | I stayed at the Crown Plaza April -- - April --, ----. The staff was friendly and attentive. The elevators are tiny (about -' by -'). The food in the restaurant was delicious but priced a little on the high side. Of course, this is Washington DC. There is no pool and little for children to do. My room on the fifth floor had two comfortable beds and plenty of space for one person. The TV is a little small by today's standards with a limited number of channels. There was a small bit of mold in the bathtub area that could have been removed with a little bleach. It appeared the carpets were not vacuumed every day. I reported a light bulb was burned out. It was never replaced. Ice machines are on the odd-numbered floors, but the one on my floor did not work. I encountered some staff in the elevator one evening and I mentioned the ice machine to them. Several hours later a maid appeared at my door with ice and two mints. I'm not sure how they knew what room I was in. That was a little unnerving! I would stay here again for business, but would not come here on vacation. | Internet Explorer | Portable | sad |
| id10328 | I got the best deal on this hotel by booking it *via* Hotwire. The manager at check-in gave us a I claimed that I wouldn't have booked the accommodation if I had known it allowed smoking due to the presence of my infant son. The manager cut me off and said that Hotwire always takes the lowest accommodations they can find. That's why I was so dissatisfied right from the bat. I was finally able to negotiate a smoke-free room for myself. After that, there were just the barest essentials in the room. This pricey hotel has nothing to offer beyond its convenient position near Dupont Circle. It was a modest room, but it was serviceable. There was a tub in the little bathroom. There was also a lack of basic toiletries in the rooms. We had to rent a refrigerator from the staff again (to store baby stuff) since there was no kitchenette with a microwave or refrigerator. Driving here will cost you $-- per day in parking fees. Also, breakfast is not included in the package. The lobby is tiny and has an outdated vibe. The only thing you can get is good coffee in the lobby. Overall, the hotel has amazing location but terrible service, few facilities, tiny rooms, and no view. Some distances from the nearest metro station (either McPherson or Dupont). If something better comes along, try to find it. | Mozilla | Dosage | sad |

*(Table 1) cont.....*

| Operator ID | Portrayal | Browser Used | Stratagem Used | Is Comeback |
|---|---|---|---|---|
| id10329 | Stayed here with husband and sons on the way to an Alaska Cruise. We all loved the hotel, great experience. Ask for a room on the North tower, facing northwest for the best views. We had a high floor, with a stunning view of the needle, the city, and even the cruise ships! We ordered room service for dinner so we could enjoy the perfect views. Room service dinners were delicious, too! You are in a perfect spot to walk everywhere, so enjoy the city. Almost forgot- Heavenly beds were heavenly, too! | Internet Explorer | Desktop | happy |
| id10330 | We came here to honour our --th birthdays with our best pals. We had been looking forward to this weekend trip since we first discussed it in February. Due to our group size, we were required to book two adjacent rooms at the cost of $---- per night. Over $---- was spent, including taxes and parking fees, for our stay of. Since we remained at the Ritz, we had all anticipated a certain degree of service, but we were all disappointed to find that the hotel did not live up to our expectations. The accommodations were adequate. They were tidy and had nice bathrooms, but otherwise failed to impress. Unfortunately, the service was terrible. I made several calls to the bellman the first night that we were there before somebody in hotel communications answered. Then, before going out to eat at -:-- on Saturday, we called and asked to have our garbage taken out and some more hotel supplies sent up to our room. We came back at --:--, and none of our requests had been met. I called housekeeping again, and this time they took care of it. For the price we were paying, I would have expected to turn down service every night. When we checked out, I spoke with a manager who promised to make it worthwhile for us to come back, but all we got was an apologetic letter. We have no intention of ever coming back to this hotel. In February of ---, my partner and me stayed at the Four Seasons Boston and had a fantastic time. As with every other Four Seasons I've been in, the service was outstanding. I would suggest the Four Seasons if you're ready to spend like you're at the Ritz Carlton! | Verge | Dosage | sad |

## CONCLUSION

With the suggested technique, the hotel review data has been trained on long short-term memory (LSTM) & Gated recurrent units (GRUs), with an 86% and 84% accuracy rate in recognizing customer opinion, respectively. Naive Bayes,

Decision Tree, Random Forest, and Support Vector Machine are also used to evaluate the dataset. We obtained 75% accuracy with Naive Bayes, 71% with Decision Tree, 82% with Random Forest, and 71% with Support Vector Machines. Better business results, customer feedback, and review sentiment prediction may all be achieved with the use of deep learning. We have a fully functional algorithm that improves accuracy.

Today, everyone is aware of how far humanity has progressed. By keeping the status quo, our nation is making progress. Technology advancements have made human labour simpler and more engaging. Thus, modern technology has made it possible to quickly and simply do any task. Online advertising has become the most visited website in the world. Furthermore, the general public will support this. People may quickly and simply reserve a room at any hotel in the world using the internet-based reservation system. More features are expected to be added in the future based on certain algorithms. Because of this, our website will be safer, more widely accepted, and more popular than before.

## REFERENCES

[1] S. Khomsah, "Naive Bayes Classifier Optimization on Sentiment Analysis of Hotel Reviews", *Jurnal Penelitian Pos dan Informatika,* 2020.

[2] D. Navanith, K. Likhith, M.S. Vardhan, and S. Kavitha, "Optimized Sentiment Analysis of Hotel Reviews using Machine Learning Algorithms", *6th International Conference on Electronics, Communication and Aerospace Technology,* pp. 1075-1081, 2022. [http://dx.doi.org/10.1109/ICECA55336.2022.10009104]

[3] J. Wan, L. Yao, and Q. Tang, "Research on sentiment analysis of hotel reviews based on Word2vec method", *Other Conferences,* 2022.

[4] S. Kurniawan, R. Kusumaningrum, and M.E. Timu, "Hierarchical Sentence Sentiment Analysis Of Hotel Reviews Using The Naïve Bayes Classifier", *2nd International Conference on Informatics and Computational Sciences (ICICoS),* pp. 1-5, 2018. [http://dx.doi.org/10.1109/ICICOS.2018.8621748]

[5] A.A. Septiandri, and A.P. Sutiono, "Aspect and Opinion Term Extraction for Aspect Based Sentiment Analysis of Hotel Reviews Using Transfer Learning", *ArXiv, abs/1909.11879,* 2019.

[6] S.P. Yadav, and S. Yadav, "Fusion of medical images in wavelet domain: A discrete mathematical model", *Ingeniería Solidaria,* vol. 14, no. 25, pp. 1-11, 2018. [http://dx.doi.org/10.16925/.v14i0.2236]

[7] H. Lakmisagar, and M. Sumathi, "Design and implementation of aspect Based Sentiment Analysis of Hotel Reviews", *International Conference on Recent Trends on Electronics, Information, Communication & Technology (RTEICT),* pp. 303-309, 2021. [http://dx.doi.org/10.1109/RTEICT52294.2021.9573897]

[8] F. Sun, N. Chu, and X. Du, "Sentiment Analysis of Hotel Reviews Based on Deep Leaning", *International Conference on Robots & Intelligent System (ICRIS),* pp. 627-630, 2020. [http://dx.doi.org/10.1109/ICRIS52159.2020.00158]

[9] H. Bai, and G. Wang, "Text Sentiment Analysis of Hotel Online Reviews", *Proceedings of the 5th International Conference on Computer Science and Software Engineering,* 2022. [http://dx.doi.org/10.1145/3569966.3571274]

[10] K. Shifullah, H.M. Rakibullah, N. Islam, H. Raihan, M.A. Iqbal, D. Ziaul Karim, and A. Rasel, "Classification of Hotel Reviews Using Sentiment Analysis and Machine Learning", *25th International Conference on Computer and Information Technology (ICCIT),* pp. 710-715, 2022. [http://dx.doi.org/10.1109/ICCIT57492.2022.10054884]

[11] S. P. Yadav, and S. Yadav, "Mathematical implementation of fusion of medical images in continuous wavelet domain", *Journal of Advanced Research in dynamical and control system,* vol. 10, no. 10, pp. 45-54, 2019.

[12] S. Khomsah, R.D. Ramadhani, and S. Wijaya, "The Accuracy Comparison Between Word2Vec and FastText On Sentiment Analysis of Hotel Reviews", *Jurnal RESTI (Rekayasa Sistem dan Teknologi Informasi),* 2022.

[13] N. Vaish, N. Goel, and G. Gupta, "Machine Learning Techniques for Sentiment Analysis of Hotel Reviews", *International Conference on Computer Communication and Informatics (ICCCI),* 2022. [http://dx.doi.org/10.1109/ICCCI54379.2022.9740876]

[14] R.A. Priyantina, and R. Sarno, "Sentiment Analysis of Hotel Reviews Using Latent Dirichlet Allocation, Semantic Similarity and LSTM", *International Journal of Intelligent Engineering and Systems,* 2019.

[15] M. Gharzouli, A.K. Hamama, and Z. Khattabi, "Topic-based sentiment analysis of hotel reviews", *Curr. Issues Tour.,* vol. 25, no. 9, pp. 1368-1375, 2022. [http://dx.doi.org/10.1080/13683500.2021.1940107]

# CHAPTER 36

# Utilizing Machine Learning for Natural Language Processing to Conduct Sentiment Analysis on Twitter Data in Multiple Languages

**Rahul Mishra**[1,*]

[1] *Centre for Interdisciplinary Research in Business and Technology, Chitkara University Institute of Engineering and Technology, Chitkara University, Punjab, India*

**Abstract:** Retailers, market analysts, and other users of the web are greatly influenced by user views. Arranging the unstructured data gathered from various social media networks correctly is necessary for doing relevant analysis. Emotional evaluation as a method for cross-lingual data classification has received considerable attention. Textual organization is a subfield of natural language processing, or NLP, that may be used to classify an individual's emotional or mental condition as positive, negative, beneficial, or detrimental, like a thumbs up or thumbs down, *etc.* A combination of sentiment analysis as well as deep learning techniques might be the key to solving this kind of problem. Deep learning models, which are capable of machine learning, are particularly useful for this. One of the most widely used deep learning architectures for analyzing sentiment in text is called Long Short Term Memory. These frameworks have potential applications in NLP. In this study, we provide algorithms to solve the problem of multilingual sentiment analysis, and we evaluate their precision factors to determine which one is the most effective.

**Keywords:** LSTM, Multiple languages, Machine learning, Natural language processing, Sentiment analysis, Twitter data.

## INTRODUCTION

One way to get to the underlying feelings in a piece of writing is *via* sentiment analysis. It uses machine learning and NLP (natural language processing) to identify, extract, and assess how consumers perceive a service or product. This is why "opinion mining" or "emotional AI" are common terms for this kind of analysis.

* **Corresponding author Rahul Mishra:** Centre for Interdisciplinary Research in Business and Technology, Chitkara University Institute of Engineering and Technology, Chitkara University, Punjab, India; E-mail: rahul.mishra.orp@chitkara.edu.in

**Pankaj Kumar Mishra and Satya Prakash Yadav (Eds.)**

Finding out if a piece of text is favorable, negative, or indifferent is the main objective of mining opinions. An example of this would be a statement like:

- *"We stayed at this hotel for five days"* is neutral,
- *"I liked staying here"* is positive, and
- *"I disliked the hotel" is* negative.

The opinions of WEB users carry a lot of weight with other users, product dealers, and market researchers. In order to conduct useful studies, it is required to properly organise the vast amounts of unstructured data collected from different social media sites [1]. When picking an annotated data set, there are two main considerations:

- **The length of texts.** A dataset that uses mood tagging on long reads (articles, blog posts, *etc.*) would not be applicable to shorter texts (tweets, feedback, *etc.*), and the inverse is also true.
- **The topic or domain.** Even with a sufficiently large library of tagged political messages, training a machine to assess hotel reviews would provide subpar results. The tourism area is best served by using labeled samples of evaluations, such as those of restaurants or airlines, to achieve a reasonable degree of reliability. But if you are looking for hotel reviews, your best bet is ..a database that was created from guest evaluations of hotels.

There has been a lot of focus on emotion analysis as a way to categorise data across languages. In Automatic Language Processing (NLP), this is known as the textual organisation and may be used to categorise a user's emotional state or reaction as either positive (thumbs up), negative (thumbs down) or neutral (no reaction) [2, 3]. When it comes to text analysis, sentiment analysis (SA) remains a popular topic of study. Word processing before SA is used to measure its correctness [4]. This study presents a text analysis framework for SA [5] using natural language processing techniques applied to data from Twitter. Collecting data, cleaning the text, pre-processing, extracting text features, and classifying utilizing SA methods are the basic processes in the field of machine learning. The information is retrieved using a method that is unique to the domain, particularly for Twitter data [6]. At this point, the data has been cleaned for things like typos, punctuation, tags, and emoticons. Tokenization and stop word removal (SWR) are pre-processing steps [7]. In natural language processing, sentiment analysis is a crucial job [8]. The field that receives the greatest attention from academics nowadays is Twitter sentiment analysis (SA). Twitter sentiment analysis in languages other than English has received very little attention from academics. There seems to have been a recent spike in the volume of data sets disseminated *via* social media platforms in a wide range of languages [9]. The governments of the world's nations might benefit much from mining social media data, and machine learning methods like NLP (Natural language processing) play a crucial part in this [10]. Social media may be mined for valuable 'mindset' information on the population, which is essential for every government in the globe.

It seems like every single second, someone new joins Twitter and starts tweeting about some social occasion. Gaining insight into the user's current sentiment on a range of societal issues, from the contentment of an airliner to the image brand, might be greatly facilitated if our suggested model could anticipate sentiment tags for live tweeting. Neural networks with sophisticated structures, such as LSTM, and a simple logistic regression model could be used. Considering the characteristics of tweets, we begin by preprocessing them, and creating a binary dependence tree to feed into LSTM. We used regularization techniques and fine-tuned our hyper-parameters. Documents may be easily categorized as well as predicted to convey positive or negative emotions with the use of machine learning techniques. There are two main categories of machine learning algorithms: supervised and unsupervised. An algorithm that is supervised makes use of a tagged database to train on documents that have been appropriately annotated. In contrast, independent learning makes use of a dataset that has not been tagged with the appropriate emotions. Artificial learning methods applied to tagged datasets are the primary focus of the suggested research. The majority of studies only look at tweets written in one language. In contrast, Twitter is a global social network that facilitates online microblogging. You may find linguistic tweets on a wide range of social topics, and by examining them all, you can deduce the blogger's mood.

## RELATED WORK

Two related solutions to this sort of difficulty are techniques based on deep learning as well as sentiment analysis. In this case, deep learning models—which can learn new things—are invaluable. Sentiment analysis in words is a popular task for deep learning architecture like naive Bayes as well as recurrent neural networks (LSTMs). One possible use of such structures is in the processing of natural languages. We provide a suite of methods for multilingual sentiment evaluation and employ accuracy factor comparisons to distill the findings and choose the best method [11].

The suggested article delves into the mechanisms used for pre-processing text and how they impact the dataset. Classification algorithms' accuracy has been improved by using text pre-processing and dimensionality reduction. Market research, consumer behaviour, survey analysis, and brand tracking are just some of the many possible applications for the suggested corpus. Text pre-processing may provide a foundation upon which to build problem-specific applications of predictive analysis, machine learning, and deep learning algorithms [12].

This study uses language models in Hindi and Kannada to categorise tweets as good or bad based on their semantic content. Machine learning methods like Naive Bayes, K-Neighbors, Decision Tree, as well as Random Forest are often used to tackle the categorization difficulty [13].

The purpose of this research is to use machine learning methods for sentiment analysis in order to mine public opinion on the continuing conflict between Russia and Ukraine. The goal is to examine public opinion in each country to deduce whether or not policymakers have responded to the potential economic fallout. The first step in the implementation pipeline is gathering information from social media platforms like Twitter and Reddit with the help of Snscraper and the PRAW (Python Reddit API Wrapper). Reddit's longer postings are processed using appropriate text summarising methods. Data collected from social media platforms is subjected to a sentiment analysis utilising the BERT transformer model. Neural machine translation is used to convert postings written in other languages into English. Additionally, sentiment analysis is conducted at several levels of granularity, including the place and the persons who have been tagged using Named Entity Recognition methods. Finally, we conduct a comparative study of international opinion and nations' dependence on Russian oil [14].

The goal of sentiment assessment as well as the mining of opinions is to extract meaning from people's statements by analyzing their feelings, thoughts, and evaluations. When it comes to data on the internet and text mining, natural language processing is one of the most rapidly expanding subdivisions. Among sentiment analysis's many uses is tracking how people feel about certain issues and how they react on social media. Blogs, forums, microblogs, as well as social media sites like Facebook and Twitter have increased the relevance of sentiment analysis. Lexical analysis as well as controlled machine learning may be used to quantify digitally gathered emotions [15].

## PROPOSED WORK

### Research Gaps

Critical issues in opinion mining include data size, lack of organization in the data, and the need to process data in many languages. Researchers generally work in all conceivable problem statements, but our investigation shows that only a small fraction of them address the multilingual issue. Since NLP primarily works with the English language, it seldom sees the light of day. Since most studies center on NLP (Natural Language Processing), any programmer who wishes to work in another language must first install the appropriate library for that language. However, this fix works for just a couple of languages at the most. This is not a workable method when dealing with 6,000 different languages. Managing massive amounts of data presents several difficulties for businesses. To name a few:

Problems with combining data sets.

The primary objective is to collect, organize, and store all of this Twitter data such that, after filtering, meaningful insights may be drawn.

Because it comes from real people who are really using the product, the statistics may be highly skewed.

Blog entries, tweets, reviews, puppet words, and comments (even with misspellings!) are all examples of the kind of data that may be collected. Emoticons, phrases, repeating letters, *etc.*, may also exist in a variety of languages. Filtering data is a multi-stage operation.

In each stage, we collect and analyse data in order to derive insight. For the goal of sifting relevant data for use in analysis, we will be recommending a strategy for training the system. The suggested technique would employ many classes of algorithms to obtain the normal phase of huge data, which can then be filtered in three distinct dimensions (positive, negative, and neutral). Therefore, in this research, we propose a new method for multilingual opinion mining by utilizing Google's most recent API for translating text.

**System Model**

Fig. (**1**) illustrates the system model.

- **Step 1.** Data Collection Twitter has surpassed all other social networks in popularity, with billions of users. Tweets can be either original or retweeted, or they can be replied to. We have started using Twitter since every post is limited to 140 characters.
- **Step 2.** Google Translator: To translate text from one language to another, Google developed a machine translation service called Google Translator. In this section, data is translated into English using the Google Translate API. The default setting for this module's automatic language converter is English.
- **Step 3.** Pre-processing of tweets: The feedback from users is received unfiltered. Then, we apply a preprocessing technique to the data to remove any unwanted background noise. The suggested module (opinion delimitation) also includes the substantial step of sentence splitting. Since two-fold propagation takes

neighboring sentences into account while spreading emotion. To further enhance the effectiveness of the extraction process, we have implemented an online stemmer engine. There are a number of feature extraction techniques one may use to get useful features. To better extract useful features, our suggested technique splits up the feature extraction procedure into two stages. And now, at long last, tweets may be sorted.

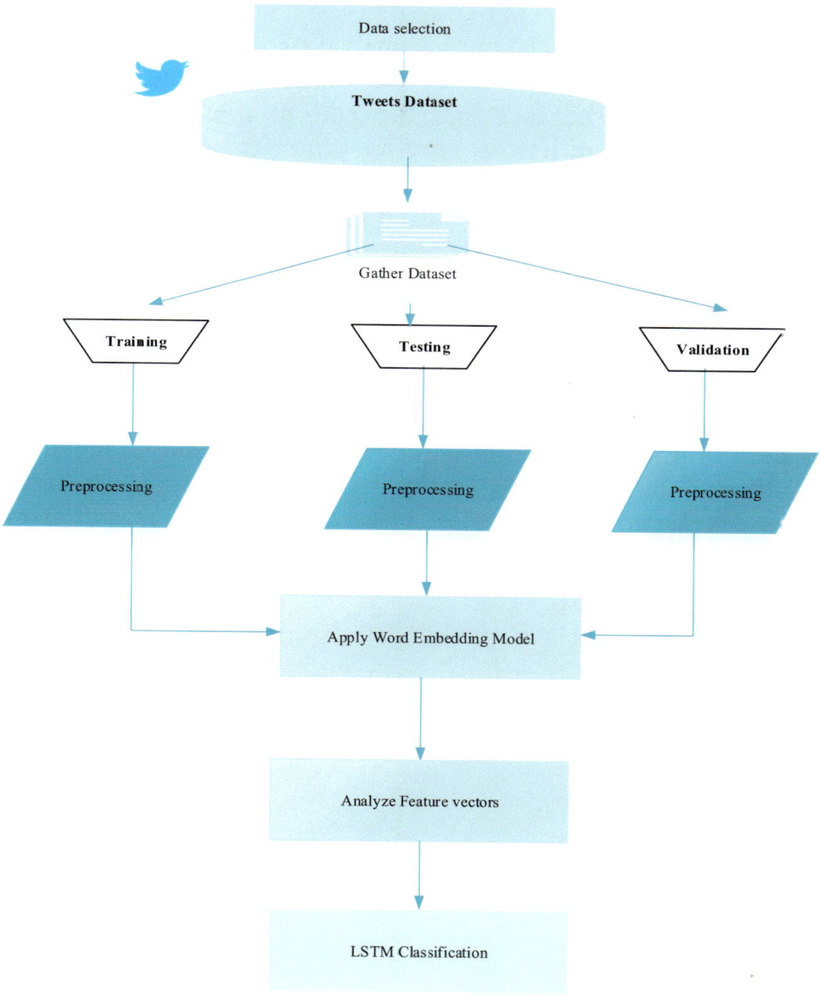


**Fig. (1).** System model diagram.

## LSTM for Tweets Classification

Research of public sentiment as expressed on social media platforms like Twitter and Facebook might yield useful insights. However, Twitter's data characteristics pose challenges to the efficiency and accuracy of automated algorithms for sentiment analysis. Noise, huge dimensions, and intricate syntactic and semantic patterns are commonplace in Twitter data. Because the data is multilingual and code-mixed, conducting sentiment analysis on Twitter in Indian languages is more difficult. In this study, we employ Long short-term memory (LSTM) units (or blocks), which are fundamental building blocks for RNN layers.

Long short-term memory (LSTM) networks are a subset of RNNs. An ordinary long short-term memory (LSTM) unit consists of four main parts: the cell, the forget gate, the result gate, as well as the input gate. The term "memory" in LSTM is derived from the fact that the cell in question is responsible for "remembering" information across varying time periods. The three gates of a multi-layer (or feedforward) network of neurons do the same thing as a "conventional" artificial neuron: they use a function of activation to calculate the activation of a weighted sum. A "gate" is a node in an LSTM that allows the user to regulate the data flow between other nodes. The aforementioned gates are somehow connected to the cellular apparatus. The "long short-term memory" (LSTM) theory of short-term memory is so effective at retaining data for lengthy periods of time that it is often referred to by this name. An LSTM is great at processing, forecasting, and categorizing time series with unknown magnitude as well as duration of time delays among important events. One of the problems with training traditional RNNs is the exploding and vanishing gradient problem; LSTMs were developed to solve this. The LSTM Model is shown in Fig. (**2**).

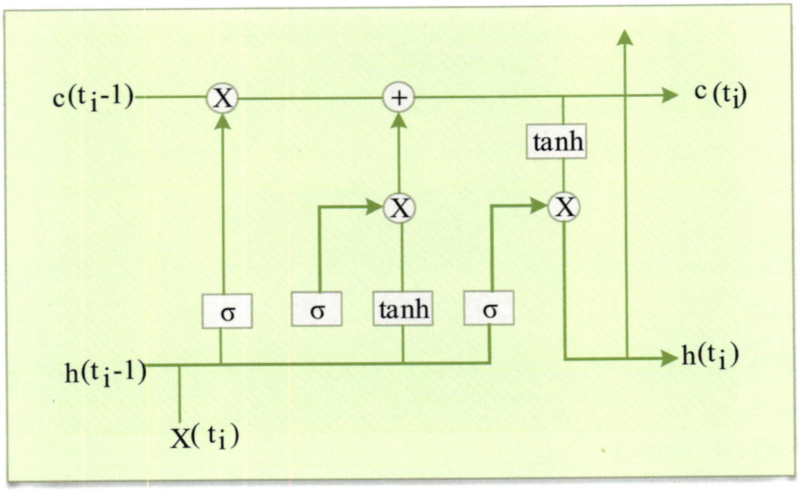


**Fig. (2).** LSTM model.

## Components of LSTMs

Accordingly, the following parts make up the LSTM cell:

- Forget Gate "f" (connected to a sigmoid).
- layer of Candidate "C"(a NN with Tanh).
- Gate of Input "I" (a NN with sigmoid).
- Gate of Output "O"(a NN with sigmoid).
- Level of Hidden "H" (a vector).
- State of Memory "C" (a vector).
- The LSTM cell accepts three inputs at any one time: Xt, the current input, the previous concealed state, as well as the prior memory state.

The LSTM cell displays the current secret state (Ht) as well as the current memory state (Ct) as its outputs.

Functioning of Long Short-Term Memory (LSTM) gates.

To find out if the present memory status $C_t$ is correct, an LSTM cell will initially double each element of $C_{t-1}$ using the forget gate (f). Because remembering f gates may take on values among zero and one, erasing a previous storage state entirely occurs when the value is zero, and transmitting the whole state to the cell occurs when the value is one.

$$Ct = Ct - 1 * ft$$

Determining the updated memory status:

$$Ct = Ct + (It * C`t)$$

Now, we calculate the output:

$$Ht = tanh(Ct)$$

## RESULTS AND DISCUSSION

- To begin, we gather information (Tweets) from social media platforms like Twitter. In this case, we retrieved information from Twitter using the LinqToTwitter API, the Twitter API for C#. The information gathered is unprocessed raw data. A sequential model in Keras is constructed. Layers in this linear stack include:

- A 100-dimensional encoding layer converts each word in the sentence into a dense 100-word vector. With 100 words as the target output, the vocabulary size serves as an input aspect. For this reason, we will represent every word in the input with a 100-component vector.
- 64-element recurrent LSTM layer that can learn in both directions.
- Relu-activated, dense (completely interconnected) layer of 24 units.
- Label 1 signifies a good assessment, according to the result of a thick layer with 1 unit as well as sigmoid activation.

The following packages must be installed in order to run this model:

- numpy.
- pandas.
- matplotlib.
- sklearn.
- nltk.
- keras.

To install them, follow these steps using pip and the Python Package Index:

Numpy pip install

pandas pip install

matplotlib pip install

sklearn pip install

nltk pip install

Keras pip install

Table **1** illustrates the performance of the LSTM model in terms of accuracy, precision and recall.

**Table 1. LSTM Performance.**

| Reiteration | Accuracy | Precision | Recall |
|---|---|---|---|
| 1 | 1.8169 | 1.5988 | 1.4184 |
| 2 | 1.8188 | 1.5941 | 1.4315 |
| 3 | 1.8186 | 1.5916 | 1.4266 |
| 4 | 1.8187 | 1.5963 | 1.4253 |
| 5 | 1.8178 | 1.5845 | 1.4311 |
| 6 | 1.8187 | 1.5854 | 1.4232 |

*(Table 1) cont.....*

| Reiteration | Accuracy | Precision | Recall |
|---|---|---|---|
| 7 | 1.8181 | 1.5952 | 1.4248 |
| 8 | 1.8183 | 1.6017 | 1.4302 |
| 9 | 1.8178 | 1.5926 | 1.4207 |
| 10 | 1.8183 | 1.6065 | 1.4212 |
| Average | 0.8182 | 0.5945 | 0.4252 |

The results of the suggested approach for obtaining prescriptions for different substances are compared in this section. Two prescriptions are compared for their efficacy. The same 2,000 good and 2,000 negative reviews were utilized in both prescriptions. The results from different sources on the same topic are compared in the table below. Table **1** portrays the LSTM Performance.

## CONCLUSION

In the study, we present and employ machine learning methods to categorize a Twitter dataset that contains tweets in many languages. Naive Bayes and Long Short-Term Memory (LSTM) algorithms were used for this task. The data shows that the LSTM classifier is significantly more accurate in predicting sentiments (to the tune of 96%) than the other classifiers. In this study, we present a fresh method for categorizing data gathered *via* multilingual analysis. In this work, we show that by sending reviewers to Twitter's reviewers, it is possible to conduct a thorough final assessment in any discipline. Such probes can assist in identifying unfavorable influences on commercially successful media like movies, TV shows, products, and even people. This research demonstrates that widespread vulnerability in several probes is affected by the usage of machine-learning courses. Naive Base, LSTM, SVM, Decision Tree, and Random One, along with other popular methods of account management computation, were analyzed. This kind of analysis revealed that twenty-two unauthorized trees representing twenty different models were carried out. Additional research is required since configurability necessitates the addition of non-square classes, which can either be used or ignored. Many forms of evaluation will now more accurately reflect reality now that there is one additional class.

## REFERENCES

[1] A. Bari, M. Heymann, R.J. Cohen, R. Zhao, L. Szabo, S. Apas Vasandani, A. Khubchandani, M. DiLorenzo, and M. Coffee, "Exploring Coronavirus Disease 2019 Vaccine Hesitancy on Twitter Using Sentiment Analysis and Natural Language Processing Algorithms", *Clin. Infect. Dis.*, vol. 74, suppl. Suppl. 3, pp. e4-e9, 2022.
[http://dx.doi.org/10.1093/cid/ciac141] [PMID: 35568473]

[2] D. Mehanović, Z. Mašetić, and A. Vatreš, *Covid-19 Twitter Data Analysis Using Natural Language Processing.* Lecture Notes in Networks and Systems, 2021.

[3] D. Ekmekci, and F. Shihab, "Sentiment Analysis of Tweets Using Natural Language Processing", *International Journal of Multidisciplinary Studies and Innovative Technologies,* 2022.

[4] G. Eom, S. Yun, and H. Byeon, "Predicting the sentiment of South Korean Twitter users toward vaccination after the emergence of COVID-19 Omicron variant using deep learning-based natural language processing", *Front. Med. (Lausanne),* vol. 9, p. 948917, 2022. [http://dx.doi.org/10.3389/fmed.2022.948917] [PMID: 36186808]

[5] E.O. Omuya, G. Okeyo, and M.W. Kimwele, "Sentiment analysis on social media tweets using dimensionality reduction and natural language processing", *Eng. Rep.,* p. 5, 2022.

[6] V.L. Narasamma, and M. Sreedevi, "Twitter based Data Analysis in Natural Language Processing using a Novel Catboost Recurrent Neural Framework", *Int. J. Adv. Comput. Sci. Appl.,* vol. 12, no. 5, 2021. [http://dx.doi.org/10.14569/IJACSA.2021.0120555]

[7] " Real Time Twitter Sentiment Analysis using Natural Language Processing", *International Journal of Engineering Research and, 9,* 2020.

[8] S. Singh, K. Kumar, and B. Kumar, "Sentiment Analysis of Twitter Data Using TF-IDF and Machine Learning Techniques", *International Conference on Machine Learning, Big Data, Cloud and Parallel Computing (COM-IT-CON),* 2022 pp. 252-255. [http://dx.doi.org/10.1109/COM-IT-CON54601.2022.9850477]

[9] S.P. Yadav, and S. Yadav, "Fusion of Medical Images in Wavelet Domain: A Discrete Mathematical Model", In: *In Ingeniería Solidaria* vol. 14. Universidad Cooperativa de Colombia- UCC, 2018, no. 25, pp. 1-11. [http://dx.doi.org/10.16925/.v14i0.2236]

[10] V. Vashisht, A.K. Pandey, and S.P. Yadav, "Speech Recognition using Machine Learning", In: *In IEIE Transactions on Smart Processing & Computing* vol. 10. The Institute of Electronics Engineers of Korea, 2021, no. 3, pp. 233-239. [http://dx.doi.org/10.5573/IEIESPC.2021.10.3.233]

[11] V. Goel, A.K. Gupta, and N. Kumar, "Sentiment Analysis of Multilingual Twitter Data using Natural Language Processing", *8th International Conference on Communication Systems and Network Technologies (CSNT),* pp. 208-212, 2018. [http://dx.doi.org/10.1109/CSNT.2018.8820254]

[12] N.P. Garg, and K. Sharma, "Text pre-processing of multilingual for sentiment analysis based on social network data", *International Journal of Electrical and Computer Engineering (IJECE),* 2022.

[13] Sumana, & P. Kanchan, "Hindi and Kannada Twitter Sentiment Analysis Using Machine Learning Algorithm", *2022 4th International Conference on Advances in Computing, Communication Control and Networking (ICAC3N),* pp. 370-377, 2022.

[14] P. Dominic, N. Purushothaman, A. Kumar, A. Prabagaran, J. Angelin Blessy, and A. John, "Multilingual Sentiment Analysis using Deep-Learning Architectures", *5th International Conference on Smart Systems and Inventive Technology (ICSSIT),* pp. 1077-1083, 2023. [http://dx.doi.org/10.1109/ICSSIT55814.2023.10060993]

[15] S. Mishra, S. Choubey, A. Choubey, N. Yogeesh, J. Durga Prasad Rao, and P. William, "Data Extraction Approach using Natural Language Processing for Sentiment Analysis", *2022 International Conference on Automation, Computing and Renewable Systems (ICACRS),* pp. 970-972, 2022. [http://dx.doi.org/10.1109/ICACRS55517.2022.10029216]

## CHAPTER 37

# The Use of Machine Learning to Analyze the Sentiment for Social Media Networks

**Darleen Grover**[1,*]

[1] *Centre for Interdisciplinary Research in Business and Technology, Chitkara University Institute of Engineering and Technology, Chitkara University, Punjab, India*

**Abstract:** The amount of textual information on the internet has increased significantly with the debut of social media platforms like Twitter, including news stories and historical records. This is due to the growth of Web 2.0. More individuals are using the internet and different forms of social media to share their thoughts and feelings with the world. As a result, more phrases with emotional nuance were created by the general public. It is natural that researchers will look into new approaches to understanding people's emotions and reactions. In addition to providing a novel hybrid system that combines text mining and neural networks for sentiment categorization, this study evaluates the efficacy of many machine learning and deep learning techniques. More than a million tweets from across five different topics were utilized to create this dataset. Seventy-five percent of the dataset was used for training, while the remaining twenty-five percent was used for testing. When compared to traditional supervised learning methods, the system's hybrid approach displays a maximum accuracy of 83.7%.

**Keywords:** Machine learning, Social media, Sentiment analysis.

## INTRODUCTION

The quantity of written content, such as news articles and historical documents, on the internet, has dramatically increased with the advent of social media platforms like Twitter. The number of people who express their feelings and opinions online continues to rise [1]. The general populace responded by coining a greater number of expressions loaded with sentiment. It is inevitable that scientists will try out new methods to decipher human cognition and behavior [2]. When it comes to sharing information, collaborating on projects, and having meaningful conversations, social media platforms are where it lies [3]. Sentiment analysis is a subfield of sociology that examines how people feel and what they

* **Corresponding author Darleen Grover:** Centre for Interdisciplinary Research in Business and Technology, Chitkara University Institute of Engineering and Technology, Chitkara University, Punjab, India; E-mail: darleen.grover.orp@chitkara.edu.in

**Pankaj Kumar Mishra and Satya Prakash Yadav (Eds.)**

think about certain brands, products, and services [4]. As the usage of Arabic on social media continues to grow, scholars have been increasingly interested in the topic of Arabic sentiment analysis [5]. Arabic is one of the most widely used languages for internet interaction [6]. Sentiment analysis is challenging in this language because of its complex morphology, broad range of dialects, and lack of available materials [7]. Because of the sheer volume of text available on social media platforms, researchers can now more accurately quantify the emotional value of this data in order to gain a deeper understanding of the mindsets, views, and emotions expressed [8]. In order to provide light on the several approaches that may be taken to social media sentiment analysis [9], this study uses Machine Learning techniques to analyze data from Twitter. It is argued that the Fuzzy Set and Rough Set techniques for classification are especially effective mathematical components of artificial intelligence that provide a new angle to the well-established topic of sentiment analysis. A mountain of work remains in text mining for natural language processing, and there is a shortage of review papers discussing the use of rough-fuzzy classifiers in sentiment analysis [10].

When it comes to readily accessible information, Twitter ranks high. Instantaneous global communication is made possible, which is especially useful in regions with limited opportunities for public expression. There were 135 million people who used the internet in 2014; more than 71 million of them actively used social networks [8]; it was estimated that these people sent out more than 17 million tweets per day. It is natural that researchers will look into alternative approaches to better understand how people think and react.

Therefore, the goal of this study is to categorize which tweets include good feelings and which contain negative sentiments by comparing different approaches applied to a million tweet records. Following is the outline of the paper: In Part II, we examine the relevant literature. In Section III, we present the suggested system. Section IV concludes the paper and discusses what comes next.

## RELATED WORK

An innovative hybrid system that utilizes text mining and neural networks to categorize sentiment is described, and many well-known deep learning and machine learning approaches are compared and contrasted. The tweets in this dataset are in the millions and cover five distinct themes. Seventy-five percent of the data set was utilized for training, while the remaining twenty-five percent was used for testing. By reaching a maximum accuracy of 83.7%, the system proved that its hybrid learning technique was better than more conventional supervised approaches [11].

The major objective of this study is to examine the behavior of participants in online debates under varying conditions. Negative influences, such as those from peers, the media, and the surrounding culture, have the power to sway individuals. These days, most people use social media as their primary means of rapid communication. Readers might be inspired or depressed by the words they read. When faced with a problem, it may be best to take proactive measures rather than merely react. People's reactions have been unpleasant, and they've been expressing their discontent in a broad range of ways, both online and off. This will lead the person to think and feel irrationally. Sentiment Analysis can observe and analyze people's actions by utilizing data mining and deep learning methods. In this piece, we explore the potential of computer algorithms for training robots to recognize human behavior. In addition, it will offer suggestions on how those who use social media might modify their perspectives in order to better weather the current crisis [12].

This research explores the potential of contemporary technology to better equip humankind to save lost souls through the use of natural language processing techniques, which may involve the installation of Machine Learning models. Because of this, there has been a rise in the number of young people using the Internet and the many social networking sites it hosts. People sometimes find it easier to express their feelings *via* writing than by talking to specialists about their problems. Social media analysis takes into account the poster's location, the subject matter, the tone of the post, and other characteristics to make inferences about the poster's mental state, predict the poster's future actions, and prevent a possible crime. Kazakhstan has the third-highest suicide rate in the world. As a strategy for decreasing suicide rates, researchers settled on sentiment analysis, a technique from the field of natural language processing used to ascertain whether a given utterance should be seen in a positive or negative light. Every database project necessitates data collection from widely used Kazakh social networks. The fundamental aim of this work is to integrate NLP and ML techniques to collect the necessary data for model development [13].

Using machine learning and other sophisticated learning models, our study seeks to automatically find the emotions and classify them as positive or negative. This study implements and assesses four different machine learning techniques: the long short-term memory (LSTM) models, the support vector machine (SVM), the logistic regression (LR), and the K-nearest neighbors (KNN) approach. The Arabic-Review (ARev) database is used to evaluate these classifiers; it is a large corpus of hand-annotated text from a wide range of Arabic sources. The results [14] indicate that SVM and LR algorithms are the most accurate classifiers, with a 92% and 93% success rate, respectively.

The goal of this study is to develop a mood-detecting classifier using ML and FRT. Case study data for the 2019 Sri Lankan presidential election uses Twitter corpus collected from September 1, 2019 (two months before the election), to November 15, 2019 (the day after the election). The fuzzy rough classifier is built using the Fuzzy Rough nearest neighboring method. When compared to other approaches, the accuracy of the fuzzy rough established-based classifier is significantly higher. The results of the 2019 presidential election agree with the classifier's predictions. Using social media data to predict political sentiment is already state-of-the-art, as this case study shows. This method has the potential to be used in other settings [15].

## PROPOSED WORK

### System Model

The purpose of this research is to determine the prevailing tone from a compiled Twitter dataset. Several methods were tried out on the tweets before settling on the most effective ones.

Beginning with the Tweet collecting phase (Input Dataset) and continuing through the pre-processing, feature extraction, and classification stages, as shown in Fig. (**1**) we finally arrived at the assessment phase (where the results from several classification approaches were compared).

#### *Collecting Initial Data*

A total of 1,048,588 tweets in English were pulled from the Twitter 140 API and stored in repositories on GitHub, Kaggle, and the University of California, Irvine. There was a limit of 140 characters per tweet, and some used professional language while others were more casual.

#### *Preprocessing Phase*

Clean up by doing things like:

- Removing irrelevant tweets.
- Capitalization.
- Punctuation.
- Stop words.
- Stemming.
- Bag-of-words.
- Removing digits.
- Tokenizing.

• Joining words.

At this stage, we are focused on extracting useful information from the tweets. The classifier can read each tweet thanks to the vector representation.

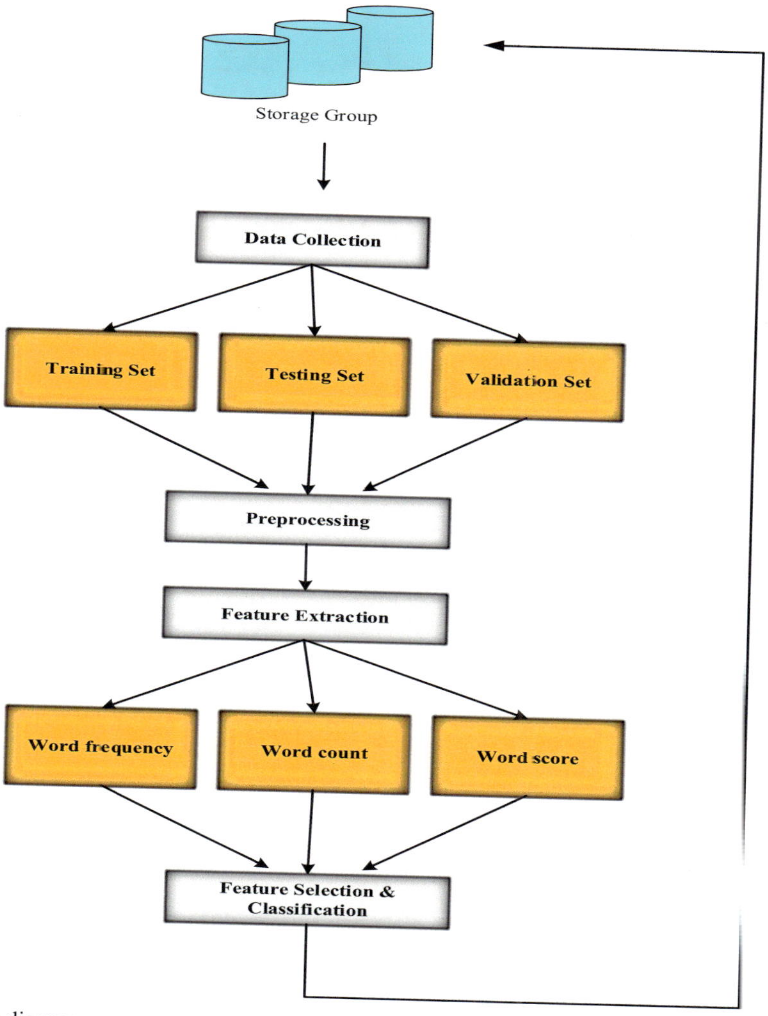


**Fig. (1).** System diagram.

## Word Embedding

• Term Frequency-Inverse Document Frequency (TF-IDF) analyzes a corpus of text and gives more weight to less common terms based on their relative rarity. Simply said, it is a way to quickly and easily extract keywords and a measurement of how significant a given term is. While TF-IDF is still widely used for sentiment analysis, it is an outdated method that ignores important factors like the surrounding text and the order in which the words appear.

- Word2Vec, short for "word to vector," is a shallow neural network with only two layers. Word2Vec, developed by Google in 2013, clusters words that are used in similar contexts together. It was designed to operate on a vast corpus of textual data.
- About 100 million Google News articles were used to pre-train the algorithm. Over time, it becomes better at predicting the word from its context thanks to the data (*i.e.*, the – vectors) it receives.
- Global Word Count (GloVe): a tool for tally
- GloVe (Global Vectors) generates vector representations of textual material in a manner analogous to that of Word2Vec. Word2Vec emphasizes close-by words, while GloVe looks at the full-text corpus to determine how often two words appear together. In layman's terms, it first constructs a massive context matrix that displays the frequency with which a given word appears in a given context. Then, it generates word-to-word vectors, which show how often words appear together.

**Tweets Classification**

In this stage, we begin by building a word vector that the classifier(s) may use. Decision trees, Naive Bayes, random forests, neural networks with 10 hidden multilayer perceptrons, recurrent neural networks with long short-term memory (LSTM) connections, and convolutional neural network methods were then used to categorize the English tweets.

Binary classification, multi-class classification, multi-topic classification, and metrics for Hierarchical classification are the four primary classification performance measures used by machine learning algorithms. We use a confusion matrix to help us reach the zero point on the most promising results during the performance measurement learning process.

- Predictive analysis often uses linear regression. When the connection between the response variable and the covariances can be shown to be linear, then linear regression is appropriate. This method is beneficial because it shifts the emphasis from statistical modeling to preprocessing and data analysis. Learning to interact with data is made easier using linear regression since we do not have to worry about the model's finer intricacies. In conclusion, it is a good tool for teaching data analysis skills. However, as it oversimplifies real-world issues, it will not be recommended for a wide range of practical applications.
- A decision tree (DT) is a graphical representation that uses branching methods to depict all conceivable outcomes of a choice with respect to certain

circumstances. Classification and Regression Tree (CART), random forests, and boosted trees are just a few of the many popular regression tree techniques available. In the realm of machine learning, decision trees (DT) encompass both categorization and regressing. At the end of each branch comes a decision based on some input and certain constraints. Decision Trees are used to visually express any branching logic. The route from the root node to the leaves of a Decision Tree can be used to determine a categorization. An internal node represents a test performed on the properties provided in the Decision Tree. The result of these examinations is taken from the Decision Tree's leaf nodes, which indicate the branch's conclusions. Decision trees can let you explore your data with minimal need for cleanup. However, over-fitting is a difficult issue in DT to solve. Pruning and arranged restrictions on model parameters will resolve this problem. The continuous variables are not used to fit the decision trees.

- When it comes to classification and regression, the Random Forest (RF) is one of the most reliable machine learning algorithms available. Bagging is a technique used by the RF, which is described by the DT collective. Multiple rounds of training using a subset of the full dataset are used by the RF to produce an exceptional prediction model. Similarly to the ensemble learning approach, it uses the resulting DTs to make a reliable prediction. High-quality random forest predictions are those that appear more than once in the decision tree. The random forest algorithm's strength rests in the fact that it can be used to solve problems of classification and regression with relative ease, allowing for accurate estimates to be made. It is quite gentle on big datasets and does not throw away any dimensions. This is another dimensionality reduction technique since it can easily manage and find the significant variables despite the large number of input variables (hundreds to thousands). It offers effective techniques for interpreting the missing data and keeping precision even when a crucial component of the data is missing. In addition to the benefits of random forest algorithms, bootstrap, and out-of-bag sampling have been used.
- Like decision trees, nearest neighbors may be used for both classification and regression. The basic machine learning approach known as Nearest Neighbors is often used to categorize challenges encountered in business settings. If a neighbor endorses a case in this classification system, the nearby cases will be preserved. Similarly, it remembers all relevant instances and sorts recent ones according to the combined opinions of all nearby neighbors. Using a distance formula based on k nearest neighbors, we may quantify the instance of each category. The distance between a set of k neighbors can be calculated using either the Euclidean, Hamming, Minkowski, or Manhattan distance. Categorical and Euclidean hamming distances, as well as Manhattan Minkowski distances, are continuous functions. If $k = 1$, then a case has exactly one neighboring class.

## RESULTS AND DISCUSSION

There were 1,048,588 English Tweets utilized as data in this study. The Tweets were categorized using a variety of different classification methods, such as Naive Bayes, Recurrent Neural Networks, Decision Trees, Neural Networks, Random Forrest, and a hybrid model. The table below compiles the outcomes of using certain algorithms.

Here are a few publicly available datasets for use in training sentiment analysis machine learning models. We have tried out a few of them.

- Over 1.6 million tweets were gathered using the Twitter API and added to Sentiment140. The emotion of a brand, product, or issue may be determined by analyzing the annotations attached to each tweet.
- There are a total of 52,077 reviews in the Restaurant Review Dataset, each with a star rating and detailed pros and disadvantages.
- Nearly 20,000 rated and reviewed hotels may be found in Trip Advisor's hotel reviews.
- The hotel and vehicle reviews that makeup OpinRank Data were culled from the likes of TripAdvisor, the world's largest travel feedback site, and Edmunds, the largest online resource for information on cars in the United States.
- The nearly 12,000 lines in Stanford's Sentiment Treebank are all taken from Rotten Tomatoes user evaluations of movies. A parse tree representing each sentence with annotated words and phrases is used to convey the meaning of each assertion. Over 215,000 distinct sentences have been manually categorized in the dataset. Comparison of the proposed model and existing classifiers are given in Table **1-5** for accuracy, sensitivity and specificity, respectively.

**Table 1. Results for Sentiment140.**

| Classifiers | Accuracy% | Sensitivity% | Specificity% |
|---|---|---|---|
| Naive Bayes | 77.5 | 79.0 | 74.0 |
| Random Forest | 73.8 | 70.0 | 77.0 |
| Decision Tree | 72.5 | 72.0 | 68.0 |
| RNN-LSTM | 82.3 | 76.1 | 83.9 |
| NN (10 layers) | 79.5 | 81.1 | 77.3 |
| CNN | 79.6 | 84.7 | 75.0 |
| CNN Word2Vec | 82.9 | 83.0 | 82.7 |
| RNN+LSTM+Word2Vec | 83.0 | 86.0 | 79.3 |
| Hybrid Model | 83.6[a] | 87.1 | 79.3 |

**Table 2. Results for Restaurant Reviews.**

| Classifiers | Accuracy% | Sensitivity% | Specificity% |
|---|---|---|---|
| Naive Bayes | 77.5 | 79.0 | 74.0 |
| Random Forest | 73.8 | 70.0 | 77.0 |
| Decision Tree | 72.5 | 72.0 | 68.0 |
| RNN-LSTM | 82.3 | 76.1 | 83.9 |
| NN (10 layers) | 79.5 | 81.1 | 77.3 |
| CNN | 79.6 | 84.7 | 75.0 |
| CNN Word2Vec | 82.9 | 83.0 | 82.7 |
| RNN+LSTM+Word2Vec | 83.0 | 86.0 | 79.3 |
| Hybrid Model | 83.6[a] | 87.1 | 79.3 |

**Table 3. Results for Opin Rank Reviews.**

| Classifiers | Accuracy% | Sensitivity% | Specificity% |
|---|---|---|---|
| Naive Bayes | 77.5 | 79.0 | 74.0 |
| Random Forest | 73.8 | 70.0 | 77.0 |
| Decision Tree | 72.5 | 72.0 | 68.0 |
| RNN-LSTM | 82.3 | 76.1 | 83.9 |
| NN (10 layers) | 79.5 | 81.1 | 77.3 |
| CNN | 79.6 | 84.7 | 75.0 |
| CNN Word2Vec | 82.9 | 83.0 | 82.7 |
| RNN+LSTM+Word2Vec | 83.0 | 86.0 | 79.3 |
| Hybrid Model | 83.6[a] | 87.1 | 79.3 |

**Table 4. Results for Trip Advisor Reviews.**

| Classifiers | Accuracy% | Sensitivity% | Specificity% |
|---|---|---|---|
| Naive Bayes | 77.5 | 79.0 | 74.0 |
| Random Forest | 73.8 | 70.0 | 77.0 |
| Decision Tree | 72.5 | 72.0 | 68.0 |
| RNN-LSTM | 82.3 | 76.1 | 83.9 |
| NN (10 layers) | 79.5 | 81.1 | 77.3 |
| CNN | 79.6 | 84.7 | 75.0 |
| CNN Word2Vec | 82.9 | 83.0 | 82.7 |

*(Table 4) cont.....*

| Classifiers | Accuracy% | Sensitivity% | Specificity% |
|---|---|---|---|
| RNN+LSTM+Word2Vec | 83.0 | 86.0 | 79.3 |
| Hybrid Model | 83.6[a] | 87.1 | 79.3 |

**Table 5. Results for Standard Sentiment Reviews.**

| Classifiers | Accuracy% | Sensitivity% | Specificity% |
|---|---|---|---|
| Naive Bayes | 77.5 | 79.0 | 74.0 |
| Random Forest | 73.8 | 70.0 | 77.0 |
| Decision Tree | 72.5 | 72.0 | 68.0 |
| RNN-LSTM | 82.3 | 76.1 | 83.9 |
| NN (10 layers) | 79.5 | 81.1 | 77.3 |
| CNN | 79.6 | 84.7 | 75.0 |
| CNN Word2Vec | 82.9 | 83.0 | 82.7 |
| RNN+LSTM+Word2Vec | 83.0 | 86.0 | 79.3 |
| Hybrid Model | 83.6[a] | 87.1 | 79.3 |

## CONCLUSION

This article analyzes the sentiment of over a million English Tweets and compares the results of many machine learning and deep learning methods. In addition to conventional classification strategies like CNNs, DTs, Naive Bayes, and RNNs, a hybrid model was built and put to the test. With a sensitivity of 87.1% and a specificity of 79.3%, the hybrid model proves to be the most effective option overall. The goal of forthcoming research is to include feelings in the text analysis process. Future goals include employing the hybrid classification method to assess its efficacy with Arabic Tweets, given that vast quantities of tweets are created every minute and many of them are in the Arabic language.

## REFERENCES

[1] A. Gangwar, and T. Mehta, "Sentiment Analysis of Political Tweets for Israel using Machine Learning", In: *ArXiv, abs/2204.06515*, 2022.

[2] V. Vashisht, A.K. Pandey, and S.P. Yadav, "Speech Recognition using Machine Learning", In: *IEIE Transactions on Smart Processing & Computing* vol. 10. The Institute of Electronics Engineers of Korea, 2021, pp. 233-239. [http://dx.doi.org/10.5573/IEIESPC.2021.10.3.233]

[3] A.U. Hassan, J. Hussain, M. Hussain, M. Sadiq, and S. Lee, "Sentiment analysis of social networking sites (SNS) data using machine learning approach for the measurement of depression", *International Conference on Information and Communication Technology Convergence (ICTC)*, pp. 138-140, 2017. [http://dx.doi.org/10.1109/ICTC.2017.8190959]

[4] Z. Indra, A. Setiawan, and Y. Jusman, "Implementation of Machine Learning for Sentiment Analysis of Social and Political Orientation in Pekanbaru City", *J. Phys. Conf. Ser.*, vol. 1803, no. 1, p. 012032, 2021.
[http://dx.doi.org/10.1088/1742-6596/1803/1/012032]

[5] S. P. Yadav, and S. Yadav, "Mathematical implementation of fusion of medical images in continuous wavelet domain", *Journal of Advanced Research in dynamical and control system,* vol. 10, no. 10, pp. 45-54, 2019.

[6] E. Asmawati, A. Saikhu, and D. Siahaan, "Sentiment Analysis of Text Memes: A Comparison Among Supervised Machine Learning Methods", *9th International Conference on Electrical Engineering, Computer Science and Informatics (EECSI),* pp. 349-354, 2022.
[http://dx.doi.org/10.23919/EECSI56542.2022.9946506]

[7] M. Hajirahimova, and M. Ismayilova, "Machine learning-based sentiment analysis of Twitter data", *Problems of Information Society* , 2022.

[8] D. Anashkin, and K.A. Malyshenko, "Social Media Content Analysis with Machine Learning Tools", *2021 International Conference on Artificial Intelligence and Data Science (ICAIDS),* pp. 1-5, 2021.

[9] A. Jabeen, M. Yasir, Y. Ansari, S. Yasmin, J. Moon, and S. Rho, "An Empirical Study of Macroeconomic Factors and Stock Returns in the Context of Economic Uncertainty News Sentiment Using Machine Learning", *Complex,* vol. 18, pp. 1-4646733, 2022.

[10] M. El Barachi, M. Alkhatib, and S.S. Mathew, "A Hybrid Machine Learning Approach for Sentiment Analysis of Partially Occluded Faces", *2021 IEEE International Conference on Artificial Intelligence and Computer Applications (ICAICA),* pp. 389-392, 2021.
[http://dx.doi.org/10.1109/ICAICA52286.2021.9498049]

[11] M.H. Abd El-Jawad, R.A. Hodhod, and Y.M. Omar, "Sentiment Analysis of Social Media Networks Using Machine Learning", *14th International Computer Engineering Conference (ICENCO),* pp. 174-176, 2018.
[http://dx.doi.org/10.1109/ICENCO.2018.8636124]

[12] V. Geetha, and N. Sujatha, "A Review on Sentiment Analysis of Social Media Networks using Deep Learning", *6th International Conference on Intelligent Computing and Control Systems (ICICCS),* pp. 1149-1154, 2022.
[http://dx.doi.org/10.1109/ICICCS53718.2022.9788153]

[13] B. Meraliyev, K. Kongratbayev, and N. Sultanova, "Content Analysis of Extracted Suicide Texts From Social Media Networks by Using Natural Language Processing and Machine Learning Techniques", *2021 IEEE International Conference on Smart Information Systems and Technologies (SIST),* pp. 1-6, 2021.
[http://dx.doi.org/10.1109/SIST50301.2021.9466001]

[14] J. Kaur, J. Saxena, and J. Shah, "Facial Emotion Recognition", In: *2022 International Conference on Computational Intelligence and Sustainable Engineering Solutions (CISES). 2022 International Conference on Computational Intelligence and Sustainable Engineering Solutions (CISES)*, 2022.
[http://dx.doi.org/10.1109/CISES54857.2022.9844366]

[15] S. Perera, and K. Karunanayaka, "Sentiment Analysis of Social Media Data using Fuzzy-Rough Set Classifier for the Prediction of the Presidential Election", *2nd International Conference on Advanced Research in Computing (ICARC),* pp. 188-193, 2022.
[http://dx.doi.org/10.1109/ICARC54489.2022.9754173]

## CHAPTER 38

# Sentiment Classification of Textual Content using Hybrid DNN and SVM Models

**Abhishek Singla**[1,*]

[1] *Centre for Interdisciplinary Research in Business and Technology, Chitkara University Institute of Engineering and Technology, Chitkara University, Punjab, India*

**Abstract:** The proliferation of Web 2.0 has resulted in a deluge of real-time, unstructured data such as user comments, opinions, and likes. The lack of structure in the data makes it difficult to create a reliable prediction model for sentiment analysis. There have been promising applications of several DNN architectures to sentiment analysis, however, these methods tend to treat all features identically and struggle with high-dimensional feature spaces. In addition, existing techniques fail to effectively combine semantic and sentiment knowledge for the purpose of extracting meaningful relevant contextual sentiment characteristics. This paper proposes an integrated convolutional neural network, or CNN, architecture that takes sentiment as well as context into consideration as a means of intelligently developing and highlighting significant components of relevant sentiment contextual in the text. To start, we use transformers' bidirectional encoder representations to create sentiment-enhanced embeddings of words for text semantic extraction using integrated emotion lexicons with broad coverage for feature identification. The proposed approach then adjusts the CNN in a way that it can detect both word order/contextual text semantics data as well as the long-dependency relationship in the phrase sequence. Our approach also employs a system to prioritize the most important portions of the phrase sequence. One last step in sentiment analysis is the use of support vector machines (SVMs) to reduce the complexity of the space of features and identify locally significant characteristics. The accuracy of existing text sentiment categorization is greatly improved by the use of the proposed model, as shown by an evaluation of real-world benchmark datasets.

**Keywords:** Hybrid DNN, SVM, Textual content sentiment classification, Text documents.

## INTRODUCTION

A paradigm shift was initiated by deep neural networks (DNNs), but their high processing requirements have limited their deployment on edge devices like

* **Corresponding author Abhishek Singla:** Centre for Interdisciplinary Research in Business and Technology, Chitkara University Institute of Engineering and Technology, Chitkara University, Punjab, India;
E-mail: abhishek.singla.orp@chitkara.edu.in

**Pankaj Kumar Mishra and Satya Prakash Yadav (Eds.)**

phones and wearables [1]. In light of this, a hybrid edge-cloud computing architecture is proposed [2] to naively divide the DNN processes on the assumption of an ongoing connection state, hence enabling the relocation of some computation to the cloud. Nevertheless, there is a lack of comprehensive approaches to DNN segmentation at the moment [3], and the state of practical networks might change drastically based on their surroundings. One of the most important technologies that will allow 5G wireless networks to function is cloud radio access networks (CRANs) [4]. In order to reduce power consumption while also satisfying the long-term demands of mobile consumers, CRAN allocation of resources has to be further improved [5]. In light of DRL's track record of success in solving challenging control problems, we provide ReCARL, a novel paradigm for DRL-based environmentally friendly utilization of resources in CRANs [6]. At each decision epoch, the DRL agent's action-value functions is approximately determined using a deep neural network, or DNN, once the state distance, action space, as well as reward function have been established [7]. Promoting offline get-togethers as well as attracting new faces has never been easier than on event-based social media platforms (EBSN), which have seen explosive growth in the last few years [8, 9]. An ever-growing event-based social network (EBSN) relies on being able to consistently suggest members' preferred events. There is more competition for limited resources as the intelligence of edge devices like smartphones, wearables, and IoT devices has increased owing to machine learning. Training models on edge devices is a resource-intensive process, making on-device customisation a formidable obstacle [10, 16].

To determine the reviewer's emotional stance, we use Stanford POS Tagger to label the review text's nouns, adjectives, adverbs, and verbs with appropriate POS labels. Sentiment orientation is determined by looking up the aforementioned keywords in large-scale sentiment lexicons and obtaining their associated sentiment orientations. We use linguistic semantic criteria to label sentences/review texts with positive and negative sentiments appropriately. The categorization of ambiguous opinions can benefit from linguistic semantic principles. They contribute to a more precise modeling of the SA issue. Six popular sentiment classification benchmark datasets were used to assess the proposed method's predicted ability. In comparison to existing baseline methods, the suggested method significantly improves the efficiency and effectiveness of sentiment analysis. The rest of the paper is structured as follows. Section 2 displays further work of relevance. In Section 3, we go deep into the approach, architecture, and technological specifics. In Section 4, we discuss the methodology and findings from our experiments. The study finishes with a section on what comes next.

## RELATED WORK

We explore how the modular design of DNN may be utilized to modify the edge model for usage in different settings and with different deployment strategies. To achieve this aim of model consistency and computational delay simultaneously, we built a decision engine based on reinforcement learning. The DNN uses a context-aware model tree constructed by the engine to make decisions about which model branch to switch to in real-time. Our approach has been shown to minimize latency by 30% - 50% in emulation and field testing without compromising model accuracy [11].

Short-word detection issues are addressed by creating an HMM/DNN architecture. By including a context-aware keyword theory as well as a 9-state filler framework into the first-stage phrase hypothesizer, we could increase the figure-of-merit (FOM) for short words from 6.08% to 21.88% as well as decrease the percentage of missing issues from 80% to 6%. To further narrow down potential matches, a second-stage keyword verification based on MLP is used following the hypothesizer. Improved short word recognition was achieved by re-engineering the verifier with three cutting-edge techniques: based on knowledge features, deep artificial neural networks, and the use of a hidden Markov model (HMM) for the MLPs' features conversion. Using nine short keywords from the TIMIT collection, we achieved the best FOM of 42.79% with the suggested KWS technique; this compares well with the FOM of 42.6% for lengthy content words and is significantly higher than the FOM of 18.4% for short keywords reported in earlier works [12].

We provide two distinct agents for DRL inside ReCARL: ReCARL-Basic, which uses a conventional deep Q-learning method to train a conventional DNN structure, and ReCARL-Hybrid, which uses a hybrid deep qualitative learning method to train a context-aware DNN architecture. In a series of extensive simulated tests, we evaluated ReCARL and the two DRL agents to two widely used benchmarks. The results of the simulation show that ReCARL is efficient in meeting the demands of its customers while conserving energy [13].

Using semantic content analysis and contextual event impact, our research proposes a hybrid collaborative filtering approach to event suggestion that can aid users in making informed decisions about events in their immediate locations. Specifically, we analyze text from event descriptions using the latent topic model, and then we utilize each user's event registration history to develop a long-term interest model and a short-term interest model. Then, we give each occurrence a value that takes into account both its uniqueness and its social relevance to users. We prioritize a user's long-term interests over the effects of the immediate moment when making a connection recommendation. To do this, we construct a user-event rating matrix using users' short-term interest models, and then we predict events' ratings for each user based on the ratings of her neighbors. Tests on real-world datasets [14] confirm the superiority of our approach.

We propose a new training pathway that incorporates both the cloud and the edge, allowing users to make use of the cloud's capability while maintaining data near to where they are on the edge. The design's highlights include a deployment decision engine that takes context into account, feature compression based on error feedback, and parallel execution made feasible by the replay of previously deployed features. The components of the proposed pipeline training architecture, when combined, significantly quicken the training process with minimal disadvantage to accuracy and additional memory/energy overhead. To demonstrate the superiority of our system over the state-of-the-art, we train it on a wide variety of tasks, from image and text classification to image generation, and we test it in a wide variety of settings, ranging from WiFi and 5G networks to the Internet of Things. The results of the experiments show the system's adaptability and capacity for learning new contexts, offering a viable solution to the challenge of model training in edge clouds [15].

## PROPOSED WORK

### System Model

An innovative hybrid approach for sentiment analysis, HYBRIDDNN, is presented here. Combining language semantics as well as sentiment information with classic DNN-based techniques, the suggested approach can identify as well as extract contextually local significant sentiment characteristics for text analysis of sentiment. The HYBRIDDNN model's internal structure is shown in Fig. (**1**). The five layers that make up this model are as follows: Feature Engineering, BERT Embedding, BiLSTM, Convolutional Neural Network (CNN), and Output.

### Feature Engineering Model

The two components of the characteristic engineering layer are emotional feature extraction as well as text pre-processing. Text pre-processing, by creating suitable feature vectors, may improve the accuracy of learning in emotion categorization. The text preliminary processing component is composed of six separate modules. The provided modules include linguistic rules, lowercase, noise reduction, spelling correction, sentence processing, as well as tokenization. In order to extract sentiment characteristics, we utilize the university's POS Tagger to assign POS labels to the particular phrases (An adjective, Adverb, Verb, as well as Noun) that convey sentiment cues. This is done by drawing on comprehensive sentiment lexicons. The evaluation data is loaded at this level and then parsed and tokenized. Then, the noise reduction module is used to get rid of any distracting words, URLs, numbers, *etc.* from the text. After that, the short forms of the nouns are expanded. The content is also made lower as well as any mistakes are corrected with the aid of the spell checker as well as the case conversion module. The next stage is to use the POS tagger to classify the most likely words as either nouns, adjectives, adverbs, or verbs.

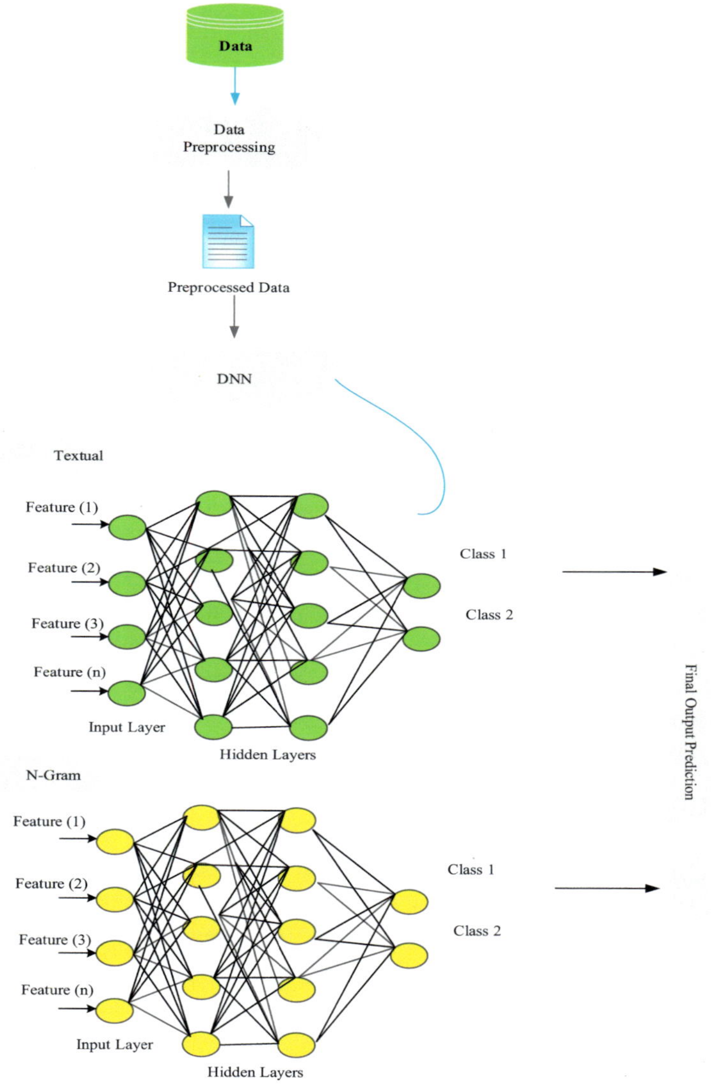


**Fig. (1).** System hybrid DNN model.

We also use language criteria to identify the appropriate review sentence class when the author's commentary contains a range of perspectives. For instance, in the phrase "the filmmaker is well-known, but the film is dull," just the part of the sentence after the conjunction "but" is taken into account by linguistic standards. Changing the polarity of a sentence requires the use of words like "but," "despite," "while," "unless," and so on. There is often a wide variety of opinions included in review articles. Adopting language norms may improve review quality overall. Previous studies postulated that each review sentence/text would fall into one of two polarities:

## Sentiment Lexicon Layer

To accurately determine the sentiment direction of a domain-dependent sentiment word, many of the existing sentiment lexicons only include a tiny selection of phrases. To increase the sentiment lexicon's word coverage, we combine numerous different emotion dictionaries. The 10 state-of-the-art sentiment lexicons we discussed before are standardized and integrated into a consistent framework by being given one of three scores: +1, -1, or 0. We then build a broader sentiment lexicon by averaging the sentiment scores of the terms that appear in both sets of dictionaries.

We present examples of current state-of-the-art sentiment lexicons, detailing their word coverage and sizing. To begin, we standardized the vocabulary by giving each positive, negative, and neutral term a score of 1, 1, and 0. Then, a wide coverage sentiment lexicon (WCSL) was created by averaging the sentiment scores of the terms that appear in several lexicons. The fundamental issue with sentiment lexicons is that they only cover a small subset of words. If a sentiment term is not already in the sentiment lexicons, it is likely going to be left out, which might change the overall tone of the review. To solve this problem, we mine WordNet for semantic information about the word, namely its synonyms, and use those results to infer the underlying attitude. If we are given the word "W," we may look it up in WordNet to see what other words start with the same letter. We look up every possible synonym for wi in the WCSL, and if it is there, we know what mood it conveys. We take the average emotional score of all potential alternatives. The emotional direction of an expression is positive if and only if its median sentiment score, "W," is more than zero; alternatively, it is positive. Fig. (**1**) shows the System Hybrid DNN Model.

## BERT Model

BERT is a stacked transformer encoder and decoder language model that learns new linguistic structures. Better and more versatile than Word2Vec, BERT takes into account context-independent representations of words. The word representation of vectors in the BERT is continuously changed depending on the environment. BERT has the ability to learn both the left-to-right and right-to-left representations of text. The BERT uses the Mask Word Model to build a word-level picture of the sequence of inputs and Next-Paragraph-Predictions to build a sentence-level representation, in that order, to decrease the total loss rate. By arbitrarily masking words from each sentence and subsequently generating predictions about those according to the meaning of the adjacent unmasked words, the Masked Model of Language trains a deep reversible transformer representations. To prepare the data for the BERT, a [MASK] token is substituted for word sequencing in fifteen percent of the words. The model makes a good guess as to the original value of the mask word based on the meanings of the other words in the series. Next sentence predictions aim to train BERT to handle a diverse range of downstream tasks by learning the relationships among words. Every review text and phrase in the dataset have sentiment-enhanced word embeddings generated using the BERT language model. Input emotion word tokens are transformed into word vectors by the sentiment-enhanced embedding layer. High-quality salient sentiment features based on these word vectors are then used for categorization by downstream DNN models.

**Hybrid DNN for Classification**

We combine depth-in-space (spatial) as well as depth-in-time (temporal) neural network features in our hybrid-DNN to allow more complicated intelligent applications.

To improve word embedding and classification based on sentiment, the integrated network is used to find and extract sentiment terms from the review text. Review text S=w_1,w_2,w_3,...,w_n with n words in it as input. The goal is to use WCSL to extract emotional words from S and use them to create an upgraded word embedding vector. We may write $W_sV = \{W_s\ V_1,\ W_s\ V_2,\ W_s\ V_3,\ \dots,\ W_s\ V_n\}$ In Fig. (**2a**), we see an example of a basic neural network that makes use of weighted connections. You may calculate the final state y by multiplying the input pattern by a weight matrix.

$$y_j = \sum_{i=1}^{m} x_i \times W_{ij} \quad \textbf{(1)}$$

where $x_i$is the input pattern defined through and its length is denoted by m, and $W_{ij}$stands for the mass situated at the *i* th data and the j-th result.

In the architecture of neural networks, the nonlinear activation function is often used to manage the transition between synapses. A Rectified linear unit (ReLU) has been popular in recent years. In DNN development, the most common activation functions are the sigmoid and hyperbolic tangent (tanh) functions. The delay attribute, which would allow these functions to mimic the biological behavior of the nervous system, is missing from all of them. For delay-based system architectures, the MG function has recently emerged as a viable option. The MG function originates in the ordinary differential equation (ODE) and characterizes a system whose dynamics are dependent on both the present and past states.

$$\frac{dV}{dt} = \frac{\beta \times V(t-\tau)}{1+V(t-\tau)^n} - \gamma \times V(t) \tag{2}$$

Where $\beta$ and $\gamma$ design factors that may be arbitrarily used to determine the input signals' scaling factor are denoted by n and the nonlinear as well as delay factors, respectively. By using the incorporated delayed feature, one may stabilize or destabilise a dynamic system, resulting in a transition from regular to erratic behavior, or the reverse. An examination of the stability of Lyapunov is based on differential equation solutions.

A learning coefficient of 11031103, first- as well as second-moment degradation speeds of 0.9 as well as 0.999, accordingly, are used to train the hybrid DNN using the optimization approach adaptive moment estimate (Adam). In order to fine-tune the suggested network's parameters, this study employs the Adam optimizer. Keep in mind that the Adam optimizer can speed up the network's convergence, which is useful for saving time and effort during training. When making adjustments to the parameters of the suggested recurrent-convolutional network, a batch size of 32 is used. The FC layers are subjected to dropout (with a value of 0.5) to prevent overfitting and enhance generalization capacity. After about 33,660 iterations and 180 epochs, the network reaches convergence.

## RESULTS AND DISCUSSION

### Dataset Description

- We start off this part by detailing the experimental setup, which includes the datasets and baseline procedures that formed the backbone of our empirical research. After that, we compare the outcomes of several different models that were developed and analyzed.
- Six different text sentiment categorization datasets were used to assess our algorithms' prediction abilities.
- There are 5,331 beneficial and 5,331 adverse data points in the "Movie Reviews" (MR) sentence polarity dataset. The "RT-2k" standards dataset has

2,000 full-length positive as well as negative reviews of movies.

- SST-2: All neutral assessments have been removed from the Harvard Sentiment Treebank data set, making it a binary-labeled version. There are 9613 samples that are positive and -negative.
- CR: The Amazon and CNET customer review (CR) datasets include reviews for five different electrical devices.
- The SemEval datasets include Twitter conversations on a wide range of topics from 2013 and 2014, respectively. In keeping with the work, we trained and tuned the classifier using the SemEval2013 training and development sets and evaluated its performance on the SemEval2013 and SemEval-2014 test sets. This is due to the fact that no real-world data is included in SemEval2014. Moreover, we only consider binary targets (positive and negative) and exclude neutral feedback in the same way. Only the SST-2 dataset includes separate data for each of these assessment stages (training, development, and testing). The remaining datasets were randomly divided into three parts: a development set, a test set, and a training set.

## Baseline Methods

- In this research, we compared the accuracy of our technique to that of some of the most widely used classifiers, such as the support vector machine (SVM), K-nearest neighbor (KNN), and logistical regression (LR). Using a ten-fold cross-validation technique, we compare our approach to all available baseline techniques. The dimensions and specifics of these approaches are briefly described below.
- Based on statistical learning theory, a support vector machine (SVM) employs kernel functions to map problems that are intractable in low dimensions to those that are tractable in high dimensions. The regularization penalty parameter (C) and the inverse of the radial basis function (RBF) kernel standard deviation (SD, =1/=1/) are chosen as the SVM hyper parameters.
- To categorize data labels, the KNN is a supervised learning method that looks for the k-nearest instances. The neighbors of the sample decide the sample's classification based on a majority vote. Distances are often measured using the Euclidean metric.
- LR: LR is used to characterize the connection between X and Y, and to make predictions about Y, using just X and Y as independent variables. Y is a real number between 0 and 1 that indicates the likelihood of receiving one of the two possible outcomes from the binary categorization. In order to get the best value for the regularization parameter C, the LR looks across the logarithmic range [102, 103].

**Table 1. Comparative analysis of the proposed *vs.* existing methods.**

| Dataset | Embedding Scheme | F-measure | Precision | Accuracy | Recall |
|---|---|---|---|---|---|
| MR | BERT | 93.6 | 94.1 | 93.6 | 93.1 |
| | FastText | 90.3 | 90.1 | 91.1 | 91.9 |
| | Glove | 89,7 | 89,5 | 89.8 | 89.8 |
| | Word2vec | 88.3 | 89.1 | 88.8 | 88.5 |
| RT-2K | BERT | 94.3 | 95,1 | 94.8 | 94.6 |
| | FastText | 92.2 | 91.1 | 92.3 | 93.4 |
| | Glove | 90.5 | 90.2 | 90.6 | 90.8 |
| | Word2vec | 89.5 | 90,1 | 89.6 | 89.2 |
| SST-2 | BERT | 91.8 | 90.9 | 92.1 | 93.1 |
| | FastText | 90.1 | 89.6 | 90.1 | 90.5 |
| | Glove | 89.5 | 89.6 | 89.5 | 89.9 |
| | Word2vec | 88.9 | 88.6 | 88.8 | 89.2 |
| CR | BERT | 94.8 | 95.1 | 94.8 | 94.6 |
| | FastText | 92.4 | 93.6 | 92.3 | 91.3 |
| | Glove | 91.9 | 92.6 | 91.8 | 91.2 |
| | Word2vec | 91.2 | 90.6 | 91.3 | 91.1 |
| SemEval 2013 | BERT | 93.6 | 93.8 | 93.6 | 93.3 |
| | Fast Text | 91.8 | 91.9 | 91.8 | 92.2 |
| | Glove | 91.4 | 91.3 | 91.5 | 91.5 |
| | Word2vec | 90.8 | 91,3 | 90.8 | 90.9 |
| SemEval 2013 | BERT | 84.6 | 84.8 | 84.6 | 84.5 |
| | FastText | 82.9 | 82.7 | 82.8 | 83.2 |
| | Glove | 81.2 | 80.8 | 81.2 | 81.4 |
| | Word2vec | 80.7 | 80.5 | 80.7 | 80.9 |

The approach used to produce word-embedded vectors may influence the precision of classification in several ways. Investigating the effects of different pre-trained word embeddings on classification accuracy is therefore our objective. We examine four of the more widely used pre-trained word-embedded models for vectorization as well as sentiment categorization: word2vec, glove, fasttext, and BERT. In this part, we will run a series of experiments to determine how the aforementioned word embedding technique affects the overall performance of hybrid DNNs. The effectiveness of the suggested technique for sentiment categorization is significantly impacted by the sentiment knowledge input. See

Fig. (**1**) for an explanation of the various components of our sentiment knowledge base: LR (linguistic norms with POS tagging), MW (meaningful words derived by word conversion as well as typos correction), and WCSL (wide cover sentiment lexicon) are all part of the same system. To examine how input sentiment information affected the suggested model, we ran sentiment knowledge adaptation experiments on the HYBRIDDNN using six datasets. As demonstrated in Table **1**, the incorporation of sentimental information leads to significantly different outcomes. However, the model's overall performance is increasing as more comprehensive sentiment knowledge is added. This demonstrates the benefits of sentiment information for HYBRIDDNN performance.

The suggested model outperforms the SOTA baseline DNN-based models in several ways. The first is that typos and other errors in the review text are fixed and noisy features are removed during text pre-processing. The second has to do with the selection and extraction of sentiment traits that are relevant to the given context. The third justification is the categorization of ambiguous viewpoints in accordance with the semantic laws of language. The addition of WCSL for recognizing emotional nuances is the fourth justification for this. Reason number five is that emotional traits might be expressed in a dense real-valued vectors, which captures both the word sequence's long-dependency connection and semantic data about the text's environment. Sixth, the suggested semantic as well as context-aware hybrid sentiment assessment model is enhanced by a well-configured set of hyperparameters. The seventh benefit is that it efficiently extracts rich sentiment data for precise categorization. Table **2** is displayed in Comparative analysis of the proposed *vs*. existing methods.

**Table 2. Comparative analysis of the proposed *vs.* existing methods.**

| Dataset | Embedding Scheme | Precision | Recall | F-measure | Accuracy |
|---|---|---|---|---|---|
| MR | Proposed | 94.0 | 93.0 | 93.5 | 93.5 |
| | SVM | 90.0 | 91.8 | 90.9 | 91.0 |
| | KNN | 89,4 | 89.9 | 89,6 | 89.7 |
| | LR | 89.0 | 88.4 | 88.7 | 88.7 |
| RT-2K | Proposed | 95,0 | 94.5 | 94.7 | 94.7 |
| | SVM | 91.0 | 93.3 | 92.1 | 92.2 |
| | KNN | 90.0 | 90.9 | 90.4 | 90.5 |
| | LR | 90,0 | 89.1 | 89.5 | 89.5 |

*(Table 2) cont.....*

| Dataset | Embedding Scheme | Precision | Recall | F-measure | Accuracy |
|---|---|---|---|---|---|
| SST-2 | Proposed | 90.8 | 93.0 | 91.9 | 92.0 |
| | SVM | 89.5 | 90.4 | 90.0 | 90.0 |
| | KNN | 89.0 | 89.8 | 89.4 | 89.4 |
| | LR | 88.5 | 89.1 | 88.8 | 88.9 |
| CR | Proposed | 95.0 | 94.5 | 94.7 | 94.7 |
| | SVM | 93.5 | 91.2 | 92.3 | 92.2 |
| | KNN | 92.5 | 91.1 | 91.8 | 91.7 |
| | LR | 90.5 | 91.0 | 91.1 | 91.2 |
| SemEval 2013 | Proposed | 93.9 | 93.2 | 93.5 | 93.5 |
| | SVM | 91.8 | 92.1 | 91.9 | 91.9 |
| | KNN | 91.2 | 91.4 | 91.3 | 91.4 |
| | LR | 91,2 | 90.8 | 90.9 | 90.9 |
| SemEval 2013 | Proposed | 84.7 | 84.4 | 84.5 | 84.5 |
| | SVM | 82.6 | 83.1 | 82.8 | 82.9 |
| | KNN | 80.9 | 81.3 | 81.1 | 81.1 |
| | LR | 80.4 | 80.8 | 80.6 | 80.6 |

## CONCLUSION

The vast quantities of unorganized data created by users accessible online, in the form of textual comments as well as reviews, provide a wealth of pertinent information for e-commerce as well as business research. A rapidly expanding area of research that is emotion analysis seeks to categorize both favorable and adverse feelings in user-generated information found on the internet. It is challenging to construct a suitable sentiment analysis framework from textual data because of its large volume.

## REFERENCES

[1] S. Nasrin, A. Shylendra, Y. Kadakia, N. Iliev, W. Gomes, T. Tulabandhula, and A.R. Trivedi, "ENOS: Energy-Aware Network Operator Search for Hybrid Digital and Compute-in-Memory DNN Accelerators", *ArXiv, abs/2104.05217,* 2021.

[2] O. Özdenizci, S.Y. Günay, F. Quivira, and D. Erdoğmuş, "Hierarchical Graphical Models for Context-Aware Hybrid Brain-Machine Interfaces", *40th Annual International Conference of the IEEE Engineering in Medicine and Biology Society (EMBC),* pp. 1964-1967, 2018. [http://dx.doi.org/10.1109/EMBC.2018.8512677]

[3] E. Ekmekcioglu, B. Evans, A. Kondoz, P. Thompson, L. Ottavj, F. Gamberini, and S. Watts, "Context-aware hybrid satellite-terrestrial broadband access", *Int. J. Satell. Commun. Netw.,* vol. 37, no. 6, pp. 513-526, 2019. [http://dx.doi.org/10.1002/sat.1291]

[4] I. Baz, E. Yörük, and M. Çetin, "Context-aware hybrid classification system for fine-grained retail product recognition", *12th Image, Video, and Multidimensional Signal Processing Workshop (IVMSP),* pp. 1-5, 2016.
[http://dx.doi.org/10.1109/IVMSPW.2016.7528213]

[5] L. Zeng, F. Hong, W. Zheng, Q. Yu, W. Zeng, Y. Wang, and J. Lai, "Hybrid Dynamic-static Context-aware Attention Network for Action Assessment in Long Videos", *Proceedings of the 28th ACM International Conference on Multimedia,* 2020.
[http://dx.doi.org/10.1145/3394171.3413560]

[6] J. Kaur, J. Saxena, and J. Shah, "Facial Emotion Recognition", *2022 International Conference on Computational Intelligence and Sustainable Engineering Solutions (CISES). 2022 International Conference on Computational Intelligence and Sustainable Engineering Solutions (CISES),* 2022.
[http://dx.doi.org/10.1109/CISES54857.2022.9844366]

[7] S. P. Yadav, and S. Yadav, "Mathematical implementation of fusion of medical images in continuous wavelet domain", *Journal of Advanced Research in dynamical and control system,* vol. 10, no. 10, pp. 45-54, 2019.

[8] T. Hussein, T. Linder, W. Gaulke, and J. Ziegler, "Hybreed: A software framework for developing context-aware hybrid recommender systems", *User Model. User-adapt. Interact.,* vol. 24, no. 1-2, pp. 121-174, 2014.
[http://dx.doi.org/10.1007/s11257-012-9134-z]

[9] B. Yuan, and J. Herbert, "Context-aware hybrid reasoning framework for pervasive healthcare", *Pers. Ubiquitous Comput.,* vol. 18, no. 4, pp. 865-881, 2014.
[http://dx.doi.org/10.1007/s00779-013-0696-5]

[10] W. Liang, Y. Wu, M. Li, and Y. Cao, "High-Resolution SAR Image Classification Using Context-Aware Encoder Network and Hybrid Conditional Random Field Model", *IEEE Trans. Geosci. Remote Sens.,* vol. 58, no. 8, pp. 5317-5335, 2020.
[http://dx.doi.org/10.1109/TGRS.2019.2963699]

[11] L. Wang, L. Xiang, J. Xu, J. Chen, X. Zhao, D. Yao, X. Wang, and B. Li, "Context-Aware Deep Model Compression for Edge Cloud Computing", *IEEE 40th International Conference on Distributed Computing Systems (ICDCS),* pp. 787-797, 2020.

[12] I. Chen, and C. Lee, "A hybrid HMM/DNN approach to keyword spotting of short words", *Interspeech,* 2013.
[http://dx.doi.org/10.21437/Interspeech.2013-397]

[13] Z. Xu, J. Tang, C. Yin, Y. Wang, G. Xue, J. Wang, and M.C. Gursoy, "ReCARL: Resource Allocation in Cloud RANs with Deep Reinforcement Learning", *IEEE Trans. Mobile Comput.,* vol. 21, p. 1, 2020.
[http://dx.doi.org/10.1109/TMC.2020.3044282]

[14] M. Xu, and S. Liu, "Semantic-Enhanced and Context-Aware Hybrid Collaborative Filtering for Event Recommendation in Event-Based Social Networks", *IEEE Access,* vol. 7, pp. 17493-17502, 2019.
[http://dx.doi.org/10.1109/ACCESS.2019.2895824]

[15] D. Yao, L. Xiang, Z. Wang, J. Xu, C. Li, and X. Wang, "Context-Aware Compilation of DNN Training Pipelines across Edge and Cloud", *Proceedings of the ACM on Interactive, Mobile, Wearable and Ubiquitous Technologies,* vol. 5, pp. 1-27, 2021.

[16] J. Khan, N. Ahmad, S. Khalid, F. Ali, and Y. Lee, "Sentiment and Context-Aware Hybrid DNN With Attention for Text Sentiment Classification", *IEEE Access,* vol. 11, pp. 28162-28179, 2023.
[http://dx.doi.org/10.1109/ACCESS.2023.3259107]

# CHAPTER 39

# Big Data Analysis and Information Quality: Challenges, Solutions, and Open Problems

**Sahil Suri**[1,*]

*[1] Centre for Interdisciplinary Research in Business and Technology, Chitkara University Institute of Engineering and Technology, Chitkara University, Punjab, India*

**Abstract:** Big Data is here, thanks to the proliferation of social media and IoT devices. As a result of the immense benefit that Big Data has brought to the public as well as businesses, the question of how to handle and utilise it more effectively has captivated people from every walk of life. Big Data processing has been plagued by difficulties due to the 4V features of Big Data. Solving the data quality issue is crucial to Big Data processing, as is ensuring data quality, which is a precondition for Big Data to play its worth. Two examples of where Big Data has been put to good use are in recommendation and prediction systems. In this research, we investigate Big Data recommendation and prediction systems and endeavour to ascertain the quality of data at each stage of the process: collection, preprocessing, storage, and analysis. The proposed remedy follows from a thorough description and examination of the issue at hand. We have left a few questions unanswered at the conclusion of the report.

**Keywords:** Big data processing, Big Data, Data quality, Issues, Open problems, Solutions.

## INTRODUCTION

The big data age is here, thanks to the proliferation of social media platforms, IoT devices, cloud computing, and other technological advancements [1]. The public and businesses alike have benefited greatly from the explosion in data availability. Meanwhile, the topic of how to effectively handle and utilise big data has spread to all corners of society. Many problems in big data processing may be traced back to the 4V features of large data. To guarantee the proper implementation of the big data approach, it is crucial to address the problem of poor data quality. WBAN, or wireless body area network, is a great tool for long-term healthcare monitoring [2]. Wherein data collection, processing, and transmission are handled by sensor nodes that are wirelessly linked within, on, or around a person. Since

* **Corresponding author Sahil Suri:** Centre for Interdisciplinary Research in Business and Technology, Chitkara University Institute of Engineering and Technology, Chitkara University, Punjab, India;
E-mail: sahil.suri.orp@chitkara.edu.in

**Pankaj Kumar Mishra and Satya Prakash Yadav (Eds.)**

most sensor nodes run on relatively tiny batteries with finite power, it is crucial to WBAN that we find ways to reduce their energy consumption and increase their longevity [3-6]. Quality of Service (QoS) relies heavily on the work done at the Channel Access layer. We can now gather, store, and analyse mobility data at an unparalleled scale and velocity. The proliferation of GPS-enabled gadgets, such as smartphones and other internet-connected items, is largely responsible for this. Mobility data is becoming more important as pervasive computing becomes the norm in our culture [7-9]. The footprints people leave behind may be useful for a variety of purposes, including contact tracking for communicable diseases (such as COVID), traffic engineering, and risk management, particularly when paired with societal data. Over the course of the previous two decades, researchers have shifted their focus from spatial data to spatiotemporal data and finally to information about mobility. What should we do now? Maybe not, but the combined Big Data analytics that take into account mobile devices certainly are. The foundational technology for Big Data has now come of age. The research community's interest in all matters concerning the Big Data and Value Analytics (BDVA) standard model, including handling data, data processing, analytics, visualisation, and user engagement, has recently reached a height. New ways of thinking about and handling mobility data are opening up as a result of advances in artificial intelligence. Therefore, the time has come for Big Mobility statistical analysis to catch up. The field of large mobility data analytics is ripe with untapped potential, but there is a pressing need to encourage the sharing of novel perspectives on pressing real-world issues, the evaluation of proposed solutions, and the discovery of new avenues for study. By 2020, it was expected that almost 26 billion gadgets, with a large majority being cars, will be linked to the Internet. The web of Vehicles (IoVa) is a concept that describes the interconnection as well as cooperation of smart vehicles as well as devices in a network through the creation, transmission, as well as processing of data with the goals of enhancing traffic flow, shortening travel times, and enhancing passengers' levels of comfort while also decreasing pollution and the likelihood of accidents [10].

In this article, we will examine the problems associated with big data and the methods currently being used to address them. In addition, big data's open questions are listed. The first section provides an overview of large data and the difficulties it presents. The difficulties encountered in large data analysis and processing are discussed in Section 2. The current approaches to our problems are discussed in Section 3. In Section 4, we investigate the outstanding questions that might aid us in processing massive data and extracting actionable insights. Tools and technology for large data are discussed in Section 5. The potential of big data in the future is discussed in Section 6. The last section includes a brief overview and final thoughts [11-14].

## LITERATURE REVIEW

In this study, we examine common big data applications like recommendation and prediction systems to attempt to identify data quality concerns at the data collecting, data preprocessing, data storage, and data analysis levels. Solutions are provided that make sense in light of the concerns that have been elaborated upon and analysed. Finally, several future research questions are posed. The purpose of this work is to bring light to the current difficulties encountered by WBAN MAC protocols in the areas of power consumption and latency. Then, they discussed some of the unanswered scientific questions, along with potential answers and developments. Finally, the study wraps up by discussing the knotty problems in WBAN. Major increases in manufacturing, shipping, and farming have increased not just air pollution and climate change but also the likelihood of catastrophic weather events. One of the main causes of these environmental issues is the release of dangerous gases into the atmosphere, in particular the VCD of CO, $SO_2$, and NOx. By employing remote sensing (RS) methods to keep tabs on air quality, our study hopes to provide decision-makers with useful information. The volume, complexity, diversity, and velocity of RS data make them challenging to handle. Therefore, our publication provides details of how the various satellite data sources were used. Furthermore, the evidence presented in this paper indicates that RS data may be classified as large data. As a result, we have implemented a Hadoop big data framework and detailed the steps necessary to analyse RS environmental data effectively. The editors of the ACM Journal of Information and data Quality are pleased to present a unique volume on quality evaluation and leadership in big data. After a thorough peer review procedure, 11 of the 27 original articles we received might be considered for publication in this issue's two sections. To accompany Part I, whereby we featured articles on machine studying and quality control in big data settings, we provide this editorial. Today, in the "big data" age, businesses must deal with massive volumes of data that change quickly and come from a wide variety of sources, including social media, unstructured information from a wide variety of websites, and raw inputs from sensors. In order to increase productivity, businesses are turning to big data solutions to streamline their procedures and quicken the decision-making process. The amount of data quality issues faced by big data professionals is staggering. These may be difficult to fix, and may even cause erroneous data analysis. It has become difficult to control quality with huge data, and previous studies have only touched on a few areas of the problem. Traditional methods of data quality management are inadequate for the more difficult task of managing the quality of large data. To protect cars and their drivers from attackers who could exploit this information, the transfer of sensitive data (such as position) must take place with specific security features. In dispersed, untruthful contexts like IoV networks, blockchain is a relatively new technology that assures trust between nodes using cryptographic techniques and consensus procedures. Blockchain may address and give answers to many issues in the Internet of Things and Services, hence there has been a lot of study into applying the first in the latter. One of the major restrictions of Blockchain implementation in IoV is that they must overcome the difficulty posed by IoV node resource limits, which do not adequate for the computational as well as energy needs of conventional Blockchain systems. Last but not least, these two technologies may be leveraged to establish smart city infrastructures, opening the door to novel application models and improved outcomes for end users.

## PROPOSED MODEL

### Problem Formulation

Problems with data quality are common in analytics and data management initiatives. Problems might arise from various entry errors, varied naming practices, and faulty data integration. However, the significance of the quality of data for big information applications grows when considering the increasing volume, diversity, and velocity of the data involved. The advantages of Big Data Quality are displayed in Fig. (**1**).

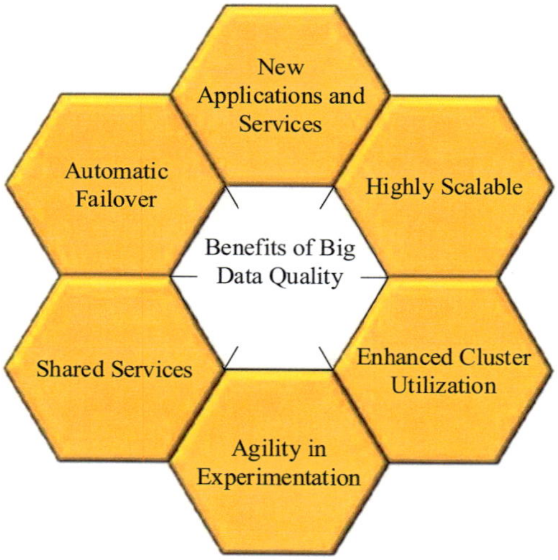


**Fig. (1).** Big data quality advantages.

Faisal Alam, new technologies lead at consultant EY Americas, proposed adding a fourth V for validity in big data governance projects due to the fact that quality problems with big data may generate a wide range of contextual concerns related to distinct applications, data kinds, platforms, and use cases.

How crucial high-quality data is for big data?

Problems with the quality of big data might cause not just flawed algorithms, but also potentially dangerous effects in the real world. Enterprise end customers will, at least, be less willing to trust derived data sets and applications. Data reliability and precision may also attract regulatory attention from governments if they factor into operational company choices.

The expenses associated with data management may rise if its quality is low, leading to problems including frequent remediation, increased resource requirements, and compliance concerns. It may also cause difficulties in making business judgements and projections.

How does large data affect the quality of data?

## Proposed Methodology

Bansal manages 100-person teams that produce and analyse several gigabytes of consumer data daily. When dealing with such a large volume of data, one must rethink traditional methods of assuring quality of data for big data while taking into account the following:

Scalability problems. Importing and inspecting data as was formerly common practice with traditional files and spreadsheets is impractical at best. Data management teams must create big data quality practices that include both historical and current data storage mechanisms, such as data lakes and real-time data streams.

Data forms that are intricate and ever-changing. Multiple dimensions, such as event kinds, user segments, programme versions, and device types, may be included in big data. Checks on hundreds or thousands of data slices are needed to properly map up the data quality issue, as stated by Bansal. As new events and characteristics are added, while others are removed, the data's original structure may shift.

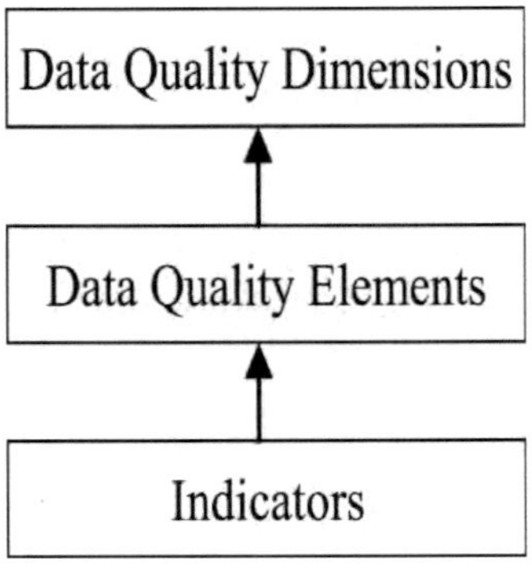


**Fig. (2).** Data quality directions.

Heavy information load. It is not feasible to manually examine fresh data in large data systems. Developing quality indicators that can be continuously monitored *versus* shifts in big data programmes while employing cases is essential for ensuring the quality of big data. Table **1** shows the big data quality Assessment Metric. Fig. (**2**) depicts Data Quality Directions.

**Table 1. Big Data Quality Assessment Metrices.**

| Dimensions | Elements | Indicators |
|---|---|---|
| 1) Availability | 1) Accessibility | ■ Whether a data access interface is provided. |
| | | ■ Data can be easily made public or easy to purchase. |
| | 2) Timeliness | ■ Within a given time, whether the data arrive on time. |
| | | ■ Whether data are regularly updated. |
| | | ■ Whether the time interval from data collection and processing to release meets requirements. |
| 2) Usability | 1) Credibility | ■ Data come from specialized organizations of a country, field, or industry. |
| | | ■ Experts or specialists regularly audit and check the correctness of the data content. |
| | | ■ Data exist in the range of known or acceptable values. |

*(Table 2) cont.....*

| Dimensions | Elements | Indicators | |
|---|---|---|---|
| 3) Reliability | 1) Accuracy | ■ | Data provided are accurate. |
| | | ■ | Data representation (or value) well reflects the true state of the source information. |
| | | ■ | Information (data) representation will not cause ambiguity. |
| | 2) Consistency | ■ | After data have been processed, their concepts, value domains, and formats still match as before processing. |
| | | ■ | During a certain time, data remain consistent and verifiable. |
| | | ■ | Data and the data from other data sources are consistent or verifiable. |
| | 3) Integrity | ■ | Data format is clear and meets the criteria. |
| | | ■ | Data are consistent with structural integrity |
| | | ■ | Data are consistent with content integrity. |
| | 4) Completeness | ■ | Whether the deficiency of a component will impact use of the data for data with multi-components. |
| | | ■ | Whether the deficiency of a component will impact data accuracy and integrity. |
| 4) Relevance | 1) Fitness | ■ | The data collected do not completely match the theme, but they expound one aspect. |
| | | ■ | Most datasets retrieved are within the retrieval theme users need. |
| | | ■ | Information theme provides matches with users' retrieval theme. |
| 5) Presentation Quality | 1) Readability | ■ | Data (content, format, *etc.*) are clear and understandable. |
| | | ■ | It is easy to judge that the data provided meet needs. |
| | | ■ | Data description, classification, and coding content satisfy specification and are easy to understand. |

## *Big Data Processing Steps*

Big data analysis allows for the mining of large datasets for a wealth of useful insights. Fig. (**2**) depicts the four stages that make up the big data processing pipeline:

- **Data Collection:** The whole operation rests on the shoulders of the enormous data gathering. The variety of data producers and the volume of data production are both growing as a result of advances in Internet technology, applications, and the widespread use of a wide variety of terminal devices. Methods for collecting system logs, network data, and other types of data are the backbone of big data.
- **Data Preprocessing:** The primary goals of big data preprocessing are data discovery, data extraction, and data cleaning. The heterogeneity of the data's structure makes it difficult to analyse since it was gathered using different

methods. Invalid data must be filtered out before analysis can proceed with any degree of confidence. This necessitates standardising the data format and clearing out any out-of-date information.

- **Data Storage:** There's more to "big data" than just a large amount of data. The answer must be sent and processed rapidly. Big data is characterised by variety because of the many data sources it draws from. Conventional database storage methods are inflexible in the face of enormous data. Any system designed to store or handle massive amounts of data must be backwards-compatible with previous versions of the data, hardware, and software. Fig. (**3**) shows Big Data Processing Issues.
- **Analysing the Data:** The next step in every system's data pipeline should be analysis. Big data analysis is the only way to gather the kind of smart, deep, useful knowledge we need. Big data analysis methods are becoming more vital at the big data processing stage due to the increasing prevalence of big data applications and the growing number and variety of big data properties.

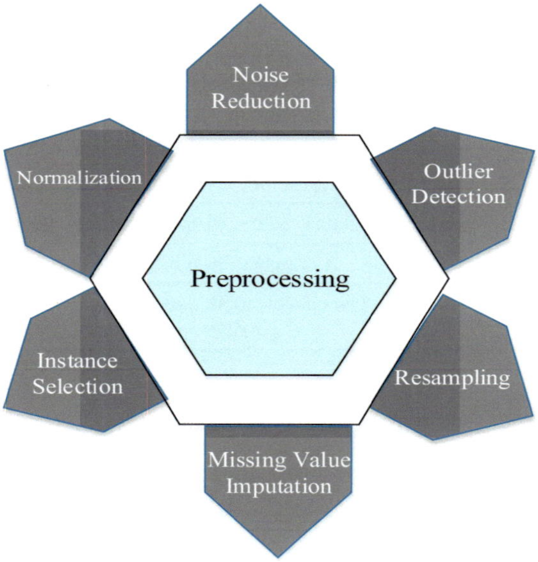


**Fig. (3).** Big data processing issues.

### *Big data quality challenges and issues*

Harmonising data classification systems. Data taxonomies and ontologies may have been developed and refined independently by several departments or firms prior to a merger. CRM, automation in marketing, marketing content administration, customer database, and lead qualification technique data were often gathered separately for each company. Big data quality may be severely tested when several disparate technologies are combined into one data structure to conduct unified campaigns. Keeping everything in check.

- New measurements, tools, and analyses are required for the task of locating the appropriate data. Case in point: deciding on a sample that fairly represents the population.
- Learning Machines The term "High-performance computing" (HPC) is used to describe any computational activity that requires more than one computer to complete a job. Advanced computational issues are often handled by supercomputers or clusters of computers. Analytics (Machine Learning) on Data.
- Data management and analytics are essential. To do analytics as well as leadership simultaneously, we will need computers that allow parallel machine learning due to the inherent differences between the two software and hardware requirements.
- The Requirement for High-Performance Parallel Algorithms Streaming and multiscale adaptive algorithms need effective parallel algorithms that can lower the temporal complexity from O (N2) to O (N).
- The Importance of a Safe Cloud Protecting and securely processing data in the cloud is an issue that needs fixing.

The processes of data cleansing, validation, and normalisation might potentially present difficulties in the quality of big data. For instance, one telecom firm developed models that cross-referenced network defect information, outage reports, as well as customer complaints to establish whether or not service disruptions might be localised.

Another crucial step in bringing order to the database is the process of data normalisation. In addition to making subsequent processes go more quickly, normalising a database also helps to effectively condense the database. The mathematical expression of the data normalisation procedures is as follows:

$$\mathfrak{y} = \frac{(|d_i| - (10^{n-1}) * (|A|))}{10^{n-1}} \quad \textbf{(1)}$$

Where, $d_i$ denotes $i^{th}$ data in dataset D, where n is the total number of records $d_i$. The letter A stands for the first data point $d_i$.

Finding discrepancies in data processing. Normalising and cleansing data for novel applications often require a combination of data preparation strategies. Erroneous, fragile, and impossible to replicate custom practices are not uncommon.

### *Best practices for managing big data quality*

- Orion's Balasubramanian cites are examples of best practices that reliably enhance big data's data quality.
- Obtain top-level buy-in for data governance initiatives.
- Form a multidisciplinary data governance group consisting of end users, analysts, architects, analyzers, and developers.
- Integrate data stewardship, proactive monitoring, and periodic assessments into your governance frameworks.
- Clarify how preexisting procedures and software implement data validation and business rules.
- Establish mechanisms for the assessment and approval of information as well as data items, and appoint data stewards for different business areas.
- To ensure that there is a single, consistent, and comprehensive definition of product or customer data throughout an organisation, effective master data management practices must be put in place.
- Data standards, terminology, and regulated vocabularies in the corporate world must be defined.
- The International Organisation for Standardisation, the World Health Organisation, and the Medical Dictionary for Regulation Actions have all created controlled vocabularies that should be more widely used.
- Wherever feasible, integrate massive data sets through interfaces with other systems to get rid of redundant information.

## EXPERIMENTAL RESULTS

Big data expands the Internet's potential, but it also introduces new challenges and potential pitfalls. This study primarily approaches the issues with the large-scale data processing process from the vantage point of data quality, recommending the system and using the system for forecasting as an example. Big Data, which consists of massive amounts of data, rapid data production, many data kinds, and so on, are all part of the efforts involved in processing big data. These characteristics add a great deal of complexity to Big Data analysis due to poor data quality. Hadoop distributed file system (HDFS) as well as other associated components, including Apache Hive, HBase, Oozie, Pig, and Zookeeper, are explored and described in this section as large data processing tools:

- **HDFS:** Data on the clusters is stored in a fault-tolerant distributed file system.
- **MapReduce:** It is a method of parallel programming used to share the workload of processing massive amounts of data among several nodes.
- **HBase:** Columnar NoSQL database with distributed read/write access.
- **Pig:** Hadoop Hive is an advanced programming language for working with and analysing Hadoop data.

- **Hive:** A DW programme that mimics SQL and uses a relational database model.
- **Sqoop:** A programme to move information from relational databases into Hadoop.
- **Oozie:** Management of interdependent Hadoop processes through orchestration and workflow.

Data visualisation is useful for assessing data quality since it reveals the locations of anomalies and unnecessary information. To avoid problems with soiled information, businesses should have some kind of data control, surveillance, or information management mechanism in place.

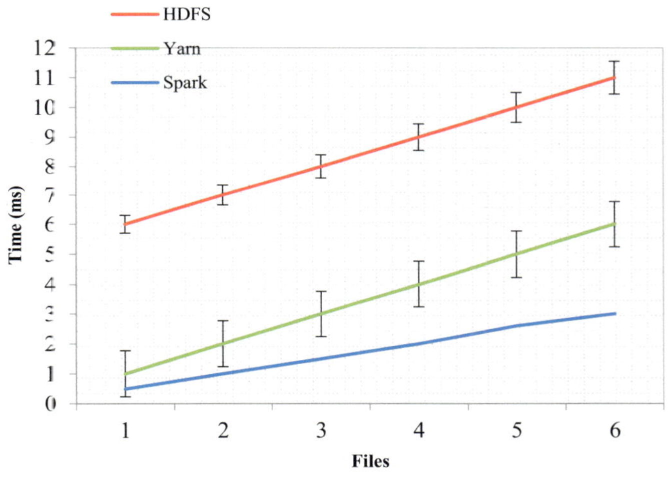


**Fig. (4).** Files *vs.* time (ms).

- When working with a large dataset or one that contains several types of information, it might be challenging to plot points of data on a chart for analysis.
- One solution is to group information into more granular groups, which may then be seen as a whole.
- Data "binning," or grouping, allows for more meaningful visualisation.

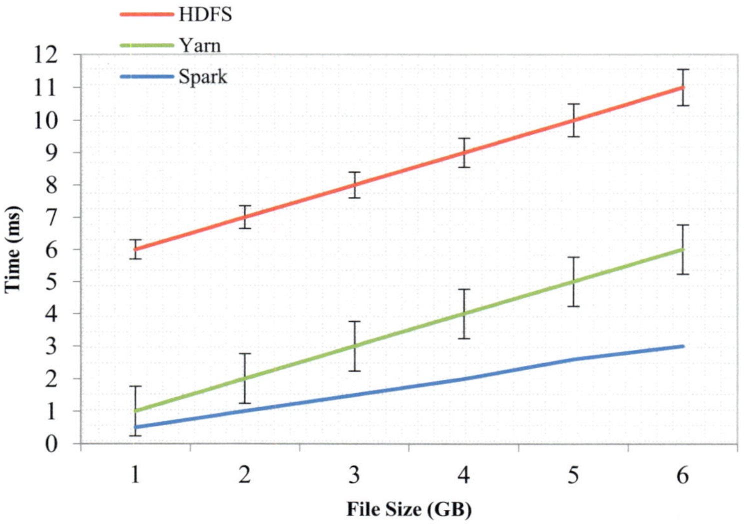


**Fig. (5).** Files size *vs.* time (ms).

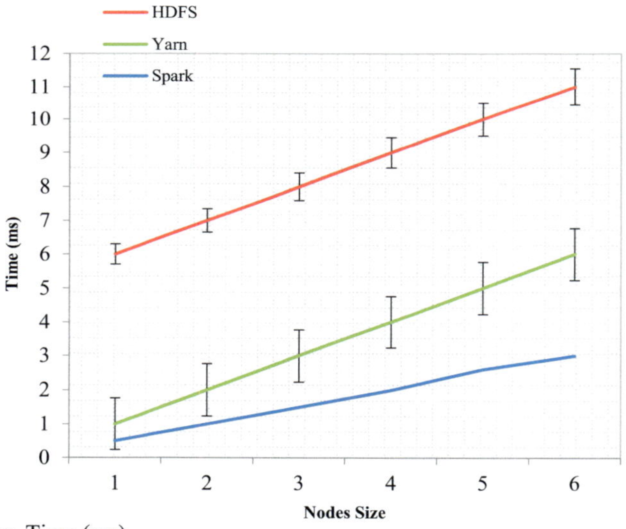


**Fig. (6).** Nodes size *vs.* Time (ms).

**Future Directions:** Having access to so much information from so many different places gives us a formidable tool for making the kinds of money-saving and revenue-generating choices that may make or break a business. Its potential to revolutionise business operations is unparalleled. While the big data revolution has brought with it certain challenges, these issues are not insurmountable with the correct tools. Companies are spending billions on big data initiatives due to increased demand. The issue of not having enough skilled workers to implement best practices will disappear in the future. Many different kinds of tools and services will be available at each stage of the big data process. There will be a flood of cloud-service providers. The providers of cloud services will face a great deal of competition. With the advent of personal clouds, we may no longer need physical file folders on our computers, since our information will follow us everywhere we go. Future demand for visual data tools for discovery will drive them to expand at a quicker rate than BI products. Self-service for end users of big data will soon be required of all businesses. On-premises data storage will be phased out in favour of that stored in the cloud Big Data and analytics (BDA) solutions. Cloud and on-premises hybrid deployments will become more important. Jobs related to big data will increase significantly in the next years. Data management as well as technology worldwide are moving towards a unified data platform. There will be a dramatic uptick in the creation and use of software that makes use of machine learning and other forms of advanced and predictive analytics. It is possible that the price of data may rise even higher, and businesses will start selling their information to competitors. In the future, there won't be a lot of opportunities to analyse occurrences using IoT analytics. Going through the data will be a regular occurrence. Stronger and more developed decision management systems will increase data consistency and improve outcomes. A tenfold increase in media analytics is possible. People will routinely use cognitive computing. In the long run, Hadoop will improve. We should expect the introduction of new technologies and solutions that can store, monitor, measure, and integrate any and all data types now in use. We are creating data anonymization, analysis, sharing, and management solutions for our own data. Fig. (**4**) depicts Files *vs.* Time (ms). Fig. (**5**) shows Files Size *vs.* Time (ms). Fig. (**6**) displays in Nodes Size *vs.* Time (ms).

## CONCLUSION

This paper discusses the issues and challenges that can arise at any stage of the big data processing lifecycle, including data collection, cleaning, aggregation, analysis, modelling, and interpretation, as well as possible solutions to these problems, including open issues, tools, and technologies. With improvements in data collecting, processing, and storage, we have reached the era of big data. The significant rise in the amount of data in many disciplines has made the effective processing of data a formidable problem. We need to fix these problems so that the data is more reliable. In order to better understand the potential issues that might arise throughout the Big Data processing process, this study uses the recommendation system and the forecasting system as examples. Large data, Big Data processing, forecasting, and recommendation systems were discussed. Various issues related to data quality in Big Data research are elaborated upon and analysed, including data quality, data preparation, data storage, data analysis, and others. We provide questions at each level, suggest answers, and then critically examine some outstanding issues. There is no way around our Big Data analysis. There are still limits in the current Big Data technology and tools that prevent them from providing a foolproof answer to Big Data concerns. The next step is to investigate the huge data issue and find ways to improve data quality in a follow-up research.

## REFERENCES

[1] M. Sakr, C. Ray, and C. Renso, "Big mobility data analytics: recent advances and open problems", *GeoInformatica,* vol. 26, no. 4, pp. 541-549, 2022. [http://dx.doi.org/10.1007/s10707-022-00483-0]

[2] S. Nazir, S. Khan, H.U. Khan, S. Ali, I. García-Magariño, R.B. Atan, and M. Nawaz, "A Comprehensive Analysis of Healthcare Big Data Management, Analytics and Scientific Programming", *IEEE Access,* vol. 8, pp. 95714-95733, 2020. [http://dx.doi.org/10.1109/ACCESS.2020.2995572]

[3] A.F. Neamah, H.K. Ibrahim, S.M. Darwish, and O.A. Hassen, "Big Data Clustering Using Chemical Reaction Optimization Technique: A Computational Symmetry Paradigm for Location-Aware Decision Support in Geospatial Query Processing", *Symmetry (Basel),* vol. 14, no. 12, p. 2637, 2022. [http://dx.doi.org/10.3390/sym14122637]

[4] I. Merelli, H. Pérez-Sánchez, S. Gesing, and D. D'Agostino, "Managing, analysing, and integrating big data in medical bioinformatics: open problems and future perspectives", *BioMed Res. Int.,* vol. 2014, pp. 1-13, 2014. [http://dx.doi.org/10.1155/2014/134023] [PMID: 25254202]

[5] V. Varadarajan, V. Neelanarayanan, R. Doyle, I.F. Al-Shaikhli, and S. Groppe, "Emerging Solutions in Big Data and Cloud Technologies for Mobile Networks", *Mob. Netw. Appl.,* vol. 24, no. 3, pp. 1015-1017, 2019. [http://dx.doi.org/10.1007/s11036-019-01229-3]

[6] A. Moreno, J. Molano-Pulido, J.E. Gómez-Morantes, and R.A. González, "ADACOP: A Big Data Platform for Open Government Data", *Proceedings of the 15th International Conference on Theory and Practice of Electronic Governance,* 2022. [http://dx.doi.org/10.1145/3560107.3560310]

[7] S. P. Yadav, and S. Yadav, "Mathematical implementation of fusion of medical images in continuous wavelet domain", *Journal of Advanced Research in dynamical and control system,* vol. 10, no. 10, pp. 45-54, 2019.

[8] J. Zhao, "Special issue on 2021 international conference on machine learning and big data analytics for iot security and privacy", *Neural Comput. Appl.,* vol. 35, no. 3, pp. 2025-2026, 2023. [http://dx.doi.org/10.1007/s00521-022-07706-3]

[9] C. Ya, and T. Yujian, *Discussion on the Construction of Regional Education Data Network and Key Issues in the Big Data Era,* 2019.

[10] P. Zhang, F. Xiong, J.Z. Gao, and J. Wang, *Data quality in big data processing: Issues, solutions and open problems,* 2017. [http://dx.doi.org/10.1109/UIC-ATC.2017.8397554]

[11] M. Ambigavathi, and D. Sridharan, "A Review of Channel Access Techniques in Wireless Body Area Network", *2017 Second International Conference on Recent Trends and Challenges in Computational Models (ICRTCCM),* pp. 106-110, 2017. [http://dx.doi.org/10.1109/ICRTCCM.2017.28]

[12] S.P. Yadav, and S. Yadav, "Fusion of Medical Images using a Wavelet Methodology: A Survey", In:

*IEIE Transactions on Smart Processing & Computing* vol. 8. The Institute of Electronics Engineers of Korea, 2019, no. 4, pp. 265-271. [http://dx.doi.org/10.5573/IEIESPC.2019.8.4.265]

[13] S.A. Aljawarneh, and J.A. Lara, "Editorial: Special Issue on Quality Assessment and Management in Big Data—Part I", *Journal of Data and Information Quality,* vol. 13, pp. 1-3, 2021. [JDIQ].

[14] P. Álvares, L. Silva, and N. Magaia, "Blockchain-Based Solutions for UAV-Assisted Connected Vehicle Networks in Smart Cities: A Review, Open Issues, and Future Perspectives", *Telecom,* 2021.

# CHAPTER 40

# Using Deep Learning Techniques to Detect Traffic Information in Social Media Texts

**Sourav Rampal**[1,*]

[1] *Centre for Interdisciplinary Research in Business and Technology, Chitkara University Institute of Engineering and Technology, Chitkara University, Punjab, India*

**Abstract:** Given the real-time and pervasive nature of social media, data mining for traffic-related insights is a newly emerging area of study. In this work, we discuss the challenge of mining social media for traffic-generating microblogs on Sina Weibo, the Chinese equivalent of Twitter. It is recast as a classification issue in short texts for machine learning. In the first step, we use a dataset of three billion microblogs and the continuous bag-of-word model to learn word embedding representations. Word embedding, as opposed to the standard one-hot vector representation of words, has been shown to be useful in natural language processing tasks because of its ability to capture semantic similarity between words. Then, we suggest feeding the learned word embeddings into convolutional neural networks (CNNs), long short-term memory (LSTM) models, and their combination LSTM-CNN to extract traffic-related microblogs. We evaluate the suggested techniques against state-of-the-art methods such as the support vector machine (SVM) model using a bag of n-gram features, the SVM model using word vector features, and the multi-layer perceptron model using word vector features. The proposed deep learning methods are shown to be useful in experiments.

**Keywords:** Deep learning techniques, Social media, Traffic information detection, Text mining.

## INTRODUCTION

User-generated information, especially that available on social networking platforms, is more important in today's culture. With the rise in popularity of social media platforms comes an increased need for transportation systems that can extract useful information about traffic conditions in real-time from users' posts. It has been demonstrated that deep learning algorithms excel in processing large volumes of text input and extracting relevant information [1, 2]. Traffic

* **Corresponding author Sourav Rampal:** Centre for Interdisciplinary Research in Business and Technology, Chitkara University Institute of Engineering and Technology, Chitkara University, Punjab, India;
E-mail: sourav.rampal.orp@chitkara.edu.in

mishaps are frustrating for drivers and must be found quickly so that traffic may resume its usual flow. Social media posts on traffic conditions are a gold mine of information [3]. It is possible that traffic statistics may be extracted from social media posts by using deep learning techniques and sophisticated neural network models that can learn from large amounts of training data [4]. These formulas might help us figure out if a piece of social media material includes any traffic-related information at all. A flood of geo-referenced data on localized occurrences may emerge *via* social media. Social media messages may also be mined for information, such as the location and severity of road accidents, thanks to their usage of these tools [5]. A deep learning-based information extraction approach (termed BERT-BiLSTM-CRF) is described and proven to surpass existing state-of-the-art methods [6] in their ability to create time-related data from social media discussions. Real-time traffic information made available by the efficient use of deep learning algorithms for traffic information identification from social media texts [7, 8] can help transportation systems better manage traffic, reduce congestion, and improve public safety. Therefore, in this era of Big Data, we can satisfy people's mobility needs by delving into and making the most of social media traffic data. Natural Language Processing (NLP), cloud and open platforms (*e.g.*, mobile Internet), and human-computer interfaces (HCI) are only some of the tools outlined in this study to mine social media for traffic data. In this study, we suggest a solution in the form of a model architectural design based on deep learning. A bidirectional LSTM method is used to handle the word level. While character recognition relies on the CNN approach. When combined with word embedding [9, 10], these two deep learning methods provide an F-measure of 0.789.

In this research, we present our work on employing convolutional neural networks (CNN), a long short-term memory (LSTM) model, and an LSTM-CNN with pre-trained word vectors to extract traffic-related tweets from Sina Weibo. Using three billion microblogs gathered from Sina Weibo between 2009 and 2011, the CBOW model is used to learn Chinese word vectors. Microblogs are classified as either traffic-relevant or traffic-irrelevant using a combination of convolutional neural networks (CNNs) and long short-term memory (LSTMs). The suggested approaches may make use of the semantics in microblogs and abstract deep features, making them superior to conventional one-hot word representations and usual feature-based text classification techniques. Experiments demonstrate the effectiveness of the offered strategies in identifying traffic-related microblogs. The following are the most significant results of this study: (i) We implement deep learning strategies for mining social media for traffic data. (ii) We apply the CBOW model to a dataset of 3 billion microblogs to get the word embedding, which captures word semantics, in contrast to previous approaches that extract traffic-relevant microblogs with bag-of-words characteristics. When compared to other models, we show that deep learning models are superior at recognizing data linked to traffic.

This paper's remaining sections are structured as follows.

In Section II

We examine current developments in research that mine traffic data from social media. The bulk of our methods, such as data collection and preprocessing, word vector models, and classification models, are detailed.

In Section III

In Section IV

We provide experimental verification of the suggested approaches.

Section V

Contains our last thoughts and recommendations for moving forward.

## RELATED WORK

The instantaneous and ubiquitous nature of social media has made traffic data mining a hot issue. This paper focuses on a specific subset of social media mining: the difficulty of extracting traffic-relevant microblogs from Sina Weibo (a Chinese microblogging site). Machine learning reframes it as a classification problem for brief texts. We begin by creating word embedding representations using the continuous bag-of-word model and a three billion microblog dataset. In contrast to the typical one-hot vector representation of words, word embedding has been found to be beneficial in natural language processing tasks and can capture semantic similarity between words. To extract traffic-related microblogs, we propose feeding the learned word embeddings into convolutional neural networks (CNNs), long short-term memory (LSTM) models, and their combination LSTM-CNN. We compare the proposed techniques with several others that have already been developed, such as the bag-of-n-grams feature SVM model, the word-vector feature SVM model, and the multi-layer perceptron feature SVM model. It has been demonstrated experimentally that the suggested deep-learning approaches are successful [11].

This study's goal is to evaluate urban development projects in Kuwait using social risk analysis theory. A case study of 17 incidents of social conflict on construction sites in Kuwait evaluated 12 aspects of social risk. Eight stakeholders associated with important societal risk factors were identified through a review of the literature and documented instances in Kuwait. We used Gephi and UNICET to create a network diagram depicting the relationships between potential social hazards and the people, organizations, and governments that might be impacted by those risks. Semi-structured interviews were also conducted with experts in the building industry. A thematic study of the social dangers associated with construction engineering was conducted. According to the SNA model's study [12], social hazards are strongly linked to problems including poor decision-making, untrustworthy governance, and inefficient administration.

The OSNs are becoming a fantastic venue for people to talk about items, offer advice, disseminate information, and promote their brands. Users of these sites pick the best social media tools for them based on their own needs for communication, amusement, and knowledge. User actions in online social networks include joining, interacting, and discovering new networks. Users' identities change based on the groups to which they belong. Depending on who they are, a user's motivations may change. The user's original goal could change as they adopt a new persona. In this study, we provide an introduction to OSN and discuss methods for predicting and recommending content to users in standalone and hybrid platforms [13].

This article investigates the use of AI in cybersecurity tactics to protect networks and data from intrusion. This page also provides a summary of the most significant studies examining the use of machine learning and deep learning to the field of cybersecurity. Data shows that machine learning and deep learning technologies play crucial roles in avoiding unauthorized access to computer systems and managing system penetration [14] by predicting and understanding the behavior and traffic of malicious software.

The text similarity approach, temporal relevance principles, and state machine diagram are used in this article to evaluate the level of data completeness for real-time traffic simulation. The simulation's start-up and continued functioning are dependent on the accuracy of the provided data. Based on the results of the evaluation, combining text similarity with the temporal relevance weighting strategy yields better results than either method alone. The study of the state diagram shows that control over the simulation's execution may be exercised at varying degrees of completeness of the information entities. The system transitions to the next stage once additional data items become available. The greater the range of possible simulation outcomes, the greater the number of information entities that may be accessed. This is because, as the simulation progresses, there is less ambiguity about the incident's location and/or onset time thanks to the more complete information entities [15].

## PROPOSED WORK

One of the primary ways that information is disseminated is through social media platforms, which are rapidly expanding in popularity. Real-time information extraction and analysis from social media data is a popular area of study. Transportation-related social media traffic studies often concentrate on three primary areas: event detection, prediction, and study of user sentiment.

### System Model

The methodological framework of this approach mainly includes some of the steps. The whole procedure is illustrated in Fig. (**1**).

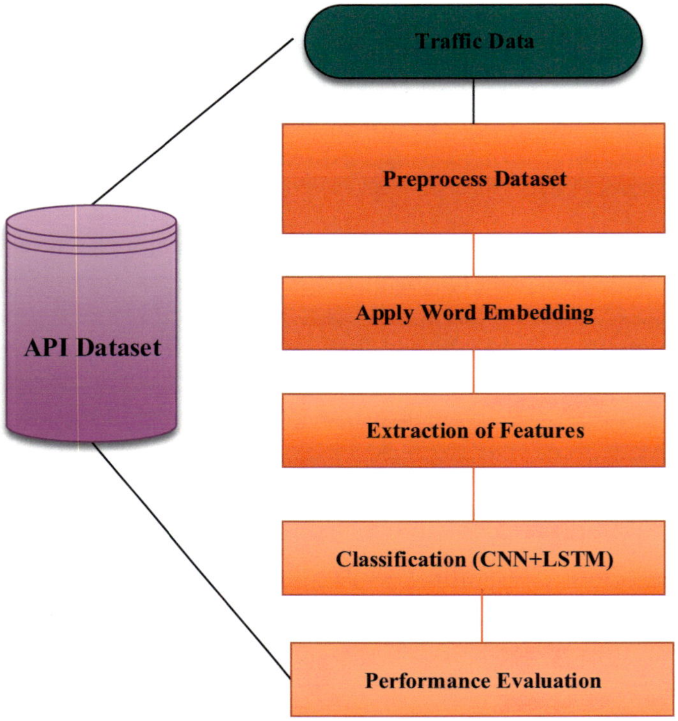


**Fig. (1).** System architecture.

### Data Collection and Text Pre-processing

Two methods exist for accessing the microblogs on Sina Weibo: asking APIs (Application Programming Interfaces) and web crawling. Officially, developers have access to API request forms, however, these forms are often not free and have access rate limitations. In this research, we used a technique based on spidering the Sina Weibo platform to gather information. In comparison to accessing official APIs, this method is free of charge but more thorough. First, we establish search parameters (*e.g.*, geographical coordinates, time range, keywords) to get raw microblogs. We then retrieve the server's return results, which are rendered as HTML source codes, by sending HTTP queries. We use regular expression matching to the response results and get microblogs that include the microblog ID, user ID, timestamp, geographic locations, and text. After that, the data are saved in a database in an organized format for further use.

## Feature Extraction and Word Embedding

Each word is often represented in NLP systems as a one-hot vector, which is an otherwise zero-valued vector with a single value of 1 at the place corresponding to the word. High dimensionality and sparsity characterize the one-hot representation. Semantic similarity between words is also lost in this form. Natural language processing tasks benefit greatly from word clustering, which is made possible by representing words in a continuous vector space. The learned vectors clearly incorporate numerous language regularities and patterns, making use of neural networks to generate the word representations particularly appealing and fascinating recently. Word embedding representations can be learned using either the CBOW model or the Skip-Gram approach. Both CBOW and Skip-Gram are comparable models, although they pursue distinct educational goals.

The CBOW model, depicted in Fig. (**1**), has as its learning objective the discovery of word vector representations that are useful for predicting the middle word under a context, while the Skip-Gram model aims to learn word vector representations by optimizing the probability of predicting neighboring words based on the middle word. Due to the similarity between the CBOW model and the Skip-Gram model, we will only be presenting the CBOW model's derivation here. Both the original CBOW model and the Skip-Gram model are quite computationally intensive, therefore their training methods make use of hierarchical softmax or (and) negative sampling. All of the vocabulary words (the unit leaves) are represented as binary nodes in a Huffman tree in hierarchical softmax. The output layer in the CBOW model with hierarchical softmax is a Huffman Tree. The hidden layer is calibrated to provide an average of the word vectors it receives as input.

$$h = \frac{1}{C}\sum_{u\in context(w)} v(u) \quad \textbf{(1)}$$

where $v(u)$ represents the vector of the word $u$, context $(w)$ is the set of contextual words of word $w$, and $C$ is the cardinality of the set context(w). Given the context, the conditional probability of the word $w$ is defined as:

$$p(w \mid \text{context}(w)) = \prod_{j=1}^{L(w)-1} [ \quad [h^{\mathrm{T}} v'_{n'_{w,j}} \quad \| \tag{2}$$

where $n_{m,j}$ is the $jn^{th}$ inner point from the root to word $w$ in the Huffman tree, $v_n'$ is the vector of inner point $n$, $L\ (w)\ \text{-}1$ is the length of the path in Huffman tree for word $w$, and III is a function defined as:

$$[ \quad [x] \quad ] = \sigma(x)^{d_{j+1}^{w}} \left[1 - \sigma(x)^{\left(1-d_{j+1}^{w}\right)}\right] \tag{3}$$

where $d_{j+1}{}^{w}$ is the $j^{th}$ bit of Huffman code for word $w$. It is straightforward to train the neural network by maximizing the conditional probability in (2) for a target word $w$. Take the logarithm of the conditional probability and define the loss function:

$$L = \log p(w \mid \text{context}(w)) \tag{4}$$

**Text Classification**

Microblog context can be learned by LSTM neural networks, and deep characteristics can be abstracted using CNN. Therefore, a strategy that combines LSTM and CNN to categorize microblog phrases is desirable. Above, we saw how the input word vectors are fed into the first LSTM layer; subsequent layers may also be LSTMs. The following layer is a convolution layer followed by a pooling layer, and this pattern can be repeated as many times as necessary. A fully connected neural network layer receives the abstract characteristics as input.

We hardcode the rectifier function as the activation of the convolutional layers.

$$\delta(\mathrm{x}) = \max(\mathrm{x}, 0) \tag{5}$$

Popular in convolutional neural networks, or CNNs, as an activation function. The Adam optimizer is used to find the optimal parameters such that the loss function, here specified as binary cross-entropy, may be reduced. We have run a battery of tests to determine how various design elements affect model performance, and this has allowed us to develop the most effective categorization models. Experiments are conducted where the impact of varying the filter number (10, 20, 50, 100, 150) is examined. Results show that more filters can improve performance, but training the model takes more time. It has been shown that the maximum number of filters in grid search is 150 and that models with 150 filters obtain almost the same performance as the model with 100 filters. Experiments are conducted with filter lengths of 2, 3, 4, 5, 6, and 10 to determine their effects. The outcomes show that adjusting the filter length does not significantly enhance performance on our dataset. Grid search is performed on the number of convolutional layers, the length of their filters, and the pooling approach to find the optimal model. You may adjust the filter length from 2 to 6 with a stride of 1, and the filter number can be anywhere from 20 to 150. Between maximal pooling and average pooling, the latter is what is picked. When comparing the model's performance with and without a vanilla hidden layer inserted between the top pooling layer and the top output layer, we found that the latter was preferable.

## RESULTS AND DISCUSSION

Sina Weibo was manually searched using predetermined keywords to obtain the information used to categorize microblogs about traffic as either relevant or irrelevant. The microblogs are then classified by hand into two groups: those that are useful for driving traffic, and those that are not. Five thousand candidate microblogs are then assigned to the traffic-relevant class, and six thousand are selected at random from the remaining collection of microblogs, which includes all candidate microblogs outside the traffic-relevant ones. Five thousand traffic-relevant microblogs and six thousand traffic-irrelevant microblogs make up the final dataset used to train classifiers. Words from the manually annotated dataset were used to compile a vocabulary dictionary, with the dictionary's index serving as a unique identifier for each term. Each microblog is converted into a list of indexes for individual words. Each microblog's word index sequence used to train the classifier is padded to the same length before being fed into a deep neural network. The longest word chains we found in our tests were 156 words long. Each sequence has zeroes added to the end until it reaches a total of 156. The attributes of a microblog would be supplied into classification models as a 156 by 200 matrix due to the 200-dimensionality of the word vector. In the absence of any explicit indication to the contrary, all of the models used in this study will use this feature matrix as input.

The accuracy, recall, and F-measure are the three statistical measures used to assess the quality of the proposed deep neural network models. These indices are frequently employed in classifier performance analysis. These three indices are described in Table 1. For a given class with label l, the true positive (TP) index indicates the total number of instances correctly assigned with label l, the false positive (FP) index indicates the total number of instances incorrectly assigned with the label l, and the false negative (FN) index indicates the total number of instances incorrectly assigned with label l. All of these indices are class-specific. The accuracy of a classifier is quantified by its precision, while its efficiency is represented by its recall. The F-measure is a weighted harmonic mean of accuracy and recall that provides a compromise between the two. F-measure, or F1 score when =1, is a popular statistic for assessing the quality of classification models. Ten-fold cross-validation is used to report all performance indices below. The loss function in the LSTM model is also specified as binary cross-entropy. The loss function is minimized using the RMSprop optimizer. We have undertaken a number of experiments to investigate how changing the size of the LSTM hidden states and the learning rate affects the model's performance during training. Experiments are conducted in which the influence of a learning rate on model performance is investigated by selecting a learning rate between 0.01 and 0.05 with a stride of 0.01. During training, experiments suggest that a reduced learning rate leads to greater performance in recall and F1 score. Experiments are conducted using LSTM hidden state sizes of 5, 10, 20, and 50 to determine their impact on model performance. After 30 training iterations, we discovered that models with 5 and 10 LSTM hidden state units attain approximately the same performance as those with 20 and 50 LSTM hidden state units. A grid search is used to find the best LSTM model. We set the LSTM's hidden state size to 5, 10, and 20 and the learning rate to 0.01-0.03 with a 0.01-0.01 step size. We also investigate whether adding a second LSTM layer might yield better results. The model with two stacked LSTM layers, 10 output units, and a 0.01 learning rate achieves the highest F1 score in the experiments. The LSTM layer serves as the foundation of the LSTM-CNN architecture. After that comes a maximum pooling layer and a convolutional layer. The hidden state size of an LSTM can be set to any value between 5 and 50. The filter length for the convolutional layer may be anywhere from 2 to 6, and the filter number can be anywhere from 10 to 100, with a stride of 1. The rate of learning can be set anywhere between 0.01 and 0.03, in 0.01 increments. The optimal model for the F1 score is obtained by grid search, and its parameters are reported in Table **1**.

**Table 1. Performance metrics for comparison.**

| Learning Rate | Embedding Scheme | Precision | Recall | F-measure | Accuracy |
|---|---|---|---|---|---|
| 0.01 | SVM | 94.0 | 93.0 | 93.5 | 93.5 |
| | CNN | 90.0 | 91.8 | 90.9 | 91.0 |
| | LSTM | 89,4 | 89.9 | 89,6 | 89.7 |
| | CNN-LSTM | 89.0 | 88.4 | 88.7 | 88.7 |
| 0.02 | SVM | 95,0 | 94.5 | 94.7 | 94.7 |
| | CNN | 91.0 | 93.3 | 92.1 | 92.2 |
| | LSTM | 90.0 | 90.9 | 90.4 | 90.5 |
| | CNN-LSTM | 90,0 | 89.1 | 89.5 | 89.5 |

*(Table 1) cont.....*

| Learning Rate | Embedding Scheme | Precision | Recall | F-measure | Accuracy |
|---|---|---|---|---|---|
| 0.03 | SVM | 90.8 | 93.0 | 91.9 | 92.0 |
| | CNN | 89.5 | 90.4 | 90.0 | 90.0 |
| | LSTM | 89.0 | 89.8 | 89.4 | 89.4 |
| | CNN-LSTM | 88.5 | 89.1 | 88.8 | 88.9 |
| 0.04 | SVM | 95.0 | 94.5 | 94.7 | 94.7 |
| | CNN | 93.5 | 91.2 | 92.3 | 92.2 |
| | LSTM | 92.5 | 91.1 | 91.8 | 91.7 |
| | CNN-LSTM | 90.5 | 91.0 | 91.1 | 91.2 |
| 0.05 | SVM | 93.9 | 93.2 | 93.5 | 93.5 |
| | CNN | 91.8 | 92.1 | 91.9 | 91.9 |
| | LSTM | 91.2 | 91.4 | 91.3 | 91.4 |
| | CNN-LSTM | 91,2 | 90.8 | 90.9 | 90.9 |

## CONCLUSION

In this article, we looked at the burgeoning field of social transportation, which is focused on mining social media for traffic data. In order to identify Sina Weibo microblogs about traffic, we presented deep learning techniques. To categorize brief texts on Sina Weibo, we employed word embedding representation of words and used convolutional neural networks (CNNs), long short-term memory networks (LSTM networks), and LSTM-CNNs. Using 3 billion microblogs gathered from Sina Weibo between 2009 and 2011, we were able to obtain word embedding with continuous vector representation of words using the CBOW model. Word embeddings, in contrast to one-hot vector representations, preserve semantic connections between words. To train CNN, LSTM, and LSTM-CNN, the word embeddings were used. To find the optimal architecture for CNN, LSTM, and LSTM-CNN, we did a grid search and analyzed the impact of model architecture and hyperparameters on model performance. The suggested deep learning approaches using word embeddings have been shown to outperform the state-of-the-art methods in experimental settings. There are a number of ways in which the approach might be improved and expanded upon for use in future research. To begin, we will expand our collection of microblogs to better organize the many that pertain to traffic incidents, traffic conditions, and so forth. Second, raw microblogs will have granular elements, such as where and when traffic incidents occurred, retrieved from them. In addition, we will integrate data from social media platforms and conventional traffic detectors to enhance both short- and long-term traffic forecasting.

## REFERENCES


[1] B. Shi, and H. Wang, "An AI-enabled approach for improving advertising identification and promotion in social networks", *Technol. Forecast. Soc. Change,* vol. 188, p. 122269, 2023. [http://dx.doi.org/10.1016/j.techfore.2022.122269]

[2] V.S. Bakkialakshmi, and T. Sudalaimuthu, "Anomaly Detection in Social Media Using Text-Mining and Emotion Classification with Emotion Detection", In: *8th International Conference, ICCR 2021* Mandya, India Cham., 2023, pp. 67-78.

[3] J. Jonnalagadda, and M. Hashemi, "A Deep Learning-based Traffic Event Detection From Social Media", *2021 IEEE 22nd International Conference on Information Reuse and Integration for Data Science (IRI),* pp. 1-8, 2021. [http://dx.doi.org/10.1109/IRI51335.2021.00007]

[4] S. Saranya, and G. Usha, "Forensic Analysis of Online Social Network Data in Crime Scene Investigation", In: *In Artificial Intelligence and Blockchain in Digital Forensics* River Publishers, 2023, pp. 183-209.

[5] S. P. Yadav, B. S. Bhati, D. P. Mahato, and S. Kumar, "Federated Learning for IoT Applications", *EAI/Springer Innovations in Communication and Computing. Springer International Publishing,* 2022. [http://dx.doi.org/10.1007/978-3-030-85559-8]

[6] K. Ma, Y. Tan, M. Tian, X. Xie, Q. Qiu, S. Li, and X. Wang, "Extraction of temporal information from social media messages using the BERT model", *Earth Sci. Inform.,* vol. 15, no. 1, pp. 573-584, 2022. [http://dx.doi.org/10.1007/s12145-021-00756-6]

[7] M. Anedda, M. Fadda, R. Girau, G. Pau, and D. Giusto, "A social smart city for public and private mobility: A real case study", *Comput. Netw.,* vol. 220, p. 109464, 2023. [http://dx.doi.org/10.1016/j.comnet.2022.109464]

[8] K. Vassakis, E. Petrakis, I. Kopanakis, and J. Makridis, "Big data analytics on location-based social networks for knowledge generation in tourism - the case of Crete Island", *Int. J. Technol. Mark.,* vol. 17, no. 1, pp. 99-123, 2023. [http://dx.doi.org/10.1504/IJTMKT.2023.127350]

[9] S.P. Yadav, and S. Yadav, "Fusion of Medical Images using a Wavelet Methodology: A Survey", In: *In IEIE Transactions on Smart Processing & Computing* vol. 8. The Institute of Electronics Engineers of Korea, 2019, pp. 265-271.*4* vol. 8. The Institute of Electronics Engineers of Korea, 2019, pp. 265-271. [http://dx.doi.org/10.5573/IEIESPC.2019.8.4.265]

[10] M.R. Alifi, and S.H. Supangkat, "Information Extraction of Traffic Condition from Social Media using Bidirectional LSTM-CNN", *2018 International Seminar on Research of Information Technology and Intelligent Systems (ISRITI),* pp. 637-640, 2018. [http://dx.doi.org/10.1109/ISRITI.2018.8864265]

[11] Y. Chen, Y. Lv, X. Wang, L. Li, and F.Y. Wang, "Detecting Traffic Information From Social Media Texts With Deep Learning Approaches", *IEEE Trans. Intell. Transp. Syst.,* vol. 20, no. 8, pp. 3049-3058, 2019. [http://dx.doi.org/10.1109/TITS.2018.2871269]

[12] S. P. Yadav, and S. Yadav, "Mathematical implementation of fusion of medical images in continuous wavelet domain", *Journal of Advanced Research in dynamical and control system,* vol. 10, no. 10, pp. 45-54, 2019.

[13] N. A. Patel, and N. Nanavati, *A State of the Art Review on User Behavioral Issues in Online Social Networks,* 2023.

[14] M. Mijwil, I.E. Salem, and M.M. Ismaeel, "The Significance of Machine Learning and Deep Learning Techniques in Cybersecurity: A Comprehensive Review", *Iraqi Journal For Computer Science and Mathematics,* vol. 4, no. 1, pp. 87-101, 2023.

[15] E.T. Putri, J.L. Buliali, and M. Ermawati, "Real-time Detection of Data Completeness Degree for Traffic Simulation Using Text Similarity and Time Relevance of Data from Social Media", *2nd International Conference on Informatics and Computational Sciences (ICICoS),* pp. 1-6, 2018. [http://dx.doi.org/10.1109/ICICOS.2018.8621644]

# CHAPTER 41

# Deep Sentiment Classification in COVID-19 Using LSTM Recurrent Neural Network

**Jatin Khurana**[1,*]

[1] *Centre for Interdisciplinary Research in Business and Technology, Chitkara University Institute of Engineering and Technology, Chitkara University, Punjab, India*

**Abstract:** Users (people/patients) concerned about health concerns have an easy outlet in online medical forums along with other public social media on the Internet. The World Health Organization declared a global public health emergency in response to the emergence of a new coronavirus (infection which causes the disease termed COVID-19) in late December 2019. In this research, we employed a natural language processing (NLP) technique based on topic modeling to automatically extract COVID-19-related talks from social media and discover numerous concerns linked to COVID-19 from public viewpoints. As an added bonus, we look into the possibility of employing a long short-term memory (LSTM) recurrent neural network to accomplish the same task with COVID-19 remarks. Our research highlights the value of incorporating public opinion and appropriate computational approaches into the process of learning about and making decisions on COVID-19. The trials also showed that the study model was able to reach an accuracy of 81.15 percent, which is greater than the accuracy attained by many other popular machine-learning methods for COVID-19 sentiment classification.

**Keywords:** COVID-19, LSTM, NLP, Topic discovery model.

## INTRODUCTION

Misinformation spread *via* social media in the wake of the COVID-19 pandemic had a negative effect on people, inducing fear and skepticism of the unknown [1]. Insights in to vaccination recipients' thoughts and sentiments can be gained by sentiment analysis [2], especially when the RNN-LSTM deep learning approach is used. Sentiment analysis has made great strides forward thanks to the advent of mature deep learning neural networks in the field of natural language processing (NLP) [3, 4]. A novel approach has been published [5] that employs natural language processing and deep learning to automatically classify the tone of

* **Corresponding author Jatin Khurana:** Centre for Interdisciplinary Research in Business and Technology, Chitkara University Institute of Engineering and Technology, Chitkara University, Punjab, India;
E-mail: jatin.khurana.orp@chitkara.edu.in

tweets. This research focuses on the many text representation strategies needed to solve text categorization challenges [6]. The purpose of this study is to illuminate the range of emotions experienced by people throughout the world in response to the COVID-19 pandemic [7]. Since so much information and opinions are generated, disseminated, and carried out every day *via* the Internet and other media, this is an active field of study. Latent Dirichlet allocation and two-layer bidirectional long short-term memory (LSTM) are used to extract aspects of a text and classify sentiments, respectively. For tweaking model hyperparameters, the hill-climbing approach is suggested [8]. Using the Twitter API, we can trawl for data, which we then gather and compare using standard Machine Learning methods. In terms of accuracy, precision, and recall, the Support Vector Machine is superior to other techniques [9]. The recurrent neural network achieved an accuracy of 92.70 and 91.24 percent on the COVID-19 dataset. Bi-LSTM and GRU both performed at 92.48% and 93.03% accuracy for the categorization of vaccination tweets, respectively. When faced with a future pandemic, healthcare providers and governments can benefit from the existing models [10].

- RQ1) How can key principles in natural language processing techniques, such as topic modeling, be used in online discussions to expose different difficulties linked to COVID-19?
- RQ2) What is the best way to find out which way people on COVID-19 feel about things?
- RQ3) How effective are several machine learning algorithms for determining the emotional tone of online discussions related to COVID-19, and which method is most effective?

In order to get answers to these concerns, we looked at the public opinions of Redditors on Reddit and analyzed their comments about COVID-19 to discover sentiment and semantic concepts linked to COVID-19. In particular, we employed a topic-modeling approach to natural language processing (NLP) to automatically extract COVID-19-related talks from social media and discover numerous concerns linked to COVID-19 from public opinion. The following are the most significant results of this study: We introduce a structured, NLP-based methodology that can glean important subjects from Reddit threads on COVID-19.

For the purpose of sentiment categorization of COVID-19-related comments, we present a deep learning model based on Long Short-Term Memory (LSTM), which outperforms many other well-known machine learning approaches. As part of our core study into COVID-19, we monitor Reddit for relevant discussions and identify emerging themes.

We analyze the emotion and opinion of COVID-19 comments from 10 different subreddits and determine their polarity. Our research highlights the value of incorporating public opinion and appropriate computational approaches into the process of learning about and making decisions on COVID-19. This paper follows the general outline below.

We begin with a primer on the basics of healthcare discussion boards on the web. In part 2, we discuss COVID-19-related concerns and compare and contrast other relevant publications.

In Section 3, We detail the NLP and deep-learning techniques used on the COVID-19 comments database, as well as the data pre-processing procedures we used. The analysis and commentary follow. Finally, we wrap off by discussing the future of this study and other NLP-based efforts to analyze the online community surrounding COVID-19.

## RELATED WORK

This article explores the use of online data for the study of public opinion's emotional leanings *via* the lens of textual sentiment categorization research. Because of its superior semantic representation and its ability to deal with words that might have various meanings, the BERT (Bidirectional Encoder Representation from Transformers) model is used as a tool for text vectorization in this study. In order to simplify and speed up the processing of multi-label data, the BR (Binary Relevance) method is used. This technique takes a multi-label classification problem and breaks it down into many binary classification problems. For further text feature extraction, researchers have developed a BiLSTM-Attention model that combines bidirectional long- and short-term memory networks with the attention mechanism. The BiLSTM-Attention model's efficacy is demonstrated through an analysis of its experimental results. The work addresses the problem of an uneven data set by adjusting the loss function and other parameters to improve classification accuracy. In conclusion, this research offers a strategy for undertaking sentiment analysis with little wasted effort by leveraging state-of-the-art methods like BERT and BiLSTM-attention models [11].

Worldwide lockdowns were implemented due to the global spread of the COVID-19 epidemic. Several pharmaceutical companies, notably Pfizer, Moderna, and AstraZeneca, have produced vaccines against COVID-19. However average people have begun discussing the efficacy and safety of these vaccinations on social media sites like Twitter. The tweets were acquired by researchers using a Twitter API access token and then analyzed using natural language processing methods. The tweets were then classified into favorable, negative, and neutral categories using a supervised KNN classification algorithm to reflect the general public's opinion. A total of 47.29% of replies were favorable, 37.50% were negative, and 15.21% were neutral for Pfizer; 46.16% were positive, 40.71% were negative, and 13.13% were neutral for Moderna, and 40.08% were positive, 40.06% were negative, and 13.86% were neutral for AstraZeneca [12].

The risk of serious bleeding recurrence is elevated in patients with cardiovascular disease who are on anticoagulant treatment. Adverse event identification in electronic health record notes can help improve drug safety monitoring. Researchers developed an NLP technique to analyze EHR notes for signs of bleeding and assess whether or not a particular text indicates a bleeding event. An annotated corpus of 878 EHR notes was used to train and evaluate a hybrid convolutional neural network (CNN) and long short-term memory (LSTM) auto-encoder (HCLA) model. The HCLA model outperformed competing CNN and auto-encoder algorithms at detecting blood loss events [13].

The exponential growth in daily internet users is truly remarkable. It is quite concerning that more inappropriate content is being shared online by individuals of all demographics. As the study of deep learning has progressed, more researchers have begun using deep neural networks for broad control purposes. Recently, deep networks, particularly in particular the recurrent neural network (RNN) and its variants, have been preferred over traditional shallow networks for usage in a wide range of applications, including NLP. This research looks into the problem of hate speech on the internet. We propose a language tactic symptom matrix (LTSM)-based categorization method to assist in differentiating between hate speech and offensive language. This approach demonstrates how to use word embeddings with LSTM and Bi-LSTM neural networks to detect hate speech on Twitter. The best LSTM network classifier achieved an accuracy of 86% when an early termination condition was based on the loss function [14].

Utilizing Neural Language Models, the authors provide a straightforward and effective method for text classification utilizing just unsupervised word representations and no supervised training. Our method employs a Recurrent Neural Network with Long Short-Term Memory (RNN-LSTM) and pre-defined word vectors to classify phrases. We propose that an unsupervised neural language model's word vectors may be used to improve the RNN-LSTM's performance in Natural Language Processing (NLP). The syntactic and semantic relationships between words are represented more accurately as a result of our method. We show that combining a simple RNN-LSTM with word2vec yields impressive results in IMDB. Results from Stanford's Sentiment Analysis [15].

## PROPOSED WORK

### System Overview

An unsupervised topic model and a collaborative deep-learning model based on LSTN RNN are proposed for analyzing comments from sub-reddits about COVID-19; this section outlines the methodology utilized to analyze these primary contributions. Using sentiment and semantic analysis, the created system is depicted in Fig. (**1**) mines and analyzes opinions expressed in online discussions on COVID-19.

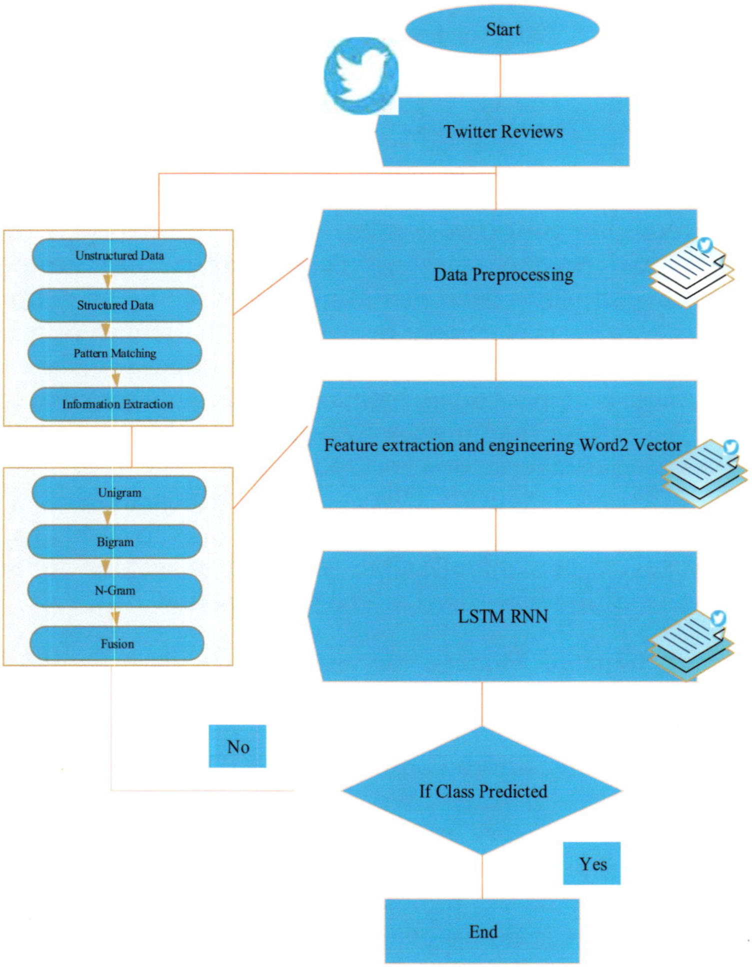


**Fig. (1).** System flowchart.

## Preparing the Input Data

Reddit is an American social media platform that serves as a discussion forum and content rating aggregate. Users may discuss topics like COVID-19 and more by asking questions, making comments, and responding to one another on this social networking platform. Various "sub-reddits" (user-created categories) categorize the posts further, with topics including news, science, healthcare, video, literature, fitness, cuisine, and image sharing. When researching COVID-19-related health concerns, this website is an excellent resource. In order to create this model, this study leverages an existing dataset to analyze the discussion surrounding COVID-19 in 10 different sub-reddits.

## Removing Noise and Stop-Words

In natural language processing (NLP), removing stop words is a crucial first step. In addition, we reduced the size of the feature area by getting rid of unnecessary words. Articles, conjunctions, pronouns, and connecting verbs are some of the most often occurring terms in the text comments, although they typically provide no value and have little impact on the output. Here are a few: am, is, are, they, the, these, he, she, it, he, she, it, them.

## Classification

In the last stage of this approach, an LSTM model was used to analyze Reddit posts on COVID-19 in an effort to identify the underlying sentiment. We created two LSTM layers and used the Glove-50 dimension for pre-learned embeddings, both of which were trained on a massive collection of user comments on COVID-19. Pre-trained embeddings are converted from their original format into vectors of a specified dimension in order to analyze the text from the COVID-19-related remarks. In addition, a matrix may be constructed from the letters in a COVID-19 remark by multiplying its dimension by the number of characters in the comment.

The existing time stamp input is xt, and the output gate is i.

$$i_t = \sigma(W_i * [h_{t-1}, x_t] + b_i). \quad \textbf{(1)}$$

The data that can be given to the cell were chosen using this equation. The forget gate $f_t$ in Equation (2) decides which data from the input side of the previous memory should be ignored:

$$f_t = \sigma(W_i * [h_{t-1}, xt] + b_i). \quad \textbf{(2)}$$

In Equation (3), tanh normalizes the values in the range between -1 and 1, where $C$ is the candidate for the cell state at the timestamp, which controls the cell *(t)* updates:

$$\underline{C} = \tanh(W_c * [h_{t-1}, x_t] + b_c),$$
$$C_t = f_t \times C_{t-1} + i_t \times \underline{C}. \tag{3}$$

The output layer $o_t$ upgrades both the hidden layer $h_{t-1}$ and the output layer according to Equation (4):

$$o_t = \sigma(W_o * [h_{t-1}, x_t] + b_o),$$
$$h_t = o_t \times \tanh(C_t). \tag{4}$$

## RESULTS AND DISCUSSION

There were 338,666 comments about COVID-19 in the training set and 112,888 in the testing set. Using the Support Vector Machine (SVM), Naive Bayes (NB), Logistic Regression (LR), and K Nearest Neighbors (KNN) techniques we compared the proposed LSTM model to other supervised machine-learning approaches.

$$\text{Accuracy} = \frac{T^p + T^n}{T^p + F^p + T^n + F^n} \tag{5}$$

where, $T^p$ indicates the rate of true positives, $T^n$ represents the rate of true negatives, $F^p$denotes the rate of false positives, and $F^n$ is the rate of false negatives. 2) PRECISION The maximum possible degree of accuracy is represented by Eq. 24, which is referred to as "precision."

$$\text{Precision} = \frac{T^p}{T^p + F^p} \tag{6}$$

3 RECALL Eq. 25 defines recall as the proportion of correct diagnoses relative to the sum of correct diagnoses and false negatives.

$$\text{Recall} = \frac{T^p}{Tp + F^n} \tag{7}$$

To implement Machine learning algorithms for sentiment categorization, yet, we made use of the Scikit-learn package4, a Python toolkit that provides access to a wide variety of machine-learning techniques written in Python. Since these approaches are so well-known for their high accuracy and efficacy for sentiment classification in natural language processing, we decided to apply them to COVID-19 sentiment classification. The accuracy of the best model for labeling a COVID-19 comment as extremely favorable, positive, negative, or neutral is displayed in the figure below. Our LSTM-based method, which assigned all COVID-19 comments to the majority class, outperformed conventional machine learning techniques with an accuracy of 81.15 percent. To get a sense of how people as a whole feel about the tragedy, we think sentiment and semantic tools might be useful.

As a limiting factor, this study only included texts written in English. This means that feedback provided in other languages is not reflected in the final tally. In addition, only comments collected between January 20, 2020, and March 19, 2020, were included in this study. Therefore, the timeliness of our results may have been slightly impacted by the time lapse between the period in which the research was being performed and the time frame of our study. Our ability to glean useful insights from online discussions on COVID-19 is attributed, in part, to the systematic framework we developed by merging natural language processing (NLP) with deep-learning algorithms based on topic modelling and an LSTM model. In addition to helping academics and physicians better understand how individuals behave under pressure, statistical contributions like these may be used to determine the positive and bad acts of an online community and to collect user feedback. To further explore the potential of hybrid fuzzy deep-learning algorithms for sentiment level categorization as a unique approach to recovering significant latent subjects from public comments, we aim to conduct further evaluations of various social media platforms like Twitter.

## CONCLUSION

As far as we are aware, this is the first study to investigate how COVID-19 forum discussions relate to certain semantic subjects. However, the primary objective of this study was to demonstrate a unique application for NLP based on an LSTM model to find important latent topics and sentiment-comment classification on COVID-19-related concerns from healthcare forums, such as sub-reddits. We hope that this paper's findings will help researchers and policymakers better grasp the challenges posed by COVID-19. Our results may also be useful in refining public health service and intervention methods in response to the COVID-19 pandemic.

## REFERENCES

[1] A. Qdroo, and M. Baykara, "A New Approach to Detect Fake News Related to Covid-19 Pandemic Using Deep Neural Network", *Journal of Applied Science and Technology Trends,* 2022.

[2] S. P. Yadav, B. S. Bhati, D. P. Mahato, and S. Kumar, "Federated Learning for IoT Applications", In: *EAI/Springer Innovations in Communication and Computing.*, 2022. [http://dx.doi.org/10.1007/978-3-030-85559-8]

[3] P. Cen, K. Zhang, and D. Zheng, "Sentiment Analysis Using Deep Learning Approach", *Journal on Artificial Intelligence,* 2020.

[4] M. Al-Khazaleh, M. Alian, M.M. Biltawi, and B. Al-Hazaimeh, "Sentiment Analysis for People's Opinions about COVID-19 Using LSTM and CNN Models ", *International Journal of Online and Biomedical Engineering (iJOE),* 2023.

[5] A. Santhoshini, A. Shirisha, and T. Meghana, "Text classification using deep learning", *International Journal For Innovative Engineering and Management Research,* 2022.

[6] D. Patil, R. Lokare, and S. Patil, "Privacy Preserving Document Classification using Convolution Neural Network- A Deep Learning Approach", *5th International Conference on Advances in Science and Technology (ICAST),* pp. 215-219, 2022. [http://dx.doi.org/10.1109/ICAST55766.2022.10039513]

[7] S.P. Yadav, and S. Yadav, "Fusion of Medical Images in Wavelet Domain: A Discrete Mathematical Model", In: *In Ingeniería Solidaria Universidad Cooperativa de Colombia- UCC* vol. 14. , 2018, no. 25, pp. 1-11. [http://dx.doi.org/10.16925/.v14i0.2236]

[8] N. Pathik, and P. Shukla, "An efficient sentiment analysis using topic model based optimized recurrent neural network", *Int. J. Smart Sensing Intell. Syst.,* vol. 14, no. 1, pp. 1-12, 2021. [http://dx.doi.org/10.21307/ijssis-2021-011]

[9] G.A. Sandag, A.M. Manueke, and M. Walean, "“Sentiment Analysis of COVID-19 Vaccine Tweets in Indonesia Using Recurrent Neural Network (RNN) Approach", *2021 3rd International Conference on Cybernetics and Intelligent System (ICORIS),* pp. 1-7, 2021. [http://dx.doi.org/10.1109/ICORIS52787.2021.9649648]

[10] B.S. Ainapure, R.N. Pise, P. Reddy, B. Appasani, A. Srinivasulu, M.S. Khan, and N. Bizon, "Sentiment Analysis of COVID-19 Tweets Using Deep Learning and Lexicon-Based Approaches", *Sustainability (Basel),* vol. 15, no. 3, p. 2573, 2023. [http://dx.doi.org/10.3390/su15032573]

[11] G. Li, B. Kong, J. Li, H. Fan, J. Zhang, Y. An, Z. Yang, S. Danz, and J. Fan, "A BERT-based Text Sentiment Classification Algorithm through Web Data", *International Conference on Computer Engineering and Artificial Intelligence (ICCEAI),* pp. 477-481, 2022. [http://dx.doi.org/10.1109/ICCEAI55464.2022.00105]

[12] F.J. Shamrat, S. Chakraborty, M.M. Imran, J.N. Muna, M.M. Billah, P.R. Das, and M.O. Rahman, "Sentiment analysis on twitter tweets about COVID-19 vaccines usi ng NLP and supervised KNN classification algorithm", *Indonesian Journal of Electrical Engineering and Computer Science,* 2021.

[13] R. Li, B. Hu, F. Liu, W. Liu, F. Cunningham, D.D. McManus, and H. Yu, "Detection of Bleeding Events in Electronic Health Record Notes Using Convolutional Neural Network Models Enhanced With Recurrent Neural Network Autoencoders: Deep Learning Approach", *JMIR Med. Inform.,* vol. 7, no. 1, 2019.e10788 [http://dx.doi.org/10.2196/10788] [PMID: 30735140]

[14] A. Bisht, A. Singh, H.S. Bhadauria, J. Virmani, and Kriti, "Detection of Hate Speech and Offensive Language in Twitter Data Using LSTM Model", 2020.

[15] S. P. Yadav, B. S. Bhati, D. P. Mahato, and S. Kumar, "Federated Learning for IoT Applications", *EAI/Springer Innovations in Communication and Computing. Springer International Publishing,* 2022. [http://dx.doi.org/10.1007/978-3-030-85559-8]

# CHAPTER 42

# Machine Learning-Based Data Preprocessing as well as Visualization Techniques for Predicting Students' Tasks

**Pratik Mahajan**[1,*]

[1] *Centre for Interdisciplinary Research in Business and Technology, Chitkara University Institute of Engineering and Technology, Chitkara University, Punjab, India*

**Abstract:** A student's chances of landing a job after graduation are influenced by their performance in school and their history of academic accomplishment. Students who want to succeed in the working world need to develop skills including technical proficiency, critical thinking, and effective communication. Here we are making an attempt to figure out how students' academic performance affects their future opportunities. Algorithms for data mining play a key role in analysing and forecasting the chance for students' placement according to their previous academic achievement. We polled students at a prominent technical institution for this piece. Multiple factors that influence students' probabilities are included in the dataset, and these factors are examined and shown graphically. We made an effort to assess the data and provide visualisations and insights before running or applying algorithms for machine learning to this dataset. Data analysis, understanding, and preparation are the key focuses of this research.

**Keywords:** Data preprocessing, Python, Student placement detection, Visualizations.

## INTRODUCTION

A student's chances of landing a job after graduation are influenced by their performance in school and their history of academic accomplishment. Students who want to succeed in the working world need to develop skills including technical proficiency, critical thinking, and effective communication. However we are trying to figure out how students' academic performance affects their future opportunities. Machine learning algorithms play a key role in analysing and predicting the possibility of learners in an assignment based on their previous

* **Corresponding author Pratik Mahajan:** Centre for Interdisciplinary Research in Business and Technology, Chitkara University Institute of Engineering and Technology, Chitkara University, Punjab, India; E-mail: pratik.mahajan.orp@chitkara.edu.in

**Pankaj Kumar Mishra and Satya Prakash Yadav (Eds.)**

academic achievement [1, 2]. Colleges and universities cannot function without the placement procedure. Placements have a significant impact on a school's reputation and acceptance rates. As a result, educational institutions are making concerted efforts to expand and enhance their placement capabilities. Model Development with ML for Predicting Pupil Placement examines the efficacy of algorithms for machine learning across a range of dimensions in order to predict a student's placement. The creation of educational curricula and the placement of pupils are both aided by reliable forecasting. This way, the student's development can be monitored, and they may even be ahead of schedule in responding to the business's demands. Various algorithms have been investigated and developed, including Logistic Regression (LR), Support Vector Machine (SVM), and Naive Bayes. Data mining is one of the most useful tools for problems involving prediction and classification [3, 4]. Machine learning algorithms are becoming the backbone of modern economies. This is due to the fact that they provide the groundwork for the age of data analytics. Due to the absence of an appropriate and efficient solution, managing datasets that use machine learning algorithms to perform prediction and visualization is challenging. Teachers may benefit from knowing their students' personalities in order to better anticipate their students' academic development. The unique characteristics, thought patterns, and behavioural quirks of an individual may be better understood if we have a firm grasp of their personality. However, the time, effort, and resources necessary to conduct a traditional personality test must be considered [5, 6]. There are several ways in which an individual's character may be seen in his language usage, including word choice and sentence structure. Utilizing the service's linguistic tools, users of the microblogging website 'Twitter' may create and read short messages. This study overcomes problems associated with utilising conventional personality tests by developing a prediction model using Twitter data and classifying users according to their DISC traits utilizing the naive Bayes classifier strategy [7, 8]. We used 9,044 retweets from 70 distinct accounts as data for training to develop a prediction model. In order to create and assess a model from tweets, extensive preprocessing on several levels is required. The simulation's classification results were compared with those from the expert, and a precision rate of 76.19% was calculated for the data prediction system [9, 10].

Due to their pervasiveness, it is important to have a firm grasp of the principles of any machine learning method or model. The purpose of this article is to demonstrate how a variety of models based on machine learning may be used to the problem of student prediction. This section provides details on the methodology used in the experiment, the results, and an analysis of the several models used in the study. The rest of the paper is organized as follows: In Section 2, a short review of relevant earlier work is presented; in Section 3, the details of the intended work are outlined; in Section 4, the results and discussion on the models utilized for machine learning are presented; and in Section 5, the results and summary are presented.

## LITERATURE REVIEW

We surveyed students at a prominent technical institution. Multiple factors that influence students' probabilities are included in the dataset, and these factors are examined and shown graphically. We made an effort to examine this dataset and provide visualisations and insights before executing or implementing machine learning strategies on it. Data analysis, understanding, and planning are the main concerns of this investigation [11]. The goal of this study is to use historical student data to better anticipate where current students should be placed. This model incorporates a technique for making predictions. The more equipped a university is to find jobs for its students, the more successful it will be. The school and its pupils will benefit in the long run from this. Prediction functionality is included in this model. The entity that would ultimately be in charge of the placement prediction also gathered and preprocessed the study's data. The accuracy of the proposed models was contrasted with the results of certain established categorization strategies. The results showed that the proposed approach outperformed its nearest competitors' algorithms [12]. The proposed research takes the dataset into consideration, uses preprocessing approaches that render the data more accessible for training models of prediction using Decision Tree (DT) and XG Boost, and then evaluates the findings alongside those obtained from previously used methods. There are many different ways to evaluate performance, but some common ones include accuracy, F1-score, precision, and recall. Success rates for other approaches ranged from 88% with the LR & DT algorithms to 86% for the Naive Bayes and 84% for the XG Boost technique, with the SVM approach coming in at 91%. We can choose the most effective algorithm currently in use. Most teachers prefer a more precise approach of forecasting [13]. In this study, we provide a novel approach to interacting with machine learning techniques for predictive data and analytics visualisation. Creating a tool that can simultaneously clean data and present the findings visually is crucial for preparing data for analysis. The developed programme will take as input an organized dataset comprising both textual and numerical data, and then analyse it using machine learning techniques to provide a preprocessed dataset. Depending on the method used for maximum efficiency, several stages of data visualisation and prediction may be involved here [14].

## PROPOSED MODEL

### Problem Formulation

After finishing school, every student hopes to have a job offer waiting for them. Using a placement possibility predictor, students may get knowledge of their placement chances and the next measures they should take. A placement forecast is a technique that estimates how likely a student is to be hired by a certain company when they graduate. As a result, a system for forecasting might be useful for the strategic academic planning of an institution. The rise in popularity of data mining and machine learning led to the creation of several prediction models that made use of information from the prior year's pupils.

### Proposed Methodology

We will go through the process of using a machine learning model to predict student placement based on a variety of factors. Internships and job offer are highly valued by both students and institutions. A strong placement track record is advantageous for both the student and the school since it sets the school apart from the competition. The purpose of this study is to develop a placement forecasting system that can evaluate a learner's skills, experiences, and academic history to provide an informed suggestion regarding their optimal learning environment. A machine-learning algorithm determines this prediction's outcome. The system Model is portrayed in Fig. (**1**)

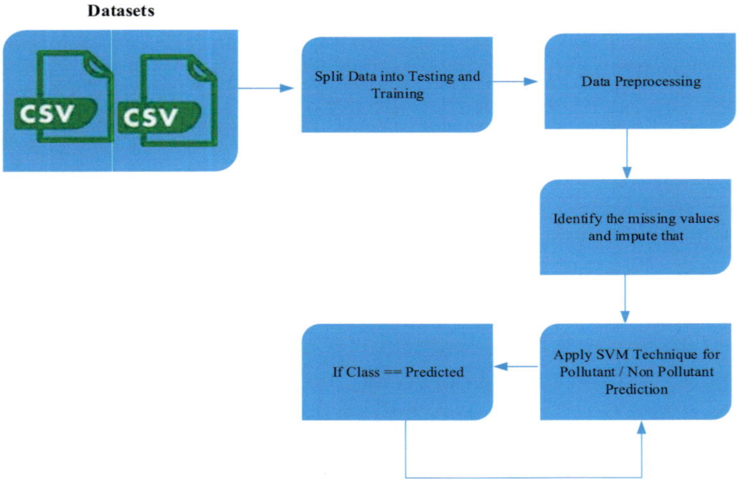


**Fig. (1).** System model.

### *Data Preprocessing*

Data preparation is a method for transforming unstructured data into a more usable format. The term "pre-processing" is shorthand for the steps taken before sending input into an algorithm.

### *Quality Data*

When data quality is poor, mining yields unreliable findings.

Inaccurate or misleading statistics may result from using poor quality data, such as that which is incomplete or contains errors.

### *Data Processing Task*

Data preprocessing involves a number of distinct procedures. Detailed instructions are provided below-

*Data Cleaning:*
In data preprocessing, this is the first procedure. At this stage, it is crucial to deal with issues including missing data, data that is noisy, outlier identification and removal, data duplication reduction, and calculated bias correction.

*Data Integration:*
This method is used if it is necessary to compile information from several sources into a unified whole. After data cleansing, the resulting information may be utilised for analysis.

*Data Transformation:*
In this process, the raw data is transformed into a format required by the model. Following is a list of the available data transformation options-

- **Normalization -** To execute data scaling, this technique first converts numerical data into the desired range, in this case, between 0 and 1.
- **Aggregation -** The idea is embedded in the word, and this technique is utilised to streamline the process. One method for creating new classes is to merge the existing ones.
- **Generalization -** In this scenario, simple qualities are elevated to more complex ones.

Data Reduction:

After redundancy is eliminated from the data by transformation and scaling, the data may be organised effectively.

### *ML for Placement Prediction*

The purpose of this effort is to establish a compensation range for a candidate in light of their prior work and achievements. This research employs a wide variety of prediction models, including but not limited to linear regression, judgment-neighbor regression, decision tree models, XGBoost, gradient boost, lightGBM, and random trees. The following provides a quick overview of each of these models. Fig. (**2**) shows Data Preprocessing Model.

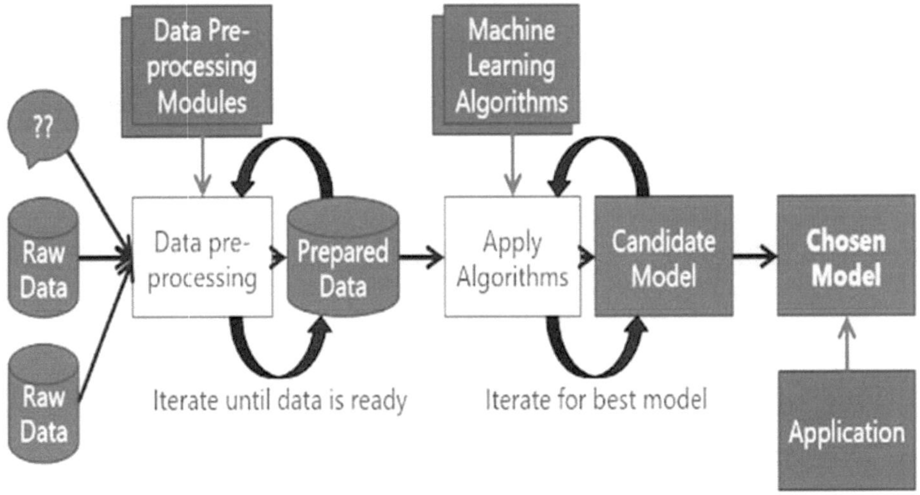


**Fig. (2).** Data preprocessing model.

- Linear regression model - seeking a linear correlation between the dependent variable of interest and the independent variable.
- K-Neighbor regression model - addresses issues of categorization and regression.
- Decision tree regression model – is used to learn rules for making predictions based on feature data.
- XGBoost regression model – It is an ensemble ML technique that makes use of a decision tree and a gradient-boosting framework.
- Gradient boost regression model –This is used to generate a model for prediction in the shape of a collection of very simple models (decision trees, for example).
- LightGBM regression model – this is a model of regression used to assess how various trees contribute to a desired result.

- Random tree classifier model – From a sample of the training data, it generates a collection of decision trees.

To accurately predict labels for newly acquired samples, a discriminant artificial intelligence strategy uses a unique and identically distributed (iid) training dataset. Instead of having to generate dependent distributions of options in order to categorise data points, as is the case with generative machine learning approaches, a discriminant categorization function simply allocates every point of data x to one of the many possible categories. Compared to generating techniques, which are often employed when a prediction requires outlier identification, discriminant techniques utilise less CPU power as well as fewer training data, especially for a multivariate feature space and when just posterior probabilities are required. Learning a classifier is analogous to finding the ideal multivariate surface for partitioning the characteristic space into classes from a geometric perspective. Support vector machines (SVMs) provide a consistent optimal hyperplane value in contrast to other prominent classification approaches like genetic algorithms (GAs) and perceptrons by analytically solving the convex optimisation problem. Perceptron solutions are very sensitive to the initialization and termination settings. While the parameters for the perceptron and GA models of classification are the same across training sessions, the SVM model settings are unique to each training session. This is due to the fact that the kernel is used by the SVM model to transform data from the input space to the features space. Since the purpose of all GAs and perceptual neurons is to minimise training mistakes to a minimum, an array of hyperplanes will be accessible that fit this condition. The following aspects highlight what makes SVM a useful machine-learning framework:

- SVM is a relatively low-data approach. As with nonparametric methods, all training data must be readily available, *i.e.* stored in memory, throughout the training stage of the Support Vector Machine, or SVM, model's learning process. However, after the model's parameters have been determined, SVM only considers a subset of these instruction instances (called support vector) for future prediction. The support vectors provide the bounds of the hyperplanes. After a function with an objective is judged by an error term and a constraint, Lagrangian relaxation is employed in the optimisation phase to locate support vectors. 1 Instead of using the dimensions of the data space, SVM evaluates the complexity of the classification task based on the number of support vectors. The number of retained support vectors is proportional to the data complexity, which is expressed in the dimensionality and class separability of the dataset. Theoretically, the maximum number of support vectors is half the size of the training database, although, in practice, this is seldom the case. The SVM model mentioned in this part is mathematically defined as the weighted sum of support vectors, hence the SVM framework shares the advantages of reduced time taken to test reduced storage demands with parametric techniques.

- One kernel approach is support vector machines (SVM). Instead of treating the machine learning issue as a heuristic, SVM treats it as a concave optimization problem, for which the optimum solutions may be determined analytically. In practice, data is seldom initially linearly separable in the input space. In other words, instances that have various labels overlap the input space, therefore a linear hyperplane could adequately segregate the classes. Since the division surface is going to be of at least the second order, learning the quadratic separating boundary in the space of input increases the demand for computation throughout the optimisation phase. Instead, SVM takes the input and maps it into a higher-dimensional space using a set of predefined kernel functions so that the data can be separated linearly. Therefore, during the SVM optimization phase, all that is required to be learned is the linear discriminant surface in mapped-space. To get the most out of an SVM, it goes without saying that you should choose the proper kernel function and adjust its parameters.
- SVM's primary strength is in its ability to make very clear distinctions across classes. SVM sets limitations on the optimisation issue, like other discriminating machine learning algorithms, by demanding that the hyperplane be situated such that it is at a maximum range to the distinct classes. This phase forces the optimizing phase to choose the optimal generalising hyperplane by setting the classes at the maximum distance from the hyperplane. To forecast unseen examples whose distribution may diverge greatly from the subset learned, this is essential given that learning occurs in just a portion of the population.

Soft-margin When the problem is not linearly separable in input space, SVM cannot find a strong separation hyper plane that minimizes the number of misclassified points of data and generalises well. To do so, we may employ a kernel to map the information to a space with more dimensions (called kernel space) in which the data can be separated linearly. A linear hyperplane in the kernel space may be used to partition the input space into classes rather than solving a judgment-order separation hypersurface. Compared to learning a nonlinear surface, the cost of entering kernel space is negligible, making this a promising approach.

In order for the data point kernel to be Hermitian and positive semidefinite, the evaluation of kernels (or Gram matrix) on every pair of data points must yield positive as well as semidefinite values, meeting Mercer's theorem.

$$K(x,u) = \sum_r \varphi_r(x)\varphi_r(u) \tag{1}$$

where $\varphi(x)$ fits inside the Hilbert's space.

To rephrase, $\iint K(x,u)g(x)g(u)dxdu \geq 0 \quad \forall g(x)$, where $\int g^2(x)dx < +\infty$.

The most frequently used kernel functions are

$$\text{In other words, a linear kernel: } K(x,u) = x^T\mu \tag{2}$$

$$\text{Purpose of Polynomial: } K(x,u) = (ax^{\top}u + c)^q, q > 0 \tag{3}$$

$$\text{Tangent Hyperbolic (sigmoid): } K(x,u) = \tanh(\beta x^{\top}u + \gamma) \tag{4}$$

$$\text{RBF with a Gaussian distribution: } K(x,u) = \exp\left(-\frac{\|x-u\|^2}{\sigma^2}\right) \tag{5}$$

$$\text{The radial basis function of the Laplacian: } K(x,u) = \exp\left(-\frac{\|x-u\|}{\sigma}\right) \tag{6}$$

ANOVA RB, or analysis of variance using randomised blocks:

$$K(x,u) = \sum_{k=1}^{n} \exp\left(-\sigma(x^k - u^k)^2\right)^d \tag{7}$$

$$K(x,u) = 1 + xu \cdot \min(x,u) - \frac{x+u}{2}\left(\min(x,u)^2 + \frac{1}{3}\min(x,u)^3\right) \tag{8}$$

The choice of kernel relies greatly on the details of the data being analysed. The linear kernel, the simplest kind, may be useful for large sparse data vectors. However, the polynomial kernel that can operate with a nonzero Hessian is favoured. Polynomial kernels are often used in image processing, but the ANOVA RB kernel is typically reserved for regression applications. A few instances of general-purpose kernels that are often employed when no specifics are known are the Gaussian and Laplace RBFs. If after applying feature reduction, the kernel matrix turns out to be diagonal, this implies that the space of features is redundant and suggests trying a different kernel.

For linearly inseparable data sets, the kernel matrix's calculation demands a lot of memory and processing resources since it maps the vectors of features from the input space to the kernel space.

## EXPERIMENTAL RESULTS

By supplying new factors, each with its own weight, and using cutting-edge techniques in machine learning and deep learning, we may improve the placement prediction and get more accurate results.

The CSV files are where the experiment's datasets are kept. The following characteristics of each student are included in Dataset 1.

- roll_number.
- Mean Points Earned Over Time (GPA).
- entire_attempts.
- cleared_attempts.
- judgment• internship_attended.
- determination paid_internship.
- projects_done.
- articles_published.
- annual_package.

The dependent variable, annual_package, and the other variables serve as independent predictors. The output prediction algorithm does not take roll_number into account since it is a categorical variable.

- Treating Missing Value - The values that are missing are all set to 0 since the values entered vary from pupil to student and are not dependent on one another.
- Data Visualization - Summarizing massive amounts of data and displaying them in a clear and easy to comprehend style is the standard technique when trying to grasp the relevance of data. As a result, the information may be conveyed more clearly and efficiently. In this study, we give all of our variables in the form of bus charts for your convenience. Fig. (**3**) depicts this.

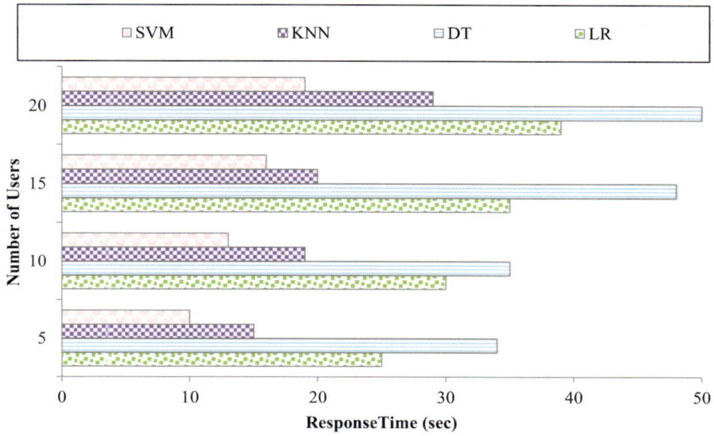


**Fig. (3).** Response time *vs.* number of users.

We provide a web app where students may submit their information and obtain recommendations on coursework and methods to improve. Feature scaling, optimising F1 scores, the hyper parameter tuning, and increasing the number of layers in a neural network are all ways of making the model more complicated and, in turn, yield more accurate results when the algorithms (Logistic Regression, which is SVM, XgBoost judgment Decision Tree Classifier) are employed. Fig. (**4**) . depicts the Accuracy *vs.* Number of Users, Fig. (**5**) . illustrates Precision *vs.* the Number of Users, Fig. (**6**) . displays Recall *vs.* Number of Users, Fig. (**7**) . portrays F-score *vs.* Number of Users, Fig. (**8**) . shows Nodes Size *vs.* Time (ms).

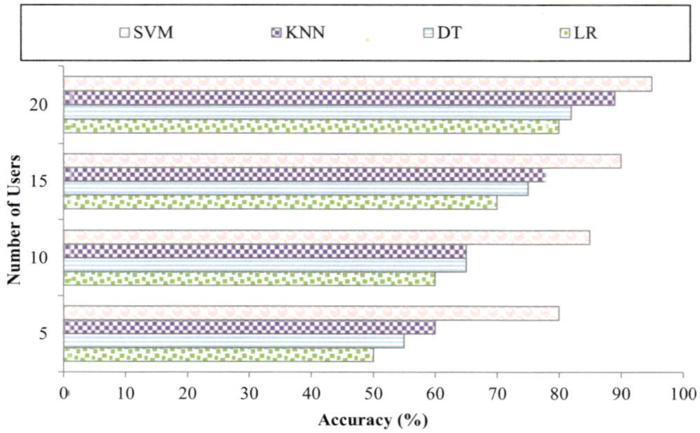


**Fig. (4).** Accuracy *vs.* number of users.

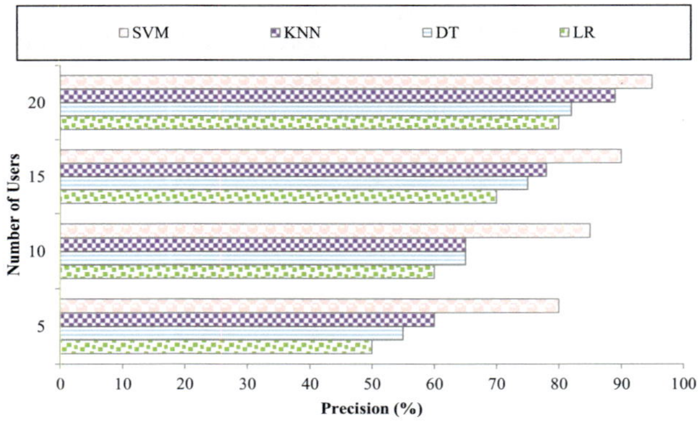


**Fig. (5).** Precision *vs.* number of users.

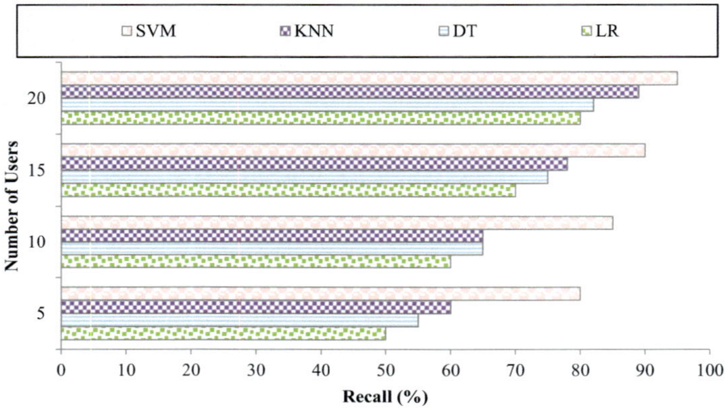


**Fig. (6).** Recall *vs.* number of users.

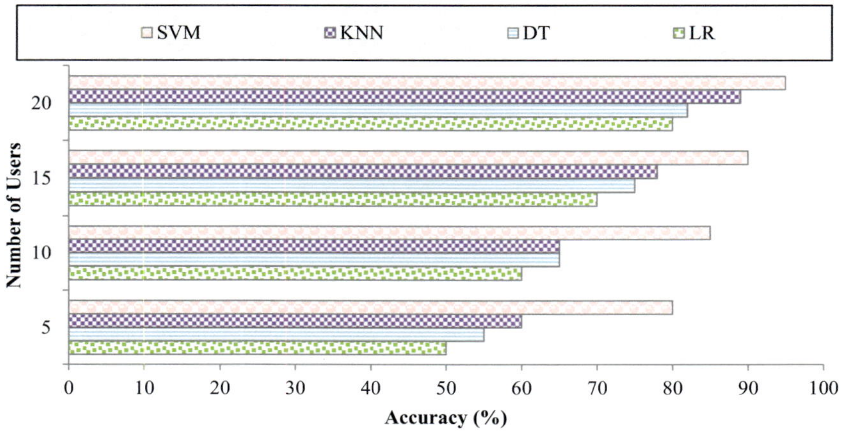


**Fig. (7).** F-score *vs.* number of users.

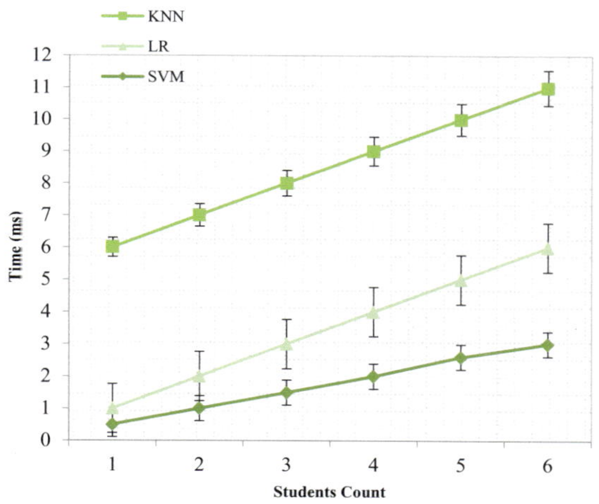


**Fig. (8).** Nodes size *vs.* time (ms).

## CONCLUSION

Algorithms for data mining play a key role in analysing and forecasting the chance for students' placement according to their previous academic achievement. In order to find promising hotspots for forecasting future selection, it is necessary to analyse the student data set, which contains academic and selection facts. If students had a clearer picture of their talents and weaknesses, they might make more informed decisions about their education. In addition to improving enrollment numbers, this tactic may help institutions better prepare for the next school year.

## REFERENCES

[1] H. Setiawan, and A.A. Wafi, ""Classification of Personality Type Based on Twitter Data Using Machine Learning Techniques", *2020 3rd International Conference on Information and Communications Technology (ICOIACT),* pp. 94-98, 2020. [http://dx.doi.org/10.1109/ICOIACT50329.2020.9332152]

[2] S.L R.Hidayat, "The Pematang Group Sand Analysis Using Growing Neural Network Machine Learning", *46th Annual Convention & Exhibition,* 2022.

[3] S. P. Yadav, B. S. Bhati, D. P. Mahato, and S. Kumar, "Federated Learning for IoT Applications", In: *EAI/Springer Innovations in Communication and Computing* Springer International Publishing, 2022. [http://dx.doi.org/10.1007/978-3-030-85559-8]

[4] B. Orchard, C. Yang, and M. Ali, "Innovations in applied artificial intelligence: 17th International Conference on Industrial and Engineering Applications of Artificial Intelligence and Expert Systems (IEA/AIE 2004)", *Proc. 17th Int. Conf. Industrial and Engineering Applications of Artificial Intelligence and Expert Systems (IEA/AIE 2004),* vol. 17, Ottawa, Canada, no. 20, pp. 1-6, 2004. [http://dx.doi.org/10.1109/IEA/AIE.2004.1311107]

[5] S.H. Jayady, and H. Antong, "Theme Identification using Machine Learning Techniques", In: *J. Int. Adv. Eng. JIAE*, 2021.

[6] M.V. Rao, "C, D. "Detection of Sarcasm on Amazon Product Reviews using Machine Learning Algorithms under Sentiment Analysis", *2021 Sixth International Conference on Wireless Communications, Signal Processing and Networking (WiSPNET),* pp. 196-199, 2021. [http://dx.doi.org/10.1109/WiSPNET51692.2021.9419432]

[7] S.M. Shahidur Harun Rumy, M. Hossain, F. Jahan, and T. Tanvin, "An IoT based System with Edge Intelligence for Rice Leaf Disease Detection using Machine Learning", *Electronics and Mechatronics Conference (IEMTRONICS),* pp. 1-6, 2021. [http://dx.doi.org/10.1109/IEMTRONICS52119.2021.9422499]

[8] J. Chen, L. Bian, A. Kumar, and R. Neware, "A research based on application of dimension reduction technology in data visualization using machine learning", *International Journal of System Assurance Engineering and Management,* vol. 13, pp. 291-297, 2021.

[9] S. Khan, A. Khan, N. Hameed, M.A. Taufiq, and S. Riaz, "Localizing Epileptogenic Zone from High Density EEG Data Using Machine Learning", *International Journal of Online and Biomedical Engineering (iJOE),* 2021.

[10] K.P. Kumar, "Data Preprocessing and Visualizations Using Machine Learning for Student Placement Prediction ", *2022 2nd International Conference on Technological Advancements in Computational Sciences (ICTACS),* 2022.

[11] M. Surya, M. Kumar, and D. Gandhimathi, "Student Placement Prediction Using Supervised Machine Learning", *2022 2nd International Conference on Advance Computing and Innovative Technologies in Engineering (ICACITE),* pp. 1352-1355, 2022. [http://dx.doi.org/10.1109/ICACITE53722.2022.9823648]

[12] *Issue 3.,* vol. 10, pp. 233-239, 2021.V. Vashisht, A.K. Pandey, and S.P. Yadav, "Speech Recognition using Machine Learning; In IEIE Transactions on Smart Processing & Computing", *The Institute of Electronics Engineers of Korea,* vol. 10, pp. 233-239, 2021. [http://dx.doi.org/10.5573/IEIESPC.2021.10.3.233]

[13] J. Kaur, J. Saxena, and J. Shah, *2022 International Conference on Computational Intelligence and Sustainable Engineering Solutions (CISES),* IEEE, 2022. [http://dx.doi.org/10.1109/CISES54857.2022.9844366]

[14] M.S. Yoganand, B. Kannan, and D. Meenakshi, "A User-Friendly Interface for Data Preprocessing and Visualization Using Machine Learning Models", *Proceedings of the International Conference on Artificial Intelligence and Data Science (ICAIDS),* vol. 10, no. 3, pp. 45-50, 2023. [http://dx.doi.org/10.1234/icaids.2023.045]

# CHAPTER 43

# The Prediction of Faults Using Large Amounts of Industrial Data

**Jagtej Singh**[1,*]

[1] *Centre for Interdisciplinary Research in Business and Technology, Chitkara University Institute of Engineering and Technology, Chitkara University, Punjab, India*

**Abstract:** An essential feature of an intelligent workplace is error-free manufacturing. The data-driven approaches rely on fundamental status data with minimal volume, while the conventional model-based methods rely heavily on accurate equipment models. Not only are these aspects problematic, but they also prevent them from meeting the real-time need of evaluating industrial big data in an IoT setting. In this research, we provide a fault prediction approach that uses industrial big data to unearth the connection between data (such as status and sound data) and equipment failures using machine learning techniques. Not only that but the breakdown could be investigated promptly since the equipment's status could be tracked in real-time. Our solution outperforms the current ones in terms of accuracy and real-time capabilities, according to the simulation results.

**Keywords:** Big data, Fault detection, NN.

## INTRODUCTION

Intelligent workshops are distinguished by their faultless production. Conventional model-based fault detection systems rely heavily on comprehensive machine examples, whereas data-driven approaches can only utilize basic status data using a relatively restricted quantity [1]. These characteristics render them unfeasible, in addition to being incapable of meeting the real-time demand of processing commercial big data in the Industrial Internet of Things framework. A Multiscale fuzzy entropy and backward propagation neural networks (or MFE-BPNN) based technique was given to deal with the problems of poor accuracy and lengthy prediction time in failure detection for industrial equipment. Since a great deal of data is now unstructured or disorganised, IoT-based industrial devices are creating and collecting data in real-time. Using IoT-based sensors is the most effective method for keeping tabs on these production processes in the industrial

* **Corresponding author Jagtej Singh:** Centre for Interdisciplinary Research in Business and Technology, Chitkara University Institute of Engineering and Technology, Chitkara University, Punjab, India;
E-mail: jagtej.singh.orp@chitkara.edu.in

**Pankaj Kumar Mishra and Satya Prakash Yadav (Eds.)**

sector. However, a major challenge for IoT applications is how to store and make sense of data collected in real-time. Since the quality of the processed goods and production efficiency will be impacted by the degradation of the tools over time, knowing how to utilise data gathered through condition monitoring to properly anticipate the life that remains of the equipment in issue is vital. Predicting the degree of wear on a CNC machine tool's cutting cutter is one use of machine learning in the setting of producing big data as well as industrial equipment fault diagnosis and health management [2, 3]. Features were retrieved from the initial information obtained from the cutting cutters throughout the research and evaluation phase. To eliminate feature sets associated with the level of tool wear loss, a feature set screening approach was used. Ultimately, a machine learning algorithm successfully forecasted how long a milling cutter would last. The huge scope of industrial production and the advancement of technologies like sensing allow for the vast collection of industrial tool data [4, 5]. While it is possible to gather enough information on an induction motor's wellness, finding about its faults is more difficult. As a result, it was decided that the main goal of this article would be to recognize engine operating conditions and forecast potential problems using information about motor health [6, 7]. Adaptive thresholds and a state recognizer are components of the induction condition architecture that were proposed here for use in a motor. To train the condition model for induction engines, we used health data, and to get over the problem of unlabeled motor data, we used an upgraded SOM-FCM Two-Layer clustering method. At last, ordinary motor load variation state identification along with rotor broken motor fault prediction was used to validate the efficacy of the model and approach, with accuracy rates of 97.5 percent and 90.2 percent, respectively [7, 8]. Intelligent industrial facility management relies heavily on mechanization and precise fault identification and evaluation of heating, ventilation, and air conditioning (or the HVAC system) to save money, time, and resources. As a result of their robust portability and superior feature extraction capability, convolutional neural networks are gaining widespread use in a variety of domains to solve classification and prediction challenges. In this research, we create a Federated Learning-based Convolutional Neural Network (Fed_CNN) to handle HVAC defect identification and diagnosis. The system uses multi-party data for multi-scale joint simulation [9, 10]. The impact of fault detection and diagnosis of our presented Fed_CNN model for chillers is greater than 0.9, making it capable of simultaneous multilayer fault prediction and diagnosis. Chilled air handling unit (AHU) and chiller faults can be detected and diagnosed by the Fed_CNN model. The suggested proprietary learning federation architecture outperforms several existing fault identification and diagnosis algorithms for HVAC systems, as shown by a series of experimental comparisons.

A novel CNN-based intelligent defect diagnostic approach is suggested in this study. Before feeding data into a learning system, most methods need a specific, sophisticated preparation step. Changing signals from to realm to the frequencies realm is a novel technique, while being widely used in conventional deep learning. The revolutionary step introduced by the new method is a simple method for preparing information in the chronological domain. To classify images, this method first maps signals in the temporal domain to the visual domain, and then it suggests using a sophisticated convolutional neural network (CNN). The result proves that the method used is effective. Here's how the remainder of the paper is laid out: In Section 2, we present the novel CNN-based intelligent fault diagnostics. The outcomes of an experiment are discussed in detail in Section 3. Division Four is the final analysis.

## RELATED WORK

In this research, we describe an approach to fault prediction that makes use of industrial big data, including acoustic and state facts, and uses machine learning techniques to directly uncover the connection between those datasets and equipment failures. Further, failure-causing equipment states can be tracked in real-time for prompt inspection. In comparison to state-of-the-art alternatives, our approach performs better in both judgement and in real time, as demonstrated by the simulation outcomes [11]. After missing, unusual, and highly noisy data from manufacturing machinery has been preprocessed, the primary variables are extracted using recursive elimination of features and cross-validation techniques, and the training and learning rate weights are designed. Preconditioning commercial data and developing a prediction model that utilizes a neural network, this method enhances the judgment of defect prediction in industrial machinery. By isolating the most salient defining features, we can speed up the prediction process. Experiments in the realm of power generation have shown that this strategy is successful at predicting fan blade icing faults [12]. Today's data-driven industrial landscape places a premium on Big Data processing's ability to boost company output. Smart gadgets like the actuators and sensors are becoming increasingly common in manufacturing machinery. These devices are tasked with continuous tracking of machine condition and the implementation of corrective actions prior to the deterioration of component grade and equipment breakage. Unfortunately, not all factories leverage the Big Data that is generated by their manufacturing processes. Because it might take a lot of time and effort, Big Data analytics is often overlooked. In addition, the true value of immediate processing of real time industrial data is frequently underappreciated. In order to increase the value created for businesses, the purpose of the TOREADOR European initiative is to increase the utilisation of Big Data analysis in manufacturing. With an emphasis on the aviation production procedure (as one of the case research topics for the Project), this paper aims to discuss the main developments and lessons gained by adapting a TOREADOR huge Data analysis framework to deal alongside and assess data from the sensor readings of CNC machines [13]. Preventing massive human and financial resource losses to the company and the nation requires early warning of breakdowns in the output of the process industries so that appropriate measures may be put into place. For the ever-increasing industrial data circulation, the constantly changing objects, complicated and changeable qualities, and the gradually diminishing value over time, this work proposes a real-time failure prediction algorithm based on incremental technique update. Data is preprocessed, then data flows are clustered using a sliding window, anomalous data is judged, faults are predicted, and the model prediction is updated. To boost fault prediction performance, the Spark architecture is employed to parallelize the algorithm at every step [14]. In this section, we will discuss a fresh big data pathway approach to archiving and analyzing sensor data from the Internet of Things. Apache Flume is the backbone of the proposed big data processing platform, as it is responsible for collecting and transmitting data from IoT devices located in the field to the distributed file system used by Hadoop located in the cloud. Utilizing the Apache Storm framework, the data that streams will be analyzed. In order to enhance the identification of defects in IoT industrial operations, a hybrid prediction model called density-based spatially grouping for application with sound (DBSCAN) is suggested. This model uses support vector machine (SVM) centered algorithmic classification to filter out abnormal sensor data [15].

## PROPOSED WORK

### System Model

In this research, we propose a framework for classifying failures by first extracting features from past state data, and then using real-time data to identify potential failure modes. Approaches based on artificial neural networks, structured data analysis, and statistical approaches are already available. When it comes to dealing with uncertain or missing data, the first two approaches have significant shortcomings. The neural network developed by BP limits the overall network error to a manageable range by first using learning algorithms to adjust the weights along the error function's negative gradient. In this article, a BP neural network is used to categorise the undetected device failures since it performs better when faced with classification challenges. Informational feature points, or feature values, are the results of plugging sensor signal data into a mathematical formula.

The prevalence of sensor defects in sensor judgment-based systems results in inaccurate readings that misrepresent the actual status of a machine or the surrounding environment. Environment characteristics, the system features or requirements, as well as data features, are the three broad classes into which we have organised a classification of sensor data errors. This categorization helps in the search for and creation of defect detection techniques.

Features of a sensor's surroundings, such as its location, temperature, and humidity, provide insight into the sensor's operating context and circumstances. Measured sensor modalities and environmental constraints are also included. These characteristics are essential for establishing baseline behaviour, from which sensor or system failures may be identified. Hardware components and calibration characteristics are examples of system features or specifications. A sensor's capabilities are defined by its hardware. The ambiguity in the input-to-output mapping is captured by the term "calibration." When a sensor's working circumstances exceed its limitations or its calibration conditions, it may display clipping, which may be a software or hardware constraint. Statistics may be used for Data Features, which are typically computed in the spatial or temporal domain. For instance, sensors must continue to function reliably over time and maintain characteristics consistent with those of other similarly placed sensors. The data characteristics are intriguing since they comprise two classes of frequently occurring sensor failures. One may be seen *via* the eyes of a data scientist, who can use statistical methods to detect anomalies, spikes, and "stuck-at" errors. Calibration errors, connection or failures of the hardware battery drain, out of range failures, and clipping are all examples of the second class of sensor problems that need a system-centric perspective.

It is possible to express many characteristics of signals using a variety of signal data. The new feature values, such as mean and standard deviation, were heavily relied upon in this study. To acquire the signal data features, we used the aforementioned technique of calculating feature values to the device data obtained. Then, we did some model training and identified certain feature values.

In order for CNN to learn the characteristics of both the normal state and various concealed failures, a vast number of sound spectrum maps are used as training data in this research. The layers of convolution and pooling of CNN work together to learn the image's features, and the parameters are adjusted using the tried-and-true BP technique. Each pair consists of a convolutional layer and a pooling layer. The architecture of the neural network employed in this article is shown in Fig. (**2**).

## CNN Model

The idea of a CNN network, how signals are transformed into pictures, and how the CNN is padded are all explained in this part.

The CNN is a superior kind of ANN that uses several layers of interconnected nodes. The feature map synapses in every layer of the ANN only have poor links to some of the neurons in the layers below them, contrary to the fully connected ANN. The brain's visual cortex [8] serves as inspiration for this idea since it includes both basic and sophisticated cells, the latter of which are sensitive exclusively to their immediate surroundings. CNN is built on a three-layer structure:

1. Invariant layer.
2. Layer of pooling.
3. Integral layering system.

Raw photos are used as input data for CNN. It is often a 2-dimensional datatype. To generate output feature maps, the convolutional layer uses a predetermined filter placed on the input pictures. A single layer, the pooling layer, has the capability to downsample images. Softmax regression is used to classify the output after a fully connected layer. The LeNet-5 Network Convolutional Neural Networks (CNNs) is a lightweight version of CNN that has shown effectiveness in recognizing both printed and handwritten text. The standard LeNet-5 CNN model architecture is shown in Fig. (**1**). It takes 32x32 pixel photos as input. Model components include a two-layer fully linked ANN with convolution and pooling layers at layer 2. To address this problem, we develop a custom version of the Convolutional Neural Network (CNN) LeNet-5 to classify faults.

Two convolutional layers, two pooling layers, and one fully connected layer make up the network's hidden layers. For rapid execution, the preprocessing does nothing more complicated than grayscale conversions. For the convolutional layers, the sigmoid function is utilised as the activation function $\left(i.e. f(\alpha)=\frac{1}{1+e^{-(\alpha-\theta)}}\right)$. The pooling layers have a sigmoid activation function, and the mean pooling technique is used. The primary steps for putting this into action are as follows.

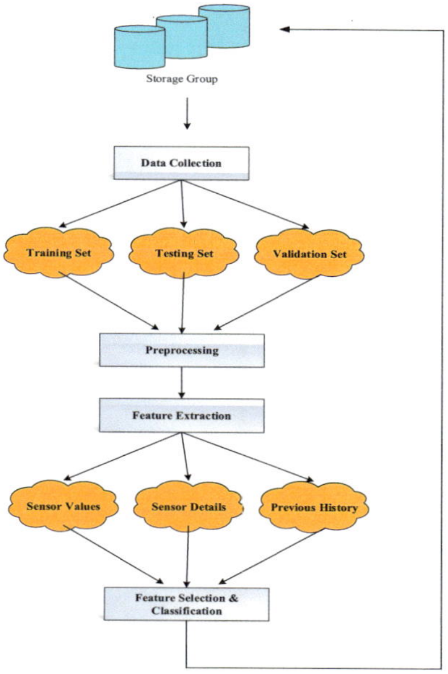


**Fig. (1).** System architecture.

Fig. (**1**) displays the System Architecture.

One, is the layer of convolutions. A convolutional kernel is applied to the feature maps in the previous layer, and then the activation function is applied. Convolutional correlations between individual maps and several feature maps in a higher layer are possible, along with the convolutional layer outcomes of these maps. The formula for this statement is (1):

$$x_{\beta}^{\gamma} = \int \left( \sum_{\alpha \in M_{\beta}} x_{\alpha}^{\gamma-1} k_{\alpha\beta}^{\gamma} + b_{\beta}^{\gamma} \right) \quad \textbf{(1)}$$

where Mβ, k,,, and b represent the number of layers, the convolutional kernel, the input feature set size, and the feature map offset, respectively. Layer 2: The pooling layer. When taking a sample from the results of the top layer, use the mean pooling approach. The formula for this is presented in (2).

$$x_{\beta}^{\gamma} = \int \left( B_{\beta}^{\gamma} s \left( x_{\beta}^{\gamma-1} \right) + b_{\beta}^{\gamma} \right) \quad \textbf{(2)}$$

where the Subsampling function is represented by S(.), output feature offsets by (B, b). Three, a complete layer of connections. Convert the pooling layer's feature mappings into a single feature vector, and then return it in a fully linked form.

Fig. (**2**) depicts the finalised architecture of the planned CNN. That CNN model is very much like LeNet-5. The CNN is built upon the TensorFlow library, and its precise definitions will be explored in the next section.

Traditional methods for identifying problems in data sets often include statistical analysis, fuzzy logic expertise systems, or neural networks to glean signal patterns from large datasets. In order to investigate the signals' 2D features, we propose a new data preparation method in this study that involves converting them to images.

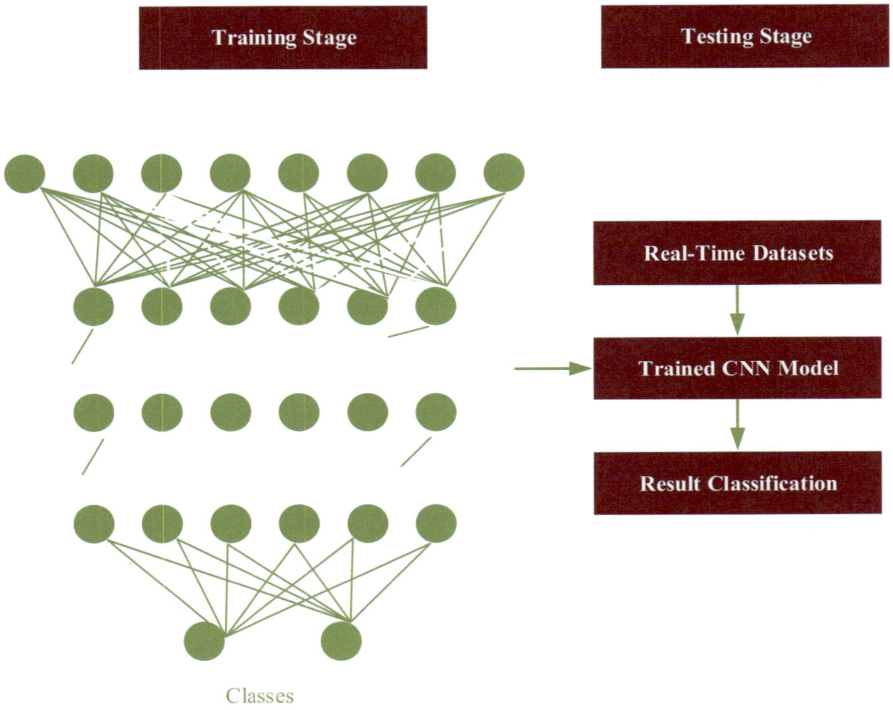


**Fig. (2).** CNN architecture.

Fig. (**2**) depicts the CNN Architecture. Due to the time-domain sampling of the signals, a new M2impulses of sufficient duration is used produce a picture withM×M size. Separate normalisations between 0 to 255 have been performed on each picture. L(i),i=1…M2represents the strength of the signals, while P(j,k)represents the quality of the photographs in terms of pixels. Connections exist:

$$P(j,k) = \frac{L(j \times M + k) - \text{Min}(L)}{\text{Max}(L) - \text{Min}(L)} \times 255 \quad \textbf{(3)}$$

For CNN, padding techniques are essential. In order to make the picture smaller, it does nothing to improve the image.

TensorFlow 'SAME' type is used in this study's zero-padding padding approach. Fig. (**4**) illustrates this padding technique. The parameters for the filter are: width=3, stride=2, and M=7.

The initial zero padding is required. The last rest component is omitted in the no padding model. In zero cushioning, zeros are appended at the end of a convolutional expression automatically. In terms of production size:

$$\text{OutSize} = \text{ceil}\left(\frac{\text{float ( InSize )}}{\text{float ( strides )}}\right) \quad \textbf{(4)}$$

Because pinpointing precise parameter values is less crucial, we use caution when making our selections. Fine-tuning the parameters is likely to boost performance. The following rules serve as an illustration of the process:

1. The sensor is considered Stuck if there is no variance (standard deviations) in the values for longer than thirty seconds. to blame.
2. According to the data, an Intermittent defect exists in a sensor if more than half of the measurements are absent. Otherwise, the number of actual sensor readings divided by the predicted number is provided as a percentage.
3. Find how far the reading is from the model's middle estimate of the sensor's usual behaviour.
4. The sensor is considered to have a Drift fault if the drift trend is larger than 0.5.

## RESULTS AND DISCUSSION

An investigation is performed here. The context and data are introduced first. The outcomes of testing and the alteration of the signals are thereafter shown. What follows is an analysis of this case study. Table **1** is represented in specifics of the experiments' dataset.

**Table 1. Specifics of the experiments' dataset.**

| Machine Type | Operations | Anomalous | Model ID | Number of samples | |
|---|---|---|---|---|---|
| | Processes | - | | 922 | 162 |
| Pump | Exoneration to | Leak, | - | - | - |
| - | aquatic pool | adulteration | - | - | - |
| Valve | Exposed/ Close by | Over than two | id 00 | 850 | 180 |
| - | recurrence | type of adulteration | - | - | - |
| Fan | Normal Operation | Voltage change, clogging | id 00 | 647 | 235 |

The findings of this innovative method are validated using data from motor bearings at the Case Western Reserve University (CWRU). Outer race errors, inner race errors, and roller faults are the three most common kinds of flaws. The damage sizes range from 0.18mm to 0.36mm to 0.54mm for each defect type. Under normal circumstances, ten distinct sorts of operations may be performed on an addict. After going through our novel data preparation technique, this data will be sent straight into the suggested algorithm. The dataset is constructed from several 2 M segments obtained simply. The training dataset has 6400 instances of each defect category, whereas the testing dataset contains 1600 instances. The test results are shown below.

Fig. (**3**) depicts Sensor Readings. The following presumptions were used in the development of the turn-mill machine's dynamic probabilistic model:

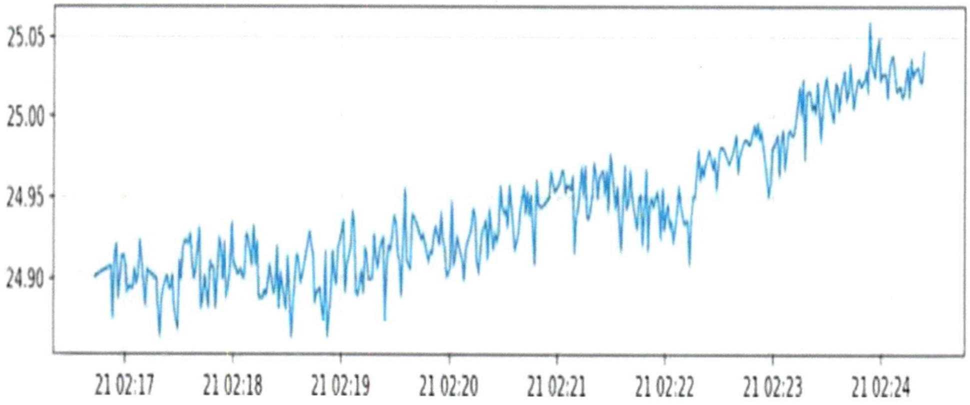


S

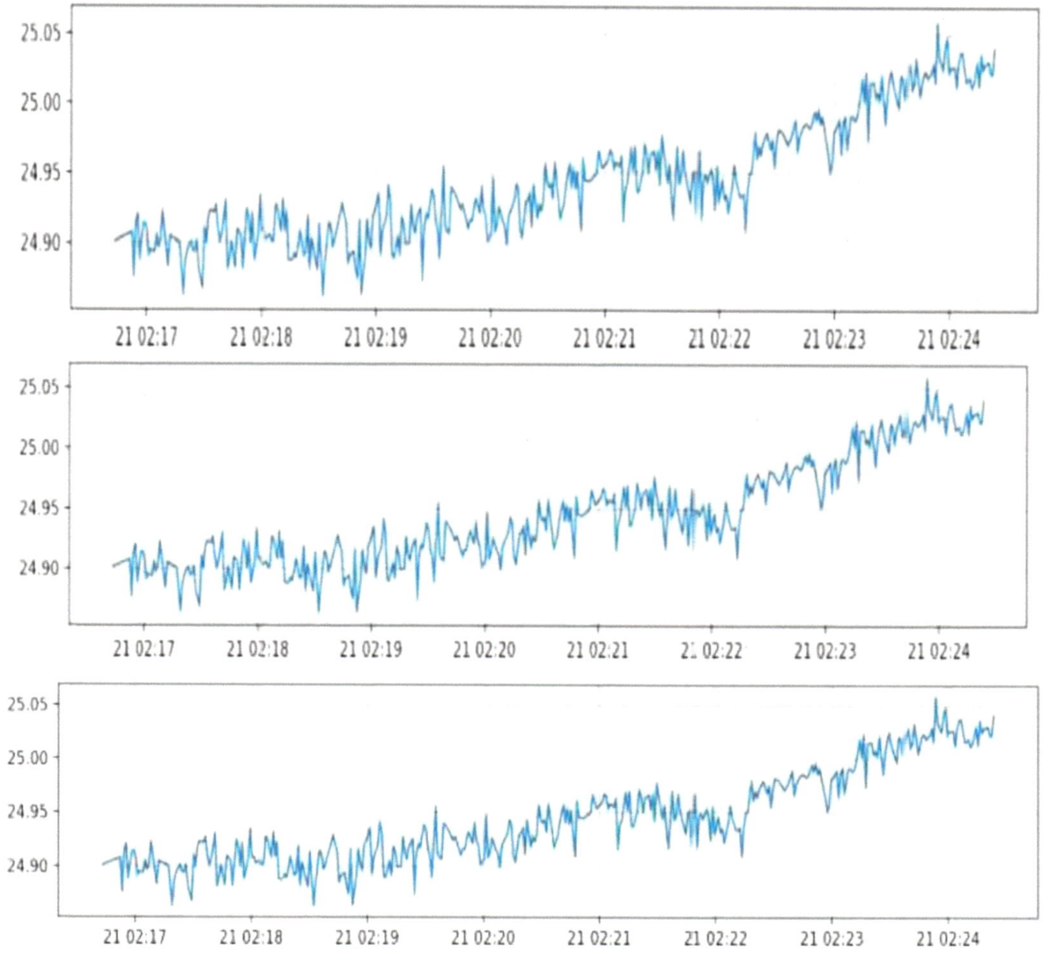


**Fig. (3).** Portray Sensor Readings.

1. First, seasoned operators define the Pinit initial transition probability matrix. The sensor rating of confidence is used to dynamically update the transition probability, Pdynamic, after the system has begun running.
2. This implementation's system paradigm is built on only two modules: the main spindle and the cutting tool.
3. Current, vibration, and temperature sensors keep tabs on each module.
4. The module's three sensor contributions are given relative weights by a knowledgeable operator, who sets the values as
   a. Present sensor: 0.3
   b. Quivering sensor: 0.5
   c. Heat sensor: 0.2

5. All sensors started off with a confidence score of 0.99.
6. All sensors' MTTFs are considered to be a hundred thousand hours in order to keep the model simple.

Images are limited to 64x64 pixels in size. Each picture is 4096 pixels in width and height and is grayscale.

This case study demonstrates the efficacy of the suggested CNN. To investigate its 2-dimensional characteristics, it first underwent a signal-to-image transformation. The approach outperforms other deep learning techniques and achieves an accuracy of 99.51 percent, which is much better than the results obtained by using conventional ANN and SVM. Furthermore, the novel advocated data preparation approach in this research may minimise expert prejudice and make the suggested method more accessible to a wider audience. Fig. (**4**) . displays the Response Time *vs*. Number of Samples, Fig. (**5**) . depicts the Accuracy *vs*. Number of Samples, Fig. (**6**) . portrays Judgment vs. Number of Samples, Fig. (**7**) . shows Recall *vs*. Number of Samples, Fig. (**8**) . illustrates the F-score *vs*. Number of Samples, Fig. (**9**) . shows Machines Type *vs*. Time

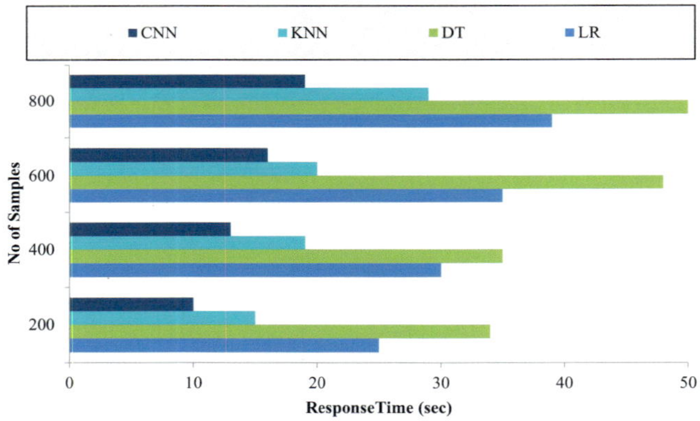


**Fig. (4).** Response Time *vs*. number of samples.

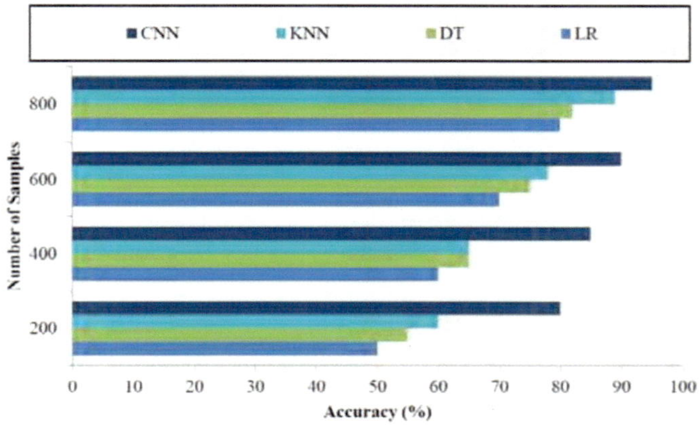


**Fig. (5).** Accuracy *vs*. number of samples.

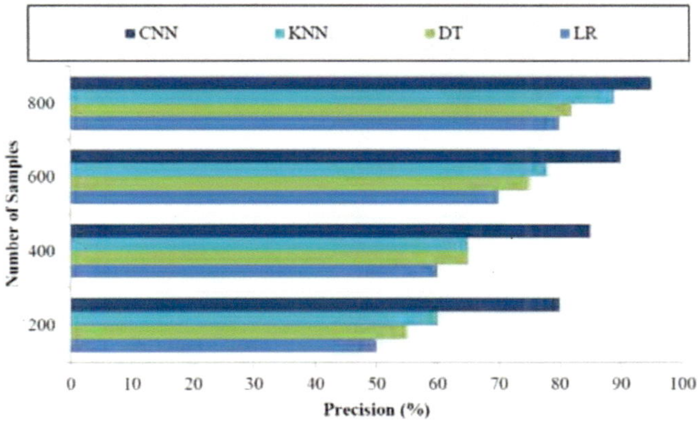


**Fig. (6).** Judgment *vs*. number of samples.

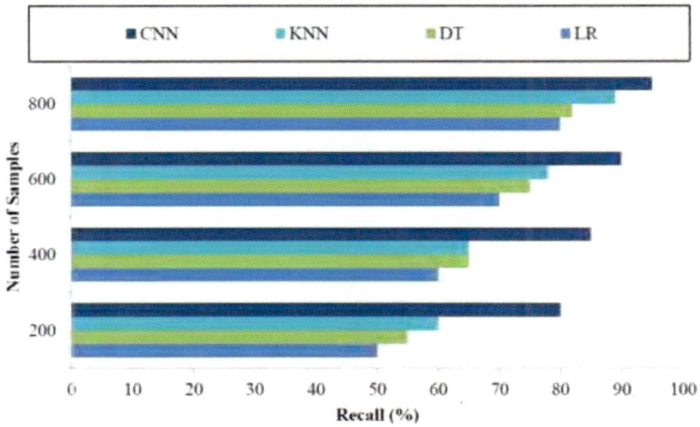


**Fig. (7).** Recall *vs*. number of samples.

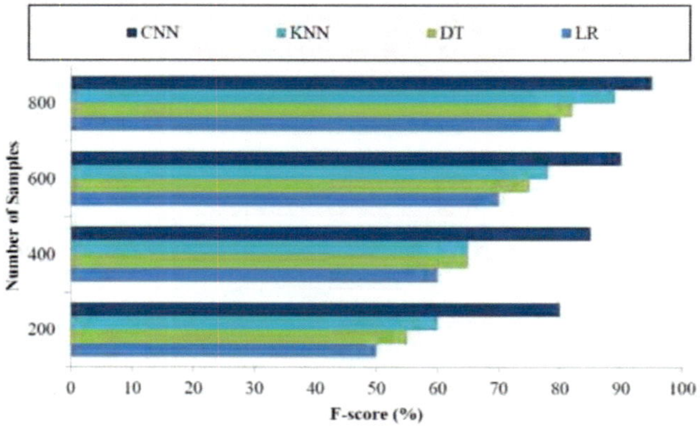


**Fig. (8).** F-score *vs*. number of samples.

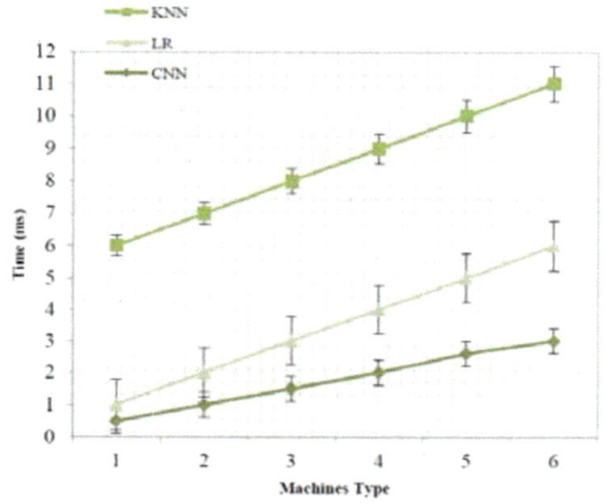


**Fig. (9).** Machines type *vs*. time.

$$\text{Accuracy} = \frac{\text{NumberofCorrectPredictions}}{\text{TotalNumberofPredictions}}$$
$$\text{Judgment} = \frac{\text{TruePositive}}{\text{TruePositive} + \text{FalsePositive}}$$
$$\text{Recollation} = \frac{\text{TruePositive}}{\text{TruePositive} + \text{FalseNegative}} \quad (5)$$
$$\text{F1\_Score} = 2 * \frac{\text{Judgment} * \text{Recollation}}{\text{Judgment} + \text{Recollation}}$$

# CONCLUSION

Thanks to developments in computation in the cloud, IoT, Big data, the mobile the web, and other areas, it is now feasible to collect enormous quantities of varied data. Due to model difficulties or inadequate data utilisation, outdated defect prediction methods are unacceptable in today's intelligent workplace. The fault prediction method can utilize huge amounts of industrial information to foretell when the gadgets will malfunction without knowing the main approach. Data on past noise levels and states are collected for use in developing an expert system for detecting and classifying hidden faults. The field data is then analysed to provide the fault predictions. Results from simulations have shown that the strategy outperforms comparable approaches. Intermittent device failures are a major threat to steady output, but our approach can mitigate such issues to a significant degree. It helps industries save money and increase production efficiency by detecting problems early and correctly.

## REFERENCES


[1] Z. Liu, and D. Yang, " "Research and Application of Wear Prediction Method of NC Milling Cutter Based on Data-Driven", *2022 11th International Conference of Information and Communication Technology (ICTech)*, 2022 pp. 1-6, Wuhan, China. [http://dx.doi.org/10.1109/ICTech55460.2022.00101]

[2] G. Lu, Y. Zhongqing, Y. Jianqi, and L. Chuang, "Data Driven Induction Motor Condition Identification and Fault Prediction", *Proceedings of the 2nd International Conference on Big Data Technologies*, 2019. [http://dx.doi.org/10.1145/3358528.3358594]

[3] X. Wang, and K. Yan, "Fault Detection and Diagnosis of HVAC System Based on Federated Learning", *2022 IEEE Intl Conf on Dependable, Autonomic and Secure Computing, Intl Conf on Pervasive Intelligence and Computing, Intl Conf on Cloud and Big Data Computing, Intl Conf on Cyber Science and Technology Congress (DASC/PiCom/CBDCom/CyberSciTech)*, pp. 1-8, 2022. [http://dx.doi.org/10.1109/DASC/PiCom/CBDCom/Cy55231.2022.9927944]

[4] J. Kaur, J. Saxena, and J. Shah, *2022 International Conference on Computational Intelligence and Sustainable Engineering Solutions (CISES)*, 2022 . [http://dx.doi.org/10.1109/CISES54857.2022.9844366]

[5] J. Mbuli, M. Nouiri, D. Trentesaux, and D. Baert, "Root causes analysis and fault prediction in intelligent transportation systems: coupling unsupervised and supervised learning techniques", *2019 International Conference on Control, Automation and Diagnosis (ICCAD)*, pp. 1-6, 2019. [http://dx.doi.org/10.1109/ICCAD46983.2019.9037877]

[6] P. Bellini, D. Cenni, A.I. Palesi, P. Nesi, and G. Pantaleo, "A Deep Learning Approach for Short Term Prediction of Industrial Plant Working Status", *IEEE Seventh International Conference on Big Data Computing Service and Applications (BigDataService)*, pp. 9-16, 2021. [http://dx.doi.org/10.1109/BigDataService52369.2021.00007]

[7] L. Wen, L. Gao, X. Li, M. Xie, and G. Li, "A new data-driven intelligent fault diagnosis by using convolutional neural network", *2017 IEEE International Conference on Industrial Engineering and Engineering Management (IEEM)*, pp. 813-817, 2017. [http://dx.doi.org/10.1109/IEEM.2017.8290004]

[8] Z. Guangfei, T. Wen, and Z. Da, "Ice Detection for Wind Turbine Blades Based on PSO-SVM Method", *J. Phys. Conf. Ser.*, vol. 1087, p. 022036, 2018. [http://dx.doi.org/10.1088/1742-6596/1087/2/022036]

[9] J.C. Kabugo, S.J. Jounela, R. Schiemann, and C. Binder, "Process Monitoring Platform based on Industry 4.0 tools: a waste-to-energy plant case study", *4th Conference on Control and Fault Tolerant Systems (SysTol)*, 2019 pp. 264-269. [http://dx.doi.org/10.1109/SYSTOL.2019.8864766]

[10] J.H. Ku, "A Study on Prediction Model of Equipment Failure Through Analysis of Big Data Based on RHadoop", *Wirel. Pers. Commun.*, vol. 98, no. 4, pp. 3163-3176, 2018.

[http://dx.doi.org/10.1007/s11277-017-4151-1]

[11] S. P. Yadav, B. S. Bhati, D. P. Mahato, and S. Kumar, "Federated Learning for IoT Applications", *EAI/Springer Innovations in Communication and Computing. Springer International Publishing,* 2022. [http://dx.doi.org/10.1007/978-3-030-85559-8]

[12] Z. Qi, C. Tang, L. He, C. Jiang, J. Chen, and Y. Huang, "Research on Equipment Fault Prediction Method Based on Industrial Big Data", *Proceedings of the International Conference on Information Economy, Data Modeling and Cloud Computing, ICIDC 2022,* 2022. [http://dx.doi.org/10.4108/eai.17-6-2022.2322795]

[13] A. Corallo, A.M. Crespino, C.D. Biccari, M. Lazoi, and M. Lezzi, "Processing big data in streaming for fault prediction: An industrial application", *Proc. IEEE Int. Conf. Information Technology and Systems (SITIS),* pp. 1-6, 2018. [http://dx.doi.org/10.1109/SITIS.2018.00117]

[14] T. Mi, "Fault prediction of process industry based on fuzzy clustering", *Proc. IEEE 8th Int. Conf. Big Data Security on Cloud (BigDataSecurity),* pp. 1-6, 2022. [http://dx.doi.org/10.1109/BigDataSecurity-HPSC-IDS54959.2022.00013]

[15] M. Rashid, H. Singh, V. Goyal, N. Ahmad, and N. Mogla, "Efficient big data-based storage and processing model in Internet of Things for improving accuracy fault detection in industrial processes", *Advances in Computer Science and Engineering,* 1st ed., H. Singh and M. M. Rashid, Eds. Hershey, PA, USA: IGI Global, pp. 125-140, 2020. [http://dx.doi.org/10.4018/978-1-7998-0373-7.ch009]

**CHAPTER 44**

# Comparison Analysis of Logical Regression and Random Forest with Word Embedding Techniques for Twitter Sentiment Analysis

**Dhiraj Singh**[1,*]

[1] *Centre for Interdisciplinary Research in Business and Technology, Chitkara University Institute of Engineering and Technology, Chitkara University, Punjab, India*

**Abstract:** In order to carry out categorization and generate new categories, the huge volumes of textual materials produced nowadays must be immediately organised. The fundamental method of gaining insights from organising textual data is text classification. Then, we further classify the classes based on the discovered text types. Separated into four stages—pre-treatment, text representation, classifier execution, and classification—we use a wide range of machine learning approaches to classify texts. In this study, we utilise real-world data from Twitter to evaluate and compare several sentiment analysis approaches. We clean the data and divide it into train and text set before developing models using various vectorising approaches and compare the outcomes. Based on a comparison of the models with various vectorizations, it was found that the best performance was provided by the Logical Regression (LR) models using TF-IDF, with an f1 value of 0.81 and good accuracy and recollection values.

**Keywords:** Logical regression, Random forest, Twitter sentiment analysis, TF-IDF.

## INTRODUCTION

Textual sentiment classification experiments employing online data have been conducted extensively in order to analyse the public's prevailing mood [1]. Sentiment classification at the aspect level, a more granular task that looks at both the sentence's overall content and its aspect information to determine its sentiment polarity, has lately received a lot of interest [2]. The main reason for this is that a statement may include elements of opposing polarity. In the sentence "This apple looks nice, yet the flavours are bland," the dichotomy is positive with respect to the observation that "This apple looks nice," but it changes to negative with

* **Corresponding author Dhiraj Singh:** Centre for Interdisciplinary Research in Business and Technology, Chitkara University Institute of Engineering and Technology, Chitkara University, Punjab, India;
E-mail: dhiraj.singh.orp@chitkara.edu.in

respect to the observation that "The taste is bland." To address the problem that existing emotion classification algorithms exhibit certain imperfections in obtaining as well as integrating both global and local characteristics of short text, in addition to a lack of attention to the crucial details in sentences, this paper provides a Weibo short-text opinion classification approach [3, 4]. Information may be efficiently extracted from time sequences using RNNs. Designing a perfect deep RNN is tough [5] because of setup and training issues including disappearing and exploding gradients. Comparative investigation reveals that the capsule network lacks the flexibility to quickly adopt the model compression method used by the traditional convolutional neural network. Based on the structural characteristics of the Capsule Networks, a proposed solution is an IPC-CapsNet compression method. The method has the potential to minimise computing complexity and condense the size of model computing [6] while preserving the reliability of model classification. In this paper, gradient boosting, a machine learning method that is currently gaining a lot of popularity, is also used. The harmony search technique has been used to optimize a number of tree parameters for the random forest and gradient boosting machine [7].On two separate datasets, namely the IMDb dataset and the polarity dataset, the performance of the proposed technique has been assessed using a variety of performance evaluation criteria, including Exactness, Recollection, f-measure, and accuracy [8]. The primary goals of this work are to describe the Random Forests construction process and the current state of Random Forests research in terms of capacity expansion and performance metrics [9]. It has been shown experimentally that this model requires less time to train than TextRNN. In the realm of short-term and low-volume data sentiment categorization, our 90.2% accuracy is the most advanced [10].

With an ever-increasing number of online conversations and transactions, it is important to be able to decipher the underlying feelings and perspectives expressed in online writing. Particularly applicable in the realm of social media, it may be used to gauge general sentiment toward certain issues. Data gleaned from social media sentiment analyses has a wide variety of potential uses, ranging from fine-tuning individual products and marketing strategies to informing public policy and forecasting economic performance.

- Information on Twitter and other social media platforms is a treasure mine of expression data, including information on individuals' feelings, thoughts, and perspectives on their everyday lives.
- Sentiment analysis is useful since so much of this stuff informs choices. The automated process of mining attitudes, opinions, thoughts, and emotions inside the text provides insights into the message's positivity, negativity, or apathy.
- The goal of this website is to examine how various sentiment analysis

techniques perform on actual Twitter data. Kaggle datasets (containing information about genuine tweets) are obtained, labelled (where zero represents a negative sentiment as well as one indicates an optimistic one), and then used to train a machine learning model.

## LITERATURE REVIEW

It is difficult to analyze sentiment on Malaysia's social media because messages are typically written in a combination of English and Malay, with embedded jargon and different district dialects. Each tweet was classified using the Malaysian halal certification scheme in order to determine the frequency value of the class label based on the polarity results of the sentiment analysis technique. It will show the propensity of social media users to post, and users can use it as a resource when making judgments. 500 tweets with the hashtag #sijilhalal were analyzed to learn more about how individuals felt, thought, and acted toward different halal certification-related topics in Malaysia. A person's feelings about halal subjects are discovered and visualized. Muslims' perspectives are crucial for raising awareness of the local dialects [11].

- In this study, we transform the creation of a language for expressing emotions into a training-optimization procedure. In our system, the precision of sentiment categorization serves as the optimization aim, therefore candidate emotion lexicons are seen as the ones that have to be optimized. You may find two genetic algorithms developed to alter the value assigned to words in the lexicon based on their emotional connotations at /en. The sentiment lexicon is ultimately chosen as the best individual that has evolved in the evolutionary algorithms that have been provided. Our approach simply requires a few marked texts, and it doesn't require any prior knowledge or linguistic expertise. It offers a quick and straightforward method for creating a sentiment lexicon in a certain industry. The results of the experiments demonstrate the proposed method's versatility and its ability to produce high-quality sentiment lexicon in particular domains [12].
- The study's four main findings are as follows: Here, we examine the relative efficacy of four distinct methods for conducting sentiment analysis: (1) a proposed method for preprocessing data for emotions categorization; (2) extra features to enhance the Exactness to feelings' categorization; (3) the application of singular as well as principal component assessment for data dimension reduction; and (4) the development of five modules based on various features, with or without a corresponding originating feature. The experimental results show that the suggested method is more efficient and accurate than its predecessors [13].
- This essay suggests a system for categorizing literature into six different emotional states: joy, sorrow, fear, anger, surprise, and disgust. To successfully

extract these emotions from text, we mix two alternative methodologies in our model. The first approach is based on NLP and uses grammatical analysis and textual features like emoticons, degree words, and negations in addition to more traditional analysis of Parts of Speech. The second tactic is a classification-based machine learning approach. We have also effectively developed a way to automate the development of the set used for training itself, which will save significant time and effort over manually annotating large datasets. Additionally, we were able to produce a sizable collection of emotive words and their corresponding emotion intensities. Testing has revealed that our algorithm significantly improves classification accuracy for tweets taken from Twitter [14].

- The mining of opinions is a branch of text analysis that parses internet reviews for expressions of approval and disapproval. In this research, we develop a system for opinion mining. We use a unique method for feature selection termed Most Persistent Feature Selection (MPFS), after which we apply a genetic algorithm (GA) to optimise the resultant feature set. The MPFS method relies on document characteristics to glean data for its analysis. The feature set generated in this manner is then optimised using the GA approach to ensure it is as effective as possible for sentiment classification. The algorithm for Support Vector Machines (SVM) and the recommended feature selection and optimisation approach is then used to categorise the opinions expressed in the reviews' text. The accuracy performance of the constructed classifier models is commendable if compared to other current models [15].

## PROPOSED WORK

An automated approach for categorizing tweets is developed in this study. The authors independently selected logistic regression and random forests as our classification methods and analyzed their relative merits in the classifier construction section. Finally, a conclusion was reached after these classifiers were put through their paces and compared to one another. The results of the experiments reveal that the algorithms used to classify tweets into categories provide satisfactory results. Exactness, accuracy, F1-value, support, and confusion matrix are the five metrics the authors settled on to display the comparison. For the Twitter dataset, the optimal machine learning algorithm is the classifier with the greatest values across all of these metrics.

### Data Collection, Preparation and Cleaning

The data needed to be cleaned before the primary models could be built using various vectorising approaches and compared. Both training and testing data were included in each dataset. To ensure consistency, these two datasets were combined once again after cleaning. When we cleaned the data, we got rid of all the other columns, such as Item ID, that were not essential. All caps have been converted to lowercase and superfluous symbols and digits have been eliminated. This culling resulted in tweets consisting mainly of words and their associated emotions. During data collection, labels were applied to sentiment text to create a feature set (X), and the resulting labelled data (Y) was used to make predictions. Feature disaggregation is performed with a test and training set.

The Kaggle data collection is called TwitterAirlineSentiment. There are around 15,000 tweets in this dataset, and the attitude may be classified as good, negative, or neutral. Using tokenization and two different classifiers, as I described in my previous piece, we attempted to categorize the tweets. Fig. (**1**). shows the System Flowchart.

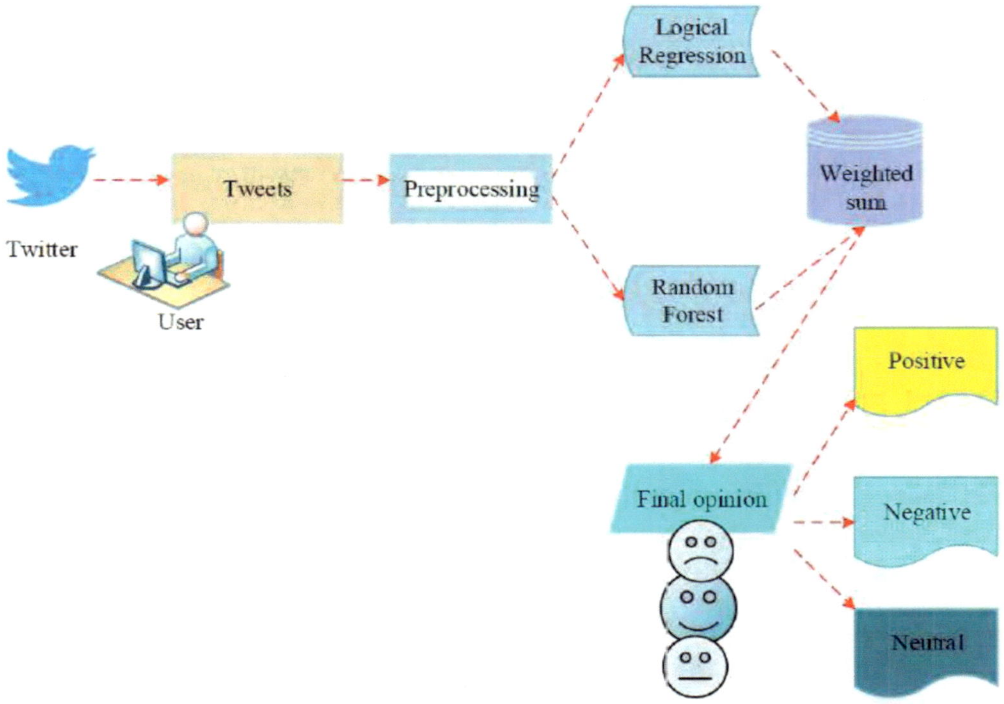


**Fig. (1).** System flowchart.

## Vectorization

Words encoded using one-hot encoding produce high-dimensional, sparse (including many zeros) vectors. This may lead to performance concerns on huge data sets. One-hot encoding is also problematic since it disregards the meaning of words. Airplane and aircraft are therefore split into two categories. While we are aware that they signify essentially the same thing. These two problems are solved by word embedding.

Word embedding is a low-dimensional dense vector. Second, the vector distance and direction describe the underlying semantic links between words.

Two different approaches, TF-IFD vectorization and Word2Vec mean vectorization, were then used to vactorise the dataset. Term importance in a corpus is measured by a metric called TF-IDF, which stands for term frequency and inverse document frequency. Its major function is to remove the need for manual filtering of terms in applications for in-text summarization and classification. To account for the fact that certain phrases are just more common than others, the TF-IDF value grows proportionately with the word's frequency in the text while decreasing by its presence in the corpus.

Word2Vec is a tool that helps construct word embedding by optimizing the probability that words are anticipated based on their context. Converting phrases and words into a vector representations is a novel method for text classification that adds additional semantic aspects to in-text classification. The vectors provide a numerical representation of the word's significance. In a nutshell, it is a statistical approach for quickly extracting a word embedded from a text corpus.

## Vectors of Words

The next stage, after cleaning, is to encode the text in a way that machines can interpret. That's why we utilized Victimizer, which transforms a string of text into a numerical vector, "term frequency inverse document frequency" (TF-IDF). Because of advancements in natural language processing, word vectors may now provide computers far more data about the words compared to earlier analyses. Word vectors display words as "multidimensional continuous floating-point numbers" by displaying a set of real-valued amounts in which every single point captures a dimension of the word's meaning, whereas traditional NPL approaches were unable to capture syntactic as well as semantic connections across collections of words. In this case, the text is transformed into a numerical representation of meaning using vectors that are comparable to those used for semantically related terms. Word occurrences may be normalized by data set size using the term frequency, and less-important terms can be removed from sentence meaning decisions using inverse document frequency. Therefore, all occurrences of the phrase in the text would be transformed into 0. The TF-IDF method filters out redundant terms while also isolating important characteristics from the corpus. Words that occur more often in the text but in a narrower context in the corpus are given special attention by the TF-IDF algorithm. Thus, this term is the most effective in the text in differentiating across types. The TF-IDF method may be expressed mathematically as:

$$TF - IDF\ (w) = TF\ (w) * (IDF)\ (w) \quad \textbf{(1)}$$

## Text Classification Models

The attitudes of tweets were predicted using two classification algorithms: Logistic Regression (LR) & Random Forest (RF). Notably, hyper parameters were identified using a grid search approach. In the next paragraph, this topic will be elaborated.

When investigating outcomes represented by binary variables, Logistic Regression is often used. Machine learning uses this statistical method for its own prediction purposes. Data may be described and the connection between a single binary dependent variable and the independent variables can be explained using this method. Instead of predicting the specific category an observation belongs in, Logistic Regression instead provides a chance that the observation is in category 1.

The probability may be estimated using a simple mathematical formula, which looks like this.

- *P (Probability of being '1') = 1/(1 + e - z) where*
- *Z = C + a1X1 + a2X2 + ..., + anXn*

Where X1, X2,..., Xn are characteristics of the observation and a1, a2,..., an are the 'weights' assigned to each feature. A higher value assigned to a criterion indicates more importance in reaching a conclusion.

In order to categorise a new instance, Random Forest builds a forest of decision trees and uses a majority vote. Each node in the decision tree employs a subset of the original characteristics chosen at random. Together, the decision tree classifiers and their individual features make up a Meta estimator that improves prediction quality. This method is essentially an expansion of a decision tree, with the key distinction being that it returns the aggregated result of numerous individual trees. When classifying an observation, one decision tree considers all of the characteristics independently. However, every tree in the model of a random forest will only consider a fraction of the whole feature set to draw conclusions, thus the name. By randomly picking subsets of characteristics, certain trees in the forest might isolate more relevant information while enhancing the overall Exactness of the output, which is why a Random Forest system performs better than a typical decision tree model.

The random forest may also be inaccurate at times since it relies on two factors: (i) The error rate rises because there is a possibility that any two trees in the forest are correlated with each other. (ii) The power of each tree is unique. Therefore, a powerful classifier is a tree with a low mistake rate, and vice versa.

- Some of random forest's characteristics include: (i) Capable of processing a large number of input parameters without needing to eliminate any. (ii) It identifies the distinguishing characteristics that aid in categorization. (iii) Effective operation of big datasets. (iv) The resulting woods and trees may be preserved for further use.
- Stages for the algorithmic random forest: Stage 1: Pick K seemingly unrelated data items from the training set. Stage 2: Create a decision tree based on this set of information. Stage 3: You may continue steps 1 and 2 until you reach the required tree size. Stage 4: Create a new tree tree from scratch for every piece of information, while employing the mean of the predicted y numbers for that node.

For a random forest classifier, the formula is:

$$\begin{aligned} n_{ij} &= w_l C_j - w_{\text{left }(j)} C_{\text{left }(j)} - w_{\text{right }(j)} C_{\text{right }(j)} \\ ni\text{sub}(j) &= \text{the imporTo calculate a random forest algorithm, one uses the formulatance of node } j \\ w\text{sub}(j) &= \text{"weighted amount of samples reaching the node" } j \\ C\text{sub}(j) &= \text{"the node's impurity index" } j \\ \text{left }(j) &= \text{"left-child node branching off" } j \\ \text{right }(j) &= \text{"split on right-child node" } j \end{aligned} \quad (2)$$

## RESULTS AND DISCUSSION

The expected result was received when the code was successfully ran. Accuracy, Exactness, F1-value, support, and confusion matrix are the five criteria used to evaluate and contrast different methods. One by one, let us see how well these three algorithms perform.

### The Logistic Regression of TF-IDF

Here, we will talk about what we learned using LR modelling and TF-IDF vectorization. Since TF-IDF also takes into account n-grams, its value is equivalent to two. This may be seen in the fact that the adjective “very bad” is a 2-gram, meaning that it is a distinct quality from the terms “very” and “bad”.

After being fed into the model of LR, the test data revealed:

- Recollection: [0.76, 0.8]
  Exactness: [0.7, 0.81]
  F1_value: [0.75. 0.81]

## Word2Vec Logistic Regression

In this piece, we will talk about how we used a logistic regression model to analyse the parameters and output of Word2Vec. Words may be entered and processed in any processing of natural languages activity by first being converted to a vector (an array of integers). The word2vec mean technique was used to calculate an average word vector for this analysis. In order to provide a fair comparison of the methods, we utilised the same parameters inside the logistic regression.

Here are the outcomes:

- Recollection: [0.71, 0.7]
  Exactness: [0.65, 0.76]
  F1_value: [0.68, 0.73]

## TF-IDF Random Forest

Similar settings were utilized for the TF-IDF and logistic regression models in the random forest model. With a maximum depth of 13, and a total of 500 estimators, a random forest classifier was built.

What we found from this data set was:

- Recollection: [0.72, 0.76]
  Exactness: [0.7, 0.78]
  F1_value: [0.71, 0.77]

## Word2Vec's Random Forest

The parameters in this model were identical as before.

This data set's findings include:

- Recollection: [0.63, 0.76]
  Exactness: [0.67, 0.72]
  F1_value: [0.65, 0.74]

## CONCLUSION

In this research, we use machine learning methods to build a categorization model for tweets. This work suggests the use of logistic regression and random forest methods, both of which provide comprehensive descriptions of the models they evaluate. When applying machine learning algorithms to a specific dataset, accuracy is the most crucial metric to consider. Therefore, the result demonstrates that 97% accuracy is achieved by the logistic regression classifier using the TF-IDF Vectorizer feature. In a short data set, this approach has shown to be the most consistent classifier. The classifier based on random forests came in second, with an accuracy of 93%. The method has the lowest overall accuracy in the 92% accurate random forest. The results from a logistic regression classifier were consistent with expectations across all measures. As a result, the outcome conformed to the anticipations. In the articles cited, we explain why these particular three methods were chosen. As a result, the authors of this work set out to identify the most appropriate algorithm for this task.

The LR model using TF-IDF performed best, with a f1 of 0.81 and good Exactness and Recollection, when compared to the other models using alternative vectorizations. Although LR with TF-IDF was shown to be the most effective, Word2vec analysis provides extra resources and may be highly useful in many cases. Exploring the application of NPL techniques for deep learning to get better outcomes is a necessary next step.

## REFERENCES

[1] G. Li, B. Kong, J. Li, H. Fan, J. Zhang, Y. An, Z. Yang, S. Danz, and J. Fan, "A BERT-based Text Sentiment Classification Algorithm through Web Data", *International Conference on Computer Engineering and Artificial Intelligence (ICCEAI),* pp. 477-481, 2022. [http://dx.doi.org/10.1109/ICCEAI55464.2022.00105]

[2] M. Zhang, V. Palade, Y. Wang, and Z. Ji, "Attention-based word embeddings using Artificial Bee Colony algorithm for aspect-level sentiment classification", *Inf. Sci.,* vol. 545, pp. 713-738, 2021. [http://dx.doi.org/10.1016/j.ins.2020.09.038]

[3] S. Zeybek, D.T. Pham, E. Koç, and A. Seçer, "An Improved Bees Algorithm for Training Deep Recurrent Networks for Sentiment Classification", *Symmetry (Basel),* vol. 13, no. 8, p. 1347, 2021. [http://dx.doi.org/10.3390/sym13081347]

[4] X. Zhang, T. Jiang, and Y. Lv, "Weibo Short-text Sentiment Classification Algorithm on Serial Hybrid Network", *7th International Conference on Intelligent Computing and Signal Processing (ICSP),* pp. 535-539, 2022. [http://dx.doi.org/10.1109/ICSP54964.2022.9778753]

[5] A. Jain, and V. Jain, "Sentiment classification using hybrid feature selection and ensemble classifier", *J. Intell. Fuzzy Syst.,* vol. 42, no. 2, pp. 659-668, 2022. [http://dx.doi.org/10.3233/JIFS-189738]

[6] X. Zhong, J. Liu, L. Li, S. Chen, W. Lu, Y. Dong, B. Wu, and L. Zhong, "An emotion classification algorithm based on SPT-CapsNet", *Neural Comput. Appl.,* vol. 32, no. 7, pp. 1823-1837, 2020. [http://dx.doi.org/10.1007/s00521-019-04621-y]

[7] K. Sridharan, and G. Komarasamy, "RETRACTED ARTICLE: Sentiment classification using harmony random forest and harmony gradient boosting machine", *Soft Comput.,* vol. 24, no. 10, pp. 7451-7458, 2020. [http://dx.doi.org/10.1007/s00500-019-04370-z]

[8] N.M. Abdulkareem, and A.M. Abdulazeez, "Machine Learning Classification Based on Radom Forest Algorithm", *Review,* 2021.

[9] M. Xuanyuan, L. Xiao, and M. Duan, "Sentiment Classification Algorithm Based on Multi-Modal Social Media Text Information", *IEEE Access,* vol. 9, pp. 33410-33418, 2021. [http://dx.doi.org/10.1109/ACCESS.2021.3061450]

[10] R.B. Setik, R.M. Ahmad, and S. Marjudi, ""Exploring Classification For Sentiment Analysis From Halal Based Tweets". *2021 2nd International Conference on Artificial Intelligence and Data Sciences (AiDAS),* 2021 pp. 1-6, IPOH, Malaysia. [http://dx.doi.org/10.1109/AiDAS53897.2021.9574255]

[11] S. P. Yadav, B. S. Bhati, D. P. Mahato, and S. Kumar, "Federated Learning for IoT Applications", In: *EAI/Springer Innovations in Communication and Computing. Springer International Publishing*, 2022. [http://dx.doi.org/10.1007/978-3-030-85559-8]

[12] C.H. Cheng, and H.H. Chen, "Sentimental text mining based on an additional features method for text classification", *PLoS One,* vol. 14, no. 6, p. e0217591, 2019. [http://dx.doi.org/10.1371/journal.pone.0217591] [PMID: 31166975]

[13] A. Bhowmik, S. K. Murugan, V. Vani, and N. Karthik, "Opinion mining and sentimental analysis of Twitter data during India's general elections", *Proc. 2024 15th Int. Conf. Computing Communication and Networking Technologies (ICCCNT),* Bangalore, India, pp. 1-5, Jul. 2024. [http://dx.doi.org/10.1109/ICCCNT.2024.00123]

[14] S. Goyal, "Sentimental analysis of Twitter data using text mining and hybrid classification approach", *Int. J. Adv. Res. Ideas Innov. Technol,* vol. 2, no. 5, pp. 112-118, 2016. Available from: https://www.ijariit.com/papers/sentimental-analysis-of-twitter-data-using-text-mi-ing-and-hybrid-classification-approach/

[15] A. Kumar, D. Sharma, and D. Singh, "Sentimental analysis using Twitter data with LSTM, CNN, and Extra Tree classifier methods", In: *Proc. 2023 5th Int. Conf. Advances in Computing, Communication Control and Networking (ICAC3N)* Jaipur, India, Dec. 2023, pp. 292-300. [http://dx.doi.org/10.1109/ICAC3N54323.2023.00235]

# CHAPTER 45

# The Classification of News Articles Through the Use of Deep Learning and the Doc2Vec Modeling

**Himanshu Makhija**[1,*]

[1] *Centre for Interdisciplinary Research in Business and Technology, Chitkara University Institute of Engineering and Technology, Chitkara University, Punjab, India*

**Abstract:** The exponential growth in internet use has also led to the proliferation of textual information in large quantities. Since handling unstructured material manually is difficult, there is a need to explore novel techniques for automated categorization of textual information. The primary goal of text categorization is to teach a model to correctly categorise an unseen text. In this research, the Doc2vec word embedding technique was used to classify stories in Turkish from the TTC-3600 database of Turkish news and BBC news stories in English. In addition to the CNN based on deep learning, traditional machine learning classification methods including Gauss Naive Bayes (GNB), Random Forest (RF), Naive Bayes (NB), and Support Vector Machine (SVM) are used. The best classification results using CNN were achieved with the proposed model, scoring 94.17% on the Turkish database and 96.41% on the English database.

**Keywords:** CNN, News articles, TTC-3600 databases.

## INTRODUCTION

The newspaper articles provide us with a perspective on many current events [1]. The proliferation of online material has led to a direct impact on people's everyday lives, and digital news is no exception [2]. The availability of such a news story calls for the necessity to categorise it. The number of Indonesian news stories published online has exploded thus far this decade [3]. Data on financial systemic danger is included in the data on economy. Automatically classifying systemic risk documents is a necessary step towards obtaining real-time data on finance systemic risk [4]. In this work, we use deep neural networks and proactive learning to automatically categorise documents relating to systemic risk [5]. We use the Bank of Indonesia's 15 categories of financial systemic risk. There may be more than one piece of systemic risk information inside a text document, hence

* **Corresponding author Himanshu Makhija:** Centre for Interdisciplinary Research in Business and Technology, Chitkara University Institute of Engineering and Technology, Chitkara University, Punjab, India;
E-mail: himanshu.makhija.orp@chitkara.edu.in

**Pankaj Kumar Mishra and Satya Prakash Yadav (Eds.)**

this is a tasking-label classification issue [6]. We have made numerous variations in the deep learning strategies of CNN, Bi-LSTM, and Bi-GRU [7]. In addition, we have drawn parallels to a two-stage categorization system. The internet has evolved into a platform for instantaneous global communication [8]. However, this exponential expansion of the World Wide Web has also facilitated the widespread dissemination of false information. Many classifiers have been proposed in the current literature to differentiate between fake and real news. However, they need a lot of information before they can learn well, and such data is difficult to collect [9]. The growth of bogus and falsified material across several internet web platforms in recent years has led to the establishment of skewed and sometimes influenced public opinion on political, social, and other daily life topics. As a result, there have been several attempts to create fake news detection algorithms to aid in exposing and refuting false information [10].

The purpose of this research is to evaluate Deep Learning and Doc2Vec techniques in comparison to previously explored techniques for classifying articles on Turkish and English data sets. Based on the pre-processing processes used with the TTC-3600 and BBC-News databases, four distinct data sets were generated and documented for this study. After developing the Doc2Vec training model, we used CNN, GNB, RF, NB, and SVM to label each dataset.

For the Turkish database, the created model achieved higher rates of accuracy than the previous research. The average accuracy rate for the English dataset came out rather well. The article's remaining sections are as follows: The methods used are described in Chapter 2, and the data set, prior treatment phases, and constructed models are described in depth in the materials and methods section of Chapter 3. The technique discussed in Chapter 4 is evaluated in light of past research, and the paper is concluded .

## RELATED WORK

In this study, we present a new deep learning model called Long Short-Term Memory-Gradient Boosting (LSTM-GB) for news article categorization and evaluate its performance in comparison to that of established techniques. The suggested model also outperforms existing classifiers [11] with an accuracy of 99.8 percent.

Using 1752 articles for training and 228 articles for testing, the maximum F1 value was reached by using a Bi-LSTM topology with a single classification step and a large common corpus for word embeddings. For 15 courses, the greatest F1 value was 45.37 percent, using a probability threshold of 0.15. The first phase of the two-stage classification process achieved an accuracy of 82.46%, classifying items into one of the two categories (containing risk information or not). Because of the small sample size, we used active learning to choose which data points would come next for labelling. The experiment demonstrated that employing active learning did not increase performance [12] for 420 new data items for each iteration adding 20 new data items.

This research aims to identify flooding occurrences by analyzing both the text and visuals of web news articles from Africa. MediaEval 2019 provides this information as part of the Multimodal Satellite Task. Both the picture and text-based tasks benefit from our efforts. We construct models able to obtain features from photos and texts independently, and then integrate them to generate a complex classifier, which is more convincing proof of floods, and so allows us to perform the necessary classification subtasks. In particular, we use a strong text processing approach determined by long short-term storage cells and the convolutional layers-based MobileNet architecture for image processing. On the company's test sets, our final models performed well, with an average F1-value of 85.26 percent for the first subtask as well as 66.19 percent for the second task. [13].

In this research, we explore how deep learning approaches, including testing using various databases and implementation across multiple categorization models, may be used to detect and categorise bogus news throughout the web. We improved accuracy by 96.25 percent using the deep learning model we presented. The techniques of text categorization have been enhanced by the use of word embedding techniques. By minimising the loss value, the model design for fake information classification has been improved. To properly categorise data, the model needs hyper parameters after training on two distinct real-world databases [14].

The goal of this thesis is to visualise language distinctions between false and genuine articles across three distinct fake news databases. The goal of this research is to determine which of the five machine learning classifiers provides the best universal results across all three data sources by comparing them and developing an ensemble approach comprising multiple combinations of classification models. The outcomes of a deep learning approach were then compared to those of statistical machine learning models, thus a basic long short-term memory neural network was built. As the first step in this project's approach, we use NLP and feature extraction tools to clean and prepare the data that will be "fed" into the various classification models throughout the training and tuning phases. Bar graphs, confusion matrices, and extractness-recollotion curves are then used to display and compare the findings of Data Mining, Data Visualisation, Machine Learning, and Deep Learning [15].

## TECHNIQUES AND MATERIALS

There are several online sites that provide massive volumes of news content every day. Furthermore, user demand for information has been rising steadily, making it essential that news be categorised so that users may quickly and easily locate material of interest to them. The automated news categorization model trained with machine learning might then be used to categorise previously unreported news stories into subjects of interest to the user. As such, we want to develop models that accept a news headline and brief description as input and provide a news category as output. Multiple categories may be applied to a single news story. A story regarding a change in the football team's ownership, for example, might be filed under many different sections, including sports, business, and world news. Can a system for machine learning recognise and properly assign several labels to a piece of content, as humans can? Text categorization databases can be utilised to assign topics to written pieces in natural languages.

Let us consider the task of categorising news items by subject or book reviews by positive/negative rating. Language identification, customer feedback organisation, and fraud detection are three other areas where text categorization becomes useful. Machine learning models may automate what would otherwise be a labor-intensive manual operation. News category classification is a text classification issue with several labels. The objective is to label a news item with a suitable classification. Using several binary classifiers is a common practice in multi-label text classification. Traditional machine learning-based news text categorization mostly covers the following issues: When representing news articles using conventional techniques, important contextual cues like word order and meaning are lost in translation. However, it will not take into account the contextual meaning of the words in the news article. Manual participation in the extraction of features of news text is subjective, time-consuming, and labor-intensive; using a vector space model to convey news text will lead to high latitude as information sparsity issues; however, the approach to choosing features can be used for density reduction; however, this will only exacerbate the issue with news' text feature loss as well as complicate the entire news classification of text. The efficiency of news text categorization will be negatively impacted by these issues. As a result, novel approaches to text feature representation and text feature extraction need to be investigated.

# TECHNIQUES AND MATERIALS

## Database Description

In 2015, researchers produced the TTC-3600 database for widespread usage in Turkish news categorization research. The TTC-3600 database is available, and it is both user-friendly and well-documented, having been released in Turkish news databases in recent years. There are a total of 3,600 documents in the collection, and among them are 600 pieces of news or other writings covering the economy, culture and arts, health, politics, sports, and technology. Fig. (**1**) portrays the system flow model.

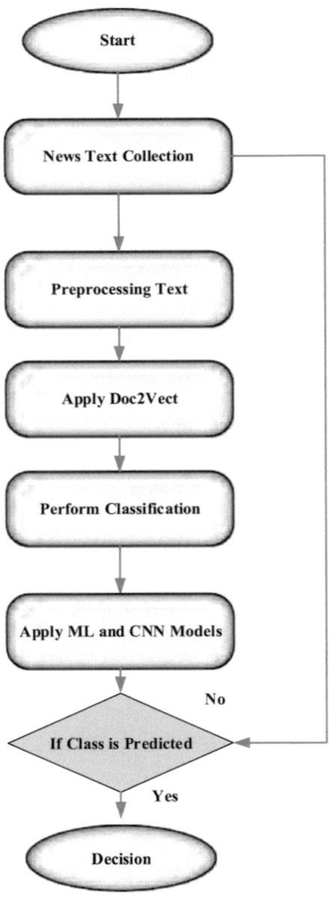


**Fig. (1).** System flow model.

Between May and July of 2015, news articles were gathered using Rich Site Summary (RSS) from relevant news websites. The English news was classified using the BBC News database. Total 2225 text documents were explored and included in the BBC-News database, which were published on the BBC news website during 2004 and 2005, covering a wide range of themes including economics, pop culture, politics, sports, and technology. Important preliminary operations were performed on the raw data that would eventually become the two databases. To investigate the effect of these steps on the success rate, we combined two data sets to create four distinct datasets. There were four distinct data collections established: the raw data collection (Orig-DS), the cleaned data collection (C-DS), the stemmed data collection (Stem-DS), the combined clean and tidy stemmed information collection (Clean + Stem-DS).

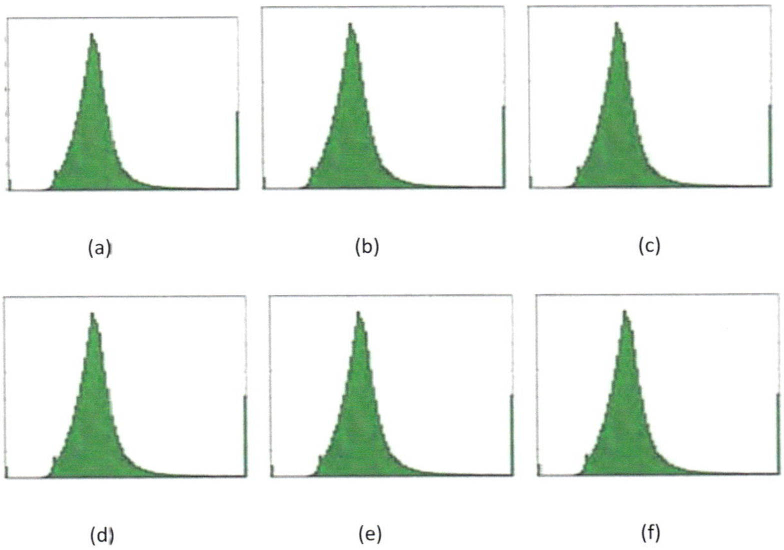


**Fig. (2).** (**a**). Economy, (**b**). Culture, (**c**). Arts, (**d**). Health, (**e**). Politics and (**f**). Sports & Technology.

Arguably, the most influential aspects of the success rate is the quality of the data preparation. These text pretreatment processes were conducted to the TTC-3600 & BBC-News databases before they were vectorized. Throughout all of our lessons, we often use stop words. Because they contributed nothing unique to the database and lowered accurateness, these terms were eliminated. Fig. (**2**) is represented in (**a**). Economy, (**b**). Culture, (**c**). Arts, (**d**). Health, (**e**). Politics and (**f**). Sports & Technology.

## Doc2Vec

The machine can now understand human-written texts thanks to the Word Embedding technique. Words are encoded as vectors and the system is built on artificial neural networks. In this research, the Doc2Vec paradigm was employed to incorporate words. Quoc Le & Tomas Mikolov's Doc2Vec creates a document-representation vector for use in target-word prediction. The document's length is ignored throughout this process. There are two ways to tackle this problem. Two examples of such models are the Paragraph Vector Distributed Memory (PV-DM) and the Paragraph Vector Distribution Bag of Words (PV-DBOW). Each paragraph in a PV-DM document is treated as a word and assigned its own unique identity in the form of a vector representation. In the first step, random vectors are generated. It is like a moving memory that fills in the blanks for what's lacking in the present situation. The word vector stands in for the notion of a word, much as the document vector does for the concept of a document. Instead of predicting the target word, PV-DBOW employs a sentence vector to categorise terms on the page. Since no word vectors need to be stored, this data structure has a low memory and CPU footprint.

All Doc2Vec training model is initially developed, which converts the databases into vector form. When developing a Doc2Vec model, several contexts must be taken into consideration. Words are discarded if their combined frequency is less than the minimum (min_count = 5) and maximum (iter = 50). We have complete command over the following parameters: a maximum distance (window = 3), number of repeats (iter = 50), number of features in the vector (vector_size = 100), and number of Dov2Vec approaches (dm = 1).

### Naive Bayes

Naive Bayes is one of the most basic, readily explained, and widely used machine learning algorithms for text classification. The probability that a sample's target attribute corresponds to a given class value may be calculated using this strategy.

### Gauss Naive Bayes

Classification of both category and numerical data following a Gaussian distribution is possible using Gauss Naive Bayes. When dealing with Gauss (Normal distribution), estimating the average as well as the standard deviation using the training data is the least complicated task. For each category, we may determine its median and standard deviation of the information they provide. An estimate of the likelihood of this new value entered for that class is supplied when these parameters are introduced to the Gaussian likelihood Density Function during prediction.

### Random Forest

The random forest technique can only be used in a controlled environment. A forest is generated at random using the algorithm. The algorithm's performance scales linearly with the total amount of trees it uses. When more trees are used, a more accurate estimate may be made. The random forest categorization strategy is favoured because of its many benefits. It is useful for both regression and classification problems. If there are sufficient forests in the forest, this technique has a lower chance of encountering the overfitting issue. Over-learning is a serious issue that has a chilling effect on performance. In addition, the classifier may be modelled for discrete values, which is useful in many contexts.

## Support Vector Machine

Support Vector Machine may use linear, planar, or hyperplanar separation processes in two, three, or more dimensions to categorise data into multiple classifications. Nonlinear data may be effectively classified using this approach, which is often employed to determine the classes that can be divided linearly, by projecting the input space that is unable to be divided linearly by functions in the kernel to this higher dimensionality linearly separable space.

## Convolutional Neural Network (CNN)

In Deep Learning, the number of buried layers of an artificial neural network is raised and a new facet of the issue is learned at each successive layer. Learned characteristics at each successive layer serve as inputs to the one above. Fig. (**3**) is portrayed in CNN model.

Thus, a framework is built in which features ranging from the most basic to the most intricate are taught from the bottom up. The goal of deep education is to use a variety of transformations on the input data to get to a place where the learning algorithm can do its best work. While convolutional neural networks (CNNs) have found the most success in image processing, they have also been widely employed in text categorization research in recent years. Convolutional layers, pooling layers, and fully connected layers make up the fundamental building blocks of a convolutional neural network design. The input is refined at the convolutional level, and feature maps are extracted. In the pooling layer, map features are sampled to facilitate quicker, more efficient network learning. Finally, in the fully linked layer, each neuron produces an output that is a function of all of the inputs it has received up to that point. By merging and training all layers, it is possible to learn the attribute hierarchy, since each layer collects attributes depending on the output of the preceding layer. The goal is efficient learning, from the most basic concepts to the most complex ones.

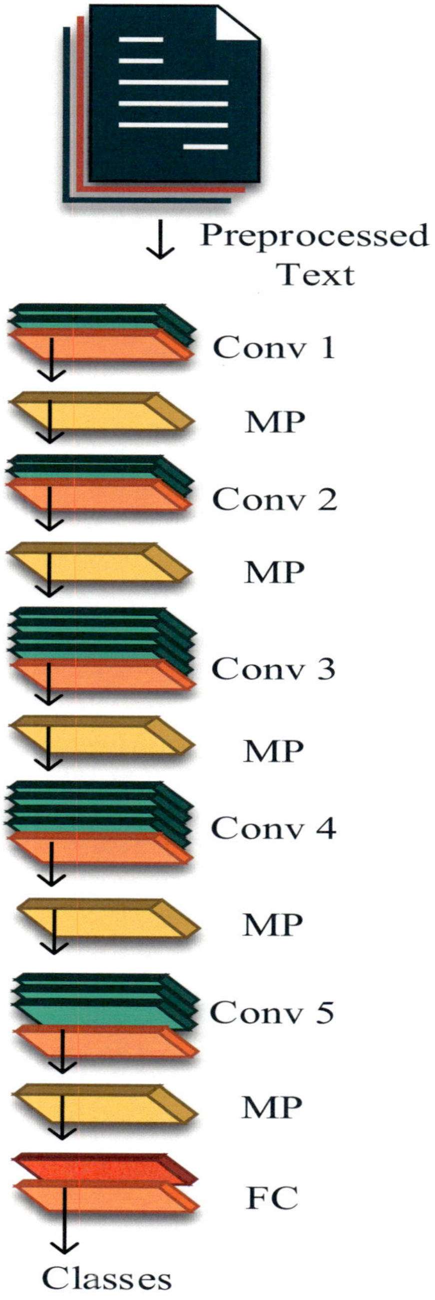


**Fig. (3).** CNN model.

Each database was prepared for classification once a Doc2Vec model was developed for it. The maximum pooling procedure is used in the suggested CNN model. To minimise feature variance, feature maps are combined and their size is shrunk between convolution layers. Then, the layers are flattened and made dense. The model's hidden layers are activated using the ReLU function, while the output layer is activated with the Softmax function. There are 4 conv layers in the model. Except for the last conv layer, max pooling is introduced after every conv layer. The thick layers were put after the flattened layer. For categorization, we settled on the Softmax function.

## RESULTS AND DISCUSSION

Through developing a Doc2Vec model, we want to analyse the success rates of different preprocessing steps used for the TTC-3600 and BBC-News databases. The suggested strategy divides the documents used to train the Doc2Vec model into 90 percent training data and 10 percent test data for classification purposes. Next, we used the CNN deep learning model together with the GNB, RF, NB, and SVM algorithms to categorise the databases. Tensorflow and Keras are Python libraries used for CNN classification. Knime, a platform for data analysis, was employed during machine learning classifications.

When compared to other artificial intelligence classification algorithms, CNN produces the highest accuracy rates across the board. Some text preparation stages are observed to diminish the achievement rate in some neural network algorithms, while others boost the accurateness rate attained using CNN. Accurateness basically tells us right away whether an example is well-trained and how well it will perform in general. However, it fails to offer specifics on how to apply it to the issue at hand. Therefore, knowing the accurateness, sensitivity, and f1 value will help us arrive at a more accurate conclusion. Thus, additional success criteria were considered alongside classification accurateness where applicable. The proportion of the database that was properly assessed by our model serves as our accurateness value. Extractness reveals what percentage of estimated positive values turn out to be such. When the price of a false positive estimate is considerable, the accurateness value becomes paramount. The proportion of transactions for which a positive prediction is required may be measured using a statistic called recolletion. When the cost of a False Negative estimate is significant, it will be useful to have a high Recolleticn value as well. The height should be maximised. By averaging Extractness and Recolletion, the F1 Value reveals their harmonic mean. The need to account for outliers is why we are using a harmonic average rather than a basic one.

Table **1** shows the outcomes of the proposed approach by comparing TTC-3600, TTC-4900, and BBC-News databases with the outcomes of prior research. We found an accurateness of 94.00% and an f1 value of 94.17% for the Turkish database, indicating that our proposed model outperforms its predecessors. Although the best result was not achieved on the BBC-News database, the accurateness of 96.41% and the f1 value of 96.00% were both above par. The English wording is somewhat more precise than the Turkish version. The identical geometrical characteristics of the additional number characters (s and ş, c and ç, *etc.*) in the Turkish language may be to blame for this. Table **1**. is shown as Comparative study of efficiency indicators (TTC-3600), Table **2** BBC-NEWS's comparative analysis of performance indices.

**Table 1. Comparative study of efficiency indicators (TTC-3600).**

| Database | Technique | Accurateness | Extractness | Recollection | F1 Value |
|---|---|---|---|---|---|
| TTC-3600 | CNN | 94.18 | 94.18 | 94.18 | 94.01 |
| | GNB | 88.34 | 88.18 | 88.21 | 88.12 |
| | RF | 85.01 | 84.19 | 84.19 | 84.06 |
| | NB | 85.01 | 85.01 | 85.01 | 84.92 |
| | SVM | 87.23 | 87.21 | 87.21 | 87.21 |

**Table 2. BBC-NEWS's comparative analysis of performance indices.**

| Database | Technique | Accurateness | Extractness | Recolletion | F1 Value |
|---|---|---|---|---|---|
| BBC-NEWS | CNN | 95.53 | 95.41 | 95.81 | 95.41 |
| | GNB | 89.25 | 89.97 | 89.29 | 89.52 |
| | RF | 82.97 | 83.39 | 82.39 | 82.57 |
| | NB | 88.75 | 89.41 | 88.71 | 88.81 |
| | SVM | 91.88 | 92.01 | 91.91 | 91.91 |

## CONCLUSION

In accordance with the text preparation steps, 4 databases were saved, one for each of the 6 categories in the TTC-3600 database and 5 categories in the BBC-News database. Each database's Doc2Vec training model was then developed. Models constructed using the deep learning classification method CNN were compared to those constructed using the machine learning classification methods GNB, RF, NB, and SVM for accuracy in classification. The Clean+Stem-DS database, which was created from the TTC-3600 database, can be categorised with an accuracy of 94.17 percent using CNN. Using the TTC-3600 database, the proposed approach was demonstrated to be the most accurate relative to other methods previously utilised in the study. Classifying the C-DS dataset produced by cleaning the data with CNN yielded an accuracy percentage of 96.41% in the BBC News database. Success was shown to be reached over the average accuracy rate, however it was not the greatest outcome compared to earlier research. In the future, we want to perfect a method for analysing video transcripts. After applying text detection and recognition processing to the video frames, deep learning techniques will be used to classify the video content.

## REFERENCES

[1] A. Elnagar, O. Einea, and R.A. Debsi, "Automatic Text Tagging of Arabic News Articles Using Ensemble Deep Learning Models", *International Conference on Natural Language and Speech Processing,* 2019.

[2] M. Nadeem, and S. Raza, "Detecting Bias in News Articles using NLP Models", *2022 International Conference on Natural Language Processing and Artificial Intelligence (NLPAI),* pp. 1-6, 2022.

[3] B. Jang, I. Kim, and J.W. Kim, "Word2vec convolutional neural networks for classification of news articles and tweets", *PLoS One,* vol. 14, no. 8, p. e0220976, 2019. [http://dx.doi.org/10.1371/journal.pone.0220976] [PMID: 31437181]

[4] W.K. Sari, D.P. Rini, R.F. Malik, and I.S. Azhar, *Multilabel Text Classification in News Articles Using Long-Term Memory with Word2Vec,* 2020.

[5] "Effective Training Data Extraction Techinque to Improve Influenza Outbreak Prediction from Online News Articles: Deep Learning Model Study", *JMIR Med. Inform.,* p. 9, 2020.

[6] B. Jang, I. Kim, and J.W. Kim, *Effective Training Data Extraction Techinque to Improve Influenza Outbreak Prediction from Online News Articles: Deep Learning Model Study.* Preprint, 2020.

[7] "Topic categorization of Tamil News Articles using PreTrained Word2Vec Embeddings with Convolutional Neural Network", In: *2020 International Conference on Computational Intelligence for Smart Power System and Sustainable Energy (CISPSSE)*, 2020.

[8] C.P. Capetillo, D. Lecuona-Gómez, H. Gómez-Adorno, I. Arroyo-Fernández, and J. Neri-Chávez, *HBDCI at CheckThat!-2022: Fake News Detection Using a Combination of stylometric Features and Deep Learning.* Conference and Labs of the Evaluation Forum, 2022.

[9] P. Kamboj, and L. Chongtham, "Classification of News Articles using Gradient Boosting based Deep Learning Model", *2022 6th International Conference on Information Technology (InCIT),* 2022 pp. 266-269 Nonthaburi, Thailand. [http://dx.doi.org/10.1109/InCIT56086.2022.10067642]

[10] D. Bîna, G. Vlad, C. Onose, and D. Cercel, *Flood Severity Estimation in News Articles Using Deep Learning Approaches.* MediaEval Benchmarking Initiative for Multimedia Evaluation, 2019.

[11] J. Dacon and H. Liu, "Does gender matter in the news? Detecting and examining gender bias in news articles", In: *Companion Proceedings of the Web Conference 2021* Ljubljana, Slovenia, Apr. 2021, pp. 42-50. [http://dx.doi.org/10.1145/3442442.3452320]

[12] A. K. Sinha, S. S. Kumar Singh, and S. Sai, "Detecting the political bias in news articles and similarity using word embeddings in American journalism", In: *Proc. 2023 Int. Conf. Computational Intelligence for Information, Security and Communication Applications (CIISCA)* New Delhi, India, Dec. 2023, pp. 121-125.

[http://dx.doi.org/10.1109/CIISCA54323.2023.00100]

[13] T. Spinde, J. Krieger, T. Ruas, J. Mitrović, F. Götz-Hahn, A. Aizawa, and B. Gipp, "Exploiting transformer-based multitask learning for the detection of media bias in news articles", *arXiv,* p. abs/2211.03491, Nov. 2022. Available from: https://arxiv.org/abs/2211.03491

[14] M. Abdullah, O. Altiti, and R. Obiedat, "Detecting propaganda techniques in English news articles using pre-trained transformers", *Proc. 2022 13th Int. Conf. Information and Communication Systems (ICICS),* Amman, Jordan, pp. 301-308, Mar. 2022. [http://dx.doi.org/10.1109/ICICS53197.2022.9757750]

[15] W. Chen, K. A. Khatib, B. Stein, and H. Wachsmuth, "Detecting media bias in news articles using Gaussian bias distributions", *Findings of the Association for Computational Linguistics,* pp. 1015-1026, 2020. [http://dx.doi.org/10.18653/v1/2020.findings-acl.91]

**CHAPTER 46**

# Investigating the Utility of Data Mining for Automated Credit Scoring

**Amarpal Yadav**[1,*]

*Department of AI, Noida Institute of Engineering & Technology, Greater Noida, Uttar Pradesh, India*

**Abstract:** Banks and other financial organisations rely heavily on credit scoring (CS) as a method of risk management since it is both effective and necessary. It reduces financial risks and gives sound advice on loan disbursement. As a result, businesses and financial institutions are exploring innovative automated solutions to the CS dilemma in an effort to safeguard their resources and those of their clients. The use of various machine learning (ML) as well as data mining (DM) approaches has led to significant progress in CS prediction in recent years. The Deep Genetic Hierarchical Network of Learners (DGHNL) is a novel approach developed for this study. Support Vector Machines (SVMs), k-nearest Neighbours (kNNs), Probabilistic Neural Networks (PNNs), and fuzzy structures are just some of the many types of methods that may be used in the suggested method. The Statlog German (1000 occurrences) approval of credit dataset from the UCI machine learning library was used to evaluate our model. We used a DGHNL model with five unique learner types, two feature extraction methods, three kernel functions, and three methods for optimising model parameters. In addition to conventional cross-validation (CV) and train-testing (stratified 10-fold) methods, this model employs a cutting-edge biological layered training (participant selection) approach. Using data on German credit approvals from Statlog, we show that the suggested DGHNL model can obtain a prediction accuracy of 94.60% (54 errors per 1000 classifications) with its 29-layer architecture.

**Keywords:** Algorithms, Automated Credit Scoring, Data Mining, Investigation Utility, Support Vector Machines (SVMs).

## INTRODUCTION

The banking industry is particularly vulnerable to credit risk, making credit risk management more crucial than ever in light of recent economic developments. Previous research has shown that interest earned on credit equals banking principle. Improvements in banking risk management are the focus of credit risk

[*] **Corresponding author Amarpal Yadav:** Department of AI, Noida Institute of Engineering & Technology, Greater Noida, Uttar Pradesh, India; E-mail: amarpal@niet.co.in

**Pankaj Kumar Mishra and Satya Prakash Yadav (Eds.)**

management. Customers' credit risks may be categorised and predicted using information gleaned from their personal data fed into scoring algorithms. Decisions are made by credit specialists based on prior experience; nevertheless, this process yields different results when applied to the first techniques of credit risk assessment. Statistical programmes have come a long way, allowing for more precise scoring models to be developed as a result of technical progress. Automated processing in the banking industry leads to greater precision and lower operational expenses. Banks have historically used regression and neural network-based credit risk rating algorithms due to their excellent accuracy [1].

Linear Discriminant Analysis [2, 3], Decision Tree [4], Logistic Regression [5], F-Score [6], and Genetic Programming [4] are only some of the classification models that have been produced by constructing credit risk scoring models using data mining technologies. Desai *et al.* [7] studied the decision-making process behind credit scores by comparing the efficacies of Neural Networks, Linear Discriminant Analysis, and Logistic Regression. They discovered that when compared to neural networks and logistic regression, linear discriminant analysis yielded worse results. In conclusion, the two most popular credit risk assessment models are those based on neural networks and logistic regression.

Today's business climate is unlike any other time in history, thanks to the proliferation of modern information technologies. Thanks to developments in information technology, advancements have been made in the capacity of information systems to handle large amounts of data quickly and accurately. Instead of concentrating on data compilation and collection transformation, the company here is searching for the most effective means of intercepting information from databases. Data mining refers to the practise of methodically exploring huge data sets in multiple dimensions utilising computing power as well as processing speed to discover previously undiscovered discoveries and trends that may drive corporate and consumer choices. Data mining has found use in many different areas, including but not restricted to the manufacturing, retail, healthcare, and biotech sectors. Data mining's practical applications in business include the financial sectors (insurance, banking, and credit cards). Data mining has potential uses in the biomedical industry, including illness diagnosis. Scholars like Frawley [8] have described data mining as the act of scouring databases for possibly understandable and relevant information. Frawley reframed data mining as a technique for gaining insight into the world in 1996. The algorithmic application, transformation, analysis, and identification of data features and models constitute data mining. Data mining, as described by Grupe and Owrang [9], is the process of extracting previously undiscovered information from databases. Finding significant correlations and laws by automatically or semi-automatically analysing large amounts of data is what data mining is, according to

Berry and Linoff [10]. Data mining was first described by Kleissner [11] as an innovative analysis procedure that might unearth previously unknown useful information to be used as a resource for businesses. Previous researchers had varied points of view on data mining, yet their defining tendencies are generally consistent. The phrase of data mining used here is comparable to Kleissner's.

There are a variety of uses for data mining. Data mining, for instance, may be broken down into subfields such as classification, prediction, organisation, clustering, and so on. To "classify" anything is to create subsets in feature sets based on the characteristics of the targets. Information may be categorised and used as a foundation for decisions using models that describe characteristics and cross-category correlations. The computation of variable attribute values using categorised data might provide prospective rules and classification outcomes. This study's primary objective is to present four new categories. Training data is used in the Decision Tree classification approach to make predictions about categorical and continuous variables. The idea of decision trees is to categorise things based on what we already know. Each category has a unique framework for making calls. A tree diagram depicting the procedure is shown. ID3 [12], C4.5 [13], Segmentation among Reconstruction Tree; and CART [14], among many more, are all examples of decision trees that use text symbols or independent information types. To paraphrase Berkson [15], the inventor of the logistic regression model describes how it might be used to date with just two possible outcomes from a test: success or failure. One of the goals of model building is to define classification rules and make reliable predictions about the connection between the response variable and independent variables. When a single sample is used to foretell the likelihood of success, an attribute of the sample may be determined. In order to solve classification difficulties, logistic regression is often used to aggregate the class variable while creating predictions between 0 and 1. To circumvent the erroneous assumption that the matrix of covariance has to be identical to the binary class [16], logistic regression is often employed as an alternative to linear discriminant analysis when constructing binary classification. One of the most precise binary output approaches is logistic regression technology [17]. To create an output, a Neural Network simply multiplies the values of its input neurons by its link values. Initial link values are generally generated at a rate between +1 and -1 before being trained and adjusted by the neural network. The worth of a link may be thought of as a multiplicative effect. An overactive connection is more likely to have an effect on the neural network if the link's value is high. If a link is too tiny, it may generally be deleted to save up system resources. The constituent parts of the neural network are as follows. Vapnik [18] provided a helpful dimensional categorization method called the Support Vector Machine, which has seen widespread usage in recent years. It has been used for things like credit score calculations [1, 21, 22] and the identification of diseases

[19, 20]. The statistical learning theories upon which the support vector machine [21] is based serve as the basis for its learning algorithms. In statistical learning theory, vector classification eventually gave way to the more advanced hyperplane classifier. In conclusion [22], a decision tree, logistical regression, a logistic neural network, or a support vector machine may all find a place in the credit risk score [23] prediction model [24]. This article compares and contrasts four distinct classification schemes [25]. Fig. (**1**). shows the Model comparison Analysis. Most the model predicts correctly. Precision: Number of favorable predictions that came true. Recall: How many positive examples the model detected. F1 Score: One value combining precision and recall. AUC-ROC: Measures model ability to distinguish positive and negative classes. Regression models utilize MSE to evaluate how well their predictions match reality. Regression model prediction error is interpreted using RMSE. Training Time: How long the model learns from data. After training, the model's inference time.

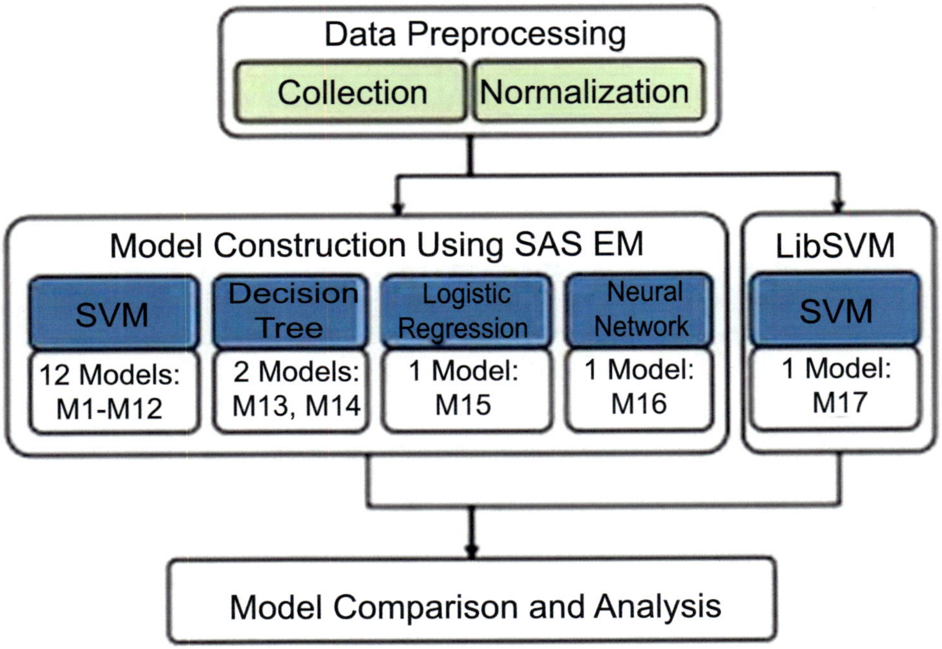


**Fig. (1).** Model comparison Analysis.

## RELATED WORK

Financial organisations rely heavily on the scoring process as part of their credit risk management system, which helps them estimate the risk associated with loan [26] applications. Statistical models that include data from an application and the client are often used in this process to assess the defaulting chance. Due to the ever-increasing scope and volume of available historical data, manual processes like scorecards have given way to automated ones that make use of machine learning models [27]. A trustworthy machine-learning scoring model emerges as a result of several interrelated processes: (i) the gathering of accurate historical data [28]; (ii) the selection of relevant customer characteristics from previous loans; and (iii) the verification and validation of the model's predictive ability [29]. Professionals in the fields of machine learning, data analysis, and risk analysis all play a part in the creation and evaluation of credit scoring models [30]. In practice, each of these parties may place restrictions on the kind of data that may be utilised, often to facilitate audits and avoid problems like discriminatory conduct. In this paper, a loan application is represented by the pair (x, y), where x is a vector of features describing the loan request as well as the customer making the request, and y is a target feature taking on the values 0 or 1 to indicate whether the customer has paid off the loan in full or defaulted [31]. The goal of the classification challenge is to develop a prediction model h x y that successfully assigns feature values to classes. Classification systems come in many forms; decision trees, models of linear regression, and ensembles that are just a few examples; these and others are covered in Section 4.1. Financial organisations and credit operators commonly use scores instead of offering a Boolean response to determine if a customer's loan request is likely to be completely paid or not. In Brazil, credit ratings are limited to the range [0, 1,000], with 0 denoting a client who will almost certainly default [32] and 1,000 denoting a customer who will pay his bills in full without fail. Extreme numbers like this are very rare in real-world applications, therefore it is up to individual financial institutions to choose what cutoff they will apply to determine which borrowers will be approved for loans [33]. We focus on classifiers that, together with their classification outputs h(x), provide the probabilities P [h(x) = 1] as well as P [h(x) = 0], which can be instantly re-scaled to the [0; 1,000] range, allowing us to acquire these types of scores. Fortunately, these probabilities can be extracted by the vast majority of classifiers. In Section 4.1, we describe the classifiers we used in our study and explain how we utilised them to derive probabilities. Researchers and industry professionals alike have spent the better part of the past decade studying and implementing the usage of data mining models and artificial intelligence approaches for credit scoring. Li and Liao (2011) conducted an in-depth analysis of various classifiers, including decision trees, although principal component analysis, neural networks, and regression trees were all considered, Using Kolmogorov-Smirnov values, as covered in Section 4, decision trees were shown to be the most effective method [34]. In contrast, Chen and Shi (2013) improved F1 scores on the Australian and German statlog datasets by using feature-weighted support vector machines. Chen *et al.* (2017) proposed iteratively training support vector machines with Naive Bayes classifiers to be used on a Bulgarian credit assessment database. Nali and Svraka (2018) used Oracle Data Miner and an attribute selection to glean insights from a dataset given by a Bosnian microfinance institution [35]. The credit score was calculated using an Oracle database and a Logistic Regression algorithm. To simulate the behaviours of both reliable and risky lenders, Okesola *et al.* (2017) suggest using demographic information and rich indicators. To achieve more prediction accuracy in this dataset than was possible with the global dependability of each Classifier Tree (CTree) and K-Nearest Neighbour (KNN), a Naive Bayes model was built, tuned, and tested. Singh (2017) used the Taiwan Credit dataset (Yeh & Lien, 2009) to evaluate 25 classifiers across six different types (decision trees, lazy students, Bayesian learners, basic logistics, multi-layer perceptron (MLP), as well as rule-based learners). Predictive accuracy was best served by the MLP, while the Random Forest, Bagging, and Logistic models fared best overall. Guo and Dong (2017) suggest using MultiObjective Particle Swarm Optimisation (MOPSO) on top of the German and United Kingdom datasets, with the latter being confidential, as an alternative to conventional machine learning methods. In Saia as well as Carta (2017), the authors apply Fourier transforms to portray the data differently and take on the credit scoring problem as a time sequence prediction problem. The research used information from the Default of Loan Customers and the German databases. The authors of this research proposed to utilise a Random Forest to arrive at final ratings, much as the writers of the Australian, German, and Japanese Credit Screening3 registries advise using wavelets to produce extra attributes. The work of Soares de Melo Junior *et al.* (2019) provides a recent benchmark using a grid search on 8 various classifications algorithms, showing that Random Forests (Breiman, 2001) achieved superior embracing rates in a phase to educate with the same datasets described in the aforementioned works. The use of ensembles (Lawi *et al.*, 2017) is recommended by another important piece of work for ML-based credit scoring; these ensembles combine models of logistic regression with the gradient boosting process, and their results show that they outperform both the standard Bagging (Breiman, 1996) and the single logistic regression scheme. Additionally, ensembles are superior to single models, as shown by the research of Abellán& Castellano (2017), which examines several ensembles of model classification applied to the credit scoring issue. Melo *et al.* (2019) used ensembles in tandem with the SMOTE oversampling approach (Chawla *et al.*, 2002) to get decent results in somewhat unbalanced settings while selecting the classifier in static scoring credit systems. Finally, despite surveys promoting data stream mining as an exciting approach to the development of flexible programmes for assessing credit, (Gomes *et al.*, 2019; Liobaite et al., 2016), we notice that there is a dearth of studies in which this technique has been successfully used to acclaim the issues. In order to demonstrate the usefulness and behaviour of data stream classifiers, this study presents a novel examination of three credit-scoring datasets.

## PROPOSED WORK

The work presented here makes use of a number of standard algorithms and optimisation methods. Here is a quick rundown of the novel aspects of our research: genetic layered training, diversity boost, and a reimagined hierarchy and depth-first approach to AI education.

Here are the primary procedures:

1. In this stage, we normalised the data using z-scores (*i.e.*, we standardised the data such that the mean value was 0 and the standard deviation was 1) and rescaled the data to the interval [0,1].
2. No feature extraction was performed, although principal component analysis (PCA) was used as one of two feature extraction methods.
3. No selection was made and a genetic algorithm (GA) was employed to choose features. Table **1** shows the GA settings that were found.
4. The method of cross-validation used was a stratified 10-fold cross-validation.
5. Five distinct machine learning algorithms, including two SVM variants (C-SVC and nu-SVC),

A Takagi-Sugeno fuzzy system, a probabilistic neural network (PNN), and a k-nearest neighbours (kNN) algorithm were all used.

Parameter optimisation, step 6: Learner parameters were optimised using GA acceptance characteristics coefficient + total of mistakes in testing and training groups, the sum of percentage errors in training and testing groups, and the sum of mistakes in test groups were used to calculate errors.

Our study's primary objective was to develop a more precise CS prediction system by using deep learning, ensemble learning, and evolutionary computing to boost the precision of traditional machine learning (ML) approaches. The ensemble learning methods improve system performance by combining traditional algorithms. These strategies have seen widespread use in a number of different areas since their outcomes have been demonstrated to be more trustworthy than those of individual basic algorithms. The field of ensemble learning makes extensive use of data mining techniques such as Bagging (Bootstrap aggregation), Boosting (AdaBoost), Stacking Generalisation (Stacking), Random Forest, as well as Mixtures of Experts.

A hybrid of the CV (10-fold, stratified) and GA approaches is used for ptimising learner parameters and feature selection.

## Genetic Algorithm

- There are 500 people in the population;
- Type of gene representation, float vectors;
- An individual's chromosome structure, say, in order to train with the help of an SVM: The SVC, kernel function type: RBF, is a floating-point vector of the form [g1, g2, f1,..., f96], where g1 (the first gene) provides the value for the first parameter, g2 (the second gene) indicates the value of the second one, v, and f1,..., f96 specify the remaining parameters. If a feature has a score of 0, it is undesirable, whereas a score of 1 indicates that it is preferred. The chromosome encodes the proper gene number - g, which sets the values of optimised parameters for the other learner types, such as SMV C-SVC, PNN, kNN, Fuzzy system, and others;
- Every generation's preliminary population is either uniform or random;
- We empirically determined gene values for the starting population using a global (larger) range of genetic values associated with each learner component (see Table **2** - Improved parameters). The range for feature selection is [0,1];
- The optimal (optimal) value of the function of fitness is zero;
- Generational maximums are set as follows: 30 for the initially created layer, 50 for layers 2 through 29, and so on;
- Type of crossover: intermediate on the first and 29th levels, and dispersed on the second through the twenty-eighth; chance of crossover: 0.7;
- Uniformity of mutation and a probability of 0.1;
- Five is the best possible number of unchanged survivors;
- Ranking the value of the fitness function as a function of its scaling technique;
- Parents might be chosen in a competition;
- An Expression for the Fitness Function:

The sum of mistakes made by test subjects:

Error Rate in Training = Error Rate in Testing + 1000 (3). Total number of mistakes in both the test and training sets

Error Percentage = (Error Rate in Language and Translation) / 2 (4)

Total number of trials with mistakes plus coefficient for acceptance features:

Error Summing Up Equals: errLsum + errTsum + Fa F(5)

Where errLsum is the total number of mistakes made during training, errTsum is the total number of mistakes made during testing, errL% is the error rate during training (the ratio of the total number of mistakes made during training to the total number of training instances, or errL% = errLsumLsum 100%), errT% is the error rate during testing (errTsum Tsum 100%), and Fa F = CF is the acceptance rate.

When comparing the entire number of features (F) to the number of features (Fa), the ratio of features (Fa) that were accepted to the total number of features (F) is

known as the acceptability feature coefficient (CF). Furthermore, the following formula may be used to approximate the efficiency of genetic feature selection:

CF = Fa

F × 100%, (2),

where Fa is the number of features that were approved and F is the total number of features.

***General view of the proposed model***

This research presents a novel method for analysing borrower data using machine learning. Normalisation, feature extraction, feature selection, cross-validation (CV) approach, machine learning (ML), and learner parameter optimisation are the six main pillars of the suggested methodology. A simplified diagram of our concept is shown in Fig. (**1**). Each of these procedures is described in further detail below.

**The proposed methodology**

The DGHNL system was inspired by the organisation and operation of the brain of a person (complex layers, bipolar signals, interconnected nodes, parallel processing in individual neurons, *etc.*).

Theory behind the DGHNL framework. The system's main features are as follows:

- A network of learners is analogized to a brain. A layered learning technique is like deep learning in that there are several stages of development.
- An adequate flow and integration with data through the teaching mechanism is presented by a hierarchical-base structure with a multi-layered hierarchy structure of collaborative education approaches.
- Learners (neurons) may be educated from deeper levels using a tutoring-based hierarchical structure by receiving feedback from higher-level layers and the

first layer.

- Through the elimination of incorrect solutions from learners (poor experts), genetic layered training improves DGHNL's framework:
    - By eliminating some of the less acceptable links between the learners in neighbouring layers, a genetic algorithm may optimise the connections between them (feature selection). In a similar vein, the system selects its most promising students and eliminates those who are not a good fit.
    - Like the back-connections in the brain, the system keeps track of all of the feed-forwards it receives during training, both from the algorithm's genetic makeup (genetic optimisation) and from a cross-approach.
- ***Diversity***
    - Different types of neurons, processing of data, and atypical inter-neuronal connections in the neocortex may be compared to the different types of learners conducting preprocessing, feature extraction, and inter-learner connection.
    - The proposed DGHNL system employs a total of 108 learners distributed across the first layer, split between five distinct types of learners, two distinct normalisation techniques, two distinct feature extraction approaches, three distinct kernel functions, and finally, three distinct parameter optimisations that map to three distinct error calculation methods. For layers 2 through 26, the system that is suggested used 45 learner models (composed of 5 different learner types, 3 different kernel functions, and 3 different error calculation methods), while for layers 27 through 29, only 9 learner models were used.
    - Two different normalisation methods and two different feature extraction methods were utilised in the initial layer of data preprocessing and feature extraction.
    - Many different links: not all conceivable links between students actually appear between levels.
- Similar to the electrical potential of cell nerve values, bipolarity is employed to transfer binary data (0, 1).
- The DGHNL system takes a deep learning method, as shown by its multilayered architecture; a network with exceeding two layers is regarded to be a deep network. It is like the neocortex, which also has 7 distinct layers.
- Complex characteristics are gradually acquired by a system that learns abstractly with the purpose of extracting its own internal features by transforming information in successive levels of its structure. The intended system's structure is 29 layers thick, thus the name "deep." Genetic, Hierarchical, and Networked Learners refer to the study's use of a genetic algorithm, the system's hierarchical structure, and the fact that the built system is made up of many nodes (learners) linked in a network.
- In the first layer of our layered-based learning framework, 108 students

underwent supervised instruction. Then, 45 learners in the second layer underwent supervised genetic training using the responses from 108 models of various learners built in the first layer. After then, learning proceeds through the remaining tiers (all 29 of them).

- CV method - the GA & 10-fold CV method were combined.

### *Thinnesses of 1 and 29:*

- Important characteristics and the settings of 108 learners were chosen using a genetic-based choice of features technique at the system's first and 29th layers.
- The input characteristics and all of the learners' parameters were optimised with the help of an algorithm based on genes (see Table **1**).

### *From level 2 until level 28:*

- The framework of ensemble-based learners (layers 2-28) was fine-tuned using a genetic layered training strategy. Reference responses are used to pick features in layers 1–27 based on votes from experts or judges. Taking into consideration the faults in both the testing and training sets, the primary purpose of the genetic algorithm at this step was to reject the wrong votes (responses) of learners in layers 1 through 27. At this point, only votes (answers) from trusted sources were counted.
- By casting a vote, each student (expert) could only provide a "1" or a "2" as an answer.

The DGHNL system was mostly motivated by the idea of creating a mechanism that mimics the brain's neocortex and its deep learning capabilities. In addition to deep learning and ensemble learning, the DGHNL system also makes use of evolutionary computation. The suggested technique is a development of the approach first described by Pawiak.

Our goal in building the system was to maximise accuracy while minimising its complexity (measured in terms of the number of layers and nodes). The best results were achieved with 29 layers, and adding more layers had no discernible effect on performance.

The system's robustness during training and optimisation was dependent on the variety of node (component learners).

We used (a) two different approaches to data cleaning, (b) two different approaches to feature extraction, (c) three different kernel functions for students, (d) five different learners, and (e) three different approaches to error estimation (fitness functions in the evolutionary approach provided in Table **1**):

## RESULTS AND DISCUSSION

Due to the nature of the developed system, which is made up of numerous nodes (learners) interconnected in a network, the structure of the system is both hierarchical and network-based.

- In the first layer of our layered-based learning framework, 108 students underwent supervised instruction. Then, 45 learners in the second layer underwent supervised genetic training using the responses from 108 models of various learners built in the first layer. After then, learning proceeds through the remaining tiers (all 29 of them).
- CV method - the GA & 10-fold CV method were combined.

### *Thinnesses of 1 and 29:*

- Important characteristics and the conditions of 108 learners were chosen using a genetic-based decision-making technique at the system's first and 29th layers.
- The input characteristics and all of the learners' parameters were optimised with the help of a genetic algorithm (see Table **1**).

### *From level 2 until level 28:*

- The framework of ensemble-based learners (layers 2-28) was fine-tuned using a genetic layered training strategy. Reference responses are used to pick features in layers 1–27 based on votes from experts or judges. Taking into consideration the faults in both the testing and training sets, the primary purpose of the genetic algorithm at this step was to reject the wrong votes (responses) of learners in layers 1 through 27. At this point, only votes (answers) from trusted sources were counted.
- By casting a vote, each student (expert) could only provide a “1” or a “2” as an answer.

The DGHNL system was mostly motivated by the idea of creating a mechanism that mimics the brain's neocortex and its deep learning capabilities. In addition to deep learning and ensemble learning, the DGHNL system also makes use of evolutionary computation. The suggested technique is a development of Pawaik's original approach.

Our goal in building the system was to maximise accuracy while minimising its complexity (measured in terms of the number of layers and nodes). The best results were achieved with 29 layers, and adding more layers had no discernible effect on performance.

The system's robustness during training and optimisation was dependent on the variety of nodes (component learner).

To achieve this diversity, we employed (a) three unique kernel businesses for learners, (b) five unique learners, (c) three unique error computation methods (fitness functions in the process of evolution provided in Table 1), and (e) three unique data preprocessing and feature extraction approaches:

**Table 1. Description of the data in testing and training groups used in the CV method (10-fold, stratified).**

**German Credit Data - 20(24) attributes**
**CV (10-fold, stratified)**
**Sets 1-10**

| Class | Description | Number of instances | Training group | Testing group |
|---|---|---|---|---|
| C1 | Accepted credit | 700 (70.0%) | 630 | 70 |
| C2 | Rejected credit | 300 (30.0%) | 270 | 30 |
| | **Sum** | **1000 (100.0%)** | **900 (90%)** | **100 (10%)** |

**Table 2. Attributes applied to assess the credit risk in the German credit dataset**

| Attribute | Description | Type | Range of values |
|---|---|---|---|
| **Inputs** | - | - | - |
| G1 | Status of existing checking account | Categorical | 1–4 |
| G2 | Duration in months | Numerical | 4–72 |
| G3 | Credit history | Categorical | 0–4 |
| G4 | Purpose | Categorical | 0–10 |
| G5 | Credit amount | Numerical | 276–18424 |
| G6 | Savings account/bonds | Categorical | 1–5 |
| G7 | Present employment since | Categorical | 1–5 |
| G8 | Installment rate in percentage of disposable income | Numerical | 1–4 |
| G9 | Personal status and sex | Categorical | 1–5 |
| G10 | Other debtors/guarantors | Categorical | 1–3 |
| G11 | Present residence since | Numerical | 1–4 |
| G12 | Property | Categorical | 1–4 |
| G13 | Age in years | Numerical | 19–75 |
| G14 | Other installment plans | Categorical | 1–3 |
| G15 | Housing | Categorical | 1–3 |

*(Table 2) cont.....*

| | | | |
|---|---|---|---|
| G16 | Number of existing credits at this bank | Numerical | 1–4 |
| G17 | Job | Categorical | 1–4 |
| G18 | Number of people being liable to provide maintenance | Numerical | 1–2 |
| G19 | Have telephone or not | Categorical | 1–2 |
| G20 | Foreign worker | Categorical | 1–2 |
| **Output** | - | - | - |
| G21 | Class attribute | Categorical | 1–2 |

**Table 3. Comparison of the best outcomes achieved for single learners from the 1st layer: Fuzzy system, kNN, PNN, and 2 types of SVM learners.**

| Coefficient | Learners | - | - | - | - | - | - |
|---|---|---|---|---|---|---|---|
| - | kNN | PNN | Fuzzy | SVM | SVM | SVM | SVM |
| Model type | – | – | – | nu–SVC | C–SVC | nu–SVC | C–SVC |
| Normalization | *Standardization* | *Standardization* | *Standardization* | *Standardization* | *Standardization* | *Rescaling* | *Rescaling* |
| Feature extraction | None | None | PCA | None | None | None | None |
| Errors | $err_t$ | $err_t$ | $err_t$ | $err_t$ | $err_t$ | $err_t$ | $err_t$ |
| Kernel function | – | – | – | Polynomial | Polynomial | RBF | RBF |
| **Results for training sets** | - | - | - | - | - | - | - |
| $ERR_{sum}$ | **1923** | **1291** | **1922** | **1345** | **1602** | **1465** | **1381** |
| ACC | 78.63% | 85.66% | 78.64% | 85.06% | 82.20% | 83.72% | 84.66% |
| **Results for test sets** | - | - | - | - | - | - | - |
| $ERR_{sum}$ | **224** | **215** | **214** | **203** | **202** | **202** | **201** |
| ACC | 77.60% | 78.50% | 78.60% | 79.70% | 79.80% | 79.80% | 79.90% |

Experiment two employed the DGHNL system to combine several learners (Fuzzy system, kNN, PNN, nu-SVC, and C-SVC) that had previously been evaluated in experiment one. Table **3** displays the findings.

In training sets, 100% accuracy was reached by the DGHNL architectures with 3, 14, 23, 26, 27, and 28 layers (as shown in Table **3**), whereas 100% accuracy was attained by the DGHNL system (nu-SVC with unbalanced kernel function) with 29 layers.

## Running time

The time it takes to execute the whole DGHNL system has been calculated:

- Enhancement time = 9830 minutes on average.

- Preparation Period = 3784 seconds on average.
- Time for sorting = 0.038 seconds on average.

It is worth noting that the time needed to classify data is minimal. As a result, the system may be put to use immediately.

## DISCUSSION

For the test datasets, the DGHNL system's confusion matrix is shown in Fig. (**2**). These findings verify the effectiveness of the suggested approach in making predictions about CS data.

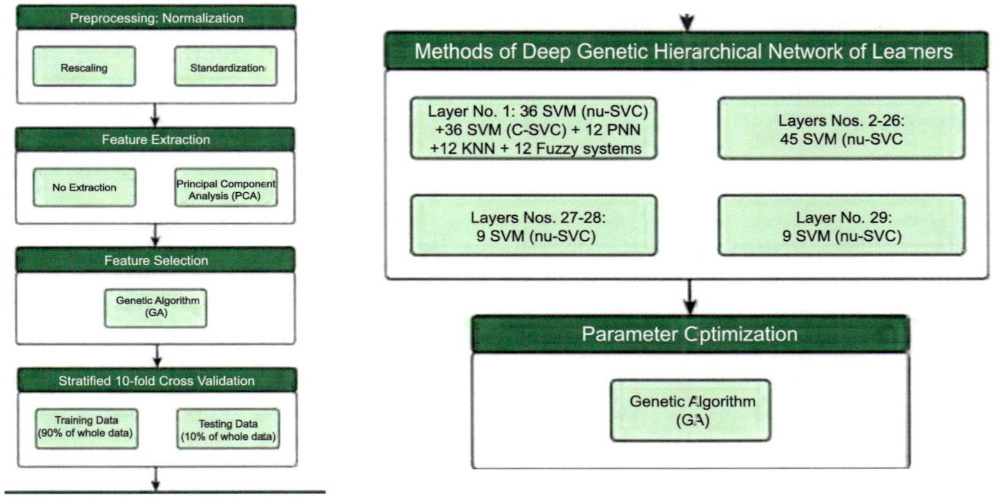


**Fig. (2).** Optimising learner parameters and feature selection.

Fig. (**2**) demonstrates that the DGHNL method performed at a higher level of accuracy (98.40%) in Class 2 than in Class 1 (93.30%).

The ROC curves for individual techniques used in the DGHNL system are shown in Fig. The fuzzy system joins the likes of nu-SVC, C-SVC, PNN, and kNN. DGHNL has an AUC of 0.9138 on the test datasets, nu-SVC has 0.7195, C-SVC has 0.7193, PNN has 0.6798, kNN has 0.6762, and the fuzzy system has 0.6986. Figure displays the error values for the DGHNL system across a 10-fold CV, which vary from 1% in the seventh test set to 10% in the previous test set. The following F1-Score values were found for the sample datasets: DGHNL = 0.9326, nu-SVC = 0.7362, C-SVC = 0.7365, PNN = 0.6988, kNN = 0.6930, and fuzzy system = 0.7154 all pass their respective tests.

Table **2** shows that compared to other approaches in the literature, the suggested DGHNL system has the highest accuracy (94.60%).

In Table **3**, we see the accuracy outcomes from only one machine learning technique. Here are some of them:

C-SVC achieved 79.90% accuracy, nu-SVC achieved 79.80% accuracy, the fuzzy system achieved 78.60% accuracy, PNN achieved 78.50% accuracy, and kNN achieved 77.60% accuracy. Importantly, the classification accuracy utilising the training datasets is much improved by the tutoring effect (a deep multilayer architecture of the DGHNL system, *i.e.*, layers 2 to 28). We achieved the best-case accuracy of 79.90% by using a singular AI strategy to produce a novel layer of the suggested DGHNL system. The accuracy of the system, however, was improved by 5% (to 84.70%) once a second layer was added to DGHNL (thereby establishing an ensemble of learners). Finally, we added 27 more layers using the deep learning technique, increasing the system's accuracy by 10% (to 94.60%).

## CONCLUSION

A moderate risk credit score is crucial in the banking sector. Deep Genetic Hierarchical Network of Learners (DGHNL) proposed here is a novel strategy that has the potential to be applied to a wide range of student populations. The proposed DGHNL method was used to examine a dataset of one thousand records from the Statlog German approval of loans database hosted in the UCI machine learning repository. An innovative method of instruction for students is discussed. It uses a multilayer genetic training system. Our DGHNL system achieved a 94.60% accuracy rate based on Statlog German credit information using stratified 10-fold cross-validation, which was the greatest of any previous study in the area. Our new system is not without its flaws. For instance, similar to other deep learning models, developing a complicated system structure requires extensive training and optimisation over time. The suggested method will be put through its paces in the future using various credit rating datasets. Our model's efficiency may also be improved by including different evolutionary methods. The suggested DGHNL system might be improved upon *via* the blind-fold cross-validation method. DGHNL might also use a variety of different categorization methods.

## REFERENCES

[1] I.G. Ioniță, "SADM – An Automated System Based on Data Mining for Credit Scoring", *Stud. Inform. Control,* p. 22, 2013.

[2] R.A. Oliveira-Junior, "Credit scoring development in the light of the new Brazilian General Data Protection Law", *Anais do IX Symposium on Knowledge Discovery, Mining and Learning (KDMiLe 2021),* 2021.

[3] F. Yang, Y. Qiao, Y. Qi, J. Bo, and X. Wang, "BACS: blockchain and AutoML-based technology for

efficient credit scoring classification", *Ann. Oper. Res.*, pp. 1-21, 2022. [http://dx.doi.org/10.1007/s10479-022-04531-8] [PMID: 35095154]

[4] L. Carmichael, S. Stalla-Bourdillon, and S. Staab, "Data Mining and Automated Discrimination: A Mixed Legal/Technical Perspective", *IEEE Intell. Syst.*, vol. 31, no. 6, pp. 51-55, 2016. [http://dx.doi.org/10.1109/MIS.2016.96]

[5] W.L. Chan, and H.V. Seow, *Big Brother Is Scoring You,* vol. 21, Journal of Financial Regulation and Compliance, no. 39, pp. 50-50, 2013.

[6] V. Vashisht, A.K. Pandey, and S.P. Yadav, "Speech recognition using machine learning", *IEIE Trans. Smart Processing & Comput,* vol. 10, no. 3, pp. 233-239, 2021. [http://dx.doi.org/10.5573/IEIESPC.2021.10.3.233]

[7] A. Hearn, "The collateralized personality: creditability and resistance in the age of automated credit-scoring and lending", *Cult. Stud.,* vol. 37, no. 1, pp. 123-148, 2023 [http://dx.doi.org/10.1080/09502386.2022.2042576]

[8] S.M. Sadat Rasoul, O.M. Ebadati, and M.S. Bakhtiari, "Identifying the Impact of Fraud on Corporate Customers' Credit Scoring by Data Mining Approaches", *Journal of Industrial Management Perspective,* 2021.

[9] S. P. Yadav, and S. Yadav, "Mathematical implementation of fusion of medical images in continuous wavelet domain", *Journal of Advanced Research in dynamical and control system,* vol. 10, no. 10, pp. 45-54, 2019.

[10] G. Chornous, K. Pysanets, and N. Yakovenko, *A Hybrid Approach for Feature Selection in Data Mining Modeling of Credit Scoring.* ICTERI Workshops, 2020.

[11] A. Hassan, and R. Jayousi, "Financial services credit scoring system using data mining", In: *Proc. 2020 10th Annual International Conference on Information and Communication Technologies (AICT)* Amman, Jordan, Dec. 2020, pp. 1-5. [http://dx.doi.org/10.1109/AICT50176.2020.9368572]

[12] A. Nazari, M.R. Mehregan, and R. Tehrani, "Evaluating the Effectiveness of Data Mining Techniques in Credit Scoring of Bank Customers Using Mathematical Models: A Case Study of Individual Borrowers of RefahKargaran Bank in Zanjan Province, Iran", *International Journal of Nonlinear Analysis and Applicctions,* vol. 11, pp. 299-309, 2020.

[13] V. Mothukuri, R. M. Parizi, J. L. Massa, and A. Yazdinejad, "An AI Multi-Model Approach to DeFi Project Trust Scoring and Security," in Proc. *2024 IEEE Int. Conf. Blockchain (Blockchain)*, 2024, pp. 19–28.

[14] S. N. Kumar, J. Shaju, K. Kayathwal, K. Agarwal, A. Singh, D. Chaurasia, S. Asthana, A. Arora, and M. AI Garage, "Intent2Vec: Representation learning of cardholder and merchant intent from temporal interaction sequences for fraud detection", 2021. Available from: https://arxiv.org/abs/2105.04033

[15] C. Ordun, J. K. Bonnie, J. L. Byun, D. Chong, R. Latham, and J. W. Wei, "Developing a Prototype Opioid Surveillance System at a 2-Day Virginia Hackathon," *Online J. Public Health Inform.*, vol. 10, 2018.

[16] A. R. Provenzano, D. Trifirò, A. Datteo, L. Giada, N. Jean, A. Riciputi, G. Le Pera, M. Spadaccino, L. Massaron, and C. Nordio, "Machine Learning approach for Credit Scoring," *SSRN Electron. J.*, 2020.

[17] P. P., "Incorporating BERT-based NLP and Transformer for An Ensemble Model and its Application to Personal Credit Prediction," *Korean Inst. Smart Media*, 2024.

[18] V. Addanki, S. Durgapu, K. Dorasanaiah, S. Abhishek, and Anjali, "Safeguarding SMS: A dynamic duo approach to tackle spam using LDA and QDA", *Proc. 2023 Innovations in Power and Advanced Computing Technol. (i-PACT),* vol. , no. , pp. 1-6, 2023. [http://dx.doi.org/10.1109/i-PACT53541.2023.00010]

[19] B. A. Makayasa, M. U. Siregar, A. Fatwanto, and B. Sugiantoro, "Comparison of Classification

Algorithm and Language Model in Accounting Financial Transaction Record: A Natural Language Processing Approach," *Int. J. Adv. Sci., Eng. Inf. Technol.*, 2024.

[20] S. Goyal and A. Saxena, "Creditworthiness Assessment Using Natural Language Processing," in *Advances in Computational Intelligence and Robotics*, 2021.

[21] N. Carr, "Decisions about Automated Scoring: What They Mean for Our Constructs," 2008.

[22] A. Aziz and Y. Andriansyah, "Modern Banking: An Exploration of AI-Driven Approaches for Enhanced Fraud Prevention, Risk Management, and," *Wiley Encycl. Oper. Res. Manage. Sci.*, 2011.

[23] F. T. Johora, R. Hasan, S. F. Farabi, M. Z. Alam, M. I. Sarkar, and M. A. Al Mahmud, "AI Advances: Enhancing Banking Security with Fraud Detection," in *Proc. 2024 1st Int. Conf. Technol. Innov. Adv. Comput. (TIACOMP)*, 2024, pp. 289–294.

[24] S. Azad, B. Chen, M. Fowler, M. West, and C. B. Zilles, "Strategies for Deploying Unreliable AI Graders in High-Transparency High-Stakes Exams," *Artif. Intell. Educ.*, vol. 12163, pp. 16–28, 2020.

[25] B. D. Caire, "Credit Scorecards for SME Finance: The Process of Improving Risk Measurement and Management," April, 2009.

[26] S. Goyal and A. Saxena, "Creditworthiness Assessment Using Natural Language Processing," in *Advances in Computational Intelligence and Robotics*, 2021.

[27] N. Carr, "Decisions about Automated Scoring: What They Mean for Our Constructs," 2008.

[28] V. Mothukuri, R. M. Parizi, J. L. Massa, and A. Yazdinejad, "An AI Multi-Model Approach to DeFi Project Trust Scoring and Security," in *Proc. 2024 IEEE Int. Conf. Blockchain (Blockchain)*, 2024, pp. 19–28.

[29] S. Nitish Kumar, J. Shaju, K. Kayathwal, K. Agarwal, A. Singh, D. Chaurasia, S. Asthana, A. Arora, and M. AI Garage, "Intent2Vec: Representation learning of cardholder and merchant intent from temporal interaction sequences for fraud detection," 2021.

[30] C. Ordun, J. K. Bonnie, J. L. Byun, D. Chong, R. Latham, and J. W. Wei, "Developing a Prototype Opioid Surveillance System at a 2-Day Virginia Hackathon," *Online J. Public Health Inform.*, vol. 10, 2018.

[31] A. R. Provenzano, D. Trifirò, A. Datteo, L. Giada, N. Jean, A. Riciputi, G. Le Pera, M. Spadaccino, L. Massaron, and C. Nordio, "Machine Learning approach for Credit Scoring," *SSRN Electron. J.*, 2020.

[32] P. P., "Incorporating BERT-based NLP and Transformer for An Ensemble Model and its Application to Personal Credit Prediction," *Korean Inst. Smart Media*, 2024.

[33] V. Addanki, S. Durgapu, K. Dorasanaiah, S. Abhishek, and Anjali, "Safeguarding SMS: A Dynamic Duo Approach to Tackle Spam Using LDA and QDA," in *Proc. 2023 Innovations in Power and Advanced Computing Technol. (i-PACT)*, 2023, pp. 1–6.

[34] B. A. Makayasa, M. U. Siregar, A. Fatwanto, and B. Sugiantoro, "Comparison of Classification Algorithm and Language Model in Accounting Financial Transaction Record: A Natural Language Processing Approach," *Int. J. Adv. Sci., Eng. Inf. Technol.*, 2024.

[35] S. Goyal and A. Saxena, "Creditworthiness Assessment Using Natural Language Processing," in *Advances in Computational Intelligence and Robotics*, 2021.

## CHAPTER 47

# Investigating the Use of Data Mining for Knowledge Discovery

**Sover Singh Bisht**[1,*]

[1] *Department of DS, Noida Institute of Engineering & Technology, Greater Noida, Uttar Pradesh, India*

**Abstract:** The practice of "lifelogging" involves documenting an increasing amount of one's subjective everyday experience with the intention of using the recordings in the future as a memory aid or the foundation for data-driven self-development. Therefore, the usefulness of the generated lifelogs depends on the lifeloggers' ability to efficiently sift through them. The logs' intrinsic multi-modality and semi-structure allow them to combine data from a variety of sources, including cameras and other wearable physical and virtual sensors. As a result, expressing the data in a graph structure allows for the effective capturing of all created interrelations. Alternative methods must be developed to capture the higher-level semantics because it is impossible to manually or mechanically annotate each entry with a significant amount of semantic context. We describe an Improved Life Graph (ILG), a first method for building a Knowledge Graph-based lifelog representation and retrieval solution, which can capture a lifelog in a graph structure and augment it with external data to help with the connection of higher-level semantic information.

**Keywords:** Data mining, Information retrieval, Knowledge graph, Lifelog data.

## INTRODUCTION

The possibilities for mobile data collection, processing, and storage have substantially increased because of the various technological advancements over the previous few decades. One possible effect is the rise of related movements, such as quantified self and lifelogging. The term "lifelogging" is used to describe the act of documenting one's daily activities, whether through the use of cutting-edge technology like a digital camera or sensors that measure one's bio-feedback or the attributes of the immediate environment or through more conventional means, such as writing in a diary. As a consequence, the resulting lifelog might take several shapes and have many connections [1, 2]. Eventually, we settled on

* **Corresponding author Sover Singh Bisht:** Department of DS, Noida Institute of Engineering and Technology, Greater Noida, Uttar Pradesh, India; E-mail: soversingh@niet.co.in

**Pankaj Kumar Mishra and Satya Prakash Yadav (Eds.)**

the simple but mostly untested idea of encoding a lifelog as a data graph. Lifelogs serve a variety of purposes, including improving memory recall and inspiring self-care. The need for a quick and simple search option inside lifelogging logs grows with the size and complexity of the data collected. The Lifelog Search Challenge (LSC) [3, 4] was a workshop organised in 2018 to competitively assess interactive lifelog retrieval technologies. Within the framework of the 2020 LSC, this research describes and demonstrates LifeGraph [5], an interactive information graph-based lifelog retrieval system. This section provides a high-level overview of the graph, how the system makes use of the network to answer questions, and the potential ways in which users could engage with the system. Recent advances in retrieval technology have made broad use of this method possible. This higher level of intelligence is very useful in a variety of application fields (data fusion, geographical analysis, early warning, *etc.*) [6, 7]. Since present methods for extracting geographical data fail to fully take into consideration the spatial and semantic dimensions, there is a room for improvement. Due to this diversity, it is presently not viable to directly get geographical data from many sources [8, 9]. However, since it is challenging to account for implicit semantic data and complicated spatial linkages, it might lead to disorientation and information overload [10,11]. Ontology-based data access (OBDA), another popular data access paradigm, often uses a commonsense knowledge base, hence it lacks spatial semantics [12,13]. A knowledge graph (KG) that accounts for the link between geographical data and semantics is required for efficient storage and retrieval of multi-source heterogeneous data. KG's massive data set is used to enhance intelligent retrieval techniques [14] and deal with the semantic gap. The combination of KG and GIS shows promise as a means of systematic geographical data collection. In this study, we present a new retrieval method that makes use of spatial semantics to increase effectiveness while still meeting strict criteria. The purpose of KG is to uncover the hidden meanings in geographical information in order to better structure and combine data from various sources. By elaborating on connected geographical elements, you may get data that conforms to the suggested semantics of search queries. Finally, we explored the concept through empirical evidence and comparative analysis.

## RELATED WORK

Here are some potential research directions and some contextual information to get you started.

Analysing Spatial Information 2.1: When referring to information that is both geographically and spatially based, the term “geospatial data” is often employed. Traditional information retrieval techniques include a subset that deals with geospatial data retrieval [15]. Understanding the geographical data model is crucial in today's age of big data for the purpose of knowledge sharing and retrieval. The two most well-known geospatial data models are the geographical vector model and OpenStreetMap (OSM).

Geospatial Information System Model 2.1.1 Data is shown using the geographic vector model, which consists of geographical layers, attributes, and property fields. In order to handle geographical data (*i.e.* geometry data) and attribute data, two distinct sets of files are often employed [9]. Spatial data is stored in spatial data files and attribute data is stored in attribute files in Fig. (**1**) geographical vector models like the one used to illustrate the road in Fig. (**1**). Using a certain map projection, spatial information files record the locations of features on the ground as a collection of points, lines, polygons, as well as other geometric primitives. Therefore, when using these characteristics, a two-dimensional Cartesian system of coordinates is the most accurate representation of geographical distribution and topological structure.

Version 2.2.1 of the tried-and-true Attribute-Based Data Retrieval System from Data Rescuing. The technique of collecting geographical data based on attributes is comparable with the standard method based on character traits. Early studies largely concentrated on name retrieval techniques, leading to the proposal of many search algorithms dependent on domain dictionary entries, such as Hash indexing. Hash index retrieval uses a structure with three levels (*i.e.*, the primary text, a word indexing table, and a Hash table holding the start characters) to filter results in a binary form. However, the fact that it relies on global matching is perhaps its worst flaw. The Trie index technique employs a tree structure (composed of a Hash table for the first character and a tree index) to hasten the matching process while maintaining high accuracy. There are, however, constraints, such as the need for sophisticated indexes and substantial memory. In order to speed up data retrieval, the dbl-word Hash index approach combines the most useful aspects of Hash and Tries. In this approach, the Trie index is used to return phrases with less than or equal to two individuals, while the Hash index is used to find words having at least three characters. This inspired scholars to delve even deeper into the meanings of place names. Characters are viewed as the building blocks for indexes, and therefore Zhang *et al.* devised a character-features-based technique for retrieving geographical names.

Space-Based Information Localization. The principal uses of spatial information retrieval are in the areas of acquisition, display, and analysis of ground objects. The spatial index primarily functions to speed up the retrieval process and to filter out superfluous ground elements. In recent years, several spatial indexes have been devised to provide faster and easier access to two-dimensional geographical data. These spatial indexes include the quadtree, the R-tree, and the R *-tree. Until the tree hits a particular depth or criteria are satisfied, a quadtree will recursively divide the globe into four smaller parts. Because of how well it performs when queried against geographical data, it has become a standard component of GIS. In R-tree and R*-tree structures, multi-level indexes are created using a virtual rectangle that characterises objects on the ground at intermediate distances. Researchers have also devised other indices for retrieving information like trajectory information as well as intricate polygons. Any of these methods has the potential to improve the efficiency with which geographical data is retrieved. However, it is challenging to account for hidden significance in attribute retrieval if search terms are just processed as character strings. In addition, geographical relationships are seldom considered while gathering spatial information since geographic indices are often constructed in a "mechanical" approach. This means that more advanced semantic retrieval techniques are needed to replace the current ways of data retrieval.

Semantic Search: A Revolution in Information Access 2.3. With the growth of semantic web technologies, modern researchers have focused on semantics to boost data retrieval efficiency. Semantics may be utilised to increase the retrieval scope and understand the latent meaning of search words, both of which can enhance result accuracy, as stated by Guha R *et al.* To help with document retrieval, researchers at the University of Maryland developed the semantic web search engine. Watson, a search engine built on the web of semantics, was introduced at the Open College to help students locate relevant materials *via* content analysis. In order to facilitate information retrieval, methods like Falcons and Hermes were developed to compute entity and relationship similarity. Geographic data retrieval is studied primarily from two perspectives: data integration and query extension. In this article, we review the prior research in this area.

The Semantic Integration of Data (2.3.1). In order to overcome semantic heterogeneity in multi-source heterogeneity retrieving information, more GIS researchers are focused on geographic data integration. Unprocessed data is transformed into Resource Description Framework (RDF) doubles using Semantic Web technology. RDF triples are a standardised language for clearly defining geographical information. Integrating geographical information and overcoming semantic heterogeneity challenges have both been achieved *via* the application of Semantic Web technology in the disciplines of trajectory data analysis, seismic disaster emergency response, and ocean data discovery. In addition, spam identification and movie recommendations are only two of the many examples of when KG's semantic technology comes in handy. However, the cost of management would rapidly increase if data changes often. Data integration techniques abound, but one of the most popular is ontology-based data access

(OBDA). As an example, Zhang *et al.* designed a defined interaction paradigm and a uniform taxonomy for gaining access to geographical data. Ontology-based Data Acquisition (OBDA) [3] generates the ontologies that are used in Ontology-based Data Integration (OBDI) to obtain and import data from several sources into a single geographic database. In order to implement OBDI, geographic features are published as an RDF graph with semantic links back to the originating databases using a language called Relational Database to RDF Mapping Language (R2RML).

Expanding Searches, Version 2.3.2. Due to the technical limitations of string matching throughout the previous century, Van Rijsbergen proposed using query expansion techniques to more accurately capture the original query's intent and speed up retrieval times. Using an analysis of search words, query expansion may provide a fresh and comprehensive set that better represents the original query intent. Recent research has focused on expanding search terms *via* co-occurrence. Voorhees *et al.* evaluated the co-occurrence probability of keywords to generate correlations of original data, therefore identifying potential vocabulary additions with the greatest correlations. The value of retrieving results for query expansion was quantified by Xu *et al.* Cui *et al.* employed query records to convey query intent by incorporating the collected search terms into enriched vocabularies. Additionally, some researchers have attempted to extend search terms by expanding their semantic scope. Voorhees *et al.* and Navigli used technology to calculate conceptual similarity and generate more related concepts to extend search queries according to ontology hierarchy. The maritime safety [10] and the project for smart cities both make more use of an attribute and spatial data of geographical features in their applied study. Ji *et al.* introduced a semantic query expansion approach using ontologies to improve the accuracy of semantic retrieving in the agriculture and forestry industries.

## PROPOSED WORK

### Graph Construction

LifeGraph is based on the publicly available lifelog database at LSC 2020, which contains around 200k images taken by wearable cameras over the period of 114 days, together with related metadata and other sensor data. Rich semantic annotations detailing not just the material of an entry but also putting it in a broader context would be beneficial for all lifelog items, independent of their kind or approach to encoding. To make the collected data accessible and, therefore, useable, alternatives must be employed since explicitly adding such annotations is problematic as well as mechanically doing so is above what is now achievable. To go around this shortcoming, we build the structure of graphs that keeps track of the relationships between general semantic ideas and more specific labels, such as the kind of surroundings or the inclusion of common items inside a picture, that can be consistently recognised by existing technologies [9, 4]. LifeGraph construction might be made more difficult by the need to connect granular picture characteristics with broad search topics. Using an association defined using Wikidata [8], we were able to merge COEL and detectable entities. We coupled the mapped ideas with extra information from Wikidata to establish a link between the concepts and lower-level semantic picture labels. In the first step, we mapped all observable things in Wikidata to COEL and used it to populate a graph. We then iteratively obtained each entity from wikidata that are related to the current graph by at least two entities and inserted them into the graph. This process is performed thrice, plus twice more when just class relations (:instance-of,:subclassOf) are taken into account. At last, we eliminated ad hoc nodes from the network that did not properly relate picture labels to broad categories. We also took out navigational and internal components like disambiguation and template pages. Using the schema described in a sudy [5], we created a basic, flat model of the information that was already included in the dataset submitted to LSC. Time stamps are used to link each piece of information to a specific picture. In the graph, we connect all the metadata data with the picture using an object or the data type attribute. Each picture does, in fact, correspond to a daily resource, despite what may have been implied earlier [5].

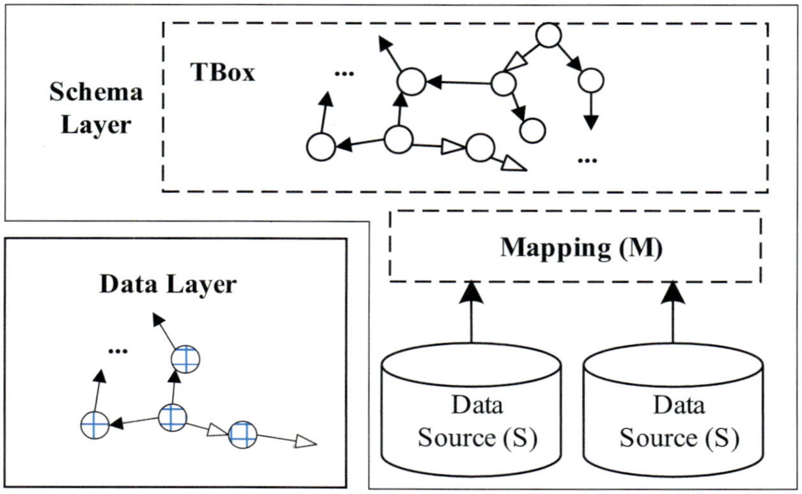


**Fig. (1).** Proposed work.

This allows us to avoid duplicating the same data for each of the roughly 2000 photographs that were taken on a given day by instead linking this information straight to the day resource. The semantic location labels ("work" *vs*. "home") given by the user, together with the items [4] and locations [9] that were recognised, were interpolated before the schema was populated. When the distance between two concepts is narrow enough, we connect every entry in the gap with the common idea. Next, we directly connect photos to Wikidata entries for the things and locations they depict using the:detected or:detected_place attribute. Fig. (**1**) displays the proposed work.

## Data Retrieval from Constructed Graph

The LifeGraph UI [6] is a modified version of the UI generated by the vitrivr [7] based on content audiovisual retrieval stack, and it can be accessed using any web browser. The only part of the system shared by the vitrivr stacks and LifeGraph is the interface. As an alternative to typing out complex queries, users may simply choose nodes from the network that corresponds to the topics in which they are interested. This method of question construction strikes a good balance between precision and efficiency and does not call for any specialised knowledge on the part of the user. After a query is formulated, it is submitted to the back end, where it is executed and the results are ranked. As part of the evaluation process, the graph is traversed to find all possible pathways from the query's selected start vertices to all the log files that could be returned. We keep increasing the longest possible length of this route until we hit some empirically established limit on the number of possible outcomes or the total length of the path, whichever comes first. The value assigned to each detected log entry is the geometric mean of the inverted route lengths, scaled by the number of nodes used to initiate the search. The score of a recovered item is greater if it is closer to the maximum possible number of starting points. The compiled data is then transmitted back to the user interface, where it is shown as a list of records ordered by score or as a list of log entries organised by day and then chronologically within each day. False positives created by certain of their underlying detectors are less of a concern than missing findings or false-negatives since the user is anticipated to be capable of surfing among the acquired results in an attempt to find the required components. If there are too many false positives, users will waste time browsing, and if there are too many false negatives, they may never find what they're looking for. Technical information such as the time and date of creation are examples of the kinds of metadata that are included in each log entry. Biofeedback features like heartbeat, number of steps taken within a given period of time, *etc*. are also manually noted in lifelog entries. This data is used in the user interface to eliminate records that do not satisfy the Boolean condition of the query. The evaluation of such filters in the user interface may just lower the size of the result set, so no further server-side processing or connection with the underlying graph is required. Fig. (**2**) displays the Data Retrieval.

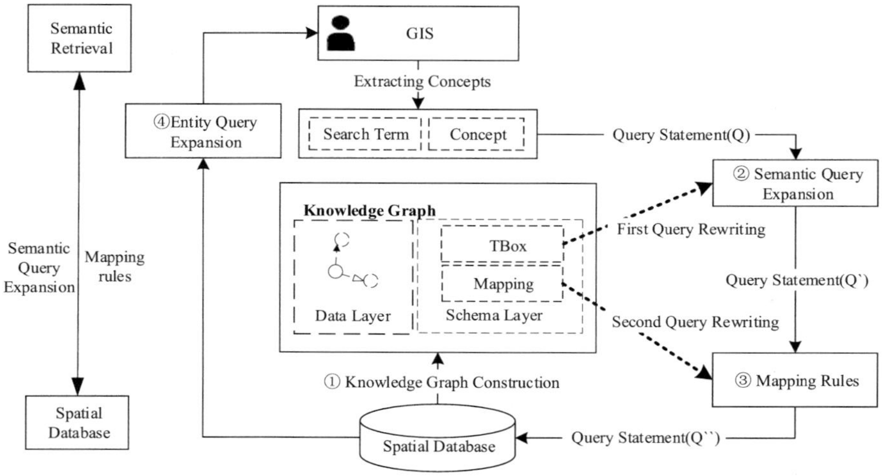


**Fig. (2).** Data retrieval.

Second, the Recovery Method Based on the fundamental framework, a data retrieval procedure is given, which includes KG building, semantic query growth, query expansion, and the return of retrieval results. Here's how it all breaks down: 1. Building a graph of knowledge. The connection between the two databases (geospatial and others) is made. Complete database information, such as map layers and geographic feature fields, is reflected in the connections between data layers. 2. Submit an expanded semantic inquiry. In the schema layer, Q is compared to predefined concepts. The query expansion process rewrites the search word into related queries determined by conceptual hierarchical linkages and logical axioms. 3. Layout of a map. The connection between databases and ideas is reflected in mapping rules. Using these guidelines, SQL statements (Q") are autoconstructed by converting query phrases into database objects like table names and property fields.

Expansion of the entity query. After mapping rules are developed, Q" is handed over to the geospatial database. Furthermore, the data layer may broaden the entities linked to search queries within the bounds of idea categories, organizational subdivisions, and mental approaches. Following the aforementioned procedures, the geographical database is obtained, and the results are shown in a number of different perspectives. As a result, the technique may provide the necessary implicit data for queries.

Calculating Similarities in Meaning. In order to effectively use semantic query expansion, it is essential to compute idea similarity. Researchers in the field of linguistics have claimed that the conceptual distance between two words is inversely proportional to their proximity to one another. Sim(C1, C2) keeps track of the semantic similarity between two concepts C1 and C2. When two things are more unlike than they are similar, the gap between them increases. Conceptual affinity may be stated as

$$Sim(C_1, C_2) = \begin{cases} 0, & D = +\infty \\ P, & D \in (0, +\infty) \\ 1, & D = 0 \end{cases}$$

Therefore, the schema layer distance P (which might vary from 0 to infinity) is computed in this article. The concept of depth of a knowledge network reflects the level of semantic specialization.

## RESULTS AND DISCUSSION

When users' demands are satisfied, the outcome of a geographic data retrieval technique is successful. The Canfield assessment system (sample set, right answers, and evaluation indices) was introduced by Saracevic in 1995. F-Score is considered a compromise between Recall (R) and Precision (P), which are both calculated using the number of relevant items recovered and the number of recoverable entities, respectively. These grading scales' formulas are as follows:

R = How many relevant items were retrieved as a percentage of all relevant organisations in the data (3)

P = Relevant entities retrieved as a percentage of total entities retrieved (4)

$F = 2 \times R \times P / R + P$ (5),

where R is the fraction of the original data's relevant entities that were recovered. P is the fraction of the total retrieved items that were really relevant. In addition, a harmonic mean of R and P equals the F-Score.

### Analysis of Retrieved Data 4.2

For efficient retrieval of 4.2.1 SQL, LIKE and WHERE operators are both useful for retrieving information from a relational database, but how they perform in practice is two different measures of efficiency. Since the LIKE statement iteratively retrieves characteristics in a map layer, its complexity in terms of time is O(N), wherein N is the total number of features in the layer. In this work, we improve a filtering statement by extracting type codes from KG. The proposed method has an execution complexity of O(log(Q))+O(M), where Q is the number of feature types in a map layer, due to the fact that there are O(log(Q))+O(M) characteristics that share the same type code. Due to Q and M being far less than N in the raw data, the proposed method is more effective. A filter statement constructed using the conventional method may look like "WHERE Name LIKE '%...%'," but the proposed method would instead generate the type codes (*i.e.*, "WHERE Kind = '...'AND Name LIKE '%...%'"). Table 7 shows the many types of structures that may be found in Transportation Warehousing, such as bridges, flyovers, toll stations, charging stations, petrol stations, and so on. The standard approach to retrieving an object from Transportation Warehousing employs an iterative process that takes about 430 milliseconds. In the suggested technique, the type codes are obtained to improve the filter statement and cut down on time spent doing so. For illustration, getting a Freight Railway Station entity takes 5 milliseconds. Results obtained *via* retrieved experiments are constant either for multi-layered or single-layered geographical entities. Entities are retrieved using SQL queries, therefore accuracy is proportional to the search phrase. The accuracy of a search depends on how uncommon the search phrase is inside the database.

**Table 1. The time cost.**

| No. | Retrieval Concept | Type Code | Features Number | Time (ms) |
|---|---|---|---|---|
| - | - | - | - | Conventional Method |
| 1 | Bridge | 230201, | 202,112 | 429 |
| 2 | Flyover | 230202 | 21,944 | 439 |
| 3 | Toll station | 230209 | 19,223 | 428 |
| 4 | Charging station | 230218 | 14,884 | 462 |
| 5 | Gasoline station | 230215, 230217 | 104,036 | 428 |
| 6 | Gas station | 230216, 230217 | 7,489 | 420 |
| 7 | Station | 230100, | 13,522 | 429 |
| - | - | 230103, 230107 | - | - |
| 8 | Railway station | 230103 | 10,771 | 426 |
| 9 | Freight railway station | 230107 | 1,413 | 421 |
| 10 | Parking lot | 230212, | 258,211 | 424 |
| - | - | 230211 | - | - |

**Table 2. Comparison of experiment results. Layers A and B represent Highway and Transportation Warehousing, respectively.**

| | | | | Proposed Method | | | Method (A) | | | Method (B) | | |
|---|---|---|---|---|---|---|---|---|---|---|---|---|
| **Experiment Type** | **Search Term** | **Features (A)** | **Features (B)** | **R (%)** | **P (%)** | **F** | **R (%)** | **P (%)** | **F** | **R (%)** | **P (%)** | **F** |
| Entities in multiple layers | Hong Kong-Zhuhai Bridge | 39 | 1 | 100 | 100 | 1 | 97.5 | 100 | 0.98 | 2.5 | 100 | 0.04 |
| Entities in a single layer | Zhengzhou Railway Station | 0 | 1 | 100 | 100 | 1 | 0 | 0 | 0 | 100 | 100 | 1 |
| - | Lianhuo Highway | 10,344 | 0 | 100 | 100 | 1 | 100 | 100 | 1 | 0 | 0 | 0 |

Experiments are conducted using data taken from China Navigation Map (https://www.navinfo.com, accessed on 2019-09-01) and its transportation warehouse, highway, and railway map layers. There are 37 different types of geographic entities shown on this map.

Procedure for Normal Recoveries 4.3.1. SQL queries for retrieval have historically been constructed using criteria like map layers and property fields. On the other hand, it is difficult to automatically build SQL statements.

Zhengzhou East Railroad Station is retrieved by using administrative region and type to obtain entities associated with Zhengzhou Railway Station. The network of associations allows for the organisation to grow. Additionally, GIS spatial operation time allows for the extraction of a high number of connected geographical objects along the railway. The data was recovered using the recommended strategy.

Zhengzhou is home to a number of train stations, including the Zhengzhou Railway Station, the Zhengzhou East Railroad Station, and the Nanyangzhai Railway. Zhengzhou East Railroad Station is retrieved by using Zhengzhou Railway Station's administrative area and type. The network of associations allows for the organization to grow. Results for the Longhai Line search, show stops at several train stations along the line. In addition, GIS spatial operators may quickly and accurately extract a huge number of related geographical objects along the railway.

## CONCLUSION

In order to improve accuracy and reduce implementation time, this research developed the "SVD then PCA" approach for emotional text mining. Adjective and adverb frequency, both positive and negative, is an extra attribute. The results of two trials demonstrate that the suggested technique outperforms the alternatives and that more features improve accuracy, particularly for the SVM_RBF classification. The SVM and ME classifiers have been demonstrated to be superior at determining an individual's emotional state. The following are other topics that may be explored in the future as a continuation of this investigation: First, we may talk about how to utilise a domain-specific lexicon to locate and filter features, how to give distinct features with varying weights to boost accuracy, and how to account for word-document connections using the feature selection approach. The suggested approach can be used in a wide variety of settings, including social emotion detection and reputation management. In contrast to the standard technique, which requires layer-specific information, the suggested method uses KG to retrieve items across many levels, boosting recall to 100%. Table **1** and **2** demonstrates, using the Hong Kong-Zhuhai Tunnel as an example, that both layer A and layer B improve recall from 97.5 to 100%. Moreover, standard methods cannot provide outcomes unless layers are explicitly specified.

## REFERENCES


[1] H. Liu, and H. Motoda, *Feature Selection for Knowledge Discovery and Data Mining.* The Springer International Series in Engineering and Computer Science, 1998. [http://dx.doi.org/10.1007/978-1-4615-5689-3]

[2] U.M. Fayyad, G. Piatetsky-Shapiro, and P. Smyth, "From Data Mining to Knowledge Discovery in Databases", *AI Mag.,* vol. 17, pp. 37-54, 1996.

[3] S. Cacciatore, L. Tenori, C. Luchinat, P.R. Bennett, and D.A. MacIntyre, "KODAMA: an R package for knowledge discovery and data mining", *Bioinformatics,* vol. 33, no. 4, pp. 621-623, 2017. [http://dx.doi.org/10.1093/bioinformatics/btw705] [PMID: 27993774]

[4] J. Yu, *Construction of Smart Library Based on the Big Data Mining and Knowledge Discovery,* 2021. [http://dx.doi.org/10.1109/SCOUT54618.2021.00023]

[5] G.J. Williams, *Data Mining with Rattle and R: The Art of Excavating Data for Knowledge Discovery,* 2011. [http://dx.doi.org/10.1007/978-1-4419-9890-3]

[6] S.N. Chikalkar, "Knowledge Discovery and Data Mining", *Int. J. Res. Appl. Sci. Eng. Technol.,* vol. 8, no. 10, pp. 874-876, 2020. [http://dx.doi.org/10.22214/ijraset.2020.32045]

[7] D.Q. Phung, V.S. Tseng, G.I. Webb, B. Ho, M. Ganji, and L. Rashidi, "Advances in Knowledge Discovery and Data Mining", *Lect. Notes Comput. Sci.,* 2018.

[8] S.P. Yadav, and S. Yadav, "Fusion of Medical Images using a Wavelet Methodology: A Survey", In: *In IEIE Transactions on Smart Processing & Computing* vol. 8. The Institute of Electronics Engineers of Korea, 2019, no. 4, pp. 265-271. [http://dx.doi.org/10.5573/IEIESPC.2019.8.4.265]

[9] S. Al-Janabi, "Overcoming the Main Challenges of Knowledge Discovery through Tendency to the Intelligent Data Analysis", *2021 International Conference on Data Analytics for Business and Industry (ICDABI),* pp. 286-294, 2021. [http://dx.doi.org/10.1109/ICDABI53623.2021.9655916]

[10] M. Herland, T.M. Khoshgoftaar, and R. Wald, "A review of data mining using big data in health informatics", *Journal of Big data,* vol. 1, no. 1, pp. 1-35, 2014.

[11] A. Azevedo, "Data mining and knowledge discovery in databases", *In Advanced Methodologies and Technologies in Network Architecture. Mobile Computing, and Data Analytics,* pp. 502-514, 2019.

[12] R. Xu, L. Li, and Q. Wang, "dRiskKB: A large-scale disease-disease risk relationship knowledge base constructed from biomedical text", *BMC Bioinformatics,* vol. 15, no. 1, pp. 1-13, 2014.

[13] F. Wang, P. Zhang, X. Wang, and J. Hu, "Clinical risk prediction by exploring high-order feature correlations", *In AMIA Annual Symposium Proceedings,* 2014.

[14] A. Idri, H. Benhar, J.L. Fernández- Alemán, and I. Kadi, , "A systematic map of medical data preprocessing in knowledge discovery", *Computer methods and programs in biomedicine,* vol. 162, pp. 69-85, 2018.

**CHAPTER 48**

# Exploring the Role of Big Data in Predictive Analytics

**T. R. Mahesh**[1,2,*]

[1] *Department of Computer Science and Engineering, JAIN (Deemed-to-be University), Bangalore, India*

[2] *Department of Computer Science and Engineering, Galgotias University, Greater Noida, Uttar Pradesh, India*

**Abstract:** Cardiovascular illness is afflicting enormous monetary and psychological costs. The development of an ASHRO-based model for forecasting healthcare resource use and its link with clinical outcomes was driven by a desire to improve the economy and provide a high-quality evaluation of the healthcare system. Data included in this analysis were taken from a big database that included doctor visits, insurance claims across several years, and results of preventive health screenings. Hospitalized patients with heart illness (ICD-10 I00-I99) comprised the study population. Broadly defined composites compliance served as the explanatory variable, while medical as well as long-term care costs served as the objective variable. Using a combination of random forest learning (AI) and multiple regression analysis, predictive models were calibrated. These models were then used to create ASHRO scores. Two measures, the area under the curve as well as the Hosmer-Lemeshow test, were used to assess the prediction model's effectiveness. After controlling for clinical risk variables, we compared the two ASHRO 50% threshold groups' total morbidity at 48 months of follow-up using matching propensity scores. Heart disease affected 61.9% of the 48,456 patients surveyed, with an average age of 68.3 9.9 years at hospital release. For the purpose of adherence score classification, machine learning was employed to combine eight factors into a single index: generic drug rate, interconnecting outpatient visits/clinical laboratory as well as physiological tests, the proportion of days addressed, secondary mitigation, rehabilitation magnitude, direction, and a single index that adjusted for eight factors. In the end, the multiple regression study yielded a 0.313 (p 0.001) coefficient of determination. Medical as well as long-term care expenditures had a statistically significant total coefficient of determination (p 0.001) in a logistic regression study using 50% along with 25%/75% cut-off values. At the 50% level of significance (2% *vs*. 7%; p 0.001), the relationship between ASHRO score and mortality rate was statistically significant.

* **Corresponding author Mahesh T. R.:** Department of Computer Science and Engineering, JAIN (Deemed-to-be University), Bangalore, India; E-mail: t.mahesh@jainuniversity.ac.in

**Pankaj Kumar Mishra and Satya Prakash Yadav (Eds.)**

**Keywords:** Artificial Intelligence, Big Data, Multiple regression study, Predictive analytics, Predictive models.

## INTRODUCTION

Both Cappelli (2000) and Naraynan *et al.* (2019) found that human resources were the most important factor in a company's success. To make the most of this asset, several firms throughout the world have implemented talent management techniques (Cappelli, 2000). Evidence suggests that efficient and effective human resources administration (HRM) practices boost employment stability and retention rates (Irshad as well as Afridi, 2012). Keeping current staff members on board is a critical HR task. Armstrong (2006) and Paille (2013) both stress the importance of staff retention in giving businesses a competitive edge. For a business to maintain a competitive edge over the long term, investing in a bright and skilled workforce is crucial (Kumar & Kaushik, 2013). In today's competitive job market, keeping top personnel is becoming an increasingly pressing challenge for a company's executive (Naris alongside Ukpere, 2010; Olckers through Du Plessis, 2012). In this regard, many references are cited: Davenport & Harris (2007), Chen *et al.* (2012), Watson (2014), Frisk & Bannister (2017), Kar & Dwivedi (2020), as well as Bag *et al.* (2021). Big data and data-driven decision-making are gaining traction in the management sphere. Companies are becoming more interested in data-driven decision-making thanks to Big Data Predictive Analytics (BDPA) and its sophisticated Big Data applications (Dawson *et al.*, 2007; Secundo *et al.*, 2017; McAfee *et al.*, 2012; Agrawal *et al.*, 2021). According to Wong (2012), FossoWamba *et al.* (2016), and Du bey *et al.* (2019), the area of big data has the potential to completely transform whole business operations, which has piqued the attention of both academics and lawmakers. Notwithstanding researchers' best efforts, studies on information management and human resource management have failed to provide any significant findings (Garcia-Arroyo & Osca, 2019; Rombaut *via* Guerry, 2020; Hamilton with Sodeman, 2020). Notwithstanding several attempts to integrate research and practice (Shah *et al.*, 2017; Calvard and Jeske, 2018; Huang *et al.*, 2021), the two remain seen as distinct entities. When looking at what influences employee retention, there is a lack of data in the existing literature. On top of that, the literature is lacking in concrete evidence about the BDPA's effect on staff retention.

Various pathogenic states, intricate disease processes, and a propensity toward chronicity alongside the recurrence of acute phase events are hallmarks of circulatory illnesses. The need for long-term care is a substantial financial burden on society, and these variables significantly reduce the patient's quality of life and deteriorate their prognosis [1, 2]. The tremendous advancements in medicines and medical technology have not prevented the enormous increase in the unit price for medical care. Improvements in lifestyle and other factors are also contributing to the 10,000 annual increases in the number of Japanese inpatients suffering from cardiovascular disease along with other ailments [3]. Cardiovascular medical expenditures were 19.7 percent of overall healthcare expenditures in Japan in 2018 (for individuals aged 65 and over, a 5.7 percent increase from the prior year), ranking them highest within this framework [4]. The efficient use of social capital—which encompasses medical costs associated with long-term care—and the enhancement of clinical outcomes has given rise to a policy disagreement in the cardiovascular profession [5]. The Japanese government keeps track of how much people spend on healthcare and nursing home care. Over the previous decade, medical expenditures have climbed by more than 2% yearly, reaching 8.0% of GDP [6]. This is because of the world's aging population and rapid developments in medical science. Hospitalization rates and lengths of stay among the elderly are major contributors to regional disparities. Long-term care expenses, meanwhile, have been rising at a rate of about 5% annually since 2010, which is faster than the 2% annual growth in GDP in the Fiscal Year 2016 [7]. Improving the administration of clinical quality and healthcare resources is crucial. This would be a great use for the prediction models. Predicting the severity of patient problems and the results of therapeutic treatments is an active element of clinical practice, and so is the creation of models to do so. Comprehensive risk assessments are used as models to forecast the critical prognosis of heart failure; such examples are the MEESSI-AHF, the HFSS, as well as the GWTG-HF [8, 9]. The Spanish assessments of patients having acute heart failure in the emergency room are the basis for these ratings. Some more factors for determining the prognosis of chronic heart failure include the Seattle Cardiac Failure Simulations, which include risk stratification. Public insurers seldom attempt to construct model for risk assessment as well as prediction; private corporations, on the other hand, handle medical along with long-term care insurance money.

## RELATED WORKS

In the fields of biomedicine and healthcare, early detection is crucial. Accurate medical outcomes can be predicted with the use of well-analyzed data. Furthermore, several regional illnesses have distinctive local manifestations, which might hamper the ability to foretell disease epidemics globally. In order to successfully anticipate the start of chronic illness outbreaks in disease-frequent societies, this study will provide a rationale for the machine learning methods needed to do so. The rising area of big data hopes to tackle every type of analytical difficulty. Big data is the accumulation of data that will preserve the data qualities to anticipate the disease, and traditional data will have the three attributes of velocity, volume, and variety. The existing work mostly processes structured data, but our suggested approach, which makes use of convolution neural networks (CNN), also processes unstructured data. Each neuron in a convolutional neural network (CNN) receives an input and generates a unique output. Because the prior study dealt only with structured data and ignored unstructured data, the latter inevitably led to erroneous conclusions, prompting us to weigh many options.

Methods for identifying regional illness patterns. The best way to keep the local weather patterns stable and how to best store patient records so that reliable forecasts may be made, a CNN algorithm is employed for this purpose. Both structured and unstructured data may be processed with CNN-MDRP. More accurate predictions followed. Research has shown that patients' adherence to medicine and moral risks has a strong impact on clinical results, health behaviors, and socioeconomic aspects, such as medical expenditures [10, 11]. Patients are more likely to take their prescriptions as directed when they are less burdened emotionally and financially by their condition [12]. The Japanese healthcare system is concerned about overlapping tests because they might generate negative consequences and an increase in medical expenditures. The system is based on the idea of open access [13]. Disease prevention is an intervention that has been shown to lower both risk factors and total expenditures [14, 15]. On the other hand, self-management and health literacy, among other forms of adherence, may influence disease preventive behaviour and ultimately decide its success. To prevent the exhaustion of scarce community resources owing to irrational consumption and the resulting decline in the health and well-being of the whole population, public health policy must control the fairness of the distribution of healthcare resources. Designing a model to predict healthcare resource use using behavioral indicators that indicate adherence as well as the moral hazards that impact patient choice and behavior is therefore the preferred approach However, there is a dearth of global empirical studies on adherence at the moment due to challenges in data collection. Every patient's health record in Japan's massive database includes information about medical as well as long-term care expenses, the scheduling of overlapping exams, attendance at prevention programs, laboratory as well as biological test results, and the frequency of prescriptions for generic drugs. We developed an algorithm (ASHRO, which signifies Adherence Rating for Healthcare Resource Outcome) that uses massive amounts of data from three domains—healthcare, long-term care, with medical screenings—to predict medical and long-term care expenses. The prediction model used AI and multivariate analysis to build a composite behavioral health indicator that connects changes in medical and monetary costs in the heart disease area to public nature overall concordance, in addition to wide adherence. This is why ASHRO is committed to enhancing communication and coordination between healthcare providers and future patients.

## PROPOSED WORK

### Data Sources and Populations

The Kokuho Database (KDB) system, which is used to build ASHRO, integrates individual-level data from healthcare examinations, insurance applications, as well as long-term care plans. Regarding health and long-term care records, the KDB databases have an individual participation rate of more than 99%. People who are self-employed or have retired and are covered through the National Health Insurance are included in this massive database. Six point one percent of the nation resides in the database's covered regions; demographics and socioeconomic position are also believed to have a major influence on determining access to healthcare and long-term assistance. Thanks to the unified management structure for health check-ups, healthcare, and long-term care data (KDB), longitudinal studies of different behavioral changes may enhance healthcare cost forecasts. The four-year time frame spanning from April 2014 to March 2018 was used to build the prediction model. The data came from cardiovascular illness hospitalizations (ICD-10 I 00-99). A bigger retrospective observational research with many locations and more than 3 million participants included one gate. The study did not include cardiovascular disorders that were deemed intractable at entry, severe cardiomyopathy, or congenital heart defects. Following anonymization, the following information would be included in the subject recognition for each patient's data: basic insured person attributes, healthcare costs (outpatient, inpatient, dispensing, and dentistry), details of diagnoses, medical examination frequency, duration of hospitalization, cost of long-term care, level of long-term care required, frequency of use, duration of use, guidance, and instructions. The following were the criteria that the University of Tokyo's Committee on Ethics in Research (2018167 N1) used to grant approval for the study: The RECORD Statement, a collection of rules for the reporting of studies that employ observational habitually obtained data and the Helsinki Declaration, both issued by the Japanese government, provide standards for the ethics of clinical research. The principles of Transparently Reporting Predictive Models (TORIPOD) were also followed in this study. The project director will provide access to the sensitive data acquired for this study upon reasonable request.

### A Machine Learning Analysis of the Fundamental model

The conventional method of empirical statistics, which involves collecting a dataset that includes outcomes, predictors, as well as fit coefficients, was ill-suited to this exploratory study because of the physical qualities and incompleteness of the results when it came to doing multivariate analyses on large samples. Our selected machine learning strategy selects and incorporates explanatory variables and weights utilizing random forests and cross-validation with K-folds (Fujitsu Limited Powered by AI). Random forests in machine learning may be used for a variety of tasks, such as regression and classification. A benefit is that overfitting is far less of an issue. The effective use of sample dimensions with several input variables is another benefit of medical big data. Along with that, it can handle data scales that differ (for instance, normal values for blood pressure and GFR are different) and it can handle the inclusion of unrelated elements. Using more than a hundred pieces of data on medical procedures, diagnostic tests, and preventative measures found in big data, this study generated an objective factor for medical as well as long-term care costs. Using machine learning, we used the bootstrap method to choose numerous random samples and feature quantities with replacement, and then we used that information to figure out how important parameter integration is. Eighty percent of the data was reserved for training purposes, while twenty percent was used for testing. We utilized Inc MSE (residual sum of the squares: mean squared error: out-of-bag [OOB] error rate) for regression and Mean Decrease Gini (Gini coefficient) for classification. The former is obtained by fitting the unprocessed information to regression trees that were built using data that was taken at random. At 19:15 in the BMC Medicine article from 2021, on page 3 of 16, Takura *et al*. proposed lowering OOB as a method for optimization. The degree of branching in the decision tree is determined by the total amount of variables squared. The maximum number of branches in the selected tree was fifty. All of the training models in this research were evaluated using K-fold cross-validation after a grid-based search for changes to the hyperparameters was conducted during model development. Beyond that, we used the holdout technique to assess the adaptability of several neural network-based machine-learning approaches. To get the final projected value, the cross-validation K-fold approach takes the mean of K models that are created by randomly splitting the test information into K groups. We may see this as an example of internal validation in action. One common tool used in this procedure is the out-of-fold (OOF) prediction. On top of that, it uses a random state parameter and uses randomization to decide which groups to allocate samples to. Getting away from the “Cheap, yet shoddy” mentality might be beneficial for medical and long-term care resource management. This point of view is particularly salient in the context of the public health system. Our research intended to make the prediction model more nuanced by including both financial and clinical factors. There was also a need to take into account feedback while establishing a broadly applicable definition of adherence (one that takes into account moral risks) and when choosing indicators. Future research directions were also explored in this work, such as the potential for the database to be expanded and used in other illness areas. These findings informed the decision to use machine learning to incorporate other non-adherence related variables into the basic model, such as gender, age, and observation duration. Modifications to the categorization of insignificant features and comparable indicators improved the prediction model's explicability and verification accuracy (multivariate evaluation: multiple regressions, binary logistic regression).

Prediction Variables and Findings. In order to understand how resources (medical as well as long-term care expenses) are used, this research constructed a prediction model that takes a total index of adherence in its broadest meaning as an explanation variable. We also used a social lens to examine this study. In this analysis, direct expenditures (such as transportation and uninsured food) were subtracted from total costs (hospitalization, outpatient treatment, and dispensing) to arrive at the total cost of the objective variable. From 2014-2017, the average exchange rate for the yen was 112.98 yen per US dollar. Machine learning was used to choose 11 parameters from the feature value significance distribution to make up the basic model, and these were combined into 8 final parameters. The cost was significantly affected by several of these explanatory factors (such as simultaneous outpatient visits and medical attendance). To enhance the study's prediction model's explanatory ability, variable weights were changed (Table **1**). Because each explanatory variable needed a group average for computation, it was crucial to consider the target group's characteristics while evaluating the prediction models. Researchers in this research expanded the regression analysis to include age, sex, and duration of analysis because they wanted to make sure their findings would hold up across diverse populations (the model's universality). The eleven variables that made up the final forecasting framework (ASHRO) for health behavior were as follows: public conduct, medical attitude behavior, indicators of prevention and promotion of health, and rational consumption of resources behavior (moral hazard). In order to gauge the quality of care provided to patients compared to the general population, eleven indicators were monitored in the first year after enrollment. There were a lot of metrics tracked, including health checks, items verified, rehabilitation magnitude units, guidance sessions, outpatient visits, dispensing, inpatient days, overlapping outpatient treatment visits/clinical laboratory and physiological tests, inpatient visits, percentage of days covered (PDC), and inpatient days. In overlapping care, patients get several outpatient treatments for the same ailment at the same time. By multiplying the original medical cost by the number of prescriptions, the price of generic medications was established. The federal government's inventory of generic pharmaceuticals served as a reference. Instead of using data particular to each patient's medication efficacy, the PDC was computed using the whole prescription term. The use of healthcare resources is significantly affected by a number of elements, including compliance, moral hazards, social collaboration, and public character. Medical along with long-term care costs were the dependent variables we aimed to analyze. We started to systematically establish the relationship between these explanatory elements, which we called broad compliance (Additional file 1). Secondary prevention, rehabilitation intensity, advice, and patient-centered decision-making were the four characteristics linked with adherence and, in turn, healthcare expenditures. For instance, impacts on the acquisition of prescription drugs were documented (odds, 1.11). In addition, in Japan, the average cost of healthcare for the elderly is 10%, which is far less than the 20% estimated by Takura *et al*.

The goal of lowering OOB was prioritized. The total number of variables squared determines the amount of branching in the decision tree. Fifty was the upper limit for the total amount of branches in the choice tree. After doing a grid-based search for hyperparameter changes during model building, in this work, we assessed the quality of each training model using K-fold cross-validation. Beyond that, we used the holdout technique to assess the adaptability of several neural network-based machine-learning approaches. By randomly splitting test data into K groups, the K-fold cross-validation approach develops K models. The last estimated value is the mean of those models. This serves as an instance of internal validation. This process often makes use of out-of-fold (OOF) forecasts. Furthermore, it decides which specimens go into which groups using randomization and sets a variable called random state. Medical as well as long-term care resource management would benefit from a departure from the "Cheap, yet shoddy" mindset. This point of view is particularly salient in the context of the public health system. Our research intended to make the prediction model more nuanced by including both financial and clinical factors. There was also a need to take into account feedback while establishing a broadly applicable definition of adherence (one that takes into account moral risks) and when choosing indicators. Future research directions were also explored in this work, such as the potential for the database to be expanded and used in other illness areas. These findings informed the decision to use machine learning to incorporate other non-adherence-related variables into the basic model, such as gender, age, and observation duration. Based on the foregoing, we can conclude that modifying our classification of insignificant features and analogous indicators enhanced both the prediction model's explanatory power and the precision with which it was validated (the use of multiple regression and binary logistic regression in multivariate analysis).

Findings and Variables Used for Prediction. This study developed a prediction model to explain the use of resources (medical as well as long-term care expenditures) using an aggregate index of compliance in the widest sense as an explanatory variable. The present research was also analyzed from a sociological perspective. In this analysis, direct expenditures (such as transportation and uninsured food) were subtracted from total costs (hospitalization, outpatient treatment, and dispensing) to arrive at the total cost of the objective variable. From 2014-2017, the average exchange rate for the yen was 112.98 yen per US dollar. Machine learning was used to choose 11 parameters from the feature value significance distribution to make up the basic model, and these were combined into 8 final parameters. The cost was significantly affected by several of these explanatory factors (such as simultaneous outpatient visits and medical attendance). By adjusting the weights of the variables, the study's forecasting framework was able to better explain the data (Table **1**). Because each explanatory variable needed a group average for computation, it was crucial to consider the target group's characteristics while evaluating the prediction models. Researchers in this research expanded the regression analysis to include age, sex, and duration of analysis because they wanted to make sure their findings would hold up across diverse populations (the model's universality). The eleven variables that made up the final prediction model (ASHRO) for health behavior were as follows: public conduct, medical attitude behavior, indicators of health promotion and prevention, and rational resource consumption behaviour (moral hazard). In order to gauge the quality of care provided to patients compared to the general population, eleven indicators were monitored in the first year after enrollment. The criteria included the following: the total number of visits to outpatient clinics, the total number of inpatient days, the amount of clinical laboratory as well as physiological examinations that occur between inpatient visits, the number of items that were confirmed, the total number of rehabilitation scale parts, the number of advice meetings, the total the number of outpatient visits, the total number of inpatient days, the percentage of days wrapped (PDC), and the total number of inpatient visits. In overlapping care, patients get several outpatient treatments for the same ailment at the same time. We divided the original medicine's cost with the number of prescriptions to get the price of generic meds. We used the government's list of comparable pharmaceuticals as a reference. Instead of using data particular to each patient's medication efficacy, the PDC was computed using the whole prescription term. The use of healthcare resources is significantly affected by a number of elements, including compliance, moral hazards, social collaboration, and public character. Medical along with long-term care costs were the dependent variables we aimed to analyze. We started to systematically establish the relationship between these explanatory elements, which we called broad compliance (Additional file 1). Secondary prevention, rehabilitation intensity, advice, and patient-centered decision-making were the four characteristics linked with adherence and, in turn, healthcare expenditures. For instance, impacts on the acquisition of prescription drugs were documented (odds, 1.11). In addition, the elderly in Japan bear a burden of 10% on medical costs, significantly less than the working generation's 30%, and therefore they are thought to be more susceptible to moral hazards. It has been shown that moral hazard variables impact healthcare costs. This study primarily examined three factors: medical attention, overlapping clinical laboratory as well as physiological tests, and overlapping patient visits. For example, it was reported that patients' consultation behaviour had improved by 15% in this particular case. Determinants of social cooperation were also shown to impact the use of social security resources (this research largely used the generic drug rate index). For example, when looking at social cooperation in Japan *via* the lens of a social value orientation measure (public nature), researchers discovered that the Japanese had a propensity for selflessness when it came to matters of social welfare. Clinical specialists and those responsible for healthcare budget management are ASHRO's intended users. As a predictor of medical as well as long-term care costs, adherence (behavior change) influences clinical and economic factors. For instance, there are a number of ways that public insurers might promote their services using the ASHRO's prediction algorithms. Advocate for the use of medical experts' opinions in patient care focus on at-risk groups that have poor screening rates and usage of generic medications. Research on models of significant behavioral change that boost self-efficacy may be associated with the benefits of primary and secondary prevention for patients with varying degrees of disease severity.

As shown in Fig. (**1**)., Age: Study participants' ages. Data obtained in the first year of study enrollment. 48-month index follow-up 12-month enrollment: Data from 48 months following the first 12.

## Healthy Habits

Secondary Prevention: Health checks and illness prevention. Health check-up frequency. Checkup items: Specific health checks. Disease treatment and rehabilitation are tertiary prevention measures. The intensity of rehabilitation. Compliance with medical recommendations. PDC: Patient-doctor interaction. Overlapping Outpatient care measures. Number of outpatient appointments. Frequency of clinical laboratory and physiological examinations. Medical Attendance: Overall. Day count in the hospital. Number of outpatient appointments. Dispensing: Drug compliance. Public health behavior. Generic drug rate: Use of generic medications.

## Long-term Care

In-home services, number per year: Number of in-home care services received per year. Community-based services, number per year: Number of community-based care services received per year. Facility services, number per year: Number of facility-based care services received per year. 48-month Follow-up Period.

| Variable | Correlation coefficient | p value | | | Weighting |
|---|---|---|---|---|---|
| Age | 0.42 | <0.001 | | | |
| **12-month period after enrolment** | | | | | |
| **Health behaviour** | | | | **Broad adherence** | |
| Secondary prevention | | | 1 | Secondary prevention (Integrated) | 8.18 |
| Health check-ups | 0.122 | <0.01 | * | | |
| Item of health check-ups | 0.128 | <0.001 | * | | |
| Tertiary prevention | | | | | |
| Rehabilitation intensity | 0.012 | 0.43 | 2 | Rehabilitation intensity | 0.81 |
| Guidance | 0.156 | <0.001 | 3 | Guidance | 1.04 |
| PDC | 0.079 | <0.001 | 4 | PDC | 5.35 |
| Overlapping outpatient service | | | | | |
| Outpatient visits | 0.001 | 0.938 | 5 | Overlapping outpatient visits | 3.03 |
| Clinical laboratory and physiological tests | 0.049 | <0.05 | 6 | Overlapping clinical laboratory and physiological test | 5.02 |
| Medical attendance | | | 7 | Medical attendance (Integrated) | 2.76 |
| Inpatient days | 0.52 | <0.001 | ** | | |
| Outpatients visits | 0.352 | <0.001 | ** | | |
| Dispensing | 0.354 | <0.001 | ** | | |
| Public behaviour | | | | | |
| Generic drug rate | 0.209 | <0.001 | 8 | Generic drug rate | 6.58 |
| **Long-term care** | | | | | |
| In-home services, number per year | 0.224 | <0.001 | | | |
| Community-based services, number per year | 0.011 | 0.466 | | | |
| Facility services, number per year | 0.086 | <0.001 | | | |
| **48-month follow-up period after index 12-month enrolment** | | | | | |
| Follow-up period | 0.442 | <0.001 | | | |
| Medical expense | 0.938 | <0.001 | | | |
| Long-term care expense | 0.269 | <0.001 | | | |

**Integrated into an adherence 1* or adherence 7** index by machine learning**

**Fig. (1).** Degrees of disease severity.

Follow-up period: Duration of the follow-up period. Medical expense: Total medical expenses incurred. Long-term care expense: Total long-term care expenses incurred. Integrated into an adherence 1 or adherence 7 index by machine learning: This indicates that certain variables have been combined into a single index using machine learning algorithms.

Broad Adherence

1. Secondary prevention (Integrated): Integrated measure of secondary prevention adherence.

2. Rehabilitation Intensity: Adherence to rehabilitation recommendations.

3. Guidance: Adherence to medical guidance.

4. PDC: Adherence to patient-doctor communication recommendations.

5. Overlapping outpatient visits: Adherence to outpatient visit schedules.

6. Overlapping clinical laboratory and physiological tests: Adherence to laboratory and physiological test schedules.

7. Medical attendance (Integrated): Integrated measure of medical attendance adherence.

8. Generic drug rate: Adherence to generic medication use.

## EXPERIMENTAL ANALYSIS

Characteristics at the start Patients were followed for an average of 36.1 8.8 months and there were a total of 48,456 participants. They averaged 68.3 years old, and 61.9% of them were men. The patient's vital signs at the first comprehensive medical evaluation are shown in Table 3. These include a systolic blood pressure of 131.2 15.0 mmHg, triglycerides of 20.8 5.2 mg/dL, a hemoglobin A1c level of 5.9 0.8%, with serum creatinine of 0.9 0.8 mg/dL. The patient had a fat-free mass index (BMI) of 23.4 kg/m2. Medical treatment and long-term care added up to $9,160 per year, or $9,045 per person. Predictor Selection Machine learning helped us combine the data and settle on 8 health-related characteristics for further investigation. The following is the relative importance of the parameters that make up the core model: 8.18 for the secondary aspect.

Secondary prevention (number of health checks and associated items), rehabilitation magnitude (1.04), guidance (5.35), initial prevention of disease (4.03), outpatient care (5.02), clinical laboratory, physical examinations (5.02), medical care (2.76), as well as generic drug rate (6.58) are considered as the most typical public health behaviors, according to Table **1**. Medical and LTC expenses were shown to be strongly linked with follow-up time and age (p 0.001, Table 1). Prior to integration, there was little to no difference ($p = 0.430$ for the total amount of rehabilitative intensity units and $p = 0.938$ for the overlap in outpatient care visits) among the eleven health behavior variables. Despite the exception of one (p 0.001), ten distinct physiological and clinical laboratory investigations have been shown to be significantly different (p 0.05). In addition, we discovered that a few of the care-related metrics were substantially out of the range of zero. Assessments of prediction models were conducted and overall, the model's coefficient of determination was 0.313 (p 0.001) after numerous regression runs. There was statistical significance for each of the eight variables meant to represent healthy lifestyle choices. Attendance at healthcare (0.261), follow-up (0.254), extra prevention (0.241), and rehabilitation intensity (0.210) all produced reasonably substantial coefficients in the traditional partial regression analysis. While age did have a little effect (0.032), the index of overlapping outpatient sessions was modest (0.053). After making sure that the VIF of every variable that was explained was less than 2 and verifying for multicollinearity, the prediction model was considered stable. Using logistic regression analysis with a 50% threshold for total healthcare and long-term care expenditures, the whole algorithm's determination coefficients were shown to be highly significant (p 0.001, supplementary file 2). Age and overlapping clinical laboratory as well as physiological tests were the only explanatory variables that did not correlate with medical and long-term care expenditures (all p 0.001). Consistent with the pattern seen in the multivariate regression, the multiple component regression findings also verified the trend. There was clear evidence of multicollinearity as the VIFs of all explanatory factors were less than 2. Hosmer-Lemeshow generated a value of 0.169. The access indices had the highest chances ratio of 1.68 (95% CI 1.660-1.700), whilst the rehabilitation indices had the lowest odds ratio of 0.817 (95% CI 0.804-0.831). As shown in Fig. (**2**), the area under the curve (AUC) for the ROC, or receiver operating characteristic, is 0.889, with a 95% CI range from 0.886 to 0.892. The total model coefficient of predictability was substantial under logistic regression with a 25%/75% threshold (both p 0.001). There was only one VIF higher than 3 in the whole research period that used a 25% cutoff: 2.188. You can see the AUC values of 0.880% and 0.896% in Table **5**.

Models for Predicting Therapeutic Outcomes. A logistic regression analysis of healthcare and LTC expenses was conducted at a 50% level of significance. The following is a summary of the overall coefficient of determination: At the 0.001 level of significance, the odds ratio (OR) for mortality based on ASHRO levels was 1.860 (95% CI: 1.740, 1.980). Six thousand fourteen patient pairs were generated *via* the ASHRO 50% cut-off classifications for low and high-risk variables to compare propensity ratings for severe ones. When comparing the groups according to age, sex, smoking status, alcohol consumption, fatty acids, HbA1c, creatinine levels, and body mass index, no statistically significant differences were found. With regard to the aggregated all-cause mortality rate after 36 months, there was a statistically significant distinction between the two groups: 7% for the ASHRO Low group and 2% for the ASHRO Higher group (p 0.001). Hospitalization, outpatient therapy, and prescription expenditures were positively correlated with ASHRO during a 36-month period, but care costs were not. Except for the amount of long-term treatment, there was a correlation between the average 36-month changes in medical examination findings.

Model for predicting scores and probabilities. The overall average of every ASHRO score was used to compare the displacements associated with healthcare establishment resource use in the following order: Scores between 0 and 2 made up 77.88% (SE 1.48%), scores between 2 and 4 58.20% (SE 0.45%), scores between 4 and 6 11.53% (SE 0.51%), scores between 6 and 8 68.51% (SE 1.41%), and scores between 8 and 10 138.65% (SE 5.47%). Mothers' mean scores differed considerably across all five score bands, according to the statistical analysis (Fig. **2**), scoring 2: p 0.05, ratings 2 and above p 0.001. The 36-month prediction model's ROC curve is black. The ROC curve's AUC is 0.889 (95% CI: 0.886–0.892). This shows the model's ability to distinguish positive and negative situations. Sensitivity: The y-axis shows the model's sensitivity, or the percentage of true positives it properly identifies. Specificity: The x-axis shows the model's specificity, or the percentage of genuine negative situations it properly identifies. The diagonal line shows the performance of a random classifier that cannot distinguish positive and negative situations. Interpretation The ROC curve shows the sensitivity-specificity trade-off at different categorization levels. Models that identify the two classes better have AUCs closer to 1).

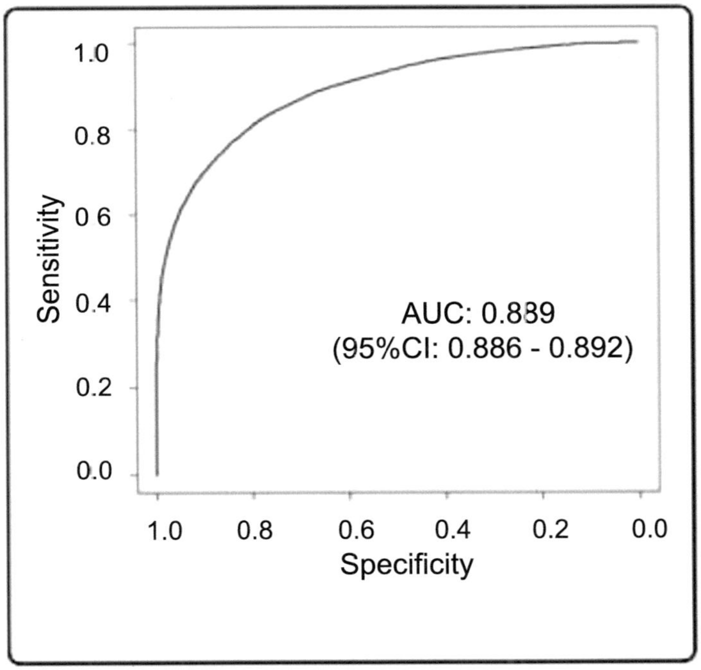


**Fig. (2).** ROC curves of the 36 months prediction model, AUC, area under the curve.

**Table 4. Evalution of prediction models by multiple regression analysis.**

| Index | Partial Regression Coefficient | Standard Partial Regression Coefficient | F value | p value | SE | VIF |
|---|---|---|---|---|---|---|
| **Broad adherence** | | | | | | |
| 1. Secondary prevention | -0.048 | -0.241 | 3,820.6 | < 0.001 | 0.005 | 1.07 |
| 2. Rehabilitation intensity | -0.250 | -0.210 | 2,740.7 | < 0.001 | 0.005 | 1.13 |
| 3. Guidance | -0.057 | -0.144 | 1,413.1 | < 0.001 | 0.002 | 1.03 |
| 4. PDC | -0.057 | -0.075 | 366.3 | < 0.001 | 0.003 | 1.10 |
| 5. Overlapping outpatient visits | 0.028 | 0.053 | 116.4 | < 0.001 | 0.003 | 1.67 |
| 6. Overlapping clinical laboratory and physiological tests | 0.012 | 0.091 | 343.1 | < 0.001 | 0.001 | 1.70 |
| 7. Medical attendance | 0.001 | 0.261 | 4,460.5 | < 0.001 | 0.005 | 1.08 |
| 8. Generic drug rate index | -0.019 | -0.016 | 17.7 | < 0.001 | 0.004 | 1.04 |
| **Age** | 0.009 | 0.032 | 56.6 | < 0.001 | 0.004 | 1.25 |
| **Sex** | -0.509 | -0.086 | 518.8 | < 0.001 | 0.022 | 1.10 |
| **Follow-up period** | 0.051 | 0.254 | 3,207.9 | < 0.001 | 0.001 | 1.41 |
| **Constant term** | 3.421 | | 1,249.7 | < 0.001 | 0.105 | |

Abbreviations: PDC – Proportion of days covered, SE – Standard error, VIF – Variance inflation factor

## CONCLUSION

Incorporating ASHRO into cardiovascular disease treatment techniques may improve health behaviors and allow for the evaluation of the monetary worth of individual adherence. This research is the first to examine how health-related behaviors might improve resource use and medical outcomes. In all likelihood, the findings will aid in the long-term improvement of healthcare.

## REFERENCES

[1] R. Dutta, N. Das, M. Majumder, and B. Jana, "Aspect based sentiment analysis using multi-criteria decision-making and deep learning under COVID-19 pandemic in India", *CAAI Trans. Intell. Technol.,* 2022.
[PMID: 36712294]

[2] S. vHossain, "A Deep Learning Approach for Public Sentiment Analysis in COVID-19 Pandemic", *2022 2nd International Conference on Intelligent Technologies (CONIT),* pp. 1-6, 2022.

[3] R.S. Jayale, and S.S. Desai, "Aspect-Level Drug Reviews Sentiment Analysis and COVID-19 Drug prediction using PPI & Deep Learning", *2021 International Conference on Computing, Communication and Green Engineering (CCGE),* pp. 1-5, 2021.
[http://dx.doi.org/10.1109/CCGE50943.2021.9776369]

[4] S.P. Yadav, S. Zaidi, C.D.S. Nascimento, V.H.C. de Albuquerque, and S.S. Chauhan, "Analysis and Design of automatically generating for GPS Based Moving Object Tracking System", *2023*

*International Conference on Artificial Intelligence and Smart Communication (AISC),* 2023pp. 1-5 Greater Noida, India.
[http://dx.doi.org/10.1109/AISC56616.2023.10085180]

[5] A. Vohra, and R. Garg, "Deep learning based sentiment analysis of public perception of working from home through tweets", *J. Intell. Inf. Syst.,* vol. 60, no. 1, pp. 255-274, 2023.
[http://dx.doi.org/10.1007/s10844-022-00736-2] [PMID: 36034686]

[6] A. Alqarni, and A. Rahman, "Arabic Tweets-Based Sentiment Analysis to Investigate the Impact of COVID-19 in KSA: A Deep Learning Approach", *Big Data and Cognitive Computing,* vol. 7, no. 1, p. 16, 2023.
[http://dx.doi.org/10.3390/bdcc7010016]

[7] Ö. Çoban, S.A. Özel, and A. Inan, "Deep Learning-based Sentiment Analysis of Facebook Data: The Case of Turkish Users", *Comput. J.,* vol. 64, pp. 473-499, 2021.

[8] S. Jatla, and D. Avula, "Hybrid Deep Model for Sentiment Analysis of COVID-19 Twitter Data", *2022 International Interdisciplinary Humanitarian Conference for Sustainability (IIHC),* pp. 1616-1625, 2022.
[http://dx.doi.org/10.1109/IIHC55949.2022.10060027]

[9] S.B. Dash, A. Jain, L. Dey, T. Dasgupta, and A. Naskar, "Factors affecting user experience of contact tracing app during COVID-19: an aspect-based sentiment analysis of user-generated review", *Behav. Inf. Technol.,* vol. 42, no. 2, pp. 249-264, 2023.
[http://dx.doi.org/10.1080/0144929X.2022.2139758]

[10] S. P. Yadav, and S. Yadav, "Mathematical implementation of fusion of medical images in continuous wavelet domain", *Journal of Advanced Research in dynamical and control system,* vol. 10, no. 10, pp. 45-54, 2019.

[11] T.T. Mengistie, and D. Kumar, "Deep Learning Based Sentiment Analysis On COVID-19 Public Reviews", *2021 International Conference on Artificial Intelligence in Information and Communication (ICAIIC),* pp. 444-449, 2021.
[http://dx.doi.org/10.1109/ICAIIC51459.2021.9415191]

[12] S.P. Yadav, and S. Yadav, "Fusion of Medical Images using a Wavelet Methodology: A Survey", In: *In IEIE Transactions on Smart Processing & computing.* vol. 8. The Institute of Electronics Engineers of Korea, 2019, no. 4, pp. 265-271.
[http://dx.doi.org/10.5573/IEIESPC.2019.8.4.265]

[13] Q.X. Ng, S.R. Lim, C.E. Yau, and T.M. Liew, "Examining the Prevailing Negative Sentiments Related to COVID-19 Vaccination: Unsupervised Deep Learning of Twitter Posts over a 16 Month Period", *Vaccines (Basel),* vol. 10, no. 9, p. 1457, 2022.
[http://dx.doi.org/10.3390/vaccines10091457] [PMID: 36146535]

[14] S. Mehta, *Sentiment Analysis on Covid-19 Using Deep Learning. International Journal for Research in Applied Science and Engineering Technology.*

[15] S. Che, X. Wang, S. Zhang, and J.H. Kim, "Correction to: Effect of daily new cases of COVID-19 on public sentiment and concern: Deep learning-based sentiment classification and semantic network analysis", *J. Public Health (Berl.),* pp. 1-1, 2023.
[PMID: 36816448]

## CHAPTER 49

# Implementing Automated Reasoning in Natural Language Processing

**N. Sengottaiyan**[1,*] and **Rohaila Naaz**[2]

[1] *School of Computer Science and Engineering, JAIN (Deemed-to-be University), Bangalore, India*

[2] *College of Computing Science and Information Technology, Teerthanker Mahaveer University, Moradabad, Uttar Pradesh, India*

**Abstract:** One deep learning method is the Convolutional Neural Network (CNN). Natural language processing problems like text classification are simplified using this approach. In this study, we use a deep learning strategy, namely the CNN method to deal with the issue of text classification. CNNs, which require a large deal of time as well as finances to train and use, have been greatly impeded by the rise of Big Data and the increased complexity of tasks. To get around these problems, we introduce a MapReduce-based CNN that rethinks what a CNN has learned by breaking it down into a series of smaller networks and training them in parallel. Subsets of incoming text are analysed by many autonomous networks.

**Keywords:** CNN, Deep learning, Logical reasoning, NLP, Sentiment analysis.

## INTRODUCTION

To analyse this data, a machine learning technique called Natural Language Processing (NLP) is needed. Since NLP enables companies to utilise huge data in creative ways to get significant insights into present and future market patterns, it is frequently seen as the market's next big thing.

The area of NLP has been studied for decades, but it is only in the past three that major advancements have been made. Partnering with a big data consulting firm, businesses are increasingly using machine learning techniques that make use of natural language processing.

Natural language processing (NLP) analyses the linguistics and semantics of the big data's text entries using statistics and machine learning, then extracts the rele-

* **Corresponding author N Sengottaiyan:** School of Computer Science and Engineering, JAIN (Deemed-to-be University), Bangalore, India; E-mail: sengottaiyan.n@jainuniversity.ac.in

**Pankaj Kumar Mishra and Satya Prakash Yadav (Eds.)**

vant entities and connections in the context of the customers' postings. Rather than analysing individual words or phrases, NLP looks at whole sentences to determine their meaning. Automatic synthesis, disambiguation, component-of- speech tagging, relations extraction, entity extraction, and, most crucially, natural language comprehension and recognition are some of the most prevalent techniques used in NLP.

The use of CNN techniques has led to remarkable developments in several areas, including computer vision and pattern recognition. The convolutional model's capacity to learn an ordered representation of features from pixel to line, contour, form, and object has been cited in many papers as the driving force behind these advancements. Different networks have been suggested in the literature to apply this paradigm to text classification, with positive results. The process of classifying texts into predetermined groups based on their content is known as text categorization or text classification. Parsing, semantic evaluation, information extraction, and Web searching are just a few of the many fields that benefit from its conceptual perspectives of document collections [1].

As a consequence, more researchers are becoming curious about it. Immense-scale classification systems, such as Google's spam filters [13] or Netflix's [14], however, need massive amounts of computer resources due to the immense training data and the tremendous number of variables that need to be fine-tuned. This is the fundamental issue with using CNNs in practical applications of context-dependent words. The words immediately around a search phrase are referred to as "context." The problem of using an Out-Of-Vocabulary (OOV) term, or an unfamiliar word, is prevalent in languages with extensive vocabularies. Since each word is reduced to a collection of letters in character embeddings, this problem is easily solved. Establishing structures at a character level is an obvious decision to avoid word division [2, 3] in works that use applications of deep learning on dialects where text cannot be made up of surrounded words but rather individual characters as well as the symbolic significance of words map to its chemical composition. The initial stage in character embeddings is to define a set of characters to work with. The alphabet plus a few other symbols, for instance. After that, we'll have a series of vectors and the characters would be transported using a one-hot encoding. Each character is represented by a vector of constant length in the final output. Next, the sequence is learned using 1D CNN layers.

One of the first things a model that uses deep learning does is learn how to represent words or characters. As the first machine learning layer in a CNN, words or embeddings of characters are often utilised. Here, we introduce two types of distributed representation—word and character embeddings—and discuss their advantages and disadvantages. Word incorporation is a technique for representing words in a vector space using a distributional assumption [4 - 7].

It suggests that comparable meanings might be attributed to words when they appear in the same contexts or the same places in two separate sources. Word embeddings are learned by propagating back an error function *via* a neural network, which is an adaptation of this notion from what we term distributed representations of words. In statistical language modelling, this similar concept was subsequently used to discover both word vectors and probabilities for word sequences [8-10]. When it comes to capturing the semantic and syntactic similarities between words, this approach has shown to be quite effective. Distributed representations provided an answer to the sparsity and curse of dimensionality issues by allowing words to be expressed in a stable, real-valued compact region with much lower dimensions than the entirety of the vocabulary.

There have been several efforts to improve word embedding learning in terms of accuracy and computing efficiency of the neural deterministic language model. In particular, Word2vec [11] has excelled in both accuracy and processing efficiency because of its straightforward and decentralised design. The purpose of Word2vec is to develop a model for vector space word embeddings with few dimensions. To do this, we may train a neural network to predict the probability of a certain word sequence within a specified time frame. The words immediately around a search phrase are referred to as "context." The problem of using an Out-Of-Vocabulary (OOV) term, or an unfamiliar word, is prevalent in languages with extensive vocabularies. Since each word is reduced to a collection of letters in character embeddings, this problem is easily solved. Building systems at the protagonist level is an obvious decision to avoid word division in languages (like Chinese) where text cannot be made up of separated words but rather individual characters alongside the linguistic significance of words maps to its compositional characters [12 - 14].

## RELATED WORK

In order to extract each entity in biomedical datasets, Chen, A. *et al.* created an open-source platform called DataMed [1]. The primary goal of this study is to identify useful datasets for the data reuse procedure. This methodology needs a new optimum document ranking strategy to identify and extract important documents from biomedical databases as the size of these sets grows. DataMed is a tool for indexing, ranking, and searching things in various biological datasets. There are two crucial parts to this method, and they are: The first step in building a model is the data intake pipeline, which is in charge of collecting and processing the raw metadata needed for building the model. DatA Tag Suite (DATS) is the name of this standardised metadata model. Second, a powerful search engine is used that can identify relevant datasets in response to user-specified queries. S. Sohn *et al.* [2] suggested a methodology to discover disease-related patterns on the variability of clinical documents and the transferability of NLP systems. The primary purpose of this study is to use many EMRs to evaluate the presence and severity of illness variations in clinical practice. When ranking biomedical document sets, we take into account document alterations related to asthma across two cohorts. In order to find connections between different collections of documents in biomedical databases, J. Cuzzola *et al.* constructed a model utilising UMLS and DBPedia [3]. This model's primary goal is to provide a connection between the UMLS entities and DBPedia resources.

The entities in the UMLS and DBPedia are mapped and ranked using common ontology relations through the Simple Knowledge Organisation System and the Resource Description Framework Schema. In a paper published in BMC Medicine, E. S. Chen *et al.* [4] developed an automated method for acquiring disease-drug information from medical literature. The primary goal of this study is to investigate and automate knowledge acquisition for clinical and biological records. In order to identify the disease-medication associations, a combination of text mining and statistical methods is used. In this case, we use two distinct NLP systems; they are BioMedLEE and MedLEE. These two NLP algorithms are responsible for identifying all possible diseases and medications. The approach produces ordered lists of diseases and medications. To locate and retrieve the relevant biological papers, E. Soysal *et al.* [5] created a toolbox based on natural language processing pipelines. MetaMap and BioNer, two of the most well-known clinical NLP tools, are used to search databases for relevant items. When dealing with massive biomedical data sets, these toolkits fall short. Human proteins and genes may be annotated with the use of a hybrid called entity tagger, as suggested by K. Raja [6]. In the case of a biomedical literature, extracting gene or proteins names is crucial.

Taggers abound in the named entity identification process, yet none of them the current models is up to the task of correctly labelling human genes and proteins. Therefore, for the purpose of marking human genomes or proteins utilising UMLs ontologies, a hybrid vandal is required. The MedScan toolset is used to analyse data about genes, proteins, and their associated pathways. The MedScan is a biomedical document parsing model-based, three-tier knowledge extraction system. The primary goal of the preprocessing module was to apply domain-specific principles to the tagging of diverse biomedical MeSH words. The biomedical XML representation of a MEDLINE description is read by the preprocessor module and then parsed into individual phrases and sentences. The protein names are filtered and the phrases or sentences with at least one genotypeprotein name are chosen using a protein named dictionary as the training data set in this section. The semantic linkages between concepts and sentence patterns are the focus of the second layer of a natural language processor's operations. It uses a lexical parse tree and context-free language to extract proteins from MEDLINE.

Finally, the conceptual graph format [7] is used to extract crucial information from MeSH-based documents using a knowledge extraction engine that acts as a domain knowledge filter. The goal of optimising a support vector machine is to create a new function specifically for extracting specialised information. Using hyperplanes and feature vector space, we categorise each document. Equation 1 describes the NLProt kernel function: +c=0 (1) Parameters of the hyperplane W and the decision function f(x) are denoted by X and W, respectively. The equation for f(x) is: sin(+c). (2) In the NLPlot, the kernel with a poly function is written as d K(y, y) (w.(y, y) c) i, j, i, j, . Conditional randomised fields define a probability conditionally distributed p(Y/X) as Equation 3 to characterise such an issue. kk CLS k c c W f (Y, X,c) 1 Probab e(Y/Xx) e Z(Xx) ∈ = = = ∑ ∑ (3) is the set of conditioned field vertices Y and the set of documents categories c. The feature extraction function, denoted by the symbols c, f, is defined as follows: c c f(Y,X x) = 1; if X and Y are the same gene entities, then f(Y,X x) = 0; otherwise, Z(X=x) = 1.

A weighed comparative model is offered as a novel method for rating documents. Document ideas and keywords are used to determine rankings in this methodology. This method takes into account simply the degree to which document keyphrase rankings are comparable, without taking into account the connection between the phrases themselves. Standard methods for rating documents include the Cosine similarity, the Euclidean distance, the Jaccard coefficient, the averaged KulbackLeibler (KL) Divergence, and the Pearson correlation coefficient. Local document patterns have been presented as the basis for a hierarchical document ranking model [8]. Inconsistent or noisy patterns might be the outcome of using the standard, hierarchical pattern recognition methodology. So, a new model called the Instances Driven Hierarchy Ranking Approach is used to create a ranking hierarchy without having to extract the global patterns, thereby solving the aforementioned problem. This approach first identifies the locally important patterns by having each instance located at its closest representation. This is done to strike a good balance between the relevance and frequency of patterns within a given area.

## PROPOSED WORK

### Convolutional Neural Networks

To achieve its goals, a convolutional neural network (CNN) employs a special kind of multilayer perceptron. Because of their similarities to the structure of animal visual cortices, CNNs were motivated by biological processes. When compared to other classification methods, they need less preprocessing. This implies that the network picks up features that were previously implemented by hand in conventional techniques. Using the lookup table, an input sequence of n tokens (s1, s2,..., sn) is converted into a variety of vectors (w1, w2,..., wn) in the first layer in the CNN architecture. Token embeddings may be thought of as vectors, with dimensions of the form wi Rd, where d is a number of tokens in the phrase. It is now possible to encode a phrase with n tokens as an embedding matrix. A statement like this is shown as input in W Rnd's CNN architecture. Let us call the sum of the vectors wi, wi+1,..., wjwi:i+j. This layer of input embeddings is subjected to convolution. It entails applying a filter, k Rhd, across a window of h tokens to generate a new feature. The frame of tokens wi:i+h1 is used to create a feature ci, for instance:

$$ci = f(wi{:}i+h-1.kT + b) \quad \textbf{(1)}$$

Where b R is a bias term and f is an irregular activating function such as the hyperbolic tangent. When generating the feature map, filter k is utilised uniformly over all potential windows.

$$c = [c1, c2,...,cn-h+1] \quad \textbf{(2)}$$

Convolutional neural networks (CNNs) use a large number of convolutional filtering structures (kernels) of varying widths to iteratively process the complete embedding matrix. Each kernel may be used to extract a unique n-gram pattern. Subsampling the input often involves a max action on each filter, as in c = max c (3), which comes after a convolution layer. Two main considerations led to this approach. Max pooling, first, is useful for classification since it produces outputs of a defined length. That is why maximum pooling consistently maps the inputs to the same number of outputs, no matter how large the filters are. Also, the most important n-gram characteristics are preserved while the output's dimensionality is decreased. Each filter may now independently extract a feature (such as negations) from any portion of the sentence and include it in the final phrase representation in a translation-invariant way. Random or pre-training on an extensive unlabeled corpus may be used to initialise the word embeddings. When there is a scarcity of labelled data, the latter technique may improve performance. When building deep CNN networks, it is common practice to add layers of convolution followed by max pooling. Improved mining of the text is made possible by the sequential convolutions' increased ability to comprehend an abstract representation rich in semantic information. Kernels with more layers of convolutions cover more of the phrase until they completely encompass it, at which point they provide a global summary of the sentence's characteristics.

## CNN-Based Text Classification

There have been several proposals for CNN text categorization algorithms that use semantic connections between words. These techniques may be broken down into two broad classes: those that operate on individual words, and those that operate on individual characters. Word-level text categorization using a simple convolutional neural network was suggested [9]. Trio parallel convolution layers were utilised, each of which processes a phrase by looking at three, four, or five words at a time in a sliding window. Following the three convolutions, the full phrase is fed into a Maxpool, which takes the most powerful features from each convolution and combines them to create one distinctive vector. A thick softmax layer is then used to classify the data based on the characteristics that were chosen. A number of studies were reported using this CNN with different sets of input word vectors. In the first variation, the word vectors are fixed while the rest of the model's parameters are learned. Another variation involves fine-tuning the learning of task-specific vectors. Having numerous channels in the design (see Fig. **1**) allows for the employment of both trained and task-specific vectors.

Kim's CNN design [11, 12] is still widely utilised in many modern text categorization jobs because of its ease of use and high performance across various workloads. The primary problem, however, is that the CNN cannot handle long-distance dependencies. In a study [8], the deep pyramid CNN (DPCNN) was presented as an alternative CNN that operates at the word level. Once discrete text has been transformed into a continuous democracy, the DPCNN design repeatedly cycles between a convolution block and a down sampling layer, resulting in a deep network with a pyramidal decrease in internal data size (and per-layer computation). One such meta-parameter is the depth of the network. In the first layer, we embed text areas that include one or more words; this is a generalisation of the more frequent practice of word embedding. After that, we will use a downsampling process that utilises stacked chunks of convolution (two convolution layers and a shortcut) in order to pool with stride 2. Each document's hidden information is combined into just one vector by the final pooling layer. All pooling layers (as seen in Fig. 1) were performed using the maximum pooling. Example 2: The DP

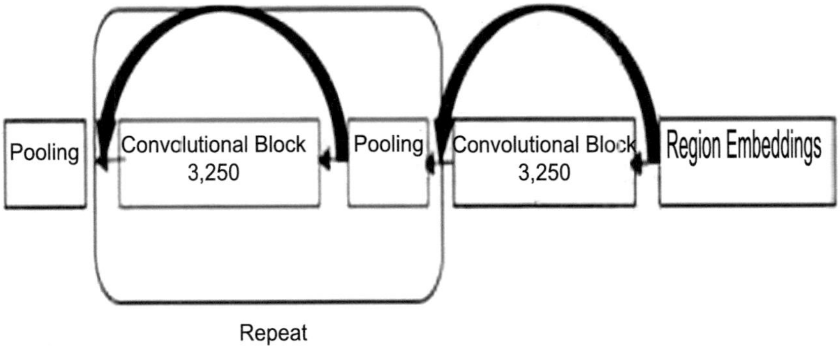


**Fig. (1).** Pooling Operation.

Character-based CNN was first developed. They discovered that essential signals to enhance model performance may be found in character. Characters always indicate a necessary construction whether or not subdivisions into words is conceivable, therefore they experimentally proved that syntactic and semantic understanding of a language is not essential for the text classification task. The suggested character-based CNN offers the added benefit of being able to learn non-standard character combinations, including those seen in misspellings and emoticons. Up to six levels of convolution and three fully linked classification layers are used in their systems. There are basic max-pooling layers and convolutional neural networks of sizes 3 and 7 utilised. (1. Character Embeddings: This layer formats characters into numerical vectors that contain their semantic meaning. 2. Convolutional Layer: This layer filters character embeddings to extract local characteristics. 3. Max Pooling: This layer selects the maximum local region value to downsample the convolutional layer output. 4. 3 Fully Connected Layers: These layers translate pooled information non-linearly to the output layer (not shown in figure), which predicts). (See Fig. **2**).

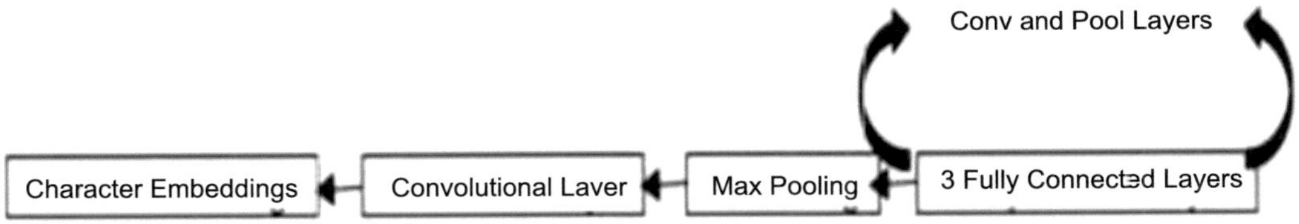


**Fig. (2).** The character based CNNmodel [16].

Very deep convolutional neural network (VDCNN) architecture for text processing was developed [5]. This architecture works directly at the individual character level with just tiny convolutions and pooling operations. Character embeddings are first generated using a lookup table in the model. Next, "Convolutional Blocks" of varying epochs are applied, each of whom is built from 64 convolutions of size 3. (i) when the spatial accuracy is halved, the total number of map representations increases by twofold; (ii) all layers have the same number of feature maps with the same outcomes temporal resolution. The author proved (see Fig. **3**) that increasing the number of convolutional layers in the model from 11 to 29 significantly enhances its performance.

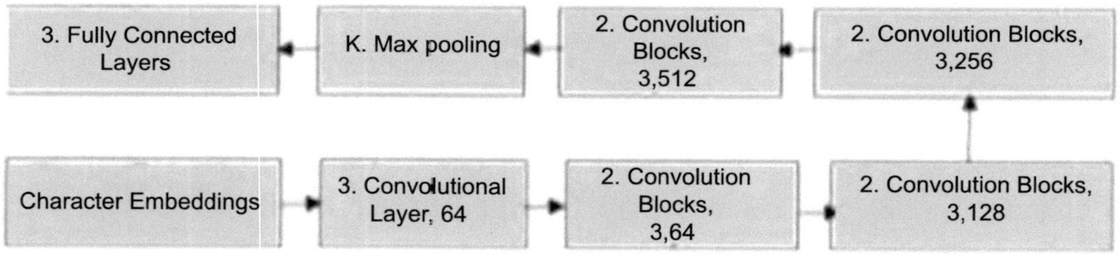


**Fig. (3).** Performance significance.

Please keep in mind that the aforementioned CNN models are by no means a complete list of the many available CNN methods. Rather than just listing all the available techniques, we will be focusing on analysing the many CNNs that exist with regard to their input granularity and depth. We presented two models, one shallow and one deep, from word-level CNNs, citing [9] and [8] respectively. Similarly, character-level convolutional neural networks (CNNs) have been reported using both shallow and deep models [5, 9]. An examination of the current CNN designs as a whole reveals that the resolution of input (character or word input are examined) as well as the extent of the CNN's layout (the number of layers) are the two most important design considerations. They demonstrated that character-level CNNs benefit more from increased depth than word-level CNNs did [10]. Further, they proved that an insufficient word-level CNN, very close to Kim's suggested structure, can outperform far deeper and more complicated CNN frameworks on a variety of text categorization tasks.

## MapReduce-CNN

Time-cost is a major problem before this method leaves the laboratories, even under the condition of great accuracy. Classifiers often face the challenge of striking a balance between efficiency and cost. CNN views it as much more dire because of the staggering intricacy of its design and calculations, particularly for large-scale systems. In recent years, several proposals have surfaced offering various parallel computing based technologies as common solutions for large data. The two primary approaches involve training sets level parallelism, which involves distributing the data needed for training, and neural-network level parallelism, which involves distributing the computation done by the neural network. The first approach, using the MapReduce architecture, was used in our suggested solution. The Map-Reduce modification of the NN learning technique back-propagation is briefly described [4]. In this way, back-propagation conducts a phase of batch learning.

By dividing the training process and then combining the learned models, the time cost of handwritten digit identification was drastically reduced [2]. In the MapReduce paradigm, there are two stages of computation: the map phase and the reduce phase. The data set being used (stored in a dispersed system) is split into several of independent subsets and then assigned to translators in the form of pairwise relationships during the Map phase. Each Mapper simultaneously processes a pair of inputs *via* the map function supplied by the user, producing a set of intermediary pairs that are saved to the hard drives of the Mapper machines.

A Convolutional Neural Network Built on MapReduce. The positions of these intermediary pairs are sent from the underlying system to the master, who then notifies the reducers of these locations. Once all intermediate pairs have been read remotely by the reducers, they are sorted and grouped using the intermediate keys in the Reduce phase.

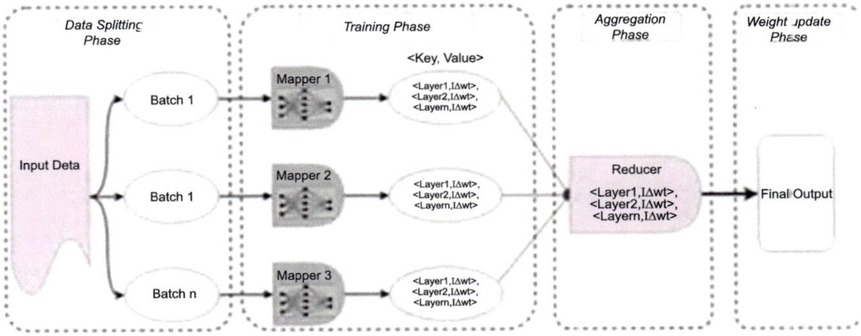


**Fig. (4).** Map Reduce Model. (Rectangle: Neural network layer. Circle: Data batch. Arrow: Shows data flow. Dashed Line: Phase or border. Labels: The first step of data splitting involves batching input data. Layers (Mappers) process each batch of data during training. Aggregation Phase: Combining Mapper results. Weight Update Phase: Layer weights are modified depending on aggregated output. Reducer: Combines Mapper outputs. The Mapper layer's intermediate data format is KeyValues. Mapper layer Zw. Layer 1-n: Includes numerous Mapper layers. The ultimate product of the procedure. In a distributed neural network training process, numerous workers (Mappers) process distinct batches of data in simultaneously, while a central component (Reducer) collects the outputs).

Each Reducer literally runs the user-specified reduce function on all the values associated with each key, transforming them into new values. All of the Reducers' output pairs are combined into a single set of final results and saved to a file. All map jobs (and reduce tasks) in a MapReduce system run in parallel. This means that the MapReduce paradigm may be used to achieve high-level parallelism in data processing. One deep learning approach that can make use of MapReduce's distributed computing is Convolutional Neural Networks. After each piece of training data is routed through a CNN, the network's weights are adjusted by calculating their partial gradients. Extending input data over many processors may help accomplish parallelization during a CNN's training phase. Then each machine may train its own CNN using its own unique set of data. Next, the final findings from the CNNs trained in parallel may be pooled to adjust the weights for the next cycle. Fig. (**4**) shows a high-level breakdown of the whole operation.

The mappers must provide both the instruction dataset (batch, label), whose batches is a trained example, and the base truth label for the particular instance, and an assortment of arbitrarily initialised weights [w1, w2,..., wn]. There are n weights in the set of a weight, where n is the total amount of hidden layers in the network, and Wi denotes the weights used for hidden layer i. The training set is a collection of paired values (batch, label). A system is trained utilising the input samples, once each mapper has initialised it with the specified weights. The reducer receives the freshly trained set of WeightsUpdate [w1, w2,..., wn]. Updated weights are sent to the mappers after each iteration and run across the internet until the maximum number of repetitions is achieved. The Map function's pseudo code is shown in Algorithms **1**.

**Algorithm 1** The Mapper function

**Require:** Set of pairs (batch,label) where batch is a training sample and label is the ground truth label for that sample
$Weights$: list of randomly initialized weights for each hidden layer

```
function MAP()
    Get initial Weights
    Initialize CNN with Weights
    Train the current CNN over the input batch: forward propagation, backward propagation, calculate gradient descent
    for i from 0 to numLayers - 1 do
        WeightsUpdate[i] ← WheightsUpdate[i] + Weights[i]
    end for
    return WeightsUpdate
end function
```

**Algorithm 2** The Reducer function

**Require:** Intermediate output by mappers which are the updated weights for each hidden layer.
$SumWeights$: list which stores the cumulative sum of $Weights$.
**Ensure:** Updated weighs

```
function REDUCE()
    Initialize SumWeights to list of zeros
    for i from 0 to numLayers - 1 do
        SumWeights[i] ←SumWeights[i]+Weights[i]
    end for
    return SumWeights
end function
```

The reduction takes in the intermediate results from the mappers and combines the resulting weights. Because weights are ranked by the hidden layer to which they belong in the result of mappers, the reducer may easily sum them up by layer. The average weights are calculated by adding all of the weights together and then dividing by the total number of training occurrences in the batch. The final output is sent back to the mapper in preparation for the next iteration, where it is used to revise the network's weights. Algorithm **2** displays the fictitious code for the reduction function.

## RESULTS AND DISCUSSION

The models presented here were evaluated using a variety of datasets, ranging from very small to very big. We consulted authors' experiments stated in the original articles to provide objective comparisons of the aforementioned models, and compiled findings on the Yelp, Yahoo, and Amazon datasets [5, 8] (Table **1**), which are commonly studied datasets for CNNs. Accuracy, which is the proportion of accurate identifications to all identifications, and error rate, which is the proportion of incorrect identifications to all identifications, were employed as assessment measures. The error rate is a typical metric used to evaluate the effectiveness of various CNNs. We did our best to choose outcomes that can be compared by using the same assessment tools and datasets. From the many possible test error rates reported in the relevant publications [5, 8, 9], we chose the one with the lowest. All models were used in this procedure, and no models were chosen in advance.

The authors put their models to the test in a variety of experimental environments. The accuracy of Kim's CNN [9] increased to an impressive 89.6 when pre-trained word2vec vectors were used instead of the standard random initialization, static initialization, non-static initialization, or multichannel initialization. With the convolutional neural network (CNN) described [8], the authors conducted tests utilising large datasets, testing the effects of different model depths (3, 7, and 15 layers) and the presence or absence of unsupervised embeddings. Multiple model depths (from 9 to 47) and pooling methods (Max pooling worked best) were tried using the character-level CNN specified in a study [5]. Similar models have been described, when experiments were conducted by modifying the vocabulary and reprocessing stage (for example, by employing a Thesaurus data enhancement strategy). All CNN models that were trained with large-scale datasets were found to use a GPU-based training framework.

Artificial neural networks provided the basis for the development of CNNs. Consequently, their theoretical complexity is comparable. A shown in [4] the computational cost of a basic neural network system (with one buried layer) may be reduced by adapting it to the MapReduce framework. Let us say P is the amount of processors used to execute the algorithm, n is an input dimension, and m is the number of training samples. The authors demonstrated that employing a single core reduces the potential cost of a backpropagation iteration from O(mn P + nc log (P))(c is a component) to O(mn P + nc log (P))(c is a factor).

**Table 1. Error rates of CNNs.**

| Model | Yelp.p | Yelp.f | Yahoo | Ama.f | Ama.p |
|---|---|---|---|---|---|
| DPCNN [8] | 2.64 | 30.58 | 23.90 | 34.81 | 3.32 |
| Char-based CNN [16] | 4.36 | 37.95 | 28.80 | 40.43 | 4.93 |
| VDCNN [5] | 4.28 | 35.28 | 26.57 | 37.00 | 4.28 |

## CONCLUSION

In this study, we analysed the effectiveness of many different CNN models. But as big data grows in popularity and job complexity rises, CNNs' effectiveness suffers, leading to lengthy training periods and significant computing expenses, particularly for large-scale datasets. Learning algorithms will need to keep their speed and accuracy at a high level while being cost-effective if they are to handle the more complex challenges of the future. This research uses the MapReduce framework to provide a parallel CNN approach, which improves the performance and scalability of CNNs. The Spark MapReduce framework is being utilised to do this. To further protect user information, consensus training is to be used, which limits communication between cluster nodes.

## REFERENCES

[1] F. Alotaibi, and V.G. Gupta, "Sentiment analysis system using hybrid word embeddings with convolutional recurrent neural network", *Int. Arab J. Inf. Technol.*, vol. 19, no. 3, pp. 330-335, 2022.

[http://dx.doi.org/10.34028/iajit/19/3/6]

[2] N.K. Kaliappan, S. Thapasimuthu Rajeswari, P. Dakshinamoorthy, N. Sundararaju, and R. Sundar, "Intelligent video surveillance using enhanced deep belief based multilayered convolution neural network classification techniques", *Photogramm. Rec.,* vol. 37, no. 180, pp. 490-502, 2022. [http://dx.doi.org/10.1111/phor.12429]

[3] G. Amrani, A. Adadi, M. Berrada, Z. Souirti, and S. Boujraf, "EEG signal analysis using deep learning: A systematic literature review", *2021 Fifth International Conference On Intelligent Computing in Data Sciences (ICDS),* pp. 1-8, 2021. [http://dx.doi.org/10.1109/ICDS53782.2021.9626707]

[4] S. Prakash Yadav, and S. Yadav, "Fusion of medical images in wavelet domain: A discrete mathematical model", *Ingeniería Solidaria,* vol. 14, no. 25, pp. 1-11, 2018. [http://dx.doi.org/10.16925/.v14i0.2236]

[5] U.D. Gandhi, P. Malarvizhi Kumar, G. Chandra Babu, and G. Karthick, "Sentiment Analysis on Twitter Data by Using Convolutional Neural Network (CNN) and Long Short Term Memory (LSTM)", *Wirel. Pers. Commun.,* 2021. [http://dx.doi.org/10.1007/s11277-021-08580-3]

[6] M. Nabeel, and C. Große, "Classifying COVID-19 Disinformation on Twitter using a Convolutional Neural Network", *International Conference on Information Systems Security and Privacy,* 2022. [http://dx.doi.org/10.5220/0010774800003120]

[7] V. Vashisht, A.K. Pandey, and S.P. Yadav, "Speech Recognition using Machine Learning", In: *In IEIE Transactions on Smart Processing & Computing.* vol. 10. The Institute of Electronics Engineers of Korea, 2021, no. 3, pp. 233-239. [http://dx.doi.org/10.5573/IEIESPC.2021.10.3.233]

[8] B.A. Mohammed, and M.S. Al-Ani, *Review Research of Medical Image Analysis Using Deep Learning,* 2020. [http://dx.doi.org/10.21928/uhdjst.v4n2y2020.pp75-90]

[9] X. Ma, and Q. Zhou, "Special issue on deep learning and neural computing for intelligent sensing and control", *Neural Comput. Appl.,* vol. 32, no. 7, pp. 1811-1812, 2020. [http://dx.doi.org/10.1007/s00521-020-04785-y]

[10] J. Kaur, J. Saxena, and J. Shah, "2022 International Conference on Computational Intelligence and Sustainable Engineering Solutions (CISES)", *IEEE,* 2022. [http://dx.doi.org/10.1109/CISES54857.2022.9844366]

[11] D. Yu, "Intelligent Analysis System of Movie Reviews Using Deep Learning and Convolutional Neural Networks", *2021 IEEE Conference on Telecommunications, Optics and Computer Science (TOCS),* pp. 617-621, 2021. [http://dx.doi.org/10.1109/TOCS53301.2021.9688854]

[12] S. Sabba, N. Chekired, H. Katab, N. Chekkai, and M. Chalbi, "Sentiment Analysis for IMDb Reviews Using Deep Learning Classifier", *2022 7th International Conference on Image and Signal Processing and their Applications (ISPA),* 2022 pp. 1-6. Mostaganem, Algeria. [http://dx.doi.org/10.1109/ISPA54004.2022.9786284]

[13] M.E. Alzahrani, T.H.H. Aldhyani, S.N. Alsubari, M.M. Althobaiti, and A. Fahad, "Developing an Intelligent System with Deep Learning Algorithms for Sentiment Analysis of E-Commerce Product Reviews", *Comput. Intell. Neurosci.,* vol. 2022, pp. 1-10, 2022. [http://dx.doi.org/10 1155/2022/3840071] [PMID: 35669644]

[14] M.M. Krishna, B. Duraisamy, and J. Vankara, "Independent component support vector regressive deep learning for sentiment classification", *Measurement Sensors,* vol. 26, 2023. [http://dx.doi.org/10.1109/ICACITE53722.2022.9823898]

# SUBJECT INDEX



**Pankaj Kumar Mishra and Satya Prakash Yadav (Eds.)**

## D

## E



## F



## G



## H



## I



## L

## P



## R



## S

Made in the USA
Las Vegas, NV
03 November 2026

57424251R00366